We Dream Together

ANNE ELLER

We Dream Together

Dominican Independence, Haiti, and the
Fight for Caribbean Freedom

Duke University Press   Durham and London   2016

© 2016 Duke University Press
All rights reserved

Typeset in Quadraat and Avenir by Westchester Publishing Services

Library of Congress Cataloging-in-Publication Data
Names: Eller, Anne, [date] author.
Title: We dream together : Dominican independence, Haiti, and the fight for Caribbean freedom / Anne Eller.
Description: Durham : Duke University Press, 2016. | Includes bibliographical references and index.
Identifiers:
LCCN 2016024763 (print)
LCCN 2016025626 (ebook)
ISBN 9780822362173 (hardcover)
ISBN 9780822362371 (pbk.)
ISBN 9780822373766 (e-book)
Subjects: LCSH: Dominican Republic—History—1844–1930. | Dominican Republic—Politics and government—1844–1930. | Dominican Republic—Colonization. | Dominican Republic—Relations—Haiti. | Haiti—Relations—Dominican Republic. | Caribbean Area—History—Autonomy and independence movements.
Classification: LCC F1938.4.E45 2016 (print) | LCC F1938.4 (ebook) | DDC 972.93/04—dc23
LC record available at https://lccn.loc.gov/2016024763

Cover art: Adapted from "Emboscada de los insurgentes en Santo Domingo," El Mundo Militar, 20 December 1863, 404.

This book was published with the assistance of The Frederick W. Hilles Publication Fund of Yale University.

FOR KEVIN LEE
WHO KNOWS ALL OF THIS
ALREADY

Contents

ix	Timeline
xv	Acknowledgments
1	INTRODUCTION Roots and Branches of the Tree of Liberty
21	ONE Life by Steam: The Dominican Republic's First Republic, 1844–1861
59	TWO Soon It Will Be Mexico's Turn: Caribbean Empire and Dominican Annexation
87	THREE The White Race Is Destined to Occupy This Island: Annexation and the Question of Free Labor
117	FOUR The Haitians or the Whites? Colonization and Resistance, 1861–1863
144	FIVE You Promised to Die of Hunger: Resistance, Slavery, and All-Out War
178	SIX The Lava Spread Everywhere: Rural Revolution, the Provisional Government, and Haiti
207	SEVEN Nothing Remains Anymore: The Last Days of Spanish Rule
229	EPILOGUE Between Fear and Hope
237	Notes
335	Bibliography
369	Index

Map 0.1 Map of the Dominican Republic and Haiti. By Annelieke Vries.

Timeline

c. 1474	Anacaona born in Yaguana, chiefdom of Xaragua, Ayiti
1500	Spanish authorities declare the island a Crown colony, Santo Domingo
1502	First Africans brought in slavery to Santo Domingo
1508	Indigenous rebellion in Higüey
1545	Maroon communities reach about seven thousand
1585–86	Siege of Santo Domingo by Sir Francis Drake
1605–6	Spanish authorities forcibly resettle colonists toward the southeast
1664	France names a governor in the west of the island, Saint-Domingue
1697	Treaty of Ryswick recognizes Saint-Domingue (west) and Santo Domingo (east)
1721	Revolt in Santo Domingo's Cibao valley against trade prohibitions with Saint-Domingue
1777	Treaty of Aranjuez fixes borders and authorizes trade
1791	Revolutionary fighting begins in Saint-Domingue
1793	Abolition won in Saint-Domingue
1795	Spain cedes Santo Domingo to France, midfighting
1796	Major rebellion at Boca Nigua sugar mill in Dominican territory

1801	General Toussaint Louverture reaches Santo Domingo; 1801 constitution affirms abolition
1802	Arriving French forces pursue Louverture, reestablish slavery in Santo Domingo
1804	Haiti proclaims independence
1805	Haitian emperor Jean-Jacques Dessalines invades Santo Domingo after direct threats from the French governor in the east
1806	Haiti fractures into a northern republic (kingdom, 1811) and southern republic
1808–9	Dominican rebels and allies expel French administration, reinstate Spanish flag
1810s	Multiple rebellions and conspiracies in Santo Domingo
1820	President Jean-Pierre Boyer reunifies Haiti
1821	Dominican independentists proclaim the Independent State of Spanish Haiti
1822	Unification of the whole island begins; Boyer abolishes slavery in the east for a second time
1825	France demands an "indemnity" to cease its aggression toward the island
1838	Haiti and France renegotiate payments; abolition in British Caribbean islands
1842	Major earthquake devastates Cap-Haïtien and other towns
1843	Reform movements threaten Boyer; Dominican politicians ponder French annexation; Boyer flees
1844	Unification ends, Dominican Republic proclaimed; antislavery rebellion and repression in Cuba
1840s	Restrictive labor codes passed in Danish West Indies, other nearby islands
1854	Dominican treaty with United States fails over popular opposition

1856	Haitian emperor Faustin Soulouque rebuffed from an invasion attempt on the east, his last
1857	Cibao politicians rebel against the administration in the Dominican capital
1859	President Fabre Nicholas Geffrard restores republican government to Haiti
1861	Spain annexes Dominican territory as the province of "Santo Domingo" once more

Figs. 0.1 and 0.2 Monuments to guerrilla fighters, Santiago de los Caballeros. Photos by author, 2008.

Acknowledgments

This book represents the work of many over a significant expanse of time, and I can only begin to describe the debts. For different parts of this project, I relied on the support of Meriwether-Sattwa, Henry Mitchell McCracken, Fulbright-Hays, Doris Quinn, Hawkinson, and Macmillan Center writing and research fellowships. Support from the Frederick W. Hilles Fund of Yale University facilitated production. I am grateful to the diligent (and patient) interlibrary loan staff at Bobst Library, as well as the rest of its staff. In New York University's Department of History, sincere thanks to the administrative staff, Karin Burrell, and King Juan Carlos Center's employees. At the library of the University of Connecticut at Stamford, I am very grateful to Nancy Romanello, Phara Bayonne, and the student assistants. Rest in peace, Nancy Comarella. At Yale's library, I am grateful to David Gary for all of his resourceful suggestions, camaraderie, and support. Dana Lee, Essie Lucky-Barros, Denise Scott, Marcy Kaufman, Liza Joyner, and Lina Chan have been invaluable. Thank you to Noelia Ruzzante and the Centro Cultural Eduardo León Jimenes in Santo Domingo for figure 1.1 and to Bethany Wade for her pivotal assistance. My sincere thanks to Annelieke Vries and Heather Rosenfeld, who made beautiful maps, and to Santiago Castro Ventura for the cover image. I am very grateful to the staff of Duke University Press, including Lydia Rose Rappoport-Hankins, Liz Smith, and Susan Ecklund, and the careful eye and encouragement of Gisela Fosado.

 I feel so grateful and humbled to have had the chance to learn over the last decade from Ada Ferrer, whose brilliance, guidance, and scholarship are a constant inspiration. I feel deep gratitude to Michael Gomez for his training, innumerable insights, engagement, and support. Sinclair Thomson, Barbara Weinstein, and Sibylle Fischer also have been incredibly generous and have led with the example of their own projects and commitments. The warmest thanks to a brilliant multiyear cohort, which included Rashauna Johnson, Abena Asare, Franny Sullivan, Kendra Field, Michelle Thompson, Kiron Johnson, Priya Lal, Ezra Davidson, Jorge Silva, Michelle Chase, Nathalie Pierre, Evelyne Laurent-Perrault, Daniel Rodríguez, Joaquin Chávez, Jennifer Adair, Tracy Neumann, Yuko Miki, Zawadi Barskile Walker, Carmen Soliz, Claire Payton, and others, for their intellect and community building, and for laughter, memories, support, editing, and so many conversations. Over nearly the past ten years, Aldo Lauria Santiago has offered last-minute readings, structure, encouragement, and so much valuable guidance; his mentorship is above and beyond anything I might have hoped for, and I am so grateful. Without Louis (Bob) Turansky's classes, I never would have begun these studies.

I am deeply appreciative of the feedback and insight of a number of wonderful scholars, especially Neici Zeller, whose knowledge and perspective guided important parts of this project. Jessica Krug's brilliant critical insight has always been a revelation. Other generous mentors, colleagues, and friends who read chapters and offered other invaluable kinds of input and support include Grégory Pierrot, Robin Lauren Derby, Marisa J. Fuentes, Kristen Block, Dixa Ramírez, Lara Putnam, Vincent Brown, Greta Lafleur, Jason McGraw, Greg Jackson, Julie Gibbings, Matthew J. Smith, Naomi Lamoreaux, Alan Mikhail, Oscar de la Torre, Kahlil Chaar-Pérez, Ernesto Bassi, Kate Ramsey, Mike Bustamante, Jennifer Lambe, Heather Vrana, Reena Goldthree, Natanya Duncan, Martha S. Jones, Dan Magaziner, Manuel Barcia, Frances Ramos, Tamara Walker, Brendan Thornton, Alejandra Bronfman, Harvey Neptune, Christy Thornton, Melanie Newton, Caree Banton, Matthew Casey, and E. Tracy Grinnell. Special thank you to Gil Joseph, Stuart Schwartz, Joe Manning, Steve Pincus, Laurent Dubois, Thomas C. Holt, Kevin Bell, and Katherine Caldwell for reading large chunks or entire drafts and offering indispensable comments. Your input made this project so much better. Christopher Schmidt-Nowara, gone far too soon, always offered tremendous generosity, perspective, and insight. He is deeply missed. On this long project, I have had the great fortune of researching and writing alongside Juan-José Ponce Vázquez and Elena Schneider, who are great colleagues, travel partners, and friends.

For their collegueship, community-building, and perspective, my deepest thanks and affection to some not already mentioned, including Joel Blatt, Mary Cygan, Fred Roden, Ingrid Semaan, Annamaria Csizmadia, Shirley Roe, Jason Chang, Mark Healey, Mark Overmyer-Velázquez, Alejandra Dubcovsky, Edward Rugemer, Jafari Alan, Carolyn Dean, Valerie Hanson, Vanessa Agard-Jones, Ned Blackhawk, Marcela Echeverri, and Jenifer Van Vleck.

I am grateful for productive conversations with Crystal Feimster, Quisqueya Lora Hugi, Maja Horn, Kaiama Glover, Elizabeth Manley, April Mayes, Kiran Jayaram, Lorgia García Peña, Paul Austerlitz, Raj Chetty, Richard Turits, Graham Nessler, Wendy Muñiz, Melissa Madera, Natasha Lightfoot, Edward Paulino, Andrew Walker, and Charlton Yingling, among others, and I look forward to more of them to come. Kate Marsh, Kathy López, Camilla Townsend, Jason Chang, Jonathan Booth, and Jason McGraw helped me greatly with details of the emancipation map. Tanya Golash-Boza's and Sandy Placido's kindness, commitment, and activism match the brilliance of their respective projects, ni una más. In the classroom, I have learned so much from Jennifer Veras, Darlene Then, Estephanie Reyes, Clebis Grullon, Rondell López, Richard H. Ramírez, Krystal Gourgue, Christie Sillo, James Shinn, Juan Ruíz, Nathalie Batraville, Shanna-Dolores Jean-Baptiste, Emmanuel Lachaud, Emily Snyder, Brandi Waters, and far too many others to list. None of you are forgotten. Rest in peace, Jessie Streich-Kest.

The kindness, generosity, and expertise of many archivists, hosts, scholars, and friends shaped the project's research and made it possible. In Santo Domingo, my deepest thanks to Quisqueya Lora Hugi, Ingrid Suriel, Reynaldo Espinal, Antonio Báez, Oscar Féliz, Oscar Mota, Joel Abreu, Ivan Henríquez, Rosmery Fanfán, Amparo Candelario, Campo (QEPD), Raymundo González, Santiago Castro Ventura, and Roberto Cassá. Ercilia (QEPD) and Miguel Henríquez, María del Carmen González Rosario, and Belkis, Pamela, and Mundy offered so much. In San Juan, thank you to Humberto García Muñiz and the staff of the Institute of Caribbean Studies at the Universidad de Puerto Rico–Río Piedras. In Havana (and also in diaspora), I am very grateful for the camaraderie, talent, and intellect of Jorge Amado Pérez Machado, Yasser Yero Feraude, Gloria Loretta Herranz Peña and Angel Suárez, Angel (Boly) Ramírez, Maritza and Adis María, Lillian Lechuga, Pepe y Mirlay, Diarmarys Sarabaza Cuesta, Zuley Fernández, Omaida Pereira, Jorge Luís Chacón, Sandy Capote Gutiérrez, Elizabeth Fernández, and Karmen Yerith Aguilar Cruz. At the archive, thanks to Julio López, Bárbara Danzie León, Belkis Quesada Guerra, and research comrade, mentor, and friend David Sartorius. Thank you to Kak Lam Yip and Lan Jo Wu for translating the Cantonese letter in chapter 5. Thanks also to the employees of the archives in Madrid and Sevilla, to Esther González and Yurnia Montes Castro, and to Cristina Violeta Jones and Charlie at the National Archives in Washington, DC.

Some brilliant and generous friends still need mention, and I regret I cannot name every single one. Steven (Tzvi) Frankel is part of every single page. Helmus Ramírez Herranz, Gregg Parrish, Lani Milstein, Federico Torres,

Yesenia Fernández Selier, Dillon, Vladimir Marcano, Beth Krafchik, Tito Román Rivera, Margaret Urías, Michael Guerrere, Nicole Anziani, Willy Annicette, Cassie Morgan, Raquel Otheguy, Didier Lobeau, Nelcy Valdiris, Brad Rouse, A.B.B., Mary Fitzpatrick O'Rear, Jeff O'Rear, Philip Cartelli, Kara Bolduc Martínez, Wendy Toribio, Rachel Lang, Jessica Krug, Lamin Brewer, Jamel Oeser-Sweat, and Kate Caldwell: you are so wonderful, you already know that. I cannot thank Dr. David Slavit, Dr. Subinoy Das, Barbara Van-Wert, and Melanie Clark enough for giving me my life back. Fede, let's keep running and talking. Joe Murphy, I look forward to more lunches to come.

For my parents, Peter and Karen, I feel more gratitude than I can possibly express. Your love, encouragement, perspective, and insight spring from every page, just like they always have. For Michael, Stephanie, Ian, and the rest of the family (Springfield, Minnesota, ¡presente!), too, thank you for tolerating a huge project with grace and humor. Love you always.

Introduction
ROOTS AND BRANCHES OF THE TREE OF LIBERTY

Listen, then: there is an Antille
in the middle of the Caribbean sea
that gets light and life
from the sun of Liberty
—MANUEL RODRÍGUEZ OBJÍO, "Mi patria" (1868)

After dark on a late spring night in 1864, an anonymous group toppled a towering palm tree, the Tree of Liberty, in the town square of Santo Domingo. Planted by officials from Jean-Pierre Boyer's administration four decades earlier, the tree represented a celebration of Dominican emancipation, independence, and the unification of the former Spanish colony with the revolutionary Haitian state.[1] Those who won abolition in 1822 called themselves "freedmen of the Palm." The tree grew just meters from the plaza's whipping post.[2] The unification of Santo Domingo and Haiti lasted for more than two decades before it dissolved, and a mobilization in the east created a separate republic. The night the palm fell, however, independence had vanished. A colonial slave power ruled Dominican territory again, warships threatened Port-au-Prince, and fighting raged throughout the east. Spanish troops, who controlled the Dominican capital, moved into free black neighborhoods and other parts of the city to prevent protests over the tree's destruction.[3] "The tree of our glories is toppled to the ground," a Dominican poet decried, imploring, "Brave Dominicans, why do you suffer so much insult?"[4]

We Dream Together considers anticolonial struggle in an island at the heart of Caribbean emancipation and independence, Hispaniola, Quisqueya, or Ayiti.⁵ Spanish Santo Domingo was the oldest site of indigenous decimation and European colonial settlement in the Americas, as well as the first nucleus of sugar slavery and marronage. The French colony of Saint-Domingue, established in the west of the island, gave the world nearly one-third of its sugar, at a staggering human cost. Tremendous upheaval from 1791 to 1804—a collection of struggles that became known as the Haitian Revolution—swept the whole island and region into pitched battles for freedom. One might easily extend the dates of emancipation and independence fighting to include the military campaign of Jean-Jacques Dessalines in 1805, when a French governor, poised in the east of the island, threatened to capture and enslave Haitian children across the mountains. The dates of revolutionary struggle might include the 1810s, when French warships arrived repeatedly and the northern Haitian empire braced for war, as whole cities emptied at the threat of battle. They might even extend into the 1820s, as so-called indemnity payments to France for recognition and independence rocked the Haitian administration, then extended to the whole island. They might extend into the 1850s, the first time both states on the island, now separated, had anything like regular international recognition. In 1861, however, an eastern leader gave the Dominican Republic back to Spain, a slave power. Fighting was not over.

We Dream Together recounts the immense opposition to self-rule directed toward the island and a popular Dominican and Haitian mobilization, when the Dominican Republic was annexed back to Spain, to defend that autonomy at any cost. The Dominican Republic and Haiti, two countries with important postslavery peasantries born of marronage and revolution, grappled with state making as anti-emancipation voices grew the loudest, as slavers continued to ferry tens of thousands of people past their shores, and as new imperial projects deepened.⁶ Atlantic empires were in a moment of profound transition. Power shifted in the Gulf of Mexico, where plantation regimes faltered but indenture expanded, large swaths of Central America changed hands, steam power and canal projects loomed, and U.S. interests grew. In domestic contests and imperial expansion, the hemisphere was an uneven geography of slavery and precarious sites of refuge. Although Spanish authorities promised they would protect free labor in Dominican territory, administrators dreamed of new projects of agricultural production, settler colonization, and labor control. Dominican elites shared the same hopes. Rural residents, who organized their lives with their own authority networks, confronted both these domestic and occupying authorities simultaneously.

In response to Spanish reoccupation in 1861, whole communities left their homes, made new alliances, burned down their own towns, and risked their lives. They did so collectively, despite divisive elite narratives and with barely any resources. Their commitment was unrelenting, even as Spanish authorities sent a host of warships to defeat them. Over a two-year period, more than fifty thousand troops arrived from Spain, Cuba, and Puerto Rico to crush the rebels, as Spain poured millions into military offense.[7] Not even prominent military men had control over the insurgents, who grew more radical in the course of the fighting. Residents of the island, fully immersed in Civilization's assault, forged lucid, alternative solidarities. They defended self-government and community, confronting opposition from both domestic and imperial authorities. They fought, explicitly, against the reestablishment of slavery, and they understood the stakes of their battles to reach far beyond the island. In their victory, guerrilla fighting spread from the island to the rest of Spain's Caribbean empire. Many demands and solidarities of the rebellion, however, like rural freedom in Santo Domingo, quickly became obscure to record and memory beyond the island. They were written in battle, even at home.

Severing Colonial Bonds

A common refrain in the present-day Dominican Republic reminds listeners that the country was "the only one in the hemisphere" to become independent from another American state, when politicians of the territory proclaimed separation from Haiti in 1844. This aphorism is not true, of course, as Panamanians, Ecuadorians, Belizeans, Uruguayans, or others could affirm. Extrication from formal European colonialism, the settling of borders, the forming and re-forming of federations, and lasting regional divides bedeviled new national projects. In cases like Paraguay's border conflicts with Brazil and Argentina in the 1860s, nationalist mobilizations and the settling of borders caused tremendous bloodshed. Although leaders compared vociferously, Santo Domingo's conflicts were minor in comparison.[8] Regional fissures nagged, however, even grew. Economic and political divisions caused powerful residents of León to tangle with Granada, Córdoba with Buenos Aires, Les Cayes with Port-au-Prince, Santiago with Santo Domingo, Quetzaltenango with Guatemala City. Proponents of federalism tangled with centralists, regional leaders competed for power, and divisions proliferated. Leaders vied, variously and alongside their constituents and clients, for local authority or centralized government. One constitution followed another. These fissures brought Venezuela to bloody civil war in 1858, for example, in battles that often drew on questions of racism, land tenure, political rights, and the very idea of autonomy itself. Limited economic integration and independent peasantries made leaders' wishful centralization more difficult. The only way to avoid tyranny was for rule by "cumaneses in Cumaná; apureños in Apure," combatants earnestly argued.[9] Where growing U.S. aggression in the Gulf of Mexico disrupted sovereignty and divided elites, state consolidation became all the more difficult.[10]

Old colonial divides carved up and united Hispaniola. After Columbus initiated a violent process of Spanish attacks and settlement, European powers recognized the island as juridically Spanish for more than one hundred years. French adventurers reached the western part of the island in the seventeenth century; after a series of battles, Spain recognized French Saint-Domingue in 1697. In the intense colonial milieu of Caribbean empire—as imperial powers tacked back and forth for way stations, plantations, geopolitical influence, and brutally gleaned profits—division of the island had ample precedent. The Dutch and the French had divided Saint Martin (Soualiga) in two, just decades before. Many more Caribbean sites, including nearby Jamaica, had simply changed hands at the muzzle of a cannon. Symbiotically, Santo Domingo and Saint-Domingue grew together. Just as the Middle Colonies formed part of a greater slave system that connected to the U.S. South, so were the cattle, hides, and foodstuffs of Santo Domingo directly essential to the functioning of the deadly, and growing, plantations in Saint-Domingue. Dominican colonists fought to break mercantilist restrictions across the island. Like many other Caribbean plantation landscapes, the two colonies were nodes of an interdependent system.[11] By the late eighteenth century, Dominican elites sought to parlay profits into more slavery of their own. Their hopes were similar to those of the elites in Cuba, whose plantation aspirations were rising simultaneously.[12] As elite supplicants vied for state attention, ranchers and a flourishing peasantry continued to trade. The population quadrupled.[13] And then, in 1791, revolutionary fighting exploded.

Dominicans' independence unfolded over decades, propelled by this fighting. Revolution in French Saint-Domingue engulfed the whole island. Spanish authorities, after abetting western rebels for a time, hastily ceded Dominican territory to France. Toussaint Louverture, claiming a French mandate, reached Santo Domingo. Four Dominicans signed Louverture's 1801 constitution, which abolished slavery on Dominican soil for the first time.[14] After Louverture's defeat, however, two successive French generals occupied the Dominican capital, threatening newly independent Haiti. Both generals were pro-slavery, and the latter introduced unpopular new taxes.[15] In this light, one can see the 1808–9 Dominican effort to expel them and to restore a Spanish flag—even as other territories in Latin America were beginning to mobilize for independence—as a devolution of authority back to the island, a battle against French domination on both sides of the Atlantic.[16] A party of Dominicans and Puerto Rican allies, aided by British ships and Haitian munitions, expelled the French occupation. A Dominican stepped in as a Spanish figurehead. He ruled by verbal edict, and he made significant diplomatic entreaties to the independent Haitian states, now split into a northern kingdom and a southern republic.[17] For more than a decade, as Spanish authorities practically ignored the territory, colonial sovereignty eroded. Dominican conspirators regularly appealed to Haitian rulers for arms and support for the many revolts and conspiracies that ensued, and pro-unification plans emerged.[18] Dominican residents of center-island towns held ceremonies that celebrated Haitian independence.[19] Authors of a brief independence conspiracy in 1821 sought to link the territory, to be called "Spanish Haiti," to Gran Colombia, in a scheme that would have maintained slavery. Within two months, however, a wave of Dominican support ushered in Haiti's president, Jean-Pierre Boyer, into the eastern capital.[20] Boyer was a republican who had defeated the northern monarch, King Henry I. Boyer proclaimed Dominican emancipation for a second time on 9 February 1822, as the colony became part of Haiti. Officials planted the Tree of Liberty less than two weeks later.[21] The whole island was now Haiti, the only independent nation in the Caribbean. One man later remembered Dominicans everywhere expressed solidarity with their "new fellow co-citizens," independent at last.[22]

For the next twenty-two years of political unification, stability reigned. Emancipation proceeded smoothly. In the former Dominican capital, many freedmen joined the ranks of the African Battalion, two regiments of freedmen in the city who also regularly welcomed escapees from neighboring islands. Outside of the capital, where sugar plantations had endured, families reclaimed the land. Small, local, unprocessed sugar production continued. In eastern cattle country, little changed.[23] New communities of regional migrants fleeing slavery formed on the northern coast. In urban settings, it is likely that proponents of "vernacular citizenship" demanded, fundamentally, new recognition and stature.[24] Dominican elites grudgingly admitted, "Boyer's measures [were] very just," even as they complained about his policies of "spreading employment and official recognition indistinctly among people of this and that color."[25] Coffee, tobacco, and wood selling thrived, with direct encouragement from Port-au-Prince.[26] The reach of the government into rural areas all over the island, however, was minimal. As if by some miracle, the regime endured for two decades, despite the fragility of its infrastructure. Residents in most areas lived within networks that were centripetal to Port-au-Prince or Santo Domingo. Small ships traveled along the coast, because overland travel was prohibitively difficult. Travelers and migrants connected, sometimes furtively, port-town residents to islands and coasts near and far. They articulated "public rights," positive claims to authority, belonging, and legal personhood, rooted in their own autonomy and in the independence of the island itself.[27]

Years passed, and a whole new Dominican generation was born into Haiti's autocratic, but defiant, republicanism. Residents of the unified island grew up with independence and emancipation while in close contact with migrants, sailors, travelers, and traders from islands where slavery was steadfast. The freedmen regiments guarded the pacific Dominican capital the whole time, led by veteran officers of the Haitian Revolution. Haiti's constitution broadcast a welcome for people of color everywhere.[28] Groups of enslaved men and women from Jamaica arrived to the north coast in circuitous routes by small craft, hiding "under the lee of the Caicos reeds."[29] Others from Puerto Rico and the United States chose the Dominican capital and other towns, as they had done even in decades before Dominican emancipation. Purposefully eluding official notice, they left few traces.[30] Dominicans lived free and independent for sixteen years before hundreds of thousands of their neighbors won full emancipation in the British West Indies. The unified administration, meanwhile, survived despite French threats and the ominous burden of Haiti's so-called indemnity debt to France, which brought warships to Haitian shores. A veritable discursive defense industry sprang up in Haiti, defending black nationhood.[31] Dominican writers defended the administration, too.[32] Those arriving from the United States brought their own elegies about, and ideas of, Haitian freedom, as they joined and shaped various north coast communities.[33] Regionally, however, the island was entirely alone in political independence. All the islands in Dominicans' immediate political and commercial sphere—Saint Thomas, the Turks and Caicos Islands, Jamaica, Curaçao, Puerto Rico, Cuba—remained colonized, and the waters percolated with illegal human traffic. No other Caribbean territory inched toward self-rule.

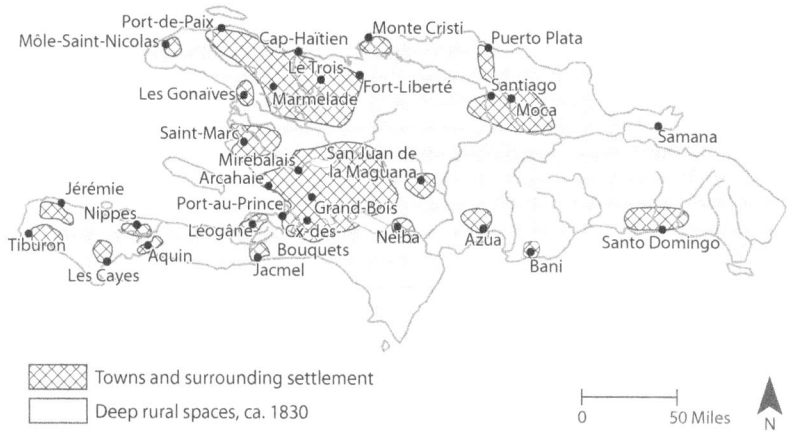

Map I.1 Map of settlement and rural spaces, ca. 1830. By Heather Rosenfeld. Adapted from Jean-Marie Dulix Théodat, *Haïti et la République dominicaine: Une île pour deux* (Paris: Karthala, 2003), 140, with the consultation of Neici Zeller and Raymundo González.

In early 1844, a small movement changed Dominican flags again, as dissidents in the east seceded and proclaimed a new state. Opponents, reform movements, and peasant opposition proliferated all over the island, from Les Cayes to Santo Domingo, fed up with Boyer's monopoly on the administration. Participants marveled at the pan-island catharsis from 1843 to 1844, during which "democracy flowed full to the brim."[34] Boyer fled the island, and the east seceded, all within a matter of months. At the time, the processes of early spring 1844 were commonly known as Separation. There was a fair amount of continuity, again, as the process unfolded. Dominican legislators merely adopted most of the articles of an 1843 joint reform constitution that almost ruled.[35] Moving forward in trying economic and political circumstances, politicians of Haiti and the Dominican Republic remained at once vulnerable and hopeful for greater integration. The nineteenth century, a journalist reported, was "the century of lights," and island elites expected it to shine on their own endeavors. "The world has taken on a new character . . . the fogs have disappeared and ignorance has taken refuge," another writer proclaimed.[36] Politicians praised Giuseppe Garibaldi, dreamed of participation in the rise of nations, and contemplated cash crop expansion. As in other states, debt, political and regional divisions, and frequent armed movements, driven by opponents with conscripted armies, challenged both administrations.[37] They warily took stock of the imperial climate, which seemed only to be worsening. "Every nation is free, as small as it might be, and has the right to make its own laws," the Dominican foreign minister proclaimed.[38]

Emancipation, Empire, and Caribbean Freedom

Caribbean independence faced more menacing scrutiny than Latin America's movements did. The liberation struggles of the Haitian Revolution unleashed an unrelenting torrent of international attention. Hemispheric master classes invoked Haiti's existence as a specter of black rebellion, and they used the moment to shore up and expand their own plantation regimes.[39] As a direct response to Haiti's independence, imperial authorities ruled surrounding islands in a state of exception.[40] After abolition in British and French islands, elites judged abolition to be a failure, compounding old discourses about the supposed dysfunction of sugar-island spaces with new layers of racist disappointment.[41] Authorities paid indemnity to slaveholders, tidily celebrated their own beneficence, restricted the rights of the emancipated, capaciously expanded indenture, and resented, judged, and excoriated the tenacious efforts of individuals and communities to carve out spaces of autonomy, even where land was scarce.[42] The fiction of experimentation, of "hopefulness," Diana Paton observes, was "itself profoundly connected to coercion and to ideas of white superiority."[43] Precisely through Caribbean emancipation, scientific racism enshrouded the putatively raceless liberal subject.[44] As plantation production declined—and postslavery peasantries grew—Britain opened up its islands to free trade, depressing prices further. Politicians began to recast the Caribbean sugar islands as an imperial burden, dependencies that a magnanimous, white empire would only have to bear as it expanded further.[45] British abolitionists envisaged Sierra Leone to be a refuge precisely in its capacity as an "anti-Caribbean" space where free labor would actually prevail.[46]

Opposition to Caribbean self-rule fed on these anti-emancipation narratives, racist pseudoscience, and an increasingly voracious imperial appetite. Scholars described neat hierarchies of race cultures and fantasized about permanent subordination. White travelers journeyed from island to island and told the same story: that the freed communities of color they encountered (or rather imagined) were "lazy," and their "wants . . . but few," their religious practice "witchcraft," their resolutions for self-governing, ultimately absurd.[47] Only force could compel these subjects to labor, imperial proponents argued. Maybe they would cease to exist entirely.[48] In the islands, political practice followed this useful pessimism. French authorities eliminated voting rights almost as soon as they were extended.[49] In Jamaica and other British possessions, white colonists deepened their commitment to empire and actively abnegated the island's self-rule. Independence, from the perspective of a white minority, was out of the question.[50] Caribbean indenture and new projects of Asian and African imperialism represented a global imperial promise that weathered, and even took strength from Caribbean abolition: unfree labor had an expanding territory, a brown or black face, and a lucrative future. As one U.S. southerner remarked, confidently, the increased interlinking of the world markets and imperial reach meant that the "civilized Nations of the Temperate Zone" would continue to profit from "tropical regions" after emancipation.[51] Powerful English figures, relentless, argued that slavery should not have been abolished at all.[52]

In the Spanish Caribbean forced labor and colonialism ruled. Sugar slavery dominated western Cuba, as planters reorganized, centralized, and expanded their holdings. Cuban planters, like their peers in the U.S. South and Brazil, had doubled down against emancipation, adopted technological innovation, expanded infrastructure, committed to the illegal slave trade, and profitably integrated brutal plantation regimes into growing international markets.[53] Colonial officials relied on elite loyalty in exchange for official undergirding of slavery.[54] Authorities made extensive inquiries into the reform and expansion of vagrancy laws, trying to draw rural and urban residents into state control.[55] In Puerto Rico, sugar and coffee production doubled from an amalgam of slave and free labor.[56] "Force could domesticate them externally, but they would continue internally to be bad citizens, disgruntled [infelices], and traitors, invisible enemies," one Puerto Rican official insisted.[57] Skepticism easily turned to persecution.[58] Nearly one in every four Cubans was enslaved, and the trade, though illegal, was massive. In Spain, abolitionist proponents amounted to "a voice in the wilderness."[59] Indenture complemented chattel trade. Spanish senator Argudín boasted that he planned the importation of forty thousand African "apprentices"; observers claimed he had struck a deal with the British to maintain slavery in Cuba until 1900.[60] Like pro-slavery advocates and imperial abolitionists alike, these authorities invoked the emancipated Caribbean as a specter. When the governor of Puerto Rico claimed that abolition led to "indolence and ruin," he directed his condemnation squarely at Haiti.[61]

Dominican separation from Haiti emerged at this precise midcentury moment of retrenchment and contest, in which Haiti faced a veritable "pro-slavery clamor," and pro-slavery entrenchment in the United States only grew louder.[62] Mapmakers and politicians of nearby Latin American nations, in their first decades of independence, increasingly distanced themselves from their own Caribbean shores, insisting that autonomy existed elsewhere. Intelligentsia in new nations like Costa Rica and Colombia invented normative Atlantic geographies, through which they drafted themselves outside of the Caribbean. Rather, they chose the "Atlantic" to bind them.[63] When representatives from Costa Rica, Mexico, New Granada, Peru, El Salvador, and Venezuela met to draft an emergency treaty meant to forestall U.S. incursion in the Caribbean and Central America in 1856, they did not invite either Haiti or the Dominican Republic, not only because they preferred not to but because neither had the formal recognition of the United States at all.[64] One African American author assessed Santo Domingo to be a dysfunctional, if fertile, space. He prescribed "Anglo-African empire" to better it.[65] Island politicians, keenly aware of the content and scope of discursive hostility, meticulously embraced Civilization's precepts. Referring to his invitation to African Americans to settle in Haiti in 1824, President Boyer wrote that he was saving them from "the alternative of going to the barbarous shores of Africa."[66] "Civilization is a fact in our days, a semiuniversal doctrine," a Dominican politician opined, agreeing—but pessimism, violence, and anxiety pursued them.[67]

The pact made by some Dominican elites in dialogue with hemispheric white supremacist and imperial pressures is infamous: effusive anti-Haitian intellectual production and racism. A vocal portion of Dominican elites blamed Haiti for their territory's ills, and they did so, from the earliest years, in explicitly racist terms.[68] Like other hemispheric elites, writers in the capital embraced dichotomous language: of progress versus backwardness, civilization versus barbarism, order versus atavism, Christianity versus fetishism, and Providence versus disorder; in the absolute weakness of their administration, they externalized the entire narrative.[69] To Dominican writers' distinct advantage, however, they conjured an external vector for their anxieties that outsiders readily embraced. A minority literate group in the Dominican capital and other towns, eager to cement distance between their national project and the west, began a furious anti-Haitian writing campaign. They excoriated Haiti's black citizenship as exclusionary; they reassured international imperial audiences of Dominican eagerness for outside (white) investment and capital. Several Haitian military mobilizations—but, overwhelmingly, the relentless poverty and precarity of the Dominican Republic itself—inflamed their sentiments. White travelers, journalists, and politicians from slaveholding societies wholeheartedly agreed with, and amplified, these Dominican elites' narrative of a race war on the island and agreed that protections against capital were backward, if not monstrous.[70] Accordingly, they demonstrated a preoccupation with the whiteness of the Dominican Republic—as a calculus for its annexionability as well as victimhood—that bordered on obsessive.[71] "The entire universe will judge between the haitians [sic] and the Dominicans," a Dominican writer unctuously agreed, and these accounts dominated new national narratives.[72]

Annexation, Belonging, and Sovereignty

Although scholars sometimes characterize Dominican annexationists as a uniquely conservative minority, politicians' recourse to outside aid and territorial cession was quite common throughout the hemisphere.[73] Annexationism embodied the crux of elite, lettered anxiety over "race," autonomy, and citizenship vis-à-vis a rural and nonwhite majority, regional divisions, a fractured partisan scene, economic difficulties, and imperial incursion. Especially in moments of economic necessity, politicians throughout the hemisphere toyed with outside intervention and territorial cession. Usually, these were short-term bargains to keep their own power against political opponents, but the projects sprang from a durable distrust of popular politics.[74] Annexation was an enduring psychological refuge and a political tactic. This experimentation was everywhere, but it was particularly enduring in the crucible of the Gulf of Mexico, where European powers, U.S. interests, and international pressures converged. Foreign reparations demands and outright aggression were common. Cuba's annexationists knew they had willing U.S. ears. Some Mexican elites, in turn, looked eagerly to the island.[75] As political turmoil and poverty plagued them, many Dominican elites decided nationhood was uncertain, even undesirable. Foreign interest in the poor territory, which began slowly, quickly grew more pronounced. Dominican annexationists were markedly omnivorous in response, offering their struggling administration every which way: to Britain, Spain, the Low Countries, the United States, Sardinia, and especially France.[76] "They know perfectly well that their republic, without any other resource than the port taxes of a few boats and the printing of continually depreciating paper money, isn't viable," one visitor to Santo Domingo asserted smugly.[77]

Spanish annexation of the Dominican Republic in 1861 tested an Atlantic empire in transition. As other scholars have observed, facile narratives of Spanish imperial decline after the 1820s preempt discussion of the political contests that followed.[78] As U.S. expansion, antislavery resistance, and the threat of Caribbean independence movements loomed, Spanish reformers realized administrative restructuring that had been debated since the independence movements several decades before, centralizing overseas administration. Constitutional representation remained in limbo, but Spain shared these debates with Britain, France, and other imperial powers that had not yet neatly codified distinctions between imperial and national subjects.[79] In settler projects on multiple continents, debates over incorporation and autonomy accelerated, vacillating between assimilation, association, and other models, as legislators circumscribed political inclusion along boundaries of lineage, "race," and culture.[80] Many Spanish liberals supported federalism, popular in new Latin American states as well, as a means to politically integrate, and save, Spain's Caribbean empire.[81] Cuban political elites looked to U.S. annexation and to the models of semi-autonomous government in the British Caribbean and Canada with pointed cupidity.[82] Simultaneously, Spanish authorities also quietly grappled with the idea of abolition in future decades. Puerto Rican plantation owners, without the capital to compete, tangled with the idea more immediately.[83] The Cuban governor, a driving force for annexation, proposed to incorporate the Dominican territory as a province without slavery, purposely to call the question of legislative unity and labor modes into debate. Once more, political impetus in the Caribbean catalyzed imperial debates.[84]

Annexationists exulted, at the same time, in a heterodox diffusion of racialist thinking, nationalist rhetoric, and imperial force. Massive territorial grabs, armed filibusters, trade imbalances, and conspiracies facilitated the urgent fraternal language on which Spanish and Dominican annexationists traded. Expansion by the United States, piratic and powerful, catalyzed urgent debates over race and political destiny among Latin American politicians, who began to identify collectively as such.[85] The language of the rights of nations, self-determination, and federalism saturated both American and Spanish political discourse.[86] Dominican and Spanish annexationists considered that a shared *raza*—a racial collective of language, religion, culture, and "blood"—offered a workable paradigm for Dominican integration, a "language of affiliation."[87] Dominican emissaries deployed fraternal narratives of Spanishness tactically in recognition missives, even as they made myriad appeals to other powers simultaneously. Just as in Central American contexts, their fraternity was a whitened one.[88] They asserted the existence of a "permanent war" with Haiti to an audience that was immediately receptive to a race-war paradigm. In response, Spanish annexationists traded on old revenge fantasies toward Haiti and lofty egalitarian promises in breezy tandem. Romantic language of racial destiny and voluntarism abetted utopian thinking and masked the violence of territorial gain. As other scholars have observed, proponents of these utopias usually indulged in free-soil claims that belied explicit plans for racial hierarchy.[89] A U.S. filibuster, meanwhile, suggested that the Dominican Republic could become "another California."[90] So the French consul dreamed of establishing a massive "immigrant empire" in Samaná.[91] Unaware of the territory's tiny and inconsistent electoral history, the Cuban governor enthusiastically swore not a single Spanish soldier would arrive until approved by universal suffrage.[92]

As with other imperial projects, discursive justifications were window dressing for economic and strategic interests that drove Spanish policy. Keen enthusiasm for renewed colonial expansion, or at least the preservation of Spanish Caribbean power, outweighed discourse about prestige, the reclamation of Columbus's island, and other florid narratives.[93] The territory's potential value in staving off U.S. interests was paramount. The Samaná peninsula was perfectly located to establish a coaling station. "Samaná is to the Gulf of Mexico what Mayotta is to the Indian Ocean," a British consul agreed. "It is not only the military, but also the commercial key of the Gulf."[94] Around the new administration, the coterie of Dominican elites gathered who ascribed to proposed projects of labor control and indenture schemes, distanced from the Dominican rural majority.[95] "I give you a people without journalists and devoid of lawyers," the Dominican president reportedly bragged.[96] Industrialists proposed a railroad "like the French have done from Puebla to Veracruz," canals and communication infrastructure "like the English have done in India," an import scheme "like Java or Mauritius," and a naval station to "block the mouth of the Mississippi."[97] Annexation was fundamentally experimental, but the Spanish officers felt confident that the moment demanded innovation. "Annexation of Santo Domingo is an event as rare as it is new . . . and it is beyond our normal rules," the Cuban governor urged. "Many of the measures we ought to adopt must also be of a most special and very extraordinary character."[98]

International imperial powers, meanwhile, ignored Dominican elites' pronouncements of Spanishness or, in fact, any narrative of Dominican agency. It was easy to imagine, in 1861, that an independent Caribbean nation might disappear. Massive territorial loss to the United States threw Mexican politics into a tailspin after 1848, Nicaraguans confronted armed conspiracies, and European groups launched a joint intervention in Mexico. These same countries deepened networks in Africa, moralized about so-called legitimate commerce, and mounted new plantation experiments. Commentators deployed toward the island the same benevolence narratives honed in other imperial sites. "The Christian and the Philanthropist must hail the event which will put Hayti under any influence or dominion," one pamphleteer declared.[99] "Dominicana has a government—so poets have empires," a U.S. man concluded, predicting their demise.[100] A French columnist urged Spanish authorities to discard the voluntary pretext. "[Spain] would do better just simply to say that she is retaking Santo Domingo because she wants to," he remarked dispassionately.[101] Finally, other European powers looked with equanimity and even approval on Dominican annexation not only because they naturalized its absorption but because, at a crucial moment of U.S. weakness, Spanish annexation might forestall several decades of U.S. expansion in the Gulf. The timing was incredibly propitious. Just months before annexation began, states in the U.S. South began to secede, one by one.

The Living Nightmare of Slavery

Beyond the capital, confronting the critical test of annexation, were the people. A small canon of early national writing, from a tiny group of elites, obscures them relentlessly. As Raymundo González observes, elites' "antipeasant, racist mindset" sprang from their disdain for the very formation of the Dominican peasantry itself, which was born, in many areas, from an independent rural maroon population who worked on the margins of cattle society or entirely for their own subsistence.[102] Elites were studiously silent on race not only out of putative republicanism but precisely in defiance of Haiti's privileging of black citizenship. The relentless invective directed toward Haiti for its defense of black sovereignty compounded their silence further; Dominican elites defined the nation as the purposeful absence of these discussions.[103] As Haitian heads of state issued periodic invitations for African American migrants, Dominican ministers secretly wrote to agents in New York demurring any new schemes of black migration.[104] Rumors of black migrants' arrival spurred alarm among officials, who wanted migrants from the Canary Islands, Spain, or another European country.[105] A submerged wave of popular politics burgeoned in the rural areas and towns, which elites minimized and denied as they gambled with foreign powers and renarrated Dominican identity. Politicians regularly ignored popular antiracism and anti-imperialism, even when it led to public protests, as they toyed with slave powers on a razor's edge. Writers admitted that popular warnings about reenslavement, for example, were an *"eternal ghost . . . the nightmare of slavery,"* but insisted they were a ridiculous relic, "from the time of Boyer."[106]

Most Dominicans left no written response. There was no planter class fastidiously observing them, no logbook, no epistolary archive. There was no archivist even of the Dominican government for the first fifteen years of separation.[107] Rural residents lived outside of documentation regimes as they made lives from woodcutting, hunting, livestock, honey and wax, and limited coffee production.[108] Contraband, slow and small-scale migration, and the lived geographic linkages to nearby island towns and coasts produced little record. Transportation between any of the regions was difficult, usually undertaken by horse or mule. Carts, even small ones, were largely limited to the towns, further impeding trade.[109] Communities relied more on orality than the written word, personal distribution of justice rather than bureaucratic dissemination, local networks more than state ambit and resources, interpersonal obligations more than contracts, usufruct rights versus titled ownership, subsistence rhythms more than other parameters of time, and so on. As for labor, their governing logic was more the moral economy of a day's manual labor than "labor discipline" in any industrial iteration, slow or seasonal production and storage more than accumulation or capitalization, and a relative nonspecialization of labor, except perhaps along gendered lines. Like other peasantries with limited market production, there was little tying them to administrative centers.[110] Their dispersal was a purposeful, centuries-old marronage.[111] As a contemporary observed from one central valley town, they were the children of slavery.[112]

We Dream Together explores a political consensus shared by this rural majority, and also by many in towns: vigilance over emancipation outside of plantation spaces, anticolonial commitment, keen understanding of the racism that surrounded them, and discourses of community and pride they articulated in response. Although they left no writing, seeking "collective biographies and community studies" reveals the many intersecting frames of a precarious entente.[113] Dominican autonomy emerged out of decades of revolutionary fighting and struggle, of small-scale regional migration, interchange, and constant domestic conversations, vigilance, and esteem. Throughout the territory, Dominicans' commonsense assumptions differed gravely from the small group who held power in the capital. Understanding of emancipation and independence was grounded in generations of conversation and interchange, at the heart of popular sentiment, and directed to defense of the whole island against outside hostility, which many understood to be constant.[114] Scholars of annexation often analyze it in nationalist terms. These interpretations tend to downplay domestic discussions about racism, which elites refused to record, as well as Dominicans' engagement with the ongoing battles over emancipation throughout the Caribbean.[115] As with many rural would-be citizens throughout the hemisphere, Dominicans shared a commitment to relative egalitarianism, general rights to political decision-making in one's community (a personhood more expansive than bourgeois citizenship), and a hybrid assemblage of positive rights, including that of military belonging.[116] The most important of these rights was probably the right to the means of subsistence (that is, independence and land), and for many it also included a certain degree of autonomy from the reaches of a formal state. With annexation, their articulation became clear.[117]

The middle chapters of this book detail the immediate conflicts that Dominicans confronted in the new occupation, as the colonial project immediately betrayed Spain's fraternal promises. In the face of material scarcity and subsistence labor, administrators constantly produced colonial difference in narrative and practice. Their registers were marvel, classification, and disdain.[118] Officials passed a series of reforms that were abrasive and alien, and the frank racism of everyday officials betrayed their explicitly race-blind mandates. Both parties felt they had preexisting knowledge of each other, and neither was pleased. The occupation was intimately linked to plantation slavery. The captain general of Cuba planned it, Spanish troops who had recently been stationed in Cuba guarded it, Cuban coffers funded expansion, and secret slaving missions buzzed the island's north coast as the Cuban governor celebrated the inauguration of Jefferson Davis.[119] Even when the project was only a rumor, widespread rejection and anticolonial sentiment were evident in Dominican territory. One early small uprising over enslavement, quickly crushed, ought to have warned authorities of the conflicts to come. Legend grew around the man who had led the small revolt in the next two years after his trial and execution; residents said that he was very old, blind, heroic.[120] Within weeks of the first renewed rebellion, fighting exploded across the territory. Popular anticolonialism, republicanism, citizenship language, and ties of solidarity with Haiti flooded public discourse against the Spanish, which became known as the War of Restoration.

The rebellion gave voice to rural politics, trenchant critiques of colonial despotism, and republican and democratic ideas that outpaced feasible implementation. As in many rural uprisings, including the Haitian Revolution, authorities had little inkling of the scale of the battle before them.[121] Everyone commented, in awe, on the popular nature of the war. "The current revolution was the masses rising up, dragging the rest with them," a town resident marveled.[122] The Dominican former president supposed that the mobilization was a military one, that he could simply neutralize the uprising by going after prominent opponents. He was wrong; the rebellion was more massive and more total than anything that had come before in his lifetime.[123]

Fear of reenslavement, particularly, electrified the whole territory. These slavery discussions, which Spanish authorities characterized as "rumor," were rather a precise window into the living discussions of autonomy, an unwritten assessment of Caribbean emancipation as news of other contests reached Dominican shores, and only lastly a response to the precipitously arrived new state.[124] They were ubiquitous, and the fighting spread like a whirlwind. Whole families left towns and refused to return. Rebels barely had munitions, but they were willing to burn their own towns to destroy Spanish advantage. The Spanish were exasperated. "In Santo Domingo one fights against invisible enemies," one lamented, "chasing ghosts."[125]

Rebels had heterogeneous tactics, allegiances, and goals. The war had no front line. As in other Caribbean contests, Dominicans and their allies resisted the Spanish troops in local networks that were constantly shifting, with very little outside help.[126] They called on decades of experience. Mobilization—even the very language of it—called on the island's shared military history.[127] Average soldiers who had previously fought for separation came to call for reunification.[128] Prominent generals espoused a range of ideologies. Like other midcentury leaders, their language was capacious, often contradictory, with ample space for pragmatism.[129] As with the loyalists, there was a portion of the rebel leadership who clung to an absolute silence on race, who insisted any mention of it was "unprincipled," that their fight was one of raceless national liberation.[130] All these leaders made overtures to the Haitian president, however, calling on his republicanism. Members of the newly formed Provisional Government extolled, "Liberty! Liberty! Poetry in every language!"[131] As the fighting continued, a more radical leadership grew to share popular irreverence toward civilizationist claims, and their anticolonial vocabulary became more explicit. Their overtures to Haiti, especially, reflected a "black recognitionist" discourse.[132] They praised the real democracy of Restoration ranks, called for direct suffrage, and moved to forge lasting alliances with other anticolonial activists. Other leaders, in horror, sought to topple them.

Dominicans and their Haitian allies defeated the Spanish in 1865, with the rapt attention of regional neighbors and increasing anticolonial ties. One Spanish senator invoked the Haitian Revolution and recent rebellions in India when he called, in vain, for a massive troop surge to crush them.[133] News of Spanish defeat spread even faster than in earlier decades, as prisoners, travelers, missives, elegies, newspapers, sailors, and returning troops circulated descriptions of Hispaniola's triumph. Dominican rebel leaders traveled, too, reaching Curaçao, Saint Thomas, Venezuela, New York, Grand

Turk, Haiti, Mayagüez, and numerous other ports. Together with other anticolonial activists from other islands, they acted with a keen sense of a heroic and historic present. The fighting inaugurated a period, much like Latin American independence that preceded it, that was "improvised and reactive . . . [a] time of macrosocial change."[134] Plans for an independent Caribbean federation bloomed. The fraternity that bound them was hybrid and multiple.[135] Rulers came and went; some stayed long past their welcome. Rebels often found themselves in outright antistate alliances. But new anticolonial alliances formed; imperial pressure constantly renewed them. Coastal towns served as vital regional outposts centuries after their outsize importance in the construction of Caribbean empire.

The Dominican War of Restoration coincided with, and contributed to, a renewal of emancipation energy, won through tenacious, constant fighting. As independence and antislavery fighting began in Cuba, Hispaniola provided concrete and ideological refuge in a deeply transcolonial space.[136] Intra-Caribbean migration accelerated, as thousands left for seasonal work, and steam travel, for some residents, made the Caribbean smaller by increments.[137] Even those who were not supporters of pan-Caribbean federation readily admitted its feasibility. "The idea of the 'Antillean League' can be realized one day, the day that Great Britain gives its permission . . . , so the Spanish Government should open its eyes," predicted one prominent Dominican liberal.[138] Idealists rallied for political "regeneration" and fraternal, voluntary alliances that could bridge political divides, defeat logistical difficulties, and overturn absolutism. Technological changes like the telegraph abetted their sense of the possible. "This is quite an era in [the] West Indian story," a visiting Jamaican man remarked.[139] In a hard won moment, optimists felt like all tides might rise, that Providence and progress might uplift everyone.[140]

Independence and Sacrifice

Independence came at a high cost. Imperial threats and state fragility kindled the new political experiments. As with other new states, on Hispaniola there were "a number of competing utopias," political frames that ranged from regional autonomy, to larger federations, to projects of sheer personal ambition.[141] Coalitions of guerrilla fighters trickled apart as the fighting ended, as individuals and families returned to their homes in a devastated landscape. In the division and exhaustion on Dominican soil, a wealthy, prominent political figure, a familiar face, handily reclaimed power. Once again there was a widening of the distance between popular visions and the praxis of those at the helm. Foreign attention, and loan offers, loomed. There existed a "mercantile oligarchy, that has never been Dominican, and has always used any means to realize its traitorous plans," one veteran protested, in exasperation.[142] After Restoration fighting, opponents of annexation still felt the danger acutely. The scope of their imagination sprang not just from optimism but also from the relative insecurity of the two nations themselves, and possibility took root not only from a hostile international climate but also from internal regionalism, separatism, fracture, and repression. Many idealists lived lives of almost constant fighting. In "stable . . . instability," life went on.[143]

Popular solidarities, forged by Dominicans, Haitians, and their neighbors, faced concrete and discursive opposition. Dominican elites renarrated the fighting even as it was happening. Within forty years, an unrecognizable narrative expunged all of the uncertainty, all plural visions, and all of the contests of the period. A small group of writers supplanted them with tales of the heroism of a single blond-haired, blue-eyed man who was barely in Dominican territory at all during these decades, Juan Pablo Duarte.[144] They re-remembered separation from Haiti as cataclysmic and the devotion of the Dominican public to nation as unwavering and inevitable.[145] In the gendered memory production of military glory, authors redrafted women's signal contribution to Restoration fighting into larger narratives of abnegation.[146] Through the eyes of an exile narrative, in fact, the nation became a morality tale of tragedy, sacrifice, and obedience for most Dominicans.[147] Outsiders minimized and marginalized the guerrilla war, too, in decades that followed. With independence and pan-Caribbean organizing famously described as "Cuba and Puerto Rico, two wings of the same bird," the geographic body, in the form of Haiti and the Dominican Republic, sustains the wings without mention.[148] In the wake of these willful counternarratives, authors work hard to recover the neglected historiographical space for Haitian political thought in the east, when elites sought to silence it most avidly.[149] Popular memories eluded this erasure, refused silencing, and frustrated the discipline of these unitary narratives. So Dominican authorities must have worried, when they arrested a group of men and women for commemorating the War of Restoration with vodou rites during Trujillo's dictatorship sixty years later, in the heart of the capital.[150]

Being alive on Hispaniola in those decades, on either side of the island, kindled a constant and vigilant defense of autonomy itself. President Boyer's Tree of Liberty on Dominican soil—adopted, embraced, toppled, mourned, forgotten—exemplifies the vibrant faith in autonomous citizenship, born of the revolution, that emerged on both sides of the island and endured across generations, but that always faced incredible contest. In a critical moment in a fight for self-rule, many Dominican rebels overwhelmingly rejected divisive narratives that had brought about annexation itself. In their solidarity, enduring and obvious, Haitian citizens helped them frankly, repeatedly, generously, and simply because their own survival was also at stake. It was a collection of battles that escaped the control of the leaders for a time. In the political and military contests that followed, these active negotiations continued. Investment, capitalization, and industrialization loomed, but neither the rate, nor the authors, nor the impact was predetermined. One writer described the pitched struggle that persisted: "Tyranny and liberty fight each other tenaciously and fiercely: the first are all the forces of hate and desperation, the second, love for the homeland and hope for the future."[151]

ONE

Life by Steam

THE DOMINICAN REPUBLIC'S FIRST REPUBLIC, 1844–1861

"*The people are miserable:*—true, but not as much as in the Haitian time," a journalist in Santo Domingo argued in late summer 1846, two years after Separation. "*Paper money has no value:*—it has more than that of the Haitians," the author persisted.[1] In the Dominican capital, columnists condemned Haitian politics in order to externalize political scrutiny and to deny the dire, authoritarian political drama that was unfolding in Santo Domingo at the same time. They allowed themselves considerable hyperbole. "We have a liberal Constitution and an honorable and patriotic leader who executes it punctually," one writer boasted, hopefully. He claimed that the newly separated east would have reduced military forces and civil rights for all citizens.[2] Instead, repression and insecurity mounted. "The public is groaning in misery," another admitted.[3] Soldiers mocked the new Dominican motto ("God, Country, Liberty"), changing it to "God, Country, Slavery, and Lean Meat."[4] Residents of the capital marked the anniversary of the constitution signing with "embarrassing coldness and indifference," and one man compared the new republic to someone slowly dying of fever.[5]

Over a series of months between 1843 and 1845, as President Jean-Pierre Boyer's power collapsed, Haiti fractured into two administrations. In chaotic and depressed circumstances, the men who held on to the reins of power in the east, the newly independent Dominican Republic, were largely the same southern elite who had worked with the Unification regime. The first Dominican president, Pedro Santana, rose to power at the head of an army of loyal followers from his home province, and his prestige made him a "true feudal seigneur," contemporaries observed.[6] Buenaventura Báez, the man who emerged to be Santana's primary political rival, was a large landowner. Well traveled and wealthy, Báez was a high-level politician who easily weathered the changes in flag. Separation came easily, but consolidating a new state proved difficult. In the Dominican capital, a tiny electorate rallied around the administration, but censorship, exile, and executions cooled the atmosphere. Alternating terms in power, Santana and Báez controlled the administration with heavy hands. Both invoked a war powers clause of the constitution, Article 210, for autocratic license. They used the clause domestically, restricting freedom of the press, relentlessly pursuing critics, and trading off power in a continuous pattern of usurpation, corruption, and revenge.[7] Reformers had little recourse but to complain about "the plague of parties."[8]

Most Dominicans, meanwhile, lived far from the capital, independent and dispersed. No export bonanza or internal migration brought them in closer contact, nor could authorities in Santo Domingo generate resources with which to expand their administration.[9] Internal travel was treacherous, and small boats, *yolas* or *balandras*, were the only practicable way to reach other coastal towns.[10] After decades of flag changes and rural independence, power had devolved "from one to many": to regional military networks, family units, religious brotherhoods, tobacco, wood, and cattle trade, and, only lastly, to the nominative southern administration.[11] As Separation unfolded, the idea of a new republic did not extend beyond a handful of towns.[12] Residents might have considered themselves at various points "Haitian-Spanish," "Dominican-Spanish," or even "not Spanish nor French nor Haitian"; more likely still, they embraced local identities that were more salient.[13] Residents of the north coast were deeply tied with Cap-Haïtien, surrounding islands, and the Atlantic. In the Cibao, politicians wealthy from tobacco trade pulled away from the capital. They wanted a federalization of power, or to relocate the government totally. In the center of the island, the unpopularity of Haiti's emperor stymied solidarities for a time, but residents were hardly faithful. In the new state, domestic flashpoints became more critical with each passing year.

This chapter details how citizens made their lives between foreign powers and political revolution. Even in the capital, few people thought autonomy was possible.[14] British, French, U.S., and Spanish authorities intervened constantly in Dominican affairs. They jockeyed for competing concessions, supported various protectorate, citizenship, or colonization schemes, manipulated treaty negotiations, meddled in domestic political struggles, demanded indemnities, sent warships as implied menace, and generally intervened aggressively for their own interests, all while withholding recognition.

As capital city figures made increasing bargains with these powers, residents engaged in active debates about identity and citizenship. Feeling anxiety over the future, Dominicans in multiple sites responded to these developments with steady vigilance, frequent protests, and warnings of slavery. From rural, center-island spaces, where decades of trade, travel, and political connection tied them to Haiti, military men occasionally drew a handful of local residents into intrigues to reunite the island. As years passed, the very fragility of the Dominican administration, wracked with political competition, economic crises, and growing imperial aggression, made these pacts more urgent. The grip of the capital was loosening.

Reform and Separation, 1843–1846

Unification of the whole island, which began in early 1822, lasted under the rule of President Boyer for two decades. After abolition in Unification's first days, many lived life much as before.[15] In towns, the administration had an uneven impact. The government employed several hundred officials in the Dominican capital and dozens in other towns. Much of the quotidian administration continued in Spanish.[16] Prominent Dominicans like Manuel Joaquín Delmonte earnestly and unctuously praised the regime. "Let us all toast to the day that the knot that binds us gets tighter," he urged, from a Masonic lodge called "Perfect Harmony" in Azua.[17] Black regiments in and around the capital, which predated Unification, enjoyed larger ranks and status.[18] Black Dominicans forged "the tightest of bonds" with arriving Haitian soldiers and administrators, one traveler remarked.[19] In the Cibao valley, Dominican tobacco merchants and others benefited from stability and government support.[20] In rural areas, the reach of the state was minimal.[21] As years passed, however, and as outside observers heaped noisy judgment on Boyer's regime, fissures grew.[22] Boyer's autocratic style, the political and economic burden of a so-called indemnity debt to France, regional divisions, and a plurality of other grievances rankled an increasing number of political opponents.[23] Dominican periodicals later blamed a parasitic administration and a bloated administrative and military class.[24] Boyer's aides had sheltered him from rumblings of discontent for years, the journalists argued.[25] By the early 1840s, a significant group in the Dominican capital had begun to support separation, Delmonte and other former Unification supporters included. In the west, anti-Boyer voices grew louder simultaneously.

A natural disaster accelerated the fracture, heralding a providential reckoning. A massive earthquake struck the heart of Haiti on 7 May 1842. It seemed like the apocalypse. In towns across the island, "not one stone was left on top of the other," an observer wrote in horror. The calamity destroyed homes, churches, and businesses and left thousands more on the brink of collapse. Visible devastation surrounded the living. On the northern coast, from Port-de-Paix to Monte Cristi, a wall of seawater flooded over residents. Rivers overflowed, and the deluge covered whole fields. Violent aftershocks "frightened and made the people more desperate." The island's capital, Port-au-Prince, burned day and night on end.[26] "I will tell you the horror, the death, the tears, the endless havoc into which the miserable nation of Haiti has sunk," an eastern poet wrote. "What confusion! What horror! What fright!" He wrote of religious fear and of the "reckless pride" of his compatriots, swallowed up in a horrible din.[27] A hurricane followed that summer. Port-au-Prince burned again in the beginning of the new year.[28]

Boyer's regime, already on the precipice of collapse, quickly crumbled. Political "excitement . . . spread like a contagion to every nook," observers reflected.[29] Earnest island liberals, Dominican separatists and annexationists, ambitious military figures of varying allegiances, prominent southern Haitian families, and growing rural opposition in the western south all vied for power. A handful of Dominican nationalists had recently returned to Santo Domingo from San Juan, inspired by liberal discontent and pro-independence murmurings in the late 1830s.[30] They joined a secret society in the capital, the Trinitarios, whose members were a small group of urban elite with insular family and geographic ties.[31] Their critiques were moderate but increasingly nationalist in elocution. Other plans proliferated, including renegotiating the terms of Unification. Dominican commentators remembered the possibilities of the moment acutely. "It seems to me that Boyer knew best the true path of happiness for all Haitians," one Dominican wrote, decades later. "He was only wrong about one thing: not having founded the union of the two pueblos on a more equal and advantageous base, for example a confederation," he concluded.[32]

From different sites, anti-Boyerists tried to salvage a federation. In Les Cayes, Haitian and Dominican reformers formed the Society of the Rights of Man and Citizen, demanding wide-ranging government changes.[33] At a constitutional convention in Port-au-Prince, Puerto Plata deputy Federico Peralta y Rodríguez spoke frankly of "atrocious oppression . . . and total ruin" of many prominent families—his frankness already revolutionary—but also expressed enthusiasm for proposed reforms, "so liberal and democratic"

Fig. 1.1 Domingo Echavarría (1805–1849, attributed), "Terremoto en la isla de Haití," 1842. Colección bibliográfica J. R. Marquez, Santo Domingo.

as they were. He and others hoped for serious constitutional changes.[34] Reformers tried to save the union, drafting a Haitian-Dominican Constitution that was unmistakably liberal, according much more power to the legislative branch, abolishing presidency-for-life, and reducing the army. They hoped to maintain and strengthen island unity, proposing a trilingual national school (English, Spanish, and French).[35] In Santo Domingo, meanwhile, Haitian opposition leaders Alcius Ponthieux and General Étienne Desgrotte plotted together with Dominican Trinitaria members to take the fort of the capital in the spring of 1843, but no mobilization materialized. In solidarity, whole regiments deserted Boyer's unpopular campaign against the southwestern conspiracy.[36] Boyer fled for Jamaica in February 1843, ending more than two decades of rule.

As months passed, however, political turmoil increased. General Charles Rivière-Hérard increasingly presided over the reform convention and maneuvered to impose his authority, proclaiming himself president. He received, and then imprisoned, Trinitario emissary Ramón Mella, as he moved to squash other reforms. Southern Haitian peasants protested his betrayal and mobilized independently; the movement became known as the Piquet Rebellion.[37] A popular song rebuked the presidential usurper:

> President Rivière was cross-eyed!
> He thought he was the king!
> He thought he was the king!
> He thought he was the king![38]

Dominican commentators expressed dismay. An editorial critiqued Rivière's January 1844 Constitution and scolded him for his excesses, calling him a "dictator who only use[d] the liberal title of president."[39] "[Without our cooperation] the revolution would not have been more than a crazy plan," another disillusioned Dominican columnist reflected. "And what was our prize . . . ? What were the considerations, the improvements, the guarantees, for our unalienable rights? Dark dungeons in Port-au-Prince!"[40]

French interference loomed as many Dominican politicians grew divided between separation or a French protectorate. From Port-au-Prince, a prominent southern Dominican, Buenaventura Báez, tried to sabotage other movements. He warned Rivière of Dominican opposition and furiously tried to conspire for a French protectorate instead, continuing to do so after he became the mayor of the Dominican town of Azua.[41] "Frenchified" Dominicans (los afrancesados) in Azua boasted their own flag: red and white vertical stripes, with a small tricolor in the top-left corner.[42] The strongest clarion call for total separation from Haiti was actually Azuans' demand for French annexation; authors of a separation statement from the Dominican capital simply called for provincial autonomy.[43] Meanwhile, prominent rancher Pedro Santana led a military mobilization for separation from further east, marshaling a loyal band of peons and peasants from his home province, Seybo. He wrote confidentially that he feared many Dominicans opposed separation, and may have even briefly lent his own allegiance to the French cause.[44]

French officials collaborated and encouraged Dominican protectorate plans, but they insisted that residents of the east continue to pay Haiti's indemnity. In a menacing and opportunistic stance, they lobbied for cession of the Samaná peninsula in exchange.[45] Diplomats felt confident that the plan could be secured in a matter of weeks.[46] Both Unification and protectorate advocates faltered; the indemnity was a major sticking point, even for reform proponents. Cap separatists made a last-minute call to make a new North Haiti–Dominican union—they freed all Dominican prisoners in the town, designed a new red and blue flag with a star at the center, and sent overtures proposing a federative alliance to central and northern Dominican towns—but eastern observers worried that a clash with France was imminent. Unity seemed too costly.[47]

Quietly, secession proceeded in the Dominican capital and spread piecemeal to other towns. With most western troops already departed, a group of Dominicans proclaimed Separation in Santo Domingo, fairly uneventfully, on 27 February 1844. A number of Haitian residents in the town openly supported the movement, and a handful of Dominican residents left for Saint Thomas to avoid taking sides.[48] Official secession occurred the next day, with a cordial withdrawal accord for property guarantees, respect, dignity, and "frankness and loyalty" on all sides.[49] In March, the leading men of several towns in the Cibao valley and elsewhere declared themselves in favor of an eastern republic. As news reached Haiti, President Rivière called for a mobilization. Trying to reach the Dominican capital, he occupied Azua, where Santana defeated him. Dominicans quickly defeated his auxiliary in Santiago, too, and a series of small skirmishes in border towns came to little that spring. Some central towns changed hands several times, but the encounters often involved only small groups of soldiers.[50] Southern Haitian peasants, still in a democratic mobilization of their own, observed Rivière's defeat by Dominicans with satisfaction. "The Spaniards chased him, he ran like a dog after fresh carrion!," one song rebuked him.[51] Losing everywhere, Rivière was unseated by May 1844. He, too, left for Jamaica.[52]

As Pablo Mella observes, traditional accounts maintain a conspiracy of silence about Dominican racism and class divisions, framing the uncertainty of 1844 as mere conflict between "liberal" and "conservative" factions.[53] Among the tiny formal political class there did exist a plurality of positions, of course, and regional elites in the Cibao also hoped for power. Much more salient, however, were the divides between the tiny elite who were assuming power and most Dominicans. These were the men in the capital whom most dubbed "white Spaniards," whom many residents considered almost a foreign group.[54] Defiantly, the Separation junta held whites-only meetings, and government emissaries bragged to foreign authorities that it had been whites who had led Separation.[55] At one meeting, liberal Juan Pablo Duarte proposed an amendment arguing, "The unity of race . . . is one of the fundamental principles of our political adhesion," but to his alarm, other attendees tore up the proposal.⁵⁶ At the head of the military forces, Santana aligned himself with these prominent whites, who appealed abroad for recognition, annexation, and white immigration simultaneously.⁵⁷ Santana's collusion with these elites disgusted and worried prominent military officers of color in the capital, even those who had previously supported him.⁵⁸ Town residents were abuzz that the group was considering reinstating slavery, either in a new Gran Colombia-like federation, like the pro-slavery separation movement of 1821, or through a French protectorate.⁵⁹ A colonel of the African Battalion, Santiago Basora, blocked the entry of separatist forces to the capital.⁶⁰ General José Joaquín Puello, a prominent officer from the Unification period, joined Duarte and others in spreading the alarm among soldiers and concerned citizens.

Tension between the governing group and the town's black regiments and other citizens peaked during the summer. To counter General Puello and to silence nervous town residents, Santana arrived with two thousand of his own followers from outside the city. In a tense compromise, Santana allowed Puello to keep command of the plaza, and several of the most vocal antiblack Junta members resigned.⁶¹ The governing group published a decree in July reaffirming the abolition of slavery. Later the same month uproar returned to the capital, however, when a wealthy planter arrived from Puerto Rico, intent on recapturing nine men who had escaped to freedom. The group of men, who had already joined the town's black regiment, recognized the slavemaster on the street, and a large group of armed Dominicans aided them in cornering him in a private house. The men's protectors very nearly attacked Santana, who arrived to the planter's rescue. Promising to jail him, Santana merely snuck him off in a boat under the cover of night. Santana went on the offensive, trying to neutralize the black regiments entirely. He dispatched many of them off to the border, "with extensive promises about their continuing liberty."⁶² To assuage the alarm of town residents, the Junta reiterated once more that Santo Domingo was free soil and decreed that any Dominican who mounted a slave voyage would be classified a pirate, tried, and executed.⁶³ Assuming the title of "Supreme Chief of the Republic," however, Santana expelled and exiled a number of the reformist legislators. Observers continued to report that the government, other than Santana, was all white.⁶⁴

Adding their support to the opposition, families and soldiers in the outskirts of the capital and the center-island distrusted new Dominican rule and continued to support Unification. Through July 1845, a number of men in Santa María refused to join the new Dominican forces, convinced that the project was to reestablish slavery.[65] Unification loyalists raised the Haitian flag in San Juan, Las Matas, and Bánica in 1846; authorities from the capital gave chase and made arrests as best they could. In the spring of the following year, rumors of unification intrigue in these same central towns rose again. Only "brute force" pacified the towns, an observer noted.[66] Some military officials changed sides in the ensuing months, throwing their allegiance back to Unification.[67] Arrests continued on the border and in the capital, and rumors abounded. Within the year, Santana executed several prominent Trinitarios and military men of color in the capital, including General José Joaquín Puello and his brother, Gabino, just before Christmas. The power struggle had reached a dramatic moment. All manner of town elites were satisfied with the executions, including proponents of a French protectorate. Unrepentant biographers later claimed Puello was simply "arrogant" and "hostile to the white race."[68]

By the end of the year, a small administration finally solidified around Santana, who ruled autocratically. Legislators borrowed 113 articles of the new Dominican constitution directly from the defunct Port-au-Prince reform constitution of 1843.[69] They kept much of the civil code, but they attacked civil marriage and a recent expansion of women's property rights.[70] Santana filled his cabinet largely with loyal allies. Unification authorities had appropriated church lands around the capital into state possession; Santana maintained control over these properties and simply distributed them among his supporters.[71] He pursued his opponents and perceived opponents quickly and mercilessly. Some wrote anguished poetry from exile.[72] Observers compared his government to a hierarchical "family" and his forces, who were mostly from his home province, to his "henchmen."[73] One columnist rhapsodized about Santana's "tender and sweet name," while another wrote a thinly veiled poem critical of the "abuse of a father."[74] Archbishop Thomas de Portes threatened excommunication to Santana's opponents.[75] Santana wielded his military power constantly, justifying his heavy-handed rule on the pretext of permanent war with Haiti. Observers were not convinced of Santana's feeble justification for his virtual dictatorship. "The War with the Haitians is preoccupying weak spirits and serving as a pretext to the malintentioned and egotistical, who benefit exclusively from the revolution," one Spanish official wrote.[76]

The rest of Separation was anticlimactic. A short-lived successor to Rivière, General Jean-Louis Michel Pierrot, tried to mount a campaign to take the Dominican capital. Dominican columnists appealed directly to a hypothetical Haitian readership to chide Pierrot for his hypocrisy and lament the continued fighting. Pierrot was just "a puppet chosen by Boyeristas," and serious political men were fleeing the violence, one argued.[77] Capital city writers became bellicose, even bloodthirsty. One poet rhapsodized about the "last Haitian biting the dust" in battle.[78] They told sentimental fables of Dominican unity and exaggerated Haitian excesses. Priests argued Separation was divinely ordained; papers republished their sermons.[79] The paper's editors announced that every issue of Santo Domingo's first regular newspaper, El Dominicano, would "refute the apocryphal writings" from official presses in Port-au-Prince that claimed official Haitian victories.[80] Dominican papers ridiculed hawkish propaganda for its dishonesty to the Haitian public.[81] They need not have bothered; or, rather, the whole island was in agreement. Haitian enlisted men refused to mobilize, and Pierrot's own troops overthrew him. They did so, not casually, on the 27 February 1846.[82] With the periodic border spats all but uneventful, Dominican journalists turned their focus to economic and political concerns.[83]

The new administration's economic predicament was dire and urgent. Foreign currency was the only hard specie, British and Saint Thomas merchants demanded exorbitant loan terms, the government printed reams of paper money, and even prominent men from the capital refused to lend the new administration any funds. Beleaguered elites bragged of extroversion and dreamed of foreign capital, condemning the supposed isolation of the wealthier state from which they had just emerged. Haiti's property protections, Dominican journalists and politicians argued, were as "absurd as they were ridiculous."[84] In reality, many Haitian elites shared the same capital development dreams, publishing front-page critiques of barriers to foreign investment and land ownership and promoting cash crop production.[85] Dominican policy vis-à-vis immigration and investment, anyway, remained more similar to Haitian law—or Mexican, which they also occasionally excoriated—than different.[86] Lawmakers passed a 30 percent tax on the sale of territory to foreigners, who also had to rely on individual dispensation of naturalization from the president.[87] Critically, they maintained a Unification-era policy of restricting foreign traders to wholesale activity.[88] They also left tariffs at Unification levels.[89]

Boasting of their extroversion was essentially a rhetorical exercise, one which Dominican elites could practice without particular consideration for consequences: few investors came. Meanwhile, the entire state budget hovered between $200,000 and $300,000, declining slightly over time.[90] Domestic agriculture was insufficient even to maintain the population; all manner of things were imported into towns of the republic, even staples like flour.[91]

Grass grew in capital city streets, and houses slowly crumbled.[92] The trade balance was abysmal. "In Saint Thomas *se vende pero no se compra*," journalists lamented.[93]

Geography, Racism, and Town Politics

Over the next two decades, a small group held power. Both of the republic's first long-ruling presidents were wealthy men of color. Pedro Santana was born in the rural center of the island and grew up in the cattle country of the east. The son of a military hero, he confidently justified his power as a heroic crusade, immune to outside assessment.[94] Divine vindication and a loyal army afforded him pronounced immunity to any sort of deference. Years later, he pointedly received the Cuban governor barefoot.[95] Imperial outsiders directed racism, disdain, and pity toward these presidents. White French observers could not contain themselves from commenting on the texture of President Báez's hair, nor from mocking the impoverished girls of the capital.[96] The political coterie around the executive, meanwhile, except for high military officials, was largely white. Baptized in twenty-two years of governance with the revolutionary Haitian state, these figures never publicly breathed a word against either leader along racist lines, even as small snippets of song from the capital betray how phenotype preoccupied them.[97] As power was reshuffling at the beginning of the republic, a few liberals did speak about race openly, even if seeking to "transcend" it.[98] Overwhelmingly, however, elites renounced any division and repudiated discussion entirely. Rather, they defended the republic in oblique, civilizationist terms, and many poured massive intellectual energy into didactic anti-Haitianism. Both Santana and Báez assented and collaborated extensively with these allies. There was only one press in the capital, owned by the state.[99]

Members of the small but politically dominant elite who lived in the capital were the protagonists of settler and protectorate schemes. Prominent families ruled: the Delmonte, Alfau, Bobadilla, Galván, and Guridi, among them. Many owned land around the capital and profited from the sales of mahogany in other parts of the south, as far east as Higüey. Visitors referred to "wealthy non-workers" and "patrician families"; they reported, too, on the families' "faithful" servants.[100] They established small private seminaries to educate the "higher classes of society."[101] The sugar industry near the Dominican capital had left its mark, ideologically and materially, decades after its absolute decline, but plans to revive it with Canary Islander colonization projects predated Separation.[102] The daughter of one large plantation owner, wealthy in property if not capital, ran one of the few guesthouses in the capital.[103] An intermittent diaspora of Dominican elites to Cuba during the nineteenth century—fleeing the Haitian Revolution, fleeing Unification—meant that a handful of wealthier residents in Santo Domingo had family in Havana, Santiago de Cuba, San Juan, and other sites. Others had sojourned in Havana for legal education or political exile, and they wrote poems about planning never to return. All casually avoided mentioning slavery.[104]

As scholars demonstrate in nearby republics, republican universalism both "enabled and constrained" debates over political belonging. Even as elites in the Dominican capital had to subdue overt racism in governance, it circulated in normative language, political rumors, and private sphere.[105] Travelers observed, "It is clear that the whites and the sons of Spain have the most influence, even if they have a touch of color."[106] Antiblack rhymes betrayed the limits of so-called civil discourse, and prejudices restricted patterns of settlement, as they did in neighboring islands.[107] Writers in the capital were unabashedly bold in their phenotypic hierarchies:

> For a woman to be a total beauty, she has to have:
> Three white things;—Her skin, teeth, and hands.
> Three black;—Her eyes, eyelashes, and eyebrows.
> Three red;—her lips, cheeks, and nails . . . [108]

"Spanishness" offered them a useful, and vague, vocabulary to articulate distance from Haiti. They authored battle hymns, urging, "Rise Up in Arms, O Spaniards."[109] El Dominicano's journalists sometimes called the eastern troops Spanish, sometimes Dominican, within the same piece.[110] Actual connections to Spain were few, of course, as Spain refused to recognize the republic for more than a decade. Elite affinities extended to regular adulation of the south's semirecent French connections. The richest Dominicans toasted "à votre santé," sent their children abroad for education, and continued, actively and constantly, to entertain French protectorate prospects.[111] French tutors advertised in the capital.[112] Responding uneasily to a foreign observer at a dance, a columnist wrote, "Come on, speak *franchement* (openly) with me (because as you know, Sirs, in addition to the Gallicisms we do all the time, we love mixing in a few French words, damn custom)!"[113] The most regular and important connections of the capital, meanwhile, were with nearby islands, sites of mahogany and cattle trade. Not a single European ship came to Santo Domingo's port in the first six months of 1848.[114]

Elite narrators remained purposefully elusive, maintaining a treacherous silence on racism in public policy. From the first months of the republic, columnists highlighted what they assessed as a labor shortage, an implicitly antiblack strategy shared by elites in neighboring islands.[115] "Depopulation is the principal cause of our misery," a columnist wrote in 1845, calling for an immigration commission in each province.[116] Lawmakers passed a colonization law in 1847 offering land, advances, tools, and an exemption from military service for arriving migrants. Legislators wanted them to be white, even as they had cautiously avoided mentioning race. Rather, officials simply blocked plans for migrants of color individually.[117] Similarly, individuals privately lobbied for French support, the consul alleged, by slandering the British flag as "the flag of the blacks."[118] Agents from the United States reported similar race-based, closed-door entreaties.[119] So did the Spanish.[120] As they excoriated Haiti, then, they maintained a deafening silence on race thinking domestically. Privately, Báez warned the Cuban and Puerto Rican governors that Dominicans feared foreign occupation and slavery, and that most Dominicans would not hesitate to call on Haiti for help.[121] Publicly, however, he blamed outside agitators, "slavery propagandists," for these fears. The archetype of the "slavery propagandist," or of "denaturalized" or "Haitianized" Dominicans, stood in for any elite acknowledgment of popular discourses about foreign threats and dismissed Dominican antiracist discourses.[122]

Elites challenged the legacy of the recent Haitian past and, along with it, emancipation. Legislators affirmed commitment to a free-soil republic; in fact, at popular vigilance, they affirmed it many times. In practice, however, they made and imagined bargains that would have imperiled free labor if they had been realized, from colonization schemes to protectorate appeals to slave powers. They did so repeatedly, even as they observed, evidently dispassionately, the popular opposition that such plans provoked.[123] Writers set about anti-Haitian mythmaking simultaneously, anxious to create distance from a nation, the target of so much hemispheric aspersion, which had only very recently been their own. Given the almost total lack of written patrimony—Thomas Madiou's *Histoire d'Haïti* was the only history book to circulate in the Dominican capital—the story of Dominican difference was an "extremely urgent necessity," these columnists decided.[124] Capital city journalists veered to the openly didactic, taking pains to explain anti-Haitian slurs for their audience with an asterisk.[125] They worried the public did not heed them. "No one writes here because no one reads, and no one reads because no one writes," one paper's motto fretted.[126] Even elites who were enthralled with nationhood felt deeply pessimistic of aggressive international interests and their own political opponents. "Civilization! Is the favorite word of 1855," one columnist observed, "[but] it has shielded rapacious politics on bayonet point."[127]

Anti-Haitianism, beyond appealing to North Atlantic powers, offered elites a proxy to exorcise their anxieties about their own political predicament, an outlet for impatient and proscriptive visions of development, for scorn toward popular religious and marriage practices, and for their own racism. It facilitated "raceless" republican fictions and maintained a putative domestic unity with rural and poor Dominicans, especially of color, by invoking a target that was simply, elusively, external.[128] Elite unease toward rural Dominicans—over whom they had precious little influence—was usually oblique, but it was constant. Columnists criticized small farming plots as an "excuse for laziness," critiqued poor Dominicans' work habits, and praised the "absolute obedience" of soldiers.[129] Adopting a script of a Haitian "other," they made accusations of "relaxed habits," a supposed lack of religion, "libertine" cohabitation, and so on, hoping to discipline common Dominicans simultaneously.[130] Legislators passed vagrancy laws, although they were probably as unenforceable as those of the Unification period.[131] Authors argued that domestic vagrancy was "the seed of so many vices" and a deterrent to both local development and international investment.[132] They urged the creation of civic honors for productive domestic laborers, a practice the Haitian government already embraced.[133] When discussions veered to leisure and religion, tensions mounted perceptibly. Anxious commentators tried to "deport" merengue back to Haiti, calling it "horrible" and "loathsome."[134] One columnist described the dance: "When a merengue starts, ¡Holy God! One man grabs the other one's partner, the other one runs around because he doesn't know what to do, this guy grabs the arm of a young woman . . . everything is confusion. . . . Could that be agreeable to anyone?"[135] Columnists acknowledged familiarity with unease. In one imagined Spanish-Kreyòl dialogue, a Dominican character remonstrates a Haitian man for allegedly allowing himself to be abused by his leader. At the close of the conversation, the Dominican man bitterly rejects the latter's offer of a *guangá* (a "disgusting talisman . . . of horsehair, salt and ashes," the character claims derisively), but the bilingual conversation—in all its political, religious, and linguistic context—is perfectly understood by both parties.[136]

Poorer Dominicans lived alongside the wealthy in the capital, which was as isolated from the north as "two different countries" but tied to cattle plains and woodcutting in the nearby south.[137] The town was materially poor, with few stores and paltry regional trade.[138] Because foreign merchants could only be wholesale traders, however, a local market did flourish.[139] Traders brought inland products—fruit, corn, root vegetables, and small amounts of tobacco, raw sugar, and coffee—downstream by two-person canoes for consumption in the capital and shipped logwood out of the country. On the banks of the Ozama, a small market bustled for hours.[140] In Santo Domingo and other towns where individuals confronted prejudice and structural inequalities, it is probably true that some individuals sought to assimilate the privileges of whiteness and anti-Haitianism, but it is also certainly true that residents of color proffered explicit discourses of esteem, including total rejection of these norms, in direct response. Dominicans of color sometimes used "white" as a simple shorthand for "foreigner," similar to usage in Haiti.[141] During Unification, anonymous poets celebrated the upending of racist order in the capital.[142] Another unknown poet offered reassurance to black Dominican listeners who endured inequality, promising that someday, "the omelet would flip to the other side."[143]

A number of distinct Afro-Dominican organizations shaped the capital landscape. The black regiments remained a separate force years after independence, receiving a "large number" of men escaping from slavery in Cuba, Puerto Rico, and other islands into their ranks as soldiers and officers.[144] Churches, brotherhoods like the Cofradía of San Juan Bautista, and mutual aid societies blossomed.[145] African American migrants, who arrived in the 1820s at the invitation of President Boyer, maintained a sizable mutual aid society and English-language Methodist church in the capital in the 1850s.[146] The small capital outlay required to participate in the market meant that African American women from Baltimore and other sites integrated themselves easily into the public space of the town as vendors, selling fruits and other wares. They joined others on the streets of the town who were curious about news from abroad and ready to debate with travelers about slavery. They asked visitors for news of their former homes, but they also informed witnesses of the horrors they had suffered there.[147] Travelers reported that black Dominicans were loath to serve as servants, and that when elites sought replacements from Saint Thomas and other islands, these individuals promptly chose independent living as well. One white U.S. traveler called them "impertinent."[148]

Unlike the group in political power, most capital residents felt a deep wariness toward European powers. Spanish warships had demanded that islanders salute their flag in the 1830s, and many residents felt an uneasy "fear of the uniformed" (*miedo a los uniformados*).[149] When a Spanish ship docked in 1846—on its way to Cap-Haïtien to demand reparations—townspeople left "joys of *mardi gras* to watch in somber silence," distrustful of the few Spanish authorities who disembarked, an observer remarked.[150] Spain's slaveholding projects were always close to Dominican shores. The French consul maintained that foreign interference would inspire "serious resistance," fears of slavery, and calls for Haitian reunification in the capital.[151] Years later, the British consul reported much the same.[152] At least since the 1820s, men and women from Puerto Rico are on record as having reached the Dominican capital; how many elusively crossed the Mona passage in smaller crafts to other sites, perhaps with their whole families, is difficult to estimate.[153] Secret antislavery societies, organized by Ramón Emeterio Betances and other Puerto Rican activists, may have ushered an increasing number to Dominican shores. An unknowable number of Cubans arrived, too, on the northern coast and in the capital. The British consul remarked in 1861 that many had "enjoyed liberty for many years."[154] One Chinese tailor slipped out of Cuba on a passport to Jamaica, heading instead to Santo Domingo.[155] The governor of Puerto Rico warned that migrants of "very advanced political opinions and of very dangerous tendencies" sought out Dominican soil, probably precisely to win this freedom.[156]

Outside the capital, the landscape bore witness to a long history of sugar slavery and of independent black settlement. San Carlos, an *extramuro* community less than two kilometers northwest of the old city, lodged many traveling day laborers and others passing through to the southern wood markets, Baní, and other towns.[157] The settlement had a small wooden church and about a hundred huts made with palm leaves, distinct both in their manner of construction and in their purposeful arrangement amid vegetation. As much for its distinctive construction as for the residents' skin hue, the community had "the most marked aspect of an African people of Zambeze [sic] or Lake Nianza [sic]," a Spanish soldier supposed.[158] Its "original and happy" arrangement contrasted with the "European taste and aspect" of the nearby capital.[159] To the west, five small rivers converged to San Cristóbal, long a site of large estate sugar production. In 1822, residents seized a plantation that had enslaved 145 people, transforming it into small-scale production of raw sugar and rum, which they continued to trade in Santo Domingo, along with various foodstuffs.[160] Los Mina, chartered as a free black town in the late seventeenth century to receive people fleeing slavery from Saint-Domingue, was just east of the capital. Monte Plata, to the north, housed one of the black regiments whose members had opposed Separation. For those returning to the capital from Monte Plata, foreboding landscape lay ahead: the Pass of the Dead and then the Cold Sugar Mill (Yngenio Frio). Maroon settlements endured farther west. Afro-Dominican residents of La

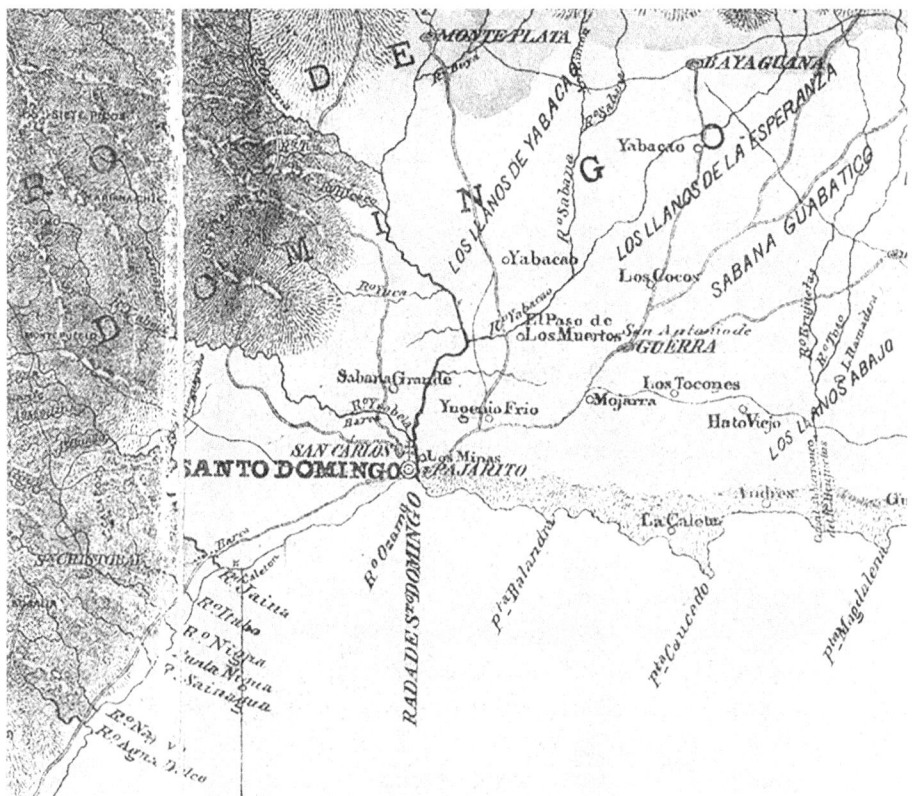

Fig. 1.2 Detail from Wm. M. Gabb's "Geological Map of the Republic of Santo Domingo," 1872.

Vereda, a settlement outside of Baní, preferred and cultivated selective isolation throughout the colonial period and all of the nineteenth century.[161] A small, fairly endogamous elite lived in town.[162] North of Baní, members of a maroon enclave founded San José de Ocoa. Paths were so tight and arduous that animals could barely pass, much less rest. "One false step or the twist of a girth would have thrown us into eternity," a traveler marveled.[163]

Almost a week's ride distant was the Cibao valley, the most populous, prosperous, and agriculturally intensive Dominican region. Travelers took pains to assert the whiteness of the people they spoke to in the Cibao, and the often-repeated pronouncements of "whites of the earth" also emanate from their reports.[164] The largest town, Santiago de los Caballeros, boasted a bustling artisan and retail class that had benefited from Haitian protectionism.[165] A small urban elite, *la gente de primera*, claimed roots in Spanish colonial families, even if their prosperity was quite recent. Pedro Francisco

Bonó reflected that his grandmother, "of one of the richest classes of planters [of Saint-Domingue] . . . drank to France with every pore" after she arrived to Santiago in exile.[166] Elites lived in the town center but also in rural areas, alongside poor families. Lack of capital meant that landowners acquiesced to informal sharecropping or squatting rather than waged work.[167] In the towns, liberal writers imagined isolated, noble, bronzed peasants, the poorest of whom were "ugly, but strong and healthy."[168] Mythical figures like the black *comegente* ("people eater") haunted public consciousness in the Cibao valley, embodying the wealthy region's troubled and inchoate relationship to the island's revolutionary past.[169] Residents had strong commercial ties, mostly via the north coast but also overland, connecting them to Cap-Haïtien, a richer city than most Dominican port towns. Wealthy men like Teodoro Heneken traveled regularly to the commercial and political centers of the island, Santiago de los Caballeros, Puerto Plata, Cap, and the two capitals.[170]

Cibao politicians, easily richer than many in the southern capital, felt Santana's and Báez's subjugation acutely, but they could not easily rally popular support. Báez dismissed the province, writing, "El Ozama thinks, Cibao works."[171] A flourishing literary culture grew in Santiago and other towns, along with progressive societies and Masonic lodges.[172] The members were men educated in Havana, Paris, London, and occasionally Philadelphia; they took a dim view of what they perceived as the provincialism and antidemocratic impulses of Báez and Santana and southern oligarchs generally.[173] Anti-Santana songs, stories, sayings, and *décimas* (short poems) abounded. The presidents' repeated printing of paper money caused deflation that devastated tobacco merchants.[174] Markets, roads, and rivers led north, to the *línea noroeste* (northwest line) of settlement and trade of tobacco, fine woods, and other products. *Recueros* (muleteers) and *prácticos* (guides) managed to travel these routes well enough, but urban Cibao residents' integration even with surrounding tobacco cultivators was not extensive.[175] Tobacco production led to centripetal settlement patterns in the surrounding countryside. Farms could be scattered around the areas of best soil; tobacco was light, transportable, and slow to rot. One historian estimates that an individual cultivator could produce anywhere from four hundred to two thousand pounds of tobacco a year, with fairly rudimentary technology.[176] The material culture was meager, and most rural cultivators probably relied on horses to counteract the physical isolation, even in Santiago's immediate surroundings. Overland travel south, meanwhile, was so arduous that most news from the capital reached, circuitously, from the northern coast. There were no places to sleep except for "the big bed" (the ground) or a hammock, and many horses, already expensive, could not weather the trip.[177]

Residents of Puerto Plata were a keenly cosmopolitan public. Migrant and commercial networks linked them regularly to Europe, the north coast of Haiti, the Turks and Caicos, Saint Thomas, southern Florida, and other sites. A free port since 1756, Puerto Plata earned the nickname "la Novia del Atlántico" (the Bride of the Atlantic) for the town's intense macroregional connections. Many residents were bi- or trilingual.[178] Germany dominated the tobacco trade, but the roster of ships that sailed in and out of the Puerto Plata—which funneled lumber and Cibao tobacco to Denmark, Bremen, and other primarily European sites—was considerable. At about two or three ships per day, it amounted to nearly ten times the traffic of the southern capital.[179] For regional trade, British and Danish vessels traded various goods for Dominican foodstuffs. The Turks and Caicos, which traded salt, depended completely on this exchange.[180] People came, too. Migrants from Saint Thomas, Tortola, Nassau, Providenciales, Grand Turk, Jamaica, Saint Kitts, Nevis, Martinique, Guadeloupe, the United States, Germany, France, and elsewhere trickled into Puerto Plata, Monte Cristi, and other north coast towns. A profusion of monikers like "el Inglés" (the Englishman) or "la isleña" (the islander) highlights the ready manner with which these migrants were received, and visitors described black migrants who earned a steady living in town as boatmen, laundry women, carpenters, and other professions.[181] Hundreds of African American émigrés came to Puerto Plata, establishing multilingual schools, churches, and mutual aid societies. Groups came at Boyer's invitation, through waters long familiar to Franco-Haitian corsairs.[182] Others escaped to freedom in following years. Individuals arrived from South Carolina and Georgia, often through the Keys, leading bookkeepers to record all of them as Floridian.[183] Trade and travel united the north coast. Cap-Haïtien was just one day's sail away. Monte Cristi residents sent wood along for resale in Puerto Plata, but they also engaged in an intense cattle and goat trade westward, to northern sections of Haiti.[184] People sometimes relocated along the coast after major life events. Theresa Smith, for example, moved back to Cap-Haïtien from Puerto Plata after her husband's passing.[185]

Regional migrants fleeing slavery also built communities alongside Dominicans in the Samaná peninsula. Faithful groups established an African Methodist church as early as the 1780s. When President Boyer issued an invitation for African American émigrés in 1824, hundreds made a permanent home in Samaná, in settlements like Protestant Heights, Free Fort, and Palenque.[186] Where the migrants to many other sites had eventually moved to nearby towns, on the peninsula, many chose farming, shipbuilding, and other activities.[187] In relative isolation, they made a community, working on sixteen-acre plots. By midcentury, the peninsula was sparsely populated—fewer than two thousand people—but it boasted a healthy trade of foodstuffs to the Turks and Caicos.[188] Like Puerto Plata, the community was actively multilingual. Town residents and visitors conversed in English, Spanish, and Kreyòl.[189] Probably the most regular regional news arrived from the nearby British islands, although the healthy salt-cowhide trade and a small stream of migrants connected them to Puerto Plata as well. Residents kept in contact with family and pastors in Philadelphia and other North American cities. Community residents remained Protestant, sometimes marrying with Turks and Caicos Islanders. They wrote to U.S. congregations praising the freedom of religion. "We enjoy our homesteads, and our freedom of worship, in neighborly peace," one parishioner reported.[190]

Filibuster intrigue, slave ship traffic, and imperial threats made north coasters very attentive to regional politics and vigilant about anticolonialism and antislavery. Puerto Plata authorities rushed into action when a suspected slaver docked in their harbor, for example. Against the protest of Spanish merchants, town officials immediately embargoed the vessel and sent the captain to Santo Domingo to stand trial, where he and his crew were convicted.[191] Despite their relative isolation, Samaná residents were keenly aware of foreign designs on the peninsula percolating in the capital and nearby waters.[192] An 1822 French expedition betrayed interest in the strategic peninsula that was decades old.[193] In the 1840s, French diplomats argued that a series of specious debts ought to justify their occupation of the peninsula, and they sent warships on numerous missions there.[194] By the 1850s, U.S. envoys angled for plans of their own. They very nearly negotiated for perpetual rent and a free port. The British and French sent warships; negotiations summarily ceased.[195] More than a few recent community members—like "Norberto [Ebora] el isleño, María la isleña"—became mixed up in anticolonial organizing in Puerto Plata and elsewhere.[196] Many maintained their first citizenship. In 1854, a group of Samaná residents traveled all the way from the peninsula to the capital to oppose a proposed U.S. treaty. Santana meant "to trick the population of color to subjugate them to slavery," they warned.[197]

New Terms for the Dictionary: Rural Identities and Politics

Many, if not most, Dominicans resided far from the coasts and towns, where they lived in rich autonomy and material paucity. Perhaps 8,000 lived in the capital, per one estimate, and about 12,000 lived in the rest of the towns of the country.[198] About 200,000 other Dominicans, more or less, lived dispersed in expansive rural areas, with perhaps just 7.4 inhabitants per square mile in 1860, compared with Puerto Rico's 169.[199] Almost everywhere but the Cibao, land pressure was very low. "The population of the African race are so spread out at points that one can travel large distances without the one hut in which to take refuge from the sun," a Spanish traveler complained in 1860. Few roads, dense vegetation, and rain-choked waterways made his travel even more difficult.[200] Little long-distance overland transport meant that most rural communities thrived in relative isolation. Since the colonial period, Dominicans of color sought respite from exploitation through rural pursuits, including ranching.[201] Scholars like David Barry Gaspar have emphasized the separate social and psychological space carved out even in the most intense modes of plantation slavery by the enslaved. This independence and selective impenetrability would have been even more pronounced in the autonomous rural contexts of postslavery Santo Domingo.[202] Narratives of national identity and difference forged in the capital amounted to a foreign construct, or simply an additional lexicon. In describing themselves, rural Dominicans throughout the territory might have invoked a discourse of relationship rather than describe a unitary identity.[203] More likely still, within their community they were endowed with plural histories and plural identities.[204] Mostly, they governed themselves.

Rural Dominicans, even the most poor, lived semi-independently. Even near the capital, just one month's work woodcutting afforded three months' leave.[205] Others took cattle-trading paths leading west into Haitian territory, as they had for more than a century. In highlands, rural dwellers subsisted on various tactics of slash-and-burn farming, animal grazing, capture of semiferal pigs and other animals. Semisedentary *monteros*, who lived in this way, might also work for a family who raised cattle without dramatic stratification.[206] Those who lived in service to a landowner did so in exchange for land use and other rights, rarely for salary.[207] Some looked to wealthier families for credit, employment, or godparentage. In the south particularly, large landowners involved in lumber and cattle held considerable influence over poorer area residents.[208] Even in those areas, however, the extent of available land greatly eased dependency. Residents had free-ranging pigs and cattle of their own, and they often cleared different lands every few years. Sometimes women managed farm plots as men traveled.[209] Common lands were usually not clearly delineated, but negotiation and the idea of community belonging and usufruct were avenues of access.[210] The system of common land use rights, *terrenos comuneros*—which had flustered President Boyer in his attempts to commercialize agriculture in the 1820s—remained well into the twentieth century.[211] Only products near natural ports or small-scale transport of rivers moved longer distances. Pack animals could carry tobacco and cacao, light but valuable, and livestock moved themselves. Sugar in Azua and lumber in northern and southern pockets were the other products that traveled by mule or small boat, without refinement. Agriculture did not transform substantively from the early nineteenth century, nor would it for decades.[212]

In their obligations, eastern rural residents probably behaved similarly to rural residents of other islands, leaving jobs when they felt they could live independently for a while.[213] Rural dwellers' party allegiances may have been more stable than party politics in towns, as land patronage was readily available.[214] As other scholars have argued, although caudillo literature has shied away from personalistic explanations, there was nothing at all illogical about either president's personal appeal, as far as the influence of either actually extended. Reciprocity, mythogenic appeal, and the language of "moral preservation" sustained them.[215] In decentralized and capricious circumstances, the idea that a powerful individual, not a distant state, might disseminate justice was an appealing recourse.[216] Fear also governed, as rivalry led to displays of public violence. "Santana was very popular among rural leaders and the masses of the countryside. . . . Many thousands viewed him with respect and even more saw him with fear, true terror," observed Alejandro Guridi, a onetime supporter of Santana.[217] In center-island areas, rumors circulated that Báez's supporters, too, had superhuman capacities, including magical bullets.[218] In every situation, however, the relative abundance of land abated inequality and increased rural Dominicans' leverage. A general aversion to state interference—only irrelevant and possibly costly or disruptive—probably typified the attitude of many. While some might have been caught up in the to-and-fro of caudillo anglings, others likely abstained from the enterprise. "He did not follow any government at all," several neighbors later observed of a day laborer who had been accused of rebellion.[219]

Rural residents constructed for themselves a different moral universe, with different political imperatives from the politicians of the capital. They embraced an epochal and moral sense of time: the Haitian Revolution, for example, ended "the time of the whites"; others remembered "when the whites hung" or made a future prophecy, "when the whites hang."[220] Similarly, villains and heroes could transcend temporality. The legend of Don Melchor, greedy slave owner from San Cristóbal who met his end falling from the sky as he tried to reach heaven, endured from the 1500s as a cautionary tale.[221] Fighting, emancipation, natural disasters, migration, illnesses, drought, pests, famine, and the arrival of strangers punctuated political beliefs and epistemologies, even as labor modes and technologies remained fairly constant. Interpersonal connections ranged from autarky, to ties between extended families, to bonds of formal patronage. Some communities may have valued periodic redistribution from their more prominent members.[222] Authority sprang from multiple reserves, from the geographically close to the celestially distant. Settlements may have remembered their founders with special veneration; it is likely, furthermore, that residents based their claims to local belonging on a genealogy of kinship.[223]

Distinctiveness and independence were fundamental to the language of everyday life. Dominican residents of southern coast towns were fascinated by what they saw as the extreme, even supernatural, solitude of the nearby mountain areas. Town residents claimed to have captured *biembienes*—several maroon individuals so isolated that they supposedly had no language—in the 1860s.[224] One traveler to the center of the island marveled at distinctive rural vocabulary: "New terms for the dictionary! Here, to say there were a bunch of things or many people: *había pila*. For a gathering of troops, *embarbascáos*. For saddlebags, *cerones*, for jacket, *celeque*, to say that anyone could do something, *esgarita*, to do something on purpose, *expresmente*, for rolls, *güalimones*, for the flies in these areas, *prieta*, to catch someone by surprise, they caught him *nete*."[225] French and Kreyòl loanwords and regionally specific rural vocabulary demonstrated wholly distinct cultural inflections, from region to sparsely populated region. One scholar has argued for as many as eight different regions whose geography and agriculture all distinguished them from the next in the center of the island alone.[226] Well beyond enduring maroon settlements in the central mountains, rural residents believed that *biembienes* populated the hills, sometimes characterized as ominous creatures, sometimes human. Biembienes' name evoked an invitation of the people who had escaped slavery in decades past: "*Come! Come!*"

The administration's reach was small. Although the constitution called for five regional courts, just two existed, in Santo Domingo and Santiago de los Caballeros, and their records were minimal. No one translated the civil code out of French after Separation, and given the dispersal of the population and the costs of traveling, many cases dragged on extensively.[227] Most rural residents likely resolved their disputes beyond formal proceedings. The wealthy administered justice extrajudicially as well, "without soiling our hands with these expensive nuisances—courts and prisons."[228] Government legislation was similarly informal. In the capital, charisma and military prowess had supplanted written dicta since the days of Juan Sánchez Ramírez ("all seems to have been by [his] verbal order," a contemporary observer marveled in 1811).[229] Buenaventura Báez and Pedro Santana, similarly, governed largely by decree. As the earliest arriving Spanish-Cuban officials lamented in 1861, "no fixed legislation" ruled, leaving citizens in the hands of these authorities.[230] The executive dictated law according to his inclinations, even as he paid lip service to popular will.[231]

Military authority reached somewhat further. Most served irregularly, often by conscription, which many resented.[232] "Al pobre no lo llaman para cosa buena" (the poor person is never called on for good things), one writer later ventriloquized.[233] There were few funds to pay soldiers, so local administrators rewarded men with rank and commissions.[234] Borrowing structure from the Haitian National Guard, regional divisions were self-ruled and decentralized, and soldiers still used some French commands.[235] "Each division general is a little president of his own province, and pronounces any odious decree, 'in virtue of Article 210,' even though that power is only conceded to the president," an observer claimed.[236] The Dominican army boasted at least 330 officers by 1861, probably many more, and officers had special rights, both for logging and to distribute wholesale goods brought in by foreign merchants.[237] Those at the highest ranks at times ruled abusively in towns. "He doesn't respect married women, girls, maidens, nor honorable men nor any class of person," read one complaint about a habitually drunk general, "and he is a disturber of the peace wherever he arrives."[238] Rank-and-file soldiers probably enjoyed much less prominence. They probably made claims to military sacrifice as a mode of political belonging, rather than a language of rights.[239] As with other armies, however, political elites valued their obedience.[240] "Our former life was the life of a soldier, or the life of a citizen who armed himself," one journalist in the capital remarked, "but here on out . . . that should change."[241] Journalists frequently lamented the burden of military expenses on the administration's meager budget.[242]

Spiritual knowledge informed Dominican life intensely. Popular religious practice differed from the doctrinal "fervent Catholicism" of urban elites, but it was by no means less integral to daily life.[243] Religious brotherhoods, in fact, were an important rural social network, and members administered them largely outside of clergy supervision.[244] In homes, popular practice probably had more of what some sociologists have termed a "matriarchal core," which not only venerated female figures such as the Virgin Mary but also afforded spiritual importance to female practitioners in general, as devotees, ritual experts, or simply women of faith.[245] The practice of *promesas* and personal altars, wakes and processions for deceased community members, and religious festivals and pilgrimages connected individuals directly to divinities and to each other. Collective rites and the veneration of a regional patron saint were important organizing principles.[246] Annual pilgrimages to the Virgin of Altagracia in Higüey united the faithful across the territory.[247] All of these modifications of priest-centric practice—from the authority of regional brotherhoods to practices of divination—disseminated alternative authority among community members. Like Obeah in other islands, Dominicans embraced epistemologies of justice that were parallel to and independent of bourgeois discourses of legality.[248] Religious fraternal societies (*cofradías*) existed as rural orders just as they did in towns, like the black Brotherhood of Saint Antoine in the Cibao valley. "These blacks have always lived in a state of independence . . . which has never permitted [officials] to collect any goods from them," an official complained in 1806.[249] Scholars would judge the 1844 invocation "Viva la República Dominicana y la Virgen Maria!" to be a "naive and charming cry," but the marriage of the two was not surprising.[250]

In their faith, Dominicans and Haitians shared overlapping lexicons, in a connection so fundamental that Dominicans and Haitians venerated the Virgin of Altagracia together for centuries.[251] Call-and-response music and liturgy, an emphasis on the Holy Spirit, and emotional conversion experiences characterized practice across the island. All-day dances on saints' days and other festivals embodied joyous or mournful expressions of faith.[252] Drumming added an important ritual element in some areas, including *palos de muerte* (to commemorate the deceased) and *fiestas* or *bailes de palo* (to celebrate saints' days).[253] Disapproving outsiders remarked that Dominican celebrations became raucous and that "singing and shouting" after baptisms was common.[254] One might seek to clean up or improve one's luck, bind a spouse or lover, gain protection from a *resguardo*, and seek the aid (or vengeance) of the deceased.[255] Many faithful performed special veneration for saints, like San Miguel, whose importance crossed pantheons, and Erzulie, Ogou, and marasa twins also appeared.[256] Especially in center-island areas, one might have appealed to papabocó or papalúa ritual experts, and some eastern faithful accorded special authority, or "generative potency," to western practitioners.[257] That authority might transcend time and space, even individual bodies, in what one scholar describes as "traveling spirithood."[258] Dominican families' mourning rituals—nine-day funeral vigils and rites like *baquiní* for deceased infants—evoked those in Jamaica, Colombia, Puerto Rico, and elsewhere.[259] The repetition of these rites, one year and seven years after the death, underscore the central importance of ancestors. Figures like *la jupia* and *la ciguapa* (*taína* spirits who roamed the fields), *nimitas* (glowing firefly-like creatures who watched over the living), and potentially malevolent creatures like *barsélicos*, *galipotes*, *zánganos*, and *bacás* all embodied the vibrant connection between the Dominican countryside's human inhabitants and other life.[260] At harvest time, Dominicans performed labor in some areas with the collective help of neighbors and extended family. Their collective work songs, *convite*, echoed *konbits* of the west.[261]

In different commercial and familial circuits, Dominicans traveled to Haiti often. Whole families traveled regularly from Puerto Plata and Santiago to Cap-Haïtien, for example. José del Carmen Rodríguez's wife was Haitian, and she had family throughout Haiti, whom she had not seen in eighteen years. José, his wife, their four children, and "un peón" made the trip to visit her relatives, perhaps to stay.[262] Some had left spouses and parents in Haiti and hoped to return. One fourteen-year-old boy, Rudolfo Ovidio, wanted to meet his mother's family. Nicasio Jiménez reported that his wife's mother and sister had been living in Haiti "ever since the Separation," when he intended to visit them nearly twenty years later.[263] Some moved multiple times in their life, like José Maria Sanchez, who moved from Higüey to Cap, overland, via Dajabón, as a child. He later settled elsewhere in the center of the island, farther to the south.[264] Southern residents traveled to the northern coast by ship, as Anna María LaPlace did, leaving Santo Domingo for Cap-Haïtien, for reasons of family.[265] Haiti's government paper published acts of naturalization. Dominican women could contract their own naturalization in the west.[266] North-coast commercial trade in both directions was brisk. Meanwhile, small-scale Haitian merchants, *pacotilleurs*, regularly traveled all the way to Higüey, selling their goods to country people along their route.[267] In the porous southern center-island region, migration was as old as the maroon communities that had welcomed fleeing slaves in the colonial era and the cattle trade that still burgeoned. Settlement patterns amounted to living geographic memory of the semirecent past.

Residents of the border or, more accurately, the center-island region in the south, were aware of but strategically removed from political projects of the island capitals. Relatively less direct travel connected the island capitals,

Fig. 1.3 A grave in Jacmel. Biencité Santana's given and family names suggest he was one of many who had family from both sides of the island.

which could take as long as two weeks in unfavorable conditions. News of Santo Domingo often arrived in Port-au-Prince via relay in Saint Thomas or Turks and Caicos Islands, and vice versa. By contrast, bustling cattle and wood trade connected the "deep south" (sur profundo) with the west, and coffee came eastward. By midcentury, there may have been some international enclaves of individuals and families engaged in wood selling on both sides of the island for decades.[268] "Free trade across the border" continued to be a primary negotiation concern in 1850s treaties.[269] In some center-island areas, settlement was shifting. In the nearly ninety years since the Treaty of Aranjuez had fixed borders on the island, decades-long demographic shifts blurred the boundaries of ethnicity and community. Hinche or Hincha, in the north-central area of the island, slowly transformed, becoming more Haitian, a pacific shift that became obvious at Separation. Several decades later, a man recalled that Separation had provoked something of a land grab, with wood sellers quickly coming forth with specious titles to continue to do business as they had before.[270]

In the center of the island, both governments had a collection of military outposts, but little more. In areas of so much commingling, "nation" was as much a tactic as it was a community. Residents' identity and filiation overlapped, intermingled, and transformed. Travelers and residents regularly negotiated differences, perhaps through humor, where they were not irrelevant.[271] Towns like Neiba were founded on a centuries-long history of marronage from the west. Expressions for the fundamental language of everyday life—words for hunger, fear, markets, scandals, and so on—easily blended center-island Kreyòl and center-island Spanish.[272] Town residents of San Juan de la Maguana, and others to the north, lived off cattle trade to Haiti. For cattle traders, Port-au-Prince was much closer than Santo Domingo.[273] Not particularly loyal to the east (much less "anti-Haitian"), peasants, cattle rustlers, and military men of central and central-southern regions of the island presented a direct challenge to political authority. Whole towns had reputations for fluid and charged allegiances. Neiba was of "well-known poor disposition," a French consul observed in 1847.[274] Neiba's "denaturalized citizens . . . threaten the country with anarchy," one Dominican paper warned, a decade later.[275] Haitian authorities also conceived of the region as a space for criminals, and they accused the Dominican government of supporting cattle rustling.[276] Dominican authorities returned the accusations, and they repeatedly complained that lower-level Haitian military officials sought to spread "letters of seduction" to Dominican military officials and other residents.[277]

Political schemes in the center-island area never ceased. Santana's opponents repeatedly fled to the area to regroup.[278] Local military men espoused goals that ranged from personal military ambitions, to vague declarations of subregional autonomy, to outright opposition to the Dominican state and proposals of reunification with Haiti. Capital city papers described their actions as "criminal" or "denationalized." Some became infamous; their nicknames—"el Quirí," "Cabulla," and so on—well known to authorities and the public alike. Their goals were similar to those of the ambitious separatists and prominent local leaders in Haiti and other state periphery sites throughout the Caribbean. Officers invoked national rivalries for their own purposes and argued that their services, rather than any ethnolinguistic claim, afforded them belonging in the national structure they chose to support.[279] Historian Ismael Hernández Flores argues that the youth of the region moved on from any rancor that had touched the region in 1844, quickly returning to centuries-old patterns of community, trade, and political collaboration.[280]

Provocation, Instability, and Revolution

Economic crises, diplomatic aggression, popular discontent, and political violence constantly plagued the new republic. France, Spain, and the United

States all withheld recognition, seeking leverage for concessions, especially the cession of the Samaná peninsula.[281] Britain, the first to recognize the republic in 1850, actively sought to stymie other treaties. To forestall U.S. influence, collect debt, or simply because it did not please their sensibilities that two "negro states" be divided, both British and French agents occasionally lobbied for reunification of the island.[282] These authorities were nakedly interventionist in Dominican local politics, too. Their favor fell to the caudillo they perceived to be more receptive to concessions. The French tended to favor Báez for his repeated (although far from exclusive) annexation entreaties. U.S. agents decided Santana would give them the concessions they sought, and one Spanish diplomat initiated a citizenship scheme that offered tantalizing (and disruptive) political immunity. Commercial agents from the United States, a growing presence, fantasized about large-scale land speculating and colonization. As they became more ambitious, these agents complained that the Dominican Republic was too "semicolonial" even to contract concessions without European nations intervening.[283] Sometimes the agents' machinations proved so outrageous that Dominican authorities, in exasperation, arrested them.[284] Dominican officials and other prominent figures, anxious, responded with annexation and protectorate overtures. Chaos grew.

By the close of the 1840s, the capital city administration was in crisis. The treasury was empty, despite ten printings of paper money.[285] The French consul alleged that a protectorate plan had near-unanimous support; indeed, the Dominican Congress may have secretly passed a resolution.[286] Haiti's new president, Faustin Souloque, looked on, with French worries of his own. His political opponents were demonstrating for democratic reforms, along the lines of the revolution that had occurred in France the previous year. Despite repression and executions, their opposition continued, and rumors of the French-Dominican protectorate provoked him further.[287] He insisted on the indivisibility of the island. The British consul egged him on, proposing a plan that would reunite the island while leaving Dominican governors and military forces intact.[288] Although his overtures were mostly bellicose, Souloque also tried to appeal directly to Dominicans, highlighting the racism of Santana's administration.[289] He invoked the memory of General Joaquín Puello, killed by Santana for his opposition to early Separation plans.[290] He reminded Dominicans, too, of the disastrous incident of the men fleeing Puerto Rico and the pro-slavery complicity of Santo Domingo officials.[291] He called Dominicans "our brothers of the east," which journalists particularly loathed and resented.[292]

A few months into the French treaty negotiations, Soulouque launched an ill-fated campaign in Dominican territory. He held Azua for a little more than two weeks; his subordinates engaged in smaller conflicts in several center-island towns.[293] Santana met him near the southern town of Baní, soundly defeating him. The aggression was so unpopular in Port-au-Prince that Soulouque's opponents were purposely silent, expectant that the mobilization would bring his downfall.[294] Tightening his grip instead, Soulouque named himself emperor. Dominicans led a small naval offensive against Haiti in 1849, burned Anse-à-Pitres, and attacked one other town, but both sides quickly demobilized.[295] The French consul was not chastened in the least. He dreamed of a "white trade" to Samaná, in new French settlers, and wrote to Dominican legislators promising it.[296] French authorities continued to lobby for both administrations to pay Haiti's indemnity, and they did not recognize the Dominican Republic for several more years.[297] British and French diplomats intervened as "mediators" in the peace that followed. Dominican ministers found few complaints too small to report.[298]

Santana's victory, easily won, gave him a temporary burst of popularity, but he quickly squandered it. He persecuted political rivals and eviscerated constitutional reforms. An "infernal party spirit" reigned.[299] Some journalists asserted Santana was a "magic name for the country"; others, that he was "fratricidal and ferocious."[300] "What a country we live in!" a columnist complained, when Santana exiled another newspaper editor.[301] Authors of a new paper, La Acusación—perhaps the most roundly critical of all antidemocratic tendencies in the city—leveled themselves squarely at Santana, accusing him of appropriating 16 million pesos fuertes and warning that the "thieves" might soon spirit away the remaining 300 million. The editor earned himself a beating.[302] Papers turned to satire and allegory. El Dominicano mocked a fictional "Don Chameleon," who threw his allegiances wherever jobs were to be found.[303] A play, entitled "The Conspiracies, Seen from One Side," depicts characters motivated by jealousy, arrogance, ignorance, and self-interest.[304] In a satirical dream sequence, El Oasis depicted a society where a "Pueri-Cracia" ruled, with a constitution ordering the deportation of all men and women over age thirty, polygamy, continuous revolution, the beating of foreign consuls, and constant conflict between legislative and executive branches. Meanwhile, military men had license to "do absolutely whatever they wanted."[305]

U.S. filibusters soon came to the island in earnest, joined by a diplomatic corps who supported their ambition. Although Dominican officials supported white American migration, incoming proposals were not agricultural projects but rather armed filibuster operations, intending to attack Cuba. One Georgia operation associated with a failed Narciso López expedition offered "8,000 migrants" for Dominican settlement. President Báez was so suspicious that he warned the outfit that Spanish troops were prepared to defend the northern coast if necessary. The French consul also offered ships.[306] Tensions ran high. The French consul predicted that north coast residents would "revolt and unite with Haiti" if French troops, meant to forestall U.S. filibusters, arrived precipitously.[307] Báez passed regulations restricting migrants' ports of arrival, preventing the disembarkation of guns, and demanding proof of employment within two months.[308] New proposals continued cropping up; the Dominican government opposed them, one by one, and sent secret agents to investigate.[309] Several years later, swashbuckling Texas veteran William Cazneau arrived aboard the USS *Columbia*, intending to draft a recognition treaty. He followed his ardently pro-filibuster wife, Jane Storm Cazneau, to the republic. Both harbored eager and aggressive settlement plans. Jane Cazneau wrote effusively that Dominican land for sugar and coffee could be had for just three dollars an acre, compared with forty or fifty dollars in Cuba.[310] Privately, she suggested armed colonization.[311] In exchange for recognition, William Cazneau demanded cheap rent of Samaná. British, French, and Spanish agents worked furiously to oppose him, docking warships in Samaná and the capital.

Dominican popular opposition to U.S. plans was acute and growing. Cazneau's proposal was so wildly unpopular in Samaná that demonstrators traveled to the capital to make their opposition plain. A Spanish observer remarked, contentedly, "Samaná has not been sold because there is a fear of revolution of the people of color."[312] In the capital, the treaty collapsed, too. Controversy about Article 3, under whose provisions Dominicans would be subject to U.S. laws, ostensibly put Dominicans at risk for enslavement upon visiting Baltimore and other southern ports. Under intense public pressure, the Dominican Congress soundly rejected it, Cazneau refused to alter it, and the negotiation was brusquely dropped.[313] Cazneau blamed opposition in Santo Domingo on "adept . . . and malicious" Haitian propaganda, trying to minimize or dismiss the obvious discontent in the town.[314] The "liberty . . . to treat the colored Dominican Consul as it treats any other negro, was too large a bone for the Dominican Congress to swallow. . . . General Cazneau is distressed, Mrs. Cazneau is mortified," the *New York Times* reported.[315] The Spanish consul expressed satisfaction that joint diplomatic action had helped to block the treaty negotiations. "I hope that the Dominican government will be demoralized," he wrote.[316] They were not. Diplomats continued talks for a naval station in Samaná as the United States sent warships to Port-au-Prince on the pretext of private debt collection.[317]

In this tempest, Soulouque mounted a second, final, disastrous campaign in late winter 1855, opposed by his own troops and the majority of the Haitian public. He imprisoned southern peasant activists, and as opposition popped up in other towns, he restlessly looked eastward.[318] Dominican newspapers knew he was trying to occupy restive high-ranking opponents.[319] The French consul in Haiti, Maxime Raybaud, goaded Soulouque in favor of unification. Raybaud then menaced Dominican officials with the suggestion that forced reunification or U.S. occupation was imminent.[320] Santana promised a fight to the death.[321] Capital city journalists furiously refuted Soulouque's propaganda about solidarity and unification, but they were much more calm.[322] Soulouque was "pumped up by a little devil, by sycophants, or maybe by liars who wanted to see his downfall," Dominican paper El Oasis asserted drily.[323] Other than a six-day occupation of one center-island town, Soulouque and supporting generals made few gains. Haitian soldiers hated the expedition, and they chided the emperor in song, "ça pa zaffair a nous" (it's not our cause).[324] Even before a second and final encounter, Dominican journalists reported confidently that "perfect tranquility reigns on the borderlands" and warned Soulouque he would soon lose power.[325]

Soulouque's last foray into Dominican territory did not disrupt Dominican domestic struggles very long, nor did it forestall growing U.S. aggression. A major uprising challenged him in Les Cayes, and U.S. adventurers claimed a small, uninhabited island off the coast for their own guano exploitation.[326] News of filibuster aggression in Nicaragua filled Dominican and Haitian headlines.[327] Dominican capital city officials, undeterred, never relented to U.S. negotiations, as U.S. officials demanded more coaling concessions. Meanwhile, Santo Domingo residents protested nightly in the capital at the house of U.S. agents. Cries of "Down with the Yankees!" could be heard on the streets. The U.S. flag had to be raised out of reach of those throwing rotten eggs. The Dominican capital was in disorder.[328]

Revolution brewed. By the summer of 1856, papers lamented that Santana was exiling people "by the thousands" and executing others without trial.[329] He made a spectacle of having the condemned dig their own graves.[330] One poet ventriloquized Santana: "Blood, always seeking blood! . . . Men hate me: I hate them!"[331] Other authorities, including the archbishop, threw their support to his rival.[332] Spanish consul Antonio María Segovia allowed Báez supporters to register as Spanish citizens in order to claim political asylum. In a popular rhyme, an anonymous person celebrated:

I'm not scared of Santana
Or the Alfau brothers
Just of Segovia
'Cause I'm matriculated.[333]

Critics lamented their impotence to quell the disorder as Santana lost his grip. The country was "lost to disorder and anarchy, plagued by hypocrites and demagogues," one writer argued, gravely, and he observed that common people were suffering the most of all from the unrelenting disorder.[334] The economic crisis continued unabated, as inflation brought nearly 80 percent devaluation each year on average, from 1847 to 1855.[335] A priest lamented, "Whoever . . . looks at the history of our country . . . will cry over its disasters."[336] Santana hurriedly retired to his ranch, ending a term he had originally claimed would last another ten years. After a brief interlude, Báez again ascended to the presidency. He, too, filled the Senate with his supporters, ordered his rivals' arrest and exile, and called for multiple printings of millions of pesos. England, France, and Spain refused the new exchange rates. Adopting the voice of a foreign lender, an anonymous Dominican author penned a poem called "Another Pirate":

My till is my treasure
My God is interest
My happiness is when I calculate
Five percent each month.[337]

Dutch creditors were so unpopular that one was nearly murdered on the street in the capital, just steps from the British consul's door.[338] Baez's printing of paper money had left the exchange rate at 4750 pesos to one dollar.[339] Particularly for tobacco merchants of the Cibao valley and northern coast, inflation made prices intolerable.[340]

In the summer of 1857, merchants and liberals of Santiago de los Caballeros and surrounding towns of the Cibao valley threw their lot into revolution. "REVOLUTION! CONSPIRACY!" screamed El Eco's headlines in the capital.[341] Delegates drafted a constitution in Moca, calling for an end to the death penalty, extensive civil liberties, more government control of the army, term limits, and other reforms. They named a provisional president, to serve in a new capital, Santiago.[342] The leaders could not easily mobilize local cultivators, who favored Báez's paper money policies. Cibao's agriculture-intense valley had less of a tradition of military mobilizations, anyway, even if local peasants had been supportive.[343] Only one man could mobilize a familiar and loyal following, and, so, the Cibaeño leaders called on Santana to command a siege of the capital. France and Britain docked warships in the harbor, and Spain clamored to do the same. The British consul in the capital and the vice consul in Puerto Plata openly supported the rebels.[344] The *Moniteur Haïtien* published a letter from the besieged capital that read, "We do not know when this war will end, nor what the result will be; . . . The picture of everything is so sad, my pen cannot paint it. Dominicans are divided among themselves. The dead! The injured!" Famine and pillage were coming, the writer warned.[345] After months of desperate standoff, Báez capitulated and fled the country. A "bloody struggle divides us," he inveighed.[346] The Cibaeños lost, too, however. Santana easily wrangled power back from them, replacing the reform constitution with a familiar, draconian one.[347]

Unrest and the Eve of Annexation

Patience for the constant foreign intrigue wore thin. "*Fulano* [that guy] (and there are lots of those guys) today is involved in French politics, tomorrow he's English, and the next day you have a Russian," a writer complained.[348] Furious editorials railed against the Spanish matriculation scheme. One author commented acerbically, "Where are *fraternity, equality, and liberal laws* . . . where one must craft a document of *limpieza de sangre*?"[349] Nearly eight hundred in the capital had taken Spanish citizenship, opponents claimed. Supporters dismissed opponents as "Boyerists."[350] "It has been a long thirteen years . . . [and] if people are demoralized, it is not by the matriculation, but because of the country's failures," another writer countered.[351] Writers tired of escapist Europhilic sentiment amid the disorder and chaos. In an editorial entitled "Spirit of the Times," an author condemned the frivolities of his small readership for their "damned craze . . . to do everything *by steam* and in accordance with the fashions of overseas." He warned them, "Well, if by some misfortune the course of things doesn't change, and becomes more laughable, then we'll just also have to live *by steam*, so that we can leave this treacherous world as fast as possible and go enjoy all the good stuff of the next in the sky."[352] A poet mocked Santo Domingo elite citizens who pretended to European birth, similarly:

> Upon seeing my friend Lola
> With a fancy black skirt and a fan
> I asked her, ¿are you Spanish?
> And the *manola* answered me
> Yes, me born in Potorico[353]

Many residents of the Dominican capital continued to demonstrate their opposition to U.S. interests. They detested the U.S. commercial agent, Jonathan Elliot. For some months, he had been suffering daily harassment; the final straw, he reported, was a young man menacing his wife at her parents' home. Before the end of the year, he wrote hurriedly to request a passport to leave with his family and servants, "by first opportunity that offers."[354] Capital residents continued to protest, however. In the summer of 1858, a U.S. commander condemned "nightly mobs" issuing "abuse and threats" about their "inimical feelings against the Agent and the flag of the United States."[355] He demanded a twenty-one-gun salute for the "public abuse" before leaving. The next year, a U.S. outfit tried to seize an island off the coast for guano exploitation, the second to have done so in as many years. The matter caused a massive uproar in the press.[356] Across the island, Jane Cazneau described constant unrest in Puerto Plata. She blamed annexation rumors on town residents of color.[357]

Despite popular opposition to colonization and protectorate plans, Santana's inner circle pushed forward. Columnists continued to support the idea of colonists for cash-crop products, and Dominican officials reached a migration agreement in Paris in April 1857.[358] When migrants arrived in Samaná that fall, the Dominican government sent some shipments of food, as promised.[359] The attempts were disastrous. Illness killed many of the new arrivals, and French authorities advised the remaining colonists that it would be wise to forfeit the project.[360] An even more ambitious coterie nevertheless dreamed of larger transformations. Santana's vice president, General Antonio Abad Alfau, and his brother, General Felipe Alfau, lobbied for both a protectorate and an indenture revolution simultaneously. The Alfaus and their supporters wanted contract laborers from India and China.[361] They wrote enthusiastically about the hundreds of Canary Islanders and Spaniards who arrived from Venezuela, fleeing social unrest.[362] The Spanish consul added his approval, noting that they had begun setting up plantations near the capital.[363] In a secret meeting with Cuban authorities in 1860, Antonio Abad Alfau argued that Dominicans loved Spain—especially the "most notable"—and suggested that Santana was considering declaring annexation unilaterally. Santana's machinations for Spanish annexation were an open secret.[364]

Conditions continued to deteriorate. Santana soon printed 10 million more pesos; the public refused to accept them. British, French, and Spanish warships all threatened military action.[365] Santana responded by printing millions more.[366] His officials rushed to sign long-term mining, wood, and guano concessions with French companies in exchange for up-front payments.[367] A flood of political exiles arrived in Haiti, Curaçao, Saint Thomas, and Venezuela as censorship and repression continued. Some men cited their Spanish matriculation to avoid military service, long after the whole affair had ended; others deserted to British ships.[368] Santana used his army to pursue Báez supporters in Azua.[369] In an 1860 debate, participants made veiled judgments about Santana through a debate about Julius Caesar. "Some say the great crime of Caesar was to have killed the Republic," one participant observed, testily. "A fairly specious paradox. Can a cadaver be assassinated?"[370] "The life of a tyrant is never long," a poet warned. In front of Santana, a liberal priest gave a defiant sermon, threatening, "The people always begin with a murmur, and end by toppling their tyrants."[371] December 1860 began with an attempt on Santana's life.[372]

Libertad, Igualdad . . .

At the close of the 1850s, echoes of the 1843 mobilizations rumbled across the whole island and in rebel networks as far as Venezuela, Saint Thomas, and Curaçao. Port-au-Prince burned in 1857, inflation soared, and open rebellion began in the north.[373] Rebellion spread from Gonaïves as foreigners evacuated. A collaborative Dominican and Haitian surge supported the anti-Soulouque revolution. "Dominicans recently made a revolution, or what they more pompously called a *combined movement* among the island residents," to instate General Fabre Nicholas Geffrard, a hostile Spanish official recorded.[374] A career officer, Geffrard had participated in Soulouque's 1856 campaign. Among his Dominican supporters in the center-island area and in exile, all was obviously forgiven. Francisco del Rosario Sánchez, himself a veteran of 1844 Separation struggles, allied with Geffrard to overthrow Soulouque. Rumors abounded about Emperor Soulouque's assassination, and in January 1859, he departed for Jamaica as Boyer and Rivière had done.[375]

Geffrard's republicanism electrified the public. Citizenship language was everywhere. The *Moniteur* promised that the revolution would "regenerate the country and make it retake its place among the peoples who are friends of civilization," reestablishing liberal institutions immediately.[376] Lawmakers took to wearing special hats to emphasize that civilian rule would replace military power at last.[377] Town politicians praised Geffrard's democratic commitments. "*We promise to bury ourselves beneath the ruins of the country before living in slavery.— We furthermore promise to obey nothing but the empire of law and never to the despotic will of any individual*," one group of citizens effused.[378] The new president offered immediate conciliatory gestures to the east. He condemned his predecessor's aggressions in ringing terms. Quickly, his ministers drafted a five-year treaty. All the while, political refugees fled Santana's repression. Often their first stop was Port-de-Paix or Cap, both easy to reach on the northern coast. Occasionally, they continued on to the Haitian capital to seek audience with high political officials.[379] By 1860, Sánchez was in exile in Saint Thomas but organizing opposition to Santana. He and other activists had Geffrard's frank support.[380] Geffrard praised the rebels publicly and urged that they sought "fraternity and conciliation." He also warned that many were discussing annexation rumors, raising the alarm as far as Curaçao.[381]

Anti-Santana figures, military authorities, their families, and allies mobilized, meanwhile, in the center of the island. They celebrated the new democratic regime in the west and opposed mounting rumors about annexation in the east.[382] News that center-island residents and these political figures wanted "indivisibility of territory" quickly reached the Dominican capital, and the border percolated with "unusual intensity."[383] Authorities mandated that all communication between the two nations cease. Already that spring, Dominican officials tried to restrict the travel of any foreigner who had been in the west, a measure that irritated the foreign consuls.[384] General Valentín Alcantara, a Dominican officer who had switched to serve the Haitian army ten years earlier, found a new "denaturalized" ally: Domingo Ramírez y Parmantier.[385] In a manifesto with a handwritten Spanish heading of the Haitian motto, "Libertad-Igualdad," Ramírez addressed his compatriots:

Our efforts have as their goal

1. To remove ourselves from the ferocity of Santana, whose bloody character pardons neither women nor children.
2. To extricate ourselves from the shocking misery in which his ignorant administration has submerged us.
3. To return to their destiny an infinite number of noble Dominicans kept in cruel ostracism by his tyranny.
4. To break the chains of the great mass of our co-citizens, shackled by that despot.
5. To impede Santana, whose relationships with foreigners, enemies of our race, threaten to alienate our territory from us and compromise our liberty and political existence.
6. To unite ourselves under one sole flag, so that the country can be indivisible and strong through the fusion of all of us.

These goals, as you see, are not just laudable; rather, they are the fundament of our common prosperity—the fate of our family—the guarantee of a future for our children!

Co-citizens, you have nothing to fear![386]

Santana himself rounded up loyal men to crush the movement.

Santo Domingo's officials refused to acknowledge the rebels' political goals. They dismissed the rebels as "ambitious men," "robbers," or "traitors," and they demanded that the Haitian government provide restitution for the whole affair. To foreign consuls, the Dominican foreign minister insisted that a total ban in communication with Haiti would prevent further disorder.[387] He claimed a "general mobilization in all of the Republic" had crushed Ramírez's "totally infamous and criminal treason," and that "the Dominican soldier . . . was always ready to fight the Common enemy," a willful misunderstanding of Ramírez's own identity.[388] Another minister admitted, uneasily, that the movement was Dominican.[389] Puerto Plata's residents warned each other that slavery was to be reestablished.[390] Capital city officials responded to the growing unrest only by declaring that spreading slavery rumors was a capital crime.[391] The common enemy was not very clear at all.

TWO

Soon It Will Be Mexico's Turn
CARIBBEAN EMPIRE AND DOMINICAN ANNEXATION

At eight in the morning on 18 March 1861, a small group of Dominican officials lowered the national flag from government buildings in Santo Domingo as a few hundred observers, mostly Spanish, watched. "*Españolismo* lives," effused a Spanish diplomat.[1] Although the republic had been separated from Spain for nearly forty years, Pedro Santana insisted that the annexation was voluntary. The Spanish official with whom the Dominican president had been most closely in communication—an activist governor of Cuba, Captain General Francisco Serrano—emphasized his agreement and support. Only after the ceremony did both officials send word to the governor of Puerto Rico and to Queen Isabel II and her ministers in Spain. Annexation was a fait accompli. Preparations had been the talk of Havana for months. "This project is discussed publicly in cafés, *paseos*, in every house; . . . no one doubts its quick and total completion," a Havana resident remarked. He was unreservedly ambitious, bragging, "Spain should not limit her aims to the Dominican Republic; it needs the whole island, and the Haitian Republic will be invaded before long." He urged Spain to be inspired by its recent victory in northwestern Africa toward more wars of conquest. "The deplorable political situation of the United States," where southern secession had already begun, offered a particular opportunity for other powers. The man predicted more Spanish expansion imminently, boasting, "soon it will be Mexico's turn."[2]

Santana and his ministers had a fair amount in common with supporters of French intervention in Mexico, which unfolded almost simultaneously. Both were a small, mainly conservative elite who were tired of political fighting, wary of the populace, and eager for outside military resources to secure order. They hoped a foreign monarch would centralize the political administration, defeat opponents, and offer strong defense to external threats. They shared ready economic extroversion, but also strong local political commitments.[3] They were nationalists after a fashion, believing that political order, under a foreign monarch, might create more local meritocratic government appointments than successive fractious administrations.[4] The strategy of asking for a protectorate in exchange for limited territorial concessions was nothing unusual, of course; it was an emergency recourse for embattled leaders throughout the hemisphere. The exaggerated political chaos of the Gulf, however—where U.S. power was entering rapidly— made both annexation projects real.[5] Their ease with monarchism was nothing uncommon, either. From Haiti to Brazil, it was a common state-making strategy of the moment, one that was challenged by republicanism but had ample liberal language of its own.[6] After succession battles in the 1830s, Queen Isabel II herself initially represented a symbol of the victory over absolutism in Spain, where moderate liberals enjoyed electoral power.[7] Observers, meanwhile, were surprised but hardly shocked about either annexation, which occurred with the United States deeply preoccupied. Most predicted the Spanish would move into Haiti, too.[8]

This chapter details how Spanish officials, working with Santana and his allies, came to incorporate Santo Domingo as a free-soil Spanish province. For more than fifty years, Spain's remaining overseas possessions—Cuba, Puerto Rico, and the Philippines—had been in legal limbo, outside of constitutional rule. Centralized, militarized government ruled the islands instead, and "special laws" to reincorporate them never materialized, forestalled both by political divides on the peninsula and by the question of slavery.[9] Cuba's governor, a powerful Spanish authority, believed Dominican incorporation might precipitate liberal reforms throughout the empire. Various Spanish politicians and writers, meanwhile, toyed with unstable discourses about federation, sometimes racial, sometimes moral, sometimes political, sometimes all of these. They intermingled fraternal and racist missives toward Santo Domingo, always with added aspersion for Haiti. "Blacks are in Haiti and not in Santo Domingo," a Madrid journalist insisted.[10] Dominican elites indulged and reciprocated them. Beyond these inconsistent narratives of inclusion, real pragmatism drove Spanish officials in the Caribbean. They envisioned a territory that could forestall U.S. advances and host new projects of labor indenture, already dawning in sites around the Atlantic.

Antillean Geopolitics and Spanish Empire, 1840–1861

By the mid-nineteenth century, both the newly independent states of Spanish America and Spain had definitively emerged from the wake of the wars of independence. The American republics were increasingly integrated in global markets, and their administrations grew.[11] In Spain, General Leopoldo O'Donnell led the moderate Liberal Union Party, which won a majority in the Cortes and presided over a period of political peace. Simultaneously, peninsular liberals finally succeeded in centralizing colonial administration, after years of debate. In 1851, legislators created the General Overseas Directorate (Dirección General de Ultramar), which later gained full ministry status as the Overseas Ministry (Ministerio de Ultramar).[12] Cuba's captain general post was a powerful and important one; multiple Spanish generals solidified their political careers in Havana to return to top positions in Spain. Cuba was Spain's most important possession and the economic heart of Spanish empire.

An unsteady diplomatic rapprochement between Spain and its former colonies grew across the Atlantic, fueled by a transforming imperial climate in Latin America and the Caribbean. As direct investment, loans, and military intervention increased, politicians of the new republics responded collectively to strengthening outside threats in a manner that sometimes drew them, at least discursively, closer to Spain.[13] As the U.S. presence in the region grew stronger, Central American liberal elites called on racial solidarity in murky but insistent terms. They extolled *raza hispana*'s putative racial inclusion (although, crucially, not qua equality but rather via miscegenation) and as a loose aggregate of cultural attributes through which to insist on difference from a potential aggressor, "the Yankee race."[14] Participating republics invited Spain to the 1847 Lima Congress that pondered defensive federation, and Spain finally signed treaties of recognition and peace with a number of the new nations.[15] Journalists of *El Museo de Ambas Américas* and *La Revista Española de Ambos Mundos* sought to tighten Atlantic relations.[16] Spanish politicians embraced the miscegenation tropes, invoking them as a "white legend" for their colonial endeavors.[17] Privately, Spanish diplomats were often derisive about the new states, mocking their civil strife. The political opponents in Venezuela were "more atrocious than savage tribes," the Spanish consul in Santo Domingo reported derisively.[18] In public, however, Spanish commentators waxed poetic about the fraternal possibilities. "Yes, we have lost our rich colonies in America, but there are still millions of men that ought to be our natural allies, given that they are united with us by the intimate and solid ties of religion, custom, language, and civil legislation," the consul argued, concluding, "Spanish politics should impede at all costs that the *raza ibero-americana* be absorbed by the *raza yankee*."[19]

Near Spain's Caribbean possessions, U.S. expansion was growing both incrementally and through dramatic aggression. Many islands bought foodstuffs from the United States, and U.S.-bound exports also increased. By mid-century, U.S. markets consumed two-thirds of Puerto Rico's sugar.[20] The 1850 Clayton-Bulwer treaty, which negotiated canal rights through Nicaragua, seemed to signify the peaceful consolidation of joint U.S.-British commercial hegemony in the Gulf region. Britain avariciously consumed cotton from the U.S. South, its financiers supported railroad projects expanding westward, and many eagerly predicted growing U.S. influence, even eventual control, over its nearby neighbors.[21] Massive watershed events, like the War of U.S. Intervention (the "Mexican-American War") and filibustering in Nicaragua, posed dramatic military threats. Even political overtures bore aggressive and meddlesome undertones. Presidents Polk and Pierce tried to buy Cuba, and some northern politicians supported the plans, despite the complications that expansion posed.[22] Pro-slavery advocates gleefully calculated that new slave states could be carved out of the acquisition, despite Spanish officials' defiant reply that they would "rather see the island sink."[23] Outright extralegal expeditions plagued Cuban authorities during the 1850s. The filibuster efforts of Narciso López—whose third invasion attempt ended in defeat in November 1851—enjoyed minority support among some Cuban elites. Disappointed supporters attacked the Spanish consulate in New Orleans when he was captured and executed. Faced with commercial and military aggression, the Spanish Crown was outraged. "Anglo-Americans easily put down roots wherever they manage to get a foothold," a Spanish diplomat complained.[24] "Two rival races are fighting for the new world," Madrid's *La América* agreed.[25]

Massive domestic inequality on the islands—the contests of plantation slavery—made Spanish officials all the more paranoid about retaining control. The conspiracies they feared reflected the ubiquity of the resentment they imagined, their unwillingness to afford agency to domestic resistance, and their preoccupation with what they imagined to be race imperialism. Authorities warned colonial whites that "race war" would result from domestic or international conflict; they imagined "machinations . . . of destroying the white race" at every turn.[26] Authorities feared that individuals were plotting in Curaçao, Jamaica, Saint Thomas, Trinidad, Venezuela, and elsewhere to join Haiti in an unnamed "Machiavellian abolitionist plan" or independence conspiracy.[27] Years later, the Spanish minister from Washington reported that free and enslaved blacks of various societies from New Orleans (including some Dominican émigrés), New York, and Philadelphia and "those who had been expelled to Mexico" were planning a "simultaneous strike" on Cuba and Puerto Rico, also aided by the British government.[28] Others wrote credulous reports of Haitian emperor Faustin Soulouque receiving aid from Africa and Britain, organizing thousands and thousands of troops for an assault on Cuba.[29] Caribbean officials petitioned constantly to increase Cuba's and Puerto Rico's military defenses. A "certain tone of anguish" characterized their repeated letters to Directorate officials in Madrid.[30] In response to a number of real and perceived threats, Puerto Rican and Cuban officials pleaded for more troops and argued that the islands' defenses were woefully insufficient. Undisciplined troops, lack of supplies, poor infrastructure, meager funding, and a lack of ships usually topped the complaint list. Their refrain—a "permanent complaint," in the words of one historian—rarely met with satisfactory response from the metropole.[31] In response to filibuster threats, Cuban officials relied on secret agents in a number of U.S. cities for counterintelligence. Governor Juan de la Pezuela re-formed the militia of color in the island, disbanded since 1844.[32] Power concentrated in the office of the captain general, and conservatism reigned.[33]

These same Caribbean authorities lent a sympathetic ear to Dominican petitions. Peninsular Spanish officials had virtually ignored Santo Domingo in its last days as a colony, sending paltry funds just twice between 1809 and 1821. Their attitude reflected, in the words of Luís Álvarez, "the politics of manifest indifference."[34] Authorities in Cuba and Puerto Rico, however, periodically considered reannexation, sending exploratory missions without directives from Madrid. In the decade after Santo Domingo joined Haiti in independence, an official traveled from Cuba several times, taking a small delegation to Port-au-Prince to discuss the possibility of the devolution.[35] Haitian officials must have greeted the entreaty exceedingly coolly, but the envoy leader hoped for "further friendly negotiations" in the future.[36] The Puerto Rican captain general sent along a letter of approval with a Dominican annexation petition to Madrid in 1847, and the next governor, General Juan Prim, also wrote to Madrid to suggest that annexation would be a strategically sound policy.[37] Madrid officials were slower to be convinced. Spain had virtually no commercial interests in Haiti or the Dominican Republic, and peninsular authorities generally viewed protection requests with a mixture of distaste and disinterest. Too many international complications—and little material gain—would arise from annexation, they concluded. In response, Dominican envoys appealed directly to Caribbean officials, making entreaties in Cuba from 1843 through 1845, to Puerto Rico in 1845, again to Puerto Rico in 1846, and so on. So many of these island-to-island missions were conducted that the queen passed a royal order insisting that the Caribbean officials consult with the peninsula before they took any actions whatsoever.[38]

After the massive U.S. expansion of the late 1840s, however, peninsular authorities began to direct their attention more acutely to growing U.S. interests on Hispaniola. The northern Dominican coast—Puerto Plata and Samaná Bay in particular—was a likely center of filibuster organizing. The Puerto Rican governor sent an alarmist report in 1852 that a massive filibuster immigration scheme to Hispaniola was underfoot.[39] A coded royal order authorized the governor of Cuba to work with Báez and the governor of Puerto Rico to disembark Spanish troops in the republic should it be necessary. Spain would have to take great precautions in mounting a military response, the report cautioned. If they seemed like an invading force, the "emancipated peoples from both sides of the island, fearing the reestablishment of slavery, would rise up against the government itself and call on the Haitian Empire, thus establishing race war," the author fretted.[40] "Rare is the boat that enters [Curaçao] that doesn't bring adventurers of all nations seeking passage to Haiti or Santo Domingo," another informer reported.[41] Spanish authorities named a secret agent to keep an eye on the republic, commissioned major reports on the state of the island, and ordered further news to be sent regularly to Washington, DC, and Cuba.[42] Spanish officials sent home reports that filibusters planned to take Haiti as well and suggested it would be done easily.[43] The rumors were inchoate: that the French might help reunification (this one was plausible), that reunification would make the island into a "refuge" to thousands of U.S. filibusters (this one was far less likely), and that Haiti would mount some sort of filibuster campaign of its own (this one tapped old fears of imagined Haitian imperialism).[44] Officials worried that the Haitian government itself was "making great sacrifices" to attract Dominican émigrés and other "adventurers of all nations" for unspecified anticolonial ends.[45] With just three hundred men and propaganda, Haitian agents could "revolutionize the island of Cuba," authorities fretted.[46]

With U.S. treaty attempts in 1854, Spanish authorities considered the U.S. threat even more concrete. The U.S. diplomatic corps in Santo Domingo had impeccable filibuster credentials, and they were dedicated and aggressive. Jane Storm Cazneau reached Santo Domingo in 1853 after more than a decade of pro-slavery and pro-expansion advocacy, as well as tours and boosterism in Texas, Mexico, and Cuba. She wrote for the *United States Magazine and Democratic Review*, the *New York Sun*, and a number of other periodicals under a pen name.[47] She knew infamous filibusters Narciso López and William Walker personally and used her connections with Secretary of State William Marcy to secure her husband's position as special diplomatic envoy to the Dominican Republic.[48] The British and French consuls conspired to oppose Cazneau's 1854 treaty proposal; even though it collapsed, Spanish authorities sprang into action. Spanish secret agents to the Dominican Republic began to report directly to Cuba as well as Madrid, and Cuban and Puerto Rican officials chose diplomatic staff for Santo Domingo at long last.[49] Spain's first commercial agent, Eduardo San Just, arrived in Santo Domingo in 1854. Recent events had only "awoken the Spanish spirit and lively enthusiasm of the inhabitants to repel all the hordes of adventurers from the North who invade this privileged soil," San Just rhapsodized confidently; he added, "The North American question is totally dead for now."[50] Still, concern over the United States' pending treaty (and the alleged concession of the Samaná peninsula) spurred Spain into signing a treaty of recognition in 1855. The treaty authors remonstrated that the territory—the "favored jewel of Columbus"—must be "kept in the command of the RAZA that TODAY populates them, NEVER passing, in whole or in part, to the hands of FOREIGN RAZAS."[51]

Spain finally recognized the republic in 1855 and sent diplomatic staff to both parts of the island, without recognizing Haiti. For all its coercive fraternal language, Spanish diplomacy was totally brusque and tactless. The Spanish consul in Santo Domingo intervened so aggressively to disrupt ongoing negotiations with the United States that even the British consul, himself only recently opposed, expressed chagrin. Privately, San Just permitted even more hostility. He wondered if Santana's administration could "even be called a government" and claimed he was surrounded by "blacks from Seybo, half-naked." The "Dominican government, *if you can even call it that*, is totally demoralized," he reported, with some satisfaction.[52] He was so rude to Dominican officials that they registered a complaint with the Spanish secretary of state.[53] The newly named emissary to Haiti, Manuel Cruzat, was far worse. Besides being involved in British intrigue that supported Haitian reannexation of the Dominican Republic—"even though I blush to admit it," he managed—his approach was generally blundering and malicious.[54] Seeking an audience with the emperor, Cruzat instead sent his secretary, who "barely [spoke] French, and not a word of Creole," and who subsequently refused to take off his hat in Soulouque's palace when ordered to do so by a functionary.⁵⁵ Cruzat demanded reparations by Haiti's foreign minister for what allegedly happened next: the emperor himself appeared in the window, Cruzat claimed, and allegedly insulted the secretary, "What a person, that fucking white man doesn't want to salute my palace!"⁵⁶ "Haitians hate the entire white race," Cruzat complained.⁵⁷ The Spanish secretary of state, irritated—he had explicitly told Cruzat to take pains to avoid incident, given the sensitivity of relations between the slave power and Haiti—instead recommended Cruzat's decommission.⁵⁸

The first Spanish consul, Antonio Maria Segovia, reached Dominican soil in late 1855, marking a new escalation of Spanish intervention. Fearing that political divisions in Santo Domingo would inevitably invite U.S. intervention, Segovia proposed a protectorate scheme in which military and foreign policy matters would be under Spanish control.⁵⁹ A protectorate was a fairly typical political construction, one that Spanish contemporaries praised. Just a few years later, proponents compared Mexican protectorate plans favorably with Britain's protectorate in Greece and Belgium. Forfeiture of sovereignty might actually "secure . . . independence" by bringing political order and preventing U.S. aggression, Spanish writers argued.⁶⁰ Felipe Fernández de Castro, the same official who had made missions from Cuba to regain Santo Domingo from Haiti in the 1820s and 1830s, penned "Proyecto de pacificación de los Estados Hispanoamericanos" from London in 1857, with the idea of a Hispano-American confederation. He was heartily in support of Dominican annexation, arguing that forfeiture might combat ambitious opportunists within the country and also help reduce poverty.⁶¹ Segovia's proposal in Santo Domingo gained no traction, but his matriculation of Dominicans as Spanish citizens did. El Oasis, a capital city paper that was fiercely critical of sitting president Santana, ran advertisements for the matriculation throughout the spring and summer of 1856. The consul dismissed all opposition in the capital as mere "calumny."⁶²

Through the late 1850s, a number of incidents rattled Spanish nerves about U.S. intent and collaboration on Hispaniola. Diplomatic ties brought a more regular flow of information to both neighboring islands. In the spring of 1859, the newly arrived Cuban governor, Francisco Serrano, warned other authorities that a thirty-five-person expedition of U.S. filibusters had arrived in Haiti with their eyes trained on Cuba, and the Haitian navy seized a Spanish ship suspected of trafficking slaves.⁶³ News followed that another handful of Cuban exiles arrived in Port-au-Prince the following month.⁶⁴ Serrano, meanwhile, was listening attentively to pro-annexation advocates. Mariano Álvarez, the new Spanish consul in the Dominican Republic and an advocate of annexation, submitted an extensive report that piqued Serrano's interest; the two officials corresponded throughout the year. "There is no country in which nature offers more resources, nor where inhabitants are in a worse state," Álvarez proclaimed.[65] Álvarez saw tremendous prospects for trade and regional strategic advantage, extolling the virtues of Samaná Bay as a fueling station and suggesting that agriculture and the cattle trade—particularly with the plantations of Cuba—could be easily stimulated.[66] Lumber and fine woods (especially mahogany), coal, cotton, tobacco, sugar, coffee, cacao, and mineral resources might all follow, he argued. A handful of wealthy Dominicans, Canary islanders, and Venezuelan émigrés were already planning "large plantations of coffee, sugarcane, and other seeds" on the riverbanks near the capital, he continued.[67] He estimated that annexation could be realized with just two thousand troops and a number of civil servants.[68] Other reports echoed his.[69] For the moment, however, the Crown remained impervious. "We consider all independent republics our best friends," it demurred to one such entreaty in 1859, "so I will limit myself to wishing that your republic might prosper."[70]

Mythmaking of a Faithful Populace

As negotiations between the Cuban governor and Dominican officials escalated in 1860, Santana and his ministers offered a streamlined, two-part annexation argument: the threat of Haiti and fidelity to Spain. Serious revisionism was necessary. In previous decades, Dominican annexationists had been wildly omnivorous in their petitions. Dominican foreign minister Manuel Joaquín Del Monte was as ready to sign away sovereignty to a French protectorate in 1843 as he was to support Spanish annexation in 1861, for example.[71] In the interim, the French consul reported, quite reasonably, that Santana was "a man of a very French heart."[72] An annexationist minority in the Cibao valley steadily preferred the United States, but they were simply too distant from the southern machinations.[73] U.S. speculators were close to important officials in the capital, too. Lobbying with her husband, Jane Cazneau bribed officials regularly. The Cazneau house was "*always so full of officers that he seems almost a member of the Government,*" one journalist observed.[74] Despite professions of fidelity, Santana was not particularly close with the Catholic Church, either. He kept its lands, seized during unification, to distribute to his allies, and he battled with the archbishop. The new interim archbishop, Fernando Arturo de Meriño, hated annexation and Santana equally.[75] Nor was there anything like an imminent threat from the west. Years after Soulouque's resounding defeat, Geffrard had sought a treaty for peace and trade between the two states the very moment he rose to the presidency, roundly critiqued the policy of his predecessor, and redoubled his dedication to domestic reforms.[76] Dominican reporters knew this, and they had long since turned their attentions to domestic political instability and pressing economic concerns. "Haiti is not thinking of invading the Dominican Republic, nor any similarly exaggerated idea," the Spanish consul in Haiti confirmed.[77]

Both Santana's allies and local Spanish officials were invested in new narratives. As his presidency was collapsing, again, in 1860, Santana's petitions sounded desperately urgent. Haiti was "an oppressor who made it its task to destroy [Santo Domingo]," he insisted.[78] The new Spanish consul, Mariano Álvarez, was an indefatigable ally, colluding closely with both Santana and his vice president, Antonio Abad Alfau. As Alfau's brother, also a high-ranking general, traveled to Madrid to lobby for guns and material support, the annexationist coterie focused their attention on the Cuban governor, escalating a letter-writing campaign that lasted all year. In a secret meeting with Cuban authorities, Alfau suggested that Santana was considering declaring the annexation unilaterally.[79] Meanwhile, Consul Álvarez produced a massive report. Like other Spanish officials in Cuba and Madrid, he emphasized annexation as a means to forestall U.S. aggression, an argument that was almost totally absent from Dominican elites' petitions. He readily accepted a general paradigm of race war, however. His report described the whiteness of Dominicans ("eight-tenths" and "all Catholic," he specified, except for "one miserable Methodist church for the black Americans") alongside the strategic value of the territory itself.[80] "Two enemy races covet this precious Antille," he maintained.[81]

On the question of Dominican fidelity to Spain, extensive rewriting was necessary. Álvarez and Alfau discussed the history of the country at some length. Together, they rewrote the previous forty years, arguing for an ever-faithful populace who remembered Spain's "paternal affection" fondly. Both of them insisted that the country's unique independence process demonstrated Dominican faithfulness to Spain. The 1821 "Brief Independence" (in which a junta in the capital simply declared Santo Domingo to be part of Gran Colombia, several months before the 1822–44 unification with Haiti) had been the work of an "ambitious and traitorous" few, both argued. Unlike other young republics that had broken violently with Spain, the Dominican Republic had, "on the contrary, been the model of fidelity and love to the afflicted Metropole," Álvarez told the Cuban governor.[82] If the 1821 independence, which lasted two months, was treason or a fluke, neither man could easily account for unification with Haiti, which lasted peacefully for twenty-two years. There was no space for the Unification period in annexation history, so both men ignored it. The Spanish consul jumped ahead to an entirely fanciful account of 1844 separation from Haiti, alleging that Dominicans hoped "it was an opening for the return of Spanish sovereignty that they had so desired."[83] Forty years after independence, many expressed "constant desire to tighten relations," he asserted.[84] Alfau added a hint of elitism to these claims, praising the "most notable of the population" for their Spanishness.[85] Álvarez continued to write letters to the governor and to meet with Cuban officials through the end of 1860 and the beginning of 1861, capitalizing on short visits of Cuban ships.[86]

To cement support for annexation, Governor Serrano commissioned another report from a high-ranking officer in Havana, who submitted a hyperbolic tale of Dominican Spanishness, with ample racist marginalia.[87] Brigadier Antonio Peláez y Campomanes began the memoir with (what he considered to be) praise, reporting, "There are sons of Spain here who preserve our customs with purity."[88] Even as Peláez tried to emphasize what he perceived to be laudable aspects of Dominican society (i.e., loyalty, whites, anti-Haitianism), he could not contain explicit antiblack venom. The report continued with the traditional narrative of the republic's 1821 separation—but Peláez embellished his version to make José Núñez de Cáceres, the principal author of Brief Independence, not just an ambitious traitor but a "miserable black." He assured Governor Serrano that the population was "half white" and insisted that they were "noble, hospitable, proud of being Spanish." Segovia's mistake in allowing some Dominicans to matriculate as Spanish citizens in 1856 was not the policy itself, Peláez argued, but having allowed black Dominican men to register for Spanish citizenship.

Seasoned in Cuba, Brigadier Peláez indulged extensively in tropes and fantasies of black submission. The idea of Dominican loyalty played easily into elite loyalist fantasies in Cuba and Puerto Rico, the idea that affective bonds of "Spanishness" could override and sublimate massive social inequalities. Although Dominicans were overwhelmingly free people of color, the officer rushed to emphasize that these Dominicans shared deep and visceral affinity for Spain. "I have heard elderly people [of color] recall, on the brink of tears, the happiness and tranquility that they enjoyed with Spain," he rhapsodized.[89] He invented a servile "poor, black man," who carefully saved a Spanish coat of arms through all the years of Haitian rule. "Valiant, docile, and submissive, they recognize in whites more capacity and knowledge for leadership and only aspire not to be repressed," he fantasized. "Despite twenty-two years of unification with Haiti, the *pardos* and *morenos* of Santo Domingo preserve the language and customs of their former masters," he continued, as though black Dominicans were recently arrived from Africa.[90] He insisted, too, on a common "hatred" for Haiti.[91] Pleased with the brigadier's report, Governor Serrano charged Peláez with leading the forces into the newly recolonized territory.[92]

One last figure remained for reinvention: Santana himself. Santana, the same head of state who had been "far too horrible, even for ridicule" and surrounded by "blacks from Seybo, half-naked," according to the former Spanish consul, became a capable collaborator.[93] Consul Álvarez cast him as a pliant partner who listened to Spanish advice; he was an "astute and wise *campesino*," he remarked with satisfaction.[94] Santana was "the guarantee of security for the country" in a critical situation, the consul concluded, and other authorities agreed.[95] A subsequent report in Madrid summarized Santana's arguments, calling the risk of Haitian and U.S. incursion "more critical each day." Although not ignorant of Santana's claims to military heroism and amenable to his narratives about the "constant threat" of Haiti, these officials made their security priorities clear. The "more formidable enemy . . . appearing as a disarmed friend" was the United States, the official assessed: "[U.S.] success, sooner or later, cannot be fought . . . even if all the Dominicans are Spanish at heart."[96]

Santana's annexation address of 18 March 1861 cemented narratives of sanguine fidelity. "Our national glories are inherited from the grand and noble lineage to which we owe our origin," he began. He continued, "Numerous, spontaneous, and popular missives have arrived in my hands; . . . today you hope that what your loyalty has always desired might come to pass. Religion, language, beliefs, and customs, all we preserve with purity . . . ; and the nation to which we are so tied today opens her arms as a loving mother who gathers up her son, lost in the tempest in which his brothers have perished." The entire weight of annexation now lay on Núñez de Cáceres's shoulders alone. "Only the ambition and resentment of one man separated us from the mother country," Santana announced. Before becoming enveloped in civil war like "those other disgraced republics . . . [Spain] will give us the civil liberty that her *pueblos* enjoy [and] will guarantee us natural liberty," he argued. All laws of the former republic were to be respected. In the new state of peace, "She will protect us . . . making one people, one united family, as we always were . . . raising the flag next to the cross that Columbus dug in these unknown lands," he concluded. "Long Live the

Queen! Long Live Liberty! Long Live Religion! Long Live the Dominican People! Long Live the Spanish Nation!"⁹⁷

Annexation in the Shadow of Slavery

By the 1850s, the idea of political federation, including protectorates, circulated throughout the Spanish empire. The Cuban elites' dissatisfaction with exclusion from power had drawn a significant minority into support of U.S. annexation in the previous decade. One plan from 1851 proposed local autonomy under a reduced Spanish authority in response.⁹⁸ One Puerto Rican author called for a partial decolonization of sorts, an evolution of Caribbean holdings into a loose moral Spanish federation; authorities prevented his work from circulating on the island.⁹⁹ Federation was a common plan on the peninsula as well. Contemporaries proposed renewing political federation between Spain and Portugal, constructing binational infrastructure and education.¹⁰⁰ Liberal commentators, in support of Dominican annexation, pointed out that Cuba and Puerto Rico's lack of integration into the Spanish constitution was a "most dangerous inequality."¹⁰¹ When General Serrano reached Cuba in 1859, he married the daughter of a rich Cuban family, revived the idea of white Cuban representation in Madrid, and hinted that his own executive post might at long last be curtailed.¹⁰² The Cuban governor hoped that Dominican annexation would be the first step in a more centralized legal regime and a transformation of the Caribbean empire from "simple colonies that produce benefits, more or less," to a resurgent, united Overseas Spain.¹⁰³ Spain would make Caribbean residents feel "truly Spanish," on the path to "total assimilation . . . slowly and gradually procured," Serrano urged. He had "profound conviction" that the humiliation caused by legal differences prevented progress.¹⁰⁴ With a stronger moral and cultural foothold, Spain could move beyond the three largest Antilles to extend its influence to "the bosom of Mexico" and beyond.¹⁰⁵

Proponents of Dominican annexation vacillated between narratives of inclusion and exclusion in the same work, even in the same sentence. Mariano Torrente's *Política ultramarina* (Overseas Politics, 1854) argued hard for Dominican annexation to preserve Spanish familial ties in the Caribbean, even as the author viciously condemned emancipation and distanced himself from Dominicans themselves.¹⁰⁶ A longtime official in Cuba, Torrente dismissed the British and French islands as failures and was bald in his antiblack racism and support for imperial aggression in Africa. "In every emancipation system, there are the same evils, the same vices, and inevitable ruin," he spat.[107] He unequivocally condemned Dominican subsistence labor and cast doubt on individuals' capacity to transcend it. He warned that the majority of Dominicans—"who are all of color," he interjected—demonstrated "the laziness typical of proletarians, *because one cannot obligate them to work.*" He mystified material scarcity in the territory, complaining, "They prefer to go around in rags, eat nothing more than sugar and plantains, which are obtained with very little labor."[108] After reviewing at some length the changing dynamics of power and commerce with the United States and Britain, Torrente clearly supported annexation of the Dominican Republic, even as he periodically claimed neutrality.[109] Just three hundred men would be necessary if the government were to want to take Santo Domingo as a protectorate, he urged, dismissing the idea of international opposition. "Our rights over that country are undeniable," he wrote. "No nation could justly allege that it had the right to intervene in what can be called purely a family question."[110] Quickly, his language shifted from familial metaphors to possessive ones. "Anglo-Americans . . . cannot detain us in any way, " he persisted, "as it is only a matter of the legitimate owner of an errant or lost resource coming back to collect it in light of his indisputable right to do so."[111]

Torrente reconciled Dominican annexation with the imminent end of the slave trade and new controls of free people of color. "The slave trade debate . . . has taken . . . the direction of speculation and politics," he began, in his report for Dominican annexation. The trade had already effectively ceased, with some exceptions, to Puerto Rico. More than a thousand enslaved Africans and Afro–Puerto Ricans were sold from Puerto Rico to Cuba in the late 1840s. "An island with only 50,000 slaves . . . will not fall apart," the governor announced. He did not tolerate open abolitionist discourse on the island, but he felt fairly confident about the island's potential course. "There are enough free workers here to replace them," he wrote, "I hope the exodus continues."[112] An expanding coffee economy raised prices on the coast and drove rural Puerto Ricans to formerly uninhabited interior lands. Their participation in coffee cultivation slowly tied them into systems of credit that bound them more to the coast and the colonial state.[113] Authorities and planters used vagrancy decrees, meanwhile, to push others onto export-oriented farms. Workers were supposed to carry a passbook (*libreta*) that established their occupation, listed their debts, and attested to their conduct.[114] Spanish authorities and planters in Cuba also sought to control free Cubans of color, whose numbers doubled from 1846 to 1861.[115] East Asian contract laborers first arrived in Cuba in 1847; nearly 125,000 arrived in the next two decades.[116] Torrente's proposal for Santo Domingo, similarly, was indentured African and Asian immigration, to be supervised by Spanish settlers. The indentured workers could "cover the most urgent cultivation needs," while the abolitionists "could calm down and be sure their wishes had been fully realized," he wrote.[117] White colonists would oversee everything, and would settle as a "bronze wall" against Haiti and U.S. filibusters. "The greatest degree of prosperity would soon result," he urged.[118]

Six years after Torrente's report, Governor Serrano placed heavy emphasis on Dominican consent as annexation began precipitously. A royal order from December 1860 authorized Serrano to take whatever measures necessary to protect the Dominican Republic from foreign invasion. Despite condemnations of annexation from Madrid, the governor felt the order gave him ample leeway to proceed.[119] Another military delegation brought back reports of annexation's "voluntary" nature after discussions with Santana's officials.[120] Meanwhile, Santana wrote to Governor Serrano announcing that he planned to effect the turnover to Spain no later than February 1861; later, one of his ministers pushed the date to March.[121] At Serrano's directive, Santana's officials solicited signatures of approval in a number of towns throughout the territory. Thirty-three towns and two military posts remitted signatures, totaling about 4,000 signatures out of the republic's population of about 200,000, or about 2 percent of the country's citizens.[122] A total of 636 men signed in the capital. By contrast, only 140 did so in Santiago de los Caballeros. The majority of the proclamations, twenty-two out of the thirty-five, were straightforward acknowledgments of reincorporation with little else added; they amounted to a pro forma acknowledgment of Santana's coup. Just seven of the thirty-five statements mentioned Haiti—allegedly Santana's primary reason to seek Spain's protection—whereas others focused on agriculture, political peace, and legal reform.[123] Significantly for annexation's future, two towns, distant from each other—Barahona and La Vega—reminded the Crown of their promise to leave the republic's laws intact, mentioning explicitly the continued abolition of slavery.

In Puerto Rico, the governor acted altogether startled by the news, which was sent not by the Cuban governor but preemptively in the form of a letter hand delivered by a Dominican official.[124] Santana "has told me the details . . . and asked for forces and money," Rafael Echagüe noted. But, he continued, distinctly irritated, "As the Governor of Cuba has been the authority elected by Her Majesty to deal with General Santana relative to this delicate negotiation, as the circumstances [of the matter] have been completely strange . . . , and as I have received no communication, neither from the Government of Her Majesty nor from the indicated Governor, not even in case an eventuality of this sort might present itself, . . . I cannot adopt any resolution whatsoever."[125] He declined to send aid to Santana but resolved to write the Cuban governor immediately.

Although news had not yet reached Madrid either, the annexation project was quickly expanding. From Santo Domingo, Mariano Álvarez wrote to the Ministry of State immediately, and Serrano did so as well. The Cuban governor's 26 March letter to Spain emphasized security; Spanish troops must move in immediately in order to solidify authority, he argued. He urged metropole officials, "Now that we are involved, isn't our honor at stake?"[126] In the summer of 1861, he sailed to Santo Domingo himself to confront firsthand the political realities of the newly annexed territory. In fact, Serrano and his Havana-based officials threw themselves immediately into the details of the annexation. All Spanish officials involved in the initial annexation and occupation accepted these basic premises that Dominican envoys had laid out: that the laws of the republic be respected, that the rampant and almost worthless paper money be amortized, and that slavery remain absolutely abolished. The task at hand was to reconcile these stipulations—particularly the slavery clause—with Spanish overseas law, and to do so quickly. In June 1861, Governor Serrano named José Malo de Molina, an auxiliary (*suplente*) of Havana's municipal government, as a special commissioner charged to submit a report on the government and social organization of the extinguished republic; he finished less than a month later and presented it to the governor in Havana in September.[127] Malo de Molina averred that he had gathered data as best he could given the constraints of time and the immensity of the task. "If the subject were not so urgent, perhaps I would tear up these smudged pages," he wrote.[128]

Both Malo de Molina and Governor Serrano pondered the issue of legislative reform for the new colony. As the Madrid newspaper *Crónica de Ambos Mundos* asked, "If it is true that the same special laws that govern Cuba, Puerto Rico, and the Philippine Islands [will apply]—that is, dictatorial ones—how will Spain respond to the votes and wishes of the residents, who, according to the letter of general SANTANA, want to *adopt the liberties of the Spanish people as their own*?"[129] "It is beyond doubt that the Dominicans are anxious to establish Spanish legislation as soon as possible: but which legislation should this be?" Malo de Molina asked.[130] Another writer suggested that Havana be the capital of a three-island federative government.[131] Havana's elite would have supported such a plan. In anticipation—or at least desire—of more legislative power in the empire, Cuban authorities had gone so far as to name four potential senators to Madrid in the event that their representation might be recognized.[132]

None of the federative options answered the question of legal freedom in Santo Domingo. "There is no doubt that the principal desire of those inhabitants is to be equal to the Peninsula, not just because they solicited it at the time of incorporation, but also because it would be positive and infallible proof that slavery would not be reestablished, as some suspect, and as the Haitians have tried to convince the people of color and others who are discontented [with annexation]," Malo de Molina wrote.[133] Serrano concurred that Cuba's code would not do,

> with the supposition that the race of color has limited civil rights, and absolutely no political ones, . . . applied to a country where *pardos* and even pure *morenos* have occupied and occupy high posts in administration and the military, and in which the *everything for everyone* of liberal governments has been known here for so long. . . . Is it feasible to establish, for example, a personal legislation that allows the sentence of flogging for one race, the law that excludes all participation in public office, and all their ramifications, in a country whose social dictionary has erased the word servitude, and in which there is a perfect and absolute leveling among its inhabitants, no matter what their origin?[134]

"The Majesty's wish is that . . . the province be ruled by the same laws as the other overseas dominions, especially by those of Cuba," Serrano wrote, but he warned the sovereign that "if such a thing were to happen, it would be to introduce an element of distrust, motivating malcontents . . . to make false interpretations." The "most essential difference" between the island and its colonial neighbors lay in its social norms; the "same strong and numerous race . . . kept in constant domination" by the laws of Cuba was "interlaced with the white in Santo Domingo, making it impossible, or at least not without great difficulty, to mark the dividing line that law and custom maintain in Cuba and Puerto Rico," Serrano argued.[135]

Despite royal edicts from May 1861 to the contrary, therefore, both Governor Serrano and Commissioner Malo de Molina concluded that metropolitan law should rule in the newly annexed territory. Peninsular law would suit the territory just fine, Malo de Molina insisted, advising Serrano to disregard earlier recommendations he had made to the contrary. Without slavery and a "diversity of castes," the issue would not arise, he asserted.[136] Serrano was equally optimistic, even pointed, in his recommendation for metropolitan law. "I see the annexation of Santo Domingo as a providential event that presents Spain with the necessity of thinking of the means to resolve for itself the grave question that is today being aired in the United States of America, and whose solution must have a very direct influence on the destiny of Cuba," he wrote.[137] The application of the civil code of Spain in Santo Domingo, "already published so that it may be practically studied, will be perhaps opportune," Serrano argued. "I do not think there would be a big problem with testing them. . . . Few times has such an opportune situation emerged for a test of this kind: Santo Domingo is a totally virgin populace in this aspect."[138] "Sooner or later the laws with no political character have to be made extensive to [Cuba and Puerto Rico]," he continued. Colonial reforms already made Cuban law so similar to metropolitan law, he asserted, that "just one step would produce perfect equality."[139] Certainly, there existed "inconveniences" in Cuban and Puerto Rican society, he admitted (with wild understatement); testing the law in free territory would be the perfect first step to reforms in all of Spain's Caribbean islands.[140] The mood among the Cuban officials was euphoric.[141]

The First Jewel in the Spanish Crown: The Debate in Madrid

> Noble and humanitarian work! How much blood and money the overseas possessions have cost Spain! How many sacrifices Spain makes even today in the deadly islands of Africa! How much did the continent of America cost her, and how liberal and giving has Spain been! How much has Spain been a true mother to those who gather at her lap in the shadow of her glorious flag!
> —FRANCISCO SERRANO

For several decades, Spanish imperial policy had grown more ambitious by increments. In 1844, Spain reclaimed the west-central African island of Fernando Po (Bioko) from the British. A handful of unsuccessful settler projects to the island—including a small group of illegally transported African men, women, and children (*emancipados*) who sought to leave Cuba—followed shortly thereafter.[142] Members of the O'Donnell administration were ready, even eager, to launch joint imperial military expeditions. Spanish troops fought alongside French forces in Cocinchina (Nam tiến) beginning in 1858. They were involved in the joint expeditionary force that arrived in Mexico in 1862 as well, although the expeditionary leader protested after Napoleon III's plans to instate the Austrian archduke became clear. Spain was unilaterally aggressive as well. The so-called War of Africa (1859–60), a one-year conflict with Morocco over the borders of the North African Spanish towns of Melilla and Ceuta, enjoyed wild popularity in Spain. Other confrontations stopped short of conquest; Spanish warships aggressively demanded reparations for their merchants or for other perceived slights in Port-au-Prince, Monrovia, and other ports.[143] After Dominican annexation, similar conflicts over reclamations escalated to the seizure of the Chincha Islands as putative payment, bringing outright conflict with both Peru and Chile.

In April 1861, however, when news of Dominican annexation first reached Spain, official reception was initially tepid. Despite repeated entreaties from Dominican officials, both members of the Unión Liberal government and the queen herself had explicitly rejected the idea of annexation in late 1860, the latter suggesting a one-year moratorium on consideration of the matter until November 1861.[144] In fact, the queen denied Governor Serrano's request to send more troops to fortify the island, although the news reached Havana after Cuban boats had already sailed.[145] Prime Minister Leopoldo O'Donnell also had Caribbean government experience: he served as governor of Cuba from October 1843 to February 1848, during the height of the repression of antislavery mobilization. He had resolved near the end of his tenure in Havana that Spain should avoid even the smallest reforms, "even those that appear insignificant." "Alarming concessions have been obtained by simple reforms [that have been] exploited in ways that were not foreseen," he insisted; rather than open up any window for such dangerous reforms, Spain ought merely to send its "most capable and active governors."[146] Any sort of social disorder would yield "the triumph of the colored castes, but if the evil is certain and the danger possibly imminent, the remedy is easy and known[;] it is enough to conserve the status quo with the most scrupulous measures," he insisted.[147] O'Donnell had opposed Dominican annexation entreaties since the 1840s, arguing that Spain should merely cultivate good sentiment in the republic, while "avoiding compromises of any kind."[148]

Madrid's vibrant newspaper sphere reflected only tepid interest in repeated Dominican entreaties throughout 1860. The progressive and democratic press did not even consider that annexation was a possibility and discounted it entirely.[149] When news arrived of Santana's and Serrano's actions, a number of journalists expressed literal disbelief at the event, insisting instead that the Cuban governor must have been merely protecting Spanish soldiers in the area.[150] Journalists voiced serious doubts about the strategic wisdom of the project. The moderate newspaper El Contemporáneo noted, "The news that we have about the origin and unfolding of such an important event is so scarce . . . we do not know the role of the Spanish government, nor has any information at all been gathered that guarantees us the unanimity of the movement."[151] Moderate *La Época* published a number of condemnations, fretting that relations with other Latin American republics would become "impossible" if they, too, were to fear any such usurpation of sovereignty.[152] The government should take necessary "precautions and guarantees to make clear that the annexation is not an act of ambition by Spain," another writer opined.[153] The moderate paper *La España* suggested that some sort of a confederation would be a cheaper, more optimal option for Spain, a position it continued to hold for months, even after the debate had been resolved by the queen.[154] Finally, writers at *El Clamor Público* worried about the cost of such a project and reminded their readers that Spain needed development of its own. An author argued that Spain ought to direct all its resources to internal development "before thinking of extending its territory with acquisitions of dubious utility." Spain's own industry was "meager and backward," the author argued, and domestic infrastructure should be the primary focus.[155] Nearly two-thirds of Spain needed colonization of its own, another concluded.[156]

Journalists cast pointed skepticism on Santana's motives and demanded more proof of unanimity on the part of the Dominican people. The issue of popular consent was key. The Dominican leader was being pragmatic, not sentimental or nationalist, and he had acted because he had "no other means of salvation," they argued.[157] *La Época* warned that the move might have stemmed from party intrigue.[158] A number of periodicals, then, suggested that a plebiscite ought to be effected before Spain accept the annexation as legal. Not surprisingly, vocally skeptic *La Época* urged O'Donnell's government not to take "any definite steps in the question of annexation, nor even protectorate, . . . until the sentiments and needs of the island are perfectly clear."[159] The *Correspondiente de España* optimistically assured its readers that a plebiscite would settle the matter, writing, "In no way will Spain reject the annexation, when they have the conviction that it is the result of a general and spontaneous vote of the people and their legitimate authorities."[160] It must have seemed, of course, that no such measure was forthcoming. Democratic *La Discusión* complained scathingly, "There is an extremely important difference between president Santana cheating the liberty and independence of a people for his advantage and the Dominican people themselves asking for annexation."[161] Even after the queen made an official decree recognizing annexation on 19 May, *La Discusión* persisted in demanding approbation by universal suffrage. "That way future complications would be avoided," the editorial insisted.[162] As the fact of the queen's approval sank in, such complaints fell on deafer ears.

As the fact of annexation set in, Spanish papers became pragmatic, echoing the uncertainty of Cuban officials about the legislative status of the new colony. The progressive press, clearly unacquainted with Santana's strong-arm political style, wondered aloud if annexation would curtail political liberties in the former republic. They hoped instead that the annexation might foster more self-government and representation in the region, perhaps even representation in the Cortes. Colonial reform was absolutely on the agenda. *La Discusión* urged that the former republic be admitted with all the same rights as a Spanish province and observed, "If this requires us to be more liberal with Cuba and Puerto Rico, let's be so, the time has come."[163] *Las Novedades* concurred, arguing that annexation marked a "propitious occasion" in order to make metropolitan rights more general in the Caribbean.[164] The moderate press, however, toed a more conservative line. Authors were very much opposed to political reforms, citing not only the precedent of past independent movements but also the authors' own investment in the plantation economies of Cuba and Puerto Rico.[165] More political rights to Cuba and Puerto Rico "would reduce them to the miserable state in which the Mexican state finds itself today," editorials argued. Rather, Spain should just send its best and brightest legislators, *La España* concluded, echoing O'Donnell's own proclamations from the Caribbean more than a decade before.[166] As for Santo Domingo, moderate papers urged that a protectorate status ought to be conferred instead. Any liberal tendencies would thus be detained on the island, and slavery, a "social necessity," would meet far fewer legal complications.

As 1861 progressed, the Spanish press nevertheless soon stirred from its relative ambivalence on the Santo Domingo question to proffer increasingly enthusiastic support. Narratives began to depict the territory as an untapped resource: Santo Domingo was a "magnificent portion of the New World" whose generosity, nobility, and patriotism "overshadowed Spanish ministers' recalcitrance."[167] Its natural resources and strategic Samaná Bay would render it not only an important Spanish stronghold against growing U.S. interests but also a potentially profitable one, Madrid newspapers argued. Many cited the annexation as an act of mercy toward a threatened state destined to be swallowed by Haitian or—"worse for us, though not for the Dominicans"—Yankee imperialism.[168] Not to accept the annexation offer would be to invite U.S. incursion and imperil Cuba.[169] *El Contemporáneo* now found the annexation to be a "necessity" and urged "Columbus's island should not be abandoned again by Spain."[170] Despite their misgivings in April, the bulk of the press became largely supportive of the apparently "spontaneous" nature of the event.[171] Revisionism came full circle in an article by La América, which argued that not to accept Dominican annexation in fact would be a violation of liberal principles:

> The novelty of the annexation, was neither as unexpected nor as unforeseen as some think. . . . It is very strange that the liberal theories that predominate today in educated nations are not being applied to the Dominicans' resolution. . . . It is clear that the Dominicans are fully within their rights to rid themselves of their sovereignty. . . . Spain would be unjustified in the eyes of humanity, if it were to ignore the cry for help from a people in whose veins the same blood runs, whose religion and language are the same as ours, and who is nothing more, in effect, than a ramification of our own family.[172]

Echoing Félix de Bona's aspirations of cultural confederation, the papers brimmed with optimism about the possibilities of the remarkable precedent.

In quick succession, the "African War" in Morocco and Dominican annexation caused something of nationalist fervor to be whipped up over the prospect of new imperial gains for Spain.[173] Florid elegies of Spain's past achievements and the language of heroism and civilization permeated the national press. The "drunkenness of a war in Africa [and] a new adventure in Mexico on the old and glorious routes of Hernán Cortes" sparked romantic reveries about Santo Domingo, the "Land of Columbus," as well.[174] Discourses about these exploits, of course, lent themselves to exaggeration and fancy; historian Francisco Febres-Cordero Carrillo argues that their "rhetoric of action" was intended principally to "anesthetize the middle class, who lacked the means of effective political participation."[175] Nonetheless, borrowing from the British lexicon of empire, one newspaper reported thusly on the new annexation of Santo Domingo: "The event could not be more felicitous, and we congratulate the Queen of Spain, the Nation, and the Ministry. . . . In just over a year, the Monarchy in which [once] the sun never set, dismembered by revolution, has considerably broadened its limits in Africa and America."[176] Politicians envisioned nothing less than an adjustment in the balance of power in the hemisphere.

A number of Cubans—creole and Spanish born—offered to serve in the Morocco campaign, petitioning for passage from Cuba with "the ardent desire . . . to march into battle for the holy Spanish cause."[177] One spectator from Havana urged the creation of a voluntary battalion of free men of color, a plan that he saw as "economical" but also in the interests of "the aggrandizement of the Spanish name," particularly "should the war take on another aspect after Tetuán's occupation."[178] A pamphlet from Barcelona—which would later circulate in newly annexed Santo Domingo—proclaimed, "The Africa War is one of the most glorious pages in the history of the Spanish nation in the present century. Everything is great and memorable: the justice of our cause, the enthusiasm of all the classes of the country, the valor and suffering of our soldiers, the intelligence and bravery that guide them to victory, which is the triumph of the Christian Civilization over Islamism and barbarity."[179] The *Times* says Haiti will soon be annexed, we say "let it be so," *La Época* proclaimed. "With all of la Española, discovered by Isabel I and recuperated by Isabel II, the strength of the Spanish in the Antilles is unmatched."[180] Dominican elites praised the Morocco campaign, too. Rhapsodized the official Spanish paper in Santo Domingo, "Every Spanish bullet carried an idea."[181]

On 19 May 1861—a little more than two months after Pedro Santana proclaimed annexation and ordered a 101-cannon salute to the Spanish flag in Santo Domingo—the Spanish Ministry of State officially approved the measure.[182] "Her Majesty's Government could not ever be indifferent to the fate of the Spanish part of Santo Domingo," the decree read. "To abandon her to foreign intrigue, expose her to the invasions of an enemy race, would have been a very grave political error, and a total forgetting of honor and even humanity."[183] Assured that the act was "spontaneous," "unanimous," "in perfect harmony with the sentiments of all of the population," and even "against the will" of its closest collaborator, Francisco Serrano, the Crown promised to act "for the growth and prosperity of its overseas provinces, benefiting from the benefits of peace and institutions in harmony with modern civilization."[184] "Señor Santana" (who was in fact acting governor from the outset) should announce the news to all the authorities and influential people of Santo Domingo, the report concluded. When the Spanish Parliament convened after a six-month recess in November, the queen reiterated the same now-familiar arguments: that annexation was spontaneous, that a glorious role awaited Spain in the former republic and the rest of the Spanish world, that political independence had wreaked dangers in young republics, and so on.[185] Some representatives bristled at the fact that annexation had been declared in their absence, but news of the event had already been circulating in Cuban and Puerto Rican newspapers for months. Thus, one of the "first Jewels in the Spanish Crown" was officially incorporated by a vote of 200 to 80.[186]

On the issue of legislating the new colony, a royal decree announced a compromise: the criminal and commercial codes of Spain would provisionally rule, but the civil code was to continue to be governed by laws from the former republic, admitting custom and traditional practice.[187] Of slavery, the Crown wrote that it was "one disastrous thing of many that afflicts societies, but a necessary one in some regions. It will not be extinguished in Cuba nor in Puerto Rico, but neither will it be established in Santo Domingo nor consented to in any form. Santo Domingo finds itself between two Spanish provinces governed by special laws as per the Constitution of the Monarchy."[188] Some modifications might be necessary, the proclamation admitted, but it insisted that the constitutional distinctions would remain firm. In Santo Domingo, Pedro Santana's response, passed along to the Ministro de Guerra y Ultramar together with Governor Serrano's and Malo de Molina's reports, seemed to presage a peaceful transition to this new administration.[189] The "too-embarrassing case" of Dominican legislation being written in a "strange language" necessarily called for its replacement by Spanish law, he agreed.[190] So, too, did the glowing missive of the newly named regent of the Real Audiencia, Eduardo Alonso Colmenares, laud the changes in government at great length; he announced that the legislative body would take up the Supreme Court cases of the "extinguished republic" right away.[191]

Félix de Bona, president of the Free Society of Political Economy in Madrid, rushed to publish a text that announced a new era in race-based federation. Believing the annexation to be voluntary, he called the reincorporation "of extraordinary importance . . . the only example in history . . . [with] immeasurable transcendence" and with the potential to spark "a moral confederation . . . of the Spanish race on both continents."[192] He proposed a convention of Spanish American nations, where Spain could have "a pacific and conciliatory influence, an honorary presidency, and without threatening in the least the autonomy of each State . . . an economic union" that would in turn foment "the strength of the *raza*."[193] "Races, like nations and individuals, have an instinct for their self-preservation," de Bona argued, and would gain both freedom and strength through confederation.[194] "Races, like nations and individuals, benefit from the right to live and exercise their industry," he continued.[195] This utopic fraternity was not based on imperial dominance, de Bona claimed; "it does not suit us to enlarge our dominions in America, because it does not suit us to *dominate* anywhere," he insisted.[196] He continued, "We don't have the strength to dominate, and even if we did, it would be insanity to spend it on an unproductive and hateful domination."[197] Spain would be a guarantor of justice and security, beginning in Santo Domingo.

International Reception of Dominican Annexation

By February 1861, Haiti's government paper, Le Moniteur Haïtien, began publishing alarming annexation rumors circulating from neighboring islands.[198] L'Abeille de la Nouvelle-Orléans reported that it seemed Spain had purchased Santo Domingo and predicted that Spain would be a "dangerous neighbor."[199] In the weeks that followed, the Port-au-Prince papers published responses from Paris, Liverpool, London, Jamaica, and a number of U.S. cities. The Massachusetts legislature passed a resolution unanimously condemning the annexation. From Jamaica, the Morning Journal impugned an "unscrupulous" Dominican president and decried, "The news presages nothing less than the annihilation of the Haitian nationality."[200] Haiti's Moniteur reprinted critical opinions that predicted French and British opposition, as well as early signs of confusion from Madrid papers.[201] President Geffrard issued a formal protest when news of the annexation definitively arrived; Kingston's Gleaner republished Geffrard's protest in its entirety. "Haiti and Jamaica are the only two countries in the world where blacks and their descendants are permitted to exercise their rights," the paper asserted, gravely. Absent other foreign intervention, they urged Geffrard to resist.[202]

Less than one month after Dominican annexation was declared—surely the news had barely reached U.S. shores—a Confederate attack on Fort Sumter summoned an ever-increasing conflagration. It was in this moment of circumstantial opportunity that Dominican annexation slipped onto the international stage; Spain hoped it would cause as little disturbance as possible. Given their impossible preoccupation, U.S. complaints "might as well be directed at the sky," one Madrid newspaper exulted.[203] Anyway, the annexation fit with the aggressive colonial imagination of the moment. A French paper, La Presse, found Spain's "voluntary" premise a bit disingenuous and predicted some opposition, without summoning much outrage.[204] Observers even speculated that Spain might subsume Haiti under the Spanish flag as well. "It will now be for Spain to prove the sincerity of its pledges and to develop the riches of this noble island," one British observer wrote, blandly.[205] Le Siècle concluded that France might have just as much claim to the island and supposed Spain "might soon [have] a tour of Mexico!"[206]

On the ground in Santo Domingo, members of Santana's government marked annexation without a hitch. The French consul was not invited, and the Spanish consul awaited instruction. In fact, the act of annexation bore Santana's signature alone; he did not solicit a single consul signature. The French consul allowed as how his only instructions had been to prevent cession to the United States, and he predicted immediate recognition from Paris.[207] Even U.S. opportunist and sometime commercial agent Joseph Fabens considered that the project had "begun well." He felt his commercial pursuits might even be abetted by the change in flag. He praised the idea that they might be inviting in U.S. settlers: "How suggestive these facts! What amazing significance in them! Young Spain, breaking through her traditional meshes of intolerance and oppression, at one bold leap . . . !"[208] British consul Martin Hood admitted he was sober, remaining "perfectly quiet" in the matter.[209] He was skeptical of popular reception of the change of flags in the capital, which took place "in complete silence, it was really a melancholic spectacle: men and women were crying; no applause or even an audible whimper . . . and no one shot guns," he claimed.[210] He predicted the territory's difficult economic situation was likely to continue and remarked with concern that he would continue to verify the status of any residents of the territory who had escaped from slavery from neighboring Cuba and Puerto Rico.[211]

From Union officials and observers, reception of the annexation was resoundingly chilly but ultimately muted. Annexation represented a flagrant violation of the Monroe Doctrine and directly opposed U.S. interests in Samaná, authorities observed. New secretary of state William E. Seward took office in March 1861 and urged Lincoln to stir from the inaction of President Buchanan on the Dominican matter. He submitted strongly worded memos from the president to Spain's representative in Washington, Gabriel Tassara.[212] Nevertheless, President Lincoln explicitly forbade him from issuing a direct ultimatum to Spain. U.S. officials in Madrid did issue protests, but no action whatsoever was taken.[213] "I say, fix your own house," the former consul to Santo Domingo reported from New York, smugly.[214] A number of newspapers—the *Chicago Tribune* and the *New York Times* among them—expressed disbelief at the events and called for action in defense of the Monroe Doctrine.[215] James Redpath's *Pine and Palm* gathered protests from readers and news of opposition elsewhere, protesting that the event was "of great importance not only for American commerce, but for the interests of freedom in general, and more particularly, of the races of color in the Americas."[216] Despite Seward's urging and popular opposition across the U.S. press, however, the Union was simply too occupied in the secession struggles at hand. Other times, the occupation did not figure into press coverage at all. In a largely disparaging article from 1862, the *Atlantic Monthly* called Spain's exploits in Morocco "a silly affair" and bristled at Spain's "entitlement" toward its former colonies, even as it assessed that Spain was "now demanding for their country admission to the list of the Great Powers of Europe."[217] Although published nearly a year after annexation, the article, inscrutably, did not mention Santo Domingo at all. At least if Spain retook Mexico, the territory might be a bulwark against the "lawless spirits of the South . . . only one step below the devil," the author supposed.[218]

Disgraced Spanish diplomat Manuel Cruzat—he of the Haitian diplomacy debacle in 1855—provoked a strong reaction from the British consul several weeks after annexation. Serving as the diplomatic secretary to Rear Admiral Rubalcava, who had arrived with military forces from Cuba, Cruzat spoke cavalierly to British consul Hood. Spain did intend to reintroduce slavery, he remarked casually, and owners of fugitive slaves from Cuba and Puerto Rico escaped to the former republic would have "a perfect right" to reclaim them as property.[219] Hood was flabbergasted. "If Spanish rule is enforced of considering all children of slaves as the property of their masters, there will hardly be a single black or coloured person in the country who will be safe from persecution," he wrote. A flurry of high official communication was exchanged, including repeated promises from Spanish prime minister O'Donnell himself, and British officials' fears were allayed somewhat. "His Excellency further said that public feeling in Spain was against the Slave Trade," even if O'Donnell claimed its suppression could not be effected "before measures for substituting other labor were matured," Lord Russell reported.[220] As a country "naturally inclined to peace, and systematically addicted to commerce," Britain's main concern was to avoid foreign conflict, Russell averred.[221] "The formal and repeated declarations of Marshal O'Donnell that under no circumstances will slavery be introduced . . . have removed the main cause which would have led HMG to view the proposed annexation with dislike and repugnance," the British consul agreed. Given that the other major powers also seemed to be quiescent, and that Britain held itself "as a Power naturally inclined to peace, and systematically addicted to commerce," the consul concluded that peaceful recognition was undoubtedly the best route.[222]

As weeks passed, general response grew more and more positive. British journalists were sanguine about the prospect for an emancipated Spanish Caribbean empire. The *Quarterly Review*, a London journal, outlined a bright future for Spanish government and economy in which imperial projects such as the annexation of Santo Domingo played an important part. Constitutional government and a growth in national revenue in the 1850s were ample evidence of Spain's upward trend, the author praised.[223] He disapproved of Spain's recent military expeditions into Morocco—an acquisition of territory that the *Review* judged superfluous to Spain's economic advancement—but was enthusiastic and effusive about the annexation of Santo Domingo.[224] Clearly unfamiliar with the history of the republic, the writer made a number of errors in describing its recent history; nonetheless, he concluded that the annexation—as Spanish officials insistently claimed—had been a "free and spontaneous act of the President and people" and as such was "one of the most remarkable events of an age full of startling changes and surprises."[225] The Spanish government has given the most satisfactory pledges that slavery shall not be reintroduced, he concluded; "indeed, the reintroduction of slavery . . . is morally impossible." This free labor experiment reflected the growth and optimism of Britain's ally, the journal argued. "It will be for the Spanish Government now . . . to develop the riches of this noble land. A great experiment will soon be in progress in the attempt to raise tropical produce by free labour. We believe it will be a successful one. It must, should it so prove, effect an entire revolution in the present colonial economy of Spain. There will no longer be even a pretext for conniving at the slave trade, and the gradual extinction of slavery within the Spanish dominions will be assured."[226] Of Spain's role in the emancipated republics of Latin America, the author writes, "It is natural that Spain should, in her renovated strength, turn her thoughts towards those vast countries. . . . The resumption of her ancient dominion [in Mexico], after the recent annexation, . . . may appear to be within her grasp." He predicted Haiti might follow.[227]

In the face of such limited opposition, it seemed that all was well with the new annexation project. Santana and Cuban officials echoed choruses about the event's spontaneity and support. The *Gaceta de la Habana* reprinted these promises and marveled at annexation's auspicious nature for Spanish empire.[228] Congratulations arrived from Spanish authorities in Manila by midsummer, praising, too, the voluntary demonstration of fidelity by the Dominican people.[229] U.S. influence was at an ebb; only eight U.S. ships reached Dominican ports from January to November 1861, and William Cazneau wrote to Secretary of State Seward that Spanish officials planned on controlling the Mona passage tightly.[230] Elsewhere, hemispheric observers watched the developments with concern. Peru issued a formal proclamation condemning the annexation, and petitioners gathered more than thirty-seven hundred signatures in Jamaica.[231] President Geffrard of Haiti would soon follow with a statement of condemnation. For the moment, however, it seemed that a new era in Spanish colonialism—of the "utmost satisfaction and glory"—was at hand, beginning in the Caribbean.[232]

THREE

The White Race Is Destined to Occupy This Island

ANNEXATION AND THE QUESTION OF FREE LABOR

As they reached Santo Domingo from Havana, a Spanish naval commander took pains to issue a reminder to his troops as they disembarked from the steamship:

1. As slavery does not exist here, and all citizens are equal in rights, the class of color enjoys the same consideration as the white.
2. As a natural consequence of the above: that in the island there are men who are generals, leaders and officials who are colored and white; but they must all be given equal respect and consideration that royal orders and the respective hierarchies afford them.

He admonished his troops to observe "prudent and caring conduct with the residents, avoiding disputes, and winning, at all cost, the affections and admiration of the Dominicans." He urged that high officers were to be absolutely inflexible in inculcating their subordinates with the gravity of this responsibility.[1]

A simple edict, of course, could do little to alter the mentality of arriving Spanish troops, authorities, and would-be colonists disembarking from Cuban ships. The whole project, precipitously realized, was somewhat haphazard. They "embarked, with no orders, no proclamation, like filibusters sneakily united for some awful escapade," one general wrote, retrospectively. "Neither officer nor soldier knew if that territory was enemy or friend, if they arrived as masters, allies, or conquistadors," he described, "no rule of conduct, no policy warning of any of the contingencies that might immediately arise from the sudden interchange of peninsular soldier and that population of color."² Officials called the territory "the extinguished republic" (*extinguida república*), awkwardly, and authorities even inquired of archivists in Seville as to what the island most appropriately was called: Santo Domingo, La Española, or Haiti.³ In the days following annexation several foreigners briefly raised flags of their own nations in one small southern town, to the consternation of authorities.⁴ Nevertheless, Spanish high authorities stayed on message: rule of law and its equal application were to reign in the new colonial experiment. "Individuals of this race are very sensitive to their treatment by public authorities; Your Excellency should keep this in mind," the Crown reiterated.⁵ Soldiers were less guarded, writing home about their shock at the spectacle of black troops and the material deprivations of the territory.⁶ Among themselves, ministers were also less circumspect. "Under the auspices of Spain, in my humble judgment, the white race is destined to occupy this ever-green tropical island, enriching it and animating it with the triumphs of science, industry, and art," the overseas minister predicted.⁷

Authorities maintained that Dominican annexation presented a new direction in Spanish Caribbean rule: a jurisdiction without slavery or legislative distinctions of race. Despite a veneer of fraternity, however, Spanish officials felt that the annexation was an act of charity, a "generous act of the Mother Country" toward an impoverished and inferior territory.⁸ That the reestablished project was to be a free-labor "experiment"—and a province—complicated Spanish intent further. The newly arrived authorities reveled at the prospect of the "inexhaustible riches" from the "virgin land," but Dominican coffers, which had been in a state of more or less permanent economic crisis for decades, offered no immediate help.⁹ In effect, the Spanish sought to jump-start a market economy where there was almost none and to rule with Dominican local officials and Spanish high authorities; their endeavor amounted to an early effort at "hegemony on a shoestring."¹⁰ They floundered for means to make it profitable, or at least less of a drain on the coffers of Cuba, whose authorities sent 150,000 pesos in July 1861 alone. After his brief stay in the capital and several hours in the port of Samaná, the Cuban governor ordered a "complete reorganization of a tattered [*desquiciado*] . . . administration" and left.¹¹

Forced labor, transformed once by the Haitian Revolution and by second slavery, was on the precipice of another fulcrum, in which expanding markets for tropical goods intersected with a sudden crisis in the southern United States and new international projects of migration and labor control. As secession and warfare decimated U.S. cotton production, industrialists schemed for new sites to fill the void.¹² Well prior to wartime disruption, in fact, cotton's high prices made Manchester merchants impatient to foment production in more territories, an ambition that neatly reinforced imperial expansion.[13] British joint-stock cotton companies in the Caribbean proliferated overnight, including an Anglo-Spanish company in Cuba.[14] Haiti's new president, Fabre Nicholas Geffrard, committed to cotton production plans, sending officials to conduct a vast survey of potential production sites.[15] The government facilitated credit to private buyers to purchase cotton and sugar machinery and offered bounties for production.[16] Cotton was highly sought after, could be planted on all types of terrain, could be produced with reasonable start-up capital, and would improve the country's trade balance, Geffrard urged.[17] High wartime prices made cotton bounties unnecessary. Haiti's production soared from less than 700,000 pounds in 1860 to more than twice that by 1862, and samples were displayed at the Great Exhibition in London that year.[18] Meanwhile, Manchester capitalists sent cottonseed to Trinidad, Tobago, Antigua, British Guiana, Barbados, Dominica, Tortola, and a plethora of other semitropical sites.[19] Investors and authorities embraced a "myth of tropical exuberance," eager and confident that they could profit in new locations.[20]

New programs of cash-crop export and labor control, rather than being a departure from slavery, were eminently legible to Caribbean elites. In conjunction with imperial offices across the Atlantic, Caribbean officials mobilized new programs of indenture. Beginning in the 1820s, more than 430,000 predominantly young men and women arrived as contract laborers in the British Caribbean, more than 76,000 to the French Caribbean, and more than 125,000 to Cuba.[21] They arrived from different sites in Africa, only just released from having been kidnapped onto slave ships, and by contract from different Indian states, China, and Madeira. Britain occasionally jealously opposed the importation projects of other empires, but programs thrived.[22] Across the islands, in Brazil, Peru, and elsewhere, the men and women were bound to an individual employer, faced criminal charges for civil offenses (including labor discipline), and had to labor for as long as ten years to earn return passage.[23] Planters intentionally tried to isolate the newly arrived into a "cycle of coercion."[24] The very language of labor scarcity was one of division and control, of course, directed as a weapon against the independence of the emancipated. On islands where land was available, the formerly enslaved had tenaciously carved out small plots, despite all manner of restrictions.[25] Low wages, surveillance, intolerable discipline, and an aversion to economic dependence, not any sort of absolute demographic shortage, had hastened freed peoples' exodus and planters' ire simultaneously. On smaller islands with no available land, the balance of power tipped hard to planters (or, in the case of Turks and Caicos Islands, salt mine owners). Here, elites colluded with authorities to try to prevent the formerly enslaved from leaving the island at all.[26]

Even authorities who explicitly promoted cotton as a chance to "acquit" free labor looked to immigration projects and to expand control over rural labor. Haiti's secretary of state, François Jean-Joseph, concluded that both state and private plantations needed foreign agricultural laborers, and he proposed immigration bureaus domestically and in the United States.[27] Geffrard invited African Americans to immigrate; U.S.-based abolitionists James Redpath and James Theodore Holly served as formidable allies who promoted the plan widely.[28] The administration awarded free passage to those who would settle on larger plantations as sharecroppers; artisans were to repay travel costs in three months' time. About two thousand African Americans arrived, but the program dwindled after 1862; the families reported poor conditions, unsatisfactory land distribution, and other conflicts. As many as a third quickly bought return passage.[29] An isolated scheme to populate Île-à-Vache quickly collapsed not long after.[30] Disappointed but not deterred, Geffrard hoped Haitian peasants would also flock to the cotton industry, out of personal interest and an abstract patriotism. "Rural populations, I like to think, will not remain deaf to these exhortations," he remarked, "and will know to enter in a path which, while taking them individually to well-being, will bring the country to an elevated position . . . , through their industriousness and the importance of their production, . . . [and will] make them indispensable." Authorities urged district generals to encourage, without requiring, cotton production, and to submit regular reports.[31] Wealthy Haitians approved of these measures and called for sugar production, too, and even suggested seeking contract laborers from India.[32] All around the island, an elaborate geography of labor restrictions, contract labor, and other restraints emerged alongside emancipation and slavery, a map that was well known to Caribbean residents.[33]

This chapter details the quotidian details of Spanish reoccupation of Dominican territory as they planned to remake the Dominican landscape and to reorder the way its residents labored and lived. Authorities intended to make Dominicans into "productive" subjects, to formalize and commercialize peasant labor, and to bring them under the authority of the colonial state. Spanish authorities focused on the investment of new industries and public works, and individual capitalists brought them numerous petitions for cotton plantations, railroads, and a series of other projects, which ranged

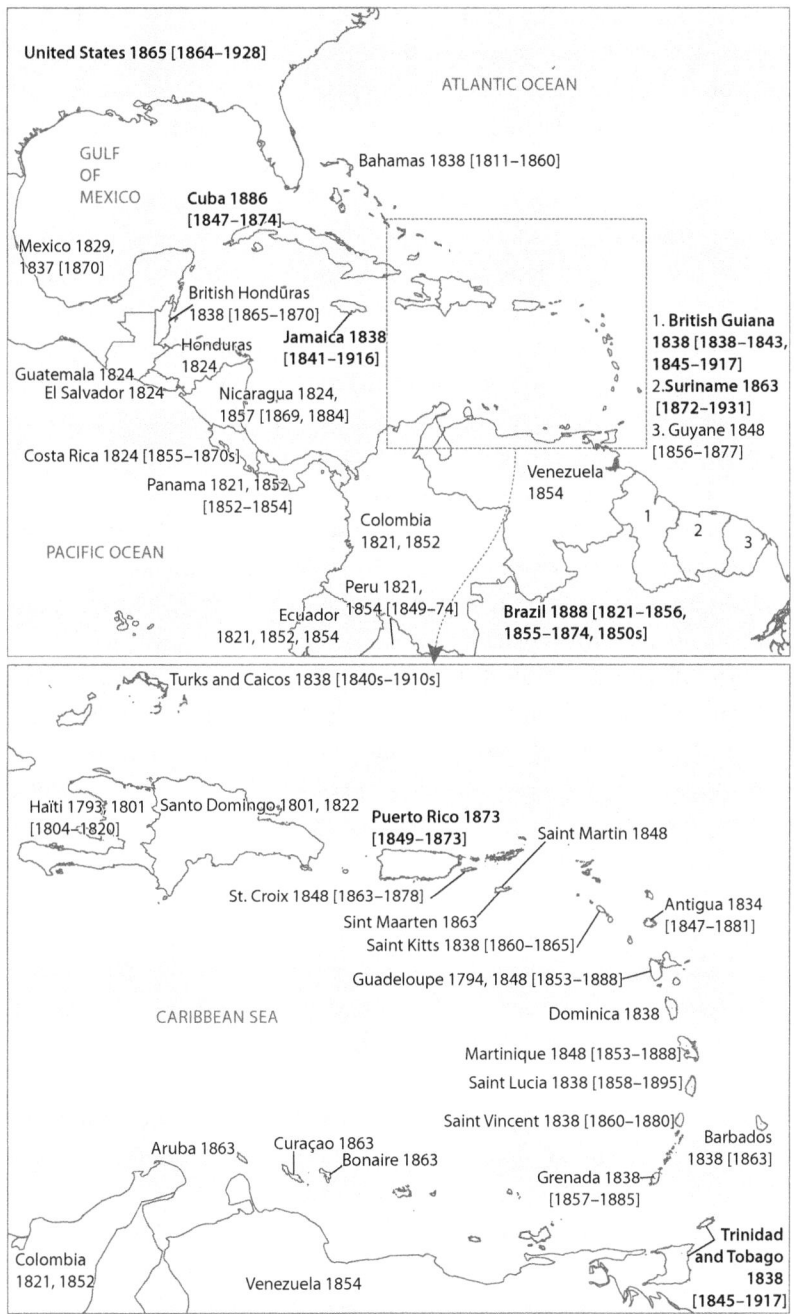

Map 3.1 Map showing emancipation dates, with major projects of indenture, labor control, or indenture emigration in brackets. By Annelieke Vries. For clarifications, see note 33.

from the mundane to the outlandish. One merchant even proposed camel transport.[34] The Crown supported these proposals, ordering land surveys and abrogating tariffs on the import of machinery. Authorities predicted that Dominicans might be willing to grow export crops for low wages.[35] Confidentially, the Crown suggested that Dominicans might be impressed into public works projects for a small wage, too, as they had "been obliged to live arms in hand and ready to serve for so long." The administration should pay for, or at least promote, projects of Spanish migration, early edicts determined.[36] A handful of established planters asked for liberated Africans or other foreign indentured laborers instead. Meanwhile, the queen passed a royal order in June 1861 that banned the arrival of free people of color to the island, intending to prevent enslaved people from Cuba and Puerto Rico from reaching the island and escaping to freedom. Santo Domingo, as a province of Spain, had a different status than its neighbors—with Dominican civil code and Spanish criminal codes set to rule—but separation from the plantation states proved immediately and fundamentally troublesome.

In Santo Domingo as in Haiti and elsewhere, discourses about free peasant labor ranged from paternalism to outright moral panic. Authorities harbored didactic fantasies that "instruction" would make emancipated or peasant individuals behave as was economically and politically convenient; they were particularly obsessed with inculcating respect—or, at least, the performance of respect—for the rule of law.[37] In Haiti, authorities codified an archetype of the rural agricultural worker (*habitant agriculteur*) as a national symbol, unequally integrated into the state. They celebrated 1 May as "la fête de l'agriculture," with equal parts pomp and moralizing. "Fathers and mothers, prepare your children from their youth for the love of work, the submission they owe the law, and the respect they owe to the authorities of the Empire!" Soulouque exhorted.[38] Geffrard's first promises were to amend the Rural Code to create a stronger rural police, local inspectors, and stronger antivagrancy strictures.[39] Authorities fretted about labor control through the lens of moral formation. "In [Puerto Rico and Santo Domingo] immorality and the lack of religious education deprive men of the essential bases to keep them in line with their duties," Puerto Rico's governor asserted.[40] White island residents fantasized that German, Irish, French, and other white laborers might "model" agricultural wage work; it was a common enough reverie that combined the preservation of a white plurality and the dream of a subordinate and docile sector of color, all at once.[41] As coercive reform "experiments" eroded in some islands, moral panic grew, about sexuality, marriage practices, religion, medicine, and all manner of imagined deviance.[42] Geffrard directed his attentions to vodou, making it a central legal target.[43] His minister proclaimed "idleness and vagabondage are a leprosy" that authorities would "work tirelessly to repress."[44] Later, his opponents would say he did not go far enough. "Surely what they are wanting then is the reestablishment of forced labor for the benefit of aristocracy, as with during Christophe," the president retorted, in frustration.[45]

Among the small southern Dominican elite coauthors of annexation— and the commercial class in the Cibao valley—a significant sector entered eager to benefit from Spanish plans for investment and labor control.[46] Dominican politicians had long argued that the country's raw potential was undeniable, a "hidden mine . . . an earthly paradise."[47] A small but enthusiastic group of elites in the Cibao mentioned development in their manifesto, hoping for an end to the inflation that had crippled the tobacco exports of the region for so long (and forced the trade into the hand of Danish and German banks). Financial reform, the idea of "sacred property," and the military tools to control unrest appealed to them greatly.[48] From the capital, elites wrote enthusiastically that reunification should henceforth "never be erased in the minds of Spaniards," and they joined authorities in celebrating Spanish arrival with ceremony and pageantry.[49] But they also subscribed, enthusiastically, to indenture schemes. When a cotton capitalist wrote asking for "ten *emancipados* per *caballería* [about thirty-three acres]," Manuel de Jesús Galván and other town council members endorsed the proposal. "It is certain that [cotton] will soon thrive in Santo Domingo," Galván wrote.[50] Prominent capital residents urged cash-crop development as a means of vindication. "The Dominican people are victims of calumny when they are supposed to be lazier than other people," Pedro Valverde explained to Spanish administrators. "Augment [their needs], as one would expect in the course of good government . . . , and their productivity will grow proportionately."[51] Valverde was eager to discipline rural Dominicans. His antivagrancy proposals were so stringent that incoming administrators thought them too harsh to implement.[52]

Before the end of 1861, major fissures became obvious. The lack of commercial endeavors was "incredible . . . in a country where sugar cane grows by itself, where coffee growers just have to plant the seed and then harvest the plants at the right time, [and] where corn grows wild," a Spanish official remarked in disbelief.[53] As the new administration floundered from lack of funds, authorities sought to privilege literate subjects and disenfranchise others, rigidify the laws in urban centers, rebuild and expand the prison system, tighten military discipline, foment free white immigration and east

Asian and African indenture, enforce strict religious reforms, and restrict the travel of free people of color to the territory. Compounding these restrictions and indignities were the often blundering, insensitive, and racist actions of Spanish authorities themselves, whose actions betrayed their experiences in the neighboring colonies and their fundamental unease with emancipated subjects. Soldiers and administrators were "accustomed" to these prejudices, one general observed, and they "did not hesitate to manifest as much."[54] Still, loyalists rallied, with new newspapers and new projects. Spanish journalists entered the discussions, arguing for open ports like that of Singapore to stimulate free trade.[55] Annexation supporters wrote to the Queen with breathless optimism, describing "the vehement desire . . . to equal, and even to exceed if possible, the progress made in neighboring Puerto Rico and Cuba."[56] "The Spanish government knows perfectly well that European immigration will not come to fertilize this fertile but hot soil," an anonymous French observer argued, and predicted slavery would soon follow.[57]

Laws Are Absolutely Lacking: Assembling the Spanish Colonial State

Troops arrived quickly. Two thousand from Havana and 800 from Puerto Rico arrived in the capital within three weeks. Nearly a thousand of them moved from the capital to Puerto Plata by steamship. A few hundred continued on to the nearby southern town of Azua.[58] The next real order of occupation was to set up a new bureaucracy. Colonial governments in Cuba and Puerto Rico had multiplied many times in size since the 1830s; colonial subjects paid taxes at rates higher than those on the peninsula.[59] Famously, infrastructure was so advanced in the plantation centers of eastern and central Cuba that the capitalists had begun a railroad system there by 1837, twelve years before construction began in the metropole itself. Frequent steam communication connected the islands to their own coastal extremities, to each other, and to the Spanish peninsula. Troops were everywhere; there were more than twenty thousand infantry in Cuba and about four thousand in Puerto Rico. The mandate for governing, however, resided in Spain and its delegates. The centralization of power was an extreme enough retreat that one political aspirant in Cuba complained, "Cuba went from being an integral part of the monarchy to becoming an enslaved colony."[60] "To be born in Cuba is a crime," complained another would-be delegate.[61] The colonial governments in the neighboring possessions were large, professionalized, and overwhelmingly Spanish.

The informality of law and government, particularly the lack of records, in Dominican territory shocked arriving Spanish authorities from Cuba. "The Government has not provided me with the data for which I have asked and which are indispensable, public archives have not been at my disposition, no collection of laws exists, nor even historical books which extend beyond the last third of the past century, [and there] are no statistics, not even approximated ones," José Malo de Molina complained. He could not procure any court records, either. Even the Catholic Church's archive was "nothing more than a few Council books, almost all illegible, and a few boxes in really poor condition," another concerned Spanish official wrote.[62] The existing laws, based on the more recent Bourbon restoration codes, had been only inconsistently translated and applied; it was "almost always an imaginary thing, and administration is more often through common sense or custom," Malo de Molina sniffed.[63] "Laws are absolutely lacking," Governor Serrano echoed, calling the overlapping legal codes an "unintelligible chaos."[64] Malo de Molina continued, "For all its written laws, the Government nonetheless has been really just verbal, and the highest-ranking officials condescend to dictating the smallest details. . . . The four Ministers of State have just one [assistant] of whom they can't even ask very much, given the stingy and insufficient state salaries. The employees are such just to avoid military service, and even high dignitaries had to dedicate themselves to commerce or another occupation to provide them with subsistence."[65] Malo de Molina fretted at the lack of credentials required to preside over the courts and other irregularities. Serrano hastily appointed the archivist of public works in Cuba to a new secretarial post in the capital.[66]

Royal orders established Santo Domingo's Real Audiencia and other parts of the administration in October 1861. As promised, the civil code of Spain ruled, replacing the French-Haitian civil code that had technically been in place since 1822 (Spanish authorities first sought to translate it into Spanish, but they repressed the publication of articles about civil marriage).[67] Municipal juntas were to govern in the small cities of the island, with five civilians and three military officials (although just six had been established by early 1862).[68] Law divided the territory into six military districts; neighboring Cuba had more than thirty.[69] The island was linked by weekly steam service to Puerto Rico and Cuba, but the ferrying of internal mail was another matter entirely. The roads throughout the republic, which were in poor condition often to the point of being impassable where they existed, presented a significant challenge. Expanding the mail system generated a tremendous paper trail in Spanish correspondence, and the budget for mail services quickly rose above 10,000 pesos annually.[70]

General Pedro Santana continued as head of state, and Spanish officials explicitly agreed that other Dominican officials would be integrated into the new colonial administration. In the first months of the occupation, it was so.[71] Malo de Molina made recommendations for two Supreme Court judges (both Dominicans of "notorious integrity"); in his report, Governor Serrano named nineteen more officials, just five of them from Havana.[72] Santana's former vice president became a field marshal, and a handful of former ministers joined the Real Audiencia.[73] Two prominent Dominicans held high civil governor positions in the capital and in Santiago de los Caballeros. Still others remained in provisional posts closely linked with Santana.[74] Appointments were contingent on a number of measures to professionalize the positions. Dominican ministers, at least in theory, were to be paid more, and they were no longer to engage in other professions while in office. Commissioner Malo de Molina drafted salaries for Royal Audiencia legislators and other governors at levels significantly higher than their current pay; eventually, the salaries were fixed to be comparable to those of Puerto Rico.[75] Judges were to serve and be housed in the same building as the Audiencia because in so doing they would "be more respectable, avoid the trouble of having to find them in their homes . . . and keep them from [undesirable living conditions] and inconvenient favors."[76]

The loyalist response, particularly in the capital, was effusive. Ten prominent Dominican residents of the capital formed an ad hoc Economic Committee to advise treasury officials. Their acceptance letters were gushing. Pedro Ricart y Torres wrote enthusiastically:

> As a loyal servant of my country and the Queen; as an enthusiastic co-participant in the political transformation that has just taken place and that opens to Santo Domingo a vast opportunity to better its luck and change the sad situation. . . . It will be my true pleasure to cooperate with my small component of insight and experience in the noble and difficult enterprise. . . . I cannot go without mentioning my feelings of gratitude that I, as a son of this soil, feel at hearing the praise you have for its inhabitants, whose self-denial, loyalty, and sacrifice ought to earn that estimation from all patriotic and educated Spaniards.[77]

The "mission was as grave as it was delicate," admonished Ricart y Torres, himself a prominent landowner and former minister of foreign relations and finance for the ex-republic. "The transition from one system of government to another by the offspring of the same mother must be conducted as smoothly as possible, in the family," he wrote. Electing the right high officials would demand selectivity, he continued, but it ought to be done "without losing sight of public opinion or of honorable men who have made great sacrifices over many years to regain the autonomy of this brave pueblo that owes its name, religion, language and civilization to the same *raza* in whose arms they return."[78]

An expeditionary brigade had gathered on the island by late spring 1861, which included Spanish soldiers from the peninsula, Cuba, and Puerto Rico; there was also a Militia of Color, origin not recorded. Spanish troops arrived in the capital, San Cristóbal, Azua, Samaná, Puerto Plata, Santiago de los Caballeros, and Samaná, constituting a standing force of ten thousand. Even the capital, however, had housing that was barely sufficient for half of a battalion. Soldiers were forced to split off into the convent, the basements of the courthouse, fort, and palace, and other temporary shelter. In Samaná they stayed in seventeen huts (*bohíos*); in Puerto Plata, they took refuge in two government houses and another rented one.[79] Provisions were no easier. "They are forced to import everything, even bricks," one diplomat reported. Flour was imported from the United States, "all manner of merchandise" arrived from Europe, and medicines were exceedingly difficult to procure. Prices were high; a saddle cost 150 pesos fuertes, "even as the fields are full of cattle," he observed grimly.[80] "The people of the country maintain themselves generally on wild plants [*viandas*] and free-range pigs," an officer explained, and "articles of primary necessity are not just in shortage, but the few that are around are sold at really outrageous prices." The corps sought additional supplies from Cuba, Puerto Rico, and Saint Thomas, but the official asserted "the troops and even the Commanders and Officers have suffered hunger and privation without measure from this matter."[81] To incoming administrators, the capital city was a sorry sight. Even the archbishop's house and the Convent of Santa Clara were in ruins, and the government buildings were little better.[82] Few houses had much furniture at all; most people made do with very little.[83] Coconut-oil lighting had only barely been introduced the year before; outside of the capital, most of the rest of the cities and towns probably went dark at sundown.[84]

Dominican Soldiers and the Classification Committee

Regulation of the military presented a particularly thorny problem for arriving Spanish authorities. Working-class men from all over Spain comprised the incoming troops, many of whom had already been stationed in Cuba and Puerto Rico for a number of years. Discipline for common infractions—misspending petty cash, drunkenness, gambling, sleeping outside of the barracks, insubordination, fighting, and other common misdeeds—was strict.[85] An anonymous letter from a soldier of the King's Regiment pleaded with Brigadier Antonio Peláez to review the harsh punishments its commanding officers inflicted. "It is a matter of nothing less than killing us or making us desert," he implored.[86] A circular forbade beating the soldiers with *palos*; it "humiliates rather than corrects the soldier," authorities admonished.[87] About ten thousand troops ultimately arrived from the neighboring islands and from Spain. Authorities stationed the steamship *Tetuán* in Samaná, and temporarily deployed eleven other warships to the east of the island.[88] If the militia of color were among the troops recently arrived from Havana, it seems that they did not stay long, and it is evident that Governor Serrano halted their commission very quickly.[89]

For a few months, the status of Dominican soldiers remained uncomfortably indeterminate alongside the newly arrived Spanish regiments. In the eyes of Spanish authorities and colonial troops, the Dominican army that these Spanish soldiers encountered could hardly be called an army at all. "All Dominican men were soldiers" in the conflict-ridden period of the First Republic, Spanish authorities observed grimly, and their discipline—relative to that of the Spanish regiments—was poor.[90] The regular practice of leaving ranks to attend to home duties irked officials so much they offered a ten-peso reward for remission of these men, whom they considered deserters.[91] Military titles were effectively honorary, the arriving officials asserted. "Dominican generals didn't know anything other than to rise up against one another to take power of the government," a general sniffed.[92] Immediately lurking behind Spanish resentment was their dismay at seeing men of color in positions of authority. "The soldier of the Spanish race couldn't comprehend that a black or a *mulato* was really a general or colonel," he observed, and a "great number of generals and chiefs" were men of color.[93] Some fought with Santana in the border conflicts that broke out in May and June of that year. The campaign proved to be a taxing first meeting between the two groups of soldiers. High-ranking officials perpetually praised the Spanish troops for their exemplary conduct; they had faced difficult conditions with "superior discipline . . . fraternizing with the residents and in everything laboring with such prudence and tact," the Cuban governor claimed.[94] Behind these reports, however, a number of incidents probably caused officials to scramble to reform the Provisional Guard during the hot summer of 1861. Plans to create a standing army of Dominicans collapsed by August.[95] It is likely that Spanish officers never wanted to integrate Dominicans into the forces at all, unless as separate standing militia of white and nonwhite regiments (as in Cuba and Puerto Rico). More likely still, they had not considered the prospect at all.

During the summer months—while the status of Dominican soldiers remained in limbo—conflict between Spanish officers and the rank and file proliferated. The regiments seem to have been led separately during the summer campaigns of 1861, but a few Dominicans appear to have been integrated directly into Spanish regiments in auxiliary roles. There, the harsh discipline of the Spanish officers—likely in a climate of racist distrust—created a volatile atmosphere. Harsh punishments, in particular, grated on observers. Twenty-year-old Enrique Padilla, a young, literate Dominican who was serving as a porter for the military command stationed in Azua, faced charges of "speaking heatedly to various soldiers of the Provisional Guard, trying to influence them with principles contrary to subordination," for example.[96] The young defendant had intervened when he saw an officer from the Crown Regiment punishing a bugle player, probably a Dominican. The brigadier accused Padilla of walking up to the soldiers and

> bitterly criticizing the punishment, saying among other things that he would have liked to have seen [the guard] try that with him, and that soldiers shouldn't have to suffer like that, adding some more insults to said officer of the Crown. The [brigadier himself] approached them, unsure of what he was hearing, sure that there could not possibly be such irresponsible nonsense being said. But he heard [Padilla] repeat them, loudly so that he would hear it; in fact he started shouting as he tried to leave. At that time the [brigadier] told two soldiers to arm themselves to arrest him.

"I saw him give the bugle player a big smack [plantazo] with a sword," Padilla explained defiantly, admitting to all the charges. "If it had been me treated like that, I would have reacted very differently," he continued. Another witness had come to his support, Padilla testified, exclaiming, "May God let that sword break!"—to which a defiant Padilla added, "May his heart stop instead!" (¡que había de ser el corazón y no el sable!). Spanish authorities felt unsure how to adjudicate Padilla's insubordination. The prosecutor (himself a lieutenant of the Crown Regiment) reserved judgment on the case, passing it on to Captain General Pedro Santana. "He should be severely punished according to royal law, but as we must consider him ignorant of these laws . . . it could not have been out of malice," the fiscal concluded. Another officer, also in Azua, wrote to the Spanish officials to complain about a certain Agustín Feliz (whose alias, "Prieto," probably indicates he was dark-skinned). Spanish superiors were frustrated with Feliz, who "never wanted to obey his officers . . . and has just been rebellious."[97]

By the fall of 1861, Spanish military authorities demoted the great bulk of Dominican soldiers. First, authorities separated Dominican soldiers into a new body, the Provincial Reserves. A Classification Committee began to review Dominican soldiers' rank and status. In order to be in the active reserves, an individual had to present to the commission a service sheet (*hoja de servicio*) describing his military feats and any other supporting documents. The decision would be based on "aptitude, service, and other circumstances," the commission announced vaguely. Authorities assiduously avoided mentioning race in any written description of the committee, although it could not have escaped notice that all of its own members were white.[98] As the committee continued its revisions, it expanded those disqualified to include those of "advanced age or poor health, [with] lack of instruction, poor capacity, more civil than military."[99] Of the first 227 applicants the commission reviewed—mostly captains and other subordinate officers, but some generals as well—it gave fewer than half active status. The committee declared the rest "passive," usually because the men could not read or write. This decommissioning extended to those who asserted they had been active soldiers since the 1840s, some of whom retired rather than suffer declassification.[100] On a very selective basis, high-ranking officers from the reserves could apply to Madrid to solicit integration into the principal corps of Spanish forces.[101] For his part, Santana faithfully related all the generals and other high-ranking officers in the different provinces. In a different handwriting, however, someone added three generals' names and the following observation: "de color."[102]

In a matter of months, Spanish officers created a three-tier hierarchy: Spanish troops, active reserves, and passive reserves. All members of the reserves were prohibited from wearing Spanish uniforms. Active reserves earned twice as much as those who had the misfortune of being made "passive," but Spanish men of the equivalent rank earned considerably more. Authorities published the (de)classifications from the "old Dominican army" (*antiguo ejército dominicano*) on the front pages of the *Gaceta de Santo Domingo* for months in late 1861 and 1862, which must have been embarrassing for those who were being publicly decommissioned, even as the loyalist press celebrated the regularization effort.

Good Subjects, Honorable Citizens: Catholic Religious Reform

Santana claimed it was a "dear wish of the Dominican people to fix the disgraceful situation of religious practice," and arriving officials agreed.[103] A perceived lack of formal religiosity among rural residents should not have surprised these officials, who were themselves arriving from a prosperous but relatively impious plantation state. In Cuba, outside of urban centers like Havana and Matanzas, residents also lacked brick-and-mortar churches, in part because plantation owners sought to be free from the church's meddlesome influence.[104] "The country people of Cuba . . . are not very religious," a traveler passing through Cuba in the late 1850s wrote. He allowed himself some condescension: "Most of them learn a few prayers by heart, which they repeat without understanding their import. This does not prevent, however, images of the Virgin and of saints being in every house."[105] The material culture of the most remote areas of Santo Domingo might have been more barren still. The Dominican Catholic Church was in a state of disarray. It had been without an archbishop since the spring of 1858. Just twenty-eight parishes served the entire territory, of which five were totally vacant for lack of funds. Only three—Puerto Plata, Santiago, and San Cristóbal—had acting high officials.[106] There was no church council, no convent, and "no hope of one," the acting ecclesiastical governor reported grimly.[107] The Dominican clergy displayed an "exaggerated superstition. . . . [and were] poor and ignorant generally" but with significant power over the populace, another wrote. He and other Spanish observers described rural priests who shirked their duties, demanded large fees for travel and services, practiced freemasonry, openly had mistresses, and married.[108] Dominican writers, long in irreverent dialogue with these men, crafted tales that imagined the assassination of intractable priests.[109] The priest who held Mass in the capital to celebrate annexation probably had children.[110] Officials conceived proselytization and the regularization of Catholic practice essential. Promoting Catholicism was promoting Spain, the Cuban governor observed; peninsular officials agreed.[111] In the capital, loyal prominent citizens felt eager to lend a hand; Don Miguel Lavastida even ceded some of his property to the church to construct a chapel commemorating the first Catholic Mass on the island.[112]

Authorities fretted that Dominican families lived in "tremendous libertinism."[113] Most Dominicans living outside of towns were not confirmed, and young children went without clothing.[114] One general claimed that "adolescents strolled nude on the streets of the capital, and . . . illicit unions abounded."[115] The behavior of women in the capital especially troubled him. "Young daughters of the family enjoyed a grand liberty to leave the paternal house—which would in Spain be inconceivable—going about with whom they wanted most and who seemed the most opportune," he remarked in horror.[116] Single women, he continued, "were not embarrassed to live maritally with a man," and "the word infanticide had no application in Santo Domingo." He disapproved heartily of civil marriage. Polygamy, even incestuous marriages, revealed how "relaxed and perverted" the nation was, he accused.[117] Drinking, prostitution, and "rampant immorality" plagued his flock, a priest reported.[118]

The Protestant population, especially in Samaná and Puerto Plata, troubled Spanish authorities. As many as one-third of all the residents of the Samaná peninsula were Protestants of color from the United States.[119] Congregations maintained contact with Methodist and Anabaptist churches in the States, as well as British Wesleyan missionaries.[120] When the minister in Samaná died, parishioners sought a U.S. replacement (although he did not stay long). Samaná congregants had built a large, wooden chapel atop a small hill, where they met multiple times a week. In Puerto Plata, there were different sects, which also met regularly on Sundays—all-day services—and one or two midweek nights, and they held baptisms, marriages, and public burials regularly. Their public meetings and house visits brought them into close contact with Catholics, a cleric wrote, contemptuously, and they freely offered Spanish-language books, pamphlets, and flyers "to pervert them." The pastors "have worked and continue to work to spread their errors among the Catholics, inviting them to listen to the sermons and take part in their ceremonies, impregnated with error and Heresy," the official concluded. "Most painfully," he noted, they had a public school "to teach Heresy to the innocent children."[121]

Authorities proved deeply divided on how to treat open practice of Protestants and Freemasons. Catholic-only territories were "a fundamental law of monarchy . . . with no exception whatsoever," the acting church head noted, suggesting that open practice disrespected Spain's "historical glories, our venerated traditions, our habits, our customs," and that it could lead to "dangerous ideas . . . and insurrection."[122] He promised that he would labor tirelessly to abolish the "grand abomination" from Dominican soil, replacing it with "the unity of religion for which our fathers fought." "Since Spain has retaken this country, the old order should disappear," he insisted, including "tolerance of cults." Other authorities were more circumspect, noting that prohibition could provoke problems of international relations and public order. The matter remained undecided for two years—at one point, superior Spanish authorities even declined to comply with church officials. As "one of the most delicate issues of all consequences of annexation, I cannot comply [with banning the public celebration of non-Catholic faith]," the governor wrote. He cited the intervention of the British consul in Samaná as evidence of international complications.[123] In the last months of 1862, orders from Spain arrived to persecute Protestant practices; again, officials on the ground in the capital quickly decided against it and wrote to northern town officials to that effect.[124] More word came in February 1863 insisting that all subjects should be Catholic; banishment or imprisonment loomed for infractors.[125] For the moment, however, the residents could continue to practice openly. Masonic lodges received no such consent, and authorities ordered them closed.[126]

A new archbishop, Bienvenido Monzón, arrived with a certain amount of pomp in the summer of 1862. The *Gaceta Oficial* republished the dual-language—Latin and Spanish—royal order that celebrated his disembarkation. Like-minded men accompanied him; individual clerics resident in Santiago de Cuba, Puerto Rico, Cartagena, and Spain solicited passage and assignment in the new colony.[127] Monzón ordered honors distributed to local prominent Dominicans, but he refused to assign them to positions of high authority. Of the eleven proposed high church officials, all were Spanish, and only three had experience from the neighboring islands. Monzón urged authorities to copy recent reforms in Puerto Rico in its new Spanish neighbor.[128] Even before his arrival, a few Dominican officials wrote for permission to marry; Monzón was not satisfied.[129] "I soon realized that the institution of the family, the primary element of every society, was being degraded and illegitimized by the remnants of the so-called civil marriage of the French code (adopted during the republican era) and also by the practice of keeping concubines," he wrote.[130] The leading story in June's second installment of *La Razón* announced the end of civil registries for marriage and the nullification of all parts of the French civil code to that effect.[131] For the first time in decades, the church was relatively flush with cash for repairs; the archbishop's salary alone was 14,000 pesos fuertes.[132] The reforms promised to forge "good subjects, good heads of family, and good and honorable citizens," one official observed.[133]

Labor, Capital, and Profit

"There is no country where nature offers more resources, nor where the inhabitants are in a worse state," one Spanish official wrote in the year before annexation.[134] When the Cuban governor Francisco Serrano arrived from Havana in the summer of 1861, he agreed. "The people are living in such a way that it can even be called miraculous," he marveled. "Uncultivated lands, virgin forests with plants still just as the explorers found them, sparse population, barely any production, industry dead, commerce almost unknown . . . [and] miserable paper money."[135] Serrano's parting recommendations—fortification of the Samaná peninsula, regularization of the government, and economic reform—signaled a fairly ambitious plan for state reorganization of the former republic intended to orient it toward commercial agriculture. "It pains me to see such magnificent terrain, much more fertile than those rightly praised in the Island of Cuba . . . without one generous heart to rebuke the unhappy Dominicans," wrote another Havana official paternally.[136] Authorities began a flurry of small projects in early months, including new wooden houses in Monte Cristi, a new dock in Santo Domingo, and the groundwork for more infrastructure projects.[137]

Officials implemented a mixture of Cuban and Puerto Rican legislation. They decided that direct taxation of residents would be too onerous, opting for sales and other indirect taxes instead, including the lottery, which they noted was popular.[138] Dominican goods became "national" products, along with goods from the rest of the empire.[139] Serrano and other officials urged the regularization of rural landownership, creating registries where possible.[140] Officials looked into the idea of cargo shipments between Cuba, Santo Domingo, and Puerto Rico, and special attention was given to plans for strengthening the defenses of Samaná, which was to be a free port.[141] A steamship connected Santo Domingo to Saint Thomas twice a month; Samaná was linked into a Veracruz–Puerto Rico–Havana route by early fall.[142] Twice-monthly service was supposed to connect the island to Cuba and Cádiz.[143] Travel to Havana on the *Pájaro del Océano* or *Cuba* was available to all those who could buy a ticket on their biweekly voyages. While the lack of pharmacies meant that prohibitively high prices of medicine persisted, military health officials offered civilians basic medical training.[144] Joaquín Manuel del Alba, *intendente* of Puerto Rico, assumed the position of *comisario regio*, where he would serve for the next two years, charged with assessing the financial status of the island and the extent of paper money.[145]

News of the annexation caused a relative stir of excitement among residents in other Spanish territories, mostly over the idea of new investments, large and small, that might be made in the colony. Even as Serrano, Santana, and Molina waited for approval from Spain, news of annexation produced immediate interest. A handful of priests requested transfer to Santo Domingo from Sevilla, Puerto Rico, and Santiago de Cuba, and at least sev-

Fig. 3.1 Industrialists sent many pamphlets, like this one about shelling coffee beans, to Spanish administrators. Journalists at *La Razón* regularly published on industry proposals.

eral individuals requested that their pensions be transferred to Santo Domingo.[146] A handful of wealthy Venezuelans, fleeing political unrest, set up plantations on the Ozama River.[147] A British subject sought to profit from "abandoned" lumber in the center-island region.[148] Others proposed canals, lighthouses, a bridge over the Ozama River in the capital, and gas lighting for all the towns of the island.[149] One wealthy man proposed building a café in the ruins of the capital city theater; another proposed a submarine telegraph cable; Don Vidal from Santiago de Cuba proposed a covered market; and various British capitalists proposed different railroad developments (at least one of which was approved).[150] Some small-business owners applied for licenses for businesses that were already running—suggesting perhaps greater official scrutiny—as Dr. Guillermo Gothburg did for his small pharmacy in Puerto Plata.[151] Other small-scale plans abounded: fabric making, an icehouse (*nevería*), printing presses, and so on. Not every small project gained approval; officials denied a rum maker license on moral grounds, for example, despite the "extremely backward" state of distilling.[152]

Large-scale projects like coal mining, cotton production, and the fomenting of tobacco cultivation generated huge amounts of official documentation as officials responded to the proposals of interested capitalists and directed their own surveys.¹⁵³ Spanish authorities were very interested in Samaná's coal, and they sent teams of military engineers to inspect possible mining sites. The standards and licenses were to mirror Cuban legislation, but experts arrived from Puerto Rico and Spain as well.¹⁵⁴ Several financiers competed for rights to introduce new cotton-processing technology, and the Cotton Association of Manchester offered to send numerous informational leaflets, translated into Spanish.¹⁵⁵ Another individual requested reimbursement for importing strains of tobacco into Puerto Plata, as had been requested by royal order.¹⁵⁶ Repeated royal orders directed officials to explore the possibility of cotton cultivation, compared agricultural conditions with those in Puerto Rico, and so on.¹⁵⁷ Enthusiastic planters recopied and sent Cuban edicts back to Spanish authorities, asking for the same concessions and promising future profits for Cataluña's cotton mills.¹⁵⁸ Well into the thick of conflict in 1864, mining development efforts and other fomentation schemes, particularly cotton, never ceased.

Immigration and Indenture

Most export agriculture proposals to the Crown involved immigration, too. The plans of new colonists in Santo Domingo in 1861 involved semifree contract labor, moralization schema, and, invariably, white supervision. The Spanish media wrote approvingly of such plans, suggesting that "freed blacks, African prisoners, Chinese coolies, and Irish settlers" would all be ideal laborers for the colony.¹⁵⁹ Specifics varied. A cotton capitalist sought tools and *emancipados* to labor on his land; he deferred to the "wisdom of the government" on how to proceed. His own land, already planted, could be "a small example of the richness and fertility of this virgin land," he urged, adding that "with a little manpower, the land could produce torrents of richness."¹⁶⁰ The proposal of another cotton planters' association urged, "the island was a source of inexhaustible riches that only needed the strength of . . . colonization based on the principles of morality, police, and order" to thrive.¹⁶¹ The proposal suggested that black laborers were adapted to the hot climate and that, under watchful white rule, they would bring the province prosperity. "One thousand or more apprentices of the African nation . . . are the only race who can make Antillean soil productive," the letter writer argued. These "apprentices" would be signed "of their own spontaneous will" to ten- to fifteen-year contracts cultivating cotton and tobacco, "under the same conditions and regulation that Asian colonization has taken place in the neighboring island of Cuba." To oversee the indentured Africans, the company promised to bring in one "Spanish head of family . . . individuals of good customs, morality, and intelligence" for every ten contract laborers. The association could pay for machinery and nominal taxes for each Spanish colonist, he boasted, as long as land was provided for ten years for free.

One individual's ambitious railroad proposal to connect the Cibao valley forty miles to the northern coast exemplifies the "racial knowledge" that typified the proposals authorities received. The railroad industrialist effused antiblack sentiment and fantasies of "coolie" docility. For the hard labor of construction, he called for ten thousand indentured men and women "from Calcutta, Hong Kong, or Cuba," specifically because of the perception that Asian laborers would stay separate from black Dominicans and would also thus serve as a racial bulwark against Haiti.[162] He maintained that these subjects would be more adapted than European emigrants to the climate, and that they might have "convincing moral and political influence" for the entirety of the colonial endeavor, not just the proposed regional railroad. In Cuba, these laborers had "consistently demonstrated that they are not to be confused with the enslaved African race," one high official insisted, concurring.[163]

From the very first days of the reoccupation, Spanish officials and private white industrialists called for large-scale white immigration, too, most often to oversee indentured nonwhite laborers. Authorities liked the idea of Spanish immigration particularly. Individual Spanish settlers might apply for support, and authorities passed laws welcoming white settlers identical to Cuba's.[164] The Spanish consul to Haiti proposed a project of immigration of two to three thousand white individuals from within the "Spanish" community of the U.S. South, especially Florida and Louisiana. He suggested that the government award each family a substantial plot of two to three hundred *caballerías* of land—ostensibly vacant—along with materials to build houses, the state honors afforded to colonizers, and a ten-year reprieve from any kind of tax. The government should also furnish Asian contract laborers as aides, "given that they are already acclimated."[165] The Overseas Ministry quizzed Santana on which professions might be the most useful for potential Spanish émigrés. Authorities felt no compunction telling Santana, himself a man of color, that the white race was going to be the motor of the colony's progress. It was "of utmost necessity that the population be increased: luckily, the conditions of the country allow that the white race fulfill this most important need," one official informed him.[166]

Outside capitalists proposed similar schemes of white immigration. William Cazneau, the U.S. agent, proposed a colonization plan of one thousand white families under ten to fifteen years of indenture. "Under the direction of proper superintendents," they would cultivate sugar, cotton, tobacco, and rice, "those species of tropical products for which the fertile soil of Santo Domingo appears so remarkably adapted."[167] The laborers—to "be of an orderly and well-disciplined class"—would follow Spanish law, Cazneau assured his readers. The settlers should be housed on "unappropriated public lands" near the capital, with one square league afforded to each one hundred male laborers between the ages of sixteen and fifty. The advantages of a white settlement project were not just economic, Cazneau wrote, "but also a wholesome example to the existing population of the province . . . able, industrious, and well disciplined." López and Company was one of the companies that sought compensation from the Crown for individual passengers, although they were remonstrated to seek individual approval first.[168] Spanish authorities expressed suspicion at U.S.-led projects, however, and it does not seem that any came to fruition.[169]

Discipline and Leisure

In addition to immigration and indenture schemes, authorities were centrally concerned with inducing Dominicans to labor. Vagrancy preoccupied Spanish authorities and their loyalist allies. In a letter to the arriving authorities, Pedro Valverde described the "drunken scandal and disorder" caused by male vagrants and of "prostitutes and corrupt women whose licentious life significantly affects . . . public morale."[170] Vagrant men eluded prosecution by citing their occasional (weekly or monthly) day labor gigs; the women usually hid behind claims of being washerwomen, pastry sellers, cooks, or servants, Valverde complained. Under the existing laws, vagrants spent a few days in jail in lieu of the fine (that they could not pay); then they returned to the streets once more. New laws proposed that all vagrants be presented to the police, where they would be given work, provided they were of age, and beggars were to seek a license proving disability.[171] Valverde sought harsher sentences still. He wanted three-time vagrants to be deported to Samaná for one year. Valverde also argued that foreigners should have a guarantor to vouch for them, just like in Puerto Rico, followed by steadily renewable provisional licenses—available at a small fee—for the first year of their residence. They should be deported outright for vagrancy, he continued.[172] Valverde's zeal was praised by other authorities, if not the specifics of his plan. Sending vagrants to nearly deserted Samaná would "simply put them in a place where they could not work, rather than inculcate in them the desire to do so," one reply concluded, expressing caution about the rights of foreign residents who antedated Spanish reoccupation.[173]

In August 1861, Santana signed into law an extensive antigaming bill, which legislators borrowed directly from codes in the neighboring islands. "It has come to my attention . . . that there are frequent meetings of people of all classes to engage in the pernicious vice of game playing," the bill began. "I am responsible to Her Majesty Our Queen (God protect Her) . . . to repress and correct this vice." The ordinances banned all games, even legal ones, from most public businesses, on the penalty of a fine of 250 pesos. Public officials, civic or military, faced the same stiff fine; others owed sixty pesos, all doubled for repeat offenses. Loss of businesses and even exile loomed for three-time offenders. Finally, the bill laid out explicit instructions for registration of the offenders' names and steps to prosecution.[174] The fines had to be paid in pesos fuertes, not paper money, authorities emphasized.[175] Other provisions extended the ban to all games of luck, *rayuela* (hopscotch), dogfighting, gaming during work hours, prostitution, and even boisterous behavior during theater performances. Some new provisions, like the banning of clothing to impersonate public officials or of masks (outside of festivals), represented clear security concerns. Other strictures sought control of leisure, especially in public and semipublic spaces. Cockfights could only be held with a license. Dances, too, required licenses, and the *holandés, danois, tango,* and *tambulá* dances were of particular concern. Along with *jodú*, they caused "frequent scandal," authorities alleged, and were to be held by permission only.[176] *Jodú* remained totally prohibited. Some provisions, like Article 69—which banned "using dress that pertains to another sex, class, or category that is not one's own"—arguably implied legal distinctions that were not supposed to be operative in the colony at all.[177]

New statutes created new costs, supervision, and the threat of fines. School administrators, merchants, street vendors, and other small enterprises required licensing. Female cooks, washerwomen, and sweets and fruit sellers were to register with their local municipality.[178] Midwives who wanted to continue to practice their skill were to present themselves to the newly formed Medicine Committee, where they would pay twenty pesos for the title. In addition, the women were expected to report the sex of the baby, the address, and other details immediately or face a stiff fine.[179] Family heads were expected to independently report their household numbers as well. Even visiting sailors were expected to register with authorities.[180] Residents were further expected to adhere to a number of public health provisions (from dampening their stoops twice daily during dry spells to adhering to a ban on throwing laundry water into the street), and public nudity, even for small children or when bathing animals in the river, was explicitly prohibited. Architects were to vet blueprints with authorities. The new, albeit small, force of watchmen in Santo Domingo and other towns implemented these laws and increased state contact with town residents. In Santo Domingo, they enforced minor rules (such as one stating that doors to the street should open inward), announced the time hourly, and conducted a rudimentary census of the city center, counting 686 brick houses and 767 huts.[181]

Authorities intended to rebuild and expand the colony's prison system. The first change was literally nominal, as town jails across the island acquired names like "The Royal Prison of Azua." The conditions in the territory's few prisons were atrocious, reflecting their absolute lack of resources since the republican period; the arrival (and imprisonment) of Spanish soldiers exacerbated the problem of space, conditions, and supplies.[182] In Santo Domingo, prisoners complained of the rations, which were only a half pound of raw meat and five platanos a day amid gloomy, humid conditions and terrible smells. After repeated inquiries, authorities nominated a full-time commissioner to monitor the conditions.[183] In Santiago de los Caballeros, prisoners had survived during the period of the republic on fifty *papeletas* (the devalued paper currency) and family aid. After 1861, prisoners received one peseta daily, but the amount was wholly insufficient for imprisoned peninsular soldiers, who had no family to bring them meals. Officials observed that they were obliged to beg for money as they cleaned the streets and performed other menial tasks.[184] After months of delay, the allocation was increased.[185] Blueprints for new prisons, civil and military, arrived from Madrid for Samaná and other sites.[186] Still, officials continued to ask that money for prisoners' upkeep be paid in advance, so paltry were the rations and unhealthy the conditions of the jails, and complaints continued into 1863 and 1864.[187] Some individuals languished for a year or more in detention with no trial.[188]

Slowly, the population transformed to include a segment of prisoners serving long sentences from elsewhere in the Spanish empire, ideal candidates for the reintroduction of prison labor on public works projects. The Cuban governor ordered a brigade of a hundred prisoners to rebuild government buildings in the capital almost immediately.[189] The Samaná peninsula in particular—strategic as it was for ships arriving from Spain and Havana—became a veritable center of prisoners from various corners of the Spanish empire. It housed prisoners from Cádiz, Puerto Rico, and Cuba serving long sentences; they were destined to work in mines and on the fortification of the bay itself.[190] The first East Asian prisoner ordered to Samaná was probably twenty-three-year-old "Antonio" from Macau, who had already begun to serve a ten-year sentence in Cuba for the murder of another man on a plantation. He was transferred to Santo Domingo in the fall of 1861.[191] More Chinese prisoners arrived in groups of twenty or thirty.[192] The East Asian prisoners in Samaná did not have enough to eat, especially given the "rude" nature of their prison labor, Santana wrote.[193] A handful escaped immediately after they arrived, and their capture often entailed serious bodily harm.[194] In Azua, as in Samaná, sometimes foreign prisoners fled together with Dominican nationals, who likely were able to serve as guides for the group; Spanish officials gave pointed phenotypic descriptions of such escapees.[195] Documentation is sparse regarding the specific public works projects on which prisoners were made to work, but it is clear that officials in the capital, including antivagrancy champion Pedro Valverde, came to rely on prisoners' labor and even squabbled over their allocation to different projects.[196] More than six hundred prisoners crowded Samaná's prison by fall 1863.[197]

A General Organ of the Interests of the Country: Dominican Loyalists and the New Press

Authorities and supporters of annexation collaborated on two publications that were meant to inform and propagandize to the public about the Spanish presence. The first, *La Gaceta de Santo Domingo*, published official government proceedings and decrees and announced the arrival of "illustrious" Spanish authorities (although it was printed by private presses for months until the state printer became operational).[198] Although the *Gaceta*'s journalists primarily reprinted perfunctory summaries of official business, certain government proceedings received particular attention. The *Gaceta*'s editors painstakingly reprinted in biweekly installments all of the civil code that had been approved for Santo Domingo, for example, and it was so voluminous that it filled more than six months' worth of columns.[199] Likewise, they reprinted the "Decree of Police and Governance" over more than a month's time. The back page informed those interested of steamship comings and goings, books for sale, or other minor commercial activities. For five pesos fuertes, one could purchase the French civil code; the Spanish penal code cost just one peso fuerte. Other leisure reading included an illustrated *War in Africa*, detailing Spanish exploits, and *The World as It Will Be in Year 3000*, by Émile Souvestre. A short one-week loop connected inhabitants of four different stops in Cuba and three in Puerto Rico, Saint Thomas, and the capital of Santo Domingo on steam liners such as the *Pájaro del Océano* and the *Cuba*. The three islands were more connected than they had been in forty years.

The second official paper, La Razón, was decidedly more polemic. The former El Oasis editor, Manuel de Jesús Galván, billed it as "the General Organ of the Interests of the Country," and its pro-annexation stance was aggressive.[200] La Razón's writers followed an official line: that annexation was the spontaneous will of the Dominican people, that Spain was generous to accept them back into her maternal arms, that Haitian provocation was the root of Dominican instability, and that annexation promised a new era of prosperity for the colony and its residents. The "deplorable state" of the country had made it "absolutely impossible to conserve . . . our sick and poorly realized nationality," La Razón argued, and articles focused in particular on internecine struggles in republican Venezuela as an analogy.[201] Echoing official proclamations, the paper promised major public works and urged solidarity with the colonial projects in Cuba and Puerto Rico, "brother" islands in the shared Spanish family.[202] Journalists published "Noticias Nacionales" that were often news tidbits from Málaga and other Spanish cities. Beyond fraternal *hispanidad*, annexation was a motor of progress, columnists argued. Other prominent Dominicans joined the pro-Spanish effort. Wealthy writer and businessman Francisco Javier Ángulo de Guridi asked to publish a "political, industrial and literary" journal in Santiago de los Caballeros.[203] A private citizen asked (and was granted) permission to print and sell copies of major Spanish edicts.[204]

La Razón's writers sought to make polemic links between Spanish identity, progress, and a community of "civilized nations." Writers extolled Spanish imperialism elsewhere, celebrating that the "unhappy blacks of Manila [had been] brought to Christianity" and praising Spain's victories in North Africa.[205] The paper republished José Ferrer de Couto's reincorporation missives in weekly installments that lasted well into the spring. De Couto, a decorated Spanish authority living in Cuba by the time of the occupation, was a tenuous ally at best—he would later write scathing condemnations of the colonial project, Dominican government, and people of color more generally—but in his early pamphlets, his enthusiasm was unbridled. Adjunct to the pro-Spanish missives, writers at La Razón took up a familiar central objective, that of distancing Dominican identity from Haiti. Just as Galván's and others' newspapers had done in the First Republic, the journal repeatedly took aim at Haiti. Once again, Haiti's perceived exclusivism—limiting foreign residents to coastal cities, preventing them from acquiring controlling amounts of Haitian land—distanced them from the community of civilized nations (including Spain), editorials argued.[206] Haitians were "governed by a tyrannical, exclusivist, and savage constitution, have convinced themselves that conviviality [el trato social] is a violation of human rights," one writer accused, "without ever realizing that that isolation, that incommunication deprives them."[207] It amounted to nothing less than "ingratitude ... an inhospitable instinct toward the rest of humanity," the author scoffed. La Razón taunted President Geffrard for his opposition to annexation and insisted, "We are sons of Spain!"[208]

A Sacred Decree ... A Categorical Prohibition

For all of the public proclamations about Santo Domingo as the "free" Spanish colony, not only was isolating the colony from slavery difficult, but the attitude of some Spanish authorities was chillingly cavalier. For example, the Spanish consul in Haiti allegedly suggested not only that fugitive slaves from Cuba and Puerto Rico would be sought out and apprehended but that slavery would be reestablished, and even the descendants of slaves could be reenslaved. Although his statements flew in the face of the actual annexation statutes, they reflected the ease with which some Spanish authorities imagined such an eventuality.[209] Other Spanish authorities wrestled—often secretly, in classified documents—with the problem of unequal status between their three Caribbean colonies. They decided that Santo Domingo should be kept as separate as possible from its plantation neighbors. Meanwhile, repeated public decrees promised that abolition was a "sacred guarantee ... a categorical prohibition."[210]

In June 1861, fearing that enslaved men and women might flee to Santo Domingo, the Queen issued a royal order banning the entry into Santo Domingo of free people of color from Cuba and Puerto Rico. Such self-emancipation was a very reasonable fear for Spanish authorities, given the record of people doing just that from Puerto Rico, Martinique, British islands, and the U.S. South during the previous several decades.[211] A local committee to verify a person's status would likely have been unpopular, impossible, or both. In fact, a secret edict insisted that under no circumstances could any search be conducted for escaped slaves who might have taken refuge in Santo Domingo, because it would stir tremendous panic among Dominicans.[212] Initially, Dominican authorities did not support the new prohibition of free travelers of color, arguing that the race-based ban was unnecessary and even alarming. Santana argued that the matter was "of utmost transcendence and offensive to public morality, [capable of] causing all manner of distrust."[213] Allowing free people of color to enter the colony would "give the men of color of this Province a better guarantee by calming the spirits of the suspicious," he urged, "whose fears, even if they stem from lamentable ignorance, were no less easy to spread by malevolent men among the simple masses of that part of the population." At the Dominican governor's insistence, it does seem that the provision was temporarily suspended in the fall of 1861.

Quickly, however, the prohibition proved necessary to prevent a practice that officials had not foreseen: wealthy colonists and authorities, arriving from Cuba and Puerto Rico, trying to sneak enslaved people into Santo Domingo, one by one. Government officials and Spanish officers often arrived with their families, and sometimes they brought domestic servants whose status was questionable.[214] One such case, of María Lucas Soto, reached the desk of authorities. Soto, abused by her female mistress after their arrival from Puerto Rico, fled and sought help. Upon examination of her case, authorities determined that "a number of other families have subsequently arrived in the capital with individuals of color as maids. . . . A [possible] pretext for better hiding slavery." Authorities averred that it was "essential that authorities redouble their zeal and adopt strict measures on a matter of so much transcendence."[215] Soto's abusive mistress managed to have her case dropped for lack of evidence, but Dominican officials observed that Soto was to "enjoy the full rights of liberty and the legal guarantees of all people *sui generis*" in Santo Domingo.[216] Authorities all over the island received a firm reminder that both men and women of color were strictly prohibited from entry and that all maids were to be presented to authorities as soon as they disembarked, so that officials could examine their passports. A royal order from Spain on 4 December 1861 reiterated the ban. Nevertheless, incidents continued in which slave owners employed "noticeably altered passports" in attempting to sneak in enslaved women as family members.[217] Dominican officials responded with concern. Sometime in the fall of 1861, Santana changed his position to support the ban himself; in fact, he even argued that it should be extended to include people of color arriving from Curaçao.

Violations, however, continued occurring at the very highest levels of colonial administration. Malo de Molina himself—the same commissioner charged by the Cuban governor to study and ingratiate himself into the transitioning administration—flagrantly ignored the law. Civil governor Pedro Valverde, a Dominican of some standing, who had received royal honors for his role in annexation, protested that Malo de Molina and another Cuban official had traveled with maids without notifying authorities.[218] When Valverde sent word to the two men to send the women to the government offices for paperwork inspection, Malo de Molina responded defiantly: if Valverde wanted to meet his maids, he retorted, he should come to his house personally.[219] Valverde, himself a prominent man, bristled at this hostile comportment. "I would have punished this discourtesy and the disrespect that it represents as it merits, if it had not fallen on no less than the Fiscal of Her Majesty," he protested. He was indignant of the challenge to his station. "I know how to fulfill the job with which Her Majesty the Queen (God protect her) has deigned to distinguish me, and I will execute it even at the price of my life, which I would happily sacrifice as long as it were in the fulfillment of my obligations and respecting the highest authority," he insisted. Santana delicately encouraged Valverde to persist in inspection, although the resolution is not clear. The matter was handled quietly, and the prohibition against free people of color definitively reinstated.

It is difficult to determine how the expanded travel ban was or was not enforced; probably, it was targeted primarily at white Spanish travelers arriving in the capital with an entourage, or at individual migrant travelers of color reaching the northern coast. Certainly it could not have been directed at every Dominican of color who traveled to and from the island; it seems likely that the regular travelers to Saint Thomas and Curaçao must have been granted some sort of individual pass, for example, or were otherwise able to easily establish their residence and status. Poorer, more infrequent, and more inexperienced travelers must have had a more difficult time, however. In one such instance, Julieta Enriquez, described as a *parda* originally from Curaçao, discovered to her dismay that she could not return to her children in the fall of 1862. When attempting to return from a sojourn in Curaçao, she was detained upon arrival in Puerto Plata. Subsequently, she was sent to Mayagüez—a Puerto Rican town, where she likely knew no one, far from her family, and where slavery persisted—to wait for nearly a month for permission to reenter Santo Domingo, while officials verified the existence and whereabouts of her two children. Although she was finally allowed to reunite with them and return to her home, the ordeal must have been arduous and traumatizing for the entire family.[220]

As 1861 wore on, high-ranking officials wrote missives that betrayed their hostility. Spanish authorities arriving in the colony should be men "already proven in these countries," of good reputation but also "without or cured of those reservations . . . commonly held against people of color, for the repugnance they inspire in us when we arrive from Europe . . . to consider them inferior and despicable," one official wrote. Betraying his own biases, he urged arriving Spanish authorities to be ready for "the customs and tendencies of the inhabitants, be experienced in the evil arts of some, know how to animate and bear their carelessness, their laziness, [and] their lethargy."²²¹ Such "indigence" highlighted "a most desolate inertia, the most total indifference to the joys and benefits of a social life that spurs advancement, and the natural delay and passive resistance to all improvements as a result," the Cuban governor echoed.²²² They had lost "their habit and love for work," an incoming governor claimed, "leading the fields to be so abandoned, that it is difficult to find more than pure forests designated for cattle and pig raising."²²³ His report made his plans and prejudices evident: "If the cultivation of tobacco and cotton are to be fomented on a large scale, many hands are necessary, because the natives are more deplorably apathetic than can be imagined."

FOUR

The Haitians or the Whites?
COLONIZATION AND RESISTANCE, 1861–1863

For the new administration to have any chance at survival, one major obstacle loomed: Haitian opposition and anticolonial organizing on Dominican soil. President Fabre Geffrard's connections with republican idealists, anti-Santana figures, and center-island generals made his immediate military mobilization a real possibility. Among Geffrard's Dominican collaborators was Francisco del Rosario Sánchez, who was a self-taught lawyer, military man, and one of the few men of color in the foundational Trinitario society of the Dominican capital. An idealist, Sánchez was no stranger to Santana's ire. Released from prison in August 1859, he quickly traveled to Saint Thomas. In January 1861, he and others issued a proclamation from Saint Thomas condemning annexation.[1] At some point, he returned to Hispaniola, taking refuge in Port-au-Prince. In late spring, he finally arrived at the center of the island. Santana could not know the specifics of Sánchez's months of communication with President Geffrard, but he almost certainly recognized the center-island campaigns for what they were—a collection of republican, nationalist, anticolonial alliances, with capable military leadership—and he was determined to crush them. With all the might of Spanish forces, Santana relentlessly pursued the small rebel groups. Within a few weeks, he overtook Sánchez and executed him. Santana blamed Haiti alone for the mobilizations, and the capital city paper agreed. "The dark propagandists of the Haitian idea . . . who try to justify or exculpate the invaders are wasting their time," La Razón insisted.[2]

The massive demonstration of Spanish military power effectively silenced open collaboration and resistance for a time, and months of apparent peace followed. In the capital and other towns, some prominent individuals weathered the political transition without much interruption, perceiving immediate financial and political opportunities. As property owners, they benefited by renting buildings to the administration, continued to forward development proposals, and sometimes served in the local administration.[3] The most optimistic speculated that Spanish rule would bring respite from party politics and, along with it, progress, peace, and order. Capital city writers pointed to the unrest and bloodshed in nearby republics and counted themselves lucky that political peace might finally be at hand.[4] These individuals liked Catholic orthodoxy and the language of order. They used a familiar vocabulary to condemn domestic and foreign opponents of the new regime, calling opponents disorderly, uncivilized, traitorous, or Haitian, just as they had in previous decades. Without writing about it explicitly, they embraced Spanish racial taxonomies. As months passed, some whites in the capital and other towns began to indulge their prejudices more openly.[5] A handful of prominent Dominican families drafted *limpieza de sangre* documents for daughters who married Spanish officials.[6] Poets wrote odes to Cuba.[7] When they condemned and ridiculed Geffrard that spring in the columns of *La Razón*, Spanish journalists joined them, producing an effusion of antiblack invective that reverberated on both sides of the Atlantic.[8]

Many residents of towns across the territory, on the other hand, hated the occupation from its first moments. In Sabaneta, a man cut the Spanish flag into little pieces at once.[9] The officer who announced annexation in the capital was assaulted a few days later.[10] In Puerto Plata, preannexation alarm gave way to immediate tension. It was the last town in the territory to witness a transition ceremony; officials waited, cagily, for hundreds of troops to arrive the night before.[11] A priest absconded with and hid the lowered republican flag. The next day, someone raised Haitian colors; just as quickly, they also disappeared.[12] An observer noted Puerto Plata's residents treated the arriving troops "with the utmost coldness and marked disgust, [and] they contemptuously gave them the nickname 'the whites.' "[13] In and outside of the capital city, a Spanish soldier provided a similar account, describing whole black communities—"the descendants of . . . slaves," he decided—who manifestly demonstrated their distaste at the change of flag.[14] "These are not the Spaniards I knew: they are very white," another capital resident remarked, disapprovingly.[15] As more troops arrived quickly, fugitivity was a central tactic. Samaná residents wrangled approval to worship in the woods, for example, and the governor even gave them lumber to build the chapel.

Other opponents to the arriving officials were left watching and waiting, furious.[16]

As months passed, paltry infrastructure, lack of funds, and interpersonal conflicts dealt successive blows to the loyalties of many others. From declassification to the daily comportment of Spanish administrators and soldiers, racism, scarce resources, and disenfranchisement contributed centrally to public discontent. Spanish appointees replaced Dominican interim officials, and Santana could not exercise patronage as he had promised. Meanwhile, many active reserve soldiers remained faithful to superior officers, who took up a career with the Spanish. As months passed, relationships deteriorated, however, sometimes violently. In the Cibao, the military governor was so hostile that he became legend. "¡Más malo que Buceta!" (Worse than [Brigadier] Buceta!) became an invective for a particularly cruel, arrogant, or volatile authority; everyone hated him, and even other Spanish authorities were galled by his behavior.[17] Spanish officials tended not to participate in the daily life of towns, even public ceremonies and church festivals.[18] In the capital, one woman's florid poetry praised the occupation, but observers claimed that there was "no cordiality" between Spanish and Dominicans, and that many in the capital were distressed and fearful.[19] They were "sadly submitted" in the capital, one observer claimed, explaining that with all of the shortages and unrest of recent years, "the people were of an ill humor to start with."[20] Still, an apparent calm persisted.

Summer, 1861

Although Spain still refused to recognize Haiti, President Geffrard issued an official protest against Spanish occupation on 6 April 1861. "Our brothers of the East have been tricked," he wrote, observing solemnly, "[and] the survival of one people is intricately tied to the survival of the other."[21] Santana had broken treaty mandates, Geffrard warned, giving Haiti "a complete freedom of action," and a duty, to restore the island's security. "We . . . declare that we continue to have feelings of brotherhood and our most sincere sympathies for this population," Geffrard wrote, carefully explaining that the Dominican people had been "surprised and tricked." In Spanish, he warned Dominicans directly: "Santana is disposing of you *en masse*."[22] Weeks passed, and Geffrard's condemnations continued, which Port-au-Prince journalists published alongside extensive coverage of outside disapproval. Geffrard considered Santana a cynic and a traitor. He referred specifically to the deep roots of "antinational designs" in the east, citing decades of intrigues.

Santana was a criminal by his own constitution, the president argued, and he proceeded to cite all seven constitutional articles in question.[23] Some weeks later, Haiti's government paper printed excerpts of a Dominican annexation pamphlet, which also detailed a litany of crimes. The pamphleteer called on fellow Dominicans to unite in common cause with Haiti. "The interests of the two peoples are compromised . . . it is time to fight with what weapons remain," the Dominican author urged.[24] Slavery rumors spread in Port-au-Prince and other towns.[25] Geffrard issued a simultaneous call to arms: "To arms, Haitians . . . Freedom or Death!"[26] "Our climate, our geographical and political position vis-à-vis foreign [powers], our preservation, our needs and our hopes are the same," another Haitian writer commented. "This annexation, it is the cannon of alarm, it is the poison, it is death: yes, it is death."[27]

Simultaneously with Geffrard's call, a handful of veteran Dominican generals launched coordinated campaigns that they had been planning for months. Francisco del Rosario Sánchez praised Haiti's "wise and just Republican cabinet" in his proclamations that spring. "I am persuaded that this Republic, against whom yesterday we fought for our nationality, is today just as dedicated as we are so that we might preserve it," he wrote.[28] A small, mixed group of rebels gathered in the tiny center-island town of Las Caobas, not far from Mirebalais. Some had only recently returned from Curaçao, Saint Thomas, and various towns in Haiti, where anti-Santana organizing had gained great urgency. General José Maria Cabral, veteran of partisan politics and exile, addressed his followers with an exhortation, which the *Moniteur Haïtien* promptly published: "The country is in danger, and we cannot save her without a revolution. [The president] has sold the Republic. . . . ¡Tomorrow we will be slaves! . . . We must rise up in the name of liberty, to the cry of ¡Viva la nación!"[29] As the rebels mobilized in the center of the island, Santana himself went after them, leading several thousand Spanish soldiers in hot pursuit. Two battalions of Spanish troops from Puerto Rico, two from Spain, a number of Spanish volunteers, and a militia of color from Cuba arrived to join them.[30] Cabral and his followers retreated into Haitian territory, but others were not so lucky. Near Las Matas, Santana ordered the execution of Sánchez, whom he knew very well. At Santana's orders, and despite the protest of Spanish officers, troops executed nineteen other men in a horrible manner on the afternoon of 4 July 1861; some were shot, others beaten, and others killed with machetes.[31] "The first stories of the atrocities . . . are beyond belief," the French consul reported. "These poor men asked to be judged before a military tribunal made up of Spanish soldiers and wrote a plea to the Queen. All was denied."[32] Authorities in Madrid were just as shocked.[33]

It is difficult to determine exactly who participated in the small campaigns, although it seems to have been Dominican officers, a number of Haitian soldiers, Dominican refugees living in Haiti, and center-island residents, who both expected and warmly received the arriving troops.[34] Domingo Ramírez, who had proposed reunification in 1860, was on the front lines.[35] Of the very few firsthand documents that survive from the rebellion itself, one is a simple letter from a woman in Neiba, Ramona Recio, to a certain "Juan Florian" in Haiti. Her "suspicious" letter, seized by Spanish authorities, and the subject of her interrogation, referred cryptically to a "burro that ought not be sold, but rather be turned over to her brother"—code for a firearm, perhaps?—but the matter was dropped after a brief interrogation.[36] Other surviving clues are more explicit. Segundo Mateo was prototypical of residents' alliances, general mobility, and support for the anti-Spanish campaign. Mateo had been born in Dominican territory but resided twelve years in Hincha (or Hinche), then governed by Haiti. He worked both with a local Haitian commander, carrying weapons, and for Cabral, as a spy against Spanish authority in San Juan de las Matas. The arriving troops, he reportedly confessed, were composed both of Haitian regiments and of "Haitianized Spaniards" (*españoles haitianizados*).[37] Geffrard may have pressured some Dominican refugees to make their way to the campaign or lose the salaries they had been collecting from the Haitian state.[38] Someone got hold of a Spanish flag that had been seized in the center-island fighting and brazenly dragged it through the mud in front of the Spanish delegation in Port-au-Prince.[39] Families trickled back into the center-island towns only slowly. A total of 207 people returned over the next eight months. Most were "Trinidad," "Acosta," and "Pérez," but there were a number of "Divals" and "Dilils" as well.[40] Many others stayed in Haiti, perhaps fearful of reprisals.[41] Despite Spanish persecution, a few ethnic Haitians did return to their homes in the east; the elderly Borni Beliard and his family came back to Guayubín, for example, after his conduct was universally vouched to have been "good."[42] The residents "do not want to be Spanish citizens," the Crown complained.[43]

Delighting in a narrative as old as the republic, annexation authorities repeatedly insisted that the rebellion was only Haitian. "The Haitians fled Neyba and Las Matas like cowards!" a writer at *La Razón* proclaimed.[44] Those few Dominicans who had been involved in the "humiliating defeat," journalists argued, were "merely a handful of misfits with the exaggerated pretentions of the descendants of Toussaint."[45] Cabral, Sánchez, Ramírez, and their followers "are, [like Judas], Haitian men who have renounced their faith, honor, and country," the writer of another editorial continued accusingly, arguing that they sought the destruction of the country and should be disowned.[46] Pro-annexation journalists followed up with an indulgent, racist press offensive. A writer rhapsodized about an unnamed young Dominican who had been canonized as a Spanish patriot for having saved a Spanish flag from the "Haitian hordes."[47] Madrid journalists were even more overt, unleashing a torrent of slurs.[48] The defeat of the "cowards" had been easy, loyalist writers concurred. "We will see if the Haitians doubt now the spontaneity of Dominicans in the annexation," one editorial exulted.[49] *La Razón* writers went so far as to embrace rumors of French reoccupation of Haiti—albeit dubious, they admitted—with glowing prose.[50] Dominicans were "working energetically with [the Spanish] . . . to reject the invasion of their black neighbors," Madrid papers agreed.[51] "Let us throw up our voices to give most fervent thanks to Divine Providence!" a proclamation attributed to Santana exhorted. "We are children of the same August Mother of all Spaniards . . . of all Spaniards born in Europe, America, Asia, and Africa!"[52]

Military reprisal was fast and brutal, directed squarely at Port-au-Prince. Spanish agent Manuel Cruzat arrived in late April and tried to force his way into having an audience at the presidential palace.[53] He demanded that Geffrard immediately renounce opposition, recognize annexation, expel any conspirators, and pay an indemnity for his call to arms. In fact, the Spanish actions of that summer very nearly destabilized the government in Port-au-Prince. On 5 July 1861, six Spanish steamships appeared in the harbor of Port-au-Prince, causing "great sensation."[54] General Joaquín Rubalcaba, the commander of Havana's naval forces, demanded 200,000 pesos fuertes, one hundred cannon shots in salute of the Spanish flag, and assurances of no further disturbances within the Haitian territory, all to be satisfied within forty-eight hours. Geffrard refused his demands and declared martial law. As hours passed, citizens became frantic, storing valuables and heading miles outside of the city.[55] The situation was so tense that Spanish authorities urged foreigners to evacuate; the Spanish press wrote almost gleefully about the terror and the tension of the peasant residents of the surrounding area. After five days of mediation with the British and French consuls, Geffrard consented to saluting the Spanish forces and negotiating compensation.[56] One month later, Spanish authorities demanded an additional 25,000 pesos fuertes as indemnity for damages caused in the Dominican towns of Las Matas, Neiba, and Cercado, a "most moderate" sum, the Spanish Crown announced.[57]

Seeking to protect his republic, Geffrard acquiesced to all signs of conciliation. He ordered Cabral and a handful of others out of Haiti, and they quickly absconded to Saint Thomas.[58] In Port-au-Prince, residents quietly criticized both Geffrard's capitulation and his quick recourse to martial law, and they feared more Spanish aggression was to come.[59] The *Moniteur Haïtien* was forced into silence. A report on Jamaicans' opposition to annexation was buried on the second page of a July paper, and a later issue praised Geffrard for having navigated "difficult and delicate" negotiations with Spain.[60] Months later, a journalist nearly echoed the Spanish line: that 1861 border troubles had caused "complications," he wrote, but that they were "smoothed out by the wisdom of both governments." The writer pointedly returned to domestic questions of agricultural development and education.[61] The "indemnity" the government was to pay received passing mention.[62] Geffrard was in a difficult diplomatic position, and he faced increasing domestic opposition. He clung to constitutionalism and pronounced clemency to conspirators who cropped up in various towns, but he also warned that unauthorized small vessels, milling about the coast, would be treated as pirates.[63] In the Dominican capital, meanwhile, the summer executions had chilled the populace. Santana's brutality ruled tenuously once again.[64]

Alarming Reports, Not at All Satisfactory: The Erosion of Spanish Optimism

Although calm was reestablished in late summer, Spanish frustration grew. General Santana, author of annexation and Spain's first collaborator, proved a troublesome and frustrating proxy who rarely fulfilled his duties as Spanish authorities would have liked. Publicly, Cuban governor Serrano referred to him positively, but in an "internal and most confidential report," he recounted a very different opinion. "Alarming reports, not at all satisfactory," had been arriving about Santana's cruelty, and soon the Cuban governor himself became convinced that the Dominican caudillo was "an almost insuperable obstacle to the organization of the territory."[65] Through maneuvering and violence, Santana was in command of a "completely loyal" party of followers on whom he rained patronage. He and his followers "have so exaggerated their pretensions . . . and ambition for salaries and posts, that it constitutes a great obstacle for continuing to organize [the administration]," the visiting governor reported. "They want the top posts and refuse the lower ones that have been generously offered them," he complained.[66] Furthermore, Santana was implacable with his Dominican enemies. He tried to block former opponents from government posts, even denying their reentry to the country on an individual basis.[67] Serrano had arrived in Santo Domingo determined to declare total amnesty, a measure that he quickly learned Santana opposed.[68] Santana's favoritism and strong-arm tactics extended as far as the clergy; Santana urged that prelate Moreno del Cristo be removed for being anti-Spanish, but Serrano determined his motivations to be wholly personal.[69] "Underhanded machinations [stemming] from political enmity and envy," Serrano concluded, disapprovingly.[70] The regente of the Real Audiencia, Eduardo Alonso y Colmenares, was even more critical. He accused Santana and his coterie of purposely provoking conflict with officials in order to regain lost popularity; he was uncooperative and narrow-minded, Alonso accused. The behavior and corruption were alarming, he continued, and advocated that Santana's replacement should be immediate.[71]

Whether Santana's resignation in mid-1862 was due to fevers and rheumatism, as he claimed, or to increasing Spanish pressure is not clear. He was obviously unhappy; he had tried for months to resign, writing repeated requests. A critical observer remarked that he had profited from the sale of supplies to Spanish troops in hard currency and sought to retire to the east with his earnings.[72] Certainly, too, he was no longer the pragmatic Spanish choice for captain general. Spanish authorities admonished Santana to defer to Governor Serrano regarding any foreign policy concerns, including Haiti.[73] Santana retreated from official business—as he had been wont to do throughout the First Republic. "Off with his cattle," one Spanish general sneered.[74] At other times he was irascible and withdrawn, "complaining about every decision that is not his," one confidential report accused, observing, "He only wants to govern with the arbitrariness, violence, and exclusivity of the Republican era, with different names."[75] To remove him without controversy, Serrano suggested he be called to Madrid, "under a plausible pretext of meeting his August Sovereign."[76] Not long after Serrano's visit, Santana retired to his Seibo ranch permanently, anyway. "If his ailments were in part responsible for his resignation, it is no less certain that his impotence versus the near absolute control of . . . an upstart bureaucracy in the process of replacing his intimate collaborators was a decisive factor," historian Luis Álvarez observes.[77]

As 1862 proceeded, so did a progressive increase in Spanish replacements for government positions. New captain general Rivero acknowledged that a dramatic replacement of partisan and problematic appointments would be "extremely impolitic in the eyes of the country," but he proposed to neutralize the appointments by adding army officers "of recognized skill and talent" as secretaries.[78] Other professionals faced new restrictions. Prior to the Spanish administration, public defenders in the republic had needed only proof of upstanding status and a two-year apprenticeship. Spanish commissioners suggested that the legal ranks be weeded out significantly. Only those who had been practicing law for fifteen or more years could continue; others would need to pass an examination, and in some cases, an additional apprenticeship.[79] Authorities disqualified three former members of the Dominican Supreme Court in this manner.[80] A handful of prominent *letrados* sought licenses to continue in their public clerk (*escribano público*) posts, but candidates arriving from Puerto Rico supplanted them.[81] As the administration stabilized, Spanish authorities methodically purged the prominent Dominicans who had overseen the transition. Spanish bureaucrats Victoriano García Paredes and Mariano Cappa replaced Fernandez de Castro and Miguel Lavastida in their high-ranking posts, leaving them only a semiofficial advisory capacity.[82] Manuel Cruzat—former consul in Mobile, Galveston, and disastrously in Haiti—became the director of mail. Eduardo Alonso y Colmenares, a Madrid-educated lawyer, became the regente of the Real Audiencia. Dominican officials Pedro Ricart y Torres, Miguel Valverde, Pedro Curiel, and others were ousted in subsequent months.[83]

Logistical and economic problems plagued the new administration. Few public works projects began. As an interim measure, authorities instructed local officials to use proceeds from fines for municipal funding, but they were insufficient, onerous to citizens, and only slowly disbursed.[84] The administration never repaid wealthy loyalists for their out-of-pocket support in crushing the 1861 revolts. Salary complaints were common.[85] "It seemed like the [Spanish] government had forgotten the town," a frustrated observer proclaimed in one center-island town, citing repeated requests for military supplies and nearly six months in pay arrears.[86] Administration costs mounted: thousands to repair the few standing government buildings, payments for renting of private homes and furniture, and other start-up expenses. Some of the expenditures highlight the formalistic costs of Spanish return: 81 pesos to celebrate the entry of the royal seal, 27 pesos for new flags in Puerto Plata, 430 pesos to relocate a woman living near a sixteenth-century chapel marked for restoration, and other incidental costs.[87] Officials proposed purchasing the land on which the island's first Mass was celebrated and finding and restoring Columbus's house in Santo Domingo, historically dubious but symbolically significant projects.[88] The new watchmen forces cost 14,000 pesos in the capital alone and almost 34,000 pesos island-wide.[89] Treasury authorities, meanwhile, were frustrated with the difficulty of organizing First Republic documents, and could not precisely ascertain what constituted state property.[90] Madrid officials were very critical of the accounting going on in Santo Domingo generally.[91]

Slow official responses aggravated everything. The lack of regular steamship service made governing difficult, officials complained.[92] Mail took about a week to arrive from the east to the capital, and about the same amount of time to get from the northern coast to the capital by boat, but it took almost two weeks to reach Santo Domingo from the territory's most important town, Santiago. Authorities in Santiago de los Caballeros complained about the slow speed of correspondence.[93] Mail from Santo Domingo to Madrid regularly took as long as two months. Santana asked Spanish authorities to send ships directly to the capital, as the roads were so poor crossing the island to Samaná that dispatches took a long time to arrive. His request was denied on the basis that the route amounted to too much of a diversion from Havana, obviously a priority destination.[94] Administrators waited on funds and instructions, but the chief postal administrator, like others, quit to find more lucrative employment.[95]

Some posts simply went unfilled. Try as they might, officials could not fill the position of minister of justice. Although notification of the post's creation was mailed to the colony's mayors in January 1862, a number of them replied that they had never received word, even six months later. Exasperated, capital city officials reissued a thirty-day call: baptized Catholic men with robust constitution, twenty-five years or older, and "certified of good morality and conduct" were welcome to apply, it urged, and the edict was to be read and repeated in important public places. "We read the edict," the Azua mayor reported months later in late summer, "but there is absolutely no person who could possibly be a candidate." The Puerto Plata mayor also complied, "but no one solicited the post," he regretted. The post was provisionally filled—more than a year later—by a French citizen living in the capital, who later deserted, leaving for Saint Thomas under an assumed name. Anyway, funds were short and would have to be borrowed from Puerto Rico. No further records suggest what exasperated officials did next.[96] Even the prized port of Samaná—where a new mayoral position was tentatively created in late 1861—could not find any notaries at all to perform secretarial duties there.[97] In the capital, meanwhile, the Royal Audiencia begged the Crown for more money—repeatedly arguing that the administration of justice could not possibly be administered with so few personnel.[98] Elsewhere, officers criticized the pace of public works projects. An officer in Azua complained of the impossibility of finishing barracks there, "whether because of the loss of materials, or the slowness of the laborers who are not sustained by anything other than the Government's ration." He asked for funds to be able to pay them according to their progress, with the hope of speeding things along.[99]

Spanish troops were not prepared for the conditions under which they met the rebels in the spring of 1861, and conditions were difficult generally. With more troops arriving in Azua from Havana in mid-June, conditions during the summer campaign "against Haiti" were unimaginably bad, the Cuban governor reported. According to authorities on the ground,

> It is impossible from all angles to form a worthy idea of the difficulties one fights against in this country for the simplest thing. I will leave out the housing of troops in a town composed of insufficient barrack-huts, in such poor condition that when it rains it is as if one were in open country. I will not tire Your Excellency by describing the Hospitals where it has been necessary to put two sick men in the same bed for days, nor will I report the scarcity of articles of the first necessity, nor the high cost of living, not even how it is necessary to travel three leagues and more amid heavy rainfall and overflowing rivers to provide forage for the horses. Your Excellency will easily understand everything when I simply tell you that since the moment of arrival I have been buying burros at any price, and despite Santana's presence and help, it has not been possible for me to buy more than forty—and that after having left Santo Domingo twenty-five days ago.

The horses were tired, he reported, and oxcarts difficult to find. "With respect to the depopulation of the country and the poor condition of roads I will just tell Your Excellency, that in more than twenty *leguas* from Azua to San Juan de la Maguana, there are just six miserable huts [*bohíos*] in three spots, hours apart on the road. . . . Often there is no other remedy than sleeping on the ground, and the forest is too dense for hammocks," he lamented.[100] As always, however, Spanish authorities were eager to underscore the harmony between Spanish troops and the Dominican peasants they encountered. The Spanish soldiers had faced the adverse conditions with such "superior discipline . . . fraternizing with the residents and in everything laboring with prudence and tact, that it is the admiration of the country," the Cuban governor insisted.

Arriving Spanish settlers fared worst of all. There was confusion over who would cover the costs of arriving Spanish families, especially if their deals had been struck before annexation was official. They arrived in small groups from port cities like Cádiz; often, expeditions of larger groups failed in planning stages.[101] Officials agreed that white labor was necessary and resolved to adhere to pro-*colono* statutes from the neighboring islands, but they quibbled on land allowances and other costs. After the settlers arrived, they fared overwhelmingly poorly. Some of them sought government aid immediately; others tried to return to Spain.[102] Widows, orphans, and the sick were left stranded. A number who were reported to be dying in Samaná had no money to return to Spain. Future colonists must not be sent in the height of the summer, which had caused so high a mortality rate "that they were terrified of all the island residents," one report warned.[103] The projects were so unsuccessful that a royal order in March 1863 allowed widows to return to Spain.

Spanish authorities endeavored on a good faith mission to redeem the paper money of the republic for pesos fuertes, just as Dominican politicians had negotiated. Authorities began the program slowly, however, and they quickly ran into problems.[104] First, the Classification Panel found that it was difficult to know if the paper bills they were receiving were real; they considered it simply impossible to validate them all.[105] In fact, the Crown issued paper IOUs of its own, papers that were themselves subject to rampant falsification and inflation.[106] When redemption began, the panel offered to redeem paper currency with copper. As paper money was already not accepted, small merchants scrambled to exchange the copper for silver or gold, often at unfavorable rates.[107] Just one year in, Puerto Plata was abuzz with discontent. The state of the town was "alarming," Santana reported, and the discontent centered on the paper money. The tone of the pamphlets circulating—railing against the "Despotic Spanish Government" and demanding "the blood of the traitor of he who sold us as vengeance"—gave ample reason to make him nervous.[108] Poorer individuals often could not get authorities to accept their money, sometimes in so deteriorated a condition that it was in multiple pieces. One anonymous letter writer later observed, "This disgusted the masses, as the measure, on top of being arbitrary, discredits their limited means." [109] Currency gained some stability, but the cost of living rose along with it, raising the price of daily goods in the capital by 20 percent almost immediately, and more in the long term.[110]

At the end of Santana's tenure, the colonial government was in dire financial straits. Railroad, canal, highway, and bridge plans were on hold, and Samaná's mine awaited an engineer. Even Santo Domingo's port could not be dredged until further notice, nor could a much-needed railroad connecting the tobacco fields of the Cibao to port cities be constructed.[111] The public works department had only an inspector at present and an annual budget of fewer than 40,000 pesos. Money was "a delicate subject"—there existed a "total lack of capital . . . to make large-scale industry"—and so contributions from Cuba ought to continue for a time, the incoming governor argued. He would study the tax system as ordered—but in the meantime, it was vital that the stipends from Cuba came with "strict regularity, as in this island there is not a single resource, nor a merchant to whom one could appeal in the case of urgency." Santo Domingo officials asked the Cuban treasury to cover its summer costs in 1862, but neither the 120,000-peso stipend requested for August nor the 200,000 pesos for September arrived.[112] The captain general of Santo Domingo would have to take a pay cut by 1863, the overseas minister warned.[113] Cuban governor Serrano was gone, too, retiring, as Santana had, for health reasons.

As the new captain general, Felipe Rivero, began his tenure, however, official Spanish sentiment was stubbornly optimistic. Rivero himself assured the Spanish Overseas Ministry that he was taking careful notes and reading the reports of "very authorized people who have had the chance to study and learn the nature and character of the inhabitants."[114] Religious reform would continue apace. Despite early failures with Spanish settlers, he urged that more rural laborers and Asian laborers ought to be drafted. General Santana retired with laurels and a healthy half-pay salary, honored with the "Grand Cross of the Royal American Order of Isabel the Catholic" and the title of "Marques of Las Carreras," recalling an 1849 battle with Haitian troops.[115] Dominican officials also wrote approvingly of Santana's replacement by Rivero.[116] Apart from a few minor incidents, the country was tranquil, authorities wrote. "Dominicans, embrace your new father!" Santana wrote before taking leave of the capital. "Peace and happiness await," the arriving Spanish governor reminded the public, arguing that a new era of prosperity was to be gained through their voluntary obedience.[117]

Conflicts with the Spanish State

To the average Dominican resident living somewhat near a larger town, the arrival of the Spanish troops and administrators steadily impacted daily life. Spain's first visibility was military; nearly three thousand troops had arrived by 5 April. The larger state—government spending grew in Santo Domingo from 241,000 pesos in 1860 to more than twice that figure within two years—brought Spanish priests, Spanish civil and military governors, and new Dominican authorities to the payroll.[118] Although much of the budget was funded by Cuban coffers, at least some of it came from residents themselves; the income exacted from Dominicans doubled from 1860 to 1862.[119] Merchants felt the impact first. It was they who suffered new licensing fees, faced difficulties exchanging the paper currency from the former republic, and—as rebellion broke out—saw few of the capital improvements for which they had so greatly hoped. Those authorities who had served in Cuba in particular were arriving from a colony with a large civil and military structure. "You can go nowhere in Cuba without meeting soldiers," a resident of the neighboring colony complained.[120] While residents of the biggest urban centers—the capital, Santiago de los Caballeros, Puerto Plata—probably felt the expansion most immediately, therefore, others received Spanish *alcaldes* and low-level Dominican officials (*alcaldes pedáneos*) charged with spreading Spanish law to the smaller towns.[121]

Few authorities were as famously unlikable as Brigadier Manuel Buceta, charged with governing the Cibao province from its capital, Santiago de los Caballeros. Buceta was irredeemably heavy-handed, authoritarian, and condescending, driving even prominent, loyal Dominicans to disgust. Alejandro Ángulo Guridi, the son of Dominican parents who had left the island in 1822, raised and educated in Puerto Rico and Havana, was such a subject. Guridi had returned to the island in 1852, involving himself in liberal politics and pro-immigration schemes, and supported annexation on the grounds it would usher in peace, with prosperity soon to follow.[122] When Spanish officials began arriving, therefore, he and other loyalists made ideal transitional authorities; in fact, a number of them constituted the municipal government (*ayuntamiento*) that was to collaborate with Buceta in Santiago, probably the wealthiest and most important city of the east. Faithfully, Guridi and others labored to establish a new town hall, in a large house with a side room. "We decorated the tables and floors of the meeting room, made a carpet-canopy for the President's place, and hung a painting of our August Sovereign," Guridi reported. Of the result, he wrote, "Well, it is clear, Excellent Sir, that the location doesn't look like the Ayuntamiento of Madrid nor that of Havana; but everything is relative in this life," explaining, "And we are satisfied in having done everything within our means to create a meeting room for decent men who have seen those of other countries."

The conflict between Buceta and Santiago's municipal government escalated quickly. Buceta's response was indecorously haughty. Guridi explained: "Well, Excellent Sir, the first day that Sr. Brigadier Governor saw it fit to attend our meeting, he said that it was an indecency, and that it was not fit even for troops to sleep in; and why were we meeting at that time anyway, if it was not the set hour."[123] Buceta exited, threatening jail for anyone who was not present again at seven that night. When the meeting convened that evening, Buceta refused to listen to the members' reasoning on a number of legislative decisions. Guridi and others tried to remain calm. "Excellent Sir, we continued carrying out our duties without complaining, without the tiniest bit of venting escaping from our lips," he reported, both composed and exasperated. Buceta's supercilious manner was not placated. Unsatisfied with the contractor chosen by the Ayuntamiento for trash collection—neighbors had simply left refuse in the wrong street, "unused to the service," Guridi insisted—the Spanish commander ordered the trash to be piled at the door of the municipal meetinghouse, blocking its entrance entirely. Residents were abuzz—some surprised, some furious. The Ayuntamiento members, for their part, felt humiliated, and they wrote individual scathing letters to the captain general directly. "I would not be worthy of my parents' name or even my own . . . please let me quit, and tell the governor not to oppose my passport," Guridi pleaded. Governor Rivero, perplexed at the events, wrote to Buceta for more information, but it was too late. Guridi left the country again in 1863; he published the oppositional pamphlet *Santo Domingo and España* anonymously from New York the following year.[124]

Town residents often resisted paying fines to the new Spanish state, especially if they were men of military rank. In the town of Guerra, a group of a dozen men were interrogated about a game of *juego del monte* (a card game similar to poker). Town officials detained the owner of the house, Pedro Pineda, and ordered him to pay sixty pesos; the rest were to pay a smaller amount or spend some time in jail. Pineda refused to submit to his sentence. His resistance flummoxed authorities, who were unused to enforcing such statutes. The mayor—whose own secretary riddled the ensuing correspondence with numerous chirographic errors—was bewildered. "I am relating this to Your Excellency so that you might answer us as quickly as possible, saying what should be done on the matter; of course the sentence should not be illusory under any context," his report read.[125] Pineda escalated his opposition, now claiming to be a "Spanish Colonel" and insisting that he would listen only to military authority. "No matter what, [that authority] falls to me," the army commander Miguel de los Santos wrote, urging, "so I hope Your Excellency can tell me what I can do to oblige him to pay, as he has been too abusive and even now continues abusing the authorities. . . . I hope that you will have the kindness to answer me on the matter using the same porter."[126] Officials in the capital replied sternly; not only was Pineda not exempt, but the fines for all the infractors should actually be double or triple the original amount. Under some confusing circumstances, Pineda himself defiantly delivered this order of punishment from the capital back to the town. Guerra's army commander balked and asked Pineda only to pay the original amount, in installments.[127]

Passports proved complicated. A larger administration probably caused more people to worry about official passports than before, although it is difficult to state conclusively that this is so. It does seem like making one's resident status official became important, as was the case for a Bavarian merchant who applied for naturalization, despite having already been a resident for more than ten years.[128] Some individuals, like Blas C. Jiménez, had served in the military in both countries, with long-term residency both places. Jiménez had moved to Port-au-Prince without any intention of returning to the east, and there he married a young Haitian woman and raised a family, all the while as a Haitian military officer, even traveling abroad under the auspices of a Haitian passport. Authorities were perplexed as to whether he should be admitted as a Spanish citizen again. After the fighting began, first in 1861 and then steadily in 1863, travel became even more fraught. Spanish authorities insisted that the families who had left in the earliest rebellions— which they characterized as "invasions" from Haiti—had been forcibly relocated westward, for example, and they bid the eastern residents return quietly to their homes. Despite their reportedly destitute conditions and official prodding, however, they were slow to return to Spanish jurisdiction.[129] Petitions to travel westward persisted long after the fighting heightened scrutiny; residents' commercial and familial interests were simply too important. Ana Maduro asked for a passport to travel to Port-au-Prince to recoup a sick daughter she had left there in 1864, for example, and others applied for cattle trading and other business interests.[130] Dozens, if not hundreds, of ethnically Haitian residents in towns like Las Matas Cercado and Sabana Mula did not return east after fighting erupted, as both scrutiny and chaos grew.[131]

Animal impressment grated on everyone. Given the extraordinarily poor condition of the territory's roads and a lack of Spanish pack animals, the governor created a system of *bagajes* in September 1862 authorizing Spanish commanders to impress oxen, burros, and horses to carry supplies, often without recourse for their Dominican owner. An anonymous letter writer described the rude manner with which impressment was effected: "The arbitrary *bagaje* system: suffice it to say that they threw what the horses were carrying into the middle of the street (the loads of the *campesinos*), saying that the urgency of Royal Service demanded it, and that the beasts, thus embargoed, didn't always make it back to the hands of their owners."[132] In San

Cristóbal, Spanish troops were encroaching on residents' farms and seizing the animals they encountered. Not even prominent area residents were safe. One of the accusing *vecinos* was prominent military officer (and future independence fighter in Cuba) Modesto Díaz, another a former senator.[133] One reservist complained that he had waited more than three months for repayment (108 pesos) for his horse, which the Spanish forces had seized with no indication of forthcoming payment. The Spanish captain was extraordinarily curt in his reply to the query, even as he took advantage of his letter to complain of the disorder of Spain's collection of pack animals. Of forty animals borrowed, he could locate only twenty-five, he admitted, and didn't know what else to say.[134]

With new civil codes ruling the towns, other costly daily irritations emerged. Where some locals had appealed to their town officials (usually an *alcalde ordinario*) for redress during previous years, now they sometimes had to travel to court in the municipal capital, a prohibitively costly proposition.[135] In the capital, building codes seemed punitive to those who tried to set up new public establishments, and homeowners had just one year to bring their houses up to architectural and hygiene codes.[136] Merchants seeking licenses (*derechos de patentes*) in smaller towns grumbled at the fact they were to pay the same rates as the capital.[137] The revenue from fines was sufficient that in the small town of Guerra officials proposed building a church from the proceeds.[138] As months passed, authorities became well aware of how onerous the fees were for much of the population, and they admitted that they had too closely modeled the police and government codes after Cuba's ordinances. After the first year, the Consejo de Administración proposed some reforms. They called on the governor to relax or suppress ordinances about house repair and painting, animal tethering, clothes hanging, children's dress, licenses for small-time vendors, and animal impressment. Demanding a license from nearly destitute, small-time vendors "would be the same as taking away from them the only means they have from not dying of misery," the council noted, empathetically, arguing that even free licenses were a problem.[139]

Protestants in Puerto Plata and Samaná, as well as other towns, faced state discrimination. Spanish officials at the highest level vacillated on the issue of religious tolerance, and lower-level authorities bungled local relationships. In Samaná, the army seized a Wesleyan chapel that served a number of British subjects for use as an infirmary, for example, only to hastily retract their occupation at the behest of the British consul and the Spanish governor.[140] The following year, authorities in Samaná found themselves defending the

Protestant population, refusing to enforce newly restrictive measures unless they heard directly from the governor.[141] As policymakers vacillated, resident Americans felt extra hostility; they suspected Spanish hostility to their community was an extension of imperial pro-Confederate sentiments.[142] The father of a free black Methodist family of five from New York—who had been living in Samaná since at least the 1850s and who worked in the customhouse as a bookkeeper—sought protection from Spanish persecution by hoisting a British flag, but British consul Hood acerbically dismissed him.[143] Some residents fled scrutiny, even to Turks and Caicos. Others appealed to the British consulate, or even President Lincoln, for intervention and protection of their churches, schools, and civil marriages. Even the smallest day-to-day dealings, like opening a small pharmacy, became problematic for Protestants who refused to swear a Catholic oath. Archbishop Monzón was hostile to their appeals; the practitioners amounted to "diverse and contrary sects," he replied scornfully.[144] Only their central importance to the Puerto Plata merchant community, long roots in other northern towns, and the threat of international incident with the British unevenly protected them. Samaná officials were acidly critical of the Catholic priests who served the area; they also demanded more funds.[145]

Invigorated Catholic orthodoxies were widely unpopular. Santana himself opposed inquiry into masonry in the territory, for example.[146] Some of the territory's most prominent men were masons; they too faced censure from the pulpit. Authorities even forced some to hand over secret documents to church authorities.[147] Parishioners of local Catholic churches resented new fines. Marriage in the church, which had been at once fairly uncommon and free, was now an expectation and cost an onerous 250 pesetas.[148] In one instance, a local Neiba official attempted to intervene on the part of the area residents, arguing that infractions like child nudity were innocent. The incoming cleric's repression had left children "marooned in their house," the sympathetic writer urged, and he testily pointed to the priest's own shirking of his duties.[149] Even the regional authority, Eusebio Puello, concurred. The commanding clergyman was absolutely curt and unsympathetic in response. "Your protests are useless and in vain, because I will still correct the scandalous behavior of nudity and common-law marriage, not just in the church, but in the street, plazas and *montes*. . . . It is diabolical," he replied.[150] Meanwhile, the archbishop muted complaints about priestly abuses, like Bonao's drunken cleric, who had wandered the streets, naked.[151]

The measures divided local religious authorities. While some probably adopted the hardline stance of the incoming archbishop, other town clergy, even those who had initially supported Spain's arrival, resented their newfound role as tax collector for various sacraments.[152] Spanish authorities lamented the loss of their "important support," and retrospective accounts point centrally to the harsh actions of the archbishop as a source of discontent.[153] A few Dominican-born priests vocally opposed annexation from the outset, and the most prominent faced unwanted repression and deportation. Father Fernando Antonio Meriño, a longtime opponent to Santana and interim ecclesiastical governor, was an immediate opponent. He attacked the proposition at an independence day Mass in February 1861, even before Spanish arrival, and refused to take a loyalty oath to the queen or to add a prayer for the life and health of the kings at the end of Mass. His open dissent earned him immediate censure and expulsion by mid-June 1862; subsequently, he spent time in Venezuela, Puerto Rico, and Spain lobbying against annexation. In frustration, he wrote in his diary, "Damn the Spanish Government, may the Devil take them!"[154]

Women confronted all manner of new measures, civil and religious. It is likely that their low-capital ventures—fruits, vegetables, alcohol, and so on—finally gained official exemption from licenses with the code reforms of 1863. Other ordinances were not as easy to elude. Spanish zeal for reformed Catholic marriage was "double-edged empathy," as administrators sought to instill a sense of "shame" and gender differences through marriage and restricted ideals of female propriety.[155] In towns and rural areas throughout the republic, most women lived informally with their partners, a position known locally as *mancebinas*. Many poorer town couples had their own small-scale commercial enterprise, but usually both partners were very cash poor. One Neiba couple, in which the man sold small amounts of tobacco (among other endeavors) and his partner sold different kinds of liquor (or sometimes traded it in kind), was perhaps typical.[156] Spanish priests of varying disposition arrived in towns across the territory. Few archival traces reflect how women might have received and responded to their strictures. The licensing of midwifery—at a prohibitive twenty pesos—must have been an obstacle that many tried to avoid, for example.[157] Other decrees, like that requiring clothing for young children, might have been simply troublesome, frustrating, and impossible.

The logistical demands of thousands of new residents in the capital, however, presented opportunities that a number of women eagerly took. Very few wealthy families had domestic servants in the capital; it was "notorious, domestics are immensely difficult to find and charge very high day rates," authorities observed. Also, water was hard to come by. The town council recommended that cooks, washerwomen, and ironers not have to seek a license.[158] Although some of the highest-ranking officers brought with them domestics from Cuba and Puerto Rico—as the enslaved maid scandals proved early in the occupation—most arriving Spanish personnel probably entrusted their laundry to enterprising local women. The occupation sanctioned an important public presence and source of income for urban women, and the multiple-day turnover demanded considerable interaction with their clients in towns and army outposts.[159] Port cities like Puerto Plata attracted women migrants from other islands, like the young Josepha Debra, from Turks and Caicos, who moved to Puerto Plata when she was very young and "perfectly understood Spanish."[160] She and other women, usually unmarried, moved again from Puerto Plata down to the capital as washerwomen and sweets sellers, probably to capitalize on the troop and governmental concentration there. Often they moved in with other unmarried women of greater means, including Spanish residents of the capital. Some struck up relationships with the soldiers that were subject to considerable scrutiny after fighting began.[161]

Call on Me, I'm No Coward!

Even for those citizens who did not find themselves on the wrong side of any gaming law, commercial code, or sacrament, the presence of Spanish troops marked a novel quotidian reality. In smaller towns, their profile was likely minimal. However, as the troops settled into larger towns across Santo Domingo, their comportment proved to be volatile. General and later governor of Santo Domingo José de la Gándara praised the "admirable instinct . . . and inalterable discipline" of the Spanish troops for avoiding incidents as they disembarked, even as he cryptically alluded to "irregularities" in how they first treated Santana.[162] Rank-and-file soldiers and officers alike met taxing conditions—difficult travel, poor housing, makeshift hospitals—and many of the soldiers were very young, just eighteen or nineteen years old, unused to their new assignment.[163] Officers and ranking soldiers alike were frustrated that their transfer to Santo Domingo had restarted seniority clocks for promotion; often, too, their abrupt transfer meant that they had been separated from families they had already established in Cuba or Puerto Rico. A new theater company in the capital, whose directors had been excited for a new public, closed when arriving officials simply did not fill the seats as they had imagined.[164]

With its extremely sparse material culture, Santo Domingo was not the most agreeable place for transfer. In their downtime, troops were often bored. Higher-ranking officers held social events like masked balls, ostensibly with well-off Dominicans (or, at the very least, with Dominican women). "Given that in this town [Santiago] there is absolutely nothing to do, sometimes the officers got together to eat dinner or lunch [sometimes with two Dominican pharmacists]," one officer testified during an inquiry about socializing. The matter was resolved without any discipline.[165] Spanish rank and file and Dominican town residents clashed over the former's bored, and hostile, misconduct. Some incidents were as innocent or thoughtless as soldiers leaving open farm gates as they exercised, repeatedly allowing local farm animals to escape.[166] Infantrymen wandered to towns' outskirts, often for extraofficial reasons. In one criminal case, seven Spanish soldiers from three different regiments, apparently friends, were arrested on a variety of charges: patrolling a house without orders to do so, having an unlicensed firearm, and stealing coconuts and sugarcane. They were "skulking about," the official reported.[167]

An excess of enforced leisure and alcohol frequently bred conflict. In Puerto Plata, a few drunken soldiers tried to crash a family baptism party in the early morning of 18 August 1862, for example, demanding beer and saying "lots of crazy stuff" (*muchos disparates*), witnesses claimed. The house's owner informed them that the party had ended, but the soldiers proceeded to trash the home, looking for its female residents. At some point, the women of the house did emerge and began throwing rocks at the intruders. "I told them that they had no authority to enter . . . not even my husband did," Juana Silberia testified. A soldier threatened her, telling her not to "get involved in men's affairs, and that if she didn't be quiet he would break everything in the house [and] kill her." Bravely, Juana responded by pushing the menacing soldier out of the house, but when the soldiers pried the door open again, she fled to her sister's home. A policeman arrived and began to beat Juana's husband, at which point her sister María threw herself on him, ripping his uniform in several places. With several rocks in her hand, she threatened the officer, "Kill me or I'll kill you!" It seems unlikely the women ever received justice. One soldier freely admitted that the band of soldiers had been partying—three sergeants, three policemen, and two Dominican men had been drinking, then six more had joined their group, he testified. More tellingly, however, another soldier dismissively referred to the incident as a "dispute with some *morenos* in the street," and the case was never resolved.[168]

Sometimes conflicts caused a public spectacle, as when a low-ranking Dominican officer from the reserves got into a drunken fight with a Spanish sergeant in Cotuy. People poured out of the town church into the street. "All the locals who were in service for Holy Friday became very upset [se alborotaron], and all the women went running in the streets to their houses," Spanish officials reported.[169] In the southern town of Baní, a fight between "various officers" of Battalion Vitoria and several local men—"a wholly personal matter, without the smallest mention of politics," one observer argued—was resolved with minor disciplinary measures.[170] Bored and prone to overreact, soldiers at times became violent. A soldier roughly disciplined a local child for fighting, bruising the child in the process; officials admonished him not to repeat the incident.[171] One soldier was accused of a very brutal beating of an elderly shoemaker after he refused the soldier a drink.[172] Soldiers felt the division between Santana and Spanish officials acutely. One Dominican lieutenant asked Santana, snidely, "How many Captain Generals are there in the island?"[173]

Interpersonal relationships between the soldiers sometimes soured. A fight during a card game won one Spanish soldier two months in prison.[174] When a Spaniard got in a squabble over which of his fellow soldiers was to give him a shave—he spoke heatedly to one, in whispers—the resulting melee caused the death of a bystander from a stray bullet. A military judge sentenced the soldier to be shot.[175] Military judges came to doubt Spanish accusations. One Spanish sergeant testified, for example, about how a Dominican soldier, Manuel Martínez, had behaved flippantly in a church—dumping drinking water into the holy water basin and defiantly refusing to remove the cup. The sergeant described how another Dominican volunteer had joined Martínez and made physical threats against him, adding to the insubordination. Based on evidence unclear in the testimony fragment, however, the Spanish military commission was not convinced of the Spanish commander's accusations. "The superior officer forgot his responsibility not to abuse power . . . [The commission determines] that there was neither irreverence nor insubordination," the report concluded.[176]

For the numerous Dominican men who found themselves expelled from the military by declassification, the sight of Spanish troops must have been even more difficult to bear. Those who were disqualified from active service in early fall 1861 received a small pension, one half of what active reserves earned. Hundreds of others were demoted, however, not just to the Provincial Reserves (where "active" Dominicans served) but out of military service entirely.[177] They were forbidden from wearing military uniforms. For soldiers used to the privileges of rank—where pay had been inconsistent in the years of the republic, title had compensated—these expulsions threatened their livelihood and dignity. One former general reported that he had presented his papers directly to the Cuban governor Serrano, only to wait eight agonizing months to hear of his declassification. It was "a great shame for me," he wrote, and he swore "that if the Spanish Government would call me to service, I would not serve, because according to them I was not worthy of attention, nor merit, nor appreciation for classification, then she could not be worth serving."[178] Gratingly, too, favoritism reigned. Some former soldiers were integrated, but mostly those who had direct connections to Santana. Members of his immediate coterie received classification, sometimes after only a few years of service, and Santana was put in charge of the troops arriving from Puerto Rico. Even those who had been classified into the reserves felt the indignity of separation, however. In a distinct uniform, they were clothed, literally, as second-class soldier-citizens. Observers commented widely about the resentment the measure caused. It was a blow to the *amor propio* of the men, an anonymous report observed.[179]

Conflict erupted between active reservists and decommissioned men. General Marcos Evangelista had been classified as passive—certainly a tough blow for a thirty-eight-year-old, and a general at that—and, indeed, the insult was almost too much for him to take.[180] When the local government of Seybo called on all soldiers to report, he did so, ignoring that his passive status disqualified him. Upon arriving in the town plaza, he was dismissed by the military commander—"There is just a lot of enmity between us," Evangelista insisted, alluding to prior disagreements—and the general became positively irate. "The authorities of Seybo are cowards, whatever their status, and *muy habladores*, too!" he reportedly said. "When things are bad, call on me, because I'm no coward!" he allegedly yelled, drawing a machete. He refused to leave the plaza. Waving the machete, he shouted, "No one come close to me!" "My brother, drop it, let it go," another Dominican officer urged. Evangelista pushed him and raised his hands as if to strike. "I'm every bit a man," he insisted. "You think you're the only one?" queried another onlooker. Still enraged, Evangelista retreated, protesting that he was leaving of his own accord, not because he had been ordered to do so. Santana and the Spanish were losing popularity anyway, he allegedly muttered. He originally had been sentenced to deportation, but his sentence was commuted in the amnesties granted by the queen that spring.[181] Other declassified officers—Evangelista among them—joined the armed opposition to the Spanish. At least twenty-seven ranking passive officers were suspected in Puerto Plata disturbances in 1863, and some of the passive generals—Jacinto de Lora,

Gaspar Polanco, Pedro Florentino, and others—became leaders in the Restoration forces, where they joined countless more who had been demoted from the infantry and other ranks.[182]

Active Dominican officers received abuse as well. Santana himself, General Juan Suero, and General Gregorio Lora were all belittled by different individuals—in the presence of their subordinate troops—for not being white. One incident caused Suero, then governing Puerto Plata, to resign his post, and the offending soldier was only minimally disciplined.[183] Spanish generals were aware of the lack of fraternal sentiment, and they readily admitted that rank-and-file Spanish soldiers "denigrated or refused the company of men of color."[184] One Spanish soldier—a young man who had served in the "African War" in Morocco—loudly insulted Santana and other Dominican authorities as he was expelled from a dance, protesting drunkenly, "Who has seen blacks govern whites?"[185]

Which Party Are You?

Spanish aggression toward Haiti reverberated everywhere. After the "indemnity" demands, Spanish authorities dropped the pretense of conciliation and became aggressive about reclaiming central territories that had been settled by Haitian residents since the last treaty, nearly ninety years earlier. The Spanish warship *Don Juan de Austria* arrived at Port-au-Prince's harbor in March 1862. Haitian foreign minister Victorin Plésance was "disconcerted . . . , and his countenance revealed deep feeling for a moment; recomposed a bit he answered me that as soon as the President and the rest of the Ministers arrived, they would take up the matter and give me a response," the Spanish consul Mariano Álvarez reported, gleeful at the minister's discomfort.[186] Given that there had never been revisions of the 1777 treaty to reflect the shifting demographics in the communities of Las Caobas, Hinche, and San Miguel, "Spain will get what no other nation has been able to obtain from those blacks [cession of territory]," the consul gloated.[187] The Spanish emissary's invective grew daily, and his viciousness harbored ambitious territorial resolve. According to him, the "country of barbarians" had won its independence illegitimately. "This is the right by which the white race can assert possession of the west side of Hispaniola," he exulted, "and with such precedent, who can dissent against the reclamation that I have just proposed?" In his strong-arm tactics, Álvarez was in close communication with the French consul but not the British vice-consul Byron, who had married a Haitian woman. "I imagine he listens to those people more than the nation he represents," Álvarez sniffed.[188] His communiqués from Haiti were so vitriolic that they often precluded any meaningful reporting at all. He openly and frequently fantasized about conquering the whole island.[189]

Spain's threatening imperial posturing came at a particularly critical time for President Geffrard. Already saddled with the complicated political position of official neutrality on annexation, the president faced numerous political rivals. Some opponents agitated against proposed reforms to Article 7 of the Constitution; some decried conciliation with Spain (without presenting evident alternatives); others represented ambitious military families and more opportunistic political complaints. The president's opponents blocked each new measure he sought to pass through Congress.[190] A small revolt broke out in Gonaïves, and the wealthy Salomon family rallied peasant opposition in the south. Spanish diplomats were well aware that Spain was tightening the legislative bind on Geffrard and his party. The opposition also exploited the border reclamation conflict, Álvarez happily reported.[191] Geffrard sought conciliation, pardoning a number of generals involved in recent political intrigues, and even an individual suspected of collaboration in the murder of his daughter, Cora Geffrard, four years prior.[192] "Despite all this, it seems like any day now the tranquility will be broken," Álvarez continued, "the conditions for unrest exist and the enemies of the government are numerous."[193] Recent unrest promised to repeat, and the president had support only from his National Guard. "The enemies of the administration are advising the people to resist [both the Spanish presence and Geffrard]," a Spanish general observed from Port-au-Prince.[194] The president sent his family to France that spring, anticipating political turmoil.[195]

At once provocative and conciliatory, Spain's actions spread fear for Haiti's territorial integrity and the prospect of reenslavement in Dominican soil. Haitian observers speculated that Samaná Bay would help with illicit slave trading to the other Spanish possessions.[196] Confederate fighting reached the island's shores—such as when the aptly named Confederate steamship *Havana* docked outside of Port-au-Prince with seventeen Union prisoners.[197] Debt anxiety and foreign aggression fed off each other. Troubling rumors were spreading: the first, that the Spanish government had ceded the whole island to France in order to settle Haiti's debt; the second, that Geffrard was also in talks to cede the island to a foreign country. Santana blamed these rumors on Geffrard's enemies and the French consul in Santo Domingo, M. Landais, "an open party loyalist."[198] "To maintain the favorable opinion of the blacks of Haiti, and even also a part of those of this Province," Santana suggested that Spanish-Dominican newspapers ought to address these concerns directly. Spanish diplomats warned that the language used to discuss

Haiti in *La Razón* should be "as moderate and prudent as possible," and avoid accusing Geffrard of complicity. Port-au-Prince's citizens were interested and troubled by Spanish coverage, and they were "noisily disturbed," the same diplomat advised.[199] The Spanish governor was intransigent, however, and did not recoil from making new threats. He wrote to Spain, asking for more forces to defend the Cibao valley from its "600 *legua* frontier with this enemy race."[200]

Rebellion continued to brew in the center of the island and in other sites, and authorities could do very little. There were hushed rumors that opponents were pondering concessions to the United States for naval backing, or that Dominican rebel agents sought a new alliance with the Haitian state.[201] Through the fall of 1861 and into the next year, disquiet in center-island areas continued. Captain Manuel Feliz ("Quirí") and Lieutenant Manuel Feliz ("Cabulla") were disturbing public order in the region, authorities complained, perhaps responsible for the rumors that revolution was going to break out in Cibao, that the queen was seeking to jail Santana, and that Báez would soon return.[202] Authorities scrambled for more information on these men. Spies along the border predated annexation, and they remained on the payroll as the new regime began.[203] The data they managed to gather were minimal, however. Supposedly Quirí had a girlfriend or wife in a place called Juan Herrera; his nearly eponymous fellow rebel had been involved in skirmishes with the authorities near Neiba at least since June, but both men continued to elude capture well into the fall.[204] Intermittent shows of "good faith" by the Haitian government that entailed expulsion of frontier groups only served to contribute to chaos in the region, a Spanish general asserted.[205] The men regularly took refuge in Ouanaminthe, la Visite, and other center-island towns.[206] It is "of utmost importance to be vigilant of Hincha," an 1862 report insisted, continuing, "Hincha is the place where all the bad men of the east and the west of this island have gathered."[207]

Even as Haitian authorities, under pressure, collaborated in the capture of suspected conspirators, anti-Spanish alliances surfaced steadily. In Jacmel, western authorities detained a small group of travelers who had arrived from the interior of the island, claiming that the purpose of their voyage was to sell wax and buy fabric. The accused came from all corners of the eastern territory: Neiba, Santiago, Las Matas, and Higüey; they even had in their company a man from Puerto Rico. Authorities accused them of meeting up with Domingo Ramírez and his forces—rumored to be as many as four thousand—of Dominican expatriates, recent rebels, and Haitians. Their intent was revolutionary. One of the defendants, Pedro Curro of Neiba, was allegedly seeking a literate man to write a proclamation of loyalty (to Haiti) for another small town, Petritut. Curro may not have known how to read or write passably enough to draft the document himself, but other witnesses testified that he spoke capable French, had some sort of association with powerful Ramírez, and had coordinated the group's travel to Jacmel. Furthermore, other witnesses reported that he grilled a number of individuals whom he encountered: "Which party are you, Haitians or the whites?" "That's a strange question, you know I serve the Spanish," one reportedly answered, deflecting. "Haitian or Spanish?" another witness reported. Spanish authorities, unable to prove that the defendants were not in fact on a commercial venture, jailed the men for months for unauthorized travel, but party loyalties were deepening.[208]

FIVE

You Promised to Die of Hunger
RESISTANCE, SLAVERY, AND ALL-OUT WAR

Do you not hear the terrible stampede that shakes the earth?
—MANUEL RODRIGUEZ OBJÍO, "War" (August 1863)

On 9 February 1863—forty-one years to the day after Haitian Unification and emancipation began in the Dominican capital—a group of day laborers, farmers, and other residents from the outskirts of the center-island town of Neiba decided to overthrow the Spanish administration. One of the ringleaders, Cayetano Velázquez, grew up in the capital during Unification, but he moved to the interior some years later. To the others in the assembled group, which came to be about thirty or forty people, Velázquez and another man allegedly suggested that Haitian help would soon come, and that they "would become Haitian" (*se harían haitianos*).[1] Not everyone supported that particular proposal, arrestees later testified. Nevertheless, the group gathered with a range of battle cries: "Free Dominicans!" and even a "Long live Santana!" After paying house calls and amassing a paltry collection of machetes, the group marched an hour or so into the town, shot off the cannon, took over the jail from its four Dominican guards, and went after the military commander, also Dominican, managing to take him captive. They tried to convince the priest, a Spanish man from Tarragona, simply to leave town, but he refused. After just seven hours, the rebellion collapsed that same afternoon, overpowered by the town's own small outpost of reserve soldiers. One of these soldiers testified that the whole disturbance had been "a drunk's affair."[2]

A little later in February, however, the residents of two towns in the Monte Cristi province rose up as well. These rebellions were slightly larger. After overcoming the loyalist forces in Sabaneta—really just a symbolic number of troops—about eight hundred area residents marched toward Guayubín, about thirty kilometers away. There was plenty of forethought to these campaigns. More than twenty-two hundred men arriving from Haiti joined them: Haitian soldiers, area residents, and Dominican refugees. Together, they organized three informal regiments. The rebels successfully appropriated a Spanish munitions stash in the second town.[3] Other north-central towns witnessed short, nearly simultaneous local disturbances; guerrilla fighting predominated. The fighting reached Santiago, which was a different campaign proposition entirely: a large Spanish and Dominican loyalist garrison, nearly eight hundred men, guarded the city.[4] Pitched hand-to-hand combat began in the city at nightfall. Spanish troops and loyal Dominican reservists, however, managed to crush Santiago's fighting first. Next, troops were able to pacify the northwestern movement. Many fled into Haiti, but no rebellions followed.[5] As quickly as the February fighting began, it was crushed again. Authorities warily pronounced victory. Late spring and summer 1863 were exceedingly tense.

By late summer 1863, fighting began again, however, and this time the whole landscape exploded. Center-island towns were again the staging site and one of the early hearts of mobilization. In Haitian Capotille, a group of generals and five hundred men issued an official statement, the "Cry of Capotillo," naming a president of a revolutionary provisional government that had yet to exist. Even as Spanish authorities dispatched troops to chase them, however, revolution took hold in the Cibao valley and the northwest.[6] The fighting spread everywhere, and for the next two years, the battles amounted to nearly total social war. Later dubbed the "War of Restoration," widespread guerrilla activity took up more than three-fifths of the entire territory.[7] Weapons were in constant shortage. In most areas the fighting involved blocking roads and access to rivers, avoiding open spaces, and even hand-to-hand combat.[8] In larger towns, the rebels devised trenches to face off with the large standing regiments. They went further, burning Santiago de los Caballeros and Puerto Plata to the ground. The rebels regularly faced regiments of as many as five thousand men, led by prominent Spanish and Dominican generals alike.[9] And yet, the fighting only spread. Families left their homes and refused to return. The fighting, nearly general from its earliest days, sealed the fate of annexation as early as summer 1863. It was a "simultaneous and total uprising," a general later wrote, noting, soon, "the vacuum was complete."[10]

A tiny fraction of the fighters, those who were unlucky enough to get arrested, left imperfect records of rebels' heterogeneous complaints and aims.

Under duress, they told Spanish jailers and judges information they hoped would be exculpatory, or simply as little as possible. Some recounted stories of poverty and frustration. "It seemed like the [Spanish] government had forgotten [habían botado] the town," a frustrated soldier testified in one small town, citing repeated requests for supplies and describing being nearly six months in arrears on pay.[11] Some wealthier, literate town citizens wrote anonymous protest letters that were positively staid, focusing on political appointments, salaries, and the like.[12] The Provisional Government, as it came into being in the midst of the fighting, made pronouncements that were overwhelmingly nationalist in grievance. The government representatives also spoke of daily indignities, however. "The customs of a people free for many years have been tactlessly violated," their Proclamation of Independence read. "Mockery, disdain, marked arrogance, unmerited and scandalous persecution, and even execution are the final result."[13] Traveling rebels proudly represented their region. "¡Viva el Cibao!" shouted one group, far from home, as they surrounded pro-Spanish reservists in an eastern battle.[14] In the earliest fighting, it seems that residents had to rouse, even threaten, prominent citizens to take up arms. They did so in Guayubín, before firing cannon shots and proclaiming "¡Viva la república!"

Most salient of all to the bulk of the population, and what drove them from their homes, was a fear that was more than a sum of any grievances: the fear of enslavement. To the despair of Spanish authorities, "false ideas and abundant rumors" of renewed chattel slavery emptied whole towns and rural areas, well before fighting became widespread.[15] As authorities tried to keep residents calm in the intermittent early fighting, they soon discovered that the slavery prediction was durable, electrifying, and everywhere throughout the territory. The warnings were specific: fleeing Dominicans discussed explicit predictions of where boats might be docked, waiting to abscond with those captured by Spanish troops; they discussed who might be targeted and where the unfortunate ones would be sent. Such rumors were persistent and prevalent, and they held tremendous weight in the desperate anticolonial struggle. In their interpretation, they were discussions of the probable, the possible, and the potentially disastrous. These debates rested, in the words of Luise White, on "a store of historical allusions" about slavery in Dominican soil—and discussions of slavery in Haiti—that gained reinvigorated urgency with the loss of Dominican control.[16] In places like the northern coast and elsewhere, accounts about slavery and postemancipation restrictions reinforced the news that Dominicans received regularly.

Conflicts with the new administration itself made the slavery discussions more acute. As the fighting began, the hostility of the Spanish troops in battle electrified the debates, which spread everywhere.

In their practical expression, what the Spanish called slavery "rumors" were functionally the scaffolds, and justification, of a plan to revolt. "As [in] the preamble of any rural uprising, there was a true 'silent war' " that preceded the Dominican rebellion, one historian observes, an "unease" that continued to grow.[17] In the countryside, Dominicans probably held gatherings and discussions about the perils and promises of resistance for weeks, even months. Groups may have gathered to recruit, to plan, even to train. Free spaces abounded, if weapons did not. Outside of Neiba, the conspirators had gathered at the wake of a young child. Weddings, funerals, saints' days, major farm labors, even the pursuit of a criminal: all of these were collective activities.[18] The lack of weapons alone required a pooling of resources. In this collective mobilization, an intense field of speculative debate arose in which group dynamics and trust were expected and paramount.[19] In occupied towns, tensions were high. Even a cautious pro-Spanish reply to watchmen on the street could cost a nervous pedestrian an arm, one unlucky Puerto Plata man learned.[20] With incredible speed, fighting enveloped entire communities and rural landscapes. It was relentless and urgent not only because of the stakes but because those fighting knew they could not count on the formal army to help them. The rebels committed arson, destroyed records, scavenged munitions, moved on, and remained fugitives. They were prepared for total war.

As Aisha Finch establishes in rural antislavery insurgencies in Cuba, women "*shared* and helped *organize* larger critiques" of colonial abuses, they had a direct, personal relationship with the targets and geographies of resistance, and their lives were also directly at stake.[21] In the Dominican context, outside of plantation surveillance, loyalist generals tried to appeal to Dominican men that women and children swept up in the uproar were experiencing great hardship. They need not have bothered, because women committed to the mobilizations independently. During the fighting, many rural women continued to manage homestead agriculture; these labors represented continuity from peacetime practices but under circumstances for provision that were much more desperate. In battle-torn areas near towns, some left to forts, but even those who remained behind were involved in the fast-moving developments of guerrilla confrontation. As participant witnesses to an itinerant struggle, these same rural women and town dwellers created the neural pathways of revolt. Their information sent armed fighters from town to town, warned of loyalist troop movement, and speculated on the prospects, and consequences, of rebel fighting. As Stephanie Camp notes, again in a plantation context, women's in situ collaboration, and small flights, facilitated male mobility and vital information networks in the face of violence and serious provision shortages.[22] That is not to say that the women got equal recognition, even in the midst of their struggles. As in other contexts, discourses of armed heroism, and citizenship in the nation they contested, were the realm of male entitlement.[23]

At the highest levels of administration, authorities tried to dissuade and defuse the opposition movement. Although they privately discussed the rebellion as a race war, in public addresses, authorities meticulously kept to fraternal language. The arriving captain general, Felipe Rivero, made all outward signs of conciliation, firing a number of offending civil service figures, offering amnesty, and trying to strike an affable tone in his public correspondence. Santana returned to the armed forces when fighting began, and a number of prominent Dominican generals, like General Juan Suero, joined him. Although Suero had resigned after conflicts that included a racist insult, when the fighting resumed in the spring of 1863, he returned to loyalist lines.[24]

No conciliatory discourse could possibly diminish the dynamics of war, however, as military tribunals tried the rebels, sent prisoners in chains to the capital, and on ships to Havana and other sites. Repeatedly, Spanish soldiers threatened and insulted the citizens they encountered. "On occasion some white man would tell a black that if he were in Cuba or Puerto Rico, he would be a slave and would be sold for a certain price," a general later recalled, dispassionately.[25] Soldiers dropped all mask of civility, and they told anyone who would listen that the government was going to send black Dominicans to work on coffee and sugar plantations.[26] Every Dominican in the capital and other towns knew that Madrid papers were printing bitter, racist missives from administrators writing home.[27] Despite Spanish authorities' frequent dissimulation, rebels were clearly mindful of the dynamics at hand. One popular song exulted:

> The whites have already left
> from Yamasá
> What a beating they got![28]

Beginning in late summer 1863, the fighting never stopped. A rebel passport was just as succinct: "The Dominican Republic still lives—liberty or death—and a war of extermination to all Spaniards and their blood."[29]

Never More Slavery!

The first rebellion explicitly over the threat of reenslavement took place deep in the Cibao valley, only weeks after annexation began. Colonel José Contreras rallied with him a group of men, mostly day laborers, from the town of Moca. Contreras and his allies warned of reenslavement, not of a metaphorical nation, but of friends and neighbors. Spanish observers described the incident as "a mutiny of *morenos*." "If Spanish troops were to withdraw, the pillage and assassination of whites would begin immediately," one concluded.[30] A firing squad shot Contreras and three others on 19 May, the same day the annexation was officially recognized by the queen. On several occasions in later weeks, *La Razón* vehemently reminded its readers "NEVER MORE SLAVERY" while repeating the Spanish promises of annexation, protection, and prosperity.[31] All the talk that first summer was on the "Haitian" mobilization in the center of the island, which had taken place almost simultaneously with Contreras' attempted revolt. A Dominican general, loyal to the Spanish, assured the Crown that the fears of Contreras and his allies were "completely isolated" and wrote, "The state of our troops could not be more satisfactory, and their comportment is unbeatable."[32] "Dominicanos-Españoles" should be "alert to the deceitful suggestions of treason, and trust in your authorities," a Dominican official chided.[33]

Center-island residents' reluctance to return to their homes after Sánchez's and Cabral's simultaneous mobilization that summer demonstrates how widespread these assumptions about slavery were, however, even as annexation was only a few weeks old. Those families uprooted from border towns in the first rebellions of 1861 were terrified to return from Haiti, "continually given false news by the enemies . . . about the poor treatment that those of their class were being given in this territory," an official argued.[34] Hundreds of people remained across the border, anxious about returning, even after an amnesty was announced. Even after the administration offered small amounts of money, appropriated from the indemnity that officials had demanded from Geffrard, residents were only slowly returning.[35] Whole families had fled to Haiti and endured months of dislocation.[36] They continued to trickle in through early spring 1862, nearly one year after the short disturbances.[37] Some parts of the border were quite desolate. "There are barely any resources for housing and subsistence [near Las Matas]; the towns are in a calamitous state," a Spanish official reported.[38] A large handful of men allegedly involved in the 1861 Moca rebellion still languished in the poorly supplied jails a full year later; commissioners advised that they should be tried or released in the short term.[39]

Slavery discussions continued unabated throughout 1862. A slow boil of unease simmered on the island. As soon as Santiago's military governor had left town, "revolutionary enemies of Spain" immediately tried to sway the morale of the city's residents, "especially the simple country people," the governor complained.[40] He described the provocation: someone, or a group of people, pointed out that the reserves were not being paid and claimed that high-ranking officials had been arrested in the capital. They were telling people, he alleged, of new policies of "all sorts of sacrifices" and "the absurd ideas of slavery."[41] The general mood in the Cibao is "alarming and hostile to the highest degree," the governor reported in December.[42] He blamed "revolutionary enemies" for the rumors that disturbed public order. Warnings of slavery and other abuses proliferated. The four thousand petitioners from Jamaica who opposed annexation—explicitly because they predicted Spain would bring slavery back to Dominican territory—fell silent, but regional eyes were still trained on the island.[43] Journalists in Port-au-Prince compiled and republished accounts of Confederate ships as they stopped at nearby islands; the Confederate *Alabama* regularly docked at Dominican ports.[44] Geffrard's opponents stoked anxiety, suggesting that Spain might offer Haiti to France, and that slavery would take root all over the island.[45] People discussed whether Spain would demand disarmament so that black Dominicans could be enslaved.[46] In Puerto Plata, slavery rumors had circulated for several years. As months of Spanish occupation passed, public signs and graffiti escalated rampant discussions about slavery and direct threats of violence. Fully three months before fighting began in other towns of the north, one prisoner warned his jailers that "this February, the streets will run with Spanish blood."[47] A massive illegal slaving vessel, which almost certainly passed the northern Hispaniola coast, made headlines in Havana that same month.[48] In the capital, authorities continued to check passports of women arriving as domestics, vigilant of slavemasters' attempted smuggling practices.[49]

After the February 1863 uprisings, Rivero suspended civil law and proclaimed the entire island in a state of siege, and a long spring of repression began. In the Cibao, no gatherings larger than three people were permitted after dusk, on the penalty of being shot.[50] The governor created military tribunals to adjudicate the fate of alleged conspirators.[51] As the commissions handed out sentences—hefty jail time and the death penalty—some officials felt uneasy. For one, some of the alleged participants were being condemned in absentia. "It is impossible to defend men I haven't even met," the Spanish *defensor*, a lieutenant, noted with concern.[52] Sabaneta was "new and unenlightened [sin luces] . . . only recently introduced to the law," another defender argued; he insisted that even the town council members were "rustic and simple laborers" with no formal education.[53] In the capital of the Cibao, Santiago, officials were in a less lenient mood. Members of the city council itself had clearly been involved in the conspiracy, and authorities arrested a number of them as they tried to board ships in Puerto Plata. Military officials decreed that active members of the Reserve Forces caught with suspected rebel conspirators would be shot.[54] A firing squad shot five Dominican men at seven in the morning on 26 April, "in perfect order . . . despite the large crowd of both sexes who had gathered to witness the execution," an authority grimly noted.[55] Authorities executed two more reservists the following week. Martial law, instead of restoring order, caused panic; Cibao residents who had returned to their houses were so alarmed that they fled again. "The towns are practically deserted," Governor Rivero admitted.[56]

Spanish administrators did not raise the specter of race-based conflict openly; they merely called for all Dominicans to remain calm and wrote dismissively of popular fears. Authorities argued that the February 1863 battles were of little importance, and that the country was on a "progressive march."[57] Privately, however, Spanish observers perceived the conflict as a race war. In court cases that summer, a Spaniard claimed that among the "acrimonious enemies" of Spain were implacable race enemies. A certain Santiago "el Francés" reportedly received a promotion in the rebel ranks for "having killed many whites," the witness insisted.[58] In the Cibao valley, "prominent citizens" resisted the incoming rebels, Spanish authorities claimed, and they were violently assaulted, burned, targeted, and killed. "It is supposed that the current rebellion is a race one, since the rebels who have been seen are black, and those against whom the excesses have been committed are whites, counting among those victims some whites: but the lack of details on the matter impede me from confirming this," their report speculated.[59] Governor Rivero pleaded for more troops. He also asked for a new budget for secret police, but funds from Havana arrived very slowly.

The slavery rumors gained further strength and specificity that spring. Many of Santiago's citizens fled to the countryside, where they remained for weeks, until a decree offered amnesty. In one specific incantation, rebels told each other that the Spanish were first slitting the throats of Dominican men and then capturing Dominican women and children, selling them into slavery. Nearly three hundred people hid from authorities on the border. Rejected from asylum in Haiti, they had built a makeshift fort out of cut wood, ready to defend themselves to the last. Luckily, the Spanish officers took note that many of the families were unarmed and dispersed the group instead by diplomatic means. "Elderly people, women, and children, truly a disconsolate portrait," an official reported of the return march, appalled.[60] The Dominican loyalist general in Santiago, José Hungria, sent an envoy to talk specifically with the prominent black landowners of the northwest, the Fermin brothers, Furey Fondreu, and a handful of others. Using them, he hoped to convince rural Dominicans not to fear reenslavement.[61] Another Dominican leader urged Santiagueros "of all colors and conditions" to obey Spain. "Let us reject such vile rabble [canalla] and group together, blacks and whites, in the shadow of Law . . . and have some patience," he insisted.[62] June edicts repeated slavery's total abolition. Hungria was satisfied with the pacification.

Meanwhile, Santiago's military tribunals of spring 1863 created greater tensions in the city. Authorities insisted on a profound racial taxonomy. They grilled witnesses about the "condition, class, and color of the insurrectionists" and sometimes borrowed terms (like *criollo*) that made little logical sense in the Dominican context. The form of the trials produced another very specific stratification; as a matter of practice, Spanish officers and wealthy merchants testified first, then any Dominican reserve soldiers, then common Dominican men, and finally, any women. In the Santiago trials, the most prominent witnesses against the rebels were prominent Dominicans. Some, like the Grullón family, were wealthy merchants. Others, like Pedro Francisco Bidó, were part of the Spanish government itself.[63] Often Spanish authorities recorded reservist soldiers within proceedings as "laborers," suggesting that the latter category was a blanket categorization for many Dominican men, whose "condition" (as free men), in the scribes' view, also merited constant notice.[64] Following this ontology, Spanish witnesses and wealthy Dominican merchants encouraged dichotomous and color-specific interpretations of the participants. They were "almost all day laborers from the countryside, blacks, with the exception of a few dark *mulatos*," one such observer testified.[65] Spanish authorities diminutively referred to one witness, Dionisio "el Inglés"—probably a free man of color from one of the British islands—as "morenito."[66] When a white man stood accused of joining the rebels, the Spanish officer who reported the incident expressed doubt at his origin. "We have caught a white man, who *says* he was born here," the officer reported.[67] As the trials concluded, a royal order granting sweeping amnesty reached the Cibao.[68] The captain general dissolved the military commission of Santiago and declared the state of siege lifted. He promised to be "humane but upright . . . judge me yourself," he urged. General clemency, he warned, could be offered only once.[69]

At the same time that these trials ended in partial conciliation, racist violence escalated in Santiago at the hands of Spanish authorities. Alexander Merriman, a black British subject and resident of Santiago, met the brunt of racist frustration at the hands of Spanish soldiers. Municipal authorities summoned him over a minor matter, but, as they notified him on a Sunday, he did not go. Subsequently, he lodged a complaint with authorities that the police were threatening him. The authorities' response proved profoundly hostile. They told him, "The police have a right to act as they please," and one officer proceeded to beat Merriman with the flat side of a sword on a public street, drag him, prone, to jail, and throw him into a cell, where he continued abusing him. The mayor himself threatened to order the police to "cut him to pieces and kill him, as it was his wish to finish with all the negroes," a distraught and injured Merriman reported. Nor did officials respect his claim to protection as a British citizen; the jailer persisted in national and racial slurs, stuck him in stocks, and continued to beat him severely with a stick as he was bound. Afterwards jail staff locked him in a windowless cell, even as Merriman was bleeding profusely. Only hours later, seeing how much blood he was losing, did the jailer send Merriman to the hospital, then in a critical state. His family brought him everything, as the jailers did not even supply him with water. Weeks passed, and officials filed no charges. British ambassador Hood quickly found himself frustrated at the efforts of local authorities to obstruct inquiry into the incident. More than a month passed—Hood sent the vice-consul from Puerto Plata to Santiago to investigate the matter himself—before Spanish authorities opened an inquiry. Merriman barely survived.[70]

Confidentially, Governor Rivero expressed concern for the long-term stability of the colony and asked for a massive increase in forces and funding. He called for "a very large army, capable of occupying even insignificant sites" in order to "suffocate" resistance on difficult terrain. At a minimum, a heavy presence on the frontier, improved troop transport by water, and at least six infantry divisions were of utmost necessity.[71] Two vessels, real steamships, were needed, he explained, to replace the small frigates currently fulfilling the postal tasks, most of which could not even dock satisfactorily at Dominican ports, much less quickly reach Cuba and Puerto Rico. Chronic supply and treasury shortages suddenly seemed more urgent. Funds were so short that the municipal government of Puerto Plata used 760 pesos of private money and borrowed 4,000 more for expenses.[72] The reserves were behind in their pay, and public works—"which should be what drives agriculture and commerce in the territory"—were in a "laughable state; they have not even been begun yet," the governor admitted.[73] The colony's needs so greatly outpaced funding and supplies that he found himself pressed to send a special envoy to Spain.[74] It was impossible "to sustain the interests of national decorum . . . and of the Queen" without addressing money problems, especially given Cuba's slow remission of funds, he maintained. Furthermore, many local officials were not of the "necessary aptitude," he argued grimly, although he conceded that replacing them would cause alarm. While totally decommissioning them would be impolitic, paying them a similar "passive" salary, giving them "some special commission of little importance," or pairing each with an officer of the army might provide a temporary solution, he mused. And the priests were either "totally uneducated . . . or not faithful to the Spanish cause."[75] More land and navy forces were an "absolute necessity," he repeated finally.[76]

A chaotic and volatile scene brewed in the center of the island as rebel leaders, refugee families, residents, and outlaws mingled in the frontier regions and northern Haitian towns. Despite the superficial peace and general amnesty, many did not return to their homes as the authorities intended.[77] In fact, families continued to flee to the countryside, frustrating officials who believed that enemy rumors were more likely to reach *gentes medrosas* (fearful people) outside of urban centers. "I ordered the police to stop the emigration as much as possible without alarming people and to spread news about the rebels, whether or not it was true, that will put a stop to the nonsense stories [*paparruchas*] that they tirelessly sow," one official attested.[78] A number of "the guiltiest and the most compromised" stayed around the center-island region, "uselessly pursued" by the Spanish troops, another general lamented.[79] Some of those freed from jail in the February disturbances in Santiago were reported to be robbing residents that spring—committing "all sorts of robberies, from jewelry to cattle"—and at least one murder.[80] The criminals themselves encouraged the families to remain in the highlands, "out of the fear that they will be persecuted and jailed," the governor lamented.[81]

Santiago authorities, frustrated, dispatched a group of sixty the next month to disperse or capture these alleged criminals, as well as to patrol the province for "bums, drunks, scandalous women, pickpockets," and other undesirable individuals.[82] Haitian officers at Fort Liberté promised cooperation. This banditry was the "true source of alarm" in the region, authorities concluded, although they simultaneously acknowledged that area residents were sheltering some of the suspects. Rebel leaders, meanwhile, had gone farther than many of the families likely did, spending months of hiding in Cap-Haïtien and other Haitian towns, where military officers offered them supplies, and at least one officer accompanied them to start the fighting again.[83] Chasing them, without any specific leads, the Spanish governor resolved to station troops at the northern border and in Cap-Haïtien.[84] Still, conditions were so unpredictable along the north-coast border that subsequent reports arrived via Puerto Plata and only there, despite Monte Cristi's more central location.[85] Two powerful officers, Buceta and Hungria, traversed the north of the island, leaving troops in Dajabón. Aided by collaborating Haitian authorities, they speculated about the whereabouts of Gregorio Luperón and other rebels. North-coast towns grew hostile; unnamed individuals ambushed a man named Jeronime, who had been serving as a translator for the visiting Spanish envoy, and shot him in his home.[86] By any index, revolutionary energy was intensifying.

They Will Brand Us with an Iron!

When fighting finally exploded again in August 1863, the whole northwest was already alight with insurrection rumors. The Cibao governor knew of the Grito de Capotillo weeks before it happened, and he described, probably accurately, that a thousand Haitian guns were distributed among residents in the northwest in preparation.[87] Area residents apparently hoped for even more help. As one official reported, "Around here the very hot gossip . . . that is agitating the families living here . . . is that on Monday, a fleet of twelve American steamships carrying war supplies and American and Haitian troops will arrive. Your Excellency: everyone says that this information has come from reliable sources, via letters from Haitian residents [of Monte Cristi]."[88]

As the fighting started, Governor Rivero declared a state of siege again, Puerto Rican authorities quickly sent another battalion of troops, and the steamship *Lealtad* mounted a partial naval blockade of Cap-Haïtien. However, a number of northern towns were quickly enveloped. Guayubín burned this time, causing the brutal death of various townspeople. Every day the number of rebels in the hills grew, and the fighting again reached Santiago. On 6 September 1863, the rebels set the richest town in the entire territory ablaze. A terrible fire raged through the streets. The Spanish troops began a rapid retreat toward Puerto Plata. An observer of the blaze in Santiago wrote, astounded, "By nightfall, there was already nothing left but rubble and ashes."[89]

At last, Puerto Plata exploded into fighting. Facing five hundred Spanish troops and more reserves, and more arrived to the fort from Santiago, town residents, despite their anticolonial commitments and alarm over slavery, had been slow to erupt. Officials knew almost a week in advance of the impending disorder, and a small volunteer militia of town residents, foreigners, resident Spanish merchants, and Dominicans added to the standing forces.[90] Known troublemakers had been arrested, although one of them, Gregorio Luperón, managed to make a dramatic jail break. The rebels fought with no uniforms, some with no shoes, using weapons stolen from the Spanish or ferried across the border from Haiti. They salvaged a cannon by diving in a nearby shipwreck.[91] The rebels raided government buildings, stole most of the letters and documents therein, and trashed the remaining offices. Hundreds and hundreds took up arms as the Dominican flag was raised over the governor's residence.[92] After the arrival of reinforcements from Santiago de Cuba and Puerto Rico, and after two days of heavy fighting, Spanish forces arrested dozens. Dominican general José Hungria himself oversaw the destruction of rebel trenches in a part of the town called Cafemba. He had been dispatched by a high-ranking Spanish general, with the admonition that residents of the town were the "most insolent and those who think they are invincible."[93]

Describing why they fought, one Puerto Plata rebel spoke of the fear that the Spanish intended to "brand them with an iron, to enslave them and shackle them with iron collars that restricted their head movement, to which a light would be attached to undertake their labors."[94] In light of the collars imposed on men and women laboring in workhouse gangs in Jamaica, these explicit details proved well-founded.[95] The mayor of Puerto Plata called on the help of the Alcalde Pedáneo and "all honorable people" to counteract the slavery propaganda. "The malcontents . . . are just enriching themselves from the disorder as the country becomes poorer and destroys itself," he pleaded.[96] Spanish authorities worried that "the tall tales would excite their spirits and make Dominicans fight to the death."[97] Alarming rumors in the surrounding countryside of Puerto Plata reported that the Spanish were killing everyone and burning everything in their path. The families of the town were fleeing not only to the countryside but to nearby islands as a result, the mayor reported.[98] On 4 October, Puerto Plata burned as Santiago had done. For three days, the fire raged, burning twelve hundred houses to the ground.

Homeless families scattered to the countryside or to the fort, held by the Spanish.[99] Spanish officers wrote in awe of the rebels' commitment.[100]

Townspeople joined the roving small guerrilla bands that traveled from town to town, disrupting Spanish administration where they could. It was often women who spread the news of coming insurrection; they traveled from house to house and on the roads at the edge of towns, calling on their neighbors to flee to the countryside, often just hours before the fighting began. Likewise, women spread other information that one side or the other had already won, and when it was safe to return. Still others warned those fleeing along one route to take another, as there were Spanish soldiers poised to ambush. Sometimes individuals ignored these warnings (and were subsequently apprehended).[101] Those groups on the move also relied on their knowledge of the surrounding countryside for tactical advantage, often heading off the Spanish at rivers where they might seek to water their horses. Reported a Spanish official with frustration, "The movement counts on leaders who know the terrain perfectly. And in such a mountainous country, too, one can only conclude that the immediate presence of a much larger number of troops can paralyze the progress of the revolution."[102] With limited evidence, it seems like these slavery warnings might sometimes have traveled as documents with the rebels from place to place. Cayetano Velázquez, the leader in the first, tiny Neiba uprising, was the only one in the group of townspeople who knew how to read.[103]

Beyond slavery warning letters, documents threatened and intimidated in other ways. When rebels arrived in towns, their first target was often the municipal building, where they would destroy Spanish records, and sometimes set the building alight. This action was a symbolic and concrete measure to destroy colonial authority, leaving officials scrambling to reestablish criminal cases and other paperwork.[104] "Given that the fire in Santiago has reduced it completely to ashes, it is presumable that the criminal cases, papers, and other documents of the circuit court have been destroyed," officials noted.[105] In Puerto Plata, rebels did the same, annihilating not only the files but even the furniture of the governor's offices and the town council.[106] So well known was this tactic of archive destruction that the queen issued a royal order commanding their reestablishment in reconquered municipalities in January 1864.[107] Other rebel tactics had more symbolic significance; someone killed the much-hated Brigadier Buceta's horse, for example.[108] Often, someone lowered the Spanish flag and cut it to pieces. In Guayubín, rebels confiscated an image of the Virgin Mary from the town church and paraded it about, "with the fanatic idea it might help them," the Spanish witnesses critically observed.[109] In the early 1863 Santiago uprising, too, someone took a Virgin of the Rosary and carried it through the streets.[110]

Within two months rebellion spread well to the east. In Hato Mayor, rebels proclaimed the restoration of the Dominican Republic at four in the morning on 2 October, without so much as a drop of blood spilled. Residents were convinced that the Spanish had chains and stocks sitting off the coast at the ready, and that defeat might mean the Spanish would enslave them for life.[111] They asked for volunteer reinforcements to arrive as military aid, "as friends and good Dominicans." The rebels' reclamation of Hato Mayor lasted barely five days, but fighting raged elsewhere.[112] Authorities wrote to the capital reporting heavy losses. Dominican guerrilla groups cut off Brigadier Buceta so completely from the rest of the Spanish forces—having retreated from Dajabon to somewhere deeper into Haiti—that the other Spanish commanders could only speculate about his whereabouts for nearly two weeks, and he barely escaped with his life. The valley town of Moca fell, trapping eighty Spanish troops inside the fort. La Vega soon followed, with rebel ranks there swelling as high as two thousand. In Santiago, outside of the reserves, anyone who had a weapon of any kind—even a machete—had only until noon the same day to turn it in at the fort, in exchange for a receipt.[113] Spanish authorities opened military courts in Santiago and in the capital.

Rural Dominican camps filled with Spanish captives, collaborators, and escaped prisoners. Editors of the *Boletín Oficial* proudly printed the names of forty Spaniards who had defected to rebel Dominican citizenship, either freely or after arriving at camp as prisoners of war.[114] One Spanish soldier reported that in his five-month captivity, he was verbally mistreated but paid the same wage as every other rebel soldier, in exchange for trench digging and other noncombat tasks.[115] The rebels also did not abuse the nearly five hundred other Spanish captives, he noted, although conditions did not bode well for the injured. A remarkable letter in Cantonese survives in the Cuban archive describing how some entered camp:

> The three of us walked along . . . [until] we met a *wu kwai* officer. We were glad to meet him [and] he was happy. . . . [The second] camp has Chinese people as well, and the three of us are very good here. You guys do not have to worry about us, now the *wu kwai* have 16,000 people. They eat a lot of pork and beef here. Now, we are writing you this letter to tell you that if someone comes near this area, come in the daytime and do not come at night! Please hold a green leaf stick so the *wu kwai* officers will know.[116]

Not everyone integrated into the camps peacefully. Some of the escaped prisoners were themselves quite violent men. Chinese laborer Macsimo Segundo, jailed for murder in Havana and subsequently transferred to Samaná, repeatedly assaulted other prisoners. In the Dominican camp, he refused to work, and some wanted to kill him. Under the cover of night, he fled back to the Spanish to turn himself in. Authorities remitted him back to prison in Samaná briefly, but then dispatched him to Puerto Plata to work on the fort.[117] Others continued to flee the Spanish. Another Chinese prisoner, Roberto, critically injured a Spanish prison guard in his escape to the Dominican lines. (Along with Segundo, he accounted for a total of four cases of laborer convicts fleeing in just a few weeks' time.)[118]

Santo Domingo was the stronghold of the administration. In the spring, the governor confidently announced that residents condemned rebellions with "reprobation and disgust," and he publicized the establishment of a volunteer militia in the capital composed "of good Spaniards from both hemispheres."[119] However, small acts of insubordination proliferated. One low-ranking Dominican officer, drunk, began insulting Spanish soldiers, as nearby townspeople leaving Good Friday services flocked to witness the disturbance. The priest tried to disperse the crowd. "This blind political passion of some, more or less drunks and disturbers of the peace in any time, [has transformed into] ranting against the Spanish and their government," an official warned.[120] Someone stole all the decrees that had been affixed to signs in the public square, leaving only the two closest to the guard post untouched.[121] Some of the early spring rebels had been brought to the capital city to work on chain gangs; although there is no record of their reception, the group was likely a startling sight.[122] By late spring, the Spanish were so on guard that soldiers were ordered to walk around with weapons loaded and swords tightly adjusted.[123] It was a long, hot summer in the capital; the prices of many food staples rose by 300 percent.[124]

Fighting reached near the outskirts of the city, as Dominican general Pedro Florentino faced off with Spanish general José de la Gándara. An article in *La Razón* urged calm:

> Gossip. There is no lack of it in the city, but it is absolutely rampant in the countryside. . . . Do not be fearful, our peasants, show yourselves to be deaf to the tall tales of those apostles of gossipry [*chismografía*], and come to the city without fear to sell your fruits and vegetables. Everything is calm here. No one is being detained, nor are they seizing anyone's packs, and men, women, and children enter the City daily, buy, sell, and

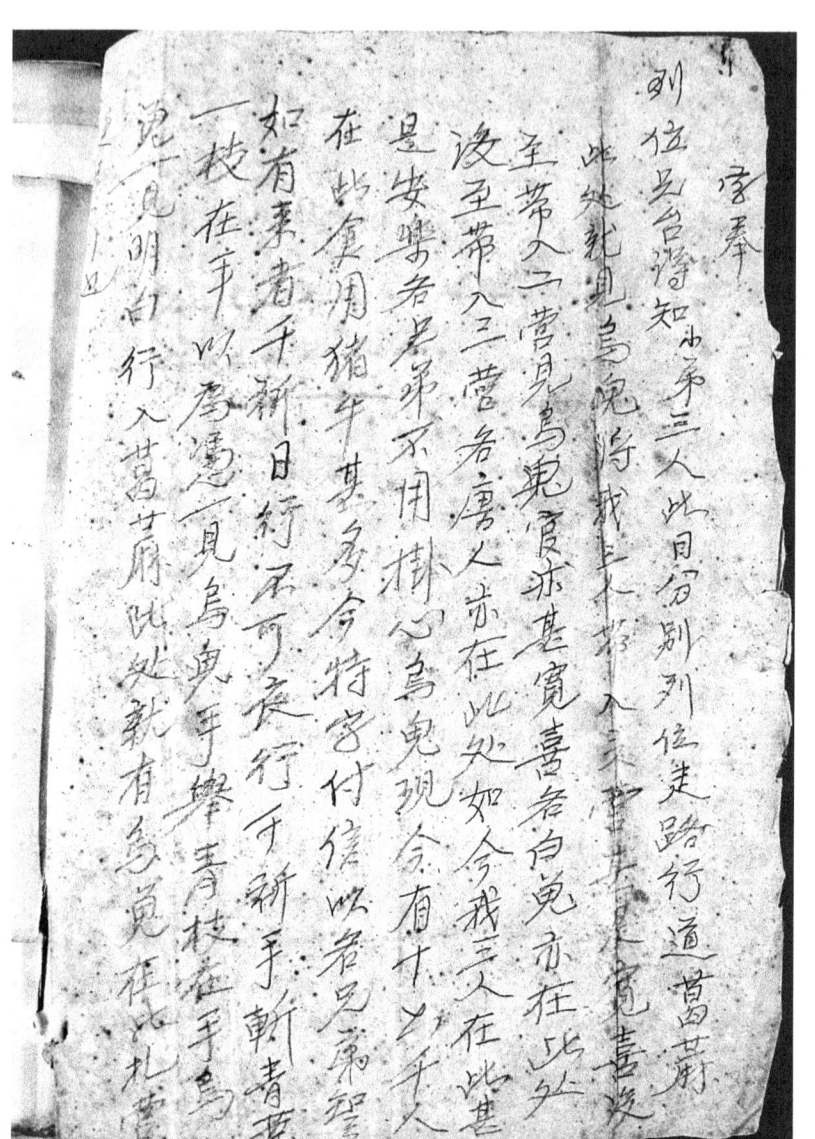

Fig. 5.1 Letter, in Cantonese, from a man who escaped a Spanish prison on the island (probably Samaná). He describes the meat-heavy rations, black officers, and welcoming conditions of the Dominican camp.

speculate, and go back to their homes calm and satisfied. Come, come without fear, because no one is impeding your entry or exit."[125]

In areas of traditional black settlement around the capital and the center-island south, Spanish troops met determined, defiant resistance and tales of great heroism. Word around the old sugar plantations and southern maroon communities held that Restoration fighter General José Melenciano, from Haina, "lado de los Naranjos," had a *resguardo* that prevented him from being killed by bullets.[126] Melenciano took his men into the Cibao region. His group was one of the few that traveled in this direction.[127] "[The division of race] is nowhere more prevalent than in the Santo Domingo Province," the Spanish governor reported, confidentially, "in the jurisdictions of San Cristóbal and Ozama, where the old sugar mills were on the Island and where the African race has the largest population. Those who were enslaved are still alive, even if elderly. Their children who knew their parents as slaves have black children of their own, and they cannot but look at the present day with horror."[128] Many around Azua and Baní burned sugar plantations, took their animals, and headed into the mountains.[129]

Men outside the capital mobilized in brazen proximity to authorities. Spanish soldiers reported "large groups of blacks" gathering at the city walls, armed with machetes.[130] Spanish authorities suspected one black Dominican man, a resident of the old *extramuro* community of San Carlos, of being "Haitian" for reasons of his dress and skin color. It seems he had donned his uniform from the Unification period. "A suspicious man, a black . . . with a Haitian-looking hat," Spanish officials recorded of the sixty-year-old Francisco de los Dolores.[131] Interrogated about where he had gotten his uniform, he insisted that it was from when he was a soldier in the time of the republic, but neither his age, his marriage, nor his "very good Spanish" could free him of Spanish suspicion.

As 1863 closed in a whirlwind of fighting, loyalists to Spain blamed propagandists, agitators, Haiti, and anyone they could for spreading slavery rumors. The authors of the branding rumor on the north coast had been "voices against whites and the Spanish," an official concluded.[132] In one instance—several years into the occupation—a young Baní man corroborated stories that claimed rebels were reading letters about slavery to the public. "They read it to most of the people in town, that the whites were going to enslave the blacks, and seeing that most people in town were leaving, I left, too," he reported.[133] Officials of all statures attempted to squelch the rumor. A colony-wide decree read: "Unauthorized men, false interpreters of public opinion . . . have transformed the rich and fertile comarcas of this island into a theater of horrible crimes. . . . Dominicans, listen to the voice that is not trying to deceive you, the one that is most interested in prosperity for this beautiful land: those who tell you that it is possible to reestablish slavery here are knowingly lying, once the Queen declared it abolished once and for all in this Province."[134] "The war has taken on an aspect of race, leaving aside political discontent or nationality," the governor wrote, "and those in Seibo and those in the Cibao have formed a common defensive mass."[135] Men and women, young and old, felt this way. "The rebellion is of the black man against the white man," he concluded.[136] "The people of Puerto Plata are very eager to fight, even though they have few munitions and are receiving even fewer," one foreign resident confirmed. "They wrap themselves in the idea that if the Spanish beat them, they will make them slaves."[137]

Forced to Fight against Your Brothers

Spanish authorities scrambled to counter the guerrilla offensives. Brigadier Buceta, humiliated, described a fantastical—and probably apocryphal—account in which he claimed he had thrown gold coins at approaching Dominicans to distract them (or at least purchase his escape).[138] Disorder in the northern valleys, the portal for tobacco commerce, deeply affected the Cibao. Merchants and growers alike suffered from the lost profits, despite a four-month debt reprieve. Authorities scrambled for prison labor to rebuild and improve area roads.[139] In Puerto Plata itself, all governing was paralyzed—surviving documents had been sequestered to the fort—but the town was largely empty, anyway.[140] A Dominican general, José Hungria, assaulted insurgent encampments, leaving piles of corpses of his countrymen in his wake.[141]

Spanish authorities and loyal Dominicans argued that the fighting sprang from factionalism or banditry. Some rebel officers were former Buenaventura Báez loyalists, and Santana heartily encouraged this interpretation.[142] Báez himself was actually in Spain (and had come to support the annexation), but pro-Spanish pamphlets excoriated him just the same.[143] Governor Rivero referred extensively to internecine party competition of the independence period.[144] "Disgraced generals, sold to Haiti and later bribed by Báez, . . . wanted to create discord," Dominican official Manuel de Jesús Galván concurred, disapprovingly.[145] In simultaneous aspersion, authorities called the movement anarchic and argued that rebels were merely following their urges for personal gain, excess, and disorder.[146] A Razón editorial challenged: "The monster of rebellion has reared its head, and we ask it anxiously: what is your goal? What do you want? What principles do you proclaim! Ay! Too soon we have the reply. . . . the goals and principles of the rebels who infest the Cibao can be reduced to this horrible formula: killing and destruction."[147] Rebels were "without cause or motive," the governor concluded. "In their vandal acts and impotent rage, they have burned the town of Guayubín . . . and they have killed unarmed and injured men . . . humanity and civilization condemn it." He appealed to the public, "These criminals—can they be called your brothers? No, because you are simple and honorable and could not be associated with arsonists and assassins. . . . You desire good for the country," he argued, concluding, "and the rebels only want to exterminate all prosperity."[148] Another loyalist urged gratitude: "Remember how afflicted we were when we sought the help of the Queen and of Spain." Of the queen's pardons in the spring, the writer chided, "The ink has not even dried on the generous amnesty decrees."[149] Santana called for "brotherhood" with peninsular soldiers and called "bravery and loyalty . . . always our only currency."[150] He urged, "Soldiers, sons of Dominican soil, you who have always heard my voice . . . you will not waver in following me!"[151] "Dominicans: when someone passes by your homes and tries to fool you, treat him like an enemy," the governor implored.[152]

The loyalist press of the capital scrambled to scold insurrection, encourage order and obedience, and sanction male responsibility. Imaginative editorials lavished praise on loyalist acts. An editorial in Razón praised "some gravely injured veterans" who offered their only mount, a "skinny horse or burro," to an ailing woman on the road from Santiago to Puerto Plata. Their masculine-heroism-cum-selflessness did not stop there; the veterans had defended a number of other women and even carried their infants, the writer recounted. A nameless soldier ("who died before we could know his name") carried a six-month-old all the way to the northern coast, the columnist continued. "It is comforting, in the presence of the extreme crimes that have been and are continuing to be committed in the Cibao, to contemplate the contrast that such a spectacle makes with the noble and humanitarian conduct of the defenders of order . . . , confident in their magnanimity," he concluded.[153] "Women and children have fallen at the mercy of the sacrilegious bullets of the rebels," another journalist proclaimed, scandalized. One poor child was shot in the arm; another "woman had an infant to her breast, and was killed exercising one of the most sanctified tasks of nature!"[154] "Mass murders, the destruction of entire towns by fire, plundering of fields, unjust imprisonment, and all acts of violence [tropelias] against all types of property, have deprived women, children, and the elderly of sustenance and reduced them to indigence, making it impossible to live if they do not seek help from the government," the governor announced in a public decree.[155]

Spanish entreaties to the rebels were similarly gendered. In Puerto Plata's diaspora, women kept families together and fed. Of the Dominicans who sought refuge in the fort in the following months, almost all the families were headed by women. Just ten adult men joined the 253 families gathered there.[156] Loyalist Dominican Antonio Alfau made a plea to a rebel general, citing his own "gentlemanly" instincts, the mothering impulses of the Spanish queen, and the familial bonds that supposedly tied the island to its former metropole:

> You are still in time to save yourselves, your beloved country, your women and children, who you have in the *montes* and who will very soon die of hunger and misery if you do not take the loyal hand I am extending to you. Spain is not an enemy of ours. . . . She is our most tender mother, who sacrifices for our happiness. . . . remember the Queen is the granddaughter of Isabel the Catholic, who gave us the religion we profess, who gave us our language, our gentle laws, who made us everything that we are. . . . Remember the unhappy women and children who you have in misery, forgotten by God; here they will be given food to eat and everything they need. . . . [But if you reject us] . . . expect nothing.[157]

To underscore his points, Alfau had his missive delivered by a woman.

La Razón and government edicts announced pro-Spanish victories and bravery as they excoriated rebel cowardice. "I rush to put these reports in your hands, for the satisfaction of all the loyal inhabitants of this Spanish Province," the notes often concluded, and Rivero preferred to sign off as "Your Captain General."[158] Government decrees were inane in their detail, announcing even the smallest spoils of war. One account of a victory reported that forces "made the insurrectionists flee in all directions, leaving us one ox and one pack horse, complete with supplies."[159] A number of Dominicans received official recognition from the Crown for their efforts. "For your loyal and noble conduct, I give you thanks in the name of the Queen, her government, and with all my heart," Rivero's decree read. He reminded the Dominicans of the queen's "untiring generosity . . . as the Mother of all Spaniards"; as for the Spanish nation itself, it was a "brother." He reiterated promises of peace and profit from the beginning of his tenure and urged Dominicans to "gain a love of work, the source of all public wealth." Justice would be swift but effective for the rebel leaders, he promised. "The rebellion will be defeated and punished. . . . Stay tranquil and loyal," Rivero appealed.[160] He wrote empathetically: "I am sorry for what has happened: authorities can never look at blood nor tears with indifference, but when they have a duty to carry out, they do so, even at the price of their emotions. This is the sad mission that social good demands of me, and I will fulfill it in the least painful way possible."[161]

Loyalist Dominicans included prominent island-born generals fighting alongside Spanish troops: José Hungria, Antonio Alfau, Eusebio Puello, Juan Suero, and Santana himself, among others. The Crown awarded Hungria the Great Cross of Isabel as recognition for his military feats; Santana had been similarly showered with laurels. Authorities published General Antonio Abad Alfau's victories in national bulletins. "Long live the Prince of Asturias! Long live the Queen!" he exhorted.[162] Valuing fealty and military discipline, loyalist officers were some of the staunchest Spanish bulwarks, and they resented the defection of other Dominican officers particularly. General Juan Suero bristled that General Gregorio de Lora had lied to his face about fidelity to Spain only the night before an attack (and was given weapons); Lora became an instrumental rebel in the Puerto Plata August movement. "I consider officers and leaders of the Reserves, who are receiving a salary either active or passive, to be defaulting on a sacred obligation," Suero penned indignantly.[163] Dominican officers' classification status remained a public debate. A general in the reserves took it upon himself to forward to the governor a list of former officers who, for "unknown reasons," had been classified as passive and thus denied military service. The men, mostly from Azua and the capital, felt that they had been needlessly "stuck with the useless men," and thus deprived of the means to buy basic goods. The petition asked for a restoration of their status and full benefits, in exchange for recognition of the "services they have offered and their faithfulness in such precarious times," the general explained. The petition was left unresolved.[164]

Pockets of loyalism to Spain, particularly in the south, buoyed the capital. Azua seemed wholly tranquil. The all-Dominican, eight-member municipal government of Azua condemned the rebels; "We come to deplore the scandalous and criminal acts that have just taken place in some parts of the Cibao, raising once again rebellion and abusing the generous pardon of our August and generous Queen," they accused. The period of the republic was "nineteen years of continual struggle, ever obstructing prosperity and order," they added.[165] The governor alleged that "all of Baní" was loyal, and that those who had fled "are back tranquilly in their houses, under the protection of the brave Army."[166] Even in the Cibao, wealthier loyalists, especially merchants, stood their ground. Some prominent families offered buildings for military use. Provincial governors organized militia of volunteers to add to the Spanish ranks, even arranging nominal pay; La Vega managed to raise seventy volunteers, for example.[167] The municipal government of La Vega criticized area rebels as "lazy, perverse, and undeserving of the title of citizen" who had "suggested such disloyal ideas" to loyal and obedient inhabitants.[168] In early 1864, Santiago itself was briefly in the power of loyalists again.[169] Businesses ran at something approximating normalcy; a few prominent Dominican merchants, like Don Juan Francisco García, were helping the Spanish extensively. It was his conviction that all the merchants wanted the Spanish government back, as did many of the residents of nearby Moca, he maintained. The governor was quick to publicly thank town councils for "loyal and patriotic" sentiments. In the capital, Josefa A. Perdomo dedicated an elegy to Rivero, expressing gratitude for his "constant wish . . . to return to us peace and prosperity." Josefa A. Del Monte replied to Perdomo, calling her lazy and ambitious. "[Queen] Isabel is waiting for you in her palace," the second poet chided.[170]

A new Spanish official, Carlos de Vargas, replaced Rivero as governor after just more than a year. Loyal observers were optimistic about his reception, despite the very compromised military situation. "There appears to be a better feeling since the arrival of the present Captain General, who appears so far to be an honorable and just ruler," the U.S. commercial agent reported.[171] In a confidential letter, the captain general expressed his grave concerns to the Overseas Ministry. "It is difficult for you to imagine, Excellent Sir, how far this extremely critical and dangerous situation can carry on," Vargas confided, praising Santana and La Gándara for fighting bravely. "I must inspire confidence in the country . . . as the first step of pacification," he wrote, "and . . . the show of adherence and cooperation from many influential men of the country . . . make me think I can achieve it." Meanwhile, though, the governors of Cuba and Puerto Rico "cannot afford to send even one more soldier," he lamented.[172] The incoming governor addressed the Provincial Reserves and Spanish forces together: "A few rebels have put this Antille, worthy of a better fate, into a terrible state. . . . They have relied on arson, robbery, assassination and horrific destruction to regain a freedom they have already been guaranteed." Protect "the peaceful and honest man, and help him immediately return to his home," he urged the troops.[173] About seventy soldiers fighting with Santana received special recognition for a particularly brutal 29 September fight at Arroyo Bermejo, and the governor promised publicly that order would soon return everywhere.

Strained resources, poor infrastructure, the demands of war, and successful guerrilla blockades crippled the administration. Public works everywhere were in "total paralysis."[174] Azuan authorities reported they had "absolutely no funds," no resources to care for the prisoners, little security, and no way to continue trials.[175] Soon, food was scarce and the town was totally empty. Rebels in and around the town burned farms, moved the livestock, and blocked supply lines. Only small amounts of food arrived by boat from the capital.[176] Government documents went unsigned for months. When towns became "empty and depopulated," authorities left some municipal posts unfilled, simply to save money.[177] Absenteeism was a problem even where government functioned. Interim regulations created sign-in logs for administrators to prove their attendance, and leaves became strictly unpaid. Troubled officials acknowledged the new restrictions but complained, in light of food scarcity and fighting, "It endangers those who are truly suffering."[178] Military officials filled empty civilian posts, sometimes poorly. When an infantry colonel became provisional governor of Samaná in the late summer of 1863—as other authorities left for the fighting in Santiago—he played fast and loose with his authority. To defend the peninsula, he selected the hundred or so "European" (presumably Spanish) convicts and gave them guns. Chaos ensued. The convicts menaced the residents, made racist threats, robbed stores, and caused many families to flee.[179] The interim governor's apparent failure to properly punish the transgressors frustrated residents further. He spent his nights sleeping on a ship off the coast, diffident and unaccountable. "I can't say this was the one and only cause of the uprising in Samaná, but I cannot think of another one to report," a reservist observed.[180]

Women in loyalist towns navigated increased tensions. As in other Caribbean towns, laundry work forged noisy, public, feminine spaces where women's labor monopoly earned them bargaining power with municipal officials, but where the public nature of their tasks could also make them targets of discursive and physical violence.[181] Laundry women found themselves before Santo Domingo's military tribunal. Sometimes, they instigated the inquest. In one case in the capital, two women (émigrées from Santiago) turned on a man, Manuel Guerrero, alleging that he had called the Spanish "whores," that he "had a pistol to shoot them all," and that he was part of a suspicious meeting. Guerrero—a bricklayer, just twenty years old, and of marginal means—retorted that he had only been detained because of the ill will the two women had for him. He had been attending wake, not a suspicious meeting, he protested, and he proceeded to name a number of people who had also been in attendance. Five washerwomen, divided in their accounts, testified at Guerrero's trial. Two reported that Guerrero yelled abusive remarks at them for attending a dance with Spanish officers, hosted at another woman's house. One of the women bragged that she had reported "the black" the next day to the same Spanish officers, for having "insulted her and spoken poorly of the Spanish." Authorities sentenced Guerrero to one month in jail, but he languished for nearly two until he was freed.[182] Other capital city women faced death threats for relations with Spanish men.[183] In the opening fighting of Santiago, rebel men shouted to a small group of women who had remained with the Spanish, "We're going to chop off your and the other four whores' heads"; another woman was murdered for her supposed treason of cohabiting with a Spaniard.[184]

Throughout the east, rebels engaged in the delicate politics of solidarity, secrecy, and trust as they tried to recruit their friends and neighbors. Letters suggested that verbal communication was best. "Let's meet so that I can tell you certain very important, secret things," one officer urged another.[185] Even discussions were not necessarily safe. In Bayaguana, authorities jailed reservist soldier José de la Cruz on suspicion of convincing his fellow soldiers to join the revolution and flee to the mountains "to meet up with the Cibaeños." One witness, Teodisio Contreras, divulged the entire conversation he had with his fellow soldier, whom he knew as Pepe. In the street at the center of town, de la Cruz had spoken to Contreras frankly, "Man, I am going to tell you something, and I think as a friend you won't give me up. And even if you do and they kill me, tomorrow there will be another person, who will kill you. I am going to join up tonight . . . come with me, or if you don't want to go, don't go, and when we arrive, I won't shoot you." De la Cruz had carefully thought about his tangled allegiances; he reassured another soldier again that "he would not harm Dominicans, just the Spanish," even if that man decided to remain loyal to the colonial forces. Unfortunately for de la Cruz, Contreras left for his barracks and told his sergeant immediately. Officials declared an embargo on de la Cruz's goods, but five months later annulled it—he had no possessions to embargo.[186] Other appeals employed similarly intimate terms. "Countryman—Brother and Friend," another writer began. "This letter doesn't seek to say anything except to say we hope that you enjoy the same feelings, and that as a result of this communication you will raise the Dominican flag. . . . Here it is reigning with high enthusiasm. Long Live Religion, Liberty, the Dominican Republic, and Perfect Union!"[187] "In all of the Cibao, the Dominican flag is flying," the writer reported. The letter bore a handwritten letterhead ambitiously announcing the return of independence: "The Dominican Republic—God, Country, and Liberty."

Fighting threatened to tear communities apart, but rebels were initially optimistic and conciliatory. In some of the early fighting in Puerto Plata, rebel commanders gave explicit orders not to shoot Dominicans fighting alongside Spanish troops, for example. Spanish authorities spread stories that the rebels were shooting loyal Dominican families, although the rumor never held much traction.[188] In Hato Mayor, a rebel letter from 1863 read encouragingly, "We have come here like brothers, and it is a revolution of principle for which we need nothing more than unity and fraternity among Dominicans." No one wanted "even a drop of blood to be spread . . . *vivan todos los dominicanos*," the letter announced reassuringly.[189] A rebel general entreated Dominicans in the reserves, "Let us not engage in a fratricidal war of hate." He continued, "I know you come forced to fight against your brothers; put down your arms or come join the ranks of liberty."[190] "Dominicans! . . . do not let yourself be seduced by the vile interests with which they try to buy your services, to make you brandish arms against your brothers and your homeland," another pleaded.[191] "Leave the lines who are assassinating your brothers," another urged a prominent rebel general.[192] "The friendship you have always shown me . . . and Christian obedience . . . [and the memory] of your noble fighting in Santiago in 1852 oblige me to write this note," one general publicly addressed General Antonio Alfau. His tone was deferential. "Even though I am not worthy of your attention, listen to what I am telling you, for no child wants bad things for his father," he urged. "But no matter what, I am a republican, and I can do nothing less than fulfill my duties as a citizen," he continued. "Santo Domingo's children do not want to fight with you nor General Santana. . . . We do not want war without fathers . . . but if you do, we will fight to the last bullet."[193] A reservist soldier in an early battle replied to such sentiments, "Everyone in Cibao should die for being traitors."[194]

As chaos swept to each town—even if it did not remain in the hands of the rebels—municipal governments' problems multiplied exponentially. In accordance with the governor's orders, all officials and prisoners from Azua evacuated to the capital city in mid-October, for example. Three months later (December), they returned, but officials from more northern cities (including La Vega) fled subsequently to the safety of the capital. Samaná, previously peaceful, was almost totally deserted by early December. As 1863 wound to a close, Spanish troops clung to the southern towns, with their eyes on the rebellious Cibao. Despite heavy fighting in nearby Llamasá, the capital remained a Spanish stronghold. Governor Vargas continued the practice of publishing victories, although his tone wavered slightly; the narrative strayed from "quick and shameful retreats" of rebels to admitting "sustained fighting." He continued to thank those loyal to the "cause of order," promising medals and praising loyalist bravery. Privately, he described a more complex situation. "Many of color join our ranks, especially from Azua and Seybo, but they stay just fifteen or twenty days, and then they leave to organize parties of bandits," he decried. Those groups troubled local residents, he claimed, "who [themselves] are gathered and armed to care for their plots and land and cannot be called enemies of ours, but neither can their loyalty be counted on."[195] Even in southern towns, flight caused the line between resident and rebel to be indistinguishable. "The Spaniards are making no progress whatever," one man observed. "Wherever they go, the people get out of their sight."[196]

Puerto Plata, strategically vital, exemplified the worst entrenchment of the conflict. As fighting cut off north-south communication, news from Santiago and Puerto Plata could reach the capital only by boat, and vice versa.[197] As Spanish forces dug in, their control did not extend much beyond the fort. Spanish troops "enthusiastically destroyed enemy trenches," Puerto Plata's mayor reported, but they could not sleep outside. Within the walls, soldiers celebrated Queen's Day, "as far as was possible, with good morale and monarchical sentiment," a commander reported; he also reported sporadic exchanges of gunfire.[198] With just a short cease-fire at Christmas, the siege and sporadic confrontations continued. Unlike in some other municipalities, officials decided that evacuating the port officials to Santo Domingo would be "embarrassing," and only the mayor made the trip. Battles continued at bayonet point around the ruins of the church. Periodic rumors of large numbers of rebels arriving from the west bolstered rebel morale, but Spanish troops dug in their heels to cries of "Long live the queen!"

The fighting swept up whole families, willingly or otherwise. Some testified to military commissions that they had been held against their will. One man who had left Puerto Plata's limits to find food on his farm was captured for two weeks, he claimed, and he suffered constant death threats and only barely escaped. Rebels took his clothing and other possessions, he lamented.[199] Area rebels gathered forces using "threats and terror," Puerto Plata officials accused.[200] Concerned parents accused disgruntled reservists of attempting to "seduce" their sons. The rebels drafted whole towns. In San Cristóbal, a handwritten decree from "the Junta of this town, in the name of the Dominican Republic" announced that all those aged sixteen to sixty were to take up arms for defense of the country, to report for duty within forty-eight hours.[201] Both Spanish and Dominican authorities pressured low-level *alcaldes pedaneos* to help recruit townspeople.[202] Rebels warned the local authorities to help the Dominican cause or "be subject to the same penalties [as traitors]."[203] A number of prominent loyalist families in the Cibao had to flee. Some traveled with the Spanish forces or fled to be with the rebels for protection. Remaining in town was physically dangerous but also presented the possibility of sedition charges.[204] Exiled men pleaded for the right to return, invoking the amnesties of early spring. "All are peaceful and honorable men . . . who want to live quietly in their homes with their families," one letter pleaded.[205] Some testified that some of their family—brothers, godfathers, and so on—had been caught up with the rebels, causing families to lose contact.[206] Given the scattered nature of the fighting, Spanish troops could not stay long in any one place, and people worried that "the grave scenes would repeat," especially pillage, as they left. Rebels grabbed what guns and munitions that remained, and then moved on themselves. Sometimes they seized the animals of locals suspected of aiding the Spanish, like one man suspected of ferrying water to the Spanish holed up in a fort.[207]

Given the fires that overtook many towns, often there was little to which people could return. Puerto Plata had burned nearly to the ground in October 1863. For the fire and for the pillaging that followed, the Spanish blamed the rebels, the rebels blamed the Spanish, and merchants and families simply faced destitution.[208] Small groups of Dominican vigilantes harassed Spanish troops who descended from the fort to protect property, Puerto Plata's mayor reported, chagrined. Because he believed there were many more rebels just outside the town, there was little to be done.[209] Baní burned that fall, too, sixty-eight buildings in all, including many of the important stores in the town. Only heavy rains saved some houses. The U.S. commercial agent observed, "No matter where the Spaniards go . . . , when the Dominicans see that they are not able to hold a place, they prefer to lay it in ashes, rather than suffer the Spaniards to take possession and hold it."[210] Small towns like Guayubín were just a collection of huts, basically defenseless, and even the Spanish admitted that the arriving rebels were kind and "humanitarian" in the early spring.[211] As the town was swept into rebellion again, however, a number of citizens died in the fires. When Spanish general La Gándara arrived in Barahona in early 1864, he found it burned and abandoned. A rebel writer lamented, "Fire, the devastation of our towns, wives without husbands, children without their parents, the loss of all of our livelihood, and finally misery—these are the fruits we have won."[212]

"Santo Domingo Don't Want Whites": Trenches Deepen

Many Dominicans remained away from their homes, and the Spanish could neither defeat the rebels nor return to everyday administration. Authorities offered a second round of political amnesty (for all but the accused "ringleaders") in August, and another as the new governor, Carlos de Vargas, took power. They bristled at what they saw as the hubris of the popular Dominican reply: few took it, few returned to their homes, and many continued to travel with the guerrilla bands that now traversed most of the country.[213] Prisoners freed by the rebels or during the chaos that swept through were in something of a predicament: they were unsure whether they could return to their homes. Because the destruction of court records had erased their legal status, former prisoners preferred the countryside, rebel lines, or even flight to foreign countries over the prospect of retrial by the Spanish. And, as one official complained, "They can hide themselves for eternity." Given these "anomalous circumstances," multiple capital city authorities argued that a tabula rasa of sorts ought to be established—not a published amnesty, per se, but rather the policy of reopening court cases only for those who newly committed themselves to the rebel cause.[214] Authorities condemned prominent rebels to death in absentia, so their exile was more certain. "All the reflections, deference, and benefits are totally useless with idiot people who are without education or civilization who have lived for decades in the woods, with only the wildest of occupations," Governor Carlos de Vargas fumed in a confidential letter.[215]

As the guerrilla opposition spread everywhere, the discipline of Spanish soldiers faltered. Newly arriving soldiers described Dominican rebels nonchalantly as "the enemy": "Long live Spain! Long live the Queen! . . . To the bayonets!"[216] Among the exhausted ground troops, however, the most common infractions came to be insubordination, obscenity, drunken soldiers leaving their posts, dereliction in prisoner surveillance, theft, fighting, dressing as a civilian, and outright desertion.[217] Murder cases occasionally gripped the military courts; a December 1863 Puerto Plata murder case, involving two soldiers from the Isabel II regiment, caused official stir as far as Havana.[218] A fight between a Spanish soldier and a Dominican cart driver in the capital proved fatal for the latter, but authorities exculpated the soldier on the grounds of self-defense.[219] One soldier, so frightened of his sentence for having shot a local man, fled the military hospital, only to be apprehended the following day.[220] Both robbery and murder seem to have increased as the fighting ground on; soldiers stood accused of stealing and reselling provisions, assaults on each other, and robberies against Dominican citizens.[221] A few of the cases in Puerto Plata and Azua involved massive theft, of the sort that might only be effected in a chaotic port town; 500 bottles of wine, 9,732 rations of *galletas*, 49,551 rations of coffee, and so on.[222] In one instance, a whole trunk of money went missing, in the amount of 9,000 pesos.[223]

Discipline of the Provincial Reserves also suffered, leaving Spanish authorities exasperated and suspicious. High-profile defection of Dominican generals put Spanish nerves on edge; among the rank and file, absenteeism was just as destructive, if more inscrutable. A considerable number deserted in the early months—in one instance, nearly five hundred people.[224] As 1863 wore on, trials for soldiers who had left the lines to return to their homes—for sojourns of varying lengths—increased. Often, it was unclear whether lax military discipline, family obligations, or rebel affiliation was to blame, and the soldiers were frustratingly negligent in the eyes of the military authorities. Deserters—in time of war, no less—faced extraordinarily strict sentences, even capital punishment. One reserves soldier, facing eight years, was only going to see his family, taking them a squash, "as he had done during times of the republic," his defense observed.[225] Townspeople came to the defense of soldiers.[226] Some claimed they had sought and gained verbal permission for leave.[227] Others claimed abduction by the rebels, a defense that could not easily be disproven. The Spanish commissions saw no easy resolution.[228] Even officers faced lengthy jail terms.[229] Some tried petitioning for release. San Carlos resident Estanislao Dusablon, a young married carpenter, entreated the governor to release him to return to his profession in order to be able tend to his family, "suffering from the hardest misery." "My poor family," he repeated.[230] Authorities were exceedingly suspicious of those who came and left repeatedly, "all while wearing the Spanish sash." "The Provisional militia are doing no other service than informing the guerrillas," one confidential report concluded bitterly, but Spanish officers could do little to prevent them.[231] A Dominican reserves lieutenant captured one spy, Daniel Rosario, as he absconded with a mule en route to tell rebels about the state of Spanish camps. The two struggled so violently that Rosario later died from his injuries.[232]

Despite public decrees that pleaded for peace, Spanish hostility and violence grew. Consul complaints left a chilling record, as the French consul and the British consul intervened repeatedly in Puerto Plata and other towns. One shooting prompted the Jamaican governor to intervene. "If these details are true . . . it amounts to premeditated assassination . . . please investigate," he urged, but the query led nowhere.[233] Spanish soldiers arrested Saint Vincent–born William Henry Abbot, a master carpenter and father of three small children, in his own house in Puerto Plata for unspecified reasons in the midst of fighting. Accusing Abbot of complicity with the rebels, a group of soldiers dragged him to the beach near the local Methodist church—all protestations of his British citizenship in vain—and murdered him without so much as a trial. In fact, Spanish soldiers forced two British day laborers to bury his body.[234] Americans like Peter Vanderhurst tried and failed to seek British protection in Samaná.[235] Dominicans, with no pretense to such recourse, confronted rising aggression.

Authorities increased surveillance as far as they could. They suspected, but could not prove, the gun pipeline from Haiti across the northwest valley.[236] U.S. steamships in Cap-Haïtien's ample port also raised suspicion.[237] Governor Rivero declared the entire island—including Haiti—to be blockaded. All printed material would be "scrupulously examined," all passengers considered suspicious, all those carrying weapons considered enemies. The governor asked for aid from the Cuban navy to survey the northern coast of the island, from Cap-Haïtien (Guarico) to Monte Cristi, and to sail its circumference where possible. Authorities sent news of the blockade to Saint Thomas, Jamaica, and other neighboring islands.[238] The governor declared that all those on ships aiding the rebels would be treated as pirates. Dominican citizens who owned gunpowder were ordered to remit it to area officials; arms restrictions varied from town to town. A colony-wide decree, citing "public hygiene" problems, announced the relocation of some prisoners to the peninsula and proclaimed that spies would be shot on sight. "They do not have the same rights [as prisoners of war do]," he announced.[239]

Spanish authorities focused their scrutiny on traditionally black communities like San Carlos and Los Mina. Officials appointed spies "of absolute trust" to investigate rumors of ferment outside of capital city walls.[240] In more frequent and more hostile patrols, Spanish watchmen pursued everyone, including priests.[241] Spanish soldiers perceived danger in houses where people of color frequently gathered, reported them to the military commission, and often engaged in outright conflict with town residents, particularly young men. In one incident, two young men were detained for two weeks simply for having left their neighborhood and returned.[242] The fighting itself seemed to make the soldiers more paranoid, more racist, and less likely to hide either of these inclinations with the mantle of civility that had framed the annexation project. In San Carlos once again, Spanish soldiers claimed they were chasing some "sospechosos" at one in the morning. One of the gunshots ended up penetrating a hut and injuring a sleeping child.[243] Spanish soldiers blamed black subjects even for their own desertions; "I was kidnapped for the night by two black men with a knife and taken to Los Mina," one Spanish soldier claimed.[244] One soldier stationed in neighboring Puerto Rico mused acerbically:

> Los negros dominicanos
> no quieren a los españoles,
> y vienen a Puerto Rico
> sin camisa y sin calzones
>
> Papá come gato,
> Santo Domingo no quiere blanco
> Papá come perro,
> en Santo Domingo no hay más que negros[245]
>
> [The black Dominicans
> don't want the Spanish,
> and they come to Puerto Rico
> shirtless and pantless
>
> Papa eats cats,
> Santo Domingo don't want whites
> Papa eats dogs,
> in Santo Domingo there are only blacks]

Tensions were high in the capital; a young man from Samaná took out his pistol and aimed it at a watchman's chest. It was unloaded, but a judge convicted the nineteen-year-old nonetheless.[246] Other young men, similarly, were detained and released with increasing frequency.

Nicolás Guzmán, a volunteer drummer in the Baní regiment, demonstrated how growing tensions over Spanish racism dovetailed with the slavery rumors, even in a loyalist town. Guzmán had been drinking with other reservists in a store when a *paisano* officer—unclear if Spanish or Dominican—entered. Guzmán offered him a drink, which the man refused on the basis of his "not being the same color" as the young drummer. "I said I drink the same as blacks, whites, and *mulatos*," Guzmán recounted, testifying he left immediately. The officer told a different story, reporting that Guzmán threatened him: "If you don't drink this, I'll pour it on you." The officer admitted his own attitude was belligerent, saying, "I replied, the only way you'll be able to pour it on me is if you behead me first." A third man separated them. In a temporary evacuation of Baní subsequently, Guzmán fled for a week with the rebels. Defending himself in court, he offered a very deliberate incarnation of the slavery rumor: a group of rebels had arrived in Baní from Maniel—that is, the historic maroon community—reading a letter about impending enslavement. They had read the letter to a gathering of most of Baní's residents. "The whites were going to enslave the blacks," he repeated, "and seeing as most of the town was fleeing, I went with them." Other accounts reported his exit was not so naive. Guzmán allegedly shouted to fleeing residents that he would shoot them en route if they joined the Spanish, who were "*sin verguenzas*," that he would continue shooting, even if it were on his knees. "*Sin verguenzas españoles blancos*," another witness quoted. The military commission ordered him summarily deported.[247]

In the context of increased tension over Spanish racism, resistance became more entrenched. Insurgents fought in extraordinarily spartan conditions. Writer Pedro Bonó observed of one group, "Barely anyone had uniforms. . . . The drummer was in a woman's shirt and no pants. . . . Many others were shirtless. . . . All were barefoot . . . no saddles, just plantain leaves covered with goat leather . . . [and they] were mostly armed with machetes and only a few guns."[248] Fathers petitioned for their sons who had been deported, as sixty-year-old Pablo Santana did for his twenty-three-year-old son, Pablo Santana de los Reyes, languishing in the Morro of Havana. The group of men who had been with young Pablo—of fifty of them, only ten had guns—could not possibly be considered guilty, his father pleaded.[249] Speculation followed those who had been deported. They were working in chain gangs, perhaps on plantations in Havana, individuals warned.[250] Slavery stories proliferated further. One reservist sergeant—indigent, despite his rank, and claiming to have lost his common-law wife to the rebels—passed on an elaborate and alarming warning. He claimed that Spanish promises were not to be believed, that the Spanish planned to burn the towns and enslave the people by embarking them onto ships. They had already taken the residents of Azua and Santo Domingo, he allegedly claimed. He died in jail.[251] A civilian, Ramón Díaz, excused his initial participation with a guerrilla group as involuntary (he joined because of threats, he alleged, and a Spanish council was inclined to agree with him), but he also admitted to becoming convinced subsequently that the Spanish "planned to ship anyone they captured to Havana, to enslave them and make them do agricultural work." The very looseness of the guerrilla ranks precipitated Díaz's capture; reservists caught him as he returned to his home in search of clothes, plantains, and water.[252]

Members of a Dominican Provisional Government, newly founded in Santiago, denied the Spanish accusation that they were using slavery as an official recruiting tactic. At the same time, they warned of slavery's salience among the people:

> We have never tried to fool the pueblo saying that the Spaniards would have them made slaves and sell them, like they do today to those *desgraciados* who they go looking for on the coast of Africa. . . . But what could stop Spain from establishing in Cuba or its other colonies all the prisons that it felt like, and send all of the inhabitants of the Dominican Republic there, if that's what they felt like doing? . . . All Dominicans should understand, then, that the Spanish government will not literally sell them as they do in Cuba and Puerto Rico to true slaves; but except for the name, the condition will be worse.[253]

It was these fears that lent incontrovertible urgency to the fighting. And so government members warned the queen, "The fight, Señora, between the Dominican people and Your Majesty's army would be totally useless for Spain; because believe it, Your Majesty, we could all perish, and the whole country could end up destroyed by war and the burning of the towns and cities, but Spanish authorities governing us again, never. . . . They clearly show that the Dominican prefers homelessness with all of its horrors, for himself, his wife and children, and even death, more than, Señora, depending on those who oppress him, insult him, and assassinate him without trial."[254] Inexorably, the resistance deepened.

SIX

The Lava Spread Everywhere
RURAL REVOLUTION, THE PROVISIONAL GOVERNMENT, AND HAITI

The year 1864 dawned with the defeat of Pedro Santana and all his men, in fierce fighting in the north. Santana retreated home to the eastern province of Seybo with two thousand followers, trying to quell an insurgency that had started there, too. He died that fall, disillusioned and frustrated.[1] In a massive military escalation, Spanish authorities brought in almost twenty thousand new troops to crush the rebellion, three thousand soldiers for the capital alone.[2] In comparison, only a few hundred Dominicans guarded Santiago, where the new Provisional Government operated. Rebels dispersed everywhere in campaigns and guerrilla battles. "Dominican society was sleeping on the crater of a volcano," poet (and Restoration fighter) Manuel Rodríguez Objío wrote. "The volcano opened its immense mouth," he described, "its flame lit up the beautiful country's sky, and its lava spread everywhere." The destruction was shocking. "Whole cities were entombed," he observed; "mountains of ash rose everywhere."[3]

As the massive mobilization swept the territory, poor country residents and laborers entered the fight decisively and in great numbers. Although documentation on prominent rural men is lacking (compared with the more extensive paper trail of wealthy figures in towns), historians suggest that many wealthy cattlemen progressed from indifference, to lending money to the rebel cause, to trying to benefit from it.[4] Like wealthier citizens in town, they worried about the popular nature of the war. "We feared that the masses [muchedumbre] didn't have anyone to moderate them," one admitted.[5] Spanish officials sought to exploit these fears, and regional sentiment, with little success. The movement was simply too popular. "I was seeking to exploit the antipathy that has always existed between those in the South and those in the North," Governor Vargas reported, but opposition was far too strong.[6] Loyalist observers commented extensively on the popular nature of the war. It was "a headless rebellion . . . a horrible hurricane . . . a crazy revolution," one priest remarked, in fear and awe.[7] Tobacco production dropped precipitously, an unavoidable blow to rebel revenue. Violent campaigns spread everywhere. Relentlessly, however, the rebellion continued to grow.

Two major political tendencies emerged in the Provisional Government, established during the first fall of fighting. The first was a studiously raceless republican nationalism, authored by prominent figures, primarily wealthy men from the Cibao, who had been part of the reform movements of the late republic. Like Mexican opponents to French occupation at the same time, they refuted the annexation in no uncertain terms, heartily exhorted republicanism, condemned Spain's tyranny, and praised independent American states.[8] Their discourse was at once anticolonial and civilizationist. In defense against the accusation of "banditry," prominent generals assured their audiences they were "Christian and civilized."[9] In defense against the accusation of "race war" (murmured on the island, shouted in Madrid periodicals), spokespeople responded with anticolonial missives to Spain that remained deafeningly silent on racism and slavery.[10] In these tracts, they wrote freely of Spanish "arrogance" and disdain—"as if we were serfs, or the indigenous conquered in the era of Columbus," contrived one—but they rarely condemned Spain's plantation present.[11] To these officials, the appropriate frame of vindication, the respectable anticolonial discourse, was nationalism. In one of Santiago writer Pedro Francisco Bonó's stories, an insurgent exclaims, "Every day I want to fight more and finish kicking out those whites"—but government members did not echo him.[12]

Leaders who were much closer to the guerrilla movements—idealistic, active, and violent men—emerged, too, embodying the radicalization of the struggle. General Gregorio Luperón, just twenty-four years old, made a meteoric, brilliant rise as a military commander from humble origins in Puerto Plata. He was among the most radical of nationalists and idealists, who, like Francisco del Rosario Sánchez, already dead for his efforts, had begun organizing when the occupation was only a wild rumor. Each revolutionary general had his own plans, command, and supply lines, leading groups of insurgents.[13] Others also quickly ascended to military leadership, including figures like Gaspar Polanco, who rose to be head of the provisional national army—"an informal mambí troop," such as it was.[14] Fissures between prominent men and these popular leaders grew until, mid-fighting, they reached fever pitch. In a coup meant to save the revolution, General Polanco ordered the execution of the president, a prominent landowner. Observers were positively scandalized; Polanco was unrepentant. Claiming the presidency on a wave of popular support, he initiated a more revolutionary government in every sense. Idealists who had served the previous administration found a new voice, too. Polanco's ministers reached farther, flooding western Puerto Rico with pamphlets as well.[15] "Citizen Presidents" ruled on both sides of the island.[16]

At the height of the fighting and revolutionary tumult, Haitian authorities continued in a bind between overwhelming popular support in Haiti for the anticolonial rebellion and the threat of Spanish might. Any overt collaboration would ally the Haitian state with a poorly armed faction of an unequal and potentially fatal fight, and Spanish warships remained docked in striking distance. Furthermore, challenges to Geffrard's hold on power compromised his ability to respond. The president's opponents called on popular opposition to his neutrality, sometimes opportunistically, to condemn him, and prominent regional politicians plotted opposition movements with growing frequency. Meanwhile, Haitian citizens in port cities and center-island towns defied all authority to collaborate with the Restoration war. Material and moral collaboration across the island was extensive, "frank and resolved," and hostile observers knew it.[17] "We cannot understand how the Spanish government can believe for one moment that the Haitian people could stay indefinitely indifferent to an issue that, as they accurately perceive, interests them as much as Dominicans," one rebel announced.[18] The northern coast, in particular, bubbled with collaborative activity, with boats hopping from Cap-Haïtien, to Monte Cristi, to Puerto Plata, to Turks and Caicos Islands, Saint Thomas, and other nearby sites.

Collaboration accelerated greatly with the demands (and radicalization) of the anti-Spanish fighting, which was unlike any military mobilization in recent memory. Urgency, opportunism, and political strife, on both sides of the island, multiplied rebel plans. Some anti-Geffrard conspirators called for the north of Haiti to ally with the rebel east. The Provisional Government called for a simple treaty of alliance, later a treaty of federation. Many other rebels, short on resources, looked to Haiti for help in any way possible. "We protest the abuses of the Spanish government . . . , impeding Haitian citizens from taking part in the Dominican cause, which is their own cause," a Dominican author chided.[19] They sent private letters describing Dominican prisoners in shackles.[20] Loyalists and Spanish called Dominican guerrilla fighters *manigüeros*, a reference to their strategic flight to rough and uncultivated land. Rebels called the Spanish *cacharros* (pot carriers), mocking them for how heavily they traveled.[21] *Manigüeros* were winning the war. In collaboration on the north coast and in newly radical elements of the Provisional Government, the egalitarian policies, antiracist patriotism, and solidarity forged in struggle grew to be something very difficult to control. After more powerful men wrested power back from Polanco and his revolutionaries, they obliquely referred to a broader "regularization" of the war effort.[22] A full-blown "reactionary clan" began to coalesce by late 1864, in opposition to the ascendant radical leadership.[23] These powerful men, already looking ahead to what they thought might be the end of the war, sought a familiar old network of patronage and hierarchy, in the figure of Buenaventura Báez. Meanwhile, however, popular collaborations and connections to Haiti only grew. The language of a heroic nationalism united them. Three years after Geffrard had resoundingly condemned Spanish occupation, a southern Dominican man carried a copy of his 1861 protest in his pocket as he fought.[24]

A "Regenerated" Republic

A group of rebel political leaders founded the Provisional Government at the center of Dominican liberal nationalist politics, the Cibao valley. "We have no doubt that our brothers in the Cibao will be the first to embrace the cause of *regeneration*," a writer had predicted in 1861, and residents of the surrounding towns saw entering the fight as "joining up with the Cibaeños."[25] Many of the prominent rebel leaders had experience in political movements of recent years and economic ties to the United States, England, and other sites.[26] Two wealthy Santiago women lent their houses to the early meetings: first, Doña Antonia Batista; next, Madame García. García, born in Haiti, was famous for the most extravagant masked balls in the Cibao valley.[27] Some had entered the annexation loyal to Spain, optimistic about party peace and economic progress. Their disillusionment was rapid, however. Almost all the members of the Santiago colonial municipal government, the same who had butted heads with Brigadier Buceta, were definitively implicated as rebels before the end of the year. Others switched ranks from Spanish to the newly reformed ad hoc government independently. Although a number of prominent Santiagueros cast themselves as fearful witnesses to early popular opposition, all of the witnesses in the March military trials in Santiago were able to carefully restate the rebel goals, months before the Provisional Government ever drafted its inaugural document. "They said they came in the name of the people . . . to reconquer the rights of free men and throw off foreign domination once and for all," one witness ad-libbed.[28]

As the government formed in late summer 1863, news traveled fast. Suspects in the Puerto Plata trials of August 1863 already knew that a letter had been sent to the queen asking for the return of the republic, probably before the letter even crossed the Atlantic.[29]

Military leaders called on a new history of the "extinguished" First Republic to redeem the territory. Their rhetoric was steeped in tales of heroism and treason. Rebel leaders and others recast 1844—once tentatively called "Separation"—as "Independence," and the previous republic achieved increasingly glorious, even mythic, proportions. "Dominicans! The homeland of the 27th of February, the country of sacrifices, calls you to her aid!" exhorted one general; many echoed his exact phrasing.[30] A number of the important Liberation Army leaders were veterans of older campaigns. Trinitario veteran Ramón Mella called to other 1844 veterans explicitly. "To my co-citizens. The Republic has called you: to arms! . . . I am a soldier of the February 27th Column, you know me, and I am here to call a few of my own," he began, continuing explicitly: "Sandoval, Lloveres, Sosa, Maldonado, Juan Suero, Valenas, Marcos Evangelista, . . . do not forget that the Republic that gave you the fame and glory that your *compañeros* have for you." Spain had already martyred many, Mella reminded veterans, invoking Sánchez but also many earlier military officers killed by Santana during the republic: "[All who have died], rise from the other side of the tomb, crying 'Revenge!' 'Revenge!' Dominicans! Listen to the patriotic laments of so many martyrs for liberty! . . . The *patria* is demanding REVENGE!"[31] Mella reminded his audience of Santana's 1845 murder of the woman who might have sewn the first Dominican flag: "And you, my friends of Santo Domingo, do not forget that Santana was the murderer of Trinidad Sánchez!" Other generals also invoked a heroic past of the republic. "Long Live the Dominican Republic . . . on Year 17 of the country," another general reminded his audience.[32]

The reinvention of a national community required a wiping clean of old caudillo loyalties. The fighting dismantled Santana's and Báez's patronage ties significantly. Báez, in Europe, was absent during the height of the fighting. Santana's network of support catastrophically disintegrated: he could not dole out the military titles and patronage as he had done prior to Spanish arrival; then the rebellion undermined him; finally, he resigned in disgrace from the Spanish administration completely. His death a short time later furthered the fragmentation of his former supporters and swelled the Restoration ranks further.[33] Certainly, anti-Santana sentiment was manifest in the rebel ranks; "¡Abajo España! ¡Abajo el Gran Pendejo!" was a common refrain. One poet suggested a sea change in popular sentiment, long in development, away from loyalties to the disgraced caudillo,

> Your children, your dear children,
> who used to worship you,
> who adored you fervently
> you must see them celebrating your ruin[34]

The Provisional Government, which personified cross-party loyalties, declared the death penalty for Santana in September 1863. After his actual death from illness a year later, a number of epitaphs excoriated him, including the following:

> Here lies a great idiot
> despotic like no other
> he did not understand his fate
> and he died like a pig
> without having done anything good.[35]

The spokesmen of the Provisional Government responded to Spanish accusations (and real vestiges) of party factionalism. Their public overtures, accordingly, were insistently nonpartisan. "We are brothers," Cabral reminded his audience in 1861, continuing, "Our arms are open to receive you . . . DOMINICANOS ALL, union, strength, enthusiasm and confidence, and I promise you that the Country will be freed.[36] "Co-citizens, a cordial welcome to all Dominicans, whatever your convictions have been, and in good faith, come take your place in the glorious lines of the *patria*," a government writer announced, invitingly.[37]

Some leaders' treatises appealed explicitly to an egalitarian nationalism. Of all the grievous elements of the occupation, "social differences, caused by, among other things, the importations of titles from Spain," were the most odious, Luperón wrote, concluding, "It is a thousand times more worthwhile to die than to be slaves."[38] Others concurred. "In Spain there are distinctions of class and trade, that is to say, inequality is consecrated," an anonymous pamphlet writer observed critically.[39] In their proclamations, the refrain was often that of the former republic—"God, Country and Liberty"—but others deepened its social implications. "Homeland, honor, and humanity," Ramón Mella exhorted, for example.[40] "DEATH OR LIBERTY," announced one general; "Liberty, Independence, Union," and "Liberty—Independence—the heroic Dominican people!" concluded others.[41] Explicitly more radical was Gregorio Luperón's version, scrawled in boldface: "INDEPENDENCE, EQUALITY, AND LIBERTY," he insisted forcefully during Polanco's administration.[42] "Free by nature, free by institutions, free, ultimately, through the conscience of our dignity—there is no human power that can sully it," Luperón concluded.[43] "FREE, we were born free, and we have broken free from Spanish oppression," a poet proclaimed. "If yesterday we were slaves by means of treachery, today the popular opinion damning those traitors makes them instead the slaves, as we cry, RESTORATION!"[44] The call to arms was universal. "All Dominicans are Soldiers of the Patria. . . . Considering that in Dominican society, there are no privileged classes, everyone without exception should wear war fatigues," the Provisional Government announced, and from age fifteen to sixty, all were expected to fight.[45]

Italy, Poland, Santo Domingo! . . . The Sublime Trilogy
of Modern Independence!

As Spanish general José de la Gándara, veteran of service on two continents, took the mantle of Spanish governor of Santo Domingo in 1864, he located the Spanish project firmly on the side of reason and civilization. Addressing his subjects with a combination of severity and strained optimism, he assured his listeners that Santo Domingo continued to be an "important province of the monarchy." Rule of law would continue to apply, for "legality is an element of progress and civilization that Spanish nationality promises you," the general maintained, "[along with] powerful resources." The rebels were outside of the law, reason, and civilization itself, he reasoned. To those who had taken up arms, the general directed a chiding message. "You have guns in your hands, but no reason in your conscience; . . . You raise a flag that has no name, that does not protect any element of liberty, peace, and civilization," he accused. "I have the duty to pacify this territory . . . and I expect to see it crowned with the success," he warned.[46] He had ample provisions, it seemed, to deliver on his threats; a royal order of April 1864 authorized the governor to use "any means in his power" to defeat the Dominican insurrection.[47]

Provisional Government authors countered de la Gándara's claims of legality and civilizing logic point by point, even as they largely accepted his premises. Nationalist, "civilized" language ruled their discourse, and they directed missives widely. In the context of British, French, and U.S. acquiescence to the reoccupation, Dominican resistance demanded not just armed struggle locally but a hemispheric defense of their right to self-determination. Representatives of the Provisional Government sought international attention and condemnation, if not aid. They dedicated the independence declaration to "God, the whole world, and the throne of Spain." Signatories announced the global import of the fight succinctly: "You have given us the mission of proving to the World, that a weak people cannot have their voice silenced by a large and noble Nation, if they are not afraid to fight for justice." "We are guided by humanitarian principles, like the rest of civilized Nations," a declaration insisted. Ulises Espaillat, serving on the Provisional Government's Foreign Relations Commission, circulated their protests to the governments of England, France, and the United States, "to make manifest to the civilized world the illegal proceedings and sinister and torturous methods [of] Spain."[48] Rebels invoked the Monroe Doctrine, prodding the war-torn United States to respond, even if only rhetorically. "[Annexation] obviously violates the Monroe Doctrine," a *Boletín Oficial* editorial implored.[49]

Provisional Government authors made pointed parallels between their struggles for national determination and those of central and southern Europe. From the safety of San Juan, Puerto Rico, Dominican author Félix María del Monte wrote a poem calling the republic an "American Poland," a "tropical siren" who would redeem herself in struggle.[50] "Italy, Poland, Santo Domingo! Here I have the sublime trilogy of modern independence!" proclaimed the *Boletín Oficial*.[51] Poets wrote elegies to Risorgimento leader Giussepe Garibaldi in particular, for his actions in Uruguay as well as the Italian peninsula. Ireland and Hungary, too, presented timely comparisons.[52] They were only reiterating what Geffrard had said two years before. His early protest questioned: "Haitians . . . could you consent [to annexation], in the nineteenth century, when Italy, Hungary, and Poland successfully regain their liberty and independence, oppressed by less terrible servitude than Spain?" "History and posterity will applaud our heroism and civilized nations will avenge our defeat and our patriotism," Geffrard had asserted. The advances of the nineteenth century rendered these claims irrevocable, Dominican authors now argued. "Liberty! . . . Who in the nineteenth century dares to ask what it is? No one; because . . . that orphaned and lonely word . . . is the bravest expression of the world's future," an editorial exulted.[53]

Rebels vaunted Haiti's and the Dominican Republic's decades-long achievements of independence. Despite invoking glorious independence in 1844, they dated Dominican experimentation with democracy to the beginning of unification with Haiti in 1822, as they chided the queen: "This people enjoyed forty years of political and civil liberty under republican rule, tolerance in religious matters, and innumerable other advantages, not least among them a National Congress and the participation in public affairs that

DEMOCRACY necessarily brings with it, a poor fit with monarchical and even colonial regimes."[54] A powerful revolution made Haiti free, and the British islands were now "calmly on the path of betterment and progress" after emancipation, an author argued in the *Boletín Oficial*. Haiti's achievements in just sixty-three years were remarkable, the writer asserted. "Thanks to the democratic system, Haiti has achieved the same level of civilization as exists in sister Republics," he concluded.[55] "Who, then, should win in this struggle? Spain, that is, the Monarchy . . . or Santo Domingo, the democracy . . . ? . . . Will the cause of humanity and civilization win?"[56] It was the colonizing Spaniards who were uncivilized. Santana might have been a "scandal to civilization" for his collusion, but it was Spain's Liberal Union government that held the most spectacular blame; it had failed to admit its "embarrassing and willful misconduct . . . in a project as *barbarous* as it is ridiculous."[57] The Dominican Republic, just like its neighbor, deserved autonomy. Annexation "of a free people to the most despotic and backward Nation of the globe" was disastrous, the authors concluded.[58] Spain has brought "misery and calamities of its own poor administration; their Government . . . has made the country move backward," the independence declaration accused. Annexation amounted to "tyranny against right, in short, barbarism against civilization."[59] It was a project "as barbarous as it is ridiculous," echoed another.[60] Poets called Spain a "prideful sultan," a barbarous "tyrant" spilling the blood of "noble Américans." "Wild despotism will never, never be able to relax . . . on heroic ground," the author warned.[61]

In official addresses, Provisional Government decrees were fairly quiet about connecting Spain's slaveholding to Spanish misrule on Dominican soil. Cuba could not remain under "a government from another century much longer," one decree announced vaguely.[62] A handful were direct in using abolitionist declarations as condemnation. "Dominicans: the day has arrived in which Spain, the only country that insists on keeping slaves, should lose her colonies in the Antilles. . . . America should belong to itself," General Ramón Mella argued.[63] Letter writers to the *Boletín Oficial* talked about local prejudice, however. "I'll take advantage of the moment to lift a great weight from my conscience," a man wrote from the capital, "as everything they write here is a big lie; everything they say about treating us well is completely the opposite." He spoke of relentless, repeated reminders from Spanish officials about how, in Spanish territories, "there cannot be black Generals and black colonels" and openly speculated about the threats to Dominican individuals in other Spanish possessions. "The only thing left to do to disrespect us more is to spit in our face," he concluded. He urged his compatriots in Santiago not to believe news of Spanish reinforcements, of the distrust and misery in the capital, and of the strength of the resistance. "Tell all them [in the Cibao] to stay strong," he wrote, "because this cannot last long . . . reconquer this country again, that's just music, not even all of Spain can do it."[64]

No, We Do Not Want Your *Lights*

Sometimes, leaders went beyond republican critiques to grapple with and articulate alternative models of civilization. "Prove to the world that you are part of the indomitable and guerrilla peoples who live civilization through customs, words, and its idea," Francisco del Rosario Sánchez began, "but who prefer liberty to all the advantages of rights." The advantages of formal rights were nothing but "golden chains," he concluded.[65] In the developmentalist furor that surrounded the island, some authors also articulated a complicated riposte to Spanish promises. Spanish authorities promised industry, commercialization, and progress. "We want this unlucky country to prosper," the first Spanish governor had proclaimed.[66] Dominican writers responded to their plans with distrust. While many in their ranks might have wished for greater capital and infrastructure—such hopes had been, after all, at the root of loyalist sentiment among a number of merchants in the Cibao and Puerto Plata—they were suspicious of Spanish-led schemes. "You want to exploit our coal, the silver and gold that is said to abound," accused an opposition pamphlet in 1861. The writer continued, "Our agriculture is not ruined. It's true that it is paltry; but that is a result of the number of inhabitants who can dedicate themselves to it. . . . *You come to rid of us of property to which we have a perfect right.*"[67] Dominican loyalist Manuel de Jesús Galván retorted:

> Well, fine: what does the author want? That the rock carbon and the iron remain permanently in their veins and beds, that is to say, hidden and denied to civilization? That's as much as can be deduced from his verbal mess. Or does he want Santo Domingo to remain as it is, with its paltry agriculture, its virgin forests, its coal deposits, without civilization ever using those elements of well-being and progress? Is that to say he wants the Dominican people to remain immobilized in disgrace . . . limited to stasis, passive in the midst of richness and in view of the progressive march of civilization![68]

Democracy, not development, was the core principle of civilization, his opponent argued. "We think it better that the small amount be split among all of our farmers than for two or three of yours to monopolize everyone's work," the *Treason* pamphlet offered testily. Moreover, the author rejected rapacious development; advancement was not worth the cost. And so the pamphlet concluded forcefully: "Spain is mistaken in her conviction, purportedly magnanimous, of the mission to bring to our soil all of the elements of civilization, judging it in a complete state of barbarism, in exchange for domination. Dominicans can tell her: No, we do not want your *lights*, because we prefer to live in the utmost degree of *backwardness*, to falling, little by little, *shining*, into the most degrading servitude."[69] Later government missives compared the nonexploitation of Dominican resources with feminine modesty, calling the territory a "respectable matron of the American world." Despite being small, "we nonetheless appear big in the eyes of the universe," the author insisted.[70] Rebel authors mocked loyalists' willful claims to monopolize civilization and reason. "We rarely read *La Razón*, unless there's nothing to do and we're in a bad mood," *Boletín* writers teased.[71]

Mass Mobilization, Alliances, and Social Mobility

Government members commented on the vast difference between the fighting and all previous political mobilizations. The liberal movement of 1858 had represented "the revolution of a few, dragging the masses along with them," one author wrote in the *Boletín Oficial*. The new mobilization was far more popular. "In the current revolution, it was the masses who rose up, dragging with them everyone else," he observed; "in this one, the educated have put themselves in service of the masses."[72] As they entered towns, rebel groups sought a pronouncement of loyalty from residents. "Thousands and thousands" signed the Act of Independence.[73] "The authorities and *vecinos* of this town and its surroundings are gathered . . . to pronounce it in favor of the Holy Cause of Independence, unanimously agreeing to raise the glorious Dominican flag,'" San José de Ocoa's statement read, and nearly two hundred signatures followed.[74]

For all the efforts of the Santiago-based Provisional Government, the dispersed anti-Spanish fighters had to be largely self-reliant. Although sometimes gathered in large numbers, rebels tended to fight in smaller guerrilla groups of several hundred or fewer, gathering provisions and materiel as they could. Dispersed amid difficult conditions, they relied both on their ties to rural families and on their own knowledge of the countryside for food. Rebels often ate the cattle and pigs that roamed free. Plantains, corn, and some meats were purchased when funds permitted, and nonperishables arrived from Haiti. "Every soldier of ours was a *montero*," Bonó wrote approvingly.⁷⁵ Munitions were a constant problem, and most of the guns were stolen from Spanish soldiers. Anywhere from seven hundred to three thousand rebels were involved in the Puerto Plata rebellion of August 1863, for example, but many reportedly had just five bullets each.⁷⁶ Others reported that as many as one in four had only blanks, while the remaining men had only two or three bullets each, rationed from Santiago. Clothing, too, was in constant shortage. In order to maintain what standing forces did exist, soldiers of the Liberation Army were to receive sixty *papeletas*.

In the chaos of mobilization, men rose to leadership ranks in the army and Provisional Government on an unprecedented scale. Officers' ranks drew from a wider swath of social classes as a result. "The War of Restoration was an event of profoundly popular roots; its leaders just as its soldiers were people from the entrails of the pueblo," Bosch writes.⁷⁷ In previous decades, caudillos had mobilized dependents for military operations, largely through patronage ties and the promises of military spoils. In the war against the Spanish, the dynamics were much more diverse. Prowess and organizing capabilities ruled. Some emerged from local notoriety to something more closely resembling prestige. Prior loyalties did not stain capable commanders; a number of military officials and administrators, only the year prior, had been loyal to (and even fighting for) the Spanish. A number of men who became national figures rose from humble origins. Gaspar Polanco, a cattle man from Guayubín, was illiterate, but he was a "capable military chief . . . and brave." Anyway, the disorder of pitched fighting and guerrilla mobilizations secured such trajectories. "On top of this, there was no one who could have given [Polanco] the position, nor was there anyone who could have denied him it," Bosch surmises.⁷⁸ Within months, Polanco became the nominal head of the army, a formal title for an informal network of combatants.⁷⁹

Some leaders, capitalizing on the extralegal spaces of the center-island region, were brutal opportunists and violent men. Juan Rondón, for example, was a career cattle rustler; authorities reported that he had accompanied his father on thievery missions on both sides of the border from a very young age.⁸⁰ In adulthood, he was at times brutally violent. Allegedly he murdered a pregnant woman from the west and sliced out her unborn baby as she died. The sensational crime was discussed throughout the center-island region. Rondón first clashed with Spanish authorities in March 1863 when, as a passive colonel, he came under suspicion of spreading alarming rumors about the meaning of the announced "state of siege" on the island. His defense was agile. Claiming to be the peón of a woman named Merced Marunga in Las

Matas, he had applied for a license to leave Higuey and return to the center of the island, instead stopping at some point in the capital; all his travels, he argued, were as an innocent dependent. Short of evidence, the commission freed him.[81] Rondón was captured in March 1864 and brought to Port-au-Prince under strict vigilance of the area commander. "Men like that cannot possibly be considered émigrés in Haiti or any other civilized country," Manuel Álvarez observed.[82] Other caudillo leaders like "El Chivo" were nothing but "vulgar criminals and assassins," Spanish authorities accused.[83] Haitian officials, too, were weary of the unrest, accusing Dominican border "criminals" of political troublemaking.[84] Other individuals simply had untrustworthy allegiances, scheming to put themselves or friends in power. Ramón Mella was so disgusted with one general that he retreated from the center of the island back to Cibao to regroup.[85]

At times leaders' cruel tactics and misconduct were so extreme that other guerrilla leaders felt compelled to intercede against, even murder, prominent transgressors. General Pedro Florentino, long established in the center of the island (San Juan de la Maguana), committed considerable atrocities in his southwestern campaigns. He murdered twenty-three people in Las Matas, evidently to take their possessions. "In the small valley near the mountain, the ground was still bloody, and the hair of the victims was still caught up in the underbrush," a horrified Spanish official alleged, noting that the bodies, left unburied, had been torn apart by wild dogs.[86] The total number of local murders allegedly committed by Florentino and his accomplices—most by machete—was 125, with most of the bodies discarded in the mountains in the same way. A number of Dominican men detained by the Spanish testified that Florentino had "forced" them to travel with his ranks; one even claimed that the general had shot his father.[87] Florentino allegedly turned over the son of a prominent Dominican general to his brother-in-law, Juan "el Ciego," who marched the captive man to a cemetery and split his head with a machete.[88] Florentino openly gave permission for looting as a way of appeasing his band of soldiers, but his authoritarian grip tightened simultaneously.[89] Harsh punishment of desertion was "of absolute necessity to save the Patria," he concluded severely. He ordered executions and authorized other officials to do the same.[90] Eventually, Florentino—"rapacious, bloodthirsty, cowardly and inept"—was apprehended and killed by the very rebel leaders he claimed to represent, including the infamous Juan Rondón.[91] Similar conflicts bubbled up elsewhere among abusive leaders and their rivals.

The trajectory of one of the most famous Restoration fighters, Gregorio Luperón—who would influence politics until just years before his death at the end of the century, even as he repeatedly refused the presidency—exemplified the political mobility that military prowess afforded brilliant strategists and leaders. Luperón, the son of a modest fruit seller (he took a version of her French-Haitian name, Duperrón, and was not recognized by his father), learned woodworking and a bit of English from his artisan master during his childhood in Puerto Plata.[92] The international itinerary of his older brother exemplified the extensive regional ties of Puerto Plata: José Gabriel Luperón fought for the Union in the U.S. Civil War, attaining the rank of captain.[93] After some scrapes with authorities and immediately opposing Spanish annexation, the younger Gregorio fled from Puerto Plata to Cap-Haïtien to New York, subsequently leaving for Mexico and Jamaica before returning to Dominican soil under an assumed identity. Sometime in the summer of 1862, he arrived amid the hotbed of conspirators south of Monte Cristi, in Sabaneta; during the next few years, he became a close personal friend and ally of Puerto Rican abolitionist and *independentista* Ramón Emeterio Betances, firebrand liberal priest Father Fernando Antonio Meriño, and other itinerant, anticolonial gadflies. With veteran general Lucas Evangelista de Peña, Luperón fought at Sabaneta in the first rebellions of the spring of 1863, earning himself a death sentence from the Spanish in absentia; he was also, crucially, at the Grito de Capotillo that summer.

Luperón's heroics at the Battle of Santiago catapulted him to military prominence—he was, by his own admission, "guerrillero improvisado"—and he led hundreds in some of the most important battles of the Restoration fighting. After Capotillo, he headed south to face Santana himself at Arroyo Bermejo later that same month.[94] His newfound prowess—and the incredible risks he engaged—might have overwhelmed him briefly; his biographers detail a moment where he almost walked intentionally into Spanish fire.[95] Luperón was literate, but "as any son of a pueblo whose parents did not have the means to pay for school," Bosch notes.[96] He consistently refused administrative posts that were offered to him. Ricardo Curiel served as Luperón's secretary during the war, and memoirs of the fighting would later be written by fellow Restorationist and friend, poet Manuel Rodríguez Objío. So sudden was Luperón's rise to prominence that in the first few months he would be looked upon with suspicion both by established political-military figures and by the new Provisional Government; he was even jailed for a short time. By early 1864, however, his authority was difficult to contest. Among the most idealistic of the politico-military leaders of the period, he would also go on to be one of the most influential for decades following, even as the depths of his anticolonial views often took him to the wrong side of the law.

Robespierre of a New Kind

The first president of the Provisional Government, José Salcedo, was a prominent and capable figure. Salcedo, born to Dominican parents in Madrid, enjoyed a profitable income in the north coast as a wood seller and landowner, with a number of dependents living on his land. People respected his stature.[97] He was also an avowed conservative Báez supporter, having even conspired against the liberal Revolution of 1857. In the first year of annexation, Spanish authorities tried Salcedo for the murder of a dependent man on his property. Whether the prosecution was motivated by his opposition to the regime or whether the trial galvanized his opposition, fighting had already begun upon his release. Salcedo arrived with men to the September fighting in Santiago, as the town was already under siege. Promptly, he assumed the presidency of the Provisional Government, less than a month old, to the irritation of some leaders. The rank and file in Santiago, too, saw it as a usurpation.[98] Over the next year, Salcedo continued to campaign as he governed. In August, he dismissed his ministry and ruled with only his personal secretary.[99] He resented Luperón and hoped to replace him with a pliant and wealthy general, a man educated in England and with merchant ties as far as Louisiana.[100] A number of unconfirmed rumors swirled around Salcedo and his small coterie: the first, that he was too conciliatory with Spanish brigadier Buceta, who attempted secret negotiations to recoup Santiago; the second, that he and his powerful allies were maneuvering to bring Báez back to the country; the third, that he was prepared to accept conditions for withdrawal that would leave Spain with control over Samaná or another north coast port. As Spanish forces regained the south, Salcedo seemed too conciliatory, calling for a return to smaller campaigns. He traveled back to Santiago to defend a friend who was suspected of pro-Báez plotting. In the capital city, Spanish authorities publicly celebrated Salcedo's cooperation over prisoner exchange. Suspicions mounted.[101]

Revolutionary figures moved to oust Salcedo. Writing as "A soldier of Capotillo" in October 1864, Luperón urged popular vigilance of all former strongmen and their annexationist collaborators. "Those men comprised a political party that we can call traitors, and since Dominican Independence, since 27 February 1844, they have worked for the ruin of their country," he accused, "those men sold their hearts and consciences to every nationality but their own." Báez was as corrupt as Santana, Luperón added stonily. "Beware, liberating soldiers of Independence, beware!" he warned, "Do not have compassion for traitors and traffickers of our freedom! Beware! Beware! Beware!"[102] Supported by other military figures, General Gaspar Polanco—who had been fighting since the siege of Santiago—assumed the presidential post. He ordered Salcedo's expulsion. Before the ousted president might even be disembarked, however, Polanco ordered him shot. Other generals, Salcedo's allies, and even some of Polanco's allies reacted with umbrage and shock. The most radical period of Restoration fighting was about to begin.[103]

The radicalism of Gaspar Polanco's administration was immediately obvious, from policy to the language of everyday governance. Under Polanco's brief tenure, "Excelencia, Señoría," and other titles were abolished.[104] Leaders addressed their fellow fighters occasionally as "los pueblos," sometimes as "compatriotas," more often still as "Dominicans," but with increasing frequency as "conciudadanos" (co-citizens or fellow citizens). So elevated was the language of citizenship that writers called the president "President Citizen Gaspar Polanco," the ministers became "Minister Citizen Rafael Leyba," and so on.[105] Not everything was a revolutionary purge; Polanco kept on Salcedo's vice president, Ulises Espaillat, as an amenable, adept, and idealistic writer and administrator. In fact, he valued civil administration. Polanco and his ministers passed a decree to fund primary school in all the communes and mount a campaign for universal vaccination.[106] "Democracy is the guiding light of the world," Espaillat wrote. "Equality of rank and rights, popular government, power exercised by the masses, abnegation, generosity, and heroism"—these were the reforms that the revolution sought.[107] Writers filled the pages of the government bulletin with praise for the French revolution, excoriation of monarchy, and an expansion of democratic practice to include the populace. "American society is by nature and necessity plebeian," one observed.[108] Unnamed authors penned odes to hard work.[109] Polanco did not draft any of those missives himself, of course, but sincere rebels who admired him and eagerly collaborated surrounded him. He and his allies committed to win the war and to revolutionize politics at the same time. Already prominent figures were wondering aloud which region might claim the seat of government after fighting ended. Polanco and his administrators urged them to focus on unity instead.[110] He redoubled military efforts. Rodríguez Objío called him "Robespierre of a new kind."[111]

The tone of Provisional Government writings directed to Spanish authorities and Dominican loyalists became irreverent. From Puerto Rico and from Spain, journalists and authorities rained invective on the Polanco administration. One Spanish political cartoonist satirized all the rebels in an imagined pidgin Spanish-Kreyòl.[112] Figures around Polanco responded with absolute defiance. Spanish authorities called Ulises Espaillat an "impenitent revolutionary."[113] Someone penned a comic opera mocking a prominent pro-Spanish priest:

> Stop lying, dear Father, and stop wielding that ancient pen . . .
> You prove that the Spanish despot has lost.
> When your ancientness offers me peace with startling quickness if I accept chains . . .
> Our olive branch is our cannon.
> Make the Ogre of Castille understand . . .
> Your letter made me double over with laughter . . .
> If your pride and brutality think they can dominate my country . . .
> You are the one who is being played with.

"*Stop playing games already*," the author taunted loyalists repeatedly, and the fighting continued.[114]

In the months before Polanco's rise, military standoffs reached a critical juncture. Dominican rebels could mount long sieges of the Spanish, but they could not defeat them, and supplies of munitions waned.[115] Spanish authorities ordered seizures of rebel goods, but the pace of seizures slowed when there were few possessions left to take.[116] The governor proved totally intractable on Spanish confiscation of pack animals, even though local officials tried to explain to him that the seizures were "the most onerous public service in the land."[117] "It must be noted that this poverty cannot be so great as supposed," he observed, in a haughty non sequitur, "given that many jobs . . . are vacant."[118] The Provisional Government enacted identical measures, decreeing that any soldier deserting—for example, seeking refuge in Haiti—would face confiscation of his possessions.[119] All manner of food—salted meat, flour, vegetables, yucca, yam (ñame), even plantains—continued to be difficult to find in many towns, as boat seizures halted trade from Saint Thomas. High prices kept many "emaciated and weakened by hunger," a U.S. observer reported gravely.[120] Dominican merchants suffered greatly, cut off from the interior.[121] Prisons and makeshift detentions brimmed with detainees in terrible conditions, as authorities converted various buildings to hold the captives.[122] Even daily meals were improbable for prisoners without family nearby. From the first fall of fighting, prisoners begged for an audience with an official who might see to it that their basic water and sanitary needs be met, as well as grant them access to a small vegetable garden.[123] Rebel prisoners were made to do all sorts of menial tasks while detained by the Spanish. Four fled at the riverbanks where they had been sent to clean the chamber pots, for example.[124] Others had to do hard labor while in shackles and chains.[125] Improbably, investors continued to send agricultural indenture schemes and other plans to authorities, impervious to the violent and hungry stalemate.[126]

In power by the early fall of 1864, Polanco pushed forward. He began with a campaign of volunteers on an impossible, symbolic mission to attack the entrenched Spanish troops in Puerto Plata. He ordered the creation of regional councils to detect pro-Spanish conspiracy.[127] Aware that inflation was hurting poorer urban citizens and desperately seeking funds, Polanco created a state tobacco monopoly, ordered "forced loans" from prominent citizens, seized goods of those who had defected to Spanish lines, and tried to promote cotton near Dajabón.[128] To Spanish authorities, Polanco's tone was unyielding. "We are not afraid of your threats," he warned. "Today all Dominicans are on the front lines for our country, and nothing you say can offend me. We are not afraid of your artillery nor all of your army, we have taken up arms to throw off your yoke, and we will defend ourselves to the death."[129] He ordered campaigns everywhere. Center-island fighting raged, and campaigns reached all the way east to Higüey. Polanco ordered those who had returned to their homes in the Cibao back out to fight. The call was immediately successful; more than two thousand men remobilized.[130] Spanish authorities also dug in. "A homicidal drama" already sixteen months long, Polanco's ministers lamented, was spilling "a precious blood, the blood of an unlucky and innocent people . . . resolved to bury themselves in the ruins and ashes piling up around them" before giving up their freedom.[131] Soon, the administration turned to Haiti for help.

A Word to the Dominicans, a Word to the Haitians

As the fighting first recommenced, the Geffrard administration had little choice but to demonstrate cooperation with the Spanish. Santana tried to forbid all communication with Haiti entirely; military and civil authorities were instructed to use extreme vigilance.[132] The *Moniteur Haïtien* announced that Dominican refugees from the border area should be marched to Port-au-Prince. "Haitian authorities have shown themselves to be completely divorced from the movement . . . and desirous of order," Spanish authorities noted with satisfaction.[133] A smattering of firings followed. Geffrard's officials dismissed Cap-Haïtien's governor for allowing rebels to gather there.

Further east on the north coast, another commanding general was fired after he received a prominent Dominican rebel. The new commander at Fort Liberté in Ouanaminthe, General Philanthrope Noël, received explicit instructions not to let anyone cross from the Dominican side without a passport signed by the Spanish governor himself, and he promised to inform Spanish authorities about the suspected whereabouts of prominent insurgent leaders.[134] Madrid officials noted with approval that Geffrard passed on confidential tips that former Dominican minister Felipe Alfau was conspiring in Paris, "as proof of his affection for Spain and her Government and of his good intentions thereto."[135] When Francisco Bonó, member of the Provisional Government, had visited Port-au-Prince, officials observed a "strict neutrality," ordering him to leave immediately.[136]

President Geffrard stuck closely to realpolitik, but there were also clear limits to his cooperation with Spain. When the Spaniards tried to land a vessel in Manzanillo Bay, individuals from the garrison there ordered them to depart. The rebuffed Spanish commander, disgruntled, sent a courier all the way to Port-au-Prince to ask President Geffrard directly for the right to land troops on Haiti's northern coast, forty miles west of the Dominican border. President Geffrard starkly rejected the officer's demand, announcing that he "could not permit one soldier to land on Haytian territory." The Spanish troops were forced to land near the trenches of the embattled town of Puerto Plata instead.[137] Rumors circulated that Geffrard was quietly formulating his own anti-Spanish schemes. Some alleged that he sought a protectorate for the east, administered by a trinational oversight federation of France, England, and Spain. The British consul had rejected it, reports claimed, leaving Geffrard in the uncomfortable position of continued collaboration. "I am trying and will try to avoid provoking any reason for complaint from the Spanish government," he reportedly explained.[138]

Semicovert Dominican-Haitian military alliances, meanwhile, could not be stanched. Haitian border officials and Dominican rebels who had gathered in the center-island area collaborated often. General José Maria Cabral was frequently in Las Caobas recruiting rebels of all flags.[139] Popular organizing was obviously gaining strength. In Puerto Plata, an individual named Filormé brought letters from Haiti, spreading word of help that was to come.[140] Domingo Ramírez had a number of rumored allies and friends in his hometown of Neiba, including high officials of relative standing, like General Pedro Nolasco. He counted on local help and even U.S. aid, according to various sources. Letter writers seeking the alliance of Haitian border officials were friendly, affectionate, and insistent. "Dear General and friend," one Dominican letter began, at the very outset of the fighting. "Considering our position today, with ten dead, because of the revolution that we have been planning . . . and the promise that you made to our dear General, Don Fernando Valerio (RIP), I find myself in the necessity of seeking your help, for protection by the army under your command, so that we can shake off and throw out from our land the Spanish standard and its armies. . . . Please remember our friend," the anonymous writer urged.[141] In a related discussion over jurisdiction and territory, the mingling expatriate groups, center-island residents, and rebels reached an agreement about some of the center-island towns, like Hinche, which had grown to be socially Haitian over the years. The new jurisdictions were to be respected, the parties agreed, in any foregoing collaboration. Rebels and local Haitian officers were supportive of these agreements.[142]

In center-island regions, collaboration with the rebellion grew relentlessly. Popular Haitian collaboration intensified after abolition in the United States, the Spanish consul claimed; Spain was now the only imperial slave power that threatened encroachment. Along the border, officials became openly recalcitrant to extradite Dominican rebel leaders and remit them to the Spanish, since the rebels themselves were simply too popular among the Haitian families living there.[143] Eastern rebels must have received the news eagerly. One Dominican loyalist general tried to mobilize the elite anti-Haitian fears of previous decades—warning that "8000 Haitians were ready to disembark" in the east as an invasion—but his tale evidently held so little salience among Dominican audiences that the rumor, for all its popularity in the 1850s, was never repeated again.[144] Rather, the west was a refuge that many used. In a conciliatory measure, the Spanish had to concede and extend amnesty to those residents who chose to remain in Haiti, trying to entice them to return. Cattle trade through San Juan, to Hinche, to Port-au-Prince continued steadily. Hincha was not well watched at all, Spanish authorities fretted.[145]

To the north, meanwhile, citizens of Cap-Haïtien only increased their support for the Dominican rebels. News of their brazen aid arrived secondhand—from a Canary Island resident in La Vega, from Tortuga via Puerto Plata, from observers in the Turks and Caicos, from rumors on the ground in northern Haiti—but it reached Spanish authorities all the same. In Cap, families offered Dominican rebel exiles housing and protection. Whole groups of Dominican exiles—not just prominent military figures but also groups primarily of women and children—arrived, often via other islands, and more convoys were expected.[146] Living in Cap-Haïtien were allies of political and military prominence like M. Macajauc, Laguerre Bart, Alexandre Pouget, and General Sylvain Salnave, all of whom were close allies with Dominican general Santiago Rodríguez or otherwise offered direct assistance at different junctures. A Saint Thomas man who regularly traveled between Monte Cristi and Cap, Huberto Marzán, sewed the flag that flew in the early battles of 1863.[147] Reports from Haiti claimed that North American ships entered and left Cap-Haïtien daily, secretly disembarking weapons for the opposition.[148] One Dominican living in Cap-Haïtien allegedly had amassed fifteen thousand locally manufactured bullets and was storing some within city limits and some in nearby Limonade.[149] Northern coast sea traffic can only be speculated. A small boat caught off the coast of Puerto Plata carried wheat, rice, rifles, lead, and a Haitian flag.[150] Whole steamships sometimes arrived, too.[151] "Credible sources" suggested that north coast authorities allowed private American ships to dock with weapons and speculated the aid "could not have gone unnoticed" by the American government, either.[152] Nameless runners ferried messages back and forth from Cap-Haïtien, and even neighboring islands, to Santiago.

Trade, and aid, in supplies and weapons flourished in the interior and on the coast. Many Dominicans who had been living in Haiti for years ferried gunpowder back through Neiba and Barahona.[153] Commanders openly sent missions in search of weapons. "Seek them from Haitian lines, but always mindful of the Country," one exhorted.[154] A supply line thrived at the center of the island; Haitian women sold soap, mackerel, codfish, flour, salt, and other supplies at Monte Cristi, Guayubín, and Hinche, receiving coffee and tobacco in barter.[155] Everyone knew of the Hinche trade, which was infamous.[156] Runners picked up supplies from the frontier and amassed them in Santiago. Mella allegedly gathered and sold ten thousand *serones* of tobacco to Haiti in exchange for war matériel in late 1863.[157] Alfredo Deetjen, born in Cap in 1824, was an important merchant and politician in Santiago de los Caballeros at the moment of annexation, and he immediately supported the creation of the Provisional Government. At the end of the year, he headed back to Cap to negotiate for more munitions. He then traveled to Port-au-Prince in search of a printing press that could spread the Dominican Provisional Government's missives. Later, ad hoc officials in Santiago used the press to print money.[158] The Provisional Government announced that the Haitian gourde would circulate in 1864; Spanish sources reported that they sought a loan from Geffrard of 1.5 million gourdes, to be distributed evenly in the north, Cibao, and the south, payable at 6 percent annual interest.[159]

President Geffrard's stance of studied neutrality, in the face of overwhelming popular support and Spanish threats, nearly brought his downfall. Spanish authorities observed the disorder with satisfaction, claiming that the president, Minister Philippeau, and other Geffrard allies feared the Dominican rebel movements as much as the Spanish did. Domestic political opponents blended blatant personal ambition with criticism of Geffrard's approach. Soulouque wrote letters from Jamaica excoriating him, as did other political exiles.[160] Prominent families rallied opposition movements in the south in 1862, in Artibonite the next year, and the north coast through much of 1864. One of the political aspirants, Sylvain Salnave, claimed common cause with the Dominican rebel fight. As Geffrard's personal guard pursued him, he fled into Dominican territory and then Saint Thomas.[161] Making a national tour in the spring of 1864, residents in Saint Marc and Gonaïves received the president coldly. "Upon his arrival, doors were closed, no residents came out to see him, and none of the prominent families attended the dance that was held in his honor," an observer alleged. The family of executed general Aimé Legros was particularly upset. Other recent reforms exacerbated the mood. As the report continued, "The rude measures that Authorities have taken to execute the ban of vodou dancing has contributed to the discontent."[162] In the capital, citizens simply matter-of-factly defied Geffrard's prohibitions. Dominicans came into town with large herds—sixty head of cattle, pairs of yoked oxen, and so on—to trade for flour and other nonperishables. They made their sales and were on their way once more, back to Dominican territory.[163]

As Dominican emissaries lobbied hard for a formal alliance, they emphasized popular support, made appeals to Haiti's internationalist leanings, and warned that a prolonged struggle could result in the absorption of Haiti. Spanish occupation "endangers true Haitian independence," one government spokesperson argued, and he warned that a protracted struggle would endanger Haitian sovereignty. Months before Polanco's administration, in a rare moment of discussing race and racism directly in the Boletín Oficial, the author made an appeal to Haiti's antiracist platform. "Haiti, more than anyone, must fight to solve the important problem of the equality of races," he began, "Haiti [is] so close to Cuba that it can, with just a small effort, hear the cries [ayes] and laments of a numerous portion of humanity that moans under the weight of the chains of slavery." The author praised Haiti, a "people so rightly proud of their own glory." Simultaneously, he warned that Dominican and Cuban independence were vital, or that Haiti would become "the slave of Spain." He suggested a common political platform, arguing for a treaty of "alliance, peace, commerce, friendship and borders, by which the political future would be assured for all the inhabitants of both parts of the island of Haiti, forever."[164]

As months passed, the Dominican Provisional Government stepped up its diplomatic efforts directly to the Haitian people. Another author in the *Boletín Oficial*, probably Espaillat, wrote "A Word to Dominicans, a Word to Haitians":

> A curious fact, proven by experience, is that the people always march ahead of their Governments. . . . There is not one Dominican who since the first days of the revolution hasn't asked himself a thousand times a day, why the Haitians do not come to help us, given that we do not have enough arms and munitions. . . . And Haitians ask themselves all the time why Dominicans do not call on them. . . . What can possibly explain this extraordinary and unforeseen reason why? It is precisely the Haitian and Dominican Governments, because there is no other way to explain such a ridiculous fact. How can two peoples composed of the same race, the same political interests, ruled by republican institutions, and who have lived together as good friends, look at each other with indifference when one of them is in danger? Is not the downfall of one the downfall of another? Is the danger of this one not the danger of that? In a word, if the Dominican people fall, does that not precipitate the fall of the Haitian Republic? The Haitian people understand that as well as we do. It seems to us that it is past time that both Governments understand . . . and unite to end foreign domination on the island of Haiti.[165]

"We profess the same political principles," another author insisted. "The elements that compose the Dominican people are identical to those that compose the Haitian people," he continued. The writer urged all Dominican men, from fifteen to sixty, to vote in the authorization of an island-wide alliance.[166]

Espaillat emphasized the popularity of the anticolonial fight and the solidarity—political and racial—that existed between Haitians and Dominicans. Support for the rebellion, he argued, amounted to a "universal sympathy" that the state could not possibly ignore. He continued: "These truths are too clear. They are within the grasp that even the most humble of Haitian society, without needing explanation. . . . Now think: ask any citizen of Haiti, any one at all, if the Government should help the Dominicans, and they will not hesitate to answer affirmatively. Is it that their logic has more common sense than the reasoning of a man of State?" His tone was frustrated, exasperated even. "What do you hope to see?" he queried, continuing, "It is a glorious struggle, how long will you remain indifferent?" "Your Excellency's co-citizens are not bothering to hide their sympathies," he reiterated. "Your neutrality is against healthy politics, natural rights, even common sense . . . It is false, illogical and absurd," he pleaded.[167] "You will excuse me when I confirm that Your Excellency's Government has caused this revolution, given that, if it did not, it should have," he wrote, arguing that the fighting was "a necessity not only for the redemption of the Dominican people, but for the rest of the Spanish colonies, and especially for the future of Haiti. . . . Your Excellency's co-citizens are not bothering to hide their sympathies to a cause that has come to be, in a manner of saying, the most natural bond that could possibly exist." Haitians and Dominicans were "united together by the tightest friendship between two neighboring peoples, who for common political and racial reasons, have been born to be brothers," he concluded.[168]

By the summer of 1864, members of the Provisional Government proposed an outright federation. Their letter to President Geffrard that June reiterated the suggestion of a treaty of goodwill, and it included a plan for political integration of the two states. Writing to the "good patriots" of the west, the rebels announced: "Even though the Dominican people have always been very protective of their Independence and their autonomy, and they remain so today, we do not fear establishing, starting now, the basis for a treaty of Federation. We are convinced that the precious gift of our sacred natural rights as free and independent people, rather than be ill-treated, will be secured, for now and for the future. For her part, Haiti should see the step as a means to protect her political existence, against any future compromise."[169] Members of Santiago's Provisional Government personally escorted the missive to Port-au-Prince.

This very same revolutionary energy—and some of the very same actors—sparked a rebellious movement in the north of the island. North coast federation plans were nothing new—they circulated in 1843, for example—but they had never gained much traction. As early as spring 1863, rumors flew that the same north coast Haitian allies who were supporting the Capotillo fight were also hoping to expel Geffrard at the same time, seeking "revolution in both countries."[170] Haitian authorities complained that Dominican agents in Cap-Haïtien were "sowing discord and spreading insults about President Geffrard, accusing him of *españolismo* and suggesting the benefits to the people of the North if they were to separate and unite with Santo Domingo."[171] Dominican rebels planned to collaborate with General Ogé Longuefosse. The conspiracy "was very far along, and Dominican insurrectionists were mixed up in it," the Spanish consul reported from Port-au-Prince. The consul summarized their common objective succinctly: "to make Geffrard fall, separate out the north [of Haiti] again, and unite it with the . . . Dominican insurrection."[172] General Longuefosse mobilized with three hundred men. Haitian authorities pursued him with a steamship and infantry.[173] Dominican captain Pablo Isidor was captured and arrested with Longuefosse after an attempt on the life of Geffrard's secretary of state and minister of war, General Philippeau. The National Guard managed to crush the budding conspiracy, but stemming ongoing opposition proved more difficult. Philippeau had two thousand men on high alert, and as many as four thousand were on call. Despite these tensions, the popularity in Haiti for collaboration with the Dominicans continued to grow.[174]

News of this revolutionary scheme almost certainly influenced Haitian officials' response to Dominican Provisional Government entreaties. Geffrard's minister of foreign affairs, Auguste Elie, firmly rejected treaty and federation plans, expelling the Dominican emissaries. "This response that you are receiving is more of a general statement than personal communication," he told them, disdainfully. "I will not mention or even try to verify if the names of your signatories, . . . you are mere inhabitants of the Spanish province, absent of any title."[175] "You understand very well, sirs, that I do not recognize in you, collectively nor individually, any political rank or legitimate authority, and that we cannot accept any proposition of yours of this or any other sort," he continued.

> According to you, the two peoples occupy two territories that in another time were just one State. Well, which brother separated from which? According to you, the two peoples are of one same race, that is also true, but which brother has looked down on the other? According to you, both peoples are motivated by sentiments of love of liberty and independence, also true, but which of the two has forfeited them? According to you, they profess the same political principles, this is also true, but which of the two has trod on them? They have, you say, the same social ideas, the same customs, the same character—look at History. Is it true, as you claim, that our interests now and in the future are identical? That is also false. The Dominican people are asking Spain again for their independence, and the Haitian people have nothing to ask.

He went on:

> Is it true, as you claim, that Haiti will secure her political future through the consolidation of this alliance, lending a hand to the Dominican insurrection? No, a thousand times no. That is also an error! Haiti is, today, a republican government freely governed by a wise, educated, and popularly elected Leader. It has never blossomed more and it does not seek anything more than to develop this nascent prosperity through order and tranquility, respecting the rights of other nations and ready to defend its own. The Government of President Geffrard seeks nothing other than to consolidate Haiti's political existence. . . . There is no one in Haiti who does not continue to feel sympathy for the Dominican people, no one who does not admire their courage and lament their misfortunes. The Government of Haiti shares those popular sentiments, but it cannot forget the duties it must perform and the sacred interests it must protect.

"In light of the current state of friendly relations between the Government of Her Majesty the Queen of Spain and the Republic of Haiti, relations whose preservation is necessary for the tranquility of this country, the Haitian Government cannot recognize any other legitimate authority in the east than that of Her Majesty," the minister wrote. Plainly, "You are trying to drag us into the danger in which you find yourselves, and that has always been a bad way to escape danger." Rather, the Haitian government would continue "strict neutrality . . . moderate and impartial conduct," the rejection letter concluded. Furthermore, Elie copied the entire exchange to the Spanish consul in Port-au-Prince, the ministry of war in Madrid, the governor of Cuba, and the governor of Santo Domingo. "He turns his back more every day, continuing in his neutrality policy that so disgusts the ungrateful Dominicans," a Spanish dispatch claimed gleefully.[176]

Despite Elie's pronouncement, Geffrard slowly increased his diplomatic involvement in the conflict. General de la Gándara met with him several times. After a long meeting outside of Port-au-Prince late in 1864, both parties agreed Haitian mediation was necessary. "His most ardent desire is that we abandon Santo Domingo, and he will help us in every way . . . to find an acceptable solution," de la Gándara observed.[177] Geffrard dispatched two emissaries to Dominican territory to discuss prisoner exchange and other terms of negotiated withdrawal. His public instructions to them were frank and conciliatory, and he lamented the bloodletting. "I would call this parricide," he remarked.[178] The two delegates embarked on a familiar cross-island itinerary: travel by small boat to a town on the northern coast, then overland travel to Dajabón. A Dominican general traveled from Santiago to receive them with a short note, in French, greeting the "citizen" emissaries. Colonel Ernest Roumain marveled at his welcome. "Impossible to tell you the friendly reception that was made for us," he wrote. "Our entry into Dajabón was practically an ovation."[179] Young men of Santiago organized a ball for them on their arrival, he continued, which took place "practically under Spanish bullets."[180] Santiago, he noted sadly, was "a heap of ruins and rubble."[181]

In war-torn Santiago, Polanco's officials met with the Haitian diplomatic envoy for nearly a month. The idealism of the revolutionary Dominican administration was on full display. During a dinner one evening, Dominican officials delivered a number of toasts: to the heroes of the Haitian Revolution, to President Geffrard, and to achieving peace. One official toasted to "social and political solidarity" that ought to reign between Dominican Republic and Haiti. Another brought up hemispheric battles over emancipation. "It is an affront to humanity that the abominable institution of civil slavery still subsists," exhorted a general, commenting on the U.S. Civil War. "I toast, therefore, to the absolute freedom of man in all the universe, and that American democracy totally uproots slavery from its breast." A priest toasted, in French, for democratic governments. A civilian toasted to the Haitian and Dominican flags "casting friendly shadows on each other, that their friendship be strong enough to defend their rights from all foreign powers who sought to uproot them."[182] Time passed as the delegation sent letters back to Port-au-Prince and awaited reply. Dominican authorities wanted to remove noxious Spanish terms from the negotiations and to modify the language of their appeal to the Crown; Geffrard, toeing de la Gándara's line, insisted on the original language and terms of the Spanish proposal.[183] In Santiago, delegates grew close as weeks passed, signing off on affectionate letters, "à vous de cœur, votre ami de cœur."[184] At the end of the delegation, Dominican officials refused many of de la Gándara's and Geffrard's proposals, but they praised the president for his efforts "for the cause of humanity," and negotiations about prisoner exchange began in earnest.[185]

Revolutionary Fever

In retrospect, many combatants considered December 1864 to be the end of the war and the beginning of an extensive diplomatic process of Spanish extrication. There was no revelry. "The country was half-dead, had exhausted its resources, only revolutionary fever sustained it," Rodríguez Objío wrote.[186] "Traitorous plants are blooming," Luperón warned Restoration soldiers, balefully, in late winter.[187] Polanco's administration lasted only ninety-eight days. His powerful opponents, who included landowners and prominent urban families of the Cibao, sought to take back the political scene from the first moments he took power. In late January 1865, they mobilized, eager for the democratic phase of the fighting to end. An armed group arrested every member of Polanco's government and put them in shackles. "No personal interest, no unworthy motive has dictated our conduct," the usurping leaders promised the public.[188] Before even naming a president, the group modified or abrogated almost every Polanco statute. They pursued Polanco supporters returning from Spanish prisons.[189] They scattered his ministers to different corners of the territory. Espaillat they sent all the way to Samaná.[190] They reinstated the 1858 Moca Constitution for a time, easily drafting a new one within the month. They tried Polanco for Salcedo's murder before an Executive Commission, found him guilty, and sentenced him to death. A new president, Pedro Antonio Pimentel, pursued Polanco's supporters as well. He called Polanco and his ilk, common men who had gained power, "engrandecidos."[191] Outgoing missives returned to a republican script. It is a revolution "purely of principles and not of race, as some have tried to claim," a new high cabinet member later insisted. Furthermore, in the wake of radicalism, he observed, "the regularization of the war was a necessity everywhere."[192]

As 1865 dawned, however, the energy of alliances, optimism, and political ferment was high. The Haitian emissary, Captain Roumain, could not refrain from marveling at the sentiment of everyone he encountered between the Cibao capital and the center of the island. "We are truly stunned by it," he effused. "These sirs, whose town offers even a more wrenching portrayal of the calamities which have desolated them, do not content themselves with lodging us and feeding us at their own expense, but they overwhelm us every day with obliging offers of all kinds." Reflecting on his experience, he promised, "We will keep the memory of the kind attention of which we have been the object for a long time."[193] Meanwhile, extraofficial collaborations burgeoned, too. So intense were the military schemes on the northern coast that some observers suspected another rebel federation might form. Observers reported new conspiracies. A Spanish report from Monte Cristi in the first month of 1865 warned that "the prolongation of the war is beginning to give the result that Dominicans and Haitians seek to unite and form an independent Republic."[194] Meanwhile, dramatically, Polanco escaped his captors and headed north, where the ferment was. In a small town on the northern coast, about a third of the way from Puerto Plata toward Haiti, he raised a special banner that depicted the Haitian and Dominican flags, intertwined. Apparently the flag was in use as far south as Moca.[195] The new Santiago administration pursued him immediately. "Residents of Santiago: the rebellion caused by the naive General Gaspar Polanco has been happily crushed," new officials insisted. "Calm your spirits and return to your laborious life."[196] But repression was not so easy. Polanco slipped into the west, and the fighting continued.

SEVEN

Nothing Remains Anymore
THE LAST DAYS OF SPANISH RULE

Writing from New York, Alejandro Ángulo Guridi—born in Puerto Rico, raised in the Dominican Republic, professionally trained in Cuba—published an open letter about Spanish defeats on Dominican soil. Even Spanish soldiers who had been seasoned in the Caribbean were succumbing to guerrilla warfare and tropical diseases, dying in great numbers. Spain was clearly losing. "Cubans! Cubans!" Guridi exclaimed. "What do you do? What do you think?"[1] Guridi traveled to Washington, DC, lobbying for independence. He moved on to New York, where he met up with a vibrant group of Latin American activists. The famous Cuban author Cirilo Villaverde edited Guridi's opposition pamphlet, *Santo Domingo and Spain*.[2] Three more itinerant stops took him to the Turks and Caicos, Saint Thomas, and Venezuela before he returned to Dominican territory. Guridi worked in tandem with Provisional Government ministers, who threw their efforts into making regional allies simultaneously. Old networks percolated with new energy. In Curaçao, exiles and allies formed a Dominican revolutionary club, defiantly flying the republican flag.[3] A wealthy Curaçao merchant was so implicated in arms sales that the Provisional Government named him an official agent; he took to addressing his notes "Citizen" and signing them "God and Liberty."[4] "Brothers in South America: Come fight in Santo Domingo and you will be fighting for the liberty of a brother people and for your own," a government writer exhorted. "Come, Come, . . . to defeat the already decrepit Spanish power, and shout with delirious enthusiasm: ¡Long live America and the republics that people it!"[5]

As the anticolonial fighting raged, Spanish authorities tried to maintain day-to-day government functioning and to restrict the local circulation of news about the war. In a rare mention of regional opposition, a writer at *La Razón* called Jamaicans' 1861 anti-Spanish petition "the machinations of clowns," but otherwise, the pro-occupation journals maintained a studious silence.[6] Cuban and Puerto Rican periodicals did the same, only mentioning boat movements and the barest of other details. To stanch local trading ties, authorities blockaded the northern Dominican coast with twenty-two Spanish ships. The captains of small crafts from Saint Thomas, Turks and Caicos, Haiti, Cuba, Puerto Rico, Curaçao, and other sites, however, simply eluded them.[7] In addition to this bustling contraband trade, human witnesses to the conflict arrived steadily to Spanish docks at San Juan, Santiago de Cuba, and Havana. Injured soldiers, arriving for treatment, described the rebels' guerrilla victories, the crumbling occupation, and the growth of the revolt. Beginning in the battles of late 1864, Cuban and Puerto Rican soldiers joined Spanish regiments, and Dominican reserve corps merged with them. Spanish, Cuban, and Puerto Rican deserters joined Dominican rebels, too, in jails as far away as Cádiz and Ceuta.

News crisscrossed the Atlantic as well. Spain's press was fractious and strident. Progressive Madrid journalists were acerbic critics of the war, especially as the fighting utterly exploded annexation's voluntary premise. Journals like *La Discusión* arrived in Caribbean ports, to the chagrin of local officials. From Santo Domingo, the captain general prohibited the paper's circulation, but *La Discusión* reached Santiago de los Caballeros all the same.[8] Provisional Government journalists reprinted key articles.[9] In Cuba, the only Spanish periodical to be admitted was a trade circular, *Comercio de Cádiz*.[10] The Cuban governor, desperate, banned discussion of abolition in Cuba in June 1862, and Spanish officials tried to enact the same ban in Spain the next fall.[11] Empire-wide censorship continued through the summer of 1865, even after the last Spanish soldier left Dominican soil.[12] Foreign observers sent news, too. Many consular agents from Hanover, Hamburg, Prussia, the United States, and Austria who had been in Puerto Plata took refuge in the Turks and Caicos Islands, where they continued to send accounts; Santo Domingo–based U.S. observers like William Cazneau and William Jaeger reported on Spanish defeats with unrepentant glee from the relative safety of the capital city, and newspapers in New York, Boston, Chicago, and other sites reprinted their accounts eagerly.[13] Critical voices from Cuba reached a Washington, DC, newspaper, for example, in a report that complained that

Cuba's colonial defenses were being "weakened to sustain a war whose results could be summarized as *defeat*."[14]

Quickly, Spanish debate over withdrawal focused as much on the dangerous example of Caribbean defeat as on cost or logistics. The original champions of annexation were gone. Serrano, the Cuban governor who was Santana's coauthor, left Cuba in late 1862; in Spain, O'Donnell's administration fell the following spring. For a short time, wealthy loyalists from Cuba and Puerto Rico offered goods and funds to help quell the rebellion, but as the fight continued, a "general disgust" grew in Havana and other sites.[15] Meanwhile, everyone, of all political orientations, civil and military, on the islands and across the Atlantic, commented on the example and significance of guerrilla warfare. Spanish military figures and politicians suggested crushing the Dominican rebels with a massive display of force. "A shameful withdrawal?" a Spanish official in Cuba asked contemptuously in 1864. "What a beautiful and useful lesson that would be for the blacks and *mulatos* of Puerto Rico and Cuba."[16] Others were more apocalyptic about an impending race war, predicting the collapse of Spanish empire and the white race if Spain admitted defeat.[17] But the progress of the fighting was undeniable. In late January 1865, the Crown initiated steps to withdrawal.

At the end of a whirlwind of fighting, and in a devastated landscape, Dominicans defeated Spain's massive mobilization without any formal alliances. Major imperial powers largely failed them. Lincoln expressed sympathy, but his government remained neutral. French officials kept totally silent. Britain finally recognized Dominicans as belligerents when the fighting was almost over.[18] Politicians from a number of South American republics, critically eying European intervention in Mexico, French intervention in the U.S. Civil War, and annexationists in Guatemala and Ecuador, expressed support for the Dominican rebels.[19] The only enduring alliances, however, were the ones Dominican rebels forged, unofficially and often secretly, with their Caribbean neighbors. Networks of trade, exile, finance, and friendship grew tighter. Meanwhile, *independentistas* in Cuba and Puerto Rico, busily organizing, watched Spain fight, and lose. Forty-one thousand Spanish soldiers, joined by twenty thousand more Cuban, Puerto Rican, and Dominican reserve soldiers, could not crush the popular resistance.[20] In Santiago de Cuba, a poet praised the victorious Dominicans and predicted the future of his own island:

Glory and honor to the American world,
the holy idea of liberty triumphs,

> ... raised and victorious
> the noble Dominican flag waves ...
> Hispaniola was the cradle of [Spain's] empire,
> and today it is the tomb.[21]

Our Cry of INDEPENDENCE! Regional and International Responses

Peruvian authorities condemned the annexation from its first days. Already embroiled in a conflict with Spain (known variously as the "Chincha Islands War," the "Spanish-Peruvian War," and the "Spanish-Chilean War"), Peruvian officials looked upon the Dominican cession with particular disapproval. They sent a circular around to other governments, condemning the act as "an attack on democratic institutions and continental security"; Nicaragua, Bolivia, Colombia, Argentina, and Venezuela all expressed support.[22] "A common peril for America," the annexation was "neither free, nor legal, nor in accordance with the Rights of Peoples, nor the practice of Nations, nor the spirit of the century," the Peruvian chancellor argued. He warned Venezuela of a possible military expedition from Cuba as well and demanded "an alliance to reject the reconquest."[23] Peru, Venezuela, and New Grenada recognized the Dominican Republic via confidential agent in July 1864; the Peruvian consul even offered to help procure arms from Curaçao to Cap-Haïtien.[24] As conflict continued off the Peruvian coast, the Peruvian president was forced out of office in November 1865, primarily for having failed to take a stronger stand against the Spanish. One Peruvian, Fruto Fuentes, participated in the fierce fighting of Puerto Plata in 1863.[25]

Venezuelans, long politically linked to Santo Domingo, were divided by their own civil war. Nevertheless, representatives of the Dominican Provisional Government were in regular contact with Venezuelan arms dealers, buying at least five thousand guns and other supplies from Coro in the summer of 1864. Caracas and other coastal cities hosted a significant and high-profile exile population, who wrote back to Dominican papers that they were eager to return.[26] Juan Pablo Duarte, in exile since the 1840s, allegedly sought guns and supplies from the Venezuelan government, to be facilitated by the commercial houses of Curaçao.[27] Manuel Rodríguez Objío shuttled back and forth from Santiago de los Caballeros to Caracas in 1863–64.[28] "Our brothers fight for the holy cause of independence. . . . [We] have common cause with those who want to sustain the integrity of the world of Columbus," a Venezuelan federalist paper praised in early 1864. "Continuous, heroic, the Dominican patriots," the editorial began, noting, "There, too, there are those who know how to love liberty." The author urged Venezuelan heads of state to send an emissary at once to Spain. "It is upon the Venezuelan Government to give this step of *americanismo*, of diligent and forthcoming friendliness," the paper reiterated, "in honor of the holy ashes of Bolívar." Perhaps Venezuelan mediation would help, the author supposed. "We are the closest to Spain and to Santo Domingo," he urged.[29]

Venezuela's own conflicts interrupted state-level diplomacy, but individuals continued to directly lobby, advocate, and even take up arms, with the Dominicans. It was a Venezuelan man, Manuel Ponce de León, who penned the Acta de Independencia on behalf of the fledgling Provisional Government; a Venezuelan general, Candelario Oquendo, became an important rebel leader.[30] Other individual Venezuelan soldiers participated in the fighting from its first days.[31] Capital city officials, suspicious, ordered all arriving from Venezuela without a passport to have someone vouch for them (a *fianza*). A small number of well-connected opponents in Madrid, such as conservative Venezuelan writer Pedro José Rojas, lobbied in Dominican favor. Other prominent Venezuelans lobbied hard for Dominican independence through the national press and in Washington; the Provisional Government thanked them officially via the Peruvian agent in Saint Thomas. "Send the titles . . . with some sentences that praise their *americanismo* . . . as thanks," the agent suggested.[32]

Residents of nearby British islands were even closer to the conflict. The Turks and Caicos Islands were reception sites for refugees and well-documented gun entrepôts.[33] The press openly favored the rebellion. Editors at the *Royal Standard and Gazette of the Turks and Caicos Islands* republished the rebel Provisional Government's protest letter to the queen and reported optimistically on Dominican gains. In the Parish Church of Saint Thomas, Grand Turk, congregants heard a sermon on the fight and took up a collection "in aid of those poor distressed Dominicans" who were living there.[34] Meanwhile, the gun trade was steady. A pair of cannons reached the rebels in Puerto Plata in 1863, followed by "war equipment, food, and supplies of all kinds."[35] British-registered ships like the *Elisa*, which ran the Turks–northern coast route, were under constant Spanish suspicion. In those instances in which the Spanish managed to intercept the ample microtrade between the two areas (Monte Cristi equally as implicated as Puerto Plata), the ships' crews alternately abandoned ship or fought back. Those unlucky enough to be jailed appealed to the British consulate for recourse. "It is obvious that one of the main causes of the war's duration is precisely the continuous sending of aid, organized in Nassau and the Turks Islands above all else," Spanish officials wrote, asking the British government to use "all direct or indirect means . . . to impede, or at least limit, the brazen and practically public sending of aid."[36] The Spanish admitted that local ship crews had been thrown into crowded cells with Dominican prisoners of war, an unpleasant and likely radicalizing experience.[37] Despite official condemnation—the British consul categorized the Dominican insurgents as rebellious Spanish subjects, and the Nassau governor agreed to forcibly return rebels—local support continued.[38]

For reasons of precedent, security, and cost, Cuba's new governor, Domingo Dulce, came to detest the annexation. He was pessimistic about the gravity of the rebellion, and he balked at the request to send five more battalions from Cuba in September 1863. "Even, by some luck, if order is reestablished," he argued, in the first weeks of fighting, "will it be the last attempt by the Dominicans to reestablish their autonomy? It is practically obvious that it will not." "The annexation was not the work of the nation: it was that of a party who dominated by terror, and who, worried for its future, negotiated for its own advantage," he wrote with lucid skepticism, continuing, "The people did not want nor pine to be governed by its old metropolis: and at every instance that has arisen to demonstrate as such, they have done so as ostentatiously as possible." The queen's "maternal benevolence . . . has bettered its miserable situation at the cost of Cuba," he allowed, but he doubted that Dominican territory, with its tiny economy and minimal infrastructure, could become profitable. And of the difficulty of the fighting, the governor was decidedly pessimistic. The guerrilla movements were "every day more powerful," he noted, and their logistical advantages were "obvious." The most dangerous aspect of the uprising, however, was the precedent it set: "These repeated rebellions, even when defeated and punished, establish a fatal example in [Cuba], where the spirit of independence began a while ago and remains robust," Dulce warned. He worried about the security of Cuba as it sent away its regiments. He suggested a show of force, "reducing the rebellious subjects to obedience, renouncing dominion of the territory of Santo Domingo, and re-establishing in it the same government . . . offering it a protectorate," he argued.[39] Upon hearing of the revolution's increasingly critical state, he reiterated his suggestion for abandonment. "A revolution that is not immediately crushed is a terrible example in the Antilles," he insisted.[40]

Despite the Cuban governor's position, administrative, financial, and military ties to Cuba and Puerto Rico made connections to Santo Domingo inevitable and constant. The Spanish consul asked for U.S. cooperation in restricting boat travel that might triangulate between Cuba, the United

States, and Santo Domingo, noting, "It is *extremely important that there be no contraband, illicit traffic, nor communication between the ports of Havana and the rebels against this Government."* There is no evidence that U.S. officials cooperated.[41] Steamship mail service, private British boats, and other vessels connected the islands. Spanish authorities wanted to build a telegraph cable between Port-au-Prince and eastern Cuba after the fighting started, without immediate result. Still, island-to-island communication proceeded regularly enough, and it had the attention of neighboring publics. Havana's *Gaceta Oficial* necessarily reported the naval blockade of Santo Domingo, for example, because it was patrolled by Cuban ships. Even as Spanish-Cuban periodicals like *El Redactor de Santiago de Cuba* sought to put the most positive possible spin on the fighting—"the roots [of the rebellion] are being destroyed in el Cibao," it reported hopefully—their point-by-point coverage of the battles themselves represented raw material for more rebellious interpretations.[42] In Guantánamo, authorities accused a Spanish merchant of holding meetings with free and enslaved people of color to read newspapers about the unfolding events in neighboring Santo Domingo. He exaggerated Spanish losses, officials accused indignantly.[43]

Soldiers and officials traveled, too. Santiago de Cuba was a key port of embarkation. Injured soldiers brought word of the fighting in person. Yellow fever massively hurt Spanish ranks, sending thousands to Cuba for treatment. Several thousand passed through eastern Cuban hospitals during the fighting, and more were sent to other sites.[44] Santiago authorities used a cannon captured from the Dominicans as a trophy of war in the atrium of the main cathedral of the town. More than fifteen hundred soldiers were present to witness its dedication on 6 June 1864, as it was paraded through the street in a military procession accompanied with fireworks. A new *danza* entitled "El Cañón" celebrated the event.[45] More Antilles-based Spanish soldiers embarked than ever before; fourteen thousand troops from the Ejército de Cuba left for Santo Domingo in the beginning of 1864. Later that year, Spanish officials both solicited volunteers from Cuba and Puerto Rico and merged the Spanish and reserve regiments. Nonmilitary Spanish officials moved back and forth between the islands, too, asking for multiple-month sojourns in their former stations of Puerto Rico and Cuba to reestablish their failing health.[46]

No neighboring official wanted to receive the Dominican deportees, whose provenance ranged from wealthy merchants to illiterate day laborers. The Puerto Rican governor wrote, not a little perturbed, that he had received a group of thirty-five men thought to be leaders of the Dominican insurrection. He immediately put them into isolation. "I have ordered them to be put in the basement of the Morro Castle, where they will be unable to communicate with the rest of the fort," he wrote anxiously.[47] Prison correspondence emanating from the lower floors of the San Juan fortress was censored carefully, for both "obscene words and [secret messages] from the gang of bandits," the governor reported.[48] These men had been arrested in a roundup in the early hours of the morning in the Dominican capital, days before. Many of them were released into Puerto Rican towns but kept under high vigilance. They were supposed to report to authorities once a day.[49] As the fighting continued, the groups of arrestees got larger. More than 150 men arrived in Vieques; hundreds passed through Havana as a way station before being sent on to the peninsula. Even when the accused did not stay in Havana, their arrival at the docks provoked commentary and gossip.[50] Among their ranks were a few Spanish men as well, such as sailor Léon Mate, sent back to Havana for his complicity in the Puerto Plata uprisings of August 1863 (the bulk of Spanish infractors, soldiers, remained within their ranks in Santo Domingo).[51] Like the Puerto Rican authorities, officials in Havana were uneasy about both the spectacle presented by and the possible communication from the insurgents. The Cuban governor suggested that deportees be sent not to the peninsula but to Ceuta.[52] Although there is no evidence that the transfer occurred on a large scale, at least a few were transferred to north Africa, and their subsequent supplication for some sort of daily support left an archival trail.[53]

Dominican families pleaded for their exiled members, and the deportees themselves entreated for mercy. From Puerto Rico, Havana, and Cádiz, petitions combined plaintive (and outraged) descriptions of the conditions of incarceration, the impossible cost of daily sustenance, and the pain of separation from their lives on the island. Some were prominent men, merchants from Puerto Plata and the like; paterfamilias supplicated for the right to return to their numerous children and grandchildren. Other prisoners were younger laborers who enlisted the help of literate men to plead their case. Juan Francisco Cuello and Domingo de Leon entreated, after five months of being locked in "tight, terrible" cells in San Juan, that they be given a chance to prove their faithfulness to Spain. They and others urged that neighbors could attest to the fidelity of their conduct. "We have never had the most remote idea against the peace and tranquility of our country . . . [and] are faithful to our Mother Country," one prisoner entreated.[54] From Cádiz, one man wrote of how he had been surprised in his home in the much-surveilled *extramuro* community of San Carlos, near the capital, precipitating a nightmarish chain of events. Escorted in shackles away from his home, into a ship, and to a cell in Havana, he was then summarily moved again, across the Atlantic. From his cell in southern Spain, he begged for clemency, some aid in the means of subsistence, and most dearly, freedom. He requested a passport "for any of the Antilles," to bring him closer to his numerous family. Authorities denied his "inopportune" request; he repeated his entreaties in subsequent months.[55] Mothers pleaded on behalf of their adult children. "It would be a grand and worthy act of Your motherly soul, to free the father of a family, today reduced to misery," one petitioned the queen pointedly.[56]

The guilt or innocence of deportees—even if loyalty were any sort of stable index in the fast-changing climes of the raging conflict—was inscrutable at best. Such was the case of Ildefonso Mella, who found himself jailed in Havana after an arrest outside of Puerto Plata. Mella had merely traveled to the eastern outskirts of the town with his daughter for fresh air, his sister and mother insisted, but damning witnesses were just as intransigent. Authorities acceded to his family's entreaties, and Mella was permitted to board a ship back to Hispaniola.[57] A number of prisoners made similarly compelling cases. One local government official wrote that his imprisonment in Cádiz was "some mistaken measure, or perhaps a victim of malintentioned persons." He explained, "The whole neighborhood can attest . . . to my constant adhesion and respect for the throne of Your Majesty." Furthermore, he had been close friends with Santana. "Your Majesty, pardon this benign old man," he concluded.[58] The Spanish were wrong about Ildefonso Mella, it turns out, and probably many others. Mella went on to be mayor of Puerto Plata long after the Spanish were gone, and his rebel loyalties proved as unshakable as his irreverence to conservative authorities in the capital city. In subsequent years, the governor of Cuba would write outraged complaints about Mayor Mella's "open sympathies for Cuban [independence] conspirators," to the defiance even of other Dominican officials.[59]

In Puerto Rico secret sites of anticolonial organizing grew. In Mayagüez, "a true *antillanista* cenacle" formed.[60] If Spanish surveillance meant that few guns could traffic through there, rebels still could. Father Fernando Antonio Meriño—a high church official, subsequently canonized as "the Father of Dominican oratory"—found himself summarily exiled to Puerto Rico for his staunch (and openly defiant) opposition of Santana. He hastily made his way to the port city, found other rebels there, and wrote to others constantly.[61] From Mayagüez on the Noche de los Muertos, he gave a dramatic sermon in the town cemetery, reporting he had seen the shadows of Hidalgo and Morelos (priests who had led anti-Spanish fighting in Mexico). Trinitario José

María de Serra lived in Mayagüez, as did Félix Delmonte, former minister of war. Delmonte was so influential in "leading political opinion astray" that he was exiled again several years later.[62] Both Delmonte and Meriño met often with Ramón Emeterio Betances, whose peripatetic activism during the years of Dominican fighting was matched only by his clandestine abolitionist and *independentista* organizing in eastern Puerto Rico itself. Betances met Luperón and José María Cabral while in exile in Saint Thomas and spent at least some of the fighting in Santo Domingo and Caracas. Moving on, he lobbied for recognition of the Provisional Government in Paris and London.[63] Much of his organizing was in secret. Years after the fighting, Dominican journalists thanked Betances "for all the generous services he privately lent the Republic in moments of the War of Restoration."[64]

Organizers in Cuba also arranged secret aid. Private boats from Cuba seem to have arrived at Samaná, instead of the commercial docks of Puerto Plata and Monte Cristi. Spanish authorities seized one such ship, carrying an inventory billed to a resident of Matanzas, for having gone off of its charter.[65] Dominican Carlos Pulien, working in Samaná's Spanish administration, was caught receiving multiple dozens of letters from Cuba that had no apparent commercial content whatsoever.[66] José Ysnaga, born in Cuba but a longtime resident in Venezuela, was "a fan of mixing himself up in political questions and a drunk," the authorities wrote, when they expelled him.[67] In New York, prominent Dominicans mingled with Cuban exiles; Cuban nationalist Juan Manuel Macías penned the 1865 pamphlet "Las Colonias Españolas y la República Dominicana" for the Sociedad Democrática de los Amigos de América, founded just the year before. The society called annexation "a bloody farce" and exulted, "No Dominican doubts the happy success in restoring free institutions."[68] Some ships sailed from New York under the rebel Dominican flag, authorized by a letter of marque from the Provisional Government. Rumors from as far as Paris linked Havana, Matanzas, New York, and Boston.[69] The Provisional Government observed and supported these covert networks. Ministers published a decree encouraging generals to purchase weapons and tighten political bonds in nearby islands.[70]

Various communities in the United States covertly organized in favor of the effort, and they connected it directly with political struggles of their own. Dominican emissary Dr. Francisco Basora made secret appeals to the Chilean mission in New York, although it is not clear if they bore fruit.[71] New York's Spanish-language newspapers began to appear in Puerto Rican ports. The authors heartily supported the Dominican rebels, Spanish authorities noted grimly.[72] Spanish authorities suspected it was Cuban exiles—and, perhaps more improbably, U.S. filibusters—who were outfitting ships in Boston. Spain seized one U.S.-registered boat with seven hundred guns, two hundred barrels of gunpowder, rice, rum, and other supplies.[73] Mostly, they speculated wildly about the amount and provenance of aid coming from the north that potentially eluded the blockade dragnet. The Spanish consul in Washington, DC, even suspected that unnamed allies were preparing a boat in Halifax, Nova Scotia.[74] Boston's vice-consul had slightly more specific information—even the names of two British and two American ships—but no one could easily intercept the boats: they were directed to Cap-Haïtien.[75] American citizens in Dominican territory tried to lobby for U.S. opposition, but to no avail.[76] English-language papers covered the conflict regularly. It was Puerto Rican and Cuban activists and exiles, however, who had immediate plans.

When Spain called for military volunteers from both islands in 1864, anti-Spanish sentiments in Puerto Rico flared. "A *Regiment of Volunteers* has been forcibly taken to assassinate their brothers in Santo Domingo," Betances decried in a pamphlet. "*Let us not be their instruments; and if they take us by force, as has been the case with others, let us go to the lines of our brothers of Santo Domingo,*" he urged. Betances invoked an indigenous history of anti-Spanish resistance. "*The jíbaros of Puerto Rico, sons de Agüeibana el Bravo, have not lost our pride,*" he wrote, "and [we] know how to prove to our tyrants, as the brave *Dominicans* are doing, that we . . . will not suffer abuse with impunity."[77] He claimed that some Puerto Rican volunteers were deserting in Dominican territory. "Some of them have dispersed and gone into hiding in the *montes*," he described, "and some have even hung themselves before agreeing to go to kill and rob our brothers." Furthermore, Dominicans were receiving these Puerto Rican deserter allies "with open arms and shower[ing them] with blessings," he claimed. Another pamphlet from 1864—the grammar and syntax of which suggest a different author who was not Betances—also called for immediate action in Puerto Rico:

> Let us not sleep: the occasion is magnificent: there are no SOLDIERS on the island, and even if there were the war of SANTO DOMINGO should have shown us that one Gíbaro with a machete in his hand is worth one hundred SPANIARDS. RISE, PUERTO RICANS!
>
> . . . our cry of INDEPENDENCE will be heard and supported by friends of LIBERTY; and there will be no lack of aid in arms and weapons to drown in the dust the DESPOTS OF CUBA, PUERTO RICO, AND SANTO DOMINGO![78]

May the Devil Take Me If I See Resolution to This

As 1865 dawned, Dominicans challenged Spanish authority everywhere. Even with the basic necessities of daily life lacking, citizens became confident that victory was near. Caricatures circulated freely, and the Provisional Government celebrated the festivities of 27 February, albeit with a ban on costumes.[79] Where the Spanish remained, tension was constant. One loyal reserves captain, drinking until dawn in the Azua encampment, suddenly turned on his superior officer at some unknown provocation, calling him and the rest of the Spanish officers present "unos pendejos."[80] A civilian man named Marcos allegedly lashed out at a Spanish soldier, also while drunk, brandishing a knife and proclaiming that "all Spaniards are robbers, pigs, traitors, and that the [*guerrillas*] were with him." "He said the Spanish were all cunning and that all they knew how to do was steal," another Spanish witness confirmed.[81] Thirty-three-year-old music professor Sebastian Morcelo admitted responding "Dominicano libre!" to a watchman's call of "Who's there?" "I meant to say Spain," he deadpanned. His brother called after him as he was being arrested, "Don't worry! There are plenty of us to save you!" The commission condemned Morcelo, who was not armed, to serve one month in jail for a simple "lack of judgment."[82] Others shared his conviction. Socorro Sánchez—a single, twenty-six-year-old, literate businesswoman in the capital—sent a letter in the care of a young bread seller to San Cristóbal seeking provisions. The content of her letter was not revolutionary, but it was irreverent in its assurance. "You [should] help me, even if it is just for the good friendship you had with your *compadre* Francisco Sánchez," she wrote. "I am his sister, and I live with his widow, we work together," she explained, "Given that the war will very soon be over, send me good sugar . . . wax, dried cowhide, and tobacco leaves." She appealed to a male cousin as well. For the communiqués, she spent late spring and early summer of 1865 in jail, as did her young messenger.[83]

Meanwhile, Spanish soldiers suffered greatly from a lack of supplies and illness. Without bread or salt, many of the Spanish troops on campaign subsisted on chunks of meat.[84] "The Spanish soldiers could be seen wandering around like squalid ghosts, supporting themselves with walking sticks and moving laboriously," a Spanish commander reflected. Where men could be dispatched to sleep, comforts were exceedingly few. Even in occupied towns, soldiers "are mostly lodged in huts in horrible condition, at grave risk to the health of the soldier and the discipline of the corps," the governor complained, but no funding for new barracks was forthcoming.[85] Endless fall rains in late 1864 dampened spirits and supplies. The treasury official asked for thousands of pesos to fix roads around the capital, where rain and heavy transit had made the roads nearly impossible, even for individuals; word arrived three months later that his request was denied until the colony's status was clear.[86] Overland, the marching was "excruciating," the governor related to the peninsula. "The rough roads, or rather paths, of this island have no resources of any kind, [troops] having to cross rivers with water up to one's waist," he continued.[87] The Dominican reservists were perhaps even more poorly provisioned. "They marched mostly barefoot, with their pants rolled up to their knees," one Spanish general wrote in his memoirs, and "others were so sick it made the camp look like a hospital."[88]

Unluckily for those who might have found themselves in serious need of medical attention, the makeshift hospitals were no place to recuperate. Hospitals were most often "nothing more than a barrack hut made from tree branches and sticks, under which refuge the sick rested, laid out on the ground," a Spanish commander observed.[89] Sickness compounded the misery. Yellow fever fatalities were high even in the summer before the fighting.[90] A mystery illness flooded hospitals in the fall of 1863; although it was mild, the governor estimated he had better send some of the sick soldiers to Cuba for treatment.[91] The U.S. agent observed that poor drainage in the capital city made it "at times a perfect graveyard."[92] The cleanliness of smaller towns would have brought little comfort to soldiers laboring and injured there; it was in the interior that scarcity was the worst. Medicine was hard to come by and expensive; improvised hospitals lacked staff, even sheets to cover the improvised bedding. "Hospital is a magic and terrible word that the soldiers instinctively reject," one report summarized, "One can well imagine the morale of the average soldier . . . , especially those recently arrived from Spain, a country with [modern supplies] . . . a disconsolate portrait. . . . Overcome with pain, they can only announce their impending end, mouthing constantly, 'I'm dying.' "[93] Typhoid fever "ran through all the housing and left barely a soldier useful" in Samaná; the hospital had burned, but staff were without the means to bleach instruments for use again, authorities remarked gravely. An anonymous complaint from a soldier protested that most in the military hospital did not have nearly enough to eat.[94] Only in larger towns did some Spanish troops receive limited aid from charitable loyal Dominicans, "without which they would have perished in the hospital," one soldier reported.[95] Others could not have been so lucky.

More Spanish troops deserted, even though soldiers faced harsh punishment. Desertion during wartime carried the threat of shooting by firing squad. One young Spanish soldier from Cartagena (serving in the Regimento de la Habana), absent for a month, pleaded that he had only left to find food, that he had been reduced to sleeping in abandoned huts, and that his consorting with Dominicans had been only out of necessity. Officials evidently took pity on the man, but he faced a decade in prison.[96] Those who had formerly been stationed in Cuba and Puerto Rico fled the most.[97] The Second Cuban Crown Regiment was not to be separated from the First Crown Regiment, the governor wrote, and they should be sent back to Cuba for reasons of discipline.[98] According to rebel pamphlets, Cuban and Puerto Rican volunteer regiments deserted at an astronomical rate.[99] Officials proposed that 1845-era Cuban penalties be brought against deserters. In Monte Cristi, the military commission surveyed the troops, asking them if they had witnessed others expressing great dissatisfaction with service, speaking with or being friends with the "enemy," facing punishment, or simply pining for their families.[100] Everything dampened morale. Occasionally, a deserter sent back an infuriating letter to his fellow soldiers, sometimes anonymously, sometimes directly. One deserter, who asserted, "The Captain knows my name very well," wrote, "A few months ago I was in your ranks, submitted to Buceta's despotism in Samaná. . . . Dominicans are just and virtuous. Everything I say to you is true, and I say it with my hand over my heart. [The Dominicans] don't need us; they have enough people, they are just trying to save us from torment. Countrymen, flee those proud and unnatural Commanders who are just trying to reduce us to ashes." He called select Dominican loyalists "scum."[101] Editors at the *Boletín Oficial* gleefully republished a letter from another Spanish soldier, insults and all:

> I am taking advantage of the short break we have to write and give you news of this famous campaign, which is nothing like the one we did in Morocco. Well, this mess is capable of irritating even a saint. One minute we go there, the next we come back. . . . May the Devil take me if I see the resolution to this. These damn *indios* are always out of sight; as soon as you see them one place they disappear, and just when we think they're defeated, they show up shooting. . . . And they're not bad shots. In fact it appears that the damn [people] have spent their whole life hunting, well when they aim, Jesus, the only thing one can do is cross oneself. . . . And that with not all of them armed. . . . What will happen, then, the day that these cunning devils get good precision weapons? . . . When will we be able to pacify such a vast country, cut off on all sides by mountains and narrow paths; populated by a damn riffraff [*canalla*] who live

just as easily in the *montes* as in a palace; who know the territory like you know your bedroom, while we cannot completely trust any who present themselves as friends. . . . And that would be nothing, if we had better superior officers, what cowards! What rogues! They are soldiers for a theater.[102]

Another soldier was even more succinct in his frustration:

> Me c . . . , c . . . , en Colón,
> en Cortés y el los Pizarros . . .
> en los Estados Unidos
> y en el seno Mexicano . . .
> por uno y otros oceanos.[103]
>
> [I s—, s— on Columbus,
> on Cortés and on the Pizarros . . .
> on the United States
> and the interior of Mexico . . .
> on this ocean and that one.]

By the spring of 1865, many troops must have felt aimless. In the capital, "some individuals who claimed to be officers of the King's Regiment" drunkenly broke down the doors of a number of single women's residences, to the chastisement of authorities the next day. Four women brought a collective case against them, and they won.[104]

The Last Days of Spanish Rule

Facing the rebellion, Madrid authorities issued policy changes month by month. In the spring of 1864, the Crown had demanded victory at any price, and de la Gándara himself hoped for thirty thousand more troops. By fall, both the queen and the general had become convinced of the futility of the fighting. Madrid authorities authorized evacuation from all of Seybo and froze any new embarkation of troops. De la Gándara was relieved at the new orders, which permitted an orderly Spanish retreat. "It frees us from expenses and embarrassment, and saves the sad remains of our most virtuous Division from complete ruin, now resting in the relatively healthy districts of Azua and Baní," he confessed.[105] All the while, however, some in Madrid forcefully argued for the continued strategic and economic value of the colony.[106] "The island of Santo Domingo is ours . . . has been ever since it opened its eyes to civilization," argued one author. He characterized the rebellion as "a handful of bandits followed by some thousands of a strange race," and concluded more decisive military action would save the endeavor. "Colonization demands great sacrifices," he insisted.[107] Manuel Buceta—perhaps the most hated military figure of the Cibao—also argued for continuing the hostilities.[108] The conservative, inveterate racist Marques de Lema gave an impassioned speech to the Senate that was quickly reprinted in pamphlet form. Point by point, he attempted to refute the pro-abandonment arguments about Dominican fidelity, cost, and futility. Nearly 40 million pesos had been spent decorating the Puerta del Sol in Madrid; "a small amount of this" could have pacified Santo Domingo, he claimed. Without sufficient resources to suffocate "*the African insurrection,*" Spain's honor had been compromised, he argued.[109] News of these debates reached President Geffrard even before the Spanish governor in Dominican soil; some suspected, probably correctly, that he rushed the news of Spanish division to the Dominican side.[110] As of 19 January, the decision to abandon Santo Domingo was irrevocable.

In a final review for the Crown of the social and political conflicts of annexation, Spain's ministers did not shy away from frank discussion of Spanish racism and slavery. "Since emancipation, Santo Domingo has held as an unbreakable canon the most complete equality not only of race and condition but also social, civil and political order," the ministers remarked. "So the *negro* and the *moreno* put on the sash of General, dress in the most distinguished uniform, flaunt the most prized insignia and decoration, and take part in the governance and administration of the island," they continued, "while the wretched of their race groan in servitude in the other Antilles, fourteen and sixteen *leguas* away." They were sober in their assessment of the impact of the failure of the project on Cuba and Puerto Rico: "The slaves of Cuba and Puerto Rico must see day in and day out their brothers in so different a condition; can it be believed for one second that this spectacle, this living provocation, would not produce dismal results in our other Antilles?" They repeated the islands' proximity again and again. "An Antille fourteen and sixteen leguas distant from the others could not govern itself with a different regimen from the others, and they in turn could not use the one Santo Domingo desired, without grave danger to their respective interests; the problem was unsolvable," they concluded finally.[111] There was nothing left to do other than to admit failure.

The ministers' withdrawal recommendation of January 1865 and the Dominican diplomatic response were emphatically principled and calm. The reincorporation had been an "act of laudable patriotism," the Spanish ministers asserted, and so its end ought "to reflect the intentions that brought it about." With measured tone, they recapped an unwavering official narrative of the project's brief trajectory: peninsular authorities had seen potential annexation as onerous, even as they sought to tighten ties with Spanish America; they accepted annexation only as a benevolent measure, and contingent on Dominican consent "not as a breach of rights, but as part of their politics," spontaneous and voluntary. Once undertaken, the project had failed because politically, socially, and religiously, the former republic was too different from the neighboring Spanish projects. What remained was an extraordinarily costly project of conquest and military occupation, "not a case of quelling a rebellion but of conquering a territory." As such, continued occupation would be fruitless and costly. Spain had spent 13.5 million pesos in four years, more than 70 percent of that from Cuba's coffers, about 10 percent from Puerto Rico, and the remaining 20 percent from the peninsula. "So much blood spilled and so much treasury wasted," the letter lamented. The next step, the ministers concluded, ought to be withdrawal.[112] Dominican emissaries, for their part, were relentlessly civil. Peace will be achieved "as Spain is an educated nation, [and] Santo Domingo is an extremely generous pueblo," one official offered.[113] "Think, Queen, where there were flourishing cities, now there are just piles of ruins and ashes," another wrote. He described a bloody scene and an exhausted people. "Blood has been running this way and that for sixteen months . . . the blood of a pueblo rudely treated, resigned to all types of sacrifices, resolved to bury itself under the mounting ruins and ashes around them," he observed gravely, "before ceasing to be free and independent." Despite the "homicidal drama," however, he insisted that there was no rancor, concluding, "Between this people and the Spanish nation, there can exist neither animosity nor hate . . . there is no fault on either side."[114]

For an awkward interim, Spanish officials in Dominican territory attempted to continue quotidian governance, with limited success. Prominent officials left steadily; the archbishop found wartime not at all to his liking, requesting evacuation as early as fall 1863.[115] Azua, still under Spanish control, had burned, but there were just sixty-five pesos in the treasury to resume affairs.[116] The government of the eastern province of Seybo retreated to the capital in February, four months after Madrid first authorized it. The evacuating officials managed to bring with them the court paperwork but not the prisoners. "Given the absolute lack of a secure jail, and the absolute lack of resources, [the prisoners] went around the City procuring their sustenance, some were armed and added to the provincial reserves," a report confessed. It continued, "At the moment of retreat there was neither the time nor the means to gather them up and bring them along." Once in the capital, the officials tried to continue with judicial paperwork, borrowing the *escribano* from La Vega, but lawyers were also lacking.[117] Also in the capital, the *Gaceta de Santo Domingo* was eerily silent on the conflict. The paper, which stuck to official announcements and was always less garrulous than its polemic counterpart, *La Razón*, barely mentioned the fighting at all in the early months of 1865, except to note honors given to some, and the freeing of Spanish and reservists from the Dominican camp in April.[118] It remained doggedly on message about projects of industry, however. In January, the paper began a multipart series on tobacco; later that month, the back page ran an ad for reprints of the famous Dominican developmentalist text *La idea de valor en Santo Domingo* (never mind that it had called for more slave importation as a central tenet).[119] The capital city administration was totally paralyzed by late spring. The governor reported a number of the government's scribes had passed to the rebels.[120] More and more prisoners and exiles were permitted to return. One man asking to return was a high-ranking general in the Dominican army, "or so he calls himself," Cádiz officials noted. A royal order from 10 April 1865 decreed that "he, like everyone," could return to the island.[121]

Evacuation preparations proceeded fairly smoothly. Prisoner exchanges were general and inclusive. Many Spanish prisoners of war were finally freed in late spring, some after a captivity of nearly two years.[122] President Geffrard continued to mediate, urging compassionate treatment of the Dominican reservists who had left Spanish ranks for reasons of necessity. They should be allowed to return to Spanish service if they so desired, he lobbied kindly.[123] The evacuation order promised "help and support" for Provincial Reserves "who had loyally and bravely supported [the Spanish] cause," but decommissioning loomed.[124] Spanish officials in the capital began ordering the recall of weapons from individuals in the Provincial Reserves in mid-May, although, true to his word, General de la Gándara oversaw the payment of Azua and Baní reservists to the very day of departure.[125] Dominican women came under intense scrutiny as Spanish officials perceived the discipline of their troops faltering further. Authorities blamed Dominican women who were "the enemies of Spain" for using "seduction" to "demoralize" the troops. Twenty-three soldiers had disappeared just from the town square of the capital in January and early February alone; women, particularly those living near the quarters, were the primary witnesses called to trial, and several found themselves in jail.[126] One woman in Azua, Petronila Núñez, was very nearly executed for her perceived influence in causing a soldier to desert. An Azua man, Honorio de los Santos, received no such pardon. "I cannot hide that it affects me greatly such severe punishments . . . but I must repress it with all the rigor of the law," the governor wrote.[127] The *Gaceta Oficial* announced De los Santos's execution in the capital.[128] Displaced Dominicans, meanwhile, asked the administration for help. Josefa Roman, an émigrée from Puerto Plata, wrote to the governor on behalf of one Guillermo Vives, former administrator of customs, also living in the capital. The ostensibly formerly wealthy man "has lost all of his goods . . . is indigent," Roman entreated for her colleague. His and many other indemnity petitions likely went unfilled, lost in the spiraling costs and chaos of conflict and the juridical limbo of slow steps made to evacuate.[129]

A small civilian diaspora left for Puerto Rico and Cuba. Some, like Juan Caballero from Cádiz, decided to move to Port-au-Prince permanently during the fighting.[130] A number of Spanish colonists, especially widows, applied for return passage to Spain. Many others requested transfer to Cuba and Puerto Rico. Some took big families, leaving immediately.[131] Among the applicants, one evacuee to Puerto Rico made a remarkable claim on the Spanish state: her freedom. In her own petition, Victoria Medina, born in Aguadilla, described how she had arrived in Santo Domingo and been kept covertly enslaved to a man named Nicolas Danbon. In her own hand, Medina described the details of her case. By May 1865, Danbon had left the capital, Medina explained, and she wanted to secure proof of her free status. Medina petitioned for a *carta de libertad*, so that she could return to Aguadilla with her family. Spanish authorities ruled her petition null, but they also acknowledged her freedom. They concluded "extraofficially" that Danbon had already granted Medina's freedom in the neighboring island, and secondly, as she was also asserting, "the mere fact of coming to [Santo Domingo] made her cease to be a slave."[132]

Departing authorities debated about Dominican émigrés. In early spring de la Gándara described the "delicate and grave question" of émigrés of color. He planned to encourage most officials and their families to settle in Curaçao and Saint Thomas. "I will inspire them with confidence in the good faith of the Government, that they will be paid their pensions regularly through the consuls, and persuading them of the benefit of living where their race is more respected, and from where they can most easily return to Santo Domingo," he wrote to the neighboring governors. "Those islands must remain *incomunicado* with Cuba and Puerto Rico," he warned.

If it proved too impolitic to order the nonwhite officials to these locations—"the white families can choose their destination," he asserted—and they chose Cuba, the general recommended they be directed to eastern areas like Baracoa, where some recent colonization projects had occurred.[133] Several months later, his restrictions for Cuba tightened further. In a private communication to a commander in Baní, he advised that loyalist Dominican colonial officials seeking reassignment outside of the island should be steered by color: to Cuba, only white Dominicans, "and even then, one must be circumspect whom will be permitted"; men of color were to be ushered to Puerto Rico, Curaçao, Saint Thomas, the Canaries, the Balearic islands (off the coast of Cataluña), Spanish outposts in Africa and Asia, or the peninsula itself, he ordered.[134] The Cuban governor did not want to receive anyone at all. He wanted the ministry to send all Dominicans to the Canary Islands, Africa, or the Philippines.[135]

When it was time to load the ships in early June, evacuation proceedings were orderly and without incident. Most troops embarked from San José de Ocoa (Maniel), Azua, and Baní. About thirty-three hundred tons of goods and supplies, seven thousand large packages (bultos), needed evacuation from the capital alone; four more ships' worth of cargo, or almost the same amount, awaited on the northern coast.[136] Some loyalist Dominicans requested transfer to Cuba well before fighting ended, even though they had never served in the Spanish state at all. Such was the case of wealthy Ramón Paredes, who wrote that he had not served militarily as he "had never been inclined to military life." His loyalty to Spain had cost him his bakery, his house, his brother, and several nieces, "just for the fact that he had always been satisfied with [Spanish] good government," he wrote sorrowfully.[137] A number of women expressed a desire to follow the Spanish troops to Cuba as well.[138] Before evacuations had even become widespread, some sneaked onto supply ships as stowaways; a few were caught "by chance," but a number of others probably escaped.[139] Of the poor people from southern towns who attempted to follow the soldiers, even to the point of trying to board the ships, de la Gándara was less empathetic. "I gave orders that absolutely prohibit the embarking of any person of that class," he observed.[140] Already in Cuba, the departed governor expressed real affection and sentiment for the reservist troops he had left behind in Azua and Baní, three days earlier. Worried about reprisals, the general took the unusual step of leaving them arms, confident that the queen would also accede to the "sincere recognition of . . . their worthiness and distinction."[141] A popular rhyme was more sardonic about their fate:

Se fueron los españoles,
¡cosa buena nunca dura!
Y quedaron los azuanos
Recogiendo la basura.[142]

[The Spanish left
¡nothing good ever lasts!
And the Azuans stayed behind
Picking up the trash.]

Santiago Was . . . Nothing Remains Anymore

Everywhere, there was devastation. Fighting "floods the city with blood and swells the land with cadavers," a newspaper lamented, in the fall after the Spanish left.[143] The injured, widowed, and homeless numbered in the thousands. In towns across the territory, bad news broke excruciatingly slowly. Some prisoners never made the return trip from Jerez to Santo Domingo, as widows like María de Jésus Gantreau sorrowfully learned. Her husband had died in custody nearly seven months earlier.[144] Elsewhere, the toll of fire alone was incredible: in the south, little but the capital was safe. Azua burned in 1863 (along with Baní).[145] Azua had burned again in early 1865, reducing seventy houses to ashes, "among them the most prominent of the population," an official observed. For residents not involved in the fighting, it amounted to a "terrible accident. . . . Azua has always shown unequivocal proof of her unwavering faithfulness," de la Gándara had written empathetically at the time.[146] Each new sweep through the towns had brought pillaging, too, as rebels gathered both supplies and personal goods.[147] San Cristóbal passed back and forth between rebel and Spanish control, suffering the ravages of fighting on multiple occasions. Life in the Cibao, the source of nearly 65 percent of the country's exports, had been totally upended. Tobacco fields were fallow, towns burned nearly to ashes, countless were homeless, and even more were wounded. A Spanish observer described the approaching flames as Santiago burned for the first time as a "whirlwind of fire," visible from a great distance in "the rich and populous capital." The man described "a horrible bonfire . . . [that] was devouring almost its entirety." The first fire to rip through Puerto Plata had lasted three whole days; it had been "an implacable war of blood and fire," an aghast witness recorded.[148] In Samaná, schools, churches, and missionary houses had burned.[149] "Santiago was . . . nothing remains anymore," mourned Rodríguez Objío of the ashes of his city in November 1864.[150] "Light ashes cover all of the homes where opulence lived; and an occasional breeze . . . mocks the mundane insanity," he marveled, in horror.

Javier Ángulo Guridi grappled with the devastation in his 1866 novel, *La campana del higo*, ostensibly set on the eve of another independence, the year 1842. An earthquake had devastated the landscape of the Cibao. Guridi described an apocalyptic rural landscape, "an indescribable scene in which nature seems to lose its equilibrium and threatens to commit massive homicide . . . even the survivors cannot cry enough tears to commiserate the absolute ruin."[151] The people, in their sober virtue, tried to show "they were all a family, not even arguing, not even a complaint or gripe among any of their infinite members," he wrote. Celestial instability had made them fearful, he explained, and they sought to avoid anything that might "cast a shadow on the tranquil sky."[152] *Higo* tells no happy tale; it is a vengeance tragedy, in which an innocent daughter, Florinda, has been assaulted. Her father becomes so obsessed with revenge that he cannot cultivate his field. "You are still not satisfied!" he cries wildly at his unseen enemy. "The hyena comes back after devouring its victim, to drink the very last drop of blood spilled on the field!"[153] The text ends with Florinda's real paramour in exile, "far from his family and his *patria*." He longs to return to Dominican soil, a "country as unhappy as it was worthy of a better fate."[154]

Slowly, however, life began again. A man in the capital city christened his new barbershop The Hills (La Manigua), in proud reference to *manigüeros*, the rural fighters. He promised that the youth of the capital would find "complete satisfaction" in his services.[155] On the streets of Puerto Plata, one man spotted his old burro, lost during the fighting, and he took it back.[156] Nearly six months after the last Spanish soldier embarked, townspeople were finally starting to return home. "We welcome back all our lost brothers," a journalist observed, softly.[157] Others started a new life away from the island. Máximo Gómez left in anonymity. Born in Baní, he was one of the loyal Dominican reservists whom Spanish authorities scattered throughout rural eastern Cuba after evacuating from Dominican soil. When independence and antislavery fighting began in Cuba in 1868, however, Gómez resolved to fight for liberation. He captured Venta del Pino in just two weeks. Another Dominican man helped free Bayamo.[158] "Everything I did in Cuba, as a fervent and humble soldier of liberty," Gómez later wrote, "I did it in the name of the Dominican people, whose eyes were fixed on me."[159]

Epilogue
BETWEEN FEAR AND HOPE

In a lucid editorial, published in the fall after the last Spanish soldier left, a writer for the Puerto Plata newspaper La Regeneración proposed a lofty plan to unite Haiti and the Dominican Republic, "born and rooted in the same soil." He called for the tightest relationship between the two republics since the Boyer administration. "Independence and freedom for both peoples are irrevocable," he wrote, discussing a new military alliance. "God has separated son from father, brother from brother, pueblo from other pueblo. But . . . can we not form an offensive and defensive alliance to conserve the integrity of our common territory, to avoid what just happened to us?" The alliance would bring security, he argued, observing, "The foreign [power] would not be able to tell which hand struck it." He suggested that the political federation include a pragmatic economic element of trade and barter for mutual benefit, "generous commerce treaties" of free trade within the island for a variety of products. Finally, the collaboration should extend to deepened diplomatic relationships and, most radically, to dual citizenship. "Can we not make the ties that must unite us tighter," he argued, "to declare that those born in the territory of the island be citizens of both independent states?" Peace, profit, and external security would result, he promised. "Let us love each other as brothers," he urged. "We will wave one flag with these words: Union, fraternity . . ." Working together, he concluded, "[we can] build between us an epoch in which man is truly a brother to fellow man."[1]

In towns throughout the territory, idealists emerging from the Restoration struggle supported a range of ambitious political reforms. They echoed wish lists from previous decades: rule of law, reduction and regularization of the army, amortization of paper money, and responsible national credit.² As an antidote both to the authoritarian political culture of previous regimes and the recent violence, abrogation of the death penalty was an easy target.³ Authors of the November 1865 Constitution, drafted in Moca, aimed for all these objectives. In addition to three branches of central government, the constitution recognized municipal power, represented by local delegates throughout the territory. Perhaps its most radical clause—one that would last through numerous constitutional changes, all the way until 2004—was the provision of jus soli, or birthright, citizenship. The jus soli provision represented part of an ambitious redefinition of the nation. Anticipating political rivalry, reformers proposed a single-party system. "The Republic is starting *a new life* and needs to be regenerated by *new ideas* that *new men* determine," one writer eagerly urged. "We dream together."⁴

Dominican anticolonial activists threw themselves into regional organizing, in familiar foreign ports and on Dominican soil. Puerto Plata emerged as a strategic and ideological center. Freemasons returned to organizing openly within months of the end of the fighting; "meeting again with frequency and enthusiasm," they founded a lodge with a singularly ambitious title: the Cradle of América.⁵ Much closer than New York for Cuban and Puerto Rican activists, Puerto Plata was also out of reach of the Dominican capital. Enthusiastic Cuban émigrés arrived in the town in such numbers that its population almost tripled in size.⁶ After independence fighting began in Cuba, Puerto Platan journalists openly ridiculed the idea of neutrality and called on the Dominican state to protect anti-Spanish revolutionaries from Cuba, in the interests of a sovereign Caribbean.⁷ The town was full of inveterate anticolonial activists, who spoke of Caribbean unity in affective and military vocabulary equally.⁸ The opening lines of a *Regeneración* editorial offered solidarity and optimism, "When oppressed peoples throw off the heavy and disgusting hand of despotism and awake from their lethargy . . . they discover in the distant horizon the outline of these fiery letters: *we are all brothers, made by the Almighty, from the same mass, from a soul made in his image: we are to love and help each other mutually, live united at all times, and we will be strong, we will be free, and we will be happy.*" Revolution was a "new existence . . . working between fear and hope," the writer began.⁹

Meanwhile, Spanish authority was collapsing. In an effort to mediate the rising *independentista* sentiment in the wake of their embarrassing defeat, Madrid authorities enacted stopgap measures—the promise of greater representation in both islands, the return of the whip in Puerto Rico—with little success.¹⁰ Island elites called for identical rights as Spaniards, but they also wanted more autonomy, not greater integration.¹¹ Abolitionist lobbying grew stronger, too. "We reformists . . . want *a single and identical Spain* on both sides of the ocean without dictators, without monopolies, and without slaves," the leader of Spanish Abolitionist Society announced in 1865.[12] From New York, the Revolutionary Puerto Rican Committee called on Puerto Ricans to follow the Dominican example immediately.[13] "Everything that has happened in [Santo Domingo], and the reasons for which it has happened, are identical to what produced rebellion in the rest of Hispanic America, and the same that might, not too long from now, cause uprising in Cuba and Puerto Rico," an observer had predicted during the fighting.[14] He was right. Just more than three years after the last troops retreated in defeat from Santo Domingo's southern coast, rebellions flared in both neighboring islands. In the interior town of Lares, far from the locus of Dominican activism in Puerto Rico's western towns, rebels raised a flag for abolition and independence modeled precisely on Dominican colors. Troops managed to crush the mobilization, but authorities conceded a path to gradual abolition at last.[15] Cuba exploded into a decade of war. Dominicans were everywhere in Cuba's rebel ranks; a few were loyalists, too.[16] Authorities invoked the specter of race war endlessly, and wealthy citizens warned each other about "the fate of Haiti and Santo Domingo."[17] French occupation in Mexico collapsed, as rebels there exulted in their own revolutionary republicanism.[18] Spanish liberals and military figures fought with, and against, each other. The queen fled the country. Everywhere there was ferment.

Following the Restoration fighting, however, old hierarchical political networks returned to the devastated landscape like a flood. In the ashes of Santiago, the Cibao-based government did not last six months. First, southern politicians challenged it, and then, after a series of intrigues, Buenaventura Báez returned. His clique relied on armed supporters, an exhausted country, and a ritual of legitimation in the capital city press. Allies at *El Monitor* announced his return gingerly; he was returning, but not as president, they claimed. As his networks solidified, editors published statements from towns across the territory with prominent citizens announcing their fidelity to the returning figure.[19] Generals signed: former president Pimentel, who had unseated Polanco's radical administration, wealthy rancher General Santiago Rodríguez, a Restoration hero, and others like him. Revolutionary words lost their meaning. Redubbed "Great Citizen," Báez assumed power as a man without rival.[20] Isolated protests occurred in towns across the country, but armed partisans of Báez praised him as the "Angel of Peace."[21] Military authority grew to be more predominant than ever—even those who had served the Spanish invoked their rank and prestige—but these networks

Fig. E.1 The Flag of Lares, modeled after the Dominican flag, first flew in October 1868. Calle Sol, San Juan, Puerto Rico. Photo by Tito Román Rivera, December 2015.

were intensely regional and fractured. Soldiers had local loyalties, and high-ranking officers made a multitude of claims.[22] "Those who were decorated with the rich crosses of Carlos III, Isabel 2 . . . ; today are called citizens instead of Sirs," one journalist observed with disgust.[23]

Social contests surrounding the island were intense. Colombian politicians explicitly attacked emancipation, and they moved to restrict suffrage.[24] In the wake of protests in the fall of 1865, known by authorities as the Morant Bay Rebellion, the Jamaican governor's forces killed, arrested, and burned homes indiscriminately. Then, in measures precisely opposite to policy in Canada and Australia, legislators dismantled Jamaica's self-rule. In Barbados, some felt that real freedom might be "put off for another time," or perhaps across the Atlantic, and a small number of Barbadians and others chose to migrate to Liberia.[25] Some left the island to indenture projects elsewhere, as intra-Caribbean migration increased.[26] As fighting began in Cuba's Oriente, exiles desperately made their way to Jamaica and Haiti to regroup.[27] On Hispaniola, the same colonial diplomats stuck around, deleteriously, immune to metropolitan political transitions. They maintained the same enduring hostility toward the island's residents that they always had.[28] Britain bombarded Cap-Haïtien in 1865. European financiers offered loans on equally interventionist terms. Their competitors were back, and stronger than ever: U.S. politicians emerged from Civil War disunion with their eyes trained, once more, on the Caribbean. As the importance of naval steam power became increasingly clear, they joined other powers that hoped for coercive territorial cessions of strategic ports and peninsulas.[29]

Aggressive foreign interest loomed over the Dominican Republic again. "The country suffers a terrible monetary crisis," a journalist observed with foreboding. Eagerly awaiting collaborators, foreign industrialists and merchant houses stood at the ready to make deals with unscrupulous heads of state.[30] "Country sellers [*vendepatrias*] still want to have their way with this people," critics remarked, in alarm.[31] In 1869, Báez very nearly managed to annex the Dominican Republic to the United States, galvanizing a new round of radical anticolonial activism on the island and in diaspora. His financial imperatives were clear: customs, coal mines, state lands, even the guano deposits offshore had been mortgaged, paper money printed and devalued multiple times.[32] Báez enjoyed support from prominent collaborators, many of whom had opposed Spanish annexation only years before.[33] The old annexationist arguments of *hispanismo* and anti-Haitianism could not serve him; his own collaboration with the incumbent Haitian president, Sylvain Salnave, was simply too close. Only political ambition and economic imperatives remained. Although the annexation measure fell well short of the two-thirds majority it needed in the U.S. Senate, Báez's opponents, and the public, were incensed and fearful.

Unlike in previous decades, however, Báez's most radical opponents were already armed, and they mobilized new alliances quickly. For the next six years, the Dominican Republic faced almost constant political unrest.[34] The U.S. threat reinvigorated activism for a defensive Caribbean alliance, and it threw prominent opponents into unrelenting military campaigns. Luperón and his allies hoped for a federation of the four states across the three islands: Cuba, Haiti, the Dominican Republic, and Puerto Rico.[35] His close friend Manuel Rodríguez Objío traveled to New York to help organize supplies; Betances joined him there, with ambitious proposals of his own. Betances saw the embattled republic at the center of an ambitious plan of "Antillean Nationality" and hoped for a Caribbean parliament with its seat in Santo Domingo. From Haiti, where he took up residence, he urged collaboration, and he met with the British prime minister and others to rally support.[36] Luperón remained in constant motion back and forth from Saint Thomas, Grand Turk, Jamaica, and the northern coast, allied with a leader of liberal political opposition in Haiti, Jean-Nicolas Nissage-Saget, to seek the simultaneous ouster of both of the island's presidents. Nissage-Saget—like Luperón himself, "profoundly anti-yankee"—authorized Luperón to impress Haitian soldiers into his anti-imperial efforts and allowed him to organize freely along the border. They fought relentlessly against the cession of coaling stations on both sides of the island.[37] "The whole republic is in a state of insurrection," observers wrote in concern.[38]

Given the unrelenting imperial climate—foreign sugar capitalists arrived within the decade—these actors' consistent, unrelenting anticolonialism was simultaneously a radical and stable philosophy. Their opposition to large-scale outside intervention, furthermore, reflected the sentiment of most of the island's residents. The interests of cottage industry producers coincided with these activists' steadfast aversion to aggressive foreign capital. "Each Dominican is a soldier and a hero," one antiannexationist wrote hopefully.[39] As citizens returned to their homes, many disappeared, once again, from historical record. Others remained mobilized, in the highlands of the Baoruco mountains, in the Cibao valley, and other sites, to fight in united bands opposing U.S. annexation.[40] From Grand Turk, a journalist marveled at the scene in Puerto Plata. "'Liberty' and 'we have beaten the whites,' these words are heard day and night," he wrote. "They despise all governments and consider themselves eminently powerful to whip them all."[41] Despite limited means, ordinary citizens offered revolutionary solidarity. Officials and town residents sent a vessel to neighbors in Grand Turk, after a hurricane, offering a ship full of aid, proposing tariff reductions, and sending well-wishes to "fellow beings in distress and want."[42] "Dominicans and Haitians, we are all brothers, brothers in origin, brothers in the days of trial," a rebel official in southern Haiti effused.[43]

Domestically, rebel efforts stood on shifting sand. Regional military loyalties, political patronage, and economic necessity frustrated stability in the capital. Each administration hoped for "a small loan, from a trusted lender," but inflation and terms were desperately unfavorable.[44] Political opponents considered armed mobilizations the only recourse. Rodríguez Objío, indefatigable friend and ally of other Restoration fighters, and poet, biographer, and historian of the Restoration fight, lost his life opposing Báez's annexation plan. Domingo Ramírez, the general who had bedeviled Santana with his reunification schemes, never returned to Dominican soil. He lived the rest of his days in Haiti, receiving and welcoming fellow travelers but never returning to another battle.[45] Years of political turmoil weighed on politicians of every political orientation. One famous old annexationist, Tomas Bobadilla, had been born a Spanish citizen. After decades of collaboration at the highest ranks in many administrations, he changed his mind in later years, after his own son defiantly opposed foreign occupation. Out of favor, he spent the last year of his life in Cap-Haïtien.[46] Poet Salomé Ureña wrote verses lamenting the "lakes of blood" spilled in her country as coups proliferated.[47] Still, fighting continued.

Even as it could no longer sustain annexationist logic, conservative anti-Haitian rhetoric emerged in Dominican politics once more. Summoned in the service of power seekers, of the "Civilized," of the cynical, those who invoked anti-Haitian discourse used it for facile patriotism where political unity flagged. The narrative reemerged among the reactionaries who struggled adamantly to regain power in 1864; they accused Gaspar Polanco of being "pro-Haitian," and they clearly understood it as a slander.[48] Writers for El Tiempo, which served as Báez's primary mouthpiece in the capital, distorted stories to meet their needs, pillorying the Haitian president until he was the caudillo's ally, for example. As ever, journalists and authorities spoke obliquely about popular Dominican-Haitian collaboration on domestic soil, dismissing all of the popular opposition to U.S. territorial cessions as the machinations of peasant rebels (cacos) who had no platform.[49] Privately to U.S. officials, Báez's aides added additional commentary, claiming the anticolonial opposition hoped "the African race [will] dominate the island.[50]

Thus diverged two histories—and two futures—for the republic. As La Regeneración wrote one history, El Tiempo wrote another. Where the journalists from the first hoped for dual citizenship born out of the collaboration of 1863–65, writers in the latter remembered Haitian collaboration of the previous period as nothing but venal self-interest. Where the first sought to foster markets in the center of the island, the second saw contraband. "The Government will take it upon itself to dictate energetic measures to repress this abuse, and it is strange that local authorities have not taken steps to prevent this problem," El Tiempo complained.[51] Luperón was "a conspirator . . . perverse and antinational," a writer accused, with "something mysterious and contrary to the true Dominican spirit." Of the rebels' desperate collaborative efforts to save the country from U.S. annexation, the journalist concluded, "The Puerto Plata movement is nothing other than an attempt to destroy national independence in favor of the Haitians."[52] In Puerto Plata, meanwhile, La Regeneración's writers pleaded for a different interpretation. "It is past time to close the disastrous period of our conflicts and begin a new era of peace and union," one urged. Hope and pessimism intermingled: "The political generation who bring with them ideas, passions, hate and rancor is disappearing. . . . [After] a foreign power's interference, a bloody revolution, a total victory, frequent bonds between the two peoples long separated, a community of ideas in the struggle, a unity of aspirations, signs of friendship, help and compassion amid the trials, must we revive old hates that should be extinguished, never to be reborn?"[53] Organization and outrage continued in the town, in the center of the island, and all across the territory. "For how long will parties toy with the destiny of *pueblos*?" another asked, demanding, "When will these wicked idols fall from their pedestals?"[54]

Notes

Abbreviations

AGI	Archivo General de Indias (Spain)
AGN-RD	Archivo General de la Nación–República Dominicana
AHN	Archivo Histórico Nacional, Madrid
AMAE	Archivo del Ministerio de Relaciones Exteriores, Madrid
ANC	Archivo Nacional de Cuba
Anexión	Fondo Anexión
AP	Asuntos Políticos
BAGN	*Boletín del Archivo General de la Nación*
BNE	Biblioteca Nacional, Madrid
BNJM	Biblioteca Nacional José Martí (Cuba)
CH	Colección Herrera
Clío	*Revista Clío, Órgano de la Academia Dominicana de la Historia*
CO	Colonial Office
Copiador	Índice General de Libros Copiadores de la Sección RREE, AGN-RD
Cuba	Papeles de Cuba
FO	Foreign Office
NARA	National Archives (U.S.)
RREE	Relaciones Exteriores
SD	Santo Domingo
s/f	sin fecha
SHM	Servicio Histórico Militar, Madrid
TNA	The National Archives, Kew (U.K.)

Introduction

1. Vicioso, *El freno hatero*, 144; Mella, *Los espejos de Duarte*, 198. Some Dominican scholars refer to the period of Unification (1822–44) as "occupation" (e.g., Núñez Grullón, *Evolución constitucional dominicana*, 17). More recent studies limit "occupation" to the first weeks of unification between the two territories during which—despite obvious support from citizens in a number of Dominican towns and a pacific reception of the transition generally—a large number of Haitian troops were present to realize the change in flag (Lora Hugi, *Transición*, 47).
2. Mella, *Los espejos de Duarte*, 197–98.
3. Castro Ventura, *La Guerra Restauradora*, 236. Spanish troops occupied San Lorenzo de los Mina and built new guard posts in Pajarito (Villa Duarte) and San Carlos.
4. José Francisco Pichardo, "A la palma de la libertad: Indignamente derribada en la noche del 9 de mayo de 1864," in Rodríguez Demorizi, *Santana y los poetas*, 342 (emphasis in original).
5. "Hispaniola" comes from the moniker that Columbus gave the island, "La Española." The etymology of "Quisqueya," reportedly an Arawak word for "mother of all lands," is more controversial, first reported by Italian historian Peter Martyr d'Anghiera, who had never traveled to the island; some emphasize that its popularity is a result of an aversion to using "Haiti" (San Miguel, *Crónicas de un embrujo*, 76). Haiti or Ayiti, conversely, was widely recorded as an Arawak name for the island meaning "mountainous land." Furthermore, it had a vibrant place in the nineteenth-century island political lexicon after its deliberate adoption by statemakers in the west in 1804 (Geggus, "Naming of Haiti"). Dominican independentists of late 1821 hoped to create "Spanish Haiti" in the east; the whole island was Haiti for a time, from 1822 to 1844. After Dominican separation, Dominican use of "Haiti" to refer to the whole island subsided, but rebels revived it during anti-Spanish fighting. Poet Manuel Rodríguez Objío pointedly gestured to a breadth of invocations, imagining, "Your former inhabitants, in patriotic cry, sometimes they called it Quisquella, sometimes they called it Haiti" (qtd. in Vicioso, *El freno hatero*, 291–92). I will use "Hispaniola," as it is the most commonly used name for the island in English. Although it lends particular credence to the imperial record, invoking that aggression is perhaps appropriate to recount the events that transpired. Where its interlocutors invoked it, I will also use "Haiti."
6. Mintz, *Caribbean Transformations*, 132–33; Casimir, *La culture opprimée*; González, *De esclavos a campesinos*; González, "War on Sugar." Bayly, *Imperial Meridian*, interprets the early 1800s as an accelerating imperial transition, rather than a lull.

7. Castro Ventura, *La Guerra Restauradora*, 160.
8. Narratives of conflict with Haiti had multiple uses. As in Argentina, Paraguay, and Brazil, willful print propagandists hoped to foment popular mobilization and national allegiance, in addition to making appeals to outside powers simultaneously (Huner, "Toikove Ñane Ŗetã!").
9. Plaza, "God and Federation," 140.
10. In the case of Nicaragua, for example, see Gobat, *Confronting the American Dream*; Wolfe, *Everyday Nation-State*; in Mexico, see, e.g., Paní, *El segundo imperio*; Ibsen, *Maximilian, Mexico, and the Invention of Empire*.
11. Tomich, *Through the Prism of Slavery*; Giusti-Cordero, "Beyond Sugar Revolutions," 58–83; Cromwell, "More Than Slaves and Sugar," 770–83.
12. Ferrer, *Freedom's Mirror*; Schneider, *Occupation of Havana*.
13. González, *De esclavos a campesinos*; Moya Pons, *Historia colonial de Santo Domingo*.
14. Dubois and Garrigus, *Slave Revolution in the Caribbean*, 36; Ferrer, *Freedom's Mirror*; Cordero Michel, *La revolucion haitiana y Santo Domingo*; Nessler, *Island-Wide Struggle for Freedom*; Yingling, "Colonialism Unraveling"; Madiou, *Histoire d'Haïti*.
15. Nessler, "'The Shame of the Nation.'"
16. Adelman, "Age of Imperial Revolution," 336.
17. Sánchez Ramírez, *Diario de la Reconquista*.
18. Paredes Vera, "La Constitución de 1812," 110; Lora Hugi, "El sonido de la libertad," 127; Eller, "'All Would Be Equal in the Effort,'" 128, 132.
19. Pierrot and McIntosh, "Henry/Nehri."
20. Dajabón, Monte Cristi, Santiago de los Caballeros, Las Caobas, Las Matas de Farfán, San Juan, Neiba, Azua, La Vega, Bánica, Hincha, and the northern port city of Puerto Plata all issued proclamations in support of the pending unification (Lora Hugi, *Transición*, 46–49; Paredes Vera, "La Constitución de 1812," 136; Janvier, *Haïti et ses visiteurs*, 601). In fact residents raised the Haitian flag in Monte Cristi, Dajabón, and Beler in November 1821, two weeks before the Colombian one was (briefly) raised in the south (Mackenzie, *Notes on Haiti*, 235).
21. Alemar, *Escritos*, 185. As a successor to Pétion, Boyer was a known entity to political observers in the Dominican capital. Fledgling periodical *El Duende* looked admiringly on Boyer's leadership skills (*El Duende*, no. 1, 15 April 1821, 1; no. 8, 3 June 1821, 1).
22. Lora Hugi, *Transición*, 46.
23. Lora Hugi, *Transición*, 73.
24. McGraw, *Work of Recognition*, 6–7.
25. Francisco Brenes qtd. in Castro Ventura, *Duarte en la proa*, 48.
26. Lora Hugi, *Transición*, 46; Jimenes Grullón, *La República Dominicana*, 132. Tobacco production nearly quadrupled in the Cibao, although farming

technology remained fairly primitive; wood exports increased significantly as well (Betances, "Agrarian Transformation," 61). Contemporary observers attested that the east-to-west cattle trade increased and that commerce from Cap, Gonaïves, Saint Marc, Port-au-Prince, and Jacmel spread to some centers of the east ("American Intrigues in St. Domingo, II," *The Anti-slavery Reporter* 7, no. 2 [1859]: 29–31).

27. Scott, "Public Rights and Private Commerce."
28. Ferrer, "Haiti, Free Soil, and Antislavery."
29. Harris, "Summer on the Borders," 152.
30. Lockward, *Documentos*, 222.
31. See, among many others, Pompée-Valentin baron de Vastey, *Colonial System Unveiled*; Bissette, *Réfutation du livre de M. V. Schoelcher*; Bongie, *Friends and Enemies*; Nicholls, "Work of Combat"; Daut, " 'Alpha and Omega' of Haitian Literature."
32. Prominent Dominican political figures explicitly condemned 1830s Spanish missions to reclaim the territory and dubbed Boyer "an angel of peace"; others penned poetry in praise of Boyer's regime (Cassá, *Personajes dominicanos*, 167; de Granda, "Un caso de planeamiento lingüístico frustrado," 209). Many pro-Boyer texts may have later been destroyed (Fischer, *Modernity Disavowed*, 181).
33. Puig Ortíz, *Emigración*; Hidalgo, "From North America to Hispaniola"; Hoetink, "Americans in Samaná"; Fleszar, " 'My Laborers in Haiti Are Not Slaves' "; Fanning, *Caribbean Crossing*.
34. Qtd. in Sheller, "Army of Sufferers," 43–44.
35. Lockward, *La Constitución Haitiano-Dominicana*.
36. "La union constituye la fuerza," *El Dominicano*, no. 1, 29 June 1855, 1; "La Historia de El Duende," *El Progreso*, no. 17, 12 June 1853, 6.
37. Pani, *El segundo imperio*, 104; Soto, *La conspiración monárquica en México 1845–6*; Andrés, "Colonial Crisis and Spanish Diplomacy," 328.
38. Índice General de Libros Copiadores de la Sección RREE, AGN-RD (hereafter cited as Copiador), 13 June 1848.
39. A small sampling of the flourishing scholarship on the immediate impact of the Haitian Revolution includes James, *Black Jacobins*; Scott, "Common Wind"; Trouillot, *Silencing the Past*; Geggus, *The Impact of the Haitian Revolution*; Dubois, *A Colony of Citizens*; Garraway, *Tree of Liberty*; Ferrer, *Freedom's Mirror*; Clavin, *Toussaint Louverture and the American Civil War*; White, *Encountering Revolution*; Johnson, *Slavery's Metropolis*.
40. Spieler, "Legal Structure of Colonial Rule during the French Revolution."
41. Brown, *Reaper's Garden*; Schmidt-Nowara, *Slavery, Freedom, and Abolition*. Planters wrote of the necessity of slavery: "For proof, look to Jamaica, San Domingo, Hayti" ("Negro Slavery," *Southern Cultivator* 20, nos. 5–6 [May–June 1862]: 110.
42. Lightfoot, *Troubling Freedom*; Besson, *Martha Brae's Two Histories*.
43. Paton, "Revisiting No Bond but the Law."

44. Among the very rich body of works, see these texts: Williams, *Capitalism and Slavery*; Holt, " 'Empire over the Mind' " and *Problem of Freedom*; Hall, *Civilising Subjects*; Rugemer, *Problem of Emancipation*; Newton, *Children of Africa*; Kazanjian, *Brink of Freedom*.
45. Hall, "Nation Within and Without."
46. Lambert, *Mastering the Niger*; for similar discourses about Liberia, see Kazanjian, *Brink of Freedom*.
47. Breen, *St. Lucia*, 240–59.
48. See, for example, Hall, *Civilising Subjects*; Brantlinger, *Dark Vanishings*.
49. Peabody, "France's Two Emancipations," 34.
50. Holt, *Problem of Freedom*.
51. Karp, "The World the Slaveholders Craved," 418. Pro-slavery voices praised the new cotton projects using indentured labor in Guiana, Trinidad, and other sites (Elliott, *Cotton Is King*, 144).
52. De Barros, *Reproducing the British Caribbean*, 28; Hall, *Civilising Subjects*, 22, 48; Rugemer, *Problem of Emancipation*, 263.
53. Ferrer, *Freedom's Mirror*; Tomich, "Wealth of Empire," 5–6.
54. Martínez-Fernández, *Torn between Empires*, 17–18.
55. Figueroa, *Sugar, Slavery, and Freedom*, 167; Picó, *Al filo del poder*, 52.
56. Laviña, "Puerto Rico," 103.
57. Figueroa, *Sugar, Slavery, and Freedom*, 36.
58. Reid-Vazquez, *Year of the Lash*; Finch, *Rethinking Slave Rebellion*.
59. Corwin, *Spain and the Abolition of Slavery in Cuba*, 153; see also Schmidt-Nowara, *Empire and Anti-slavery*.
60. Philadelphia, "Friends' Intelligencer," no. 13, 13 September 1856, 408.
61. Puerto Rican governor Rafael Aristegui to Spanish minister of state, 15 November 1844, qtd. in Febres-Cordero Carrillo, "La anexión," 80; Ruffin, *Diary of Edmund Ruffin*, 291.
62. Candler, *Brief Notices of Hayti*, 121; Rugemer; *Problem of Emancipation*.
63. Putnam, "Ideología racial, práctica social y estado liberal en Costa Rica"; Bassi, *An Aqueous Territory*. Mainland Caribbean areas—coastal Venezuela and Colombia, for example—further erased Caribbean regional connections in favor of a continental Latin American identification (Gómez, "Entwining the Revolutions").
64. Gobat, "Invention of Latin America," 1363.
65. Harris, "Summer on the Borders."
66. Dewey and Boyer, *Correspondence Relative to the Emigration to Hayti*, 11.
67. B. F. Rojas, "A los dominicanos," 11 June 1865, qtd. in Rodríguez Demorizi, *Actos y doctrina*, 394.
68. Henríquez Ureña, *Panorama histórico de la literatura dominicana*, 69. On the durability of these narratives, see, for example, Torres-Saillant, "Blackness and Meaning in Studying Hispaniola."

69. Wolfe, *Everyday Nation-State*, 171–72.
70. "Exclusivism . . . isolated from humanity," Dominican president Báez inveighed in 1850 (Lockward, *Documentos*, 133). For a contextualizing of these isolation narratives in a slightly earlier period, see Gaffield, *Haitian Connections*.
71. Out of direct imperial interests and an irrepressible urge to excoriate Haiti, outside travelers and eager capital city elites argued for flagrant contrasts on the island along multiple tacks: that there was no racism in the republic, that Dominicans were white-identifying, and that good Dominican patriots hated Haiti (Candelario, *Black behind the Ears*, chap. 1; Martínez-Fernández, *Torn between Empires*, 41–42; Eller, "Awful Pirates and Hordes of Jackals"). Their preoccupation continued unabated for decades. One author pleaded that the United States remain neutral in any island conflict, for example, but only because the story of "130,000 white Dominicans" was a "pious fraud" (Clark, *Remarks upon United States Intervention in Hayti*).
72. "Al Público," *El Dominicano*, no. 1, 19 September 1845, 1.
73. This literature often separates the annexationism of the small group in power (e.g., Álvarez López, *Dominación colonial*, 11, 33; Betances, "Social Classes," 23) from another undercurrent in the Cibao valley, less systematically discussed (e.g., Marte, *Correspondencia*, 63), or even from pro-U.S. annexation sentiment in the far eastern province of Higüey (Mayes, *The Mulatto Republic*, 18). It also tends to exaggerate the differences between politicians of the south and the Cibao, discussed more in chapter 1 (Landolfi, *Evolución cultural dominicana*).
74. Larson, *Trials of Nation Making*, 6.
75. Rojas, *Cuba Mexicana*.
76. Martínez-Fernández, "Caudillos," 574; Escolano Giménez, *La rivaldad internacional*, 68.
77. Dhormoys, *Une visite chez Soulouque*, 147.
78. Brown, "Global History of Latin America"; Sartorius, *Ever Faithful*; Schmidt-Nowara, "La España ultramarina"; Thomson, *Birth of Modern Politics in Spain*; Morillo-Alicea, "'Aquel laberinto de oficinas.'"
79. Hall, "Nation Within and Without," 181; Peabody, "France's Two Emancipations," 31.
80. Stasiulis and Yuval-Davis, *Unsettling Settler Societies*, 275; Razack, *Race, Space and the Law*, 55.
81. E.g., Colombia's 1863 Rionegro Constitution (Andrés, "Colonial Crisis," 335).
82. Escolano Giménez, "La organización de la provincia de Santo Domingo," 340; Castro Ventura, *La Guerra Restauradora*, 372.
83. Dorsey, "Seamy Sides of Abolition."
84. Cooper, *Colonialism in Question*; Dubois, *Avengers*.

85. McGuinness, "Searching for 'Latin America,' " 102; Luis-Brown, *Waves of Decolonization*, 247; Gobat, "Invention of Latin America," 1346.
86. Sanders, *Vanguard of the Atlantic World*, 4; Thomson, "Garibaldi and the Legacy of the Revolutions of 1848"; Peyrou, "Harmonic Utopia of Spanish Republicanism."
87. Coviello, *Intimacy in America*, 4.
88. McGuinness, "Searching for 'Latin America,' " 101.
89. Smith, *Freedom's Frontier*.
90. May, "Lobbyists for Commercial Empire," 408.
91. Rodríguez Demorizi, *Correspondencia*, 65; Hauch, "The Dominican Republic and Its Foreign Relations," 98.
92. R. Edwardes to Lord J. Russell, Madrid, 22 April 1861, AGN-RD: Anexión DE/000933, Expte. 6, p. 17.
93. Fontecha Pedraza and González Calleja, *Una cuestión de honor*, 5, 9, 51; Álvarez Junco, "Spanish National Identity," 321.
94. Schomburgk, "Peninsula and Bay of Samaná," 283.
95. Eusebio Soler to Gob. Superior Civil, SD, 4 July 1864, AGN-RD: Anexión 16, Expte. 1, doc. 3.
96. Qtd. in Welles, *Naboth's Vineyard*, 224.
97. Eusebio Soler to Gob. Superior Civil, SD, 4 July 1864, AGN-RD: Anexión 16, Expte. 1, doc. 3.
98. Francisco Serrano to Min. de Guerra, Havana, 6 September 1861, AHN: Ultramar 3532, Expte. 2, doc 2.
99. *Hispaniola, Hayti*, 87.
100. Harris, "Summer on the Borders," 80.
101. Qtd. in "Nouvelles étrangères," *Le Moniteur Haïtien*, no. 27, 8 June 1861, 3.
102. González, "Ideologia del progreso y campesinado," 34; González, "La figura social del montero," 79.
103. Ferrer, *Insurgent Cuba*; Lasso, *Myths of Harmony*; McGraw, *Work of Recognition*; Grandin, "Liberal Traditions in the Americas."
104. Min. de RREE to Cornelio G. Holff, RD Agente Comercial in NYC, Copiador, 4 March 1860.
105. Fr. Consul to Min. de RREE, Copiador, 4 February 1861.
106. Rodríguez Demorizi, *Relaciones dominicoespañolas*, 352; Marte, *Correspondencia*, 42.
107. Marte, "La oralidad sobre el pasado insular," 7.
108. Escolano Giménez, "La insurrección dominicana," 73. Ranches make notoriously difficult historiographical subjects, authors observe (Giusti-Cordero, "Beyond Sugar Revolutions," 67). Considering the issues of evidence about black ranching societies throughout the Atlantic World, see Sluyter, *Black Ranching Frontiers*.
109. Cross-Beras, *Sociedad y desarrollo en la República dominicana*, 54.

110. Turits, *Foundations of Despotism*.
111. González, *De esclavos a campesinos*.
112. Rodríguez Demorizi, *Papeles de Pedro F. Bonó*, 192.
113. Putnam, "To Study the Fragments/Whole," 619.
114. Vinson, "African (Black) Diaspora History, Latin American History."
115. There has been a profusion of valuable monographs about the Restoration War within this paradigm that focus, instead, on other aspects of the annexation and rebellion. One scholar writes that there was "no discrimination" during the First Republic (Castro Ventura, *La Guerra Restauradora*, 102); others disregard elite racism more obliquely, in the tendency to mystify annexationist tendencies as "backward," rather than interrogating the common goals (of indenture, of profit, or of self-preservation versus a rural majority) that an important sector of Dominican annexationists had in common with elites throughout the Caribbean (for an overview, see Febres-Cordero Carrillo, "La anexión," chap. 2). Scholars tend to mention the importance of fears of reenslavement to the rebels without further contextualization outside of the immediate antagonism of the occupation (i.e., the regional context or long-term domestic discussions of emancipation and racism). At different moments, authors have used the nationalist frame, furthermore, specifically as a vehicle of liberation. Professor, intellectual, and revolutionary Juan Bosch published his classic study of the popular rebellion, with an essay about U.S. intervention wreaking havoc on the territory, one hundred years later. "To reach the category of hero, men and women do not need to be *letrados*; what they need is the capacity to create acts," he urges, pointedly (Bosch, *La Guerra de la Restauración*, 125).
116. Mimi Sheller refers to this as a "peasant democratic ideology" (*Democracy after Slavery*, 5).
117. On the concept of articulation of solidarities in the African diaspora, see Patterson and Kelley, "Unfinished Migrations."
118. Mignolo, *Local Histories/Global Designs*.
119. Carlos Helm to Francisco Serrano, 5 March 1862, ANC: AP 53, Expte. 16.
120. Luperón, *Notas autobiográficas*, 99; Ayuso, *Historia pendiente*, 9, 94.
121. Abreu Cardet and Sintes Gómez, *El alzamiento de Neiba*, 29.
122. Qtd. in Rodríguez Demorizi, *Actos y doctrina*, 77.
123. Marte, *Correspondencia*, 90.
124. On discussions of warnings of reenslavement in other contexts, see, e.g., Hahn, "'Extravagant Expectations' of Freedom."
125. Jimenes Grullón, *Sociología política dominicana*, 131.
126. Finch, *Rethinking Slave Rebellion*, 171.
127. De la Gándara, *Anexión y guerra de Santo Domingo*, 201–2; Rodríguez Demorizi, *Del vocabulario dominicano*, 20. The Haitian president, Fabre Nicholas Geffrard, predicted the struggle. "Dominicans and Haitians are the two most indomitable peoples of the new world, and . . . the most resolute,"

he warned the Spanish. "Call Dominicans . . . , and ask each one what they have done for their country (*Le Moniteur Haïtien*, no. 12, 23 February 1861, 3).
128. Martínez, *Diccionario*, 514.
129. Sanders, *Vanguard of the Atlantic World*, 26; Smith, *Roots of Conservatism*, 79.
130. Rodríguez Demorizi, *Actos y doctrina*, 375.
131. *Boletín Oficial*, 18 December 1864, qtd. in Rodríguez Demorizi, *Actos y doctrina*, 249.
132. Fusté, "Possible Republics," 3.
133. Bermúdez de Castro y O'Lawlor, *Cuestión de Santo Domingo*, 39, 47–49.
134. Adelman, "Iberian Passages," 59.
135. Amid a valuable body of works that consider how Caribbean activists confronted constant tension between the insistent "racelessness" of republican national projects and the immediate menace of racism at home and abroad, see Fusté, "Possible Republics"; Stephens, *Black Empire*; Reyes-Santos, *Our Caribbean Kin*; Mayes, *The Mulatto Republic*; Scott, "Public Rights"; Ferrer, *Insurgent Cuba*.
136. Johnson, *Fear of French Negroes*, 2; Reyes-Santos, *Our Caribbean Kin*, 8; Chaar-Pérez, "'Revolution of Love.'"
137. Sheller, *Citizenship*, 102.
138. He continued, wryly: "In the great Confederation there will be the French of Guadeloupe and Martinique, whom I don't know; the Haitians, whom I know too well; the Cubans, whom I am getting to know, as I am seeing them in the work of destruction, which they will most probably continue after emancipation; the English of Jamaica and the rest of the British isles; and us. . . . Superb elements, of course, to construct a mixed society that ought to serve as a barrier to the aspirations and invasions of the Anglo-Saxon *raza*!" (Espaillat y Quiñones, *Escritos*, 269).
139. Hepburn, *Haiti as It Is*, 11.
140. Kachun, "'Our Platform Is as Broad as Humanity,'" 2; Hepburn, *Haiti as It Is*, 16.
141. Gómez, "Entwining the Revolutions."
142. Rodríguez Objío, *Gregorio Luperón e historia de la Restauración*, 2:192; Haitian heads of state engaged in similar "salvation diplomacy" (Adam, *Une crise haïtienne 1867–1869*, 42).
143. Dubois, *Haiti*, 169.
144. Mella, *Los espejos de Duarte*. Duarte was in exile after the first six months of Separation. He wrote mournfully of the battles that raged from exile in near-total anonymity (Castro Ventura, *Duarte en la proa de historia*, 252).
145. Mella, *Los espejos de Duarte*, 34, 38, 54.
146. Hagemann and Rendall, "Introduction," 28. On archetypes of Dominican women in the nineteenth century, see Lora Hugi, "Las mujeres anónimas," 84.

147. Mella, *Los espejos de Duarte*, 301.
148. Rodríguez de Tió, *Mi libro de Cuba*, vii.
149. Among works that consider the nineteenth century specifically, see Cordero Michel, *La revolución haitiana*; Hernández Flores, *Luperón, héroe y alma*; Torres-Saillant, "Tribulations of Blackness"; Mayes, *The Mulatto Republic*; Nessler, *An Island-Wide Struggle for Freedom*; Martínez, "Not a Cockfight"; Franco, "Remanentes ideológicos."
150. Torres-Saillant, "Tribulations of Blackness," 132.
151. "Convulsiones de los pueblos," *La Regeneración*, no. 2, 3 September 1865, 3.

1. Life by Steam

1. "Haiti," *El Dominicano*, no. 21, 5 September 1846, 81.
2. "Continuación," *El Dominicano*, no. 7, 13 November 1845, 17–18.
3. "Clamor Público," *El Dominicano*, no. 21, 5 September 1846, 83.
4. Rodríguez Demorizi, *Correspondencia*, 1:164.
5. Rodríguez Demorizi, *Correspondencia*, 2:12, 17.
6. Rodríguez Demorizi, *Correspondencia*, 1:59; these caudillo-led troops or party militias were known elsewhere as *montoneras* (Holden, *Armies without Nations*, 38).
7. Aluma-Cazorla, "Caudillo as the Post-bandit."
8. Pérez Memén, *El Pensamiento dominicano*, 25; Campillo Pérez, *Historia electoral dominicana*; Franks, "Transforming Property," 90.
9. Salvatore, *Wandering Paysanos*, 1, 398.
10. To propose to cross the island by land, "people seemed to think a man must either be crazy, or that he expected to derive some mysterious benefit from such a trip," one traveler remarked in 1870 (Hazard, *Santo Domingo, Past and Present*, 274).
11. François-Xavier Guerra qtd. in Knöbl, "State Building in Western Europe and the Americas," 72.
12. Marte, "La oralidad sobre el pasado insular," 41.
13. Marte, "La oralidad sobre el pasado insular," 34. "Spaniards" was also commonly used in Haiti at the popular level; Emperor Soulouque often simply referred to "the eastern part" (Pablo de Urrutia to Cap. Gen. of Cuba, 6 November 1858, ANC: AP 224, Expte. 13). Other scholars emphasize that leaders invoked terms of political consensus ("copatriots," con-patriotas) precisely because the idea of territorial unity was so weak (Mella, *Los espejos de Duarte*, 216).
14. Vicioso, *El freno hatero*, 333.
15. Lora Hugi, *Transición*, 130; San Miguel, *Los campesinos del Cibao*, 44.
16. After 1824, only state documents were in French, and French secretaries (*greffiers*) appeared only in the Dominican capital (de Granda, "Un caso de planeamiento lingüístico frustrado," 193, 199–201, 203; Lora Hugi, *Transición*,

48–49). In nearly all of the "Sentencias Penales de la Época Haitiana," republished in the Dominican National Archive's *Boletin General de la Nacion*, nos. 79–87 (1953–55), the cases are conducted in Spanish; the only exceptions are defendants with French/Haitian surnames.
17. Vicioso, *El freno hatero*, 139. He was also a prolific poet in favor of Boyer's regime; e.g., de Granda, "Un caso de planeamiento lingüístico frustrado," 209.
18. Pablo Alí's 31st Regiment, known as the "Batallón de los Morenos," was composed of "two Black companies that existed . . . before the emancipation of 1822." Boyer created the 32nd Regiment for the newly manumitted after 1822, and it was composed of "Africans and youth from the town" (Madiou, *Histoire d'Haïti*, 95; Mella, *Los espejos de Duarte*, 200–201). There was another specifically black regiment in San Cristóbal (Mella, *Los espejos de Duarte*, 199).
19. Porter, *Diario de una misión secreta*, 28.
20. Lora Hugi, *Transición*, 46; Jimenes Grullón, *La República Dominicana*, 132. Tobacco production nearly quadrupled in the Cibao, although farming technology remained fairly primitive; wood exports increased significantly as well (Betances, "Agrarian Transformation," 61). Contemporary observers attested that the east-to-west cattle trade increased and that commerce from Cap, Gonaïves, Saint Marc, Port-au-Prince, and Jacmel spread to some centers of the east ("American Intrigues in St. Domingo, II.," *The Anti-slavery Reporter* 7, no. 2 [1859]: 29–31).
21. Traditional narratives stress the impact of Boyer's 1826 Rural Code, arguing it had widespread, onerous effects (Moya Pons, "The Land Question in Haiti and Santo Domingo"). Again, Lora Hugi's study of Higüey is instructive. In Higüey, months passed before new officials were sworn in, and Boyer never traveled to the province. Lora Hugi demonstrates that authorities did not enforce vagrancy codes, travel passes were few, and communal land practices continued without interruption (Lora Hugi, *Transición*, 55–56, 73, 128, 130, 143). In one collection of dozens of cases from the capital, just one vagrancy prosecution emerges, in the aggravating instance of a robbery ("Causa contra Pedro Manuel," BAGN, no. 83 [1954], 402–4).
22. Schoelcher, *Abolition de l'esclavage*.
23. The indemnity provoked immediate domestic and international complications. By decree in April 1826, each commune was to furnish 3 million gourdes, an amount soon reduced by a third. Higüey's special commission, not convened until the following summer, gathered just several hundred pesos in voluntary donations; it is not immediately evident how much more was levied through taxes or tariffs. Citizens were exempted from individual taxation in 1828 (although it seems this was reinstated in 1829). Numerous adjustments highlight the pragmatic, political, and economic impossibility of paying such a sum (Lora Hugi, *Transición*, 122–24).

24. "Reflecciones Políticas sobre la cuestión de Haiti," El Dominicano, no. 4, 1 November 1845, 13. In the west, one traveler noted in 1837 that guards often overstepped their daily authority. A "dangerous military spirit" that was antidemocratic and a "fearful engine of any government" prevailed (Brown, History and Present Condition of St. Domingo, 2:268).
25. "Reflecciones Políticas sobre la cuestión de Haiti," El Dominicano, no. 4, 1 November 1845, 14.
26. Nouel, "El terremoto de 1842," 99–100.
27. Illás, "El terremoto del 7 de mayo," 67.
28. Hispaniola, Hayti, 24.
29. Hispaniola, Hayti, 30.
30. Fiallo Billini, "La construcción antillanista," n.p.
31. Espinal Hernández, "Familiaridad y consanguinidad." The group had disbanded before Separation was even realized (Guerrero, "El Pensamiento conservador," 114).
32. Pedro Bonó qtd. in Castro Ventura, Duarte en la proa, 47).
33. They drafted the Praslin Manifesto, named for the property of Charles Hérard ouside of Les Cayes (Sheller, "Army of Sufferers," 42).
34. Qtd. in Rodríguez Demorizi, Invasiones haitianas, 302.
35. "Informe del General Charles Hérard ainé," in Rodríguez Demorizi, Invasiones haitianas, 285. Fifteen delegates from Puerto Plata and other towns of the east were in attendance (Lockward, La Constitución Haitiano-Dominicana, 17; Rodríguez Demorizi, Invasiones haitianas, 286). Large landowning representatives, like future Dominican caudillo president Buenaventura Báez, lobbied hard about the limitations of landowning and citizenship; historian Franklin Franco Pichardo observes that he was preoccupying himself with the concerns of about 5 percent of the east's elite, former slave owners who had extensive property, and that the debate was therefore necessarily a "delicate issue" (El pensamiento dominicano, 97; on property and citizenship, see also Venator Santiago, "Race, Nation-Building and Legal Transculturation"). Other scholars argue that discontent was more widespread, and that "Boyer's repression generally and the marginalization of the east" ensured the popularity of Separation (Venator Santiago, "Race, the East, and Haitian Revolutionary Ideology," 112).
36. Sheller, "Army of Sufferers," 42.
37. John Baur claims that Soulouque sought their alliance in years subsequent but was unable to satisfy the demands of "sixty arpents of land each . . . and town-houses for their officers" (Baur, "Faustin Soulouque," 136).
38. Courlander, Treasury of Afro-American Folklore, 47.
39. "Continuación . . . ," El Dominicano, no. 7, 13 November 1845, 17.
40. "Haiti," El Dominicano, no. 2, 8 October 1845, 2. He was "the most ridiculous, the most despotic, the most barbarous" of all of the leaders, the paper complained.

41. Welles, Naboth's Vineyard, 68.
42. Rodríguez Demorizi, Correspondencia, 2:83.
43. Vicioso, El freno hatero, 136.
44. Mella, Los espejos de Duarte, 185. For Dominicans fighting on the Unification side, see Santana's speculative letter to that effect, qtd. in Welles, Naboth's Vineyard, 68–69.
45. Copiador, 1 January 1845; Rodríguez Demorizi, Correspondencia, 55.
46. The French consul, André-Nicolas Levasseur, reported that a small group of Haitian politicians appealed to him at exactly the same time (Brière, Haïti et la France, 292–94).
47. Rodríguez Demorizi, Correspondencia, 74, 100.
48. Guerra Sosa, "Familias Haitianas al Servicio de Nuestra Independencia"; Rodríguez Demorizi, Correspondencia, 161–62.
49. Madiou, Histoire d'Haïti, 99, 103.
50. Despite apocryphal (and widely variant) estimates of the number of men involved in these and other encounters, Haitian forces, gathered by conscription, were in decline and had been for some years (Candler, Brief Notices of Hayti, 93; Bird, Black Man, 187, 284; Cap. Cayetano Pilon to the Queen, Puerto Rico, 4 February 1845, AMAE: Política Exterior: RD 2373, Expte. s/n.; on varying estimates, compare, e.g., Rodríguez Demorizi, Guerra dominico-haitiana, 22, and Robles-Muñoz, Paz en Santo Domingo, 66). Roads across the island were often impassable for carriages and, after a rain, impassable even on foot, much less by groups of forces traveling long distances who may have been feeding themselves (Brown, History and Present Condition of St. Domingo, 2:266; Raybaud, Soulouque et son empire, 274, 308; Baur, "Faustin Soulouque," 142). Dominican reports were frank about the exceedingly small numbers of individuals involved in most incidents (even as they exaggerated tales of heroism and cowardice). Even Santana's famous 19 March 1844 battle at Azua involved just "a handful of patriots," El Dominicano acknowledged (no. 11, 28 November 1846, 43).
51. Courlander, Treasury of Afro-American Folklore, 47.
52. For more on the Haitian exile community in Jamaica, see Smith, Liberty, Fraternity, Exile.
53. Mella, Los espejos de Duarte, 58.
54. Mella, Los espejos de Duarte, 153.
55. Franco Pichardo, "Remanentes ideológicos," 83. The traveling emissary was Dr. José María Caminero, born in Santiago de Cuba, who had served as an interpreter and a politician during Unification (Martínez, Diccionario, 98; Lockward, Documentos, xliv; Logan, Diplomatic Relations, 238).
56. Franco Pichardo, "Remanentes ideológicos," 83.
57. Caminero attempted negotiations with the United States for a commercial treaty that also sought to attract white immigrants to the island (Sang Ben, La Política Exterior Dominicana, 1844–1961, 37).

58. Franco Pichardo, "Remanentes ideológicos," 85; Mella, *Los espejos de Duarte*, 191–92.
59. Mella, *Los espejos de Duarte*, 152.
60. Franklin Franco, *Los negros*, 161; Madiou, *Histoire d'Haïti*, 99.
61. Rodríguez Demorizi, *Correspondencia*, 114, 116, 135, 138.
62. Rodríguez Demorizi, *Correspondencia*, 142, 145.
63. Vega Boyrie, "La labor legislativa," 206.
64. Rodríguez Demorizi, *Correspondencia*, 2:39.
65. Lizardo, *Cultura Africana en Santo Domingo*, 68.
66. Rodríguez Demorizi, *Correspondencia*, 2:15, 21, 28.
67. "Comunicado," *El Dominicano*, no. 12, 15 February 1846, 46. Lieutenant Colonel Simon had sailed to Saint Thomas in order to defect, but he was later captured at Puerto Plata and condemned to die by a special military commission.
68. Garrido, *Los Puello*, 87, 93.
69. Lockward, *La Constitución Haitiano-Dominicana*, 16.
70. Lora Hugi, "Las mujeres anónimas," 90; Martínez-Fernández, "The Sword and the Crucifix," 74. The prominent men involved in Separation seemed to have taken the matter of women's legal recognition, recently afforded across the island, as a direct affront, a point of agreement they shared with town Catholic officials (who were fully one-fourth of the Separation manifesto's signatories). Upon his divorce from his wife, Guadalupe Heredia, José María Caminero became enraged that Haitian authorities were "partial" to her in the settlement proceedings (Lockward, *Documentos*, xliv). Subsequent Dominican administrations targeted civil marriages on four separate occasions (Lockward, *Documentos*, xliv, 135; Martínez-Fernández, "The Sword and the Crucifix," 76, 79, 82).
71. Hoetink, *Dominican People*, 89.
72. F. M. Delmonte, "Canto de un Desterrado," *El Dominicano*, no. 1, 19 September 1845, 4.
73. Mariano Álvarez to Secretario de Estado, Havana, 12 November 1860, AGI: Cuba 2266, Pieza 2, doc. s/n). Santana's party was "simply a gigantic group of 'friends' of the caudillo," historian Campillo Pérez observes (*Historia electoral dominicana*, 47); Rodríguez Demorizi, *Correspondencia*, 108.
74. *El Dominicano*, no. 21, 5 September 1846, 82; *El Dominicano*, no. 14, 18 March 1846, 55.
75. Martínez-Fernández, "The Sword and the Crucifix," 73. Portes's tyrannical inclinations extended to the persecution of Protestants on the island. He ordered that only Catholics should be able to use church bells, pursued critical missionaries, and opposed a treaty with the British that would establish religious tolerance. The British consul in Santo Domingo, Robert Schomburgk, called Portes "a Vicar General, a Jesuit, and [a] blind bigot" (Martínez-Fernández, "The Sword and the Crucifix," 73).

76. Conde de [Spiculot?] to Ramón María Narváez, Secretario de Estado y del Despacho de la Guerra, Puerto Rico, 18 January 1845, SHM: Ultramar 5646, Expte. s/n.
77. "Haiti," El Dominicano, no. 2, 8 October 1845, 6.
78. "Soneta: La Batalla de Beler: Dedicado a los heróicos habitantes del Cibao," El Dominicano, no. 7, 13 November 1845, 28.
79. "Discurso de Presbitero Sr. Andres Rosón," El Dominicano, no. 9, 1 January 1846, 33.
80. "Al Público," El Dominicano, no. 1, 19 September 1845, 1.
81. "Al Público," El Dominicano, no. 1, 19 September 1845, 1; "Mas Sobre Haiti," El Dominicano, no. 5, 13 November 1845, 19.
82. Rodríguez Demorizi, Guerra dominico-haitiana, 16, 18.
83. Even the vitriolic El Dominicano quieted down about its neighbor by late spring 1846, filling its pages instead with questions of financial reform, agriculture, and politics. Observing that political disturbances were constant, they mocked the neighboring government as "moribund" (El Dominicano, no. 3, 28 October 1845, 9; El Dominicano, no. 15, 11 April 1846, 57).
84. El Dominicano, no. 11, 28 January 1846, 42.
85. A. Monfleury, "De l'industrie en Haïti: Réponse à M. Ed. Paul," L'Opinion Nationale, nos. 10 and 11, 15 March 1862, 1; Nicholls, Economic Dependence and Political Autonomy, 11. Boyer himself may have pondered abrogating Article 7, which prevented foreign land ownership, despite popular opposition (Sheller, "Army of Sufferers," 38).
86. Blanco Díaz, Alejandro Ángulo Guridi, 2:12; Pani, "Ciudadanos precarios."
87. Britannicus (Heneken), Dominican Republic and the Emperor Soulouque, 26; Porter, Diario de una misión secreta, 19. These restrictions were despite the fact that Báez and others had pushed for nationalization reform since the late Unification period (Hauch, "The Dominican Republic and Its Foreign Relations," 41).
88. Moya Pons, Manual de historia dominicana, 363.
89. They left them at 1838 levels, to be paid half in Spanish pesos fuertes, half in Dominican paper money (Rodríguez Demorizi, Correspondencia, 151, 212).
90. Martínez-Fernández, Torn between Empires, 93.
91. Mariano Álvarez, "Memoria: Santo Domingo o la República Dominicana," SD, 20 April 1860, AHN: Ultramar 2775, Expte. 16.
92. Bosch, La Guerra de la Restauración, 15.
93. La Razón, no. 7, 15 June 1862, 1.
94. Mella, Los espejos de Duarte, 177; Martínez-Fernández, "The Sword and the Crucifix."
95. Martínez-Fernández, "The Sword and the Crucifix," 73; Welles, Naboth's Vineyard, 234.
96. Dhormoys, Une visite chez Soulouque, 72, 112.
97. On Báez's hair, see Rodríguez Demorizi, Del vocabulario dominicano, 197.

98. Juan Pablo Duarte's most famous poem expresses this desire explicitly (Rodríguez Demorizi, *Santana y los poetas*, 331–32), although scholars argue convincingly that he may have written it during the Restoration War (Mella, *Los espejos de Duarte*, 145).
99. Vallejo, *Las madres de la patria*, 75.
100. Fabens, Montgomery (pseudonym), and Kimball, *In the Tropics*, 17, 101, 181. E.g., the Alfau's property holding (Martínez, *Diccionario*, 24; Bosch, *La Guerra de la Restauración*, 28).
101. Wipfler, "The Catholic Church and the State," 193.
102. Martínez-Fernández, *Torn between Empires*, 216.
103. Porter, *Diario de una misión secreta*, 27.
104. Penson, *Reseña histórico-crítica*, 272.
105. McGraw, *Work of Recognition*, 9, 10; Rodríguez Demorizi, *Del vocabulario dominicano*, 197.
106. Torrente, *Política ultramarina*, 290.
107. Rodríguez Demorizi, *Del vocabulario dominicano*, 95, 177; Kinsbruner, *Not of Pure Blood*, 32.
108. *El Dominicano*, no. 14, 6 October 1855, 55. Determining the date of another vitriolic snippet, directed against a black woman, is difficult (Rodríguez Demorizi, *Del vocabulario dominicano*, 201).
109. "Poesia: Canción Dominicana," *El Dominicano*, no. 11, 28 January 1846, 44.
110. "Al Público," *El Dominicano*, no. 1, 19 September 1845, 1. Debates of the Spanish matriculation scheme provoked ample refutation of imprecise usage of "Spanish" within the Dominican press ("La Matrícula Española," *La República*, no. 1, 19 August 1856, 1–2).
111. López Morillo, *Memorias sobre la segunda reincorporación de Santo Domingo*, 259.
112. Advertisement of Monsieur Perrot, *El Oasis*, no. 12, 16 September 1855, 48.
113. "Costumbres," *El Oasis*, no. 1, 26 November 1854, 3.
114. Matibag, *Haitian-Dominican Counterpoint*, 117.
115. Rodríguez Silva, *Silencing Race*.
116. Authors issued a fifteen-point colonization plan the following year ("Inmigración," *El Dominicano*, no. 7, 13 November 1845, 26; *El Dominicano*, no. 19, 24 July 1846, 74).
117. Copiador, 13 October 1848, 3 April 1860, 4 February 1861.
118. Rodríguez Demorizi, *Correspondencia*, 2:161.
119. Logan, *Diplomatic Relations*, 238.
120. Antonio Alfau to Serrano, 21 July 1860, AGI: Cuba 2266, Pieza 1, doc. s/n.
121. Febres-Cordero Carrillo, "La anexión," 122.
122. Marte, *Correspondencia*, 42, 89. These terms are in use from the beginning of the nineteenth century (García, *Compendio*, 1:313).
123. France was an enduring, favored partner. Petitioners also made entreaties to Spain and authorities in its Caribbean possessions in 1843, 1844, 1845, 1846,

1848, 1850, 1851, a yearlong mission to Madrid in 1853–54, 1857, 1858, and all of 1859–60 (Torrente, *Política ultramarina*, 310).

124. "Don Cameleón," *El Dominicano*, no. 16, 2 May 1846, 62; Marte, "La oralidad sobre el pasado insular," 2, 5, 7.

125. A. J. Bautista Romane, "Fragmentos," *El Oasis*, no. 19, 4 November 1855, 75. "Mañesa is a nickname we use for our neighbors of the east," the author explained after an asterisk to his public. The editor of *El Dominicano*, the first paper after Separation, ran a regular column, "Political Reflections on the Haitian Question," in which the journal would mention or parody, and then didactically refute, articles from the Haitian press (e.g., "Al Público," *El Dominicano*, no. 1, 19 September 1845, 1; *El Dominicano*, no. 5, 13 November 1845, 19).

126. *El Dominicano*, 1845–46.

127. "The Nineteenth Century," *El Oasis*, no. 19, 8 April 1855, 75.

128. On class analyses of anti-Haitianism, see, e.g., Cordero Michel, *La revolución haitiana*, 141; Matibag, *Haitian-Dominican Counterpoint*, 18; Franco Pichardo, *Sobre racismo y antihaitianismo*; Mayes, *Mulatto Republic*; Sagás, *Race and Politics*.

129. "Continua el articulo sobre la Inmigración," *El Dominicano*, no. 6, 27 November 1845, 23; "Amor al Trabajo," *El Dominicano*, no. 23, 8 December 1855, 91; "La Obedencia pasiva del soldado," *El Porvenir*, no. 4, 29 October 1854, 3.

130. Febres-Cordero Carrillo, "La anexión," 19.

131. Franks, "Transforming Property," 54.

132. "Inmigración," *El Dominicano*, no. 14, 6 October 1855, 53–54.

133. *Le Moniteur Haïtien*, nos. 26–27, 12 June 1858, 2.

134. Ismenes, "Cuatro preguntas a Ingenuo," *El Oasis*, no. 6, 31 December 1854, 24; Ingenuo, "Al Amigo Ismenes," *El Oasis*, no. 7, 7 January 1855, 28; Emmanuel (Galván), "Quejas de la Tumba contra el Merengue," *El Oasis*, no. 8, 14 January 1855, 30.

135. "Costumbres," *El Oasis*, no. 1, 26 November 1854, 3–4.

136. I.e., a *wanga* or *ouanga*, which Boyer had also banned in the west ("Haitianaparla," *El Dominicano*, no. 25, 22 December 1855; "Variedades," *El Dominicano*, no. 26, 29 December 1855, 99–100, 103; Ramsey, *Spirits and the Law*, 58).

137. Moya Pons, *Dominican Republic*, 185.

138. Porter, *Diario de una misión secreta*, 25–26.

139. Moya Pons, *Dominican Republic*, 186.

140. Keim, *San Domingo*, 25–27.

141. Rodríguez Demorizi, *Del vocabulario dominicano*, 36; also *The Royal Standard*, 1 September 1866, clipping in TNA: CO 301/44/269, n.p.

142. Johnson, *Fear of French Negroes*, 71–73.

143. The poem vividly describes righting racist injustices: "Algún día llegará / que la tortilla se vuelva, / que los negros coman pan / y los blancos coman mierda" (Rodríguez Demorizi, *Del vocabulario dominicano*, 17). Another popular

poem pointedly responded to prejudice, "Being black is not shameful, the church wears black on [Maundy] Thursday and Holy Friday . . . on its sacred altar, and to rise up to heaven, we are all of us equal" (Rodríguez Demorizi, *Del vocabulario dominicano*, 179).

144. Lora Hugi, *Transición*, 96; Porter, *Diario de una misión secreta*, 22; Consul Hood to Lord J. Russell, SD, 21 April 1861, AGN-RD: Anexión DE/000933, Expte. 10, p. 28.
145. Guerrero Cano, *Disciplina y laxitud*, 68.
146. Lockward, *Documentos*, 222.
147. Gage, "The Market Woman of San Domingo," 717.
148. Porter, *Diario de una misión secreta*, 219.
149. St. John, *Hayti*, 85; Lora Hugi, "Las mujeres anónimas," 106.
150. Rodríguez Demorizi, *Correspondencia*, 231.
151. Rodríguez Demorizi, *Correspondencia*, 229.
152. Logan, *Diplomatic Relations*, 281.
153. *El Telégrafo Constitucional*, no. 2, 12 April 1821, 12; others reached the eastern province of Higüey by small craft, like twenty-year-old Viviana Morales and her infant daughter (Certificación de Declaración, 13 April 1837, AGN-RD: Archivo Real de Higüey 1700123 Leg. 18 Azul, Expte. 96; I am grateful to Andrew Walker for this source).
154. Consul Hood to Lord J. Russell, SD, 21 April 1861, AGN-RD: Anexión DE/000933, Expte. 10, p. 28.
155. Juan Fello to Cap. Gen. of Cuba, 7 December 1842, ANC: AP 137, Expte. 13.
156. Suárez Díaz, *El Antillano*, 28.
157. "Criminal contra el coronel de las Reservas Provinciales D. Juan Rondón . . . ," April 1863, AGN-RD: CH Tomo 11 (AGI: Cuba 1014B). San Carlos also had a large Canary Islander population.
158. López Morillo, *Memorias sobre la segunda reincorporación de Santo Domingo*, 221.
159. López Morillo, *Memorias sobre la segunda reincorporación de Santo Domingo*, 221.
160. De la Rosa Garabito, *San Cristobal en la historia dominicana*, 12; Moya Pons, *Dominican Republic*, 185.
161. Tejeda Ortíz, "El cimarronaje," 281.
162. Porter, *Diario de una misión secreta*, 74.
163. Porter, *Diario de una misión secreta*, 109.
164. Brown, *History and Present Condition of St. Domingo*, 2:286; Lockward, *Documentos*, 62–63; Porter, *Diario de una misión secreta*, 205. On the eagerness of foreign sources to echo these pronouncements, either to instantiate their claims of whiteness for the whole Dominican territory or to parody Dominicans' thinking about identity, see Eller, "Awful Pirates and Hordes of Jackals."
165. Moya Pons, *Dominican Republic*, 186–87; Landolfi, *Evolución cultural dominicana*, 69.
166. González, "Bonó, un crítico del liberalismo," 473.
167. Baud, "Patrons, Peasants, and Tobacco," 220–21.

168. Vicioso, El freno hatero, 234, 236.
169. Johnson, Fear of French Negroes, 83–90; Raymundo González, "The 'People Eater,' " in Roorda, Derby, and González, Dominican Republic Reader, 102–8.
170. Rodríguez Demorizi, Correspondencia, 157, 13. Ships left "daily" in earlier decades (Montulé, A Voyage to North America, and the West Indies, 24).
171. "Las Provincias del Cibao," La Regeneración, no. 5, 24 September 1865, 1.
172. Harry Hoetink suggests that Masonic brothers referred to each other as "frercitos" (an amalgamation of French frère and the Spanish diminutive suffix—ito), suggesting the influence of either Haitian or French sources on Dominican Masonic practices (Dominican People, 170).
173. Scholars have traditionally drawn a stark contrast between "liberal Cibao" and the traditional, "semi-feudal south" (Landolfi, Evolución cultural dominicana, 54). Several observations temper this dichotomy, however. The first is that many southern commentators desired the very same reforms—financial reform, agricultural development, fiscal reform, "a pro-business constitution," and so on—as they, too, were shut out of power (El Orden, no. 6, 18 February 1854). The second is simply the observation that many of the Cibao elites, probably an "ample majority," were themselves markedly conservative (Jimenes Grullón, Sociologia política dominicana, 138).
174. Abreu Cardet and Álvarez-López, Guerras de liberación, 22.
175. Hoetink, Dominican People, 175. Some elites supported land enclosure, but they did so in measured tones that reflected their relatively isolated position (Vicioso, El freno hatero, 234, 236); see Franks, "Transforming Property," 55–56, for titling and survey practices.
176. Main, Tobacco Colony, 38.
177. Rodríguez Demorizi, Correspondencia, 2:104; Rodríguez Demorizi, Del vocabulario dominicano, 154; Hazard, Santo Domingo, Past and Present, 186.
178. Hazard, Santo Domingo, Past and Present, 181.
179. "Puerto de Plata Estado del movimiento marítimo . . . ," Gaceta de Santo Domingo, no. 54, 30 January 1862, 3.
180. GB Consul a Min. of Foreign Affairs, 1 October 1860, AGN-RD: RREE 14, Expte. 7.12.
181. See, e.g., "Estado nominativo de los individuos llegados a este puerto desde el 1 de Octubre 1851 hasta el 1 de Julio de 1852," Puerto Plata, July 1852, AGN-RD: RREE A441, Expte. 7; Puig Ortíz, Emigración de libertos, 25–26; Hazard, Santo Domingo, Past and Present, 175, 181, 201. One report suggests that African American migrants arrived first in the 1820s, followed by migrants from the British Caribbean in the next decade (Meriño, "Expte. reservado para tratar de la aplicación . . . ," 26 September 1862, ANC: AP 53, Expte. 20).
182. Faye, "Commodore Aury"; Grégory Pierrot, personal communication, 29 April 2016.
183. Harris, "Summer on the Borders," 89; Rodríguez Demorizi, Samaná, 333; Vega, Breve historia de Samaná, 28.

184. Moya Pons, *Dominican Republic*, 187; Herrera R., *Montecristi entre campeche y bananos*, 36.
185. Theresa Smith to Cap. Gen., 1862, AGN-RD: Anexión 12, Expte. 56, doc. s/n.
186. Enrique Llansó y Oriol to Cap. Gen., Samaná, 4 Nov. 1864, AGN-RD: CH Leg. 24, Expte. 212, p. 26 (originally 36).
187. Hidalgo, "From North America to Hispaniola," 146; Fanning, *Caribbean Crossing*, 85.
188. Keim, *San Domingo*, 110.
189. Tejeda Ortíz, *Cultura y folklore de Samaná*, 75.
190. Tejeda Ortíz, *Cultura y folklore de Samaná*, 76. See also Davis, "La historia de los inmigrantes afro-americanos."
191. "Santo Domingo, Feb. 20: Seizure of a Portuguese Slaver by the Dominican Republic," *Frederick Douglass's Paper*, 22 April 1853, 1.
192. "Who Would Like to Do Some Good in Hayti?," *Christian Advocate and Journal* 29, no. 23 (8 June 1854): 91.
193. Pierrot, "The Samaná Affair."
194. Rodríguez Demorizi, *Correspondencia*, 62; Lockward, *Documentos*, 59.
195. Keim, *San Domingo*, 119.
196. "Proceso contra varios individuos acusados de complicidad en la sublevación que tubo lugar en Puerto Plata," September 1863, AGN-RD: CH Leg. 24 (AGI: Cuba 1014A), Expte. 211.
197. Lockward, *Documentos*, 233.
198. Mariano Álvarez, "Memoria: Santo Domingo o la República Dominicana," SD, 20 April 1860, AHN: Ultramar 2775, Expte. 16.
199. Martínez-Fernández, *Torn between Empires*, 90. Some contemporary estimates suggest about 260,000 in the territory (Ministers to the Queen, January 1865, AHN: Ultramar 2775, Expte. 17).
200. Felipe Rivero to Min. de la Guerra y Ultramar, SD, 19 June 1862, AHN: Ultramar 3525, Expte. 15. Pedro Francisco Bonó would comment, decades later: "Those around town are paths; those in the savanna are cattle-trails. . . . Every old Dominican who finds himself obligated to make a journey spends the evening before agitated as if it were one preceding a battle" (qtd. in Hoetink, *Dominican People*, 47).
201. Rubén Silié, "The Hato and the Conuco: The Emergence of Creole Culture," in Vega and Castillo Pichardo, *Dominican Cultures*, 140.
202. Gaspar, *Bondsmen and Rebels*.
203. Hall, *History of Race in Muslim West Africa*, 22.
204. Mamdani, *Define and Rule*.
205. González, "Ideología del progreso y campesinado," 34. On incipient labor divisions in the wood industry, see Abreu Cardet and Álvarez-López, *Guerras de liberación*, 19.
206. Vicioso, *El freno hatero*, 236.
207. Abreu Cardet and Álvarez-López, *Guerras de liberación*, 19–21.

208. Landolfi, *Evolución cultural dominicana*, 55.
209. Harris, "Summer on the Borders," 93; Vallejo, *Las madres de la Patria*, 48; González, "Ideologia del progreso y campesinado," 30–31. For similar constructs in Haitian rural life, see N'Zengou-Tayo, " 'Famn Se Poto Mitan,' " 121–22.
210. Franks, "Transforming Property," 57.
211. González, "Ideología del progreso y campesinado"; San Miguel, *Los Campesinos del Cibao*; Cassá, *Historia social y económica*; Franks, "Transforming Property"; Turits, *Foundations of Despotism*, chap. 1.
212. Hoetink asserts that metal-tipped plows were not introduced to the Cibao valley until 1898; peasants worked with wooden tools called *coas* (*Dominican People*, 5).
213. Figueroa, *Sugar, Slavery and Freedom*, 171.
214. De la Fuente, *Children of Facundo*, 191.
215. De la Fuente, *Children of Facundo*, 31, 123.
216. Smith, *The Oracle and the Curse*; Reuben Zahler, *Ambitious Rebels*.
217. Blanco Díaz, *Alejandro Ángulo Guridi*, 1:24, 131; others concurred (Marte, *Correspondencia*, 95).
218. Rodríguez, "Encroachment of Creole Culture," 116.
219. Declaración del testigo paisano Fermín Vázquez, in "Sumaria Instruido contra el paisano Manuel de Arias acusado de Sospechoso," SD, July 1864, AGI: Cuba 1012A, "Sumarias," 5v.
220. Marte, "La oralidad sobre el pasado insular," 21; Rodríguez Demorizi, *Del vocabulario dominicano*, 17, 36, 70.
221. De la Rosa Garabito, *San Cristobal en la historia dominicana*, 12.
222. On reciprocity norms elsewhere in the rural greater Caribbean, see, e.g., Williams, *Stains on My Name*.
223. Macleod, "Narratives of Belonging and Identity," 97–114. This model would be similar to recognition of the original founder (*prenmye mèt bitayson*) of a *lakou* in the west (Ramsey, *Spirits and the Law*, 68).
224. Larrazábal Blanco, *Los negros y la esclavitud*, 170. On semi-anthropomorphized beings and shapeshifting in Dominican wooded spaces of the center island, see Derby, "Male Heroism."
225. Excerpt of *El Grito de la Frontera*, spring 1857, in Sáez, *Documentos inéditos de Fernando A. de Meriño*, 70.
226. Moya Pons, "Las ocho fronteras de Haití y la República Dominicana," 441–46; García Tamayo, "Cultura campesina en la frontera norte."
227. José Malo de Molina to Cap. Gen. Francisco Serrano, 4 September 1861 (15 July 1861), AHN: Ultramar 3532, Expte. 1, doc. 2, pp. 17, 39, 43 (hereafter cited as Malo de Molina to Serrano, "Memoria").
228. Fabens, Montgomery, and Kimball, *In the Tropics*, 162.
229. José Núñez de Cáceres to Secretario de Estado, SD, 18 February 1811, AGI: Audiencia de SD 1016, Expte. s/n.

230. Francisco Serrano, *Informe de la visita a SD*, SD, 5 September 1861, in Rodríguez Demorizi, *Antecedentes*, 245.
231. Malo de Molina to Serrano, "Memoria," 17; Pérez Memén, *El Pensamiento Dominicano*, 31.
232. Lockward, *Documentos*, 214; Keim, *San Domingo*, 223.
233. Rodríguez Demorizi, *Cuentos de política criolla*, 36.
234. Martínez-Fernández, *Torn between Empires*, 93; Franks, "Transforming Property," 103. A young secret agent reported to Puerto Rican authorities that soldiers never saw pay, as public funds were "the vomit of thousands of paper bills" (Conde de [Spiculot] to Ramón María Narváez, Sec'y de Estado y del Despacho de la Guerra, Puerto Rico, 18 January 1845, SHM: Ultramar 5646, Expte. 4, "Asuntos: Operaciones de Campaña . . . 1843–1857").
235. Franks, "Transforming Property," 90; Rodríguez Demorizi, *Del vocabulario dominicano*, 20, 40.
236. Porter, *Diario de una misión secreta*, 15.
237. Febres-Cordero Carrillo, "La anexión," 232; Torrente, *Política ultramarina*, 294; Neici Zeller, personal communication, 19 August 2015.
238. Michez to Director General del Ramo de la Guerra, Seybo, 16 July 1861, AGN-RD: Coleccion Herrera Leg. 21, Expte. 174, 17.
239. Hoetink refers to the salience of military status in community prestige as a "heroic ideology" (*Dominican People*, 166).
240. Samet, *Willing Obedience*; "La obediencia pasiva del soldado," *El Porvenir*, no. 4, 29 October 1854, 3.
241. "Varias reflexiones sobre cual debe ser el espiritu publico para salvar la situación que atravesemos," *El Porvenir*, no. 2, 15 October 1854, 1.
242. *El Eco del Pueblo*, no. 18, 23 November 1856, 1.
243. Martínez-Fernández, "The Sword and the Crucifix," 70.
244. Robin Derby, personal communication, 11 August 2015.
245. Díaz-Stevens, "Saving Grace," 60–78.
246. The Cofradía del Espiritu Santo in the San Juan valley is another example (Robin Derby, personal communication, 11 August 2015).
247. "Romerias a Higüey," *El Oasis*, no. 18, 28 October 1855, 70–71.
248. Paton, *No Bond but the Law*, 184.
249. Nessler, "'The Shame of the Nation,'" 5–28.
250. Janvier, *Haïti et ses visiteurs*, 603.
251. Throughout the colonial period and unification, some Haitian faithful traveled all the way to Higüey for the annual Altagracia pilgrimage (Ramsey, *Spirits and the Law*, 6–7; Franklin, *Present State of Hayti*, 297–98; Rey, "Toward an Ethnohistory"). In western vodou, or Ginen, Erzulie Freda of the rada pantheon is identified with Altagracia; in Santo Domingo she is sometimes identified with Ezili Aíla (Alaíla) (Deive, *Vodú*, 227).
252. Austerlitz, *Merengue*, 25.
253. Guerrero Cano, *Disciplina y laxitud*, 67.

254. "Bando," in *Colección de leyes*, 150.
255. Vásquez de Díaz, *Antiguallas de Neyba*, 116; Ubiñas Renville, *Historias y leyendas afro-dominicanas*, 91; Brendan Thornton, personal communication, 4 July 2015.
256. Larrazábal Blanco, *Los negros y la esclavitud*, 190.
257. Derby, "Haitians, Magic, and Money," 520.
258. Krug, "Healing Politics and the Politics of Healing."
259. Besson, *Martha Brae's Two Histories*, 257; Davis, "Afro-Dominican Religious Brotherhoods."
260. Vásquez de Díaz, *Antiguallas de Neyba*, 322.
261. Martínez, "Not a Cockfight," 92; Vásquez de Díaz, *Antiguallas de Neyba*, 153.
262. José del Carmen Rodríguez to Cap. Gen., Santiago, 21 January 1863, AGN-RD: Anexión 12, Expte. 56, doc. s/n.
263. Gob. Militar de Santiago to José Hungria, Santiago, 7 November 1862, AGN-RD: Anexión 12, Expte. 56, doc. s/n. Other passport applicants were vague about their motives, citing only "personal reasons" (*asuntos particulares*).
264. José María Sánchez to Cap. Gen., s/f, probably 1862–63, AGI: Cuba 1025A, Expte. "Declaraciones recibidas," doc. s/n.
265. Anna María LaPlace to Cap. Gen., Puerto Plata, 15 January 1863, AGN-RD: Anexión 12, Expte. 56, doc. s/n.
266. E.g., Madame Beazley and Madame Gustave Ducastro (*Le Moniteur Haïtien*, no. 14, 9 March 1861, 1; *Le Moniteur Haïtien*, no. 15, 16 March 1861, 1).
267. Théodat, *Haïti et la République Dominicaine*, 217.
268. Referring to French national Mme. Rosette in Yuna (Copiador, 7 March 1848); for statistics on wood selling in this period, which peaked in the 1830s, see Abreu Cardet and Álvarez-López, *Guerras de liberación*, 17–19.
269. Raybaud, *Soulouque et son empire*, 277; Copiador, 6 May 1857.
270. José María Sánchez to Cap. Gen., s/f, probably 1862–63, AGI: Cuba 1025A, Expte. "Declaraciones recibidas," doc. s/n. *El Dominicano* complained of foreign interests in Hincha, writing, "Who doesn't know that [almost all] of this industry is foreign, covered with the name of some Haitian?" (no. 8, 24 November 1845, 29).
271. On the "contradictory axes" of identity construction and the idea of "copresence" in center-island regions in later decades, see Derby, "Haitians, Magic, and Money," 490, 495.
272. Vásquez de Díaz, *Antiguallas de Neyba*, 321–26.
273. Moya Pons, *Dominican Republic*, 185. Lauren Derby observes that the prevalence of these west-going networks—and relative lack of infrastructure connecting the region to the Dominican capital—endured into the twentieth century ("Haitians, Magic, and Money," 488–526).
274. Rodríguez Demorizi, *Correspondencia*, 2:22.
275. *El Eco del Pueblo*, no. 26, 1 February 1857, 101.

276. Other witnesses, including Spanish authorities, supported these claims (Philantrope Noël to Brig. Buceta, Dajabon, 15 August 1863, AHN: Ultramar 3525, Expte. 99, Anexo 6; López Morillo, *Memorias sobre la segunda reincorporación de Santo Domingo*, 82).
277. Copiador, 26 July 1850.
278. Hernández Flores, *Luperón, héroe y alma*, 97.
279. Crawford, "Politics of Belonging to a Caribbean Borderland."
280. Hernández Flores, *Luperón, héroe y alma*, 96.
281. "Formally recognizing the independence of Santo Domingo . . . is not necessary, and besides, it is convenient to reserve the weapon of recognition," one diplomat cynically observed (qtd. in Martínez-Fernández, "Caudillos," 576). A number of recent works have ably described the strong-arm diplomacy of foreign powers toward the nations of the island in this period, as well as the rabidly annexationist efforts of many Dominican elites (Febres-Cordero Carrillo, "La anexión"; Martínez-Fernández, "Caudillos"; Robles-Muñoz, *Paz en Santo Domingo*; Álvarez López, *Dominacion colonial y guerra popular*).
282. F. W. Chesson, "American Intrigues in Santo Domingo," 15 December 1858, *The Anti-slavery Reporter* 7, no. 3 (1859): 7–8.
283. Lockward, *Documentos*, xix.
284. Copiador, 21 January 1856. The government's arrest and imprisonment of U.S. agent Edward Roolt was far from the first incident of exasperation at U.S. officials' behavior: Francisco Harrison was remonstrated in 1847, Abner Burbank in 1847 and 1848, Jonathan Elliot in 1848, suspected spy Cherí Brocard in 1850, Jacob Pereira in 1856, Elliot again in 1857, an unnamed vice-agent in 1859, and so on.
285. Moya Pons, *Dominican Republic*, 190; Hauch, "The Dominican Republic and Its Foreign Relations," 59.
286. Rodríguez Demorizi, *Correspondencia*, 2:198; Tansill, *The United States and Santo Domingo*, 131.
287. Baur, "Faustin Soulouque," 135.
288. Lockward, *Documentos*, 144.
289. "[The *Moniteur Haïtien*] and other Haitian periodicals treat us like a handful of rebels who need to be subjugated again," a journalist observed (*El Dominicano*, no. 27, 5 January 1856, 105).
290. Garrido, *Los Puello*, 85.
291. Soulouque, "Carta dirigida a los habitantes del este," Port-au-Prince, 24 November 1848, in Rodríguez Demorizi, *La Marina de Guerra dominicana*, 75.
292. A. J. Bautista Romane, "Fragmentos," *El Oasis*, no. 19, 4 November 1855, 75.
293. As with the Separation campaigns, traditional accounts exaggerate the size of these encounters, and the absence of surviving newspapers from 1849 to 1850 makes rectification difficult. Several years later, just five pro-Santana officers and their supporters easily took the town, for example, despite Azua being a traditional opposition stronghold (Bosch, *La Guerra de la Restauración*,

44–45). A Dominican minister later dismissed Soulouque's mobilizations as "piratic and impotent" (Núñez de Arce, Santo Domingo, 48).
294. Rodríguez Demorizi, Correspondencia, 2:370; "The feeling of the great mass of the Haytian people towards the Spaniards of their own island, is perfectly friendly," an English man observed from Haiti, noting that Soulouque had to mobilize in secret (Bird, Black Man, 294, 308).
295. Hauch, "The Dominican Republic and Its Foreign Relations," 87; Torrente, Política ultramarina, 316.
296. Rodríguez Demorizi, Correspondencia, 2:40; Copiador, 9 June 1852.
297. Lockward, Documentos, 144.
298. The Dominican foreign minister wrote to the consuls of Britain and France and the U.S. commercial agent about a "pack" (pelotón) of Haitian soldiers, for example, or about incidents involving a single individual (Copiador, 26 July 1850, 5 February 1855). Mostly Dominican reports involved cattle theft in the center of the island. However, it seems that Dominican soldiers (or perhaps simple residents) shared responsibility. Occasionally, officials admitted that "stray" Dominican soldiers had wandered into Haitian territory and taken cattle, and sometimes Dominican officers admitted guilt, too (Copiador, 25 August 1852, 19 August 1853, 26 April 1854, 13 November 1855). Nevertheless, Dominican ministers stayed firmly on-narrative. The foreign minister complained to the British consulate that the injury of one individual was a "new aggression" that proved "the eternal predisposition of the enemy," Haiti (11 December 1851). Meanwhile, the French authorities, particularly, never stopped provoking the Haitian and Dominican heads of state in the name of "mediation," goading Dominican officials about imagined threats well into periods of indiscutible peace (French consul to For. Min., 21 November 1860, AGN-RD: RREE 14, Expte. 6, doc. 23).
299. El Oasis, no. 6, 5 August 1855, 23; El Oasis, no. 10, 2 September 1855, 37.
300. "Manifiesto de Santana contra Báez," El Progreso, no. 20, 10 July 1853; El Eco del Pueblo, no. 7, 7 September 1856, 25; El Eco del Pueblo, no. 20, 7 December 1856, 77.
301. "En que país vivimos!!," El Progreso, no. 17, 12 June 1853, 1.
302. La Acusación, no. 1, 12 November 1856, 1; Martínez Paulino, Publicaciones periódicas dominicanas, 27.
303. "Mi vecino Don Cameleón," El Dominicano, no. 17, 27 May 1846, 48.
304. "Las conspiraciones vistas de un lado," El Oasis, no. 7, 12 August 1855, 26.
305. "La Pueri-Cracia," El Oasis, no. 23, 2 December 1855, 89–92.
306. French consul to Cap. Gens. of Puerto Rico and Cuba, 14 September 1852, ANC: AP 47, Expte. 15.
307. French consul to Cap. Gens. of Puerto Rico and Cuba, 14 September 1852, ANC: AP 47, Expte. 15.
308. Cap. Gen. of Cuba to Cap. Gen. of Puerto Rico, 25 October 1852, ANC: AP 47, Expte. 15, 78.

309. Min. de RREE to J. B. Camoin, 29 January 1853, AGN-RD: RREE A441 [7/008374], Expte. 8.
310. "The Dominican Republic—The Grand Plot," *National Era*, 2 November 1854, 1.
311. May, "'Plenipotentiary in Petticoats,'" 27.
312. Juan Abril to D. José de la Concha, Cap. Gen. of Cuba, SD, 25 November 1854, AGI: Cuba 984C.
313. A Spanish observer commented snidely that he assumed a Dominican ship sailing to Baltimore to conduct treaty organizations with "a mulatto owner and a black crew" had been detained and its crew arrested (Juan Abril to Don Leopoldo Augusto de Cueto, Ministro de SMC en Washington, 23 July 1854, AMAE: Política Exterior: RD 2374, Expte. s/n). Apparently the French consul was so opposed to the treaty (for the Samaná concessions it presented, not for stipulations of racism) that he managed to have pro-treaty *El Porvenir* shuttered (Martínez-Fernández, *Torn between Empires*, 45).
314. William Cazneau, "Remitido," *El Porvenir*, no. 3, 22 October 1854, 3. Dominican officials republished his claims.
315. "Our Failure in the Dominican Matter," *New York Times*, 24 January 1855, 4.
316. Juan Abril to Cap. Gen. of Puerto Rico, SD, 6 November 1854, AGI: Cuba 984C, Expte. s/n; Juan Abril to Cap. Gen. of Puerto Rico, SD, 28 November 1854, AGI: Cuba 984C, Expte. s/n.
317. Hauch, "The Dominican Republic and Its Foreign Relations," 124; Dubois, *Avengers*, 147.
318. Baur, "Faustin Soulouque," 154.
319. *El Oasis*, no. 33, 17 February 1856, 131.
320. Moya Pons, *Dominican Republic*, 198.
321. Rodríguez Demorizi, *Guerra dominico-haitiana*, 23.
322. *El Dominicano*, no. 27, 5 January 1856, 105. For descriptions of the failed 1855–56 campaign, see, e.g., Bird, *Black Man*, 294; *El Oasis*, no. 31, 27 January 1856, 123–24.
323. *El Oasis*, no. 33, 17 February 1856, 131.
324. Baur, "Faustin Soulouque," 154. The expeditionary groups were poorly supplied, and Soulouque also often used conscription as political punishment for towns that opposed him (142). French Consul Maxime Raybaud—the very same who provoked Soulouque on numerous occasions—concurred, admitting under a pseudonym that the conflicts were "profoundly disagreeable to nineteen-twentieths of Haitians (Raybaud, *Soulouque et son empire*, 190).
325. *El Oasis*, no. 29, 13 January 1856, 115; "Vade Retro," *El Dominicano*, no. 24, 15 December 1855, 24.
326. Dubois, *Haiti*, 150.
327. "Los filibusteros," *El Eco del Pueblo*, no. 1, 27 July 1856, 3; "Revista exterior," *El Eco del Pueblo*, no. 27, 8 February 1857, 105; "Exterieur," *Le Moniteur Haïtien*,

no. 5, 8 January 1859, 4; "Nouvelles étrangères," *Le Moniteur Haïtien*, no. 47, 27 October 1860, 4; "Nouvelles étrangères," *Le Moniteur Haïtien*, no. 27, 8 June 1861, 3.
328. Hauch, "The Dominican Republic and Its Foreign Relations," 124, 128–30; Manning, *Diplomatic Correspondence*, 175.
329. "Programa Gubernativa," *El Eco del Pueblo*, no. 2, 3 August 1856, 7.
330. Eduardo San Justo to Cap. Gen. of Cuba, SD, 7 March 1855, AGI: Cuba 984C.
331. Félix María del Monte, "El General Antonio Duvergé o las víctimas del once de abril," qtd. in Rodríguez Demorizi, *Santana y los poetas*, 115.
332. Martínez-Fernández, "The Sword and the Crucifix," 77.
333. Qtd. in Rodríguez Demorizi, *Santana y los poetas*, 155.
334. *El Oasis*, no. 46, 18 May 1856, 183.
335. Martínez-Fernández, *Torn between Empires*, 93.
336. Pérez Memén, *El Pensamiento Dominicano*, 325.
337. "Otro Pirata," *El Dominicano*, no. 33, 16 February 1856, 131.
338. Consul Martin Hood to Minister Delmonte, SD, 24 April 1858, AGN-RD: RREE 11, Expte. 6, doc. 7.
339. To worsen matters, fake pesos occasionally arrived from New York and Boston (Copiador, 12 February 1855; AGN-RD: RREE 12, Expte. 19.3, 15 June 1859).
340. "La Tirania Comercial," *El Eco del Pueblo*, no. 30, 15 March 1857, 118.
341. "REVOLUCION! CONSPIRACION!," *El Eco del Pueblo*, no. 36, 10 May 1857, 141.
342. Núñez Grullón, *Evolución constitucional dominicana*, 34–37.
343. Franks, "Transforming Property," 97; Bosch, *La Guerra de la Restauración*, 28.
344. Báez, Decreto, 6 November 1857, ANC: AP 50, Expte. 22; Copiador, 21 December 1857.
345. "Extrait d'une lettre de Sto.-Domingo du 1er. mai," *Le Moniteur Haïtien*, nos. 26–27, 12 June 1858, 2.
346. Buenaventura Báez, 12 June 1858, AHN: Ultramar 3525, Expte. 4, doc. 2.
347. Landolfi, *Evolución cultural dominicana*, 87. Báez sought help from Spanish authorities in Puerto Rico on the pretext that rebellion against him was "pro-American" and annexationist (Martínez-Fernández, "Caudillos," 586).
348. "Mania de la epoca," *El Dominicano*, no. 1, 29 June 1855, 3.
349. "Matrícula de Segovia II," *La República*, no. 4, 30 September 1856, 2.
350. "Matricula Española," *El Eco del Pueblo*, no. 2, 3 August 1856, 6–7.
351. "Matricula Española," *El Eco del Pueblo*, no. 1, 27 July 1856, 2.
352. Arminio, "Espiritu de la Epoca," *El Oasis*, no. 7, 7 January 1855, 27–28.
353. Nisidas, "Epigram," *El Dominicano*, no. 8, 25 August 1855, 31. Manola means "gal from Madrid."
354. Copiador, 5 May 1857; Copiador, 25–26 October 1857 and December 1857; Jonathan Elliot to Felix María Delmonte, 25 October 1857, AGN-RD: Leg. 7/008370, Expte. 22, doc. 9.

355. M. McIntosh, Flag Officer, Commander-in-Chief, Home Squadron to President Buenaventura Báez, U.S. Flag Ship "Colorado" off SD City, 1 June 1858, AGN-RD: Leg. 11 (7/008371), Expte. 2, p. 7.
356. Moya Pons, Dominican Republic, 201–2. In April 1858 a crew from Baltimore, including fifty enslaved men, landed and tried to claim Navaza Island.
357. Lockward, Documentos, 339.
358. "Colonia Agrícola," El Eco del Pueblo, no. 23, 11 January 1857, 91.
359. Traité entre la République Dominicaine et B. Bullot, 30 April 1857, AGN-RD: RREE A441, Expte. 11, p. 9; Copiador, 26 October 1857.
360. Le Moniteur Haïtien, no. 8, 30 January 1858, 1. At any rate, the eastern republic was in the midst of being wracked by a regional civil war; the Moniteur concluded, with satisfaction, "Civil war is in a way the normal state [for] Dominicans, and nothing indicates that these matters will conclude anytime soon."
361. Lockward, Documentos, 348.
362. Min. RREE to Ministro Alfau, Copiador, 21 August 1860.
363. Mariano Álvarez to Cap. Gen. of Cuba, 20 June 1860, AGI: Cuba 2261, Pieza 1.
364. Lockward, Documentos, 349; Ministro de Guerra y Ultramar to Ministerio de Marina, 24 August 1860, AHN: Ultramar 3526, Expte. 1, pp. 9–10.
365. Moya Pons, Dominican Republic, 198; AGN-RD: RREE 12 (7/008375), Exptes. 2, 5.
366. Moya Pons, Dominican Republic, 199.
367. Lockward, Documentos, 324–25.
368. Copiador, 9 March 1857, 1 June 1860.
369. Bosch, La Guerra de la Restauración, 45.
370. Vicioso, El freno hatero, 260.
371. Vicioso, El freno hatero, 267.
372. Copiador, 5 December 1860.
373. Pablo de Urrutia to Cap. Gen. of Cuba, Port-au-Prince, 6 November 1858, ANC: AP 224, Expte. 13; St. John, Hayti, 97.
374. González Tablas, Historia de la dominación, 41 (emphasis in original); beyond the support of high-profile generals like Sánchez, prisoner lists in the capital (e.g., Le Moniteur Haïtien, nos. 39–40, 9 September 1858, 1) substantiate his observation.
375. Pablo de Urrutia to Cap. Gen. of Cuba, Port-au-Prince, 10 January 1859, ANC: AP 224, Expte. 13; Copiador, 22 January 1859; St. John, Hayti, 97.
376. Le Moniteur Haïtien, nos. 6–7, 22 January 1859, 3.
377. Mariano Álvarez to Cap. Gen. of SD, Port-au-Prince, 9 May 1862, SHM Leg. 5645, Expte. "Sobre operaciones militares en Santo Domingo . . . ," doc. s/n.
378. "Discours prononcé par le Comité central des Gonaïves de l'anniversaire de l'independance de 1er. janvier 1859," Le Moniteur Haïtien, nos. 6–7, 22 January 1859, 3 (emphasis in original).
379. Le Moniteur Haïtien, nos. 39–40, 9 September 1858, 1–2.

380. Copiador, 22 January 1861. Dominican officials sought help in his surveillance (Felipe Alfau to Min. de RREE, Madrid, 20 February 1861, AGN: RREE 14/15/16 (7/008378), Expte. 6, doc. 5.
381. *Le Moniteur Haïtien*, no. 12, 23 February 1861, 3.
382. *Le Moniteur Haïtien*, no. 12, 23 February 1861, 3.
383. Ministro de RREE a los Cónsules de Inglaterra y Francia, 23 June 1860, AGN: RREE 14, Expte. 2, pp. 6–10v; Moya Pons, *Dominican Republic*, 201.
384. S. Chedeville au Ministre des relations étrangères, 2 May 1853, AGN: RREE 6–7, Expte. 7; Copiador, 19 August 1853.
385. Without the full foreign relations log, much of the communication about events on the border remains lost. The British authorities asked to send emissaries to the "revolutionary encampment of Alejandro Gregor," for example, but no further information is recorded (Copiador, 27 September 1857). Evidently Ramírez had been given an official position in the Haitian army in the month prior and was receiving instructions from Alcantara (M. Hood to Min. de RREE, SD, 24 June 1860, AGN-RD: RREE 14/15/16 (7/008378), Expte. 1, p. 22. Alcantara had sworn allegiance to the west at least since 1850 (Rodríguez Demorizi, *Correspondencia*, 2:350).
386. "Orden del día del General de División Domingo Ramírez," Given in the General Barracks of Cercado, 12 June 18[60], AGN: RREE 14/15/16 (7/008378), Expte. 1, p. 1.
387. Ministro de RREE a los Cónsules de Inglaterra y Francia, 23 June 1860, AGN-RD: RREE 14, Expte. 2. The document cites several Dominican officials (Alcantara, Ramírez, the commander of las Caobas) and only one Haitian officer, Colonel Joseph Chateau. Nevertheless, the Dominican minister demanded 400,000 pesos fuertes.
388. M. Lavastida, "Memoria que dirige el Ministro de Guerra y Marina a S.E. el Presidente de la República," 27 February 1861, AGN-RD: Leg. DE/1371 (1861–1913), Expte. s/n. Evidently Ramírez was totally defeated, although many took refuge in Haiti (Abram Coën to Min. de RREE, Curaçao, 11 Julio 1860, AGN-RD: RREE 14/15/16 [7/008378], Leg. 15, Expte. 2, p. 19).
389. Min. de Marina to Min. de Guerra y Ultramar, 24 August 1860, AHN: Ultramar 3526, Expte. 1.
390. Copiador, 14 September 1860.
391. Martínez-Fernández, "Caudillos," 571.

2. Soon It Will Be Mexico's Turn

1. Manuel de Cruzat to Felipe Ribero (passed on to the Queen), SD, 15 August 1862, ANC: Audiencia de la Habana Leg. 245, Expte. 2; Consul Hood to Russel, 21 March 1861, AGN-RD: Anexión DE/0093, Expte. 1, p. 1. The flag was lowered the following day and not raised again for some time.
2. Rodríguez Demorizi, *Antecedentes*, 157.
3. Pani, "Dreaming of a Mexican Empire."

4. Pani, "Dreaming of a Mexican Empire," 28.
5. In Ecuador, for example, President José María Urvina Viterí offered territorial cessions to pay for British debt in 1854; five years later, Gabriel García Moreno hoped for a French protectorate not only to secure Ecuador's borders from partition by Colombia and Peru but also to forestall U.S. aggression. In 1861, a new plan to establish a monarchy in Ecuador with French help (and some territorial cessions) also never materialized, in part because Napoleon III was already involved in Mexico (Pineo, *Ecuador and the United States*, 42; Lauderbaugh, *History of Ecuador*, 57).
6. "What then is the citizen-king? . . . That is what we want, what all Brazilians want: a strong monarch who curbs the ambitions of the discontented and suppresses the fanaticism of the masses," Brazilian chroniclers proclaimed (Barman, *Citizen Emperor*, ix). Emperor Souloque, too, sought the "esteem and sympathy of civilized peoples" through "empire . . . as the signal of rebirth and order" ("PROCLAMATION. Faustin Ier, Empereur d'Haïti, au peuple et à l'armée," *Le Moniteur Haïtien*, no. 5, 8 January 1859, 1). Opponents of Napoleon III accused him of *souloquerie* even as they praised Dom Pedro II (Dubois, *Haiti*, 146; Barman, *Citizen Emperor*, 160).
7. Burdiel, "The Queen, the Woman, and the Middle Class."
8. "Astounding Intelligence," *New York Times*, 30 March 1861, 1; "Spanish Designs on the American Continent," *Chicago Tribune*, 3 April 1861, 1.
9. Spain's 1812 constitution proposed the transformation of the American colonies into representative provinces, albeit with unequal representation. Even though it excluded men of African ancestry from citizenship, Cuban planters had opposed it, associating constitutionalism with abolitionism. Implementation stalled, anyway, as independence vitiated the empire. In 1837, Caribbean representatives were expelled from Madrid's Cortes altogether. The overseas territories were ruled in a state of exception for the next several decades, despite the promise of "special laws" to bring the colonies back under constitutional rule (Fradera, "Why Were Spain's Special Overseas Laws Never Enacted?," 338, 348; Marquese and Parron, "Atlantic Constitutionalism," 184; Fradera, "Reading Imperial Transitions," 57; Schmidt-Nowara, *Empire and Anti-slavery*, 25).
10. Rodríguez Demorizi, *Antecedentes*, 152.
11. Centeno, "Critical Debates," 154.
12. Morillo-Alicea, "Uncharted Landscapes of 'Latin America,'" 31.
13. Powelson, "Nineteenth-Century Latin American Imperialism," 827–43.
14. McGuinness, "Searching for 'Latin America'"; Gobat, "Invention of Latin America."
15. Álvarez Junco, "Spanish National Identity," 321; Febres-Cordillo Carrillo, "La anexión," 101; Malamud, *Ruptura y reconciliación*, 2.
16. Delutis-Eichenberger, "National Consciousness and Shared Americanism," 10.

17. Schmidt-Nowara, *Empire and Anti-slavery*, 105; Schmidt-Nowara, *Conquest of History*, 34–42.
18. Mariano Álvarez to Francisco Serrano, SD, 20 July 1860, AGI: Cuba 2266, Pieza 1.
19. *La Epoca*, 11 July 1860, qtd. in Fontecha Pedraza and González Calleja, *Una cuestión de honor*, 45 (hereafter cited as *Cuestión*).
20. Cubano-Iguina, "Visions of Empire," 89.
21. *Cuestión*, 20.
22. May, *Slavery, Race, and Conquest in the Tropics*.
23. Martínez-Fernández, *Torn between Empires*, 22–23.
24. L. A. de Cueto to 1r Secretary of State, Washington, DC, 25 October 1851, AMAE: Política Exterior: RD 2374, Expte. s/n.
25. Qtd. in "La América," *El Eco del Pueblo*, no. 35, 3 May 1857, 137.
26. Puerto Rican governor Rafael Aristegui to Spanish Minister of State, 15 November 1844, qtd. in Febres-Cordero Carrillo, "La anexión," 80–81.
27. Febres-Cordero Carrillo, "La anexión," 92, 93; Cap. Gen. of Puerto Rico to Secretary of State and Despacho de la Guerra, Puerto Rico, 20 April 1843, SHM: Ultramar 5646, Expte. 4, "Operaciones de campaña."
28. Febres-Cordillo Carrillo, "La anexión," 109.
29. On the African-British plot, see Juan de la Peruela to Ministro de la Guerra, Puerto Rico, 5 November 1849, SHM: Ultramar 5639, Expte. "Esclavitud/Esclavos 1849–1862." On a supposed gathering force of forty thousand, see Fernando de Norzagaray to Cap. Gen. of Cuba, 23 August 1852, ANC: AP 47, Expte. 15, p. 2.
30. Febres-Cordillo Carrillo, "La anexión," 115, 118.
31. Febres-Cordillo Carrillo, "La anexión," 137.
32. Sartorius, "My Vassals."
33. Schmidt-Nowara, *Conquest of History*, 23, 27.
34. Febres-Cordillo Carrillo, "La anexión," 125; Álvarez López, *Dominación colonial y guerra popular*, 9.
35. Felipe Fernández de Castro to Ministro de Ultramar, Madrid, 3 October 1822, AGI: Audiencia de SD 970, Expte. s/n.; Felipe Fernández de Castro to Ministro de Ultramar, 26 November 1824, AGI: Estado Leg. 4, Expte. 7; Real Orden of 24 August 1829, ANC: AP 34, Expte. 16.
36. Felipe Fernández de Castro to Intendente General de Cuba, 10 February 1830, ANC: AP 120, Expte. 124. For mention of the plans for continuing negotiations, see ANC: AP 34, Expte. 39; Leg. 36, Expte. 7.
37. Torrente, *Política ultramarina*, 311; *Cuestión*, 24.
38. Cuba, 1843: AGN-RD: "Misión en Cuba 1." Puerto Rico, 1845: Cayetano Pilón to the Queen, AMAE: Política Exterior: RD 2373, Expte. s/n, doc. s/n. Puerto Rico, 1846: Febres-Cordillo Carrillo, "La anexión," 102–3.
39. Fernando de Norzagaray to Gov. of Cuba, Puerto Rico, 14 September 1852, ANC: AP 47, Expte. 15. Another report claimed that as many as five thousand

armed volunteers from Kentucky and Georgia were attempting to enter the republic under the pretext of fighting Emperor Soulouque, and that they would then quickly turn their attentions to Cuba (Expte. of the Secretary of State, 25 September 1852, AMAE: Política Exterior: RD 2373, doc. s/n).

40. Expte. of the Secretary of State, 10 November 1852, AMAE: Política Exterior: RD 2373, doc. s/n.
41. J. M. Pando to Cap. Gen. of la Habana, Curaçao, 17 November 1850, ANC: AP 44, Expte. 15, doc 1.
42. Expte. of the Secretary of State, 6 Dic. 1852, AMAE: Política Exterior: RD 2373.
43. Mariano Torrente, "Segunda memoria sobre el Imperio de Haití," Havana, 14 January 1853, AMAE: Política Exterior: Haití 2523, Expte. 1, p. 49.
44. J. M. Pando to Cap. Gen. of la Habana, Curaçao, 17 November 1850, ANC: AP 44, Expte. 15, doc. 1; J. M. Pando to Cap. Gen. of la Habana, Curaçao, 6 December 1850, ANC: AP 44, Expte. 15, doc. 6.
45. J. M. Pando to Capitan General de la Habana, Curaçao, 17 November 1850, ANC: AP 44, Expte. 15, doc. 1.
46. Min. de State to Consul gral. de España en Haiti, Madrid, 1 November 1855, AGI: Cuba, Expte. "que comprende las instrucciones dadas al Cónsul de SM en Haití, por el Gobierno Supremo . . . ," doc. s/n.
47. Her nom de plume was Cora Montgomery. Eyal, *Young America Movement*, 159; May, "Lobbyists for Commercial Empire," 383–90.
48. Greenberg, *Manifest Manhood*, 225; Caughfield, *True Women and Westward Expansion*, 132.
49. Febres-Cordillo Carrillo, "La anexión," 123.
50. Eduardo San Just to Cap. Gen. of Cuba, SD, 7 March 1855, AGI: Cuba 984C, Expte. s/n (last in box), doc. s/n.
51. Rodríguez Demorizi, *Antecedentes*, 170.
52. Eduardo San Just to Cap. Gen. of Cuba, SD, 7 March 1855, AGI: Cuba 984C, Expte. s/n (emphasis in original).
53. Copiador, 7 May 1855.
54. Manuel Cruzat to Cap. Gen. of Cuba, Port-au-Prince, 20 August 1855, AGI: Cuba 984C, Expte. "que comprende las instrucciones dadas al Cónsul de SM en Haití, por el Gobierno Supremo . . . ," doc. s/n.
55. Manuel Cruzat to L. Dufrène, Port-au-Prince, 13 August 1855, AGI: Cuba 984C, Expte. "que comprende las instrucciones dadas al Cónsul de SM en Haití, por el Gobierno Supremo . . . ," doc. s/n.
56. "Qui moun ça, sacré foutu blanc qui veut pas saluer mon palais!" Manuel Cruzat to L. Dufrène, Port-au-Prince, 13 August 1855, AGI: Cuba 984C, Expte. "que comprende las instrucciones dadas al Cónsul de SM en Haití . . . ," doc. s/n.
57. Manuel Cruzat to [unclear], August 1855, AMAE: Política Exterior: Haiti 2523, Expte. 4.

58. Joaquin Francisco Pacheco to Cap. Gen. of Cuba, Madrid, 18 November 1854, Expte. "que comprende las instrucciones dadas al Cónsul de SM en Haití . . . ," doc. s/n; Juan de Zabala to Eugenio Villevaleix (Haitian commissioner in Paris), Madrid, 4 October 1855, AGI: Cuba 984C, Expte. "que comprende las instrucciones dadas al Cónsul de SM en Haití, por el Gobierno Supremo . . . ," doc. s/n.
59. Martínez-Fernández, *Torn between Empires*, 56.
60. Sp. Foreign Minister to Cap. Gen. of Cuba, Paris, 16 September 1859, ANC: AP 51, Expte. 9.
61. Vicioso, *El freno hatero*, 250.
62. "La República y el Sr. Segovia," *La República*, no. 4, 30 September 1856, 3.
63. Francisco Serrano to Santiago governor Carlos de Vargas, Havana, 10 April 1859, ANC: AP 224, Expte. 14.
64. Cap. Gen. of Cuba to Ministro de Estado, Havana, 12 May 1859, AMAE: Política Exterior: Haiti 2523, Expte. 1; Spanish Consul Pablo de Urrutia to Minister of Foreign Relations of Haiti, Port-au-Prince, 25 April 1859, AMAE: Política Exterior: Haiti 2523, Expte. s/n.
65. Mariano Álvarez, "Memoria: Santo Domingo o la República Dominicana," 20 April 1860, AHN: Ultramar 2275, Expte. 16 and 3526, Expte. 2.
66. Mariano Álvarez, "Memoria: Santo Domingo o la República Dominicana," 20 April 1860, AHN: Ultramar 2275, Expte. 16.
67. Mariano Álvarez to Cap. Gen. of Cuba, 20 July 1860, AGI: Cuba 2266, Pieza 1.
68. Mariano Álvarez to Secretary of State, 12 November 1860, AGI: Cuba 2266, Pieza 2.
69. Ministro de Guerra y Ultramar to Ministerio de Marina, 24 August 1860, Passing on the Comandante General del Apostedro de la Havana's 10 July report, AHN: Ultramar 3526, Expte. 1, pp. 25–26.
70. Qtd. in Núñez de Arce, *Santo Domingo*, 55.
71. Hernández Flores, *Pedro Santana*, 18.
72. Hernández Flores, *Pedro Santana*, 26.
73. Abreu Cardet and Álvarez-López, 9; Marte, *Correspondencia*, 63.
74. "The Dominican Republic—The Grand Plot," *National Era*, 2 November 1854, 1 (emphasis in original).
75. Vicioso, *El freno hatero*, 267.
76. *Le Moniteur Haïtien*, no. 11, 19 February 1859, 1.
77. Pablo de Urrutia to Gob. Cap. Gen. of Cuba, Port-au-Prince, 10 July 1860, AGI: Cuba 2266, Pieza 1.
78. Pedro Santana to the Queen, SD, 18 March 1861, AGN-RD: Anexión DE/000933, Expte. 14, p. 62.
79. Ministro de Guerra y Ultramar to Ministerio de Marina, 24 August 1860, Passing on the Comandante General del Apostedro de la Havana's 10 July report, AHN: Ultramar 3526, Expte. 1, pp. 9–10.

80. Mariano Álvarez, "Memoria: Santo Domingo o la República Dominicana," 20 April 1860, AHN: Ultramar 2775 Expte. 16. Incidentally, U.S. boosterism that year returned to these same convictions. Dominicans were "Spaniards, Spanish creoles, and *some* Africans and people of color," one insisted (Courtney, *Gold Fields of Santo Domingo*, 132 [emphasis in original]).
81. Martínez-Fernández, *Torn between Empires*, 211; Álvarez to Min. de Guerra y Ultramar, 24 August 1860, AHN: Ultramar 3526, Expte. 1.
82. Mariano Álvarez to Min. de Guerra y Ultramar and Cap. Gen. of Cuba, 24 August 1860, AHN: Ultramar 3526, Expte. 1. He admitted that he had been lobbied that very day by Vice President Alfau, who had "explicitly manifested" that version of events.
83. Mariano Álvarez, "Memoria: Santo Domingo o la República Dominicana," 20 April 1860, AHN: Ultramar 2275, Expte. 16 and 3526, Expte. 2.
84. Mariano Álvarez to Cap. Gen. of Cuba, 20 and 21 July 1860, AGI: Cuba 2266, Pieza 1.
85. Ministro de Guerra y Ultramar to Ministerio de Marina, 24 August 1860, Passing on the Comandante General del Aposterdo de la Havana's 10 July report, AHN: Ultramar 3526, Expte. 1, pp. 9–10.
86. Febres-Cordero Carrillo, "La anexión," 191.
87. Memoria of Antonio Peláez y Campomanes to Gob. Serrano, Havana, 8 November 1860, AHN: Ultramar 3526, Expte. 2, doc. 2 (hereafter cited as Memoria of Antonio Peláez y Campomanes).
88. Memoria of Antonio Peláez y Campomanes.
89. Memoria of Antonio Peláez y Campomanes.
90. In fact, due to Santo Domingo's relatively capital- and sugar-poor nature, its plantations relied on island-born slaves much more than did its profitable neighbor.
91. Memoria of Antonio Peláez y Campomanes.
92. Febres-Cordero Carrillo, "La anexión," 200.
93. Eduardo San Justo to Cap. Gen. of Cuba, SD, 7 March 1855, AGI: Cuba 984C.
94. Mariano Álvarez to Cap. Gen. of Cuba, 9 August 1860, AGI: Cuba 2266, Pieza 1.
95. Mariano Álvarez to Min. de Guerra y Ultramar and Cap. Gen. of Cuba, 24 August 1860, AHN: Ultramar 3526, Expte. 1.
96. Min. de Marina to Min. de Guerra y Ultramar, 24 August 1860, AHN: Ultramar 3526, Expte. 1.
97. Pedro Santana, 18 March 1861, AGI: Cuba 2266, Pieza 2, doc. s/n
98. Schmidt-Nowara, *Empire and Anti-slavery*, 26–27.
99. Hostos, *La Peregrinación*; Alonso, "Fiction," 149.
100. Álvarez Junco, "Spanish National Identity," 320.
101. De Bona, *Cuba, Santo Domingo y Puerto-Rico*, 5.
102. Corwin, *Spain and the Abolition of Slavery in Cuba*, 132.

103. Francisco Serrano to the Ministro de Guerra y Ultramar, 6 September 1861, AHN: Ultramar 3532, Expte. 2, doc. 2 (herafter cited as Serrano, *Resultado de viaje*), 28.
104. Serrano, *Resultado de viaje*, 31.
105. Serrano, *Resultado de viaje*, 29.
106. Torrente, *Política ultramarina*.
107. Torrente, *Política ultramarina*, 162; Schmidt-Nowara, *Conquest of History*, 219.
108. Torrente, *Política ultramarina*, 144 (emphasis added).
109. "We should be sensitive to the illustrious Dominican general Mella" (who conducted a five-month European mission seeking annexation in 1854), Torrente urges (*Política ultramarina*, 344).
110. Torrente, *Política ultramarina*, 342.
111. Torrente, *Política ultramarina*, 345.
112. Dorsey, "Seamy Sides of Abolition," 112, 114. Planters and the enslaved and their families protested cabotage vigorously, but their attempts to seek legal redress were almost never successful (Dorsey, "Seamy Sides of Abolition," 109, 116). Indenture projects were proposed on the island through the 1860s but never realized (Schmidt-Nowara, *Empire and Anti-slavery*, 42).
113. Picó, *Libertad y servidumbre*.
114. Martínez-Fernández, *Torn between Empires*, 111; Santiago-Valles, "'Forcing Them to Work,'" 123–68.
115. Reid-Vazquez, *Year of the Lash*, 146.
116. Scott, *Slave Emancipation in Cuba*, 29. Just at the moment of annexation, British authorities tried to restrict the indenture trade to Cuba (López, *Chinese Cubans*, 24).
117. Torrente, *Política ultramarina*, 144, 148, 170. He proposed forty thousand be contracted immediately (237). For his critique of the slave trade, see esp. pp. 274–76.
118. Torrente, *Política ultramarina*, 336–37.
119. Febres-Cordero Carrillo, "La anexión," 189.
120. Febres-Cordero Carrillo, "La anexión," 186.
121. Febres-Cordero Carrillo, "La anexión," 193.
122. Collected in Núñez de Arce, *Santo Domingo*, 76–106.
123. Núñez de Arce, *Santo Domingo*, 104.
124. Joaquin María del Monte to Min. de Guerra y Ultramar, Puerto Rico, 27 March 1861, AHN: Ultramar 5485, Expte. 1, doc. 1.
125. Raphael Echagüe to Min. de Guerra y Ultramar, Mayagüez, 1 April 1861, AHN: Ultramar 5485, Expte. 1, doc. 2.
126. Serrano to Min. de Estado, Reservado, 26 March 1861, AGN-RD: CH Leg. 24, Expte. 198, p. 11.
127. José Malo de Molina to Cap. Gen. Francisco Serrano, 4 September 1861 (15 July 1861), AHN: Ultramar 3532, Expte. 1, doc. 2 (hereafter cited as Malo de Molina to Serrano, "Memoria").

128. Malo de Molina to Serrano, "Memoria," 70–71.
129. Rodríguez Demorizi, Antecedentes, 180.
130. Malo de Molina to Serrano, "Memoria," 17–18.
131. Ferrer de Couto, *Reincorporación de Santo Domingo a España*, 30.
132. Royal Order, Reservada, 5 April 1859, ANC: AP 224, Expte. 6, doc. s/n.
133. Malo de Molina to Serrano, "Memoria," 18.
134. Emphasis in original. "¿Es dable establecer, por ejemplo, una legislación personal que admite la pena de azotes para una raza, la ley que la escluye de toda participación en los negocios públicos, las que suponen con todas sus consecuencias, en un país de cuyo diccionario social se ha borrado la palabra servidumbre, y en el que hay una nivelación perfecta y absoluta entre sus naturales, sea el que quiera su origen?" (Serrano, *Resultado de viaje*, 12).
135. Serrano, *Resultado de viaje*, 10–11.
136. Malo de Molina to Serrano, "Memoria," 23, 25.
137. Serrano, *Resultado de viaje*, 14.
138. Serrano, *Resultado de viaje*, 17–18.
139. Serrano, *Resultado de viaje*, 32.
140. Serrano, *Resultado de viaje*, 33.
141. Febres-Cordero Carrillo, "La anexión," 200–201.
142. The Cuban government considered an abortive, small-scale resettlement scheme to serve labor "contracts" in Bioko not long thereafter, but Cuban planters pressured the state to ban emigration and retain the individuals for sugar harvest (Sundiata, *From Slaving to Neoslavery*, 52–53). In the absence of any significant Spanish population, Spanish missionaries hoped that conversion would bring local fidelity to Spain (Castillo-Rodríguez, "The First Missionary Linguistics in Fernando Po," 84). Epigraph to this section qtd. in Rodríguez Demorizi, *Antecedentes*, 245.
143. In the latter port, see, e.g., "The Growing Insolence of Spain," *New York Times*, 8 November 1861, 4.
144. Febres-Cordero Carrillo, "La anexión," 188.
145. Febres-Cordero Carrillo, "La anexión," 192.
146. Qtd. in Febres-Cordero Carrillo, "La anexión," 111.
147. Qtd. in Febres-Cordero Carrillo, "La anexión," 111.
148. Qtd. in *Cuestión*, 23.
149. *Cuestión*, 41.
150. *Cuestión*, 65, 66.
151. *El Contemporáneo*, 20 April 1861, qtd. in *Cuestión*, 65–66. *La América* echoed their concern; "the lack of explanations and insufficient time . . . do not permit us either to assess what to do or to ensure a safe outcome," they fretted (*La América*, 24 May 1861, qtd. in *Cuestión*, 65).
152. *Cuestión*, 69.
153. *Cuestión*, 69.

154. La España, 17 April 1861, qtd. in Cuestión, 69–70. "If Mexico or any other of the *regiones desprendidas* of what was Spain, came to offer themselves in the same terms that Santo Domingo did, I think all the thinking men would thank them for their offer but would not accept; we would be *desgraciados*, if for sterile pride and vanity we sacrificed our real future without having learned anything from days gone by," one editorial argued (La España, 7 July 1861, qtd. in Cuestión, 75). El Contemporáneo accused the O'Donnell government of working secretly with annexation agents in the Dominican Republic and of fostering Spanish immigration there.
155. El Clamor Público, 23 May 1861, qtd. in Cuestión, 74.
156. El Clamor Público, 10 May 1861, qtd. in Cuestión, 73.
157. La Discusión, 20 April 1861, qtd. in Cuestión, 70.
158. La Época, 24 April 1861, qtd. in Cuestión, 78.
159. La Época, 24 April 1861, qtd. in Cuestión, 80.
160. Correspondiente de España, 22 April 1861, qtd. in Cuestión, 80.
161. La Discusión, 21 April 1861, qtd. in Cuestión, 78.
162. La Discusión, 23 May 1861, qtd. in Cuestión, 80–81.
163. La Discusión, 23 May 1861, qtd. in Cuestión, 85; La Discusión, 17 May 1861, qtd. in Cuestión, 86.
164. Las Novedades, 18 April 1861, qtd. in Cuestión, 86.
165. Cuestión, 87.
166. La España, 15 August 1861, qtd. in Cuestión, 88.
167. El Contemporáneo, 27 April 1861, qtd. in Núñez de Arce, Santo Domingo, 20.
168. El Contemporáneo, 14 April 1861, qtd. in Núñez de Arce, Santo Domingo, 72.
169. Cuestión, 67.
170. El Contemporáneo, 14 April 1861, qtd. in Cuestión, 72; El Contemporáneo, 18 April 1861, qtd. in Cuestión, 57.
171. Cuestión, 58.
172. La América, 8 May 1861, qtd. in Cuestión, 79.
173. The "War of Africa" was Spain's brief military campaign in the northern tip of Morocco in 1859–60. Under the pretext of skirmishes near Ceuta, a Spanish holding since the days of al-Andalus, the Spanish Crown declared war against Morocco in October 1859. Heading up Spanish forces of more than thirty-five thousand was Prime Minister Leopoldo O'Donnell himself. After some to-and-fro, Spanish troops won a victory at Tétouan, also just across the Gibraltar Strait, about twenty miles down the coast from Ceuta. Peace negotiations won Spain some 20 million piastres in indemnity, an enlargement of Ceuta's borders as a Spanish enclave, and negotiations for another territorial cession, which secured Spanish holdings in nearby Melilla. Most significantly, the campaign piqued imperialist discourse on the national stage. O'Donnell was awarded the title of "Duke of Tetuan" for his exploits.
174. Febres-Cordero Carrillo, "La anexión," 146.

175. Febres-Cordero Carrillo, "La anexión," 146.
176. *El Pensamiento Español*, 20 May 1861, qtd. in *Cuestión*, 55.
177. Francisco J. Sarmientos y Quiñoes to Cap. Gen. of Cuba, 5 December 1859, ANC: AP 224, Expte. 20, n.p.
178. Martín de Arredondo y Oléa to Cáp. Gen. of Cuba, Havana, 24 February 1860, ANC: AP 53, Expte. 1.
179. *Juntas*, Barcelona, Imprenta de F. Sánchez, 1860, AGI: Cuba 970B, Expte. 248, doc. s/n.
180. Qtd. in Rodríguez Demorizi, *Antecedentes*, 155.
181. "España y el siglo XIX," *La Razón*, no. 13, 1 July 1861, 1. A *contradanza* entitled "La expedición de Marruecos" celebrated Spain's North African imperial exploits (Manuel, "Cuba: From Contradanza to Danzón," 73).
182. Min. de Guerra y Ultramar to Min. de Estado, 22 May 1861, AHN: Ultramar 5485, Expte. 2, doc. 1. It seems Serrano first wrote on 26 March.
183. Min. de Estado (sub-secretario) to Min. de Guerra y Ultramar, Palacio, 22 May 1861, AHN: Ultramar 5485, Expte. 2, doc. 1, p. 3.
184. Min. de Estado (sub-secretario) to Min. de Guerra y Ultramar, Palacio, 22 May 1861, AHN: Ultramar 5485, Expte. 2, doc. 1, p. 3.
185. Febres-Cordero Carrillo, "La anexión," 147–48.
186. *Cuestión*, 90, 92, 96.
187. AHN: Ultramar 3532, Expte. 3, 7 October 1861.
188. Min. de Estado (sub-secretario) to Min. de Guerra y Ultramar, Palacio, 22 May 1861, AHN: Ultramar 5485, Expte. 2, doc. 1.
189. Pedro Santana to Capitán General de Cuba, Francisco Serrano, 6 August 1861, AHN: Ultramar 3532, Expte. 2, doc. 3.
190. Santana to Serrano, *Resultado de viaje*, 2.
191. Eduardo A. Colmenares to Min. de Guerra y Ultramar, SD, 8 January 1862, AHN: Ultramar 3532, Expte. 8, doc. 2.
192. De Bona, *Cuba, Santo Domingo y Puerto-Rico*, 2.
193. De Bona, *Cuba, Santo Domingo y Puerto-Rico*, 2.
194. De Bona, *Cuba, Santo Domingo y Puerto-Rico*, 3.
195. De Bona, *Cuba Santo Domingo y Puerto-Rico*, 42.
196. De Bona, *Cuba, Santo Domingo y Puerto-Rico*, 41.
197. De Bona, *Cuba, Santo Domingo y Puerto-Rico*, 41.
198. *Le Moniteur Haïtien*, no. 12, 23 February 1861, 3.
199. Qtd. in *Le Moniteur Haïtien*, no. 12, 23 February 1861, 4.
200. *Le Moniteur Haïtien*, no. 20, 20 April 1861, 2–3.
201. Qtd. in *Le Moniteur Haïtien*, no. 25, 25 May 1861, 3–4.
202. "Questions de l'Est," *Le Moniteur Haïtien*, no. 22, 4 May 1861, 3–4.
203. *La Correspondencia*, Madrid, 20 April 1861, in Rodríguez Demorizi, *Antecedentes*, 154.
204. Qtd. in "Nouvelles étrangères," *Le Moniteur Haïtien*, no. 27, 8 June 1861, 3.
205. "The Revival of Spain," *Quarterly Review* 3 (1862): 147–75, 172.

206. Qtd. in *Le Moniteur Haïtien*, no. 25, 25 May 1861, 4.
207. [Mariano Álvarez] to Min. de Estado, 19 March 1861, AGN-RD: CH Leg. 24, Expte. 198, p. 4.
208. Fabens, *Facts about Santo Domingo*, 30–31.
209. Consul Hood to Lord J. Russell, SD, 21 March 1861, AGN-RD: Anexión DE/000933, Expte. 1, p. 1.
210. Marte, *Correspondencia*, 72.
211. Consul Hood to Lord J. Russell, SD, 21 April 1861, AGN-RD: Anexión DE/000933, Expte. 9, p. 27; Consul Hood to Lord J. Russell, SD, 21 April 1861, AGN-RD Anexión DE/000933, Expte. 10, p. 28.
212. Hauch, "Attitudes of Foreign Governments," 256.
213. Hauch, "Attitudes of Foreign Governments," 256.
214. Informa a S.E. sobre el estado de la Unión, Mariano Álvarez to Cap. Gen. of Cuba, New York, 5 April 1861, AGN-RD: CH Leg. 24, Expte. 198, pp. 51–52.
215. For example, "Spanish Filibustering in Santo Domingo," *Chicago Tribune*, 30 March 1861, 1; "Astounding Intelligence: Aggressive Designs of Spain in the West Indies," *New York Times*, 30 March 1861, 1.
216. Qtd. in *Le Moniteur Haïtien*, no. 31, 6 July 1861, 2–4. The *Moniteur* reported that on 11 April the Boston legislature passed a resolution against annexation (*Le Moniteur Haïtien*, no. 25, 25 May 1861, 4).
217. "Rehabilitation of Spain," *Atlantic Monthly*, March 1862, 360.
218. "Rehabilitation of Spain," 362–63.
219. Consul Thomas Hood to Lord J. Russell, SD, 21 April 1861, AGN-RD: DE/000933 ("Papeles relativos a la Anexión de la parte oriental"), Expte. s/n.
220. Lord Russell to R. Edwardes, Foreign Office, 7 July 1861, AGN-RD: DE/000933, s/n.
221. Lord J. Russell to R. Edwardes, Foreign Office, 14 May 1861, AGN-RD: DE/000933, s/n.
222. Lord Russell to R. Edwardes, Foreign Office, 14 May 1861, AGN-RD: Anexión DE/000933, Expte. 11, pp. 30–31.
223. "Revival of Spain," 158, 170.
224. "Revival of Spain," 170. "The military enterprise recently undertaken by Spain against Morocco is understood to have been forced upon the Government by public opinion. . . . We must, however, state our opinion that the harsh and onerous terms she imposed upon a brave but unmilitary enemy were unworthy of her generosity; and the desire evinced to acquire additional territory in Morocco is as much opposed to her true interests as it is inconsistent with the declarations made before the commencement of the war."
225. "Revival of Spain," 172. The article echoes the assertion that a plebiscite was taken (173).
226. "Revival of Spain," 174.
227. "Revival of Spain," 171.

228. *Gaceta de la Habana*, 30 March 1861, SHM: Ultramar 5645, Expte. s/n.
229. José Lemery to Min. de Guerra y Ultramar, Manila, 19 July 1861, AHN: Ultramar 5185, Expte. 24.
230. Borges, "Competencia y Anexión," 53.
231. Martínez-Fernández, *Torn between Empires*, 220.
232. *La Discusión*, 10 April 1861, qtd. in Núñez de Arce, *Santo Domingo*, 151.

3. Destined to Occupy This Island

1. Rubalcava qtd. in *Colección de leyes*, 101.
2. De la Gándara, *Anexión y guerra de Santo Domingo*, 200.
3. Director del Archivo General de Indias to Ministro de Ultramar, Sevilla, 9 April 1862, AHN: Ultramar 5485, Expte. 26, doc. 2. They also requested that pre-1821 documents that had been sent to Cuba be returned to Santo Domingo (24 November 1861, AHN: Ultramar 3537, Expte. 7), while Santana sent on copies of some of the extinguished republic's treaties to Spain (Santana to Min. de Guerra, 2 January 1862, AHN: Ultramar 3531, Expte. 14).
4. Comandante de armas interino de Barahona Angel Féliz to Cap. Gen. of SD, Barahona, 29 April 1861, AGN-RD: CH Leg. 21, Expte. 173, pp. 23–24.
5. Minuta de Real Orden (reservada), from Min. de la Guerra y Ultramar to Teniente General D. Felipe Rivero, 19 June 1862, AHN: Ultramar 3525, Expte. 14.
6. Adriano López Morillo, *Memorias sobre la segunda reincorporación de Santo Domingo a España*, vol. 1 (Santo Domingo: Editora Corripio, 1983), excerpted in Cordero Michel, *La ciudad de Santo Domingo*, 255.
7. Ministro de Ultramar to Primera Secretaria de Estado, Madrid, 2 December 1863, AHN: Ultramar 3525, doc. 109.
8. Francisco Serrano, *Informe de la visita a SD*, SD, 5 September 1861, in Rodríguez-Demorizi, *Antecedentes*, 245.
9. Cruzat to Felipe Rivero, SD, 15 August 1862, ANC: Audiencia de la Habana 245, Expte. 2.
10. Barry, "Hegemony on a Shoestring."
11. Serrano to Min. de Guerra y Ultramar, Havana, 5 September 1861, AHN: Ultramar 5485, Expte. 16, doc. 1, p. 4.
12. Beckert, *Empire of Cotton*. In the first half of the nineteenth century, European markets were a "global cotton-growing countryside . . . grown by slave labor" (226).
13. The doubling of the price of raw cotton from 1848 to 1857 had driven Manchester merchants to look to new supplies and become somewhat less enamored with laissez-faire dicta generally. Joint-stock companies to fund cotton in other parts of the empire sprang up. Ventures in West Africa included a failed cotton project in Senegal in earlier decades, an uptick of intervention in Dahomey and southwestern Nigeria, and other projects of

so-called legitimate commerce, as missionaries and imperial adventurers bedecked their ventures with a cloying humanitarian veneer. Small-scale production of cotton in West Africa dated to antiquity, but the tide of imperial imports impeded proto-industrialization; by 1850, British merchants flooded West African markets with thirty times more finished cotton goods than in previous decades (Ratcliffe, "Cotton Imperialism," 87, 91; Inikori, "English versus Indian Cotton Textiles," 89; Hopkins, *Economic History of West Africa*, 128, 137–38).

14. In Jamaica, the British Cotton Company, Jamaica Cotton Company, Clarendon Company, Manchioneal Company, and Kingston Cotton Company all "speedily formed" (Watts, *Cotton Supply Association*, 94). None were successful. In Cuba, see Watts, *Cotton Supply Association*, 93.
15. F. Jn. Joseph, Secretary of State of Interior and Agriculture, "Rapport," *Le Moniteur Haïtien*, no. 37, 18 July 1860, 1–4.
16. *Le Moniteur Haïtien*, no. 10, 9 February 1861, 3.
17. Geffrard, "Circulaire aux généraux commandant les arrondissements de la Republique," *Le Moniteur Haïtien*, no. 12, 23 February 1861, 1; Geffrard, "Arrêté," *Le Moniteur Haïtien*, no. 13, 3 March 1860, 1.
18. St. John, *Hayti*, 367.
19. Watts, *Cotton Supply Association*, 96. The British Cotton Supply Association collaborated with the Union government to disseminate seeds and machinery to the Ottoman Empire, Egypt, Palestine, and other locations (Calhoun, "Seeds of Destruction").
20. Ratcliffe, "Cotton Imperialism," 87.
21. Kale, *Fragments of Empire*, 1; López, *Chinese Cubans*, 22; David Northrup, "Indentured Indians in the French Antilles"; Renault, *Libération d'esclaves et nouvelle servitude*. My thanks to Kate Marsh for her clarification of French Caribbean statistics.
22. Marsh, "'Rights of the Individual,'" 225.
23. Works include Schuler, "*Alas, Alas Kongo*"; Rodney, *History of the Guyanese Working People*; Jung, *Coolies and Cane*; López, *Chinese Cubans*.
24. Jung, *Coolies and Cane*, 17. They were, on some plantations, "treated no better and even worse than negro slaves," the U.S. consul reported from Havana in 1855 (22).
25. Internal markets of crops like ginger, arrowroot, and banana grew incrementally alongside older cash crops, as did emancipated communities' consumption and standard of living (Thompson, *Haunting Past*, 122).
26. In 1863, nearly three thousand Barbadians left the island as indentured laborers to multiple sites; in an attempt to prevent future migrations, planters opposed political federation with the other British Islands in the next decade (Brown, "Experiments in Indenture," 44; Levy, *Emancipation, Sugar, and Federalism*). On the case of Antigua, see Lightfoot, *Troubling Freedom*.

27. F. Jn. Joseph, Secretary of State of Interior and Agriculture, "Rapport," *Le Moniteur Haïtien*, no. 37, 18 July 1860, 1–4. Specifically, they were to settle in a number of regions where land was not already subdivided into small plots.
28. Geffrard gave Redpath $20,000 to open an emigration bureau in Boston; it was decked with "mahogany splendor," probably from the island itself (Alexander, "'Black Republic,'" 70–75). See also Dixon, *African America and Haiti*.
29. Alexander, "'Black Republic,'" 75.
30. Capitalist Bernard Kock, who had been leasing Ile-à-Vache, sought fifty dollars per person for up to fifty thousand émigrés. Privately, the Haitian minister in Washington, DC, was instructed to avoid any such massive-scale migration, although he need not have worried. Smallpox, mismanagement, and corruption crippled, then ended, the project (Logan, *Diplomatic Relations*, 308–10).
31. Geffrard, "Circulaire aux généraux commandant les arrondissements de la Republique," *Le Moniteur Haïtien*, no. 12, 23 February 1861, 1. He exhorted that rural Haitians increase domestic food staple production simultaneously, to free the country from a reliance on imports.
32. Nicholls, *Economic Dependence and Political Autonomy*, 15; A. Monfleury, "Fabrication du Sucre," *L'Opinion Nationale*, no. 6, 8 February 1862, 1.
33. See map 3.1. Clarifications are as follows. Costa Rica and Nicaragua: Robinson, "Chinese of Central America," 107, 113. Panama: Meagher, *The Coolie Trade*, 272. Although abolition legislation was passed in Colombia in 1851, the legislation took effect in early 1852; the *concierto* system of apprenticeship was abolished simultaneously (Jason McGraw, personal communication, 7 November 2015). Trinidad and Tobago: Roberts and Byrne, "Summary Statistics on Indenture," 127. The earliest contract schemes under British rule date to 1806 (Allen, "Slaves, Convicts, Abolitionism," 6). Jamaica: Roberts and Byrne, "Summary Statistics on Indenture," 127; Schuler, *"Alas, Alas Kongo"*; Anderson, "The Diaspora of Sierra Leone's Liberated Africans," 117–18. British Guiana: Roberts and Byrne, "Summary Statistics on Indenture," 127. Some regional migrants arrived without contracts (pre-1846 and in 1864) (Richardson, "Freedom and Migration"; Brown, "Experiments in Indenture," 48). Barbados was a site of indenture emigration briefly (Brown, "Experiments in Indenture," 44). Saint Vincent, Grenada, Dominica, and British Honduras: Roberts and Byrne, "Summary Statistics on Indenture," 127; Robinson, "Chinese of Central America," 108. Antigua: the long dates reflect Madeiran migration more than smaller numbers from other places, which occurred in the early 1860s (Brown, "Experiments in Indenture," 42; Roberts and Byrne, "Summary Statistics on Indenture," 127; Robinson, "Chinese of Central America," 108; Lightfoot, *Troubling Freedom*, 172). Saint Kitts: 1860–65 is the period of Indian indentured migration (Vertovek, "Indian Indentured Migration," 59); Madeira Island and African migration may have been longer (Roberts and Byrne, "Summary Statistics on Indenture,"

127). The Turks and Caicos: dates refer to changes in the salt rights system after emancipation that resulted in the predominance of truck system payments and bonded debt labor through the early twentieth century (*Laws of the Turks and Caicos Islands* [London: Saunders, Otley and Co., 1862], 85–86, 415–16, 438; http://tcmuseum.org/slavery/emancipation-beyond/, accessed June 2015). Saint Croix, indenture and Labour Act restrictions: Roopnarine, "The First and Only Crossing"; Roopnarine, "Comparative Analysis of Two Failed Indenture Experiences," 207. Martinique and Guadeloupe: Marsh, " 'Rights of the Individual.' " Saint Lucia, Guyane: Vertovek, "Indian Indentured Migration to the Caribbean," 59. Suriname: the 1931 date refers to the end of penal sanction (Hoefte, "Labour in the Caribbean," 259, 262; Hoefte, personal communication, 3 January 2016). Puerto Rico: dates refer to *libreta* controls; indenture projects were popular proposals in the 1860s but never materialized (Schmidt-Nowara, *Empire and Anti-slavery*, 38; Figueroa, *Sugar, Slavery and Freedom*, 166–69). Brazil: the various dates refer to fragmented indenture schemes targeting liberated African and Chinese individuals (Mamigonian, "To Be a Liberated African in Brazil"). In 1855, Bahian sugar planters sent an emissary to China; one boatload of laborers arrived in 1855 (Meagher, *Coolie Trade*, 146, 266). In 1883, short-lived renewed Chinese indenture plans fizzled (Meagher, *Coolie Trade*, 269). United States: end dates refer to the end of the convict lease system in Alabama and may well be extended forward (for more on convict labor, see LeFlouria, *Chained in Silence*. Mexico: the 1870 date refers to debt labor in Yucatán, although there is considerable debate as to whether this constituted indenture (Levy, *The Making of a Market*, 48). Peru: Meagher, *Coolie Trade*, 40. Ecuador: Townsend, "In Search of Liberty," and Camilla Townsend, personal communication, 3 January 2016. Haiti's dates refer to the projects of *caporalisme agraire* of the earliest days of independence as well as King Henri Christophe's militarized labor control in his northern kingdom, but they do not extend to subsequent rural codes, as land distribution and flight from plantations were extensive (see, e.g., Nicholls, *From Dessalines to Duvalier*, 68; González, *War on Sugar*).

34. May, "Lobbyists for Commercial Empire," 406.
35. Felipe Rivero to Min. de la Guerra y Ultramar, SD, 2 February 1863, AHN: Ultramar 3542, Expte. 1, Doc. 4.
36. Minuta de Real Orden (reservada), from Min. de la Guerra y Ultramar to Teniente Gral D. Felipe Rivero, 19 June 1862, AHN: Ultramar 3525, Expte. 14.
37. Paton, *No Bond but the Law*, 149.
38. *Le Moniteur Haïtien*, nos. 26–27, 12 June 1858, 2. Police were to verify the travel pass (*permis de route*) of any individual in the interior (*Le Moniteur Haïtien*, no. 24, 21 May 1859, 2).
39. Geffrard, "Haïtiens!," *Le Moniteur Haïtien*, no. 11, 19 February 1859, 1.
40. Febres-Cordero Carrillo, "La anexión," 83.
41. Breen, *St. Lucia*, 306; Schmidt-Nowara, *Empire and Anti-slavery*, 33, 42.

42. Dalby, " 'Such a Mass of Disgusting and Revolting Cases' "; Fryar, "Moral Politics of Cholera."
43. Ramsey, *Spirits and the Law*, 83–90.
44. "Le secretaire d'Etat au département de l'interieur et de l'agriculture, aux inspecteurs et sous-inspecteurs de culture de la République," *Le Moniteur Haïtien*, no. 27, 11 June 1859, 6.
45. Geffrard, "Adresse au peuple et à l'armée," *Le Moniteur Haïtien*, no. 25, 20 May 1865, 1.
46. Serrano to Min. de Guerra y Ultramar, Havana, 16 August 1861, AHN: Ultramar 5485, Expte. 14, doc. 1, p. 4. "Every day they are happier to be part of the big Spanish family," he reported.
47. "Industria," *El Dominicano*, no. 1, 29 June 1855, 4; *El Oasis*, no. 2, 4 December 1854, 5.
48. Juan B. Zafra to Santana, 17 November 1862, AGN-RD: Anexión 11 (DE/1800), Expte. 21. Land privatization support: "Artículo Primero," *El Dominicano*, no. 11, 15 September 1855, 41; "División de propriedad," *El Dominicano*, no. 13, 29 September 1855, 49.
49. Eduardo Alonso y Colmenares (Regente de la RA de SD) to Min. de Guerra y Ultramar, SD, 8 January 1862, AHN: Ultramar 3532, Expte. 8, doc. 2.
50. Manuel de Jesús Galván to Cap. Gen., 20 January 1862, AGN-RD: Anexión 11 (DE/1800), Expte. 40, doc. 2.
51. Pedro Valverde to Gob. Sup. Civil, 8 Feb 1864, AGN-RD: Anexión 26, Expte. 23.
52. Gob. Sup. Civil, to Pedro Valverde, 5 September 1863, AGN-RD: Anexión 23 (000149), Expte. 11.
53. Mariano Álvarez, "Memoria: Santo Domingo o la República Dominicana," SD, 20 April 1860, AHN: Ultramar 2775, Expte. 16, p. 4.
54. De la Gándara, *Anexión y guerra de Santo Domingo*, 238.
55. Fontecha Pedraza and González Calleja, *Una cuestión de honor*, 75, 87.
56. Noel Henriquez to the Queen, London, 9 November 1862, AGN-RD: Anexión 25, Expte. 10.
57. *Les intérêts français et européens à Santo Domingo* (Paris: E. Dentu, 1861).
58. Consul Hood to Lord J. Russell, SD, 8 April 1861, AGN-RD: Anexión DE/000933, Expte. 5, p. 16; Consul Hood to Lord J. Russell, SD, 21 April 1861, AGN-RD: Anexión DE/000933, Expte. 9, p. 27.
59. The budget of the colonial state in Cuba and Puerto Rico "ballooned . . . to pay a bloated bureaucratic corps" from 1840 to 1860. Cuban and Puerto Rican taxes were high—in Cuba, as much as four times what the average peninsular resident paid (Martínez-Fernández, *Torn between Empires*, 62).
60. Qtd. in Martínez-Fernández, *Torn between Empires*, 61.
61. Martínez-Fernández, *Torn between Empires*, 63.
62. Eduardo Alonso y Colmenares to Min. de Ultramar, SD, 16 February 1862, AHN: Ultramar 3545, Expte. 1, doc. 12.

63. José Malo de Molina to Cap. Gen. Francisco Serrano, 4 September 1861 (15 July 1861), AHN: Ultramar 3532, Expte. 1, doc. 2 (hereafter cited as Malo de Molina to Serrano, "Memoria"), p. 15. Interestingly, he suggests that the Dominican government might have chosen to continue with the French codes after separation from Haiti in 1844 because they were timorous of Spanish reoccupation and slavery (14), although just one page later, he suggests that the very reason for annexation was that the populace was eager to introduce the Spanish code in 1861.
64. Serrano, *Resultado de viaje*, 5.
65. Malo de Molina to Serrano, "Memoria," 17.
66. Real Orden of 7 October 1861, AHN: Ultramar 3531, Expte. 24.
67. Real Orden of 6 October 1861, AHN: Ultramar 3532, Expte. 3; *Gaceta de Santo Domingo*, no. 92, 12 June 1862, 1; Alonso y Colmenares to Gob. Sub. Civil, SD, 14 June 1862, AGN-RD: Anexión 8, Expte. 29.
68. Expte. sobre organización y regimen municipals, 1 September 1861–14 November 1863, AHN: Ultramar 3535, Expte. 3.
69. "Organización y planta de los gobiernos, comandancias militares y de armas de la Isla de Santo Domingo," Ministro de Guerra, 26 June 1862, AHN: Ultramar 3527, Expte. 51, doc. 9. These were the five extant provinces (Santo Domingo, Santiago, Azua, la Vega, Seibo) and a new one, the commercial coast of Puerto Plata.
70. Felipe Rivero to Min. de Guerra y Ultramar, 6 July 1862, AHN: Ultramar 2785, Expte. 8, doc. 1.
71. Ministerio de Estado to Serrano, 24 April 1861, in Núñez de Arce, *Santo Domingo*, 56–60.
72. Malo de Molina to Serrano, "Memoria," 64; Serrano, *Resultado de viaje*, 51–56.
73. Other founding members included José María Morilia, a lawyer (Spanish, practicing in Havana), and Ramón de la Torre Trassierra (ex-mayor in Philippines). Real Orden of 6 October 1861, in *Gaceta del Notariado Español* (Madrid: Imprenta de D. Ramón Campuzano, 1861), 3:637.
74. Serrano to Min. de Guerra, Havana, 1 September 1861, AHN: Ultramar 3526, Expte. 3; Álvarez López, *Dominación colonial y guerra*, 78.
75. Malo de Molina to Serrano, "Memoria," 17, 45–47, 50; AHN: Ultramar Anexo 3 (3532.1 Expte. 1, doc. 5); Santana to Min. de Guerra, 7 July 1862, AHN: Ultramar 3540, Expte. 19. The mayor of Santo Domingo, making an estimated $20 a month at the time of annexation ($240 yearly) would have made $3,500 annually, according to his plan, for example.
76. Malo de Molina to Serrano, "Memoria," 51.
77. Pedro Ricart Torres to el Comisario (Joaquín Manuel de Alba), SD, 20 November 1861, qtd. in Lugo Lovatón, "La junta económica annexionista de 1861," n.p.

78. Joaquín Manuel de Alba. Convocatoria del Comisario Regio Don Manuel Joaquín de Alba, SD, 19 November 1861, qtd. in Lugo Lovatón. "La junta económica anexionista de 1861," 111.
79. Ramón Blanco to Brig. Peláez (and to Cap. Gen. of Cuba), SD, April 1861, AGI: Cuba 1006B, in AGN-RD: CH Leg. 21, Expte. 172, 1 May 1861, p. 19.
80. Mariano Álvarez, "Memoria: Santo Domingo o la República Dominicana," SD, 20 April 1860, AHN: Ultramar 2775, Expte. 16, p. 4.
81. Ramón Blanco to Brig. Peláez (and to Cap. Gen. of Cuba), SD, April 1861, AGI: Cuba 1006B, in AGN-RD: CH Leg. 21, Expte. 172, 1 May 1861, p. 20.
82. Expte. del Gobierno Político, 1 September 1861, AGN-RD: Anexión 1 (DE/1378), Expte. s/n (old #46).
83. Dhormys, *Une visite chez Soulouque*, 90.
84. Landolfi, *Evolución cultural dominicana*, 93.
85. Santana to Min. de Guerra y Ultramar, 15 June 1862, AGI: Cuba 1018 (libro), p. 108.
86. Anónimo to Gob. Militar de SD Antonio Peláez, s/f (passed on to Santana, 21 October 1861), AGI: Cuba 945, Expte. 24 (Anónimos), doc. s/n.
87. Felipe Rivero to Gob. Militar de Samaná, Reservado, SD, 10 September 1862, AGN-RD: CH Leg. 21 (1702432), Expte. 169, p. 36.
88. Welles, *Naboth's Vineyard*, 229.
89. For discussion of these militia, see Reid, "Protesting Service"; Sartorius, "My Vassals."
90. De la Gándara, *Anexión y guerra de Santo Domingo*, 232.
91. Antonio Peláez to Cap. Gen., 19 August 1861, AGI: Cuba 953, Expte. "Desertores de 1861–3."
92. De la Gándara, *Anexión y guerra de Santo Domingo*, 101.
93. De la Gándara, *Anexión y guerra de Santo Domingo*, 233.
94. Serrano to Min. de Guerra, Havana, 25 July 1861, SHM: Ultramar 5645, Expte. "Asuntos operaciónes de campaña," doc. s/n.
95. Serrano to Brigadier Don Antonio Peláez Campomanes, SD, 5 August 1861, AGI: Cuba 1006B, in AGN-RD: CH Leg. 21, Expte. 172, p. 3.
96. "Sumaria instruida contra Enrique Padilla," Azua, 12 November 1861, AGI: Cuba 1013B, pp. 4–8.
97. Coronel Comandante de Armas Angel Féliz to Governador Político y Militar de la provincia de Azua, 2 September 1861, AGI: Cuba 1022A, in AGN-RD: CH Leg. 21, Expte. 173, p. 6.
98. Libro Gral de Actas de las Sesiones celebradas por la Junta de Clasificacion de los Señores Generales Gefes y Oficiales del antiguo Ejercito Dominicano, 19 September 1861, AGI: Cuba 1018, libro 16, p. 1.
99. Álvarez López, *Dominación colonial y guerra*, 83.
100. Registro de Espedientes para la Clasificación de Generales Gefes y oficiales del antiguo ejercito dominicano, Fall–Spring 1861–1862, AGI: Cuba 1017, libro 15.

101. De la Gándara, *Anexión y guerra de Santo Domingo*, 235.
102. Pedro Santana, "Relación nominal de los Generales y Gefes del Ejercito Dominicano que al acto de la incorporación de SD a la Monarquía Española ejercían los cargos de Gobernadores y Comandantes de armas . . . ," SD, 20 December 1861, SHM Ultramar 5645, Expte. "Asunto operaciones de campaña . . . ," doc. s/n.
103. Santana to Cap. Gen. of Cuba, 8 August 1861, AGI: Cuba 2267, Expte. "Sobre la iglesia Dominicana."
104. Catholic instruction and rites posed potential costs and unwanted influence. Rather than pay for a Christian burial for enslaved men and women, sugar plantation owners found loopholes that permitted their own cemeteries; rather than church instruction for their slaves, owners managed to be named officially responsible for local religious instruction, through legislation like the Good Government Laws of 1842.
105. Demoticus Philalethes, *Yankee Travels through the Island of Cuba* (New York, 1856), qtd. in Brandon, *Santeria from Africa to the New World*, 63.
106. Eduardo Alonso y Colmenares to Min. de Ultramar, SD, 16 February 1862, AHN: Ultramar 3545, Expte. 1, doc. 12. Vacant: Montecristi, Bonao, los Alcarrizos, San Lorenzo de los Mina, las Matas de Farfán. Only Puerto Plata, Santiago, and San Cristobal had their own authorities.
107. Sáez, *Documentos inéditos de Fernando A. de Meriño*, 80.
108. De la Gándara, *Anexión y guerra de Santo Domingo*, 223; Guerrero Cano, *Disciplina y laxitud*, 59–60; Martínez-Fernández, "The Sword and the Crucifix," 83, 85.
109. Guridi, *La campana del higo*.
110. Sáez, *Documentos inéditos de Fernando A. de Meriño*, 100.
111. Martínez-Fernández, *Torn between Empires*, 215; Vicioso, *El freno hatero*, 282.
112. Lavastida to Cap. Gen., 20 July 1861, AHN: Ultramar 3531, Expte. 36.
113. De la Gándara, *Anexión y guerra de Santo Domingo*, 258.
114. Keim, *San Domingo*, 145, 155.
115. Keim, *San Domingo*, 224.
116. De la Gándara, *Anexión y guerra de Santo Domingo*, 229.
117. De la Gándara, *Anexión y guerra de Santo Domingo*, 230.
118. Martínez-Fernández, "The Sword and the Crucifix," 83.
119. Meriño, "Expte. reservado para tratar de la aplicación . . . ," 26 September 1862, ANC: AP 53, Expte. 20.
120. Hidalgo, "From North America to Hispaniola," 161.
121. Meriño, "Expte. reservado para tratar de la aplicación . . . ," 26 September 1862, ANC: AP 53, Expte. 20.
122. Meriño, "Expte. reservado para tratar de la aplicación . . . ," 26 September 1862, ANC: AP 53, Expte. 20.
123. Felipe Rivero to Regente de la Real Audiencia, 6 October 1862, ANC: AP 53, Expte. 20.

124. Leopoldo O'Donnell to Rivero, 21 December 1882, AGN-RD: Anexión 4 (DE/1383), Expte. 11; Alcalde de Puerto Plata to Regente de la RA de SD, 31 March 1863, ANC: AP 53, 20.
125. *Colección de leyes*; Martínez-Fernández, "The Sword and the Crucifix," 83.
126. De la Gándara, *Anexión y guerra*, 224.
127. E.g., AHN: Ultramar 3529, Exptes. 12–20.
128. Expte. sobre arreglo y dotación del clero, 30 April 1862, AHN: Ultramar 3545, Expte. 1, doc. 19. A few did not want to leave their Santiago de Cuba posts (doc. 20).
129. E.g., Juan Bautista Zafra to Gob. Superior Civil, 24 December 1861, AGN-RD: Anexión 11 (DE/1800), Expte. 15. At no time did these documents mention the skin color of either party (though their titles suggest they were prominent citizens).
130. Martínez-Fernández, "The Sword and the Crucifix," 82. He approved of "spontaneous" marriages occurring at the behest of arriving priests in rural areas (Estracto—Informando sobre las cuestiones que abraza la RO de 10 de Noviembre de 1864," de la Gándara to Min. de Guerra, 9 January 1865, ANC: AP 225, Expte. 2, doc. s/n).
131. *La Razón*, no. 7, 15 June 1862, 1.
132. *Colección de leyes*, 134–36.
133. Teniente Gobernador de Neyba to Cura Párroco de Neyba, 28 April 1863, AGN-RD: Anexión 27, Expte. 18, p. 2v.
134. Mariano Álvarez, "Memoria: Santo Domingo o la República Dominicana," SD, 20 April 1860, AHN: Ultramar 2775, Expte. 16, p. 4.
135. Serrano, *Informe de la visita a SD*, 245.
136. Memoria of Antonio Peláez y Campomanes to Gob. Serrano, Havana, 8 November 1860, AHN: Ultramar 3526, Expte. 2, doc. 2.
137. Bosch, *La Guerra de la Restauración*, 84.
138. The customs rules were changed to Puerto Rican (from Cuban) standards, for example (Manuel de Alba to Min. de Guerra y Ultramar, 9 January 1862, AHN: Ultramar 3528.7; approved by royal order, 12 March 1862). While treasury oversight was delegated to Cuban officials, it was determined that merchants could pay in installments, as per Puerto Rican guidelines, for example (AHN: Ultramar 3528.6, 8). Taxes: Comisario Regio de Hacienda to Min. de Ultramar, 19 February 1862, AHN: Ultramar 3528, Expte. 30. The popular Cuban lottery was introduced as an additional revenue measure (Superintendente Delegado de Hacienda de SD to Serrano, 16 October 1861, AHN: Ultramar 3528, Expte. 2).
139. Cap. Gen. of Puerto Rico to Min. de Ultramar, 12 June 1861, AHN: Ultramar 1128, Expte. 30.
140. Serrano to Santana, SD, 8 August 1861, AHN: Ultramar 3527, Expte. 4, doc. 3.
141. AHN: Ultramar online 1128:45.

142. Santana to Min. de Guerra, 28 November 1861, AGI: Cuba 1018 (libro), p. 3; "Secretaria del Gobierno," *Gaceta de Santo Domingo*, no. 50, 4 January 1862, 1.
143. "De Oficio," *Gaceta de Santo Domingo*, no. 51, 11 January 1862, 1.
144. Expte. 119 de la Junta Superior de Medecina, Cirujía y Farmacia, 18 February 1863–1864, AGN-RD: Anexión 29, Expte. 37; *Gaceta de Santo Domingo*, no. 56, 6 February 1862, 1.
145. Min. de Guerra to Joaquín Mauel del Alba, Madrid, 7 October 1861, AHN: Ultramar 3527, Expte. 57.
146. AHN: Ultramar 3529, Exptes. 13, 14, 15, June–October 1861. Pensions: e.g., AHN: Ultramar 1122, Exptes. 37–38.
147. Mariano Álvarez to Cap. Gen. of Cuba, 20 July 1861, AGI: Cuba 2266, Pieza 1, n.p.
148. Secretaria de Estado to Min. de Guera y Ultramar, 4 April 1862, AHN: Ultramar 3540, Expte. 16.
149. Minuta de Min. de Guerra y Ultramar, 5 October 1861, AHN: Ultramar 3540, Expte. 5; Minuta de Min. de Guerra y Ultramar, 29 October 1861, AHN: Ultramar 3540, doc. 10; Felipe Rivero to Min. de Ultramar, 4 February 1863, AHN: Ultramar 3540, Expte. 8; Cap. Gen. of SD to Min. de Guerra y Ultramar, 21 December 1862, AHN: Ultramar 3531, Expte. 28.
150. Gob. Superior Civil to Min. de Guerra, SD, 30 January 1862, AGN-RD: Anexión 11 (DE/1800), Expte. 34; AHN: Ultramar online 79, Expte. 23; Manuel del J. Galván (Expte. del Gob. Sup. Civil), SD, 19 August 1862, AGN-RD: Anexión 11 (DE/1800), Expte. 37; Noel Henriques to Min. de Ultramar, 29 September 1861, AHN: Ultramar 3540, Expte. 4.
151. Manuel de Jésus Galván to Gob. Superior Civil, 14 December 1861, AGN-RD: Anexión 1 (DE/1378), Expte. 31.
152. Pedro Valverde to Gob. Superior Civil, 13 October 1862, AGN-RD: Anexión 26 (DE/000152), Expte. 15. A wealthy Venezuelan immigrant initiated the Dominican Republic's rum industry in 1852 (Edwin Rafael Espinal Hernández, "Los apellidos del ron: Bérmudez," *Hoy* [Sección Sabatina: Cápsulas Genealógicas], 29 August 2009, http://www.idg.org.do/capsulas/agosto2009/agosto200929.htm, accessed 18 September 2009). For further discussion of rum, see Chez Checo, *El ron en la historia Dominicana*.
153. E.g., Pedro Santana to Sr. Intendente Gral. de Ejercito y Hacienda, SD, 23 August 1861, AHN: Ultramar 6160, Expte. 26; Ministerio de Guerra y Ultramar to Comisario Regio de SD, 7 October 1861, AHN: Ultramar 2785, Expte. 16.
154. Real Decreto de 12 Octubre de 1862, Anexión 26 (DE/000152), Expte. 13.
155. Expediente . . . del Cédula de privilegio a Don Juan A. Cohen, September–October 1861, AGN-RD: Anexión 1 (DE/1378), Expte. 16; Expte. del Gobierno Superior Civil, 13 May 1862, AGN-RD: Anexión 10, Expte. 41. Various government inquests about cotton continued (e.g., Gob. de SD to Min. de Ultramar, May 1862–September 1863, AHN: Ultramar 3542, Expte. 1, docs. 1–8).

156. Jose Rocas to Comisario Regio, 15 April 1861, AGN-RD: Anexión 24 (000150), Expte. 13.
157. Real Orden of 27 September 1863, 22 February 1864, in AGN-RD: Anexión 26, Expte. 23.
158. Don Francisco de Olazarra to Cáp. Gen. of SD, 11 January 1862, AGN-RD: Anexión 11 (DE/1800), Expte. 40.
159. From Felipe Rivero to Min. de la Guerra y Ultramar, SD, 19 June 1862, AHN: Ultramar 3525, Expte. 15.
160. Don Francisco de Olazarra to Cáp. General de SD, 11 January 1862, AGN-RD: Anexión 11 (DE/1800), Expte. 40.
161. [R. Caymare] to Ministro de Ultramar, 30 January 1862, AGN-RD: Anexión 4 (DE/1383), Expte. 20, doc. 1. The proposal, like many others of its kind, demonstrated a total unwillingness to acknowledge the other state of the island, referring instead to the "island of Santo Domingo," "bringing prosperity to the island," and so forth.
162. Eusebio Soler to Gob. Superior Civil, SD, 4 July 1864, AGN-RD: Anexión 16, Expte. 1, doc. 3.
163. Felipe Rivero to Min. de la Guerra y Ultramar, SD, 19 June 1862, AHN: Ultramar 3525, Expte. 15.
164. Cuba had a "Junta de Población Blanca" since 1817, although the numbers were somewhat small in the 1850s and 1860s. Dirección de Armamentos del Ministerio de Marina to Min. de Guerra y Ultramar, San Ildefonso, 19 September 1861, AHN: Ultramar 3526, Expte. 4; Serrano to Min. de Guerra, Havana, 7 October 1861, AHN: Ultramar 3625, Expte. 6.
165. Manuel de Cruzat to Felipe Rivero (passed on to the Queen), SD, 15 August 1862, ANC: Audiencia de la Habana Leg. 245, Expte. 2.
166. Min. de Guerra y Ultramar to Santana, Madrid, 1 August 1861, AHN: Ultramar 5485, Expte. 11.
167. William Cazneau and Joseph Fabens to Ministro de Ultramar, 2 January 1863, AGN-RD: Anexión 4 (DE/1383), Expte. 20, doc. 2. See also AHN: Ultramar 3531, Expte. 42, doc. 2 (a copy); Martínez-Fernández, *Torn between Empires*, 217.
168. E.g., Luís Ramírez to Min. de Guerra, Madrid, 6 July 1861, AHN: Ultramar 3527, Expte. 3.
169. From Felipe Rivero to Min. de la Guerra y Ultramar, SD, 19 June 1862, AHN: Ultramar 3525, Expte. 15.
170. Pedro Valverde to Gob. Sup. Civil, 28 August 1863, AGN-RD: Anexión 23 (000149), Expte. 11.
171. "Bando de Policia y Gobernación," in *Colección de leyes*, 150.
172. Pedro Valverde to Gob. Sup. Civil, 28 August 1863, AGN-RD: Anexión 23 (000149), Expte. 11.
173. Gob Sup. Civil to Pedro Valverde, 5 September 1863, AGN-RD: Anexión 23 (000149), Expte. 11.

174. Pedro Santana, Bando de 29 de Agosto de 1861, AGI: Cuba 948, "Bandos," doc. s/n. The low-level local administrators called alcaldes pedáneos were responsible for supplying the information to their superiors. The edict borrowed directly from such strict legislation as Puerto Rico's 1849 "Bando de Policía y Buen Gobierno," which restricted travel, nighttime activities, and other security measures (Martínez-Fernández, *Torn between Empires*, 66).
175. Real Audiencia to the Queen, SD, 8 January 1862, AHN: Ultramar 3532, Expte. 10.
176. "Bando de Policia y Gobernación," in *Colección de leyes*, 149; Lizardo, *Cultura Africana en Santo Domingo*, 69.
177. "Bando de Policia y Gobernación," in *Colección de leyes*, 161.
178. "Bando de Policia y Gobernación," in *Colección de leyes*, 150.
179. Expte. "Relativo a las examenes que deben de sufrir las mugeres . . . ," 24 June 1864, AGN-RD: Anexión 29, Expte. 2.
180. "Bando de Policia y Gobernación," in *Colección de leyes*, 147.
181. Benito Cuadron to Gob. Político de SD, 22 April 1863, and José Leyba to Gob. Político de SD, 26 June 1863, AGN-RD: Anexión 28, Expte. 6. Each was armed with a pistol, a light, and a whistle. Authorities instructed them to listen for insults against authority (*Colección de leyes*, 163–65).
182. Santana to Min. de Guerra y Ultramar, 15 June 1862, AGI: Cuba 1018, p. 108.
183. Eduardo Alonso y Colmenares to Cap. Gen., SD, 10 January 1862, AGN-RD: Anexión 1 (DE/1378), Expte. 12.
184. Santana to Superintendente Gral. de Ejército y Real Hacienda, 10 December 1861, AHN: Ultramar 2785, Expte. 24, Doc. 3. A soldier from the Crown Regiment, serving a ten-year sentence in Santiago de los Caballeros and without any family to send food, was among the prisoners so poor that Santana feared he would die of hunger, despite his begging for money during street cleaning.
185. Comisaria Regia de SD Joaquin M de Alba, to Min. de la Guerra y Ultramar, 12 July 1862, AHN: Ultramar 2785, Expte. 4.
186. Santana to Min. de Guerra, 30 April 1862, AHN: Ultramar 3531, Expte. 33; Real Orden of 19 August 1862, AGI: Cuba 974A.
187. Joaquín Manuel del Alba to Min. de Guerra, 10 March 1862, AHN: Ultramar 2784, Expte. 42; "Expte promovido por el Regentde de la RA relativo a la mala alimentación que se da a los presos de la Real Carcel de esta Capital," Fall 1864, AGN-RD: Anexión 27, Expte. 9.
188. Consul Hood to Cap. Gen. Felipe Rivero, 7 October 1862, AGN-RD: Anexión 4 (DE/1383), Expte. 26.
189. Serrano to Min. de Guerra, 25 July 1861, AGN-RD: Colección Herrera Leg. 21, Expte. 169, p. 20; Min. de Guerra to Cap. Gen. of SD, AHN: Ultramar 3527, Expte. 15.
190. Expte. de Ministro de Guerra, 17 October 1861, AHN: Ultramar 3626, Expte. 11, doc. 11.

191. Expediente formado para la plaza de Ministro de Justicia de Santo Domingo, August 1861–26 February 1863, ANC: AP 53, Expte. 15.
192. Min. de Guerra to Santana, 6 March 1862, AHN: Ultramar 3626, Expte. 11, doc. 13.
193. Santana to Min. de Guerra y Ultramar, 5 February 1862, AGI: Cuba 1018, p. 36.
194. Santana to Min. de Guerra y Ultramar, 5 February 1862, AGI: Cuba 1018, p. 35.
195. "Sumaria Instruida en averiguación de la fuga del confinado José Poce Camboy," October 1862, AGI: Cuba 1012B; José Hungria to Cap. Gen., 5 September 1862, AGN-RD: Anexión 28, Expte. 9.
196. Pedro Valverde to Gob. Sup. Civil, 8 January 1863, AGN-RD: Anexión 26, Expte. 33; Pedro Valverde to Gob. Sup. Civil. 28 January 1864, AGN-RD: Anexión 29, Expte. 16.
197. Cap. Gen. of Puerto Rico to Min. de Guerra, Puerto Rico, 13 November 1863, AHN: Ultramar 3626, Expte. 11, doc. 16.
198. The *Gaceta* republished Eduardo Alonso Colmenares's opening speech at the inauguration of the Real Audiencia de Santo Domingo, for example (*Gaceta*, no. 50, 4 January 1862, 1, SHM: Ultramar 5645, Expte. s/n); state *imprenta*: Expte. del Gobierno Superior Civil, 9 January 1862, AGN-RD: Anexión 4 (DE/1383), Expte. 22.
199. This began with *Gaceta*, no. 92, 12 June 1862, and continued through the end of the year (1863 has been lost).
200. Expte. del Gob. Sup. Civil sobre *La Razón*, 1861–64, AGN-RD: Anexión 1 (DE/1378), Expte. 8a.
201. "La Situación pasada y el presente IV," *La Razón*, no. 6, 6 June 1861, 1.
202. "No Oficial," *Gaceta de Santo Domingo*, no. 77, 21 April 1862, 3.
203. José Hungria to Cap. Gen., 30 July 1862, AGN-RD: Anexión 28, Expte. 4.
204. Manuel de Jésus Garcia to Gob. Sup. Civil, 14 June 1862, AGN-RD: Anexión 11 (DE/1800), Expte. 2.
205. *La Razón*, no. 19, 22 July 1861, 2–3; "España y el siglo XIX," *La Razón*, no. 13, 1 July 1861, 1.
206. José Mompou, "Presente y porvenir de Haiti," *La Razón*, no. 9, 17 June 1861, 1.
207. Mompou, "Presente y porvenir de Haiti," 1.
208. "La Situación pasada y el presente IV," *La Razón*, no. 6, 6 June 1861, 1.
209. Hauch, "Attitudes of Foreign Governments," 251. Although this statement was reported secondhand by the British consul—who might, perhaps, have had reason to stir up abolitionist anxieties—it was reportedly said by none other than Manuel Cruzat, the famously racist and difficult former ambassador to Haiti who had almost brought the country to the brink of diplomatic disaster there in the 1850s.
210. Regente de la audiencia, Don Eduardo Alonso y Colmenares to Min. de Guerra y Ultramar, s/f (spring 1862), AHN: Ultramar 3525, Expte. 13, doc. 4.

211. El Télegrafo Constitucional, no. 2, 12 April 1821; Lora Hugi, Transición, 127; Asaka, "'Our Brethren in the West Indies'"; Kerr-Ritchie, Freedom's Seekers.
212. Real Orden of 24 June 1861 (reservado), AHN: Ultramar 5485, Expte. 6.
213. Pedro Santana to Min. de Guerra, 18 February 1862, SHM: Ultramar 5639, Expte. "Esclavitud/Esclavos 1849–1862," doc. s/n.
214. Lower-ranking officers often brought their families, even when embarking from as far away as Madrid. Min. de Guerra to Min. de Ultramar, 30 January 1862, AGN-RD: Anexión 8, Expte. 23.
215. Regente de la audiencia, Don Eduardo Alonso y Colmenares to Min. de Guerra y Ultramar, s/f (spring 1862), AHN: Ultramar 3525, Expte. 13, doc. 4.
216. Regente de la audiencia, Don Eduardo Alonso y Colmenares to Min. de Guerra y Ultramar, s/f (spring 1862), AHN: Ultramar 3525, Expte. 13, doc. 3.
217. Pedro Santana to Min. de Guerra, 18 February 1862, SHM Ultramar 5639, Expte. "Esclavitud/Esclavos 1849–1862," doc. s/n.
218. The Valverdes were a prominent family in Santo Domingo. Valverde had continued in the position since the republic; he is referred to in other Spanish documents as a "persona de buenas circunstancias" and was on the list of prominent men to be rewarded with *gracias* and *cruces* after the annexation (Serrano to Min. de Guerra y Ultramar, Havana, 1 September 1861, AHN: Ultramar 3526, Expte. 3, doc. 2; Serrano to Min. de Guerra y Ultramar, 7 October 1861, AHN: Ultramar 3526, Expte. 10, doc. 5).
219. Gob. Sup. Civil to Pedro Valverde, SD, 19 February 1862, AGN-RD: Anexión 11 (DE/1800), Expte. 27, doc. 1.
220. Gob. Superior Civil de Puerto Rico to Cap. Gen. of SD, 27 November 1862, AGN-RD: Anexión 27, Expte. 25.
221. Molina to Serrano, Memoria, 63–65.
222. Serrano, Informe de la visita, 245.
223. From Felipe Rivero to Min. de la Guerra y Ultramar, SD, 19 June 1862, AHN: Ultramar 3525, Expte. 15.

4. The Haitians or the Whites?

1. News reached the Dominican capital within days (Copiador, 22 January 1861).
2. José Mompou, La Razón, no. 14, 4 July 1861, 1.
3. José de Villar to Ministerio de Ultramar, SD, 13 October 1864, AHN: Ultramar 3526 Expte. 17, doc. 10.
4. La Razón, no. 39, 25 January 1863, 1.
5. De la Gándara, Anexión y guerra de Santo Domingo, 238.
6. D. Claudio Morales to the Queen, SD, 22 December 1864, AHN: Ultramar 3543, Expte. 26. These documents are few, but they demonstrate how some urban Dominican families, probably among the more prominent (given that both parents were formally married), embraced Spanish marriage policy.

7. *La Razón*, no. 34, 21 December 1862, 3.
8. Rodríguez Demorizi, *Antecedentes*, 176.
9. Even in the capital, the ceremony had started two hours late, and the flag was removed for a time after flying just one day (Consul Hood to Lord J. Russell, SD, 21 March 1861, AGN-RD: Anexión DE/000933, Expte. 1, p. 1).
10. Bosch, *La Guerra de la Restauración*, 53; García, *Compendio*, 1:376. There was also open opposition in the small town of San Pedro de Macorís.
11. Finke, "Puerto Plata en la Gesta Restauradora," 118, 120.
12. Marte, *Correspondencia*, 72; Finke "Puerto Plata en la Gesta Restauradora," 121.
13. Finke, "Puerto Plata en la Gesta Restauradora," 123.
14. López Morillo, *Memorias sobre la segunda reincorporación*, 222.
15. Castro Ventura, *La Guerra Restauradora*, 60.
16. Tejeda Ortíz, *Cultura y folklore*, 79; Finke, "Puerto Plata en la Gesta Restauradora," 122.
17. Bosch, *La Guerra de la Restauración*, 197; de la Gándara, *Anexión y guerra de Santo Domingo*, 285.
18. Marte, *Correspondencia*, 192.
19. Vallejo, *Las madres de la Patria*, 58; Marte, "La oralidad sobre el pasado insular," 61.
20. Marte, *Correspondencia*, 193.
21. Qtd. in Matibag, *Haitian-Dominican Counterpoint*, 111.
22. *Le Moniteur Haïtien*, no. 18, 6 April 1861, 5.
23. *Le Moniteur Haïtien*, no. 19, 13 April 1861, 3.
24. "Brochure Dominicaine contre Santana," *Le Moniteur Haïtien*, no. 27, 8 June 1861, 1–2. The author was probably Manuel María Gautier.
25. Santana to Min. de Guerra, SD, 5 March 1862, SHM: Ultramar 5645, Expte. "Asuntos operaciónes de campaña," doc. s/n.
26. Qtd. in Álvarez López, *Dominación colonial y guerra popular*, 60.
27. V.F., "Quelques mots d'une patriote sur la question de l'Est d'Haïti," *Le Moniteur Haïtien*, no. 27, 8 June 1861, 2–3.
28. Hernández Flores, *Luperón, héroe y alma*, 101.
29. Rodríguez Demorizi, *Antecedentes*, 160. Cabral's words reached the *New York Times*, possibly through the advocacy of Alejandro Ángulo Guridi ("Will Spain Be Able to Retain Dominica?," *New York Times*, 3 June 1861, 4).
30. Written in the margin of Rubalcalva to Brig. Peláez (and to Cap. Gen. of Cuba), SD, April 1861, AGI: Cuba 1006B, in AGN-RD: CH Leg. 21, Expte. 172, 1 May 1861, p. 24; Febres-Cordero Carrillo, "La anexión," 212.
31. Rodríguez Demorizi, *Antecedentes*, 191; Álvarez López, *Dominación colonial y guerra popular*, 67. All of the executed were Dominican except for an American, William Morris, longtime resident of the Dominican capital (Marte, *Correspondencia*, 90). Santana's parody of military justice and horrific execu-

tion amounted to "a disgusting and indefensible tyranny," de la Gándara wrote (Anexión y guerra de Santo Domingo, 205).

32. Rodríguez Demorizi, Antecedentes, 198.

33. Spanish senator Ríos Rosas called the event a "barbarous catastrophe of extermination . . . a deplorable start to the Spanish Government in Santo Domingo (Rodríguez Demorizi, Antecedentes, 213). "A horrible event [that] produced a deep and terrible sensation throughout the country," a Madrid paper lamented (Rodríguez Demorizi, Antecedentes, 223).

34. "The rebels had widespread support in the towns, settlements, and outposts of the frontier regions; many of the inhabitants there joined the expeditionaries," Luis Álvarez López writes. "The majority of government troops also supported the rebels and joined their lines" (Dominación colonial y guerra popular, 65). Consuls reported that center-island residents called on Haiti in early March and openly supported Geffrard (Marte, Correspondencia, 63; Joquín Rubalcaba to Brig. Peláez, 1 May 1861, AGN-RD: CH Leg. 21, Expte. 172, p. 23). Some of the Haitian soldiers may have been from Geffrard's guard of tirailleurs (Lespinasse, Price-Mars, and Gutiérrez, Haïti et la restauration de l'indépendance dominicaine, 34–35).

35. Marte, Correspondencia, 90; Álvarez López, Dominación colonial y guerra popular, 57.

36. Expte. promovida por la Señora Ramona Recio," Neyba, 15 August 1861, AGN-RD: Anexión 1 (DE/1378), Expte. 18.

37. General Eusebio Puello to [Cap. Gen.], San Juan (Las Matas), 12 June 1861, AGI: Cuba 1025A, Expte. "Declaraciones recibidas," n.p.

38. M. Álvarez to Cap. Gen. of SD, Port-au-Prince, 16 April 1862, ANC: AP 224, Expte. 30, doc. s/n (see Rodríguez Demorizi, Antecedentes, 208).

39. Lespinasse, Price-Mars, and Gutiérrez, Haïti et la restauration de l'indépendance dominicaine, 34–35.

40. Eusebio Puello to Cap. Gen. Azua, 2 January 1862, AGN-RD: Anexión (DE/1381) 2, Expte. 1.2, doc. 1. Others, like Altagracia Douval, Colonel Gabino Simonó (or Simoneau), and Major José Pierre, likewise bore prototypically Spanish given names and French or Haitian surnames. Both men were with Sánchez and Cabral in spring 1861, and Simoneau was executed alongside Sánchez that July (Hernández Flores, Luperón, héroe y alma, 102; Lugo Lovatón, "Tomás Bobadilla Briones," 303).

41. "Nota de los individuos y familias que han salido de la parte de Haiti y se encuentran en sus hogares y establecimientos" and "Relación de los individuos procedentes de Haytí que pertenecieron a los pueblos de las Matas Cercado y Sabana Mula y se marcharon en esta última invasión de 1861," 11 October 1861, AGN-RD: Anexión (DE/1381) 2, Expte. 1, doc. s/n.

42. Jose Hungria to Cap. Gen. Santiago, 3 May 1862, and reply Cap. Gen. to Hungria, 23 May 1862, AGN-RD: Anexión (DE/1381) 2, Expte. 1.2, docs. s/n. He may well have been long established in the country, actually, as with the Beliards of Puerto Plata (Puig Ortíz, Emigración de libertos, 74).

43. Real Orden minuta, Ministro de Guerra y Ultramar to Min. de Estado, Madrid, 12 July 1861, AHN: Ultramar, Expte. 8, doc. 2.
44. "Huyeron los haitianos!," La Razón, no. 10, 20 June 1861, 1.
45. José Mompou, "A El Eco Hispano-Americano," La Razón, no. 11, 23 June 1861, 1.
46. José Mompou, "¡Admite disculpa la agresión haitiana!," La Razón, no. 13, 1 July 1861, 2.
47. La Razón, no. 13, 1 July 1861, 2. This story was republished in Madrid papers. See Rodríguez Demorizi, Antecedentes, 221.
48. Rodríguez Demorizi, Antecedentes, 176, 218.
49. "Huyeron los haitianos!," La Razón, no. 10, 20 June 1861, 1.
50. Manuel de Jésus Galván, "Francia y Haiti," La Razón, no. 14, 4 July 1861, 1.
51. Rodríguez Demorizi, Antecedentes, 192–93.
52. Santana, "DOMINICANOS," La Razón, no. 10, 20 June 1861, 4; and La Razón, no. 12, 27 June 1861, 1.
53. Febres-Cordero Carrillo, "La anexión," 213; Hernández Flores, Luperón, alma y héroe, 101.
54. Rodríguez Demorizi, Antecedentes, 215. Documents do in fact substantiate that the Spanish military intended to attack Port-au-Prince's defenses "to do as much damage as possible," before potentially doing the same in Jacmel and Cap-Haïtien (de la Gándara, Anexión y guerra de Santo Domingo, 212).
55. Joseph Lewis to Seward, Port-au-Prince, 15 July 1861, NARA Reg. 84, Vol. 30, 1849–60, n.p.
56. Febres-Cordero Carrillo, "La anexión," 220. The consuls urged Spanish authorities not to attack, arguing that fatal riots would ensue; Spanish authorities agreed that it amounted to attacking a defenseless town.
57. Real Orden of 12 September 1861, AHN: Ultramar 5485, Expte. 15. That sum may have been reduced (St. John, Hayti, 105), although evidence is contradictory. The Haitian government completed payment by March of the next year (Expte. de Secretario del Estado, Madrid, 24 March 1862, AHN: Ultramar 3527, Expte. 35.)
58. Rodríguez Demorizi, Antecedentes, 212.
59. Joseph Lewis to Seward, Port-au-Prince, 15 July 1861, NARA Reg. 84, Vol. 30, 1849–60, n.p.
60. Le Moniteur Haïtien, no. 34, 27 July 1861, 2; Le Moniteur Haïtien, no. 35, 3 August 1861, 2.
61. Le Moniteur Haïtien, no. 47, 26 October 1861, 1.
62. Le Moniteur Haïtien, no. 51, 23 November 1861, 1.
63. M. Álvarez to Cap. Gen. of SD, Port-au-Prince, 2 March 1862, ANC: AP 224, Expte. 30, doc. s/n; Fabré Geffrard, "Loi," Le Moniteur Haïtien, no. 11, 15 February 1862, 1.
64. Marte, Correspondencia, 95.
65. Qtd. in Rodríguez Demorizi, Antecedentes, 258.

66. Qtd. in Rodríguez Demorizi, Antecedentes, 258.
67. Santana to Sp. Consul in Haiti, 18 April 1862, AGN-RD: CH Leg. 21, Expte. 175, p. 64.
68. Serrano to Min. de Guerra, Reservada, 6 September 1861, AHN: Ultramar 3525, Expte. 1.
69. Santana to Cap. Gen. of Cuba, 8 August 1861, AGI: Cuba 2267, Expte. "Sobre la iglesia Dominicana."
70. Serrano to Min. de Guerra y Ultramar, 6 November 1861, AGI: Cuba 2267, Expte. "Sobre la iglesia Dominicana."
71. Regente de la audiencia, Don Eduardo Alonso y Colmenares to Min. de Guerra y Ultramar, Reservada, 5 March 1862, AHN: Ultramar 3525, Expte. 13, docs. 1 and 2 (26 May 1862).
72. Bosch, La Guerra de la Restauración, 175.
73. Minuta de RO de Min. de Guerra y Ultramar to Gob. Santana, Madrid, 7 October 1861, AHN: Ultramar 5485, Expte. 20.
74. De la Gándara, Anexión y guerra de Santo Domingo, 142.
75. Rodríguez Demorizi, Antecedentes, 276.
76. Rodríguez Demorizi, Antecedentes, 261.
77. Álvarez López, Dominación colonial y guerra popular, 89.
78. From Felipe Rivero to Min. de la Guerra y Ultramar, SD, 19 June 1862, AHN: Ultramar 3525, Expte. 15.
79. José Malo de Molina to Cap. Gen. Francisco Serrano, 4 September 1861 (15 July 1861), AHN: Ultramar 3532, Expte. 1, doc. 2, pp. 56–57.
80. Exptes. sobre Don Benito Alejandro Pérez et al., January–May 1862, AHN: Ultramar 3529, Expte. 20, docs. 1–8. Some of Santana's appointments to municipal posts were vetoed because the candidate was not qualified as a *letrado*.
81. March–August 1862, AHN: Ultramar 3529, Expte. 42–48.
82. Álvarez López, Dominación colonial y guerra popular, 86 (he suggests that this process sped up further still after 1863, to the point that it "seems to have affected the most enthusiastic collaborators of Santana in the annexation process"); Colección de leyes, 184.
83. Rather than name Ricart y Torres to the Tribunal de Cuentas, the accounts were passed on to Cuba (Manuel del Alba to Min. de Guerra, 30 August 1861, AHN: Ultramar 3528, Expte. 6).
84. Escolano Giménez, "La organización de la provincia de Santo Domingo," 346, 348.
85. Delayed payment frustrated many. Others asked for additional funds to feed their families (e.g., Michez to Director General del Ramo de la Guerra, Seybo, 16 July 1861, AGN-RD: CH Leg. 21, Expte. 174; Secretario de la Junta Municipal de la Vega, 6 October 1862, AGN: Anexión 11 [DE/1800], Expte. 24).

86. "Contra los paisanos Juan Isidro Rodríguez . . . ," 1863, AGN-RD: CH Leg. 24, Expte. 2025, pp. 15, 79.
87. Comisario Regio to Min. de Guerra, 1861–63, AHN: Ultramar 3527, Expte. 44; 3528, Expte. 15; 2785, Expte. 1; 2785, Expte. 2.
88. Real Orden de Min. de Ultramar, Madrid, 29 October 1861, AHN: Ultramar 3526, Expte. 7.
89. Expte. de Real Audiencia de SD, 30 April 1862, AHN: Ultramar 3542, Expte. 4.
90. Joaquín María de Alba to Cap. Gen., SD, 28 November 1861, AGN-RD: Anexión 2 (DE/1381), Expte. 19, doc. 1.
91. Manuel del Alba to Min. de Ultramar, 2 June 1862, AHN: Ultramar 2785, Expte. 20.
92. Manuel del Alba to Don Augusto Ulloa, 20 April 1862, AHN: Ultramar 3543, Expte. 27.
93. Colmenares to Cap. Gen., 25 April 1862, AGN-RD: Anexión 37, Expte. 25.
94. Min. de Guerra to Santana, 16 August 1862, AHN: Ultramar 3531, Expte. 21.
95. From Felipe Rivero to Min. de la Guerra y Ultramar, SD, 19 June 1862, AHN: Ultramar 3525, Expte. 15; Manuel Maria Reyes to Cap. Gen., 16 September 1862, Anexión 37 (000163), Expte. 15.
96. Expediente formado para la plaza de Ministro de Justicia de Santo Domingo, August 1861–26 February 1863, ANC: AP 53, Expte. 15.
97. Colmenares to Min. de Guerra, 9 September 1862, AHN: Ultramar 3533, Expte. 2.
98. Colmenares to the Queen, SD, 16 May 1862, AHN: Ultramar 3533, Expte. 5.
99. J. Obijo to Cap. Gen. of Santo Domingo, Azua, 20 August 1861, AGI: Cuba 852, Expte. "Cuarteles," doc. s/n.
100. Serrano to Min. de Guerra, Havana, 25 July 1861, SHM: Ultramar 5645, Expte. "Asuntos operaciónes de campaña," doc. s/n.
101. Serrano to Min. de Guerra, 27 July 1861, AHN: Ultramar 3531, Expte. 43; Pedro Valverde to Gob. Sup. Civil, 9 May 1862, AGN-RD: Anexión 2 (DE/1381), Expte. 11, doc. s/n; 11 February 1861, AGN-RD: RREE 14/15/16, Expte. 6, doc. 4.
102. Expediente de la Real Audiencia de SD, SD, 17 November 1862, ANC: Audiencia de la Habana Leg. 245, Expte. 2; Comisario Regio to Min. de Guerra, 31 May 1862, AHN: Ultramar 3531, Expte. 44.
103. Felipe Rivero to Min. de la Guerra y Ultramar, SD, 19 June 1862, AHN: Ultramar 3525, Expte. 15.
104. Febres-Cordero Carrillo, "La anexión," 232.
105. Junta Classificadora (Blas. De Castro) to Cap. Gen., SD, 9 December 1861, AGN-RD: Anexión 2 (DE/1381), Expte. 10.2, doc. s/n.
106. Bosch, *La Guerra de la Restauración*, 68.
107. Álvarez López, *Dominación colonial y guerra popular*, 90.

108. Pedro Santana to Min. de Guerra, SD, 29 April 1862, SHM: Ultramar 5656, Expte. 2. "In my opinion this is nothing other than a pretext for opportunists and opponents of the current Government to disturb the peace and achieve purely personal gains," Santana wrote dismissively.
109. "Reasons for the current uprising" [anonymous, s/f, probably late 1863–64], AHN: Ultramar 3525, Expte. 128.
110. Consul Hood to Lord J. Russell, SD, 21 April 1861, AGN-RD: Anexión DE/000933, Expte. 9, p. 27.
111. From Felipe Rivero to Min. de la Guerra y Ultramar, SD, 9 June 1863, AHN: Ultramar 3540, Expte. 9; Rivero to O'Donnell, 16 December 1862, AGN-RD: Anexión 4, Expte. 9.
112. Felipe Rivero to Superintendencia de Cuba, 18 August 1862, AHN: Ultramar 3528, Expte. 18.
113. Real Orden of 5 October 1861, Min. de la Guerra y Ultramar, AHN: Ultramar 3531, Expte. 27.
114. From Felipe Rivero to Min. de la Guerra y Ultramar, SD, 19 June 1862, AHN: Ultramar 3525, Expte. 15.
115. U.S. commercial agent William Jaeger estimated that his 50 percent pay was still $6,000 a year.
116. Manuel del Alba to don Augusto Ulloa, 20 April 1862, AHN: Ultramar 3543, Expte. 27.
117. "Dominicanos!," *Gaceta de Santo Domingo*, no. 102, 21 July 1862, 3.
118. Spending grew from 174,832 pesos in the first summer of occupation to 527,026 just two years later (Contaduría General de Hacienda, Cuaderno de la recaudación e inversión general de fondos, July 1861 and July 1863, BNE, Mss 12813, n.p.). As soon as sustained fighting began, expenditures ballooned to nearly 4,500,000 pesos in 1864 (Martínez Fernández, *Torn between Empires*, 214).
119. Álvarez López, *Dominación colonial y guerra popular*, 92.
120. Martínez Fernández, *Torn between Empires*, 62.
121. These low-level officials were instructed to maintain order, arrest any troublemakers and remit them to alcaldes ordinarios, prevent games and cockfighting, impede liquor sales, enforce licenses to sell animals, prevent entry without a passport, enforce cleanliness, and so forth (Victoriano García Paredes to Gob. Político de Azua, SD, 11 February 1863, AGI: Cuba 1025A, Expte. "Instrucciones a los Alcaldes Pedáneos," doc. s/n).
122. Blanco Díaz, *Alejandro Ángulo Guridi*, 1:11.
123. Alejandro Ángulo Guridi to Cap. Gen., Santiago, 17 July 1863, AGN-RD: CH Tomo 15, p. 69.
124. Even Santana had his own qualms about abusive Buceta, reporting that he was "inconsiderate and violent." Writing to the Spanish Ministry of War, the Dominican general minced no words: "The outrages committed by him . . . [make] him a tyrant in every sense of the word, provoking the honorable

inhabitants of the Cibao, accustomed to liberal treatment, with insults unworthy of his station. What Buceta has done in the Santiago province has no precedent in the history of Christian pueblos" (Pedro Santana to Min. de Guerra, 10 October 1863, AHN: Ultramar 3525, Expte. 10).

125. Antonio Castillo y Miguel de los Santos to Gob. Sup. Civil, Guerra, 14 January 1862, AGN-RD: Anexión 2 (DE/1381), Expte. 9, docs. s/n.

126. E.g., Miguel de los Santos to Gob. Sup. Civil, Guerra, 15 January 1862, AGN-RD: Anexión 2 (DE/1381), Expte. 9, doc. s/n.

127. Miguel de los Santos to Gob. Sup. Civil, Guerra, 29 January 1862, AGN-RD: Anexión 2 (DE/1381), Expte. 9, doc. s/n.

128. Passports generated a tremendous amount of paperwork. See, e.g., AGN-RD: Anexión 33, Expte. 37; Antonio Peláez to Gob. Sup. Civil, 12 October 1861, AGN-RD: Anexión 1 (DE/1378), Expte. 27.

129. Santana to Min. de Guerra y Ultramar, SD, 6 February 1862, AHN: Ultramar 5485, Expte. 24; [no sig.] to Cap. Gen. of Cuba, SD, 21 October 1861, AGN-RD: Anexión (DE/1381) 2, Expte. 1, doc. s/n; Pedro Santana to Gob. Sup. Civil, 8 October 1861, AGN-RD: Anexión 2 (DE/1381), Expte. 1, doc. s/n.

130. Ana Maduro to Cap. Gen., 11 Oct 1864, AGN-RD: Anexión 30, Expte. 5, doc. s/n.

131. "Nota de los individuos y familias que han salido de la parte de Haiti y se encuentran en sus hogares y establecimientos" and "Relación de los individuos procedentes de Haytí que pertenecieron a los pueblos de las Matas Cercado y Sabana Mula y se marcharon en esta última invasión de 1861," 11 October 1861, AGN-RD: Anexión 2 (DE/1381), Expte. 1, doc. s/n.

132. "Reasons for the current uprising" [anonymous, s/f, probably late 1863–64], AHN: Ultramar 3525, Expte. 128.

133. "Sumaria en averiguación de ciertos hechos que denuncia el comandante militar de San Cristóbal . . . ," 15 February 1863, AGI: Cuba 950B, "Causas."

134. Juan Crisostomo de Rojas to Cap. Gen., 3 June 1863, AGN-RD: Anexión 28, Expte. 1, doc. 2.

135. "Estracto—Informando sobre las cuestiones que abraza la RO de 10 de Noviembre de 1864," de la Gándara to Min. de Guerra, 9 January 1865, ANC: AP 225, Expte. 2, doc. s/n.

136. Antonio Subirá to Cap. Gen., SD, 20 July 1863, AGN-RD: Anexión 18, Expte. 17; *Colección de leyes*.

137. Apolinario de Castro to Real Audiencia de SD, 13 May 1863, AGN-RD: Anexión 29, Expte. 41.

138. [Unsigned] to Cap. Gen., 13 March 1863, AGN-RD: Anexión 11 (DE/1800), Expte. 44.

139. *Memoria informativa de las razones que ha tenido la Sección de Gobierno para alterar, modificar y aun suprimir algunas de las disposiciones del anterior Bando de Policía y*

Gobernación, y para establecer una que otra nueva prescripción, SD, 13 July 1864, AHN: Ultramar 3526, Expte. 17, doc. 3.
140. Augusto Ulloa to Cap. Gen., 2 June 1862, AGN-RD: Anexión 4, Expte. 14.
141. "Expte. reservado para tratar de la aplicación . . . ," 8 April 1863, ANC: AP 53, Expte. 20.
142. Welles, Naboth's Vineyard, 242.
143. Martin J. Hood to Peter Vanderhurst, SD, 5 April 1863, in "Espediente instruido en averiguación de las circunstancias que concurren en el paysano Pedro Richardson Vanderhorst, procedente del campo enemigo," Samaná, April 1864, AGI: Cuba 1011A, 20.
144. Juan Zafra to Gob. Sup. Civil, September 1862, AGN-RD: Anexión 8, Expte. 37.
145. Juan B. Zafra to Cap. Gen., 3 November 1862, AGN-RD: Anexión 17, Expte. 4.
146. Welles, Naboth's Vineyard, 241.
147. "Estracto—Informando sobre las cuestiones que abraza la RO de 10 de Noviembre de 1864," de la Gándara to Min. de Guerra, 9 January 1865, ANC: AP 225, Expte. 2, doc. s/n.
148. Bosch, La Guerra de la Restauración, 80.
149. Teniente Gobernador de Neyba to Cura Párroco de Neyba, 28 April 1863, AGN-RD: Anexión 27, Expte. 18, p. 2v.
150. José Barrosela to Teniente Gobernador de Neyba, s/f, AGN-RD: Anexión 27, Expte. 18.
151. Juan B. Zafra to Cap. Gen., 4 July 1863, AGN-RD: Anexión 17, Expte. 16.
152. The priest in Sabaneta even convinced the local municipal government to collect the fees for him, as he found the task too unpleasant. "Contra los paisanos Juan Isidro Rodríguez . . . ," 1863, AGN-RD: CH Leg. 24, Expte. 205, p. 14. He eventually fled ([Unclear] to Cap. Gen., SD, 7 April 1863, AGN-RD: Anexión 18, Expte. 9).
153. "Estracto—Informando sobre las cuestiones que abraza la RO de 10 de Noviembre de 1864," de la Gándara to Min. de Guerra, 9 January 1865, ANC: AP 225, Expte. 2, doc. s/n; de la Gándara, Anexión y guerra de Santo Domingo, 258.
154. Sáez, Documentos inéditos de Fernando A. de Meriño. 28. Meriño's name is sometimes recorded as Fernando Arturo de Meriño (for discussion, see Mella, Los espejos de Duarte, 233).
155. Paton, No Bond but the Law, 6.
156. Abreu Cardet and Sintes Gómez, El alzamiento de Neiba, 17.
157. Expte. "Relativo a las examenes que deben de sufrir las mugeres . . . ," 24 June 1864, AGN-RD: Anexión 29, Expte. 2.
158. Memoria informativa de las razones que ha tenido la Sección de Gobierno para alterar, modificar y aun suprimir algunas de las disposiciones del anterior Bando de Policía y Gobernación, y para establecer una que otra nueva prescripción, SD, 13 July 1864, AHN: Ultramar 3526, Expte. 17, doc. 3.

159. François, "Laundering Identities in the Americas."
160. Declaración de Josefa Debra, "Relación nominal de los desertores que han tenido los Cuerpos de la guarnición de esta Plaza [SD] . . . ," SD, 23 February 1865, AGI: Cuba 1015A, "Sumarias," 35. Josepha had been raised from an early age by one Madame Richard in Puerto Plata, perhaps a member of one of the families who had moved from Haiti during the Unification period.
161. Declaración de Guadaloupe Rodríguez, "Relación nominal de los desertores que han tenido los Cuerpos de la guarnición de esta Plaza [SD] . . . ," SD, 23 February 1865, AGI: Cuba 1015A, "Sumarias," 31.
162. De la Gándara, *Anexión y guerra de Santo Domingo*, 200.
163. Makeshift hospital from a borrowed house: Ramón Blanco to Brig. Peláez and Cap. Gen. of Cuba, SD, 1 May 1861, AGN-RD: CH Leg. 21, Expte. 172, p. 19.
164. Marte, *Correspondencia*, 192.
165. "Testimonio de la Sumaria en aberiguación de si en algunas reuniones . . . hubo indisciplina," Case 256, May 1863, AGI: Cuba 1015A, "Sumarias."
166. Pedro Valverde to Gob. Superior Civil, 22 March 1862, AGN-RD: Anexión 33, Expte. 36.
167. Causa formada a 7 individuos de los Batallones de San Marcial, Vitoria y Tarragona por encontrarse merodeando en los afueras de esta Ciudad, October 1863, AGI: Cuba 950B, "Causas."
168. "Copía testimoniada del Testimonio de la Causa instruida contra los Subtenientes D. Pedro Obanos y Alcalde, y D. Pedro García Maquina y varios individuos de la clan de tropa y carabineros de Hacienda pública . . . 18 de Agosto de 1862," Plaza de la Havana, 1867, AGI: Cuba 1015A.
169. José E. Rocas to Cap. Gen., La Vega, 5 April 1863, AGI: Cuba 950B, "Causas."
170. José P. Mayo to Cap. Gen., SD, 11 June 1863, AGI: Cuba 950B, "Causas."
171. "Sumaria Instruida en aberiguacion de unos golpes inferidos al niño (Pedro) de Doña Dolores Bernal de Valberde . . . ," SD, May 1864, AGI: Cuba 1011B.
172. "Testimonio sacado de la causa seguida Contra el Soldado de la 3º Compañía del Batallón Infantería de San Marcial José Puga Martínez . . . ," June 1863, AGI: Cuba 1012A, "Sumarias."
173. Expte. sobre Don. Tomas Botello, Manuel del Jésus Galván, SD, 3 November 1862, AGN-RD: Anexión 11 (DE/1800), Expte. 38.
174. "Contra el soldado de la Compañía de Cazadores del Batallón de San Marcial José Birrete," SD, October 1864, AGI: Cuba 1011B.
175. "Testimonio Contra el Soldado de la 5ª compañía José Cabrera y López acusado por haber pegado un tiro con un Cachorrillo del que resultó muerto el paisano Don Manuel Meta . . . ," SD, August 1863, AGI: Cuba 1012A, "Sumarias."
176. "Sumaria instruida contra los paisanos del Batallón de Voluntarios de esta Plaza Manuel Martínez y Enrique Iglesias . . . ," November 1863, AGI: Cuba 950B, "Causas."

177. Ramón Blanco to Brig. Peláez and Cap. Gen. of Cuba, SD, 1 May 1861, AGN-RD: CH Leg. 21, Expte. 172, pp. 6–7. Large and well-constructed buildings existed—constructed "in the time of Spanish domination," the officer noted—but they had gone without repair and been burned during various sieges until they were mostly "fallen, dismantled, and converted into a mountain of rubble" (18).
178. Marcos Adon to Antonio Alfau, 19 February 1864, AGI: Cuba 952, Expte. 98, "Correspondencia," doc. s/n.
179. "Reasons for the current uprising" [anonymous, s/f, probably late 1863–64], AHN: Ultramar 3525, Expte. 128.
180. It is unclear whether Evangelista was declassified because of limited literacy or not; he did manage to sign his court papers. His signature was shaky; "M" and "E" were the clearest letters, perhaps studied.
181. "Sumaria del General Don Marcos Evangelista acusado de haber proferido palabras suversivas . . . ," March 1863, AGI: Cuba 1011A. Also in AGN-RD: CH Leg. 21, Expte. 174.
182. "Relación Nominal de los Señores Gefes y Oficiales de las reservas provinciales en situación pasiva . . . ," in "Proceso Contra varios individuos de complicidad en la sublevación que tubo lugar en Puerto Plata en 27 de Agosto ultimo," 1863, AHN: Ultramar 881ª, 1ª Pieza.
183. Bosch, *La Guerra de la Restauración*, 76.
184. De la Gándara, *Anexión y guerra de Santo Domingo*, 238.
185. "Sumaria formada . . . en averiguación de la conducta de . . . Don Pedro Obanos," Case 265, AGI: Cuba 1015A, "Sumarias," 21.
186. Mariano Álvarez to Primera Secretaria de Estado (I), Port-au-Prince, 25 March 1862, SHM: Ultramar 5645, Expte. "Asuntos operaciónes de campaña," doc. s/n.
187. Mariano Álvarez to Cap. Gen. of SD (II), Port-au-Prince, 8 April 1862, SHM: Ultramar 5645, Expte. "Asuntos operaciónes de campaña," doc. s/n.
188. Mariano Álvarez to Primera Secretaria de Estado (II), Port-au-Prince, 25 March 1862, SHM: Ultramar 5645, Expte. "Asuntos operaciónes de campaña," doc. s/n.
189. Unable to assimilate the fact of the Haitian independence, he suggested that a 1795 treaty offered Spain "the right by which the white race can assert possession of the west side of Hispaniola" as well. "And with such precedent, who can dissent against the reclamation that I have just proposed?" he demanded (Mariano Álvarez to Primera Secretaria de Estado [II], Port-au-Prince, 25 March 1862, SHM: Ultramar 5645, Expte. "Asuntos operaciónes de campaña," doc. s/n).
190. Milans del Bosch to Cap. Gen. of Cuba, Port-au-Prince, 24 June 1863, AGI: Cuba 984C, Expte. "Sobre la sublevación de SD en 1863," doc. s/n.
191. M. Álvarez to Cap. Gen. of SD, Port-au-Prince, 16 April 1862, ANC: AP 224, Expte. 30, doc. s/n; M. Álvarez to Cap. Gen. of SD, Port-au-Prince, 9 May

1862, SHM: Ultramar 5645, "Expte sobre operaciones militares en SD sobre la frontera . . . ," doc. s/n.
192. Geffrard, "Proclamation," *Le Moniteur Haïtien*, no. 9, 1 February 1862, 1.
193. Mariano Álvarez to Cap. Gen. of Cuba, 22 January 1863, AGI: Cuba 984C, Expte. "Sobre la sublevación de SD en 1863," doc. s/n.
194. Mariano Álvarez to Cap. Gen. of SD, 24 April 1862, AGN-RD: CH Leg. 21, Expte. 175, 26.
195. M. Álvarez to Cap. Gen. of SD, Port-au-Prince, 2 March 1862, ANC: AP 224, Expte. 30, doc. s/n.
196. Bonneau, *Haïti*.
197. Felipe Rivero to Min. de Guerra, 4 February 1863, AHN: Ultramar 3534, Expte. 9.
198. Santana to Min. de Guerra, SD, 5 March 1862, SHM: Ultramar 5645, Expte. "Asuntos operaciónes de campaña," doc. s/n.
199. Milans del Bosch to Cap. Gen. of Cuba, Port-au-Prince, 19 June 1863, AGI: Cuba 984C, Expte. "Sobre la sublevación de SD en 1863," doc. s/n.
200. Felipe Rivero to Min. de Guerra y Ultramar, 14 December 1862, AGI: Cuba 1018 (libro).
201. Marte, *Correspondencia*, 210–12.
202. Comandante de armas Angel Feliz to Gob. interino de Azua, San Juan, 28 September 1861, AGN-RD: CH Leg. 21, Expte. 173, p. 5; Bobadilla to Comandante de Armas Angel Feliz, Barahona, 25 December 1861, AGN-RD: CH Leg. 21, Expte. 173, p. 9. Other officials worried that a certain Ponsin Rondon was in Las Matas, causing considerable disorder (Santiago Suero to Gob. Militar de Azua, San Juan, 28 December 1861, AGN-RD: CH Leg. 21, Expte. 173, p. 4).
203. Teniente Gob. de Guayabin, Santiago [unclear] to Cap. Gen. of SD, 20 October 1861, AGN-RD: Anexión 1 (DE/1378), Expte. 6.
204. F. Sosa to Santana, 14 June 1861, AGI: Cuba 984C, Expte. "promovido a consecuencia de la invasión . . . por los Haitianos."
205. De la Gándara, *Anexión y guerra de Santo Domingo*, 273.
206. Hernández Flores, *Luperón, alma y héroe*, 106.
207. M. Álvarez to Cap. Gen. of SD, Port-au-Prince, 16 April 1862, ANC: AP 224, Expte. 30, doc. s/n. (see Rodríguez Demorizi, *Antecedentes*, 208).
208. "Sumaria instruida en averiguación del tráfico y comunicaciones que con los haitianos tuvieron los paisanos Pedro Curro, Venancio Gil, Soten Sambra, Manuel Sanjuanaro, José Ramírez, Norverto Cueva, José Sánchez y José Ignacio," October 1862, AGN-RD: CH Leg. 24, Expte. 202 (AGI: 1013B).

5. You Promised to Die of Hunger

1. Abreu Cardet and Sintes Gómez, *El alzamiento de Neiba*, 46.
2. Abreu Cardet and Sintes Gómez, *El alzamiento de Neiba*, 28; "Sumaria Contra Don Nicolás de Mesa, SubT de las milicias provinciales, los paysanos

Manuel Chiquito, Cayetano Velázquez . . . ," Neiba, February 1863, AGI: Cuba 1011B, p. 99.
3. Abreu Cardet and Sintes Gómez, Los alzamientos de Guayubín, 31. Earlier on in February, a man in Guayubín could not contain his disdain for Spanish soldiers in the town. When one greeted him as a "countryman" (paisano), he replied, "Countryman of yours? . . . within five days you'll see what's coming for you" (Bosch, La Guerra de la Restauración, 86).
4. Abreu Cardet and Sintes Gómez, Los alzamientos de Guayubín, 37.
5. Abreu Cardet and Sintes Gómez, Los alzamientos de Guayubín, 8; Monción, "De capotillo a Santiago," 13.
6. Manuel Buceta to Felipe Ribero, Santiago, 8 August 1863, AHN: Ultramar 3525, Expte. 27, doc. 2; Felipe Ribero to Min. de Ultramar, 18 August 1863, AHN: Ultramar 3525, Expte. 26, doc. 2.
7. Gil, Orígenes y proyecciones de la revolución restauradora, 82.
8. Hernández Flores, Luperón, 56, 68.
9. Pérez Dionisio, "Santiago de Cuba y la Guerra de la Restauración," 113.
10. De la Gándara, Anexión y guerra de Santo Domingo, 290, 344, 347.
11. "Contra los paisanos Juan Isidro Rodríguez . . . ," 1863, AGN-RD: CH Leg. 24, Expte. 2025, pp. 15, 79.
12. "Reasons for the current uprising" [anonymous, s/f, probably late 1863–64], AHN: Ultramar 3525, Expte. 128.
13. Qtd. in Comisión Permanente de Efemérides Patrias, Proclamas (hereafter cited as Proclamas), 18.
14. "Sumaria [sobre Hato Mayor] . . . ," October 1863, AGN-RD: CH Leg. 21 (AGI: Cuba 1014A), Expte. 176, 7.
15. Real Orden of 26 February 1863, AHN: Ultramar 3525, Expte. 17.
16. White, Speaking with Vampires, 82.
17. Abreu Cardet and Sintes Gómez, El alzamiento de Neiba, 29.
18. Vallejo, Las madres de la Patria, 47; Abreu Cardet and Sintes Gómez, El alzamiento de Neiba, 19.
19. Hahn, "'Extravagant Expectations' of Freedom," 128.
20. Finke, "Puerto Plata en la Gesta Restauradora," 126.
21. Finch, "Insurgency at the Crossroads," 143. Historians have gestured to Dominican women's roles as "ignored heroes" of the fighting (Jimenes Grullón, Sociología política dominicana, 141).
22. Camp, "'I Could Not Stay There,'" 3; Camp, Closer to Freedom, chap. 5.
23. Mallon, Peasant and Nation, 78.
24. Martínez, Diccionario, 237.
25. De la Gándara, Anexión y guerra de Santo Domingo, 238.
26. Blanco Díaz, Alejandro Ángulo Guridi, 2:201.
27. "Reasons for the current uprising" [anonymous, s/f, probably late winter 1863–64], AHN: Ultramar 3525, Expte. 128.

28. "Ya se fueron los blancos / de Yamasá, ¡ay palisa! / Ya se fueron los españoles / con su banderita en popa." A "cantar de la época," anonymous, in Rodríguez Demorizi, *Poesía popular dominicana*, 89.
29. Hauch, "The Dominican Republic and Its Foreign Relations," 163.
30. Rodríguez Demorizi, *Antecedentes*, 187.
31. Santana, "DOMINICANOS," *La Razón*, no. 10, 20 June 1861, 4; *La Razón*, no. 12, 27 June 1861, 1.
32. Ministro de Estado (Tomas de Ligués) to Ministro de Guerra y Ultramar, Palacio, 28 June 1861, AHN: Ultramar, Expte. 8, doc. 1.
33. Santiago Pichardo, "Al Pueblo," Santiago, 20 June 1861, SHM: Ultramar 5645, Expte. "Asuntos operaciónes de campaña," doc. s/n. Santana was "the indefatigable caudillo of our holy cause," he concluded. He admonished, "Our cause is just, God protects it, and if it were necessary, the neighboring islands of Cuba and Puerto Rico would give us abundant reinforcements of all kinds."
34. [No sig.] to Cap. Gen. of Cuba, SD, 21 October 1861, AGN-RD: Anexión (DE/1381) 2, Expte. 1, doc. s/n.
35. *Gaceta de Santo Domingo*, no. 110, 14 August 1862, 1.
36. Domingo Lasala to "Gefe de la frontera haitiana," Neyba, 18 September 1861, AGN-RD: Anexión (DE/1381) 2, Expte. 1, doc. s/n; Gob. de Azua to [unclear], 16 December 1861, AGN-RD: Anexión (DE/1381) 2, Expte. 1, doc. s/n; Santana to Min. de Guerra y Ultramar, SD, 6 February 1862, AHN: Ultramar 5485, Expte. 24.
37. For example, Eusebio Puello to Cap. Gen., Azua, 20 February 1862, AGN-RD: Anexión (DE/1381) 2, Expte. 1.2, doc. s/n.
38. Santana to Min. de Ultramar, 19 February 1862, AGN-RD: CH Leg. 21, Expte. 175, p. 1.
39. Eduardo Alonso Colmenares to Min. de Guerra, 21 January 1862, AHN: Ultramar 3532, Expte. 12. Other individuals—like British sailor Jaime Barret, suspected of a murder of another British subject—also languished without trial. British Consul Martin J. Hood to Cap. Gen. Felipe Ribero, SD, 7 October 1862, AGN-RD: Anexión 4 (DE/1383), Expte. 26, doc. 1.
40. Felipe Ribero to Min. de Guerra y Ultramar, 9 December 1862, AGI: Cuba 1018 (libro).
41. Felipe Ribero to Min. de Guerra y Ultramar, 9 December 1862, AGI: Cuba 1018 (libro).
42. Felipe Ribero to Min. de Guerra y Ultramar, 14 December 1862, AGI: Cuba 1018 (libro).
43. "Le Grand Meeting," *Le Moniteur Haïtien*, no. 26, 1 June 1861, 1–4.
44. Jung, *Coolies and Cane*, 74; *Le Moniteur Haïtien*, no. 12, 23 February 1861, 2–3; Hauch, "Attitudes of Foreign Governments," 267.
45. Pedro Santana to Min. de Guerra, 5 March 1862, AGN-RD: CH Leg. 21, Expte. 175, p. 11.

46. Marte, *Correspondencia*, 196.
47. Copiador, 14 September 1860; Felipe Ribero to Min. de Guerra y Ultramar, 14 December 1862, AGI: Cuba 1018 (libro).
48. Joaquín de Rubalcalva, Comandancia Gral. de Marina, to Gob. Sup. Civil., 15 February 1863, ANC: AP 225, Expte. 1.
49. Pedro Santana to Min. de Guerra, 18 February 1862, SHM: Ultramar 5639, Expte. "Esclavitud/Esclavos 1849–1862," doc. s/n.
50. Bando, Achilles Michel, 25 February 1863, AGN-RD: CH Tomo 19 (AGI: Cuba 1004B), p. 27.
51. Bando, 28 February 1863, AGI: Cuba 984C.
52. "Proceso instruido contra Don Ramón Almonte, Don Isidro Jimenez, Don Manuel Tejada, Don Manuel de Jesus Vargas (presente), Don Juan Antonio Alis, . . . y Don Domingo Curiel, Oficiales de las reservas de esta isla . . . ," Santiago de los Caballeros, March–May 1863, AGN-RD: CH Tomo 11 (AGI: Cuba 1015A), 75.
53. "Contra los paisanos Juan Isidro Rodríguez . . . ," 1863, AGN-RD: CH Leg. 24, Expte. 205, p. 103.
54. "Proceso Instruida contra D. Álvaro Fernández, D. José Vidal Pichardo, D. Juan de la Cruz Ureña, D. José Cepeda, D. Ambrosio de la Cruz . . . ," Santiago, March 1863, AGI: Cuba 1014A.
55. Ribero to Min. de Guerra, 26 April 1863, AGI: Cuba 1018.
56. Ribero to Min. de Guerra, 16 March 1863, AGI: Cuba 1018.
57. Castro Ventura, *La Guerra Restauradora*, 132.
58. Declaración de D. Rafael Leandro García in "Proceso Contra varios individuos de complicidad en la sublevación que tubo lugar en Puerto Plata en 27 de Agosto ultimo," 1863, AHN: Ultramar 881[a], 1[a] Pieza, 87.
59. Real Audiencia de SD to Min. de Ultramar (copia), Madrid, 20 October 1863, AHN: Ultramar 3525, Expte. 30.
60. Ribero to Min. de Guerra, 19 March 1863, AGI: Cuba 1018.
61. Abreu Cardet and Sintes Gómez, *Los alzamientos de Guayubín*, 42.
62. Achilles Michel to Cap. Gen., Santiago, 2 March 1863, AGN-RD: CH Tomo 19 (AGI: Cuba 1004B), p. 7.
63. Don Diego Crespo was a day laborer, for example, but he had been educated at some point and was able to sign his testimony clearly ("Causa formada en aberiguación de los hechos que han tenido lugar en la insurrección de Guayubín . . . el día 22 de Febrero," March 1863, AGI: Cuba 1011A, Expte. s/n, p. 107).
64. As was the case for Pablo Rodríguez in "Proceso instruido contra el paisano José de la Cruz . . . ," November 1863, AGI: Cuba 1011A.
65. "Causa formada en aberiguación de los hechos que han tenido lugar en la insurrección de Guayubín . . . el día 22 de Febrero," March 1863, AGI: Cuba 1011A, Expte. s/n, 7v, 11.

66. "Sumaria instruido contra el paisano Manuel de Arias . . . ," SD, July 1864, AGI: Cuba, 1012A, "Sumarias," 32v.
67. "Sumaria contra el paisano D. Miguel Valverde, acusado de haber salido de esta plaza para unirse a los insurrectos, SD, 9 September 1864, AGI: Cuba 1011A (emphasis added). During his exile in Puerto Rico, interrogators of the rebellious priest Fernando Antonio Meriño were "visibly upset" at his interrogation for similar reasons, and they insisted that neither his speech nor his countenance was Dominican. "Even though [they] did not verbalize it, it is possible they thought that a white, well-dressed man who spoke Spanish well could not be Dominican," one author concludes (Sáez, *Documentos inéditos de Fernando A. de Meriño*, 28).
68. Granted in May, it reached the Cibao in late June. It extended to those who had been involved not only in the events of the spring but also in prior republican-era discord if the applicant swore loyalty to Her Highness within six months' time (Real Orden of 27 May 1863, ANC: AP 53, Expte. 25, doc. 1). Governor Rivero urged the public—excluding any ringleaders and members of the Provincial Reserves—not to worry they would be judged as rebels, and he promised amnesty for those returning to their homes within fifteen days (Felipe Ribero, "Dominicanos," SD, 29 May 1863, AHN: Ultramar 3525, Expte. 91).
69. Felipe Ribero, "Dominicanos," SD, 29 May 1863, AHN: Ultramar 3525, Expte. 91.
70. Martin Hood to Cap. Gen., 22 May 1863, AGN-RD: Anexión 19, Expte. 8, doc. 2; Marte, *Correspondencia*, 247.
71. Ribero to Min. de Guerra, 17 March 1863, AGI: Cuba 1018.
72. Administrador de Rentas al Gob. Gral, 3 March 1863, AHN: Ultramar 6159, Expte. 41.
73. Ribero to Min. de Ultramar, 20 April 1863, AHN: Ultramar 3525, Expte. 24.
74. Felipe Ribero to Min. de Guerra y Ultramar, 20 April 1863, AGI: Cuba 1018 (libro).
75. Ribero to Min. de Ultramar, 20 April 1863, AHN: Ultramar 3525, Expte. 24.
76. Felipe Ribero to Min. de Guerra y Ultramar, 20 April 1863, AGI: Cuba 1018 (libro).
77. Min. de Estado to Felipe Ribero, 12 June 1863, AHN: Ultramar 3525, Expte. 25.
78. Achilles Michel to Cap. Gen., 1 March 1863, AGN-RD: CH Tomo 19, 1004B, p. 22.
79. De la Gándara, *Anexión y guerra de Santo Domingo*, 291.
80. Ribero to Min. de Guerra, 20 May 1863, AGI: Cuba 1018; Felipe Ribero to Min. de Estado, 10 June 1863, AHN: Ultramar 3525, Expte. 25.
81. Felipe Ribero to Min. de Estado, 10 June 1863, AHN: Ultramar 3525, Expte. 25.
82. Buceta to Cap. Gen., 12 July 1863, AGI: Cuba 963, Expte. 198, doc. s/n.

83. Monción, "De capotillo a Santiago," 14, 26.
84. Ribero to Min. de Guerra, 2 June 1863, AGI: Cuba 1018.
85. Segundo Días Herrera to Cap. Gen. of Cuba, 25 August 1863, ANC: AP 53, Expte. 28, doc. s/n.
86. Mariano Álvarez, s/f [June 1863], AHN: Ultramar 3525, Expte. 95, Copia 2.
87. Manuel Buceta to Felipe Ribero, Santiago, 8 August 1863, AHN: Ultramar 3525, Expte. 27, doc. 2; Felipe Ribero to Min. de Ultramar, 18 August 1863, AHN: Ultramar 3525, Expte. 26, doc. 2.
88. Pedro Ezequiel Guerrero to Manuel Buceta, Monte Cristi, 8 August 1863, AHN: Ultramar 3525, Expte. 27, doc. 3.
89. Castro Ventura, *La Guerra Restauradora*, 155.
90. "Proceso Contra varios individuos de complicidad en la sublevación que tubo lugar en Puerto Plata en 27 de Agosto ultimo," 1863, AHN: Ultramar 881ª, 1ª Pieza, 9. The atmosphere was so alarming by late July that when the Havana port commander arrived by steamship with more than six hundred men, he boarded another ship to travel to Santo Domingo immediately, in order to inform the governor of the extremity of the situation (Segundo Días Herrera to Cap. Gen. of Cuba, 25 August 1863, ANC: AP 53, Expte. 28, doc. s/n).
91. Finke, "Puerto Plata en la Gesta Restauradora," 134.
92. "Proceso Contra varios individuos de complicidad en la sublevación que tubo lugar en Puerto Plata en 27 de Agosto ultimo," 1863, AHN: Ultramar 881ª, 1ª Pieza, 4.
93. Martínez, *Diccionario*, 237.
94. Declaración de D. Rafael Leandro García in "Proceso Contra varios individuos de complicidad en la sublevación que tubo lugar en Puerto Plata en 27 de Agosto ultimo," 1863, AHN: Ultramar 881ª, 1ª Pieza, 89.
95. Paton, *No Bond but the Law*, 43.
96. José Porrua Valdivia, Circular, Puerto Plata, 31 August 1863, ANC: AP 54, Expte. 3, doc. s/n.
97. Declaración de D. Rafael Leandro García in "Proceso Contra varios individuos de complicidad en la sublevación que tubo lugar en Puerto Plata en 27 de Agosto ultimo," 1863, AHN: Ultramar 881ª, 1ª Pieza, 89.
98. José Porrua Valdivia to Regente de Real Audiencia, Puerto Plata, 2 September 1863, ANC: AP 54, Expte. 3, doc. s/n.
99. Finke, "Puerto Plata en la Gesta Restauradora," 135–36. It was the second major fire in four months. More than forty buildings, including the customhouse, burned to the ground in July.
100. Finke, "Puerto Plata en la Gesta Restauradora," 139.
101. Declaración de D. Rafael Leandro García in "Proceso Contra varios individuos de complicidad en la sublevación que tubo lugar en Puerto Plata en 27 de Agosto ultimo," 1863, AHN: Ultramar 881ª, 1ª Pieza, 126.
102. [Sin firma] to Cap. Gen., 23 August 1863, AGN-RD: CH Tomo 15, p. 79.

103. Abreu Cardet and Sintes Gómez, *El alzamiento de Neiba*, 25.
104. Min. de Ultramar to Gob. Superior Civil, 11 January 1864, AGN-RD: Anexión 25, Expte. 7, doc. 3.
105. Román de la Torre to Min. de Ultramar, 8 October 1863, AHN: Ultramar 3533, Expte. 1, doc. 7.
106. Finke, "Puerto Plata en la Gesta Restauradora," 127.
107. Cáp. Gen. José de Villar to Min. de Ultramar, SD, 1 September 1864, AHN: Ultramar 3533, Expte. 1, doc. 24.
108. [Sin firma] to Alejandro Guridi, Santiago, 4 August 1863, AGN-RD: CH Tomo 15, p. 49.
109. "Causa formada en aberiguación de los hechos que han tenido lugar en la insurrección de Guayubín . . . el día 22 de Febrero," March 1863, AGI: Cuba 1011A, Expte. s/n.
110. "Causa formada en aberiguación de los hechos que han tenido lugar en la insurrección de Guayubín . . . el día 22 de Febrero," March 1863, AGI: Cuba 1011A, Expte. s/n, 6.
111. "Sumaria [sobre Hato Mayor] . . . ," October 1863, AGN-RD: CH Leg. 21 (AGI: Cuba 1014A), Expte. 176, pp. 8, 89.
112. "Sumaria [sobre Hato Mayor] . . . ," October 1863, AGN-RD: CH Leg. 21 (AGI: Cuba 1014A), Expte. 176, p. 8. The rebels raised the very same flag that had been lowered on the day of annexation. The flag had been on display in the church, intertwined with the Spanish one for a time, and later stored by reserve officers. Evidently the rebels had located and confiscated it to raise it again, and tried to find the Spanish one in order to burn it, but it was saved by the wife of a reservist.
113. [Sin firma], Santiago, 31 August 1863, AGN-RD: CH Tomo 15, p. 145.
114. Rodríguez Demorizi, *Actos y doctrina*, 152.
115. Testimonio de Francisco Mosqueton, 7 February 1864, AGN-RD: CH Tomo 15, p. 186.
116. Translated by Kak Lam Yip and Lan Jo Wu, who translate "Wu kwai officer" as "black officer." Ah Yeung and Ah Sung to Ah Kun, Wong Yi, and Ah Bong, September or October 1864, ANC: AP 226, Expte. 9, doc. s/n.
117. "Causa Contra el penado asiático Macsimo Segundo por el delito de fugarse . . . ," Puerto Plata, February 1864, AGI: Cuba 1012A, "Sumarias."
118. "Sumaria instruida contra el asiático penado 'Roberto,'" 4 May 1864, AGI: Cuba 950B, "Causas."
119. Bando, 2 March 1863, AGI: Cuba 984C; Rivero to Min. de Guerra, 8 March 1863, AHN: Ultramar 3525, Expte. 21.
120. "Proceso Formado contra el SubT de las RP de esta Isla Don Hilarion Puello, con motivo del desorden originado por el, en el pueblo del Cotuy," Santiago, April 1863, AGI: Cuba 1011B, Expte. s/n.
121. Mariano Cappa to Cap. Gen., SD, 25 August 1863, AGI: Cuba 950B, "Causas."

122. Hauch, "The Dominican Republic and Its Foreign Relations," 161.
123. Castro Ventura, *La Guerra Restauradora*, 59.
124. Hauch, "The Dominican Republic and Its Foreign Relations," 162.
125. "Chismes," *La Razón*, no. 72, 19 September 1863, 4.
126. Ubiñas Renville, *Historias y leyendas afro-dominicanas*, 91. Los Naranjos was a settlement of maroon families who moved there from the Neiba settlement, at the end of the 1700s (Lora Hugi, "El sonido de la libertad," 111; Yingling, "Maroons of Santo Domingo," 25).
127. Martínez, *Diccionario*, 311.
128. Carlos de Vargas to Min. de Guerra y Ultramar, Reservado, SD, 23 December 1863, SHM: Ultramar 5655, Expte. 2º Periodo Ministerio del General Lersundi, doc. s/n.
129. W. Jaeger to W. H. Seward, 10 January 1864, AGN-RD: "Correspondencia del Agente Comercial de los EEUU No. 43-52," 4.
130. "Sumaria Instruida contra el paisano moreno Manuel Guerrero y Guerrero acusado de sedicioso," SD, August 1864, AGI: Cuba 1014A.
131. "Sumaria en averiguación de los motivos que hubo para prender al moreno paisano Francisco de los Dolores . . . ," SD, September 1863, AGI: Cuba 1012A, "Sumarias," IV.
132. Declaración de D. Rafael Leandro García in "Proceso Contra varios individuos de complicidad en la sublevación que tubo lugar en Puerto Plata en 27 de Agosto ultimo," 1863, AHN: Ultramar 881ª, 1ª Pieza, 89.
133. Sumaria de Nicolas Guzman, March 1864, AGI: Cuba 1011A.
134. Carlos de Vargas, "Dominicanos!," 23 October 1863, AHN: Ultramar 3525, Expte. 33, doc. 2.
135. Carlos de Vargas to Min. de Guerra y Ultramar, Reservado, SD, 23 December 1863, SHM: Ultramar 5655, Expte. 2º Periodo Ministerio del General Lersundi, doc. s/n.
136. Carlos de Vargas to Min. de Guerra y Ultramar, Reservado, SD, 23 December 1863, SHM: Ultramar 5655, Expte. 2º Periodo Ministerio del General Lersundi, doc. s/n.
137. Juan Suero to Cap. Gen. of SD, Puerto Plata, 24 December 1863, AGN-RD: CH Tomo 15, p. 240.
138. Archambault, *Historia de la Restauración*, 77. Governor Rivero planned to dismiss Buceta to Havana; both his military tactics and his behavior as governor of Santiago had been "dubious," the governor told Madrid officials, hinting strongly at abuses to authority (Min. de Guerra to Cap. Gen. of SD, Madrid, 26 November 1863, AGI: Cuba 923B, doc . s/n de Expte. "Buceta de Villar, D. Manuel"). Although the order was annulled before Buceta ever received it, the sanctioned officer was absolutely indignant at the prospect of censure, calling the resolution "exceptionally offensive" (Manuel Buceta to Cap. Gen., 2 October 1863, AGI: Cuba 923B, Expte. "Buceta de Villar, D. Manuel," doc. s/n).

139. [Sin firma] to Alejandro Guridi, Santiago, 4 August 1863, AGN-RD: CH Tomo 15, p. 49; José Porrua to Regente de RA, 6 October 1863, ANC: AP 54, Expte. 3, doc. s/n.
140. José Porrua Valdivia, Puerto Plata, 30 August 1863, ANC: AP 54, Expte. 3, doc. s/n.
141. Martínez, Diccionario, 237.
142. A few witnesses in early revolts reported hearing cries of "Viva Báez, Viva la República, Muera España." Álvarez López, *Dominación colonial y guerra popular*, 55–56. Felipe Ribero to Min. de Guerra y Ultramar, 9 December 1862, AGI: Cuba 1018; Ministro de Estado (Tomas de Ligués) to Ministro de Guerra y Ultramar, Palacio, 28 June 1861, AHN: Ultramar, Expte. 8, doc. 1. Governor Serrano of Cuba had arrived in Santo Domingo determined to declare total amnesty, but he faithfully passed on Santana's "semiofficial" letter seeking to ban the Báez family, General José María Cabral, and a handful of others, even as he continued to suggest total clemency (Serrano to Min. de Guerra, Reservada, 6 September 1861, AHN: Ultramar 3525, Expte. 1). Santana seems to have remained fairly vigilant about not letting in individual political opponents; he denied their entry on a case-by-case basis (Santana to Sp. Consul in Haiti, 18 April 1862, AGN-RD: CH Leg. 21, Expte. 175, p. 64). Santana's successor confirmed the ban on former political opponents, ordering Spanish authorities in Saint Thomas not to issue passports to General Ramón Mella or any other prominent political refugee (Felipe Ribero to Min. de Guerra, 2 October 1862, AHN: Ultramar 3535, Expte. 2).
143. "Báez gained power, not through the sympathies of the people whom he tyrannized and dilapidated, but rather through intrigue and treachery; Santana has always occupied the Presidency based on [legitimate means]." Báez is corrupt, "*immoral, cynical and destructive*," argued Galván, the response pamphlet's author. Báez was wealthy and profited from discord, while Pedro Santana was the worthy political hero—akin to Cincinnati, Napoleon, and George Washington—who lived in poverty, he continued (Galván, "El General don Pedro Santana," 3, 12).
144. Bando, 16 March 1863, AHN: Ultramar 3525, Expte. 22, doc. 3.
145. Galván, "El General don Pedro Santana," 25.
146. Conclusion Fiscal, "Causa formada en aberiguación de los hechos . . . de Guayubín . . . el día 22 de Febrero," March 1863, AGI: Cuba 1011A, Expte. s/n, p. 224.
147. Editorial, *La Razón*, no. 70, 3 September 1863, 1 (emphasis in original).
148. Felipe Ribero, "Dominicanos!," SD, 24 August 1863, ANC: AP 54, Expte. 2.
149. Manuel Urbano Sánchez to Cap. Gen., La Vega, 3 September 1863, ANC: AP 54, Expte. 3, doc. s/n.
150. Pedro Santana, "SOLDADOS!," Monte Plata, 17 September 1863, AGI: Cuba 947B, Expte. 332.

151. Pedro Santana, "SOLDADOS!," Monte Plata, 17 September 1863, AGI: Cuba 947B, Expte. 332.
152. Bando, 16 March 1863, AHN: Ultramar 3525, Expte. 22, doc 3.
153. "Rasgos de generosidad,"*La Razón*, no. 73, 26 September 1863, 4.
154. "La Insurrección," *La Razón*, no. 72, 19 September 1863, 4.
155. Carlos de Vargas, Bando, 19 March 1864, AGI: Cuba 948C.
156. "Padrón que se forma de todas las cabezas de familia . . . ," 26 October 1863, AGN-RD: CH Tomo 15, p. 181.
157. Antonio Alfau to Marcos Adon, 16 February 1864, AGI: Cuba 952, Expte. 98, "Correspondencia," doc. s/n.
158. Felipe Ribero, Bando, 30 September 1863, AGI: Cuba 984C, "Bandos."
159. Carlos de Vargas, "Habitantes de SD," 23 January 1864, AGI: Cuba 948, "Bandos."
160. Felipe Ribero, "Dominicanos!," SD, 24 August 1863, ANC: AP 54, Expte. 2.
161. Bando, 16 March 1863, AHN: Ultramar 3525, Expte. 22, doc. 3.
162. "Habitantes de SD," 25 January 1864, AGI: Cuba 948, "Bandos."
163. "Proceso Contra varios individuos de complicidad en la sublevación que tubo lugar en Puerto Plata en 27 de Agosto ultimo," 1863, AHN: Ultramar 881ª, 1ª Pieza, 2.
164. Nicolas Pérez to Cap. Gen., 27 November 1863, AGI: Cuba 1001B, "Exptes. en suspenso," doc. s/n.
165. Ayuntamiento del Comun de Azua to Cap. Gen., 3 September 1863, ANC: AP 54, Expte. 2, doc. s/n.
166. Carlos de Vargas, "Habitantes," 20 November 1863, AGI: Cuba 948, "Bandos."
167. José Roca to Cap. Gen., La Vega, 20 August 1863, AHN: Ultramar 3525, Expte. 27, doc. 7; José Roca to Cap. Gen., La Vega, 19 August 1863, ANC: AP 54, Expte. 2.
168. Proclama del Ayuntamiento de la Vega, 27 August 1863, AGI: Cuba 947B, Expte. 332.
169. Testimonio de Francisco Mosqueton, 7 February 1864, AGN-RD: CH Tomo 15, 186.
170. "Afectuosa y sentida composición poética que dedica al ES Don Carlos de Vargas . . ." and "Contestación a la sentida composición . . . ," in Rodríguez Demorizi, *Santana y los poetas*, 317–20.
171. Wm. G. N. Jaeger to William Seward, 25 November 1863, AGN-RD: Libro US Agente Comercial.
172. Carlos de Vargas to Min. de Ultramar, Reservado, 24 October 1863, AHN: Ultramar 3525, Expte. 149, doc. 1.
173. Carlos de Vargas, "SOLDADOS!," 23 October 1863, AGI: Cuba 947B, Expte. 332.
174. Alejandro Ricart to Cap. Gen., 26 January 1864, AGN-RD: Anexión 29, Expte. 15, doc. 6.

175. De la Gándara to Cap. Gen., Azua, 15 December 1863, AGI: Cuba 950B, Expte. 77, "Causas," doc. s/n.
176. W. Jaeger to W. H. Seward, 10 January 1864, AGN-RD: "Correspondencia del Agente Comercial de los EEUU No. 43-52," 4.
177. [Unclear] to Cap. Gen., 5 July 1865, AGN-RD: Anexión 32, Expte. 5 (2006).
178. "Reglamenta interina para el régimen de las oficinas administrativas de la Provincia de la parte Española de SD," José de Villar, 22 October 1864, AHN: Ultramar 6160, Expte. 17, doc. 2; Carlos Borrajo to Sr. Admor. de Rentas de Azua, 3 February 1863, AHN: Ultramar 6160, Expte. 17, doc. 4.
179. Declaracion de Teniente Coronel de las Reservas D. Luís Bernal, in "De la sumaria instruida en averiguación de la conducta observada por el Coronel de Infantería D. Bruno Ganoso y Quesada," SD, March 1864, AGI: Cuba, 1012A, "Sumarias," 27.
180. Declaración de Luís Bernal; Declaración de Federico Quisch, in "De la sumaria instruida en averiguación de la conducta observada por el Coronel de Infantería D. Bruno Ganoso y Quesada," SD, March 1864, AGI: Cuba, 1012A, "Sumarias," 27v, 28v. Samaná's authorities moved several times subsequently, first to a healthier spot on the peninsula and later integrating their judiciary with Seibo entirely.
181. Matos Rodríguez, "Street Vendors, Pedlars, Shop-Owners and Domestics," 187–88.
182. "Sumaria Instruida contra el paisano moreno Manuel Guerrero y Guerrero acusado de sedicioso," SD, August 1864, AGI: Cuba 1014A.
183. Hauch, "The Dominican Republic and Its Foreign Relations," 163.
184. "Proceso instruido contra Don Ramón Almonte, [et al.] . . . ," Santiago de los Caballeros, March–May 1863, AGN-RD: CH Tomo 11 (AGI: Cuba 1015A), 12; murder of Juana: "Proceso contra varios individuos acusados de complicidad en la sublevación que tubo lugar en Puerto Plata," September 1863, AGN-RD: CH Leg. 24 (AGI: Cuba 1014A), Expte. 211.
185. From Lucas Peña, General en Gefe de las Fronteras, to General de División, Don Antonio Batista, "Causa formada en aberiguación de los hechos que han tenido lugar en la insurrección de Guayubín . . . ," March 1863, AGI: Cuba 1011A, Expte. s/n, 38.
186. "Proceso instruido contra el paisano José de la Cruz acusado de seducción al enemigo, a los soldados del país," November 1863, AGI: Cuba 1011A.
187. "Proceso instruido contra Lorenzo Munoz como complicado en la actual rebolucion por conductor de correspondencia enemiga," SD, September 1863–January 1865, AGI: Cuba 1012B.
188. Expte. de Tribunal Supremo de Justicia, 19 September 1863, AHN: Ultramar 3525, Expte. 31, doc. 2.
189. "Sumaria [sobre Hato Mayor] . . . ," October 1863, AGN-RD: CH Leg. 21 (AGI: Cuba 1014A), Expte. 176, 40–42 (but 41 missing).

190. General José María Cabral, "DOMINICANOS!," Las Caobas, 6 April 1861, AGI: Cuba 984C, Expte. "promovido a consecuencia de la invasión de la frontera de SD por los Haitianos," doc. s/n.
191. Proclamas, 62.
192. Ramón Mella, "Dominicanos," 16 January 1864, AGI: Cuba 973B, Expte. "306: Parlamentos," doc. s/n.
193. Ramon Mella and Marcos E. Adon to Gral. Antonio Alfau, s/f (February 1864), AGI: Cuba 952, Expte. 98, "Correspondencia," doc. s/n.
194. "Sumaria [sobre Hato Mayor] . . . ," October 1863, AGN-RD: CH Leg. 21 (AGI: Cuba 1014A), Expte. 176, 62.
195. Carlos de Vargas to Min. de Guerra y Ultramar, Reservado, SD, 23 December 1863, SHM: Ultramar 5655, Expte. 2º Periodo Ministerio del General Lersundi, doc. s/n.
196. W. Jaeger to W. H. Seward, 10 January 1864, AGN-RD: "Correspondencia del Agente Comercial de los EEUU No. 43-52," 4.
197. Expte. de Tribunal Supremo de Justicia, 19 September 1863, AHN: Ultramar 3525, Expte. 31, doc. 2.
198. Jose Porrúa to Regente de RA de SD, 21 November 1863, ANC: AP 54, 3, doc. s/n.
199. Declaración de D. Rafael Leandro García in "Proceso Contra varios individuos de complicidad en la sublevación que tubo lugar en Puerto Plata en 27 de Agosto ultimo," 1863, AHN: Ultramar 881ª, 1ª Pieza, 87.
200. [Sin firma] to Jose Roca, 27 August 1863, AGN-RD: CH Tomo 15, p. 151.
201. Bando, San Cristobal, 14 October 1863, AGI: Cuba 1003B, Expte. "Documentos cojidos al enemigo y referentes a sus movimientos," doc. s/n.
202. Alcalde Pedáneo Pedro Quintin of Santiago, and D. Juan Lafit, AP of Puerto Plata, were actually suspected of being principal insurgents in the fall of 1863, for example.
203. Bando, San Cristobal, 14 October 1863, AGI: Cuba 1003B, Expte. "Documentos cojidos al enemigo y referentes a sus movimientos," doc. s/n. Just four days later, the town fell back to the Spanish.
204. E.g., "Sumaria Instruida contra el paisano Alpolinar Megia acusado de sospechoso . . . ," Bayaguana, 7 October 1863, AGI: Cuba 1014A.
205. Don Rafael Garrido, Apolinario Megias et al. to Min. de Ultramar, 27 April 1864, AHN: Ultramar 3525, Expte. 136.
206. "Sumaria Instruida contra el paisano moreno Manuel Guerrero y Guerrero acusado de sedicioso," SD, August 1864, AGI: Cuba 1014A.
207. "Proceso contra varios individuos acusados de complicidad en la sublevación que tubo lugar en Puerto Plata," September 1863, AGN-RD: CH Leg. 24 (AGI: Cuba 1014A), Expte. 211.
208. Officially, foreign merchants blamed the Spanish for the October 1863 fires in Puerto Plata. Their immediate reclamations—for more than 100,000

pesos—continued well after Spanish evacuation (1896!). They may simply have been trying to finger a wealthier culprit; Dominican historians suggest that General Gaspar Polanco explicitly ordered arson to reproduce Santiago's calamitous disruption (Finke, "Puerto Plata en la Gesta Restauradora," 135). Spanish officers admitted the fires followed the wake of Spanish troops and asserted that they had attempted to extinguish them. The wooden constructions were simply too quickly reduced to ashes, however (En averiguación de si el incendio de Puerto Plata [SD] en Octubre de 1863 fue prendido por las tropas españolas o por los dominicanos, Havana, 1896, AGI: Ultramar 881ª, Expte. s/n).

209. Jose Porrúa to Regente de la RA de SD, 6 October 1863, ANC: AP 54, Expte. 3, doc. s/n.
210. William Jaeger, 4 December 1863, AGN-RD: Libro de Correspondencia del Agente Comercial de los EEUU.
211. Abreu Cardet and Sintes Gómez, Los alzamientos de Guayubín, 35.
212. Proclamas, 19.
213. "Some of those pardoned have returned to this City. Others have left Porto Rico (where they were imprisoned) and gone to St. Thomas and Curaçao, refusing to return while the Spaniards have possession of this island. The majority of those who returned are closing their business and intend to leave, if the Spaniards remain," the U.S. commercial agent wrote (Wm. G. N. Jaeger to William Seward, 25 November 1863, AGN-RD: Libro US Agente Comercial).
214. Cáp. Gen. José de Villar to Min. de Ultramar, SD, 1 September 1864, AHN: Ultramar 3533, Expte. 1, doc. 24.
215. Carlos de Vargas to Min. de Guerra y Ultramar, Reservado, SD, 23 December 1863, SHM: Ultramar 5655, Expte. 2º Periodo Ministerio del General Lersundi, doc. s/n.
216. Otero y Pimentel, Reflejos de la vida militar, 232.
217. E.g. of a robbery case (Puerto Plata): José de la Gándara to Cap. Gen., Puerto Plata, 30 September 1863, AGI: Cuba 950B, "Causas." E.g. of a small group of soldiers written up for delinquency (Samaná): Felipe Ribero to Comisario Regio de la Real Audiencia, 15 January 1863, AGN-RD: Anexión 18, Expte. 25. E.g. of a soldier judged guilty of robbery and assault within his own barracks (for which he was sentenced to one month in jail): "Instruido contra el Cabo 2º de la 2ª Compañía del Batallón Cazadores de Bailen No 1º Rafael Quintana . . . ," SD, 1863, AGI: Cuba 1012A, "Sumarias." One soldier, a laborer from the Canary Islands, even shouted "Nueva España!"—an oblique parallel, perhaps, to conquistador efforts in sixteenth-century Mexico and the campaign in which he found himself—he faced trial for it but was mostly exonerated for drunkenness ("Instruida contra el paisano [español] José Linares y Fernández acusado de haber dado voces de Nueva España," 10 May 1865, AGI: Cuba 1014A, Expte. s/n).

A sample month of the early fighting, November 1863: twenty-one Spanish soldiers were arrested (one for murder of a Dominican man, two for suspected murder, seven for desertion, two for insubordination, three unknown, one for drunkenness, three for robbery, two for *riñas* with paisanos). That same month, fourteen "paisanos" (Dominican troops) were arrested, two as prisoners of war; one for carrying enemy communication; two for *sospechoso*, seven for deserting Santana's ranks, one for an argument with his superior ("Relación de los presos y arrestados . . . ," SD, 4 November 1863, AGI: Cuba 950B, "Causas").

218. Causas contra dos soldados del Batallón de Isabel 2ª, Francisco Miñarro y Francisco Mesa, por el asesinato del paisano D. Lorenzo Barrera, December 1863, AGI: Cuba 950B, "Causas."
219. "Sumaria En averiguación de los motibos que ocasionó la muerte del Carretero Benito Barreto . . . ," SD, June 1864, AGI: Cuba 1011B.
220. "Sumaria En averiguación de la fuga del soldado del Batallón Cazadores de Bailen José Cabrera de los Calabozos del Hospital Militar . . . ," SD, October 1864, AGI: Cuba 1011B.
221. Libro 3, "Gral. de SD/Estado Mayor/Registro Gral. de Causas, da principio desde 1º de Nov 1864 Libro 3º," AGI: Cuba 1017.
222. E.g., Carlos Gutíerrez to Cap. Gen., Puerto Plata, 7 April 1864; Eusebio Puello to Cap. Gen., Azua, 31 October 1864; Domingo Dulce to Cap. Gen., 29 March 1865, AGI: Cuba 950B.
223. "De la causa instruida en averiguación del autor o autores del robo de una maleta en Guasa . . . ," November 1864, AGI: Cuba 1015A, "Sumarias."
224. Bosch, *La Guerra de la Restauración*, 156, 164.
225. "Sumaria instruida contra el soldado de las Reservas Juan del Rosario," March 1864, AGI: Cuba 953b, Expte. 125, "Desertores de 1864–65, Desertores en Reservas Provinciales," doc. s/n.
226. When Spanish general José Maria Pérez sent out a soldier in search of a reservist who had deserted to gather plantains, for example, angry townspeople came to the soldier's defense. Five men—laborers and farmers all—were arrested for their alleged threats to the general and held on trial as prisoners of war ("Proceso instruido contra los paisanos Miguel Rodríguez, Tomas Hidalgo, Juan Culinario y Santiago de la Concepción aprehendidos con las armas en la mano y Julio Marti acusado de insubordinación y seducción, para atentar a la vida del General de las reservas D. José Maria Pérez," January 1864, AGI: Cuba 1011A).
227. "Sumaria instruida en averiguación de la deserción al enemigo de soldado de las reservas Pedro Alcántara (a) Elías," SD, 1864, AGI: Cuba 1011A.
228. Proceso instruido contra Saturnino Castillo, acusado de deserción y complicado en la revolución, SD, January 1864, AGI: Cuba 1011A. He could not possibly have presented himself to authorities sooner because the rebels had stolen his clothing, he reported.

229. "Proceso instruido al Cáp. Don José Agustín Henríquez por habandono que hizo de la guardia de Pajarito," SD, October 1864, AGI: Cuba, 1012A, "Sumarias," 55.
230. Estanislao Dusablon to Cap. Gen. of SD, San Carlos, 14 July 1864, AGI: Cuba 995B, Expte. s/n. Sometimes mothers interceded for their sons to petition for release from military service, as Candelaria Brunel did, to call them back to support their numerous family (Candelaria Brunel to Cap. Gen., San Carlos, 5 August 1864, AGI: Cuba 995B, Expte. s/n).
231. Carlos de Vargas to Min. de Guerra y Ultramar, Reservado, SD, 23 December 1863, SHM: Ultramar 5655, Expte. 2º Periodo Ministerio del General Lersundi, doc. s/n.
232. "Sumaria Instruida con motivo de la aprehension el espia de los enemigos Daniel Rosario, el dia 14 del mes de Junio de 1864 en el Arroyo del Carreton . . . ," June 1864, AGN-RD: CH Leg. 24 (AGI: Cuba 1039B), Expte. 214.
233. Gov. Eyre to Cap. Gen. of SD, 18 May 1864, AHN: Ultramar 3525, 124; Gov. Eyre to Cap. Gen. of Cuba, 18 May 1864, ANC: AP 225:4.
234. Jose de Villar to Gob. Superior Civil, 10 December 1864, AGN-RD: Anexión 27, Expte. 15; Gov. Eyre to Cap. Gen. of SD, 18 May 1864, AHN: Ultramar 3525, 124; Gov. Eyre to Cap. Gen. of Cuba, 18 May 1864, ANC: AP 225:4.
235. Martin J. Hood to Peter Vanderhurst, SD, 5 April 1863, in Espediente instruido en averiguación de las circunstancias que concurren en el paysano Pedro Richardson Vanderhorst, procedente del campo enemigo, Samaná, April 1864, AGI: Cuba 1011A, 20.
236. Manuel Buceta to Felipe Ribero, Santiago, 8 August 1863, AHN: Ultramar 3525, Expte. 27, doc. 2; Felipe Ribero to Min. de Ultramar, 18 August 1863, AHN: Ultramar 3525, Expte. 26, doc. 2.
237. Segundo Diaz to Cap. Gen. of Cuba, Reservado, 28 September 1863, ANC: AP 53, Expte. 28, doc. s/n. For more discussion of U.S. aid, see Espinal Hernández, "Geopolítica y armamentos en la Guerra Restauradora."
238. Felipe Ribero, Bando, 5 October 1863, ANC: AP 53, Expte. 28, doc. s/n.
239. Carlos de Vargas, Bando, 27 January 1864, AGI: Cuba 948C, "Bandos."
240. Ribero to Min. de Guerra, SD, 22 August 1863, AGN-RD: CH Tomo 15, p. 82.
241. Spanish officials extensively pursued one priest from Los Mina, D. José Páez, suspected of having fled with the rebels, for example. Leaving Los Mina, they looked for him "at a place called Mandingo," but no one there admitted to knowing his whereabouts. They interviewed Maria de los Reyes Rosario, an older woman who washed his clothes, but she also refused to give information to the authorities. Although Paéz was never caught, Spanish authorities embargoed all his worldly goods in absentia ("Sumaria Instruida en averiguación del paradero del Párroco del pueblo de San Lorenzo de las Minas D. José Páez," SD, April 1864, AGI: Cuba 1011A).

242. "Proceso instruido contra los paisanos Pedro Hernández y Buenaventura Ureña acusados de haber tratado de atravesar la guardia abanzada sobre el Camino de Santa Cruz," August 1864, AGI: Cuba 1011A.
243. "Causa inferida a un niño en San Carlos por uno de los disparos hechos por los centinelas . . . ," San Carlos, 31 March 1864, AGI: Cuba 950B, "Causas."
244. "Sumaria en habeariguacion de los motivos que ocasionó la desaparición del soldado de la 2ª Compañía del 2º Batallón de Vitoria Sebastián Moreno Beltran . . . ," 20 March 1865, AGI: Cuba 1012B.
245. Frustratingly, the exact source of this poem is not given, although it was evidently written from a pro-Spanish perspective from Puerto Rico. Qtd. in Rodríguez Demorizi, Santana y los poetas, 325.
246. "Sumario En averiguación de los motivos que tuvo el sumariado Pablo Hamburgo . . . ," SD, June 1864, AGI: Cuba 1011B.
247. "Sumaria Instruida contra el voluntario del Batallón de Baní Nicolás S. Guzmán acusado de delitos . . . y por falta de respeto al Comandante de as reservas D. José Joaquín Sánchez," SD, March 1864, AGI: Cuba 1011A.
248. Qtd. in Bosch, La Guerra de la Restauración, 10.
249. Pablo Santana to Cap. Gen., SD, 17 December 1863, AGI: Cuba 953B, Expte. 112, "Deportados," doc. s/n.
250. W. Jaeger to W. H. Seward, 18 December 1863, AGN-RD: "Correspondencia del Agente Comercial de los EEUU No. 43-52," 49.
251. "Sumaria Instruida contra el Cabo 2º de las reservas de Baní, José Maria German . . . ," SD, July 1864, AGI: Cuba, 1012A, "Sumarias."
252. "Sumaria Instruida contra el faccioso Ramón Díaz," Azua, June 1864, AGI: Cuba 1011A. He received a reduced judgment of two months in prison from a Spanish judge who, perhaps charitably, agreed he was not a rebel.
253. Alerta a los dominicanos, Boletín Oficial, no. 9, 14 June 1864, in Rodríguez Demorizi, Actos y doctrina, 129.
254. Rodríguez Demorizi, Actos y doctrina, 43.

6. The Lava Spread Everywhere

1. Marte, Correspondencia, 254; Hauch, "The Dominican Republic and Its Foreign Relations," 169.
2. Hauch, "The Dominican Republic and Its Foreign Relations," 163.
3. Rodriguez Objío (spring 1864) qtd. in Vicioso, El freno hatero, 335.
4. Gil, Orígenes y proyecciones de la revolución restauradora, 80. In a passage of Pedro Francisco Bonó's unfinished novel En el cantón de Bermejo (1863), a wealthy Cibaeño offers cattle to the rural rebels; he is thanked "in the name of the nation" (Vicioso, El freno hatero, 322).
5. "Proceso Instruido contra el Ayuntamiento," Santiago, February 1863, AGI: Cuba 1011A, Expte. s/n.

6. Carlos de Vargas to Min. de Guerra y Ultramar, Reservado, SD, 23 December 1863, SHM: Ultramar 5655, Expte. 2º Periodo Ministerio del General Lersundi, doc. s/n.
7. Qtd. in Vicioso, *El freno hatero*, 277.
8. Sanders, *Vanguard of the Atlantic World*, 6.
9. Ramón Mella, "Dominicanos!," 16 January 1864, AGI: Cuba 973B, Expte. 306, "Parlamentos," doc. s/n.
10. On Madrid journalists' coverage of the conflict as it escalated, see Castro Ventura, *La Guerra Restauradora*.
11. Rodríguez Demorizi, *Actos y doctrina*, 100. One other missive makes a tepid, vague mention of "mixed races" in Santo Domingo, but the allusion is also understood to be about the island's deep colonial past, ostensibly indigenous (Rodríguez Demorizi, *Actos y doctrina*, 228).
12. Rodríguez Demorizi, *Papeles de Pedro F. Bonó*, 120.
13. Cassá, *Personajes dominicanos*, 1:357.
14. Cassá, *Personajes dominicanos*, 1:354.
15. Castro Ventura, *La Guerra Restauradora*, 408.
16. E.g., *Le Moniteur Haïtien*, no. 8, 29 January 1859, 2.
17. Min. de Ultramar to Secretario de Estado, Palacio, 22 February 1864, AHN: Ultramar 3525, Expte. 114; Abreu Cardet and Álvarez-López, *Guerras de liberación*, 127.
18. "Examen de la Anexión. Posición de Haití," *Boletín Oficial*, no. 2, 20 January 1864, qtd. in Rodríguez Demorizi, *Actos y doctrina*, 86.
19. "A los dominicanos y al mundo entero," in Rodríguez Demorizi, *Actos y doctrina*, 93.
20. Lespinasse, Price-Mars, and Gutiérrez, *Haïti et la restauration de l'indépendance dominicaine*, 117.
21. Deive, *Diccionario de dominicanismos*, 46.
22. Rodríguez Demorizi, *Actos y doctrina*, 375.
23. Hernández Flores, *Luperón, héroe y alma*, 72.
24. Carrying the pamphlet was a forty-three-year-old French merchant named Victor George, resident in Baní. The proclamation from President Geffrard was evidently from the very first weeks of annexation. George claimed, probably apocryphally, that he had merely copied it for someone who "couldn't write well in French," and that he had ignored its content ("Sumario Instruido contra el paisano D. Víctor George acusado de habersele ocupado en su poder una proclama subversiva," November 1864, AGI: Cuba 1011A, Expte. s/n).
25. Gran Traición de Santana, qtd. in Galván, "El General don Pedro Santana," 24.
26. Rodríguez Demorizi, *Actos y doctrina*, 331.
27. Rodríguez Demorizi, *Actos y doctrina*, 6; Espinal Estévez and Jiménez, *Santiago de los Caballeros*, 101.

28. Proceso Instruido contra el Ayuntamiento . . . sobre los acontecimientos que tubieron lugar . . . en la noche del 21 de febrero último, Santiago, February 1863, AGI: Cuba 1011A, Expte. s/n, 197.
29. Extrato de la causa contra Federico Scheffenberg in "Proceso instruido contra varios individuos acusados de formar parte del Gobierno rebolucionario," October 1863, AGI: Cuba 881ª, 2ª Pieza.
30. Qtd. in Rodríguez Demorizi, Actos y doctrina, 70.
31. Ramón Mella, "Dominicanos," 16 January 1864, AGI: Cuba 973B, Expte. 306, "Parlamentos," doc. s/n.
32. General José María Cabral, "DOMINICANOS!," Las Caobas, 6 April 1861, AGI: Cuba 984C, Expte. "promovido a consecuencia de la invasión de la frontera de SD por los Haitianos," doc. s/n.
33. Hernández Flores, Luperón, héroe y alma, 64.
34. Rodríguez Demorizi, Santana y los poetas, 340.
35. "Epitafio de Santana: Aquí yace un gran pollino / despótico cual ninguno / que no entendió su destino / y murió como un cochino, / no habiendo hecho bien alguno," in Rodríguez Demorizi, Santana y los poetas, 341.
36. Cabral, "DOMINICANOS!," Las Caobas, 6 April 1861, AGI: Cuba 984C, Expte. "promovido a consecuencia de la invasión de la frontera de SD por los Haitianos," doc. s/n.
37. Qtd. in Comisión Permanente de Efemérides Patrias, Proclamas (hereafter cited as Proclamas), 62.
38. Luperón qtd. in Proclamas, 89.
39. Opposition pamphlet qtd. in Galván, "El General don Pedro Santana," 18.
40. Ramón Mella, "Dominicanos!," 16 January 1864, AGI: Cuba 973B, Expte. 306, "Parlamentos," doc. s/n.
41. Proclamas, 68; Rodríguez Demorizi, Actos y doctrina, 184.
42. Proclamas, 87.
43. Luperón qtd. in Proclamas, 88.
44. "Epistle, in response to the letter written by Priest Juan de Jesús Ayala y García," remitted by Coronel Gob. Militar Interino to Cáp. Gen., SD, 25 November 1864, AGI: Cuba 965A, Expte. 213, "Impresos," doc. s/n.
45. Proclamas, 55.
46. Alocución, José de la Gándara, 1 April 1864, ANC: AP 54, Expte. 11.
47. Real Orden of 11 April 1864, AHN: Ultramar 3525, Expte. 47.
48. Ulises Espaillat to Primo de Rivera, 15 February 1864, AGI: Cuba 973B, Expte. 306, "Parlamentos," doc. s/n. Opponents sought international audience from the outset. The firebrand 1861 pamphlet "Santana's Great Treason" circulated first in Europe; it was intercepted in the customs of the capital city (Galván, "El General don Pedro Santana," 3).
49. Rodríguez Demorizi, Actos y doctrina, 84.
50. "To my homeland annexed to Spain," qtd. in Vicioso, El freno hatero, 219.
51. Boletín Oficial, 1864, qtd. in Vicioso, El freno hatero, 220.

52. Rodríguez Objío, *Poesías coleccionadas*, 55, 74.
53. Rodríguez Demorizi, *Actos y doctrina*, 246.
54. Letter to the queen, 1863, qtd. in Rodríguez Demorizi, *Actos y doctrina*, 40.
55. "Situación de Haití. La libertad de Cuba," *Boletín Oficial*, no. 3, 24 January 1864, in Rodríguez Demorizi, *Actos y doctrina*, 87.
56. Rodríguez Demorizi, *Actos y doctrina*, 88.
57. *Proclamas*, 59 (emphasis added).
58. Rodríguez Demorizi, *Actos y doctrina*, 98.
59. "A los Dominicanos y al Mundo entero" (Comisión encargada del Despacho de RREE), 28 January 1864, AHN: Ultramar 3525, Expte. 120, doc. 3.
60. *Proclamas*, 59.
61. Rodríguez Objío, "Guerra," 255.
62. Rodríguez Demorizi, *Actos y doctrina*, 88.
63. Ramón Mella, "Dominicanos," 16 January 1864, AGI: Cuba 973B, Expte. 306, "Parlamentos," doc. s/n.
64. Carta de Santo Domingo, *Boletín Oficial*, no. 11, 2 July 1864, in Rodríguez Demorizi, *Actos y doctrina*, 146.
65. 20 January 1861, qtd. in Vicioso, *El freno hatero*, 251. See the whole text in Luperón, *Notas autobiográficas*, 1:55–57.
66. Felipe Ribero, "Dominicanos!," SD, 24 August 1863, ANC: AP 54, Expte. 2.
67. Qtd. in Galván, "El General don Pedro Santana," 18 (emphasis in original).
68. Galván, "El General don Pedro Santana," 19.
69. "We don't understand such a line of argument," the response pamphlet announced (Gran Traición de Santana, qtd. in Galván, "El General don Pedro Santana," 17).
70. Rodríguez Demorizi, *Actos y doctrina*, 223.
71. "Contra La Razón," *Boletín Oficial*, no. 10, 18 June 1864, qtd. in Rodríguez Demorizi, *Actos y doctrina*, 133.
72. *Boletín Oficial*, no. 1, 10 January 1864, in Rodríguez Demorizi, *Actos y doctrina*, 77.
73. Gil, *Orígenes y proyecciones de la revolución restauradora*, 78.
74. Pedro Antonio Casimiro to Gral. Antonio Salcedo, 15 October 1863, AGI: Cuba 1003B, Expte. "documentos cojidos . . . ," doc. s/n.
75. Bosch, *La Guerra de la Restauración*, 160.
76. "Proceso Contra varios individuos de complicidad en la sublevación que tubo lugar en Puerto Plata en 27 de Agosto ultimo," 1863, AHN: Ultramar 881ª, 1ª Pieza, 9.
77. Bosch, *La Guerra de la Restauración*, 170.
78. Bosch, *La Guerra de la Restauración*, 145.
79. Cassá, *Personajes dominicanos*, 1:354.
80. Daringly, he had even stolen a prized black horse from former emperor Soulouque in the contested region of Hinche, for which he had become somewhat infamous.

81. "Criminal contra el coronel de las Reservas Provinciales D. Juan Rondón . . . ," April 1863, AGN-RD: CH Tomo 11 (AGI: Cuba 1014B).
82. Mariano Álvarez to Secretario del Estado y RREE, Port-au-Prince, 25 March 1864, AGI: Cuba 984C, Expte. "relativo a la Guerra de SD/7 Marzo/Año de 1864," doc. s/n.
83. De la Gándara, *Anexión y guerra de Santo Domingo*, 348, 373. By August 1863, de la Gándara reports, "it was a mystery to no one that the vagrants [merodeadores] of the frontier were going to convert themselves from one moment to the next into a revolutionary army" (301).
84. Philantrope Noël to Brig. Buceta, Dajabon, 15 August 1863, AHN: Ultramar 3525, Expte. 99, Anexo 6.
85. Mariano Álvarez to Secretario del Estado y RREE, Port-au-Prince, 25 March 1864, AGI: Cuba 984C, Expte. "relativo a la Guerra de SD/7 Marzo/Año de 1864," doc. s/n.
86. Mariano Álvarez to Secretario del Estado y RREE, Port-au-Prince, 25 March 1864, AGI: Cuba 984C, Expte. "relativo a la Guerra de SD/7 Marzo/Año de 1864," doc. s/n. His accomplices were his brother Cheché, Manuel Santana, his son-in-law Clemente Guzmán, and Marcoté.
87. "Sumaria Instruida contra el faccioso Ramón Díaz," Azua, June 1864, AGI: Cuba 1011A.
88. Mariano Álvarez to Cap. Gen., Port-au-Prince, 6 April 1864, AGI: Cuba 984C, Expte. "relativo a la Guerra de SD/7 Marzo/Año de 1864," doc. s/n.
89. In Azua, for example, where he had about five hundred men, he complained that another rebel commander confiscated pillaged goods from troops. They "should be returned to those who had rightfully earned it" (i.e., the soldiers), he argued (Pedro Florentino to Gral. Comandante de Armas de Neyba, Azua, 20 October 1863, AGI: Cuba 1003B, Expte. "documentos cojidos . . . ," doc. s/n). He heartily disagreed with General Angel Féliz's delegating alcaldes pédaneos to confiscate "whatever little thing [bobería] they managed to grab" through looting. "It does not seem just to me to take away from the poor wretches the tiny pillages they committed," he insisted (Pedro Florentino to Gral. Comandante de Armas de Neyba, Azua, 23 October 1863, AGI: Cuba 1003B, Expte. "documentos cojidos . . . ," doc. s/n).
90. Pedro Florentino to Gral. Comandante de Armas de Neyba, Azua, 23 October 1863, AGI: Cuba 1003B, Expte. "documentos cojidos . . . ," doc. s/n.
91. Hernández Flores, *Luperón, héroe y alma*, 46.
92. Martínez, *Gregorio Luperón*, 5.
93. Torres-Saillant, "Before the Diaspora," 258.
94. Gil, *Orígenes y proyecciones de la revolución restauradora*, 80.
95. Martínez, *Gregorio Luperón*, 12.
96. Bosch, *La Guerra de la Restauración*, 126.

97. Martínez, *Diccionario*, 445. There is some dispute about whether his parents were Spanish, or whether he was born in Baraco, Cuba, or even Monte Cristi (Rodríguez Demorizi, *Próceres de la Restauración*, 306).
98. According to Luperón, they made a "noise of disgust" (Castro Ventura, *La Guerra Restauradora*, 215). He wrote, "The belief that most of the people who were around Salcedo were *españolizados* and Spanish spies was proverbial in the countryside, and the president was aware of it, but he didn't worry about it" (263).
99. Rodríguez Demorizi, *Próceres de la Restauración*, 307.
100. Hernández Flores, *Luperón, héroe y alma*, 71.
101. Álvarez López, *Cinco ensayos*, 82; *Proclamas*, 75; Cassá, *Personajes dominicanos*, 1:363–64.
102. "Un soldado de Capotillo, al Ejercito Libertador," Santiago, October 1864, qtd. in Rodríguez Demorizi, *Actos y doctrina*, 180.
103. President Salcedo was definitely in negotiations with General de la Gándara, who tried to interceder for him, probably only throwing his allegiances more into question (Cassá, *Personajes dominicanos*, 1:364).
104. Jimenes Grullón, *Sociologia política dominicana*, 130.
105. Rodríguez Demorizi, *Actos y doctrina*, 211.
106. Álvarez López, *Cinco ensayos*, 79.
107. "Democracia," *Boletín Oficial*, 23, Santiago de los Caballeros, 26 February 1865, SHM: Ultramar 5657, Expte. "Prisioneros 1865."
108. Rodríguez Demorizi, *Actos y doctrina*, 215.
109. Rodríguez Demorizi, *Actos y doctrina*, 258.
110. Rodríguez Demorizi, *Actos y doctrina*, 231.
111. Rodríguez Objío, *Gregorio Luperón e historia de la Restauración*, 1:69.
112. Castro Ventura, *La Guerra Restauradora*, 342, 347. The cartoon was published about a month after Polanco's administration fell.
113. Castro Ventura, *La Guerra Restauradora*, 16.
114. "Epistle, in response to the letter written by Priest Juan de Jesús Ayala y García," Remitted by Coronel Gob. Militar Interino to Cáp. Gen., SD, 25 November 1864, AGI: Cuba 965A, Expte. 213, "Impresos," doc. s/n (emphasis in original).
115. Cassá, *Personajes dominicanos*, 1:362.
116. Carlos de Vargas, Bando, 19 March 1864, AGI Cuba 948C; "Sumaria Instruida en averiguación del paradero del Párroco del pueblo de San Lorenzo de las Minas D. José Páez," SD, April 1864, AGI: Cuba 1011A; Cap. Gen. to Ministro de Ultramar, 18 August 1864, AGN-RD: Anexión 34 (DE/160), Expte. 1.
117. *Memoria informativa de las razones que ha tenido la Sección de Gobierno para alterar, modificar y aun suprimir algunas de las disposiciones del anterior Bando de Policía y Gobernación, y para establecer una que otra nueva prescripción*, SD, 13 July 1864, AHN: Ultramar 3526, Expte. 17, doc. 3.

118. José de Villar to Ministerio de Ultramar, SD, 13 October 1864, AHN: Ultramar 3526, Expte. 17, doc. 10.
119. Decreto destituyendo a todo militar que abandone las filas de la Revolución, 6 November 1864, in Rodríguez Demorizi, Actos y doctrina, 217.
120. W. Jaeger to W. H. Seward, 10 January 1864, AGN-RD: "Correspondencia del Agente Comercial de los EEUU No. 43-52," 4; Gob. Interino to Gob. Sup. Civil, 31 October 1864, AGN-RD: Anexión 34, Expte. 5, doc. 3.
121. "Varios comerciantes" to Cap. Gen., SD, 31 December 1864, AGN-RD: Anexión 32, Expte. 13 (*2006). The government had insisted that those defaulting would face full fines (Cap. Gen. to José Méndez de Arcaya, 13 December 1864, AHN: Ultramar 3536, Expte. 26).
122. De la Gándara to Min. de Ultramar, 2 April 1864, AHN: Ultramar 3542, Expte. 12.
123. S. Vicioso et al. to Gob. de Puerto Plata, 15 November 1863, AGN-RD: CH Tomo 15, p. 175.
124. Eusebio Puello to Cap. Gen. Azua, 19 January 1863, AGI: Cuba 950B, "Causas."
125. Lespinasse, Price-Mars, and Gutiérrez, Haïti et la restauration de l'indépendance dominicaine, 117.
126. Eusebio Soler to Gob. Superior Civil, SD, 4 July 1864, AGN-RD: Anexión 16, Expte. 1, doc. 3.
127. Álvarez López, Cinco ensayos, 78.
128. Álvarez López, Cinco ensayos, 78–79; Rodríguez Objío, Gregorio Luperón e historia de la Restauración, 1:223.
129. Gaspar Polanco to Primo de Rivera, Puerto Plata, 8 February 1864, AGI: Cuba 973B, Expte. 306, "Parlamentos," doc. s/n.
130. Cassá, Personajes dominicanos, 1:369; Álvarez López, Cinco ensayos, 77; Rodríguez Demorizi, Actos y doctrina, 246; Rodríguez Objío, Gregorio Luperón e historia de la Restauración, 1:252.
131. Rodríguez Demorizi, Actos y doctrina, 256.
132. Orden General de Pedro Santana, 15 March 1863, AHN: Ultramar 3525, Expte. 8.
133. Secretario de Estado to Min. de Ultramar, Madrid, 2 October 1863, AHN: Ultramar 3525, Expte. 99.
134. General Simon Sam received Lucas Peña. Peña's letters to Sam suggest a certain intimacy—he suggested that Sam would "be infinitely happy" at the news of fighting, and asked for five hundred guns. However, Ouanaminthe and Dajabón were quickly changing. The Spanish had ignored Dajabón until the fighting of February, but they quickly moved troops back there. Under pressure, Sam passed on news of his meeting to President Geffrard (evidently not expecting decommission to result). Mariano Álvarez to Cap. Gen. of Cuba, 7 March 1863, AGI: Cuba 984C, Expte. "Sobre la sublevación de SD en 1863," doc. s/n. As for Peña, unfazed, he took refuge somewhere in Haiti

for the summer, returning for the fighting of August (Martínez, *Diccionario*, 375).

135. Primera Secretario de Estado to Min. de Ultramar, Reservado, 19 September 1863, AHN: Ultramar 3525, Expte. 97.
136. Federico Granados to Cap. Gen. of SD, Port-au-Prince, 18 July 1864, ANC: AP 226, Expte. 7, doc. s/n.
137. Wm. G. N. Jaeger to William Seward, 25 November 1863, AGN-RD: Libro US Agente Comercial.
138. Tomas de Ligués Baudaje to Min. de Ultramar, 3 November 1863, AHN: Ultramar 3534, Expte. 26.
139. Federico Granados to Cap. Gen. of SD, Port-au-Prince, 18 July 1864, ANC: AP 226, Expte. 7, doc. s/n.
140. Pedro Ezequiel Guerrero to Manuel Buceta, Monte Cristi, 8 August 1863, AHN: Ultramar 3525, Expte. 27, doc. 3.
141. Unsigned letter, marked "Comandancia en Gefe del Cuartel de Guayubín," in "Causa formada en aberiguación de los hechos que han tenido lugar en la insurrección de Guayubín . . . el día 22 de Febrero," March 1863, AGI: Cuba 1011A, Expte. s/n, p. 35.
142. "Sumaria instruida en averiguación del tráfico y comunicaciones que con los haitianos tuvieron los paisanos Pedro Curro, Venancio Gil, Soten Sambra, Manuel Sanjuanaro, José Ramírez, Norverto Cueva, José Sánchez y José Ignacio," October 1862, AGN-RD: CH Leg. 24, Expte. 202 (AGI: Cuba 1013B), 5.
143. M. Álvarez to Secretario de Estado, Port-au-Prince, 6 February 1864, AMAE: Tratados 439; Rodríguez Demorizi, *Antecedentes*, 190.
144. Antonio Alfau to Marcos Adon, 16 February 1864, AGI: Cuba 952, Expte. 98, "Correspondencia," doc. s/n.
145. Mariano Álvarez to Min. de RREE, Port-au-Prince, 3 June 1864, AHN: Ultramar 3525, Expte. 125, doc. 3.
146. Sec. de Estado to Min. de Ultramar, 4 January 1864, AHN: Ultramar 3525, Expte. 111, doc. 2.
147. Hernández Flores, *Luperón, héroe y alma*, 106–7; Martínez, *Diccionario*, 303.
148. Manuel Buceta to Cap. Gen., 10 August 1863, AHN: Ultramar 3525, Expte. 27, doc. 4.
149. Ylont L. H. Blot to President Geffrard, 12 August 1863, AHN: Ultramar 3525, Expte. 102, doc. 2.
150. Primo de Rivera to Cap. Gen., 29 December 1863, AGN-RD: CH Tomo 15, p. 15.
151. Carlos de Vargas to Cónsul de SMC en Haití, SD, 26 March 1864, AHN: Ultramar 3525, Expte. 125, doc. 2.
152. Ministro Plenipotenciario de SM en Washington to Cap. Gen. of Cuba, Reservado, 29 September 1863, ANC: AP 53, Expte. 28, doc. s/n.
153. Castro Ventura, *La Guerra Restauradora*, 229.

154. Pedro Florentino to Comandante de Armas de Neyba, Azua, s/f (1863), AGI: Cuba 1003B, Expte. "Documentos cojidos al enemigo y referentes a sus movimientos," doc. s/n.
155. Juan Suero to Cap. Gen. of SD, Puerto Plata, 24 December 1863, AGN-RD: CH Tomo 15, p. 240.
156. Carlos de Vargas to Cónsul de SMC en Haití, SD, 26 March 1864, AHN: Ultramar 3525, Expte. 125, doc. 2.
157. Academia Dominicana de la Historia, *Homenaje a Mella*, 19. Each serón, or woven basket to transport tobacco, carried about 100 pounds (Richard Hacker, *The Ultimate Cigar Book*, 4th ed. [New York: Skyhorse, 2015], glossary).
158. Hernández Flores, *Luperón, héroe y alma*, 102; Castro Ventura, *La Guerra Restauradora*, 228; Espinal Estévez and Jiménez, *Santiago*, 97; Juan Suero to Cap. Gen. of SD, Puerto Plata, 24 December 1863, AGN-RD: CH Tomo 15, p. 240.
159. [Sin firma] to Mr. Adolphe Grimard, 1864, AGN-RD: RREE 14/15/16 (7/008378), Expte. 2, p. 19.
160. Smith, *Liberty, Fraternity, Exile*, 110–11.
161. Smith, *Liberty, Fraternity, Exile*, 113–14.
162. Mariano Álvarez to Sec. de Estado, 8 April 1864, AGI: Cuba 984C, Expte. "relativo a la Guerra de SD / 7 Marzo / Año de 1864," doc. s/n.
163. Mariano Álvarez to Min. de RREE, Port-au-Prince, 3 June 1864, AHN: Ultramar 3525, Expte. 125, doc. 3.
164. "Examen de la Anexión," *Boletín Oficial*, no. 2, 20 January 1864, qtd. in Rodríguez Demorizi, *Actos y doctrina*, 88.
165. "Una palabra a los dominicanos," Santiago, 8 June 1864, qtd. in Rodríguez Demorizi, *Actos y doctrina*, 125.
166. "Proyecto de tratado con Haiti," Santiago, (June?) 1864, qtd. in Rodríguez Demorizi, *Actos y doctrina*, 126–27.
167. Ulises Espaillat to Min. de RREE de Haiti, Santiago, 30 January 1864, AHN: Ultramar 3525, Expte. 120, doc. 2.
168. Ulises Espaillat to Min. de RREE de Haiti, Santiago, 30 January 1864, AHN: Ultramar 3525, Expte. 120, doc. 2.
169. Qtd. in Auguste Elie al Gobierno Provisional, July 1864, AGI: Cuba 984C, Expte. "relativo a la Guerra de SD / 7 Marzo / Año de 1864," doc. s/n.
170. Felipe Ribero to Min. de Ultramar, 18 August 1863, AHN: Ultramar 3525, Expte. 26, doc. 2; Pedro Ezequiel Guerrero to Manuel Buceta, Monte Cristi, 8 August 1863, AHN: Ultramar 3525, Expte. 27, doc. 3.
171. Federico Granados to Cap. Gen. of SD, Port-au-Prince, 18 July 1864, ANC: AP 226, Expte. 7, doc. s/n.
172. Segundo Diaz to Cap. Gen. of Cuba, Havana, 16 August 1864, AGI: Cuba 984C, Expte. "relativo a la Guerra de SD / 7 Marzo / Año de 1864," doc. s/n.
173. Fede Granados to Cap. Gen. of SD, Port-au-Prince, 23 June 1864, AHN: Ultramar 3525, Expte. 127, doc. 2.

174. Segundo Diaz to Cap. Gen. of Cuba, Havana, 16 August 1864, AGI: Cuba 984C, Expte. "relativo a la Guerra de SD / 7 Marzo / Año de 1864," doc. s/n.
175. Auguste Elie al Gobierno Provisional, July 1864, AGI: Cuba 984C, Expte. "relativo a la Guerra de SD / 7 Marzo / Año de 1864," doc. s/n.
176. 1r Secretario de Estado to Min. de Ultramar, 20 March 1864, AHN: Ultramar 3525, Expte. 120, doc. 1.
177. Rodríguez Demorizi, Actos y doctrina, 197.
178. Lespinasse, Price-Mars, and Gutiérrez, Haïti et la restauration de l'indépendance dominicaine, 41.
179. Lespinasse, Price-Mars, and Gutiérrez, Haïti et la restauration de l'indépendance dominicaine, 55.
180. Lespinasse, Price-Mars, and Gutiérrez, Haïti et la restauration de l'indépendance dominicaine, 61.
181. Lespinasse, Price-Mars, and Gutiérrez, Haïti et la restauration de l'indépendance dominicaine, 70.
182. Boletín Oficial, no. 17, 26 November 1864, qtd. in Rodríguez Demorizi, Actos y doctrina, 212.
183. Lespinasse, Price-Mars, and Gutiérrez, Haïti et la restauration de l'indépendance dominicaine, 85–95.
184. Lespinasse, Price-Mars, and Gutiérrez, Haïti et la restauration de l'indépendance dominicaine, 100, 107.
185. Lespinasse, Price-Mars, and Gutiérrez, Haïti et la restauration de l'indépendance dominicaine, 111, 114.
186. Rodríguez Objío, Gregorio Luperón e historia de la Restauración, 1:259.
187. Hernández Flores, Luperón, héroe y alma, 82.
188. Rodríguez Demorizi, Actos y doctrina, 276.
189. Jimenes Grullón, Sociologia política dominicana, 140.
190. Rodríguez Objío, Gregorio Luperón e historia de la Restauración, 1:246, 268, 279; Cassá, Personajes dominicanos, 1:367, 371; Álvarez López, Cinco ensayos, 91.
191. Jimenes Grullón, Sociologia política dominicana, 132; Castro Ventura, La Guerra Restauradora, 369.
192. Rodríguez Demorizi, Actos y doctrina, 375.
193. Lespinasse, Price-Mars, and Gutiérrez, Haïti et la restauration de l'indépendance dominicaine, 72.
194. Cordero Michel, "Gregorio Luperón y Haiti," 502.
195. Cassá, Personajes dominicanos, 1:373.
196. Rodríguez Demorizi, Actos y doctrina, 400.

7. Nothing Remains Anymore

1. Castro Ventura, La Guerra Restauradora, 390.
2. Blanco Díaz, Alejandro Ángulo Guridi, 1:35.
3. Expte. de Min. de Ultramar, August 1864, AHN: Ultramar 3525, Expte. 143.

4. Jesurum to "Citizen Minister of Foreign Relations, Curaçao, 9 January 1866, AGN-RD: RREE 14/15/16 (7/008378), Expte. 7.
5. Gil, Orígenes y proyecciones de la revolución restauradora, 81.
6. La Razón, no. 12, 27 June 1861, 2.
7. Abreu Cardet and Álvarez-López, Guerras de liberación, 127, 129.
8. Villar to Min. de Ultramar, 15 September 1864, AHN: Ultramar 3542, Expte. 17.
9. Rodríguez Demorizi, Actos y doctrina, 238.
10. Castro Ventura, La Guerra Restauradora, 391.
11. Abreu Cardet y Álvarez-López, Guerras de liberación, 230.
12. Castro Ventura, La Guerra Restauradora, 397.
13. Min. de Ultramar to Sec. de Estado, 26 January 1864, AHN: Ultramar 3525, Expte. 141.
14. Expte. Ministro de Ultramar, April 1864, AHN: Ultramar 3525, Expte. 119 (emphasis in original).
15. Cap. Gen. of Puerto Rico to Min. de Ultramar, September–October 1863, AHN: Ultramar 3525, Expte. 51, docs. 1–5; Rafael Hernández de Alba et al. to Cap. Gen. of SD; Gob. Civil de Dep. Oriental de Cuba to Cap. Gen. of SD, 25 and 31 May 1864, ANC: AP 54, Exptes. 12 and 13; Castro Ventura, La Guerra Restauradora, 195, 202, 383.
16. Castro Ventura, La Guerra Restauradora, 402.
17. "Throw the Dominicans into the arms of the negroes, contributing powerfully to the fact that very soon . . . the European race, the white race, the Spanish race will be destroyed," Senator Ulloa inveighed hysterically (Yuengling, Highlights in the Debates, 9).
18. Rodríguez Objío, Gregorio Luperón e historia de la Restauración, 1:259–60.
19. Frazer, "Role of the Lima Congress," 321.
20. Castro Ventura, La Guerra Restauradora, 160.
21. Castro Ventura, La Guerra Restauradora, 403.
22. Fontecha Pedraza and González Calleja, Una cuestión de honor, 62.
23. Rodríguez Demorizi, Actos y doctrina, 232.
24. M. Valverde to Máximo Grullon, 1 July 1864, AGN-RD: RREE 14/15/16 (7/008378), Expte. 2.
25. Finke, "Puerto Plata en la Gesta Restauradora," 127.
26. La Regeneración, no. 4, 17 September 1865, 2.
27. Carlos de Vargas to Min. de Ultramar, 8 March 1864, AHN: Ultramar 3525, Expte. 46. Political opposition frustrated his more ambitious diplomatic efforts (Rodríguez Objío, Gregorio Luperón e historia de la Restauración, 1:259–60).
28. Pensón, Reseña histórico-crítica, 257.
29. El Federalista, Diario de la Tarde, Caracas, 21 January 1864, in Min. de Ultramar to Secretario de Estado, Palacio, 27 February 1864, AHN: Ultramar 3525, Expte. 116, doc. 3.
30. Bosch, La Guerra de la Restauración, 139; Proclamas, 63.

31. Finke, "Puerto Plata en la Gesta Restauradora," 141.
32. M. Valverde to Máximo Grullon, Caracas, 23 August 1864, AGN-RD: RREE 14/15/16 (7/008378), Expte. 2 (labeled Expte. 4).
33. The petition left Jamaica by late May and reached London about a month later. *Le Moniteur Haïtien*, no. 34, 27 July 1861, 2.
34. Carlos de Vargas to Min. de Ultramar, 10 December 1863, AHN: Ultramar 3525, Expte. 38. The *Gazette* dramatized the conflict further: "No one can safely venture a mile beyond the City without hearing the sharp whiz of a rifle ball uncomfortably close to his head—to say nothing worse" ("Santo Domingo," *Royal Standard and Gazette of the Turks and Caicos Islands*, 7 November 1863, 2).
35. [Sin firma] to Regente de RA de SD, 24 December 1863, ANC: AP 54, Expte. 3, doc. s/n; José de la Gándara to Cap. Gen. of Jaimaica (CC to Cap. Gen. of Cuba), 5 June 1864, ANC: AP 226, Expte. 4, doc. s/n.
36. Min. de Estado to Min. de Ultramar, Madrid, 9 August 1864, AHN: Ultramar 3525, Expte. 121.
37. El General 2º en Gefe del Ejercito y Gob. Sup. Civil to Governor Eyre, SD, 29 May 1864, AHN: Ultramar 3525, Expte. 124, doc. 3.
38. Gov. Eyre to Cap. Gen. of SD, 18 May 1864, AHN: Ultramar 3525, Expte. 124.
39. Domingo Dulce to Min. de Ultramar, 14 September 1863, AHN: Ultramar 3525, Expte. 75.
40. Domingo Dulce to Min. de Ultramar, 30 September 1863, AHN: Ultramar 3525, Expte. 77.
41. Ministro Plenipotenciario de SM en Washington to Cap. Gen. of Cuba, 19 October 1863, ANC: AP 53, Expte. 28, doc. s/n (emphasis in original).
42. "Santo Domingo," *El Redactor de Santiago de Cuba*, 10 June 1864, ANC: AP 295, Expte. 26. El Tiempo in Havana also claimed that the Spanish were winning (Castro Ventura, *La Guerra Restauradora*, 393).
43. Criminal de oficio contra Don Buenaventura Anglada, natural de Cataluña . . . para averiguar su modo de juzgar los sucesos políticos de StoDgo, 17 November 1863, ANC: AP 54, 5.
44. Pérez Dionisio, "Santiago de Cuba y la Guerra de la Restauración de Santo Domingo," 116.
45. Pérez Dionisio, "Santiago de Cuba y la Guerra de la Restauración de Santo Domingo," 114–16.
46. Eugenio López Bustamente to Cap. Gen., SD, 17 June 1862, AGN-RD: Anexión 2 (DE/1381), Expte. 18, doc. s/n.
47. Feliz Maria de Messina to Cap. Gen. of SD, 27 September 1863, AGI: Cuba 953B, Expte. 112, "Deportados," doc. s/n.
48. Cap. Gen. of Puerto Rico to Id. de Cuba, 5 October 1863, ANC: AP 54, Expte. 2, doc. s/n.
49. Rodríguez Demorizi, Blanco, and Durán, *Apuntes de Rosa Duarte*, 26.

50. [No author] to Cap. Gen., 1 November 1864, AGI: Cuba 953, Expte. 112, "Deportados," doc. s/n; Comandante Militar de Higüey [Deogracia Linares] to Cáp. Gen., 21 November 1864, AGI: Cuba 852, Expte. 97, doc. s/n.
51. "Proceso . . . de los individuos que tomaron parte en la Rebelión de Puerto Plata," September 1863, AGI: Ultramar 881, 1ª Pieza.
52. Min. de Guerra to Min. de Ultramar, 21 January 1864, AHN: Ultramar 3542, Expte. 24, doc. 26.
53. Min. de Guerra to Min. de Ultramar, 9 August 1864, AHN: Ultramar 3525, Expte. 73; Min. de Guerra to Min. de Ultramar, 22 February 1864, AHN: Ultramar 3536, Expte. 16.
54. J. F. Cuello and Domingo de León to Cap. Gen. of SD, Real Cárcel de Puerto Rico, 16 March 1864, AGI: Cuba 953, Expte. 112, "Deportados," doc. s/n.
55. José Antonio Pina to Min. de Ultramar, 18 April 1864, AHN: Ultramar 3525, Expte. 135.
56. Francisca del Castillo to the Queen, 29 March 1864, AHN: Ultramar 3525, Expte. 134, doc. 4.
57. Domingo Dulce to Cap. Gen. of SD, 29 December 1863, AGI: Cuba 953B, Expte. 112, "Deportados," doc. s/n.
58. Apolinario Megia to Min. de Ultramar, 12 February 1864, AHN: Ultramar 3525, Expte. 132.
59. Cap. Gen. of Cuba to Min. de Estado, 30 November 1874, AGI: Cuba 2266, Expte. 1874.
60. Ojeda Reyes and Estrade, *Pasión por la libertad*, 33.
61. Santana had even offered him the archbishopric in exchange for his benevolent regard for annexation, but Meriño absolutely could not be moved (Vicioso, *El Freno hatero*, 269).
62. Suárez Díaz, *El Antillano*, 50.
63. Abreu Cardet and Álvarez-López, *Guerras de liberación*, 129.
64. Suárez Díaz, *El Antillano*, 92.
65. El General 2º en Gefe del Ejercito y Gob Sup Civil to Governor Eyre, SD, 29 May 1864, AHN: Ultramar 3525, Expte. 124, doc. 3.
66. [Sin firma] to Cap. Gen. of Cuba, s/f [1864], AGI: Cuba 984C, Expte. 1864.
67. Manuel del Galván to Gob. Sup. Civil, 29 November 1864, AGN-RD: Anexión 25, Expte. 3.
68. Juan Manuel Macías, *Publicaciones de la Sociedad Demócrata de los Amigos de América* (New York, December 1864), 8, 54.
69. Domingo Dulce to Min. de Ultramar, 28 November 1863, AHN: Ultramar 3525, Expte. 81.
70. Decree, 8 August 1864, AGN-RD: RREE 14/15/16 (7/008378), Expte. 2, doc 1.
71. Abreu Cardet and Álvarez-López, *Guerras de liberación*, 129.
72. Castro Ventura, *La Guerra Restauradora*, 406.
73. Abreu Cardet and Álvarez-López, *Guerras de liberación*, 127, 129.

74. Gabriel Tassara to Cap. Gen. of Cuba, 4 April 1864, AGI: Cuba 984C, Expte. "relativo a la Guerra de SD/7 Marzo/Año de 1864," doc. s/n.
75. Gabriel Tassara to Cap. Gen. of Cuba, 22 October 1864, AGI: Cuba 984C, Expte. "relativo a la Guerra de SD/7 Marzo/Año de 1864," doc. s/n.
76. William Clark, living in Santiago, for example, had an audience with Seward himself (Castro Ventura, *La Guerra Restauradora*, 181).
77. "Abajo los Españoles!," 1864, in Suárez Díaz, *El Antillano*, 60 (emphasis in original). The Puerto Rican governor banned circulation of an eponymous poem praising the rebel cacique exactly ten years prior (Schmidt-Nowara, *Conquest of History*, 128).
78. Castro Ventura, *La Guerra Restauradora*, 407.
79. "Sección de SD" to [no address], Havana, 29 July 1865, AGI: Cuba 950B, Expte. 77, doc. s/n; Rodríguez Demorizi, *Actos y doctrina*, 286.
80. "Sumaria Contra el Cáp. de las Reservas Don Arquímedes," Azua, February 1865, AGI: Cuba 1013A.
81. "Sumaria instruida contra el paisano Marcos de Jesús . . . ," SD, May 1865, AGI: Cuba 1013A, p. 4.
82. "Sumaria Instruida contra el paisano Sebastián Morcelo . . . ," 27 April 1865, AGI: Cuba 1014A, Expte. 169.
83. "Sumaria Instruida contra el paisano José Ruiz y Doña Socorro Sánchez . . . ," April 1865, AGI: Cuba 1014A (also in AGN-RD: CH Tomo II).
84. Bosch, *La Guerra de la Restauración*, 166, 156; González Tablas qtd. in Bosch, *La Guerra de la Restauración*, 158.
85. Ribero to Min. de Guerra, 2 April 1863, AGI: Cuba 1018.
86. De Villar to Min. de Guerra, 4 November 1864, AHN: Ultramar 3546, Expte. 17.
87. Cap. Gen. to Min. de Ultramar, 19 August 1863, AGI: Cuba 1018 (libro), n.p.
88. González Tablas, *Historia de la dominación*, 121.
89. Bosch, *La Guerra de la Restauración*, 158.
90. Sheina, *Latin America's Wars*, 348.
91. Carlos de Vargas to Min. de Ultramar, 16 November 1863, AHN: Ultramar 3525, Expte. 36.
92. W. Jaeger to W. H. Seward, 10 January 1864, AGN-RD: "Correspondencia del Agente Comercial de los EEUU No. 43-52," 4.
93. Enrique Llansó y Oriol to [Cap. Gen.], Samaná, 4 November 1864, AGN-RD: CH Leg. 24, Expte. 212, pp. 32–33 (originally 42–43).
94. Anonymous to Cap. Gen., Hospital de la Plaza de Armas, 26 October 1863, AGI: Cuba 945, Expte. 24, "Anónimos."
95. "Declaración del Teniente del Batallón de San Quintín Don Miguel Muzas y Franco," 2 May 1865, in "Sumaria formada . . . en averiguación de la conducta de . . . Don Pedro Obanos," no. 265, AGI: Cuba 1015A, "Sumarias," 12v.

96. "Instruido contra el soldado de la 1ª Compañía de 1er Batallón del Regimiento de la Habana Damián Soto Martínez . . . ," December 1863, AGI: Cuba 1011B.
97. Santana to Gral. de Fort Liberté, 10 December 1861, AGI: Cuba 953, Expte. "Desertores de 1861–3"; AGI: Cuba 1017, Libro 3, "Gral. de SD / Estado Mayor / Registro Gral. de Causas, da principio desde 1º de Nov 1864 Libro 3º."
98. Felipe Ribero to Min. de Guerra y Ultramar, 20 April 1863, AGI: Cuba 1018 (libro).
99. "Abajo los Españoles!," 1864, in Suárez Díaz, El Antillano, 60.
100. "Información: Instruida en averiguación de las causas que hayan podido dar origen a deserciones . . . ," December 1864, AGI: Cuba 1015A, "Sumarias."
101. Roque Quintana to Soldiers of the Fort of Puerto Plata, 14 January 1864, AGN-RD: CH Tomo 15, pp. 198–99.
102. "Carta de un soldado español," Boletín Oficial, no. 11, 2 July 1864, in Rodríguez Demorizi, Actos y doctrina, 144.
103. Nicolás Estévanez, no title, in Rodríguez Demorizi, Santana y los poetas, 325.
104. "Sumaria en averiguación del escándalo habido en varias casas de esta ciudad, de una a dos de la madrugada del día 2 de Marzo . . . ," March 1865, AGI Cuba 1013A, Expte. s/n.
105. De la Gándara to Min. de Guerra, 8 January 1865, ANC: AP 227, Expte. 6.
106. Cayetano Martín y Oñate, España y Santo Domingo: Observaciones de simple y racional criterio acerca de lo que interesa a la nación española (Toledo: Imprenta de Severiano López Fando, 1864).
107. Joaquín Muzquiz y Callejas, Una idea sobre la cuestión de Santo Domingo (Madrid: Imprenta Dubrull, 1864), 5, 24.
108. Martínez-Fernández, Torn between Empires, 221.
109. Bermúdez de Castro y O'Lawlor, Cuestión de Santo Domingo, 7, 14, 26, 33, 41 (emphasis in original).
110. Bermúdez de Castro y O'Lawlor, Cuestión de Santo Domingo, 33.
111. Ministers to the Queen, January 1865, AHN: Ultramar 2775, Expte. 17.
112. Ministers to the Queen, January 1865, AHN: Ultramar 2775, Expte. 17.
113. B. F. Rojas, "A los dominicanos," 11 June 1865, in Rodríguez Demorizi, Actos y doctrina, 394.
114. "Exposición dirigida por el Gobierno Provisorio a SMC," 3 January 1865, in Rodríguez Demorizi, Actos y doctrina, 255–56.
115. Monzón to Cap. Gen. of SD, 7 October 1863, AHN: Ultramar 3538, Expte. 10; Blas Esparolini to Cap. Gen. of SD, 26 February 1864, AHN: Ultramar 3540, Expte. 13.
116. De la Gándara to Min. de Ultramar, 27 March 1865, AHN: Ultramar 3526, Expte. 18.
117. Antonio Corro to Min. de Ultramar, Madrid, 28 February 1865, AHN: Ultramar 3533, Expte. 1, doc. 27.

118. "Compatriotas," *Gaceta de Santo Domingo*, no. 385, 27 April 1865, 1.
119. *Gaceta de Santo Domingo*, no. 360, 26 January 1865, 4.
120. De la Gándara to Min. de Ultramar, SD, 20 May 1865, AHN: Ultramar 3525, Expte. 151.
121. Expte. sobre León Güilamo. Min. de Ultramar, April 1865, AHN: Ultramar 3525, Expte. 133.
122. Cap. Gen. to President Geffrard, 21 January 1865, ANC: AP 227, 1; "Relación nominal clasificada por clases y Cuerpos de los individuos de este Egercito que siendo prisioneros de guerra en Santo Domingo han sido rescatados," Domingo Dulce to Min. de la Guerra, Havana, 8 January 1866, SHM: Ultramar 5657, Expte. "Prisioneros 1866," doc. s/n. This partial list included 383 troops, 17 officers, and 1 commander.
123. Geffrard to Coronel Francisco Van Halen, Port-au-Prince, 21 January 1865, ANC: AP 227, Expte. 1, doc. s/n.
124. Royal Order of 19 January 1865, ANC: AP 227, Expte. 8, doc. s/n.
125. Cap. Gen. to Gob. Superior Civil, 18 May 1865, AGN-RD: Anexión 33, Expte. 16; de la Gándara to Min. de Guerra, 8 June 1865, ANC: AP 227, Expte. 6.
126. "Relación nominal de los desertores que han tenido los Cuerpos de la guarnición de esta Plaza [SD] . . . ," SD, 23 February 1865, AGI: Cuba 1015A, "Sumarias"; AGN-RD: Anexion 30, Expte. 27; Min. de Ultramar to Min. de Guerra, Madrid, 6 July 1865, AHN: Ultramar 3545, Expte. 13.
127. Cap. Gen. Orden General, 23 May 1865, AGI: Cuba 953, Expte. 125, "Desertores de 1864–65, Desertores en Reservas Provinciales," doc. s/n.
128. "De Oficio," *Gaceta de Santo Domingo*, no. 392, 25 May 1865, 1.
129. Josefa Roman to Cap. Gen., SD, 7 February 1865, AGN-RD: Anexión 35, Expte. 3. Women continued to make claims on the Spanish state, for pensions of their deceased sons and husbands and for their own missing effects (e.g., "Sumaria Instriuida en averiguación que abrasa una solicitud promovida por Doña Carlota de Sosa . . . ," January 1865, AGI: Cuba 1012B; Juana Valeria to Gob. Sup. Civil, 17 May 1865, AGN-RD: Anexión 33, Expte. 9).
130. Juan Caballero to Gob. Político de Azua, 26 September 1864, AGN-RD: Anexión 30, Expte. 5, doc. s/n.
131. E.g., Angel Rodriguez to Cap. Gen., AGN-RD: Anexión 40, Expte. 18, doc. 14.
132. "Expte sobre individuos que han sido esclavos en Puerto Rico y piden documentos que acrediten el derecho que les asiste para ser libres al regresar a aquella isla," May 1865, AGN-RD: Anexión 31 (DE/157), Expte. 29 (formerly 21).
133. De la Gándara to Cap. Gen. of Cuba and Puerto Rico, Reservado, 27 February 1865, ANC: AP 227, Expte. 8. "Your Excellencies understand the problems that the presence and dispersal of [Dominicans] could bring to both islands," he wrote. "The men of this country, born in liberty, accustomed to the enjoyment of political and civil rights . . . will bring their habits and

their haughty condition to possessions where there is slavery, serving as a pernicious example to slaves and *libertos* of their own race there. The white inhabitants of those islands, accustomed to look on the dominated race with disdain, cannot grant any consideration to black and *mulato* Dominicans, no matter that they have rank and civil and military posts; whereas these men, for their part, will not want to submit their standing to a situation that would make them extremely violent and intolerable, the cause of conflict . . . and disturbance of public order."

134. Cap. Gen. to Brig. Comandante Gral. de la Columna de Baní, Reservado, SD, 22 May 1865, ANC: AP 227, Expte. 6, doc. s/n.
135. Dulce to Min. de Ultramar, 4 April 1865, AHN: Ultramar 3534, Expte. 34, doc. 14.
136. "Estado que manifiesta los efectos del Estado que ecsisten en los diversos puntos de esta Isla ocupados por las tropas con expresión de su peso," s/f (spring 1865), ANC: AP 227, Expte. 4.
137. Ramón Paredes to Cap. Gen., 1864, AGN-RD: Anexión 33, Expte. 10.
138. Declaración de Josefa Debra, "Relación nominal de los desertores que han tenido los Cuerpos de la guarnición de esta Plaza [SD] . . . ," SD, 23 February 1865, AGI: Cuba 1015A, "Sumarias," 35v.
139. Sumaria de Cándido Sándara, 18 March 1865, AGN-RD: Anexión 35, Expte. 14.
140. De la Gándara to Min. de Guerra, 8 June 1865, ANC: AP 227, Expte. 6.
141. De la Gándara to Min. de Guerra, 8 June 1865, ANC: AP 227, Expte. 6.
142. No title, in Rodríguez Demorizi, *Santana y los poetas*, 361.
143. "Convulsiones de los pueblos II," *La Regeneración*, no. 3, 10 September 1865, 4.
144. Cap. Gen. to Min. de Ultramar, 21 July 1865, AHN: Ultramar 3546, Expte. 20.
145. William Jaeger, 4 December 1863, AGN-RD: Libro de Correspondencia del Agente Comercial de los EEUU.
146. De la Gándara to Min. de Ultramar, 27 March 1865, AHN: Ultramar 3526, Expte. 18.
147. For example, Pedro Florentino to Gral. Comandante de Armas de Neyba, Azua, 22 October 1863, AGI: Cuba 1003B, Expte. "documentos cojidos . . . ," doc. s/n.
148. Bosch, *La Guerra de la Restauración*, 128.
149. Tejeda Ortíz, *Cultura y folklore de Samaná*, 73.
150. "Santiago. Oda," 1864, in Rodríguez Objío, *Poesías coleccionadas*, 35.
151. Guridi, *La campana del higo*, 14.
152. Guridi, *La campana del higo*, 15.
153. Guridi, *La campana del higo*, 25.
154. Guridi, *La campana del higo*, 72.
155. *El Monitor*, 5 September 1865, 4; Castro Ventura, *La Guerra Restauradora*, 358.
156. Correspondencia, *La Regeneración*, no. 5, 24 September 1865, 4.

157. *La Regeneración*, no. 4, 17 September 1865, 1.
158. Garrido, *Los Puello*, 193.
159. Rodríguez Demorizi, *Papeles dominicanos de Máximo Gómez*, 3.

Epilogue

1. *La Regeneración*, no. 3, 10 September 1865, 1–2.
2. "Hacienda Pública," *La Regeneración*, no. 2, 3 September 1865, 2.
3. A.S.V. "Pena de Muerte," *La Regeneración*, no. 5, 24 September 1865, 2.
4. "Las Provincias del Cibao," *La Regeneración*, no. 5, 24 September 1865, 1.
5. "Logia," *La Regeneración*, no. 6, 6 October 1865, 3.
6. Leonardo Díaz Jáquez, "Puerto Plata y los censos de 1871, 1875 y 1879," in *Areíto, Sección sabatina del diario Hoy*, 1 September 2007, http://www.idg.org.do/capsulas/septiembre2007/septiembre20071.htm.
7. French Consul en SD to Cap. Gen. of Cuba, 17 July 1874, AGI: Cuba 2266, Expte. 1874.
8. See, e.g., Chaar-Pérez, "'Revolution of Love.'"
9. "Convulsiones de los pueblos," *La Regeneración*, no. 2, 3 September 1865, 2 (emphasis added).
10. Suárez Díaz, *El Antillano*, 66, 102.
11. Schmidt-Nowara, *Empire and Anti-slavery*, 116; Schmidt-Nowara, *Conquest of History*, 26.
12. Schmidt-Nowara, *Empire and Anti-slavery*, 1.
13. Castro Ventura, *La Guerra Restauradora*, 413.
14. Memorando a los Gobiernos de Inglaterra, Francia, E.U.A. y las Repúblicas Hispano-Americanas (12 February 1864), qtd. in Fiallo Billini, "La construcción antillanista," n.p.
15. Cubano-Iguina, "Freedom in the Making."
16. Sartorius, *Ever Faithful*, 101.
17. Ferrer, *Insurgent Cuba*, 48, 59.
18. Sanders, *Vanguard of the Atlantic World*, 4.
19. *El Monitor*, no. 13, 31 October 1865, 2.
20. Moya Pons, *Dominican Republic*, 226.
21. *El Monitor*, no. 12, 24 October 1865, 1; Jesurum to Ciudadano Ministro de Relaciones Exteriores, Curaçao, 9 January 1866, AGN-RD: RREE 14/15/16 (7/008378), Expte. 7, doc. 1; Nelson, "Crisis of Liberalism," 24.
22. Franks, "Transforming Property," 95, 103–4.
23. "They work and conspire in elections, making themselves candidates and withdrawing scandalously, making themselves military officers because they did this or that in the service of someone, using indecorous means to favor someone who is not worthy, someone who was so much of a coward he was a spy for the *Cacharros*. . . . By devil, where will you stop?" he continued ("Costumbres," *La Regeneración*, no. 3, 10 September 1865, 4).
24. McGraw, "From a Mulato Caribbean to a Black Pacific," n.p.

25. Banton, "'More Auspicious Shores'"; Banton, "Spatial Shifts and Generational Advancement," n.p.
26. Brown, "Experiments in Indenture," 44.
27. Hulme, Cuba's Wild East, 266–67; Ferrer, Insurgent Cuba, 81; Smith, Liberty, Fraternity, Exile.
28. Mariano Álvarez remained so vitriolic that even Spenser St. John found him "severe." Both predicted the end of independence for the island in the 1880s (St. John, Hayti, vii).
29. Martínez-Fernández, "Caudillos," 592.
30. La Regeneración, no. 6, 6 October 1865, 4.
31. "Costumbres," La Regeneración, no. 3, 10 September 1865, 4.
32. Moya Pons, Dominican Republic, 228.
33. Vicioso, El freno hatero, 281.
34. Sang Ben, "Contradicciones en el liberalismo dominicano," 248.
35. Qtd. in Ojeda Reyes and Estrade, Pasión por la libertad, 33.
36. Rodríguez Objío, Gregorio Luperón e historia de la Restauración, 2:162; Ojeda Reyes and Estrade, Pasion por la libertad, 37, 192.
37. Cordero Michel, "Gregorio Luperón y Haiti," 504; Welles, Naboth's Vineyard, 402; Sang Ben, Buenaventura Báez, 104. General José María Cabral, strategically allied with Luperón once again, occupied much of San Juan de la Maguana with as many as three thousand men, many among them Haitian citizens (Lundias and Lundahl, Peasants and Religion, 432).
38. David Leon to Lord Stanley, 8 January 1868, TNA: FO 23/57, n.p.
39. Qtd. in Vicioso, El freno hatero, 326.
40. Cassá, Personajes dominicanos, 1:398; Sang Ben, Buenaventura Báez, 104; Gaillard, Le cacoisme bourgeois, 45.
41. Royal Standard, September 1, 1866, clipping in TNA: CO 301/44/269, n.p.
42. Luperón to President Moir, Puerto Plata, 6 October 1866, TNA: CO 301/44/269, n.p.
43. Septimus Rameau, 1 September 1869, qtd. in Rodríguez Objío, Gregorio Luperón e historia de la Restauración, 1:371.
44. "Hacienda Pública," La Regeneración, no. 2, 3 September 1865, 2.
45. Martínez, Diccionario, 414.
46. Cassá, Personajes dominicanos, 1:182.
47. Qtd. in Vallejo, Las madres de la patria, 127; on Salomé's political engagement, see Zeller, Discursos y espacios femeninos, and Ramírez, At the Navel of the Americas.
48. Rodríguez Demorizi, Actos y doctrina, 401–2.
49. Gaillard, Le cacoisme bourgeois, 45; Cassá, Personajes dominicanos, 1:396, 429.
50. Candelario, Black behind the Ears, 51.
51. "Fronteras del Sur," El Tiempo, no. 4, 28 January 1866, 2.
52. El Tiempo, no. 3, 21 January 1866, 1–2.
53. La Regeneración, no. 3, 10 September 1865, 1.
54. Rodríguez Objío, qtd. in Vicioso, El freno hatero, 338.

Bibliography

Archives and Newspapers

CUBA

Archivo Nacional de Cuba (ANC)
    Asuntos Políticos (AP)
    Diario de la Habana
    Gaceta de la Habana
    El Redactor de Santiago
Biblioteca Nacional José Martí (BNJM)

DOMINICAN REPUBLIC

Archivo General de la Nación–República Dominicana (AGN-RD)
    Archivo Real de Bayaguana
    Archivo Real de Higüey
    Ayuntamiento de Santiago
    Colección Garcia
    Colección Herrera (CH)
    Fondo Anexión (Anexión)
    Memoria de Guerra y Marina
    Relaciones Exteriores (RREE)
    La Acusación
    Boletín del Archivo General de la Nación (*BAGN*)
    El Dominicano
    El Eco del Pueblo
    Gaceta de Santo Domingo
    El Monitor
    El Oasis
    El Orden
    El Porvenir
    El Progreso

La Razón
La Regeneración
La Républica
Revista Clío, Órgano de la Academia Dominicana de la Historia (Clío)
El Tiempo

Some of the AGN-RD collections were being reorganized during this research period; Fondo Anexión's legajo numbers changed from 2006 to 2008 to 2010, for example. The bulk of the numbers cited here refer to the most recent 2008 and 2010 numerations; wherever possible, changes are recorded in the corresponding citation.

HAITI

Simityè Jakmèl (Cimitière de Jacmel)
La Feuille de Commerce
Le Moniteur Haïtien
L'Opinion Nationale
La République

SPAIN

Archivo Histórico Nacional, Madrid (AHN)
    Ultramar
    Gaceta de Madrid
Biblioteca Nacional, Madrid (BNE)
Servicio Histórico Militar, Madrid (SHM)
    Ultramar
Archivo del Ministerio de Relaciones Exteriores, Madrid (AMAE)
    Política Exterior, Haití
    Política Exterior, Santo Domingo
    Tratados
Archivo General de Indias (AGI)
    Audiencia de Santo Domingo
    Papeles de Cuba (Cuba)

UNITED KINGDOM

The National Archives, Kew (TNA)
    Colonial Office (CO)
        301 Turks and Caicos
    Foreign Office (FO)
        23 Dominican Republic
        35 Haiti

UNITED STATES

National Archives (NARA)
Schomburg Library

Secondary Sources

Abreu Cardet, José, and Luis Álvarez-López. *Guerras de liberación en el Caribe hispano, 1863–1878*. Santo Domingo: El Archivo General de la Nación, 2013.

Abreu Cardet, José, and Elia Sintes Gómez. *El alzamiento de Neiba: Acontecimientos y documentos (Febrero de 1863)*. Santo Domingo: El Archivo General de la Nación, 2012.

———. *Los alzamientos de Guayubín, Sabaneta y Montecristi: Documentos*. Santo Domingo: El Archivo General de la Nación, 2014.

Academia Dominicana de la Historia. *Homenaje a Mella*. Santo Domingo: Editora del Caribe, 1964.

Adam, André Georges. *Une crise haïtienne 1867–1869, Sylvain Salnave*. Port-au-Prince: Henri Deschamps, 1982.

Adelman, Jeremy. "An Age of Imperial Revolution." *American Historical Review* 113, no. 2 (2008): 319–40.

———. "Iberian Passages: Continuity and Change in the South Atlantic." In *The Age of Revolutions in Global Context, c. 1760–1840*, edited by David Armitage and Sanjay Subrahmanyam, 59–82. New York: Palgrave Macmillan, 2010.

Alemar, Luís Emilio. *Escritos de Luís E. Alemar, 1918–1945*. Edited by Constancio Cassá. Santo Domingo: Academía Dominicana de Historia, 2009.

Alexander, Leslie. " 'The Black Republic': The Influence of the Haitian Revolution on Northern Black Political Consciousness." In *African Americans and the Haitian Revolution*, edited by Maurice Jackson and Jacqueline Bacon, 57–80. New York: Routledge, 2010.

Alfau Durán, Vetilio. "Hostos." *Clío* 109 (1957): 32–43.

Allen, Richard B. "Slaves, Convicts, Abolitionism, Origins of the Post-emancipation Indentured Labor System." *Slavery and Abolition* 35, no. 2 (2014): 1–21.

Alonso, Carlos. "Fiction." In *A History of Literature in the Caribbean, vol. 1, Hispanic and Francophone Regions*, edited by Albert James Arnold, 141–54. Philadelphia: John Benjamins, 1994.

Aluma-Cazorla, Andrés. "The Caudillo as the Post-bandit." Paper presented at the Latin America and Caribbean Studies Center 9th Annual Graduate Conference, sponsored by SUNY Stony Brook, New York, 9 April 2010.

Álvarez Junco, José. "Spanish National Identity in the Age of Nationalisms." In *State and Nation Making in Latin America and Spain: Republics of the Possible*, edited by Miguel A. Centeno and Augustin E. Ferraro, 307–28. New York: Cambridge University Press, 2013.

Álvarez López, Luís. *Cinco ensayos sobre el Caribe hispano en el siglo XIX: República Dominicana, Cuba y Puerto Rico, 1861–1898*. Santo Domingo: Archivo General de la Nación, 2012.

———. *Dominación colonial y guerra popular 1861–1865*. Santo Domingo: Universidad Autonoma de Santo Domingo, 1986.

Anderson, Jennifer L. *Mahogany: The Costs of Luxury in Early America*. Cambridge, MA: Harvard University Press, 2012.

Anderson, Richard. "The Diaspora of Sierra Leone's Liberated Africans: Enlistment, Forced Migration, and 'Liberation' at Freetown, 1808–1863." *African Economic History* 41 (2013): 101–38.

Andrés, Agustín S. "Colonial Crisis and Spanish Diplomacy in the Caribbean during the Sexenio Revolucionario, 1868–1874." *Bulletin of Latin American Research* 28, no. 3 (2009): 325–42.

———. "En busca de la reconciliación: La diplomacia española hacia la República Dominicana tras el fracaso de la reanexión, 1865–1879." *Revista de Estudios Históricos* 55 (2012): 157–204.

Appelbaum, Nancy P., Anne S. Macpherson, and Karin Alejandra Rosemblatt, eds. *Race and Nation in Modern Latin America*. Chapel Hill: University of North Carolina Press, 2003.

Archambault, Pedro M. *Historia de la Restauración*. 2nd ed. Paris: La Libraire Technique et Economique, 1973 [1938].

Arroyo, Jossianna. *Writing Secrecy in Caribbean Freemasonry*. New York: Palgrave Macmillan, 2013.

Asaka, Ikuko. " 'Our Brethren in the West Indies': Self Emancipated People in Canada and the Antebellum Politics of Diaspora and Empire." *Journal of African American History* 97, no. 3 (Summer 2012): 219–39.

Augelli, John P. "Nationalization of Dominican Borderlands." *Geographical Review* 70, no. 1 (1980): 19–35.

Austerlitz, Paul. *Merengue: Dominican Music and Dominican Identity*. Philadelphia: Temple University Press, 1997.

Ayuso, Juan José. *Historia pendiente: Moca, 2 de Mayo de 1861*. Santo Domingo: Archivo General de la Nación, 2010.

Banton, Caree. " 'More Auspicious Shores': Post-emancipation Barbadian Emigrants in Pursuit of Freedom, Citizenship, and Nationhood in Liberia, 1834–1912." PhD diss., Vanderbilt University, 2013.

———. "Spatial Shifts and Generational Advancement in Post-emancipation: Barbadian Families, Migration, and Political Transitions in Liberia." Paper presented at the annual meeting of the American Historical Association, New York, 3 January 2015.

Baptist, Edward E. "Hidden in Plain View: Evasions, Invasions, and Invisible Nations." In *Echoes of the Haitian Revolution, 1804–2004*, edited by Martin Munro and Elizabeth Walcott-Hackshaw, 1–27. Mona: University of the West Indies Press, 2008.

Barman, Roderick J. *Citizen Emperor: Pedro II and the Making of Brazil, 1825–1891*. Stanford, CA: Stanford University Press, 1999.

Barry, Sara. "Hegemony on a Shoestring: Indirect Rule and Access to Agricultural Lands." *Africa* 62, no. 3 (1992): 327–55.

Bassi, Ernesto. *An Aqueous Territory: Sailor Geographies and New Granada's Transimperial Greater Caribbean World.* Durham, NC: Duke University Press, 2016.

Baud, Michiel. "Patrons, Peasants, and Tobacco." In *The Dominican Republic Reader: History, Culture, Politics,* edited by Eric Paul Roorda and Lauren Derby, 217–24. Durham, NC: Duke University Press, 2014.

———. *Peasants and Tobacco in the Dominican Republic 1870–1930.* Knoxville: University of Tennessee Press, 1995.

Baur, John. "Faustin Soulouque, Emperor of Haiti: His Character and His Reign." *The Americas* 6, no. 2 (1949): 121–66.

Bayly, C. A. *Imperial Meridian: The British Empire and the World, 1780–1830.* Harlow: Longman, 1989.

Beckert, Sven. *Empire of Cotton: A Global History.* New York: Knopf, 2015.

Bermúdez de Castro y O'Lawlor, Salvador (Marqués de Lema). *Cuestión de Santo Domingo: Discurso pronunciado en el Senado.* Madrid: Imprenta del Banco Industrial y Mercantil, 1865.

Besson, Jean. *Martha Brae's Two Histories: European Expansion and Caribbean Culture Building in America.* Chapel Hill: University of North Carolina Press, 2002.

Betances, Emelio R. "Agrarian Transformation and Class Formation in the Dominican Republic, 1844–1930." *Latin American Perspectives* 10, nos. 2–3 (1983): 60–75.

———. "Social Classes and the Origins of the Modern State: The Dominican Republic, 1844–1930." *Latin American Perspectives* 22, no. 3 (1995): 20–40.

Bhabha, Homi. *Location of Culture.* New York: Routledge, 1994.

Bird, Mark Baker. *The Black Man; Or, Haytian Independence.* New York: American News Company, 1869.

Bissette, Cyrille. *Réfutation du livre de M. V. Schoelcher sur Haïti.* Paris: Ébrard, 1844.

Black, Jeremy. *Fighting for America: The Struggle for Mastery in North America, 1519–1871.* Bloomington: Indiana University Press, 2011.

Blanco Díaz, Andrés, ed. *Alejandro Ángulo Guridi: Obras escogidas.* Vol. 1, Artículos. Santo Domingo: Archivo General de la Nación, 2006.

———. *Alejandro Ángulo Guridi: Obras escogidas.* Vol. 2, Ensayos. Santo Domingo: Archivo General de la Nación, 2006.

Bongie, Chris. *Friends and Enemies: The Scribal Politics of Post/Colonial Literature.* Liverpool: Liverpool University Press, 2008.

Bonneau, Alexandre. *Haïti: Ses progrès—son avenir.* Paris: E. Dentu, Libraire-éditeur, 1862.

Borges, José Lee. "Competencia y Anexión: La República Dominicana en la órbita expansionista de los Estados Unidos en el siglo XIX." *Focus* 1, no. 2 (2002): 47–58.

Bosch, Juan. *La Guerra de la Restauración.* 9th ed. Santo Domingo: Editora Corripio 1998 [1982].

Brandon, George. *Santería from Africa to the New World: The Dead Sell Memories.* Bloomington: Indiana University Press, 1993.

Brantlinger, Patrick. *Dark Vanishings: Discourse on the Extinction of Primitive Races, 1800–1930.* Ithaca, NY: Cornell University Press, 2003.
Breen, Henry Hegart. *St. Lucia: Historical, Statistical, and Descriptive.* London: Longman, Brown, Green, and Longmans, 1844.
Brière, Jean-François. "Abbé Grégoire and Haitian Independence." *Research in African Literatures* 35, no. 2 (2004): 34–43.
———. *Haïti et la France, 1804–48: Le rêve brisé.* Paris: Editions Karthala, 2008.
Britannicus (T. S. Heneken). *The Dominican Republic and the Emperor Soulouque, Being Remarks and Strictures on the Misstatements, and a Refutation of the Calumnies, of M. D'Alaux.* Philadelphia: T. K. Collins, 1852.
Brown, Jonathan. *The History and Present Condition of St. Domingo.* 2 vols. Philadelphia: Wm. Marshall and Company, 1837.
Brown, Laurence. "Experiments in Indenture: Barbados and the Segmentation of Migrant Labor in the Caribbean, 1863–1865." *New West Indian Guide* 79, nos. 1–2 (2005): 31–54.
Brown, Matthew. "The Global History of Latin America." *Journal of Global History* 10, no. 3 (2015): 365–86.
Brown, Vincent. *The Reaper's Garden: Death and Power in the World of Atlantic Slavery.* Cambridge, MA: Harvard University Press, 2008.
Burdiel, Isabel. "The Queen, the Woman, and the Middle Class: The Symbolic Failure of Isabel II in Spain." *Social History* 29, no. 3 (2004): 301–19.
Calhoun, Ricky-Dale. "Seeds of Destruction: The Globalization of Cotton as a Result of the American Civil War." PhD diss., Kansas State University, 2012.
Camp, Stephanie. *Closer to Freedom: Enslaved Women and Everyday Resistance in the Plantation South.* Chapel Hill: University of North Carolina Press, 2004.
———. "'I Could Not Stay There': Enslaved Women, Truancy and the Geography of Everyday Forms of Resistance in the Antebellum Plantation South." *Slavery and Abolition* 23, no. 3 (2002): 1–20.
Campillo Pérez, Julio G. *Historia electoral dominicana, 1848–1986.* 4th ed. Santo Domingo: Junta Central Electoral, 1986.
———. *Santiago de los caballeros, imperecedero legado hispano-colombino.* Santiago: Universidad Católica Madre y Maestra, 1977.
Campos Johnson, Adriana Michéle. "La Peregrinación de Bayoán: Writing (and Failing) in the House of Pilgrims." *Chasqui* 30, no. 1 (2001): 64–80.
Candelario, Ginetta. *Black behind the Ears: Dominican Racial Identity from Museums to Beauty Shops.* Durham, NC: Duke University Press, 2007.
Candler, John. *Brief Notices of Hayti.* London: Thomas Ward, 1842.
Casimir, Jean. *La culture opprimée.* Delmas, Haïti: Imprimerie Lakay, 2001.
———. "The History of Haiti's Poverty." Lecture given at New York University, 10 March 2010.
Cassá, Roberto. *Historia social y económica de la República Dominicana.* Vol. 1. Santo Domingo: Editora Alfa y Omega, 2000.

———. *Personajes dominicanos*. 2 vols. Santo Domingo: Archivo General de la Nación, 2014.
Castillo-Rodríguez, Susana. "The First Missionary Linguistics in Fernando Po." In *Colonialism and Military Linguistics*, edited by Klaus Zummerman and Birte Kellermeier-Rehbein, 75–106. Boston: Walter de Gruyter, 2015.
Castro Ventura, Santiago. *Duarte en la proa de historia*. Santo Domingo: Editora Manatí, 2005.
———. *La Guerra Restauradora: Erupción del anticolonialismo en las Antillas españolas*. Santo Domingo: Editora Manatí, 2014.
Caughfield, Adrienne. *True Women and Westward Expansion*. College Station: Texas A&M University Press, 2005.
Centeno, Miguel Angel. "Critical Debates: Latin American Independence and the Double Dilemma." *Latin American Politics and Society* 50, no. 3 (2008): 147–61.
Chaar-Pérez, Kahlil. " 'A Revolution of Love': Ramón Emeterio Betances, Anténor Firmin, and Affective Communities in the Caribbean." *Global South* 7, no. 2 (2013): 11–36.
Charolais [P. L. H. Chauvet]. *Les intérêts français et européens à Santo Domingo*. Paris: E. Dentu, 1861.
Chez Checo, José. *El ron en la historia dominicana. Vol. 2, Desde los antecedentes hasta finales del siglo XIX*. Santo Domingo: Ediciones Centenario de Brugal, 1988.
Chinea, Jorge L. "Race, Colonial Exploitation and West Indian Immigration in Nineteenth-Century Puerto Rico, 1800–1850." *The Americas* 52, no. 4 (1996): 495–519.
Clark, B. C. *Remarks upon United States Intervention in Hayti, with Comments upon the Correspondence Connected with It*. Boston: Eastburn's Press, 1853.
Clavin, Matthew J. *Toussaint Louverture and the American Civil War: The Promise and Peril of a Second Haitian Revolution*. Philadelphia: University of Pennsylvania Press, 2010.
Colección de leyes, decretos y resoluciones emanadas de los poderes legislativo y ejecutivo de la República Dominicana. Vol. 4. Santo Domingo: Imprenta de García Hermanos, 1883.
Comisión Permanente de Efemérides Patrias. *Proclamas de la Restauración*. Santo Domingo: CPEP, 2005.
Cooper, Frederick. *Colonialism in Question: Theory, Knowledge, History*. Berkeley: University of California Press, 2005.
Cordero Michel, Emilio. "Características de la Guerra Restauradora." *Clío* 164 (2004): 39–78.
———, ed. *La ciudad de Santo Domingo en las crónicas históricas*. Santo Domingo: Comision Municipal para la conmemoración del V Centenario de la Ciudad de Santo Domingo, 1998.
———. "Gregorio Luperón y Haiti." In Consejo Superior de Investigaciones Científicas, *Anuario de estudios americanos* XLIX, 497–528. Seville: Escuela de Estudios Hispano-Americanos, 1992.

———. *La revolución haitiana y Santo Domingo*. 4th ed. Santo Domingo: Facultad Latinoamericana de Ciencias Sociales, 2000 [1968].

Corwin, Arthur F. *Spain and the Abolition of Slavery in Cuba, 1817–1886*. Austin: University of Texas Press, 1967.

Courlander, Harold. *A Treasury of Afro-American Folklore*. Cambridge, MA: Da Capo Press, 2002.

Courtney, W. S. *The Gold Fields of Santo Domingo*. New York: A. P. Norton, 1860.

Coviello, Peter. *Intimacy in America: Dreams of Affiliation in Antebellum Literature*. Minneapolis: University of Minnesota Press, 2005.

Crawford, Sharika. "Politics of Belonging to a Caribbean Borderland: The Colombian Islands of San Andrés and Providencia." Paper presented at the meeting of the American Historical Association, New York, 4 January 2015.

Cromwell, Jesse. "More Than Slaves and Sugar: Recent Historiography of the Trans-imperial Caribbean and Its Sinew Populations." *History Compass* 12, no. 10 (2014): 770–83.

Cross-Beras, Julio A. "Clientelism, Dependency and Development in the Dominican Republic." PhD diss., Cornell University, 1981.

———. *Sociedad y desarrollo en la República Dominicana, 1844–1899*. Santo Domingo: Editorial CENAPEC, 1984.

Cubano-Iguina, Astrid. "Freedom in the Making: The Slaves of Hacienda La Esperanza, Manatí, Puerto Rico, on the Eve of Abolition, 1868–1876." *Social History* 36, no. 3 (2011): 280–93.

———. "Visions of Empire and Historical Imagination in Puerto Rico under Spanish Rule, 1870–1898." In *Interpreting Spanish Colonialism: Empires, Nations, and Legends*, ed. Christopher Schmidt-Nowara and John M. Nieto-Phillips, 87–108. Albuquerque: University of New Mexico Press, 2005.

Dalby, Jonathan R. " 'Such a Mass of Disgusting and Revolting Cases': Moral Panic and the 'Discovery' of Sexual Deviance in Post-emancipation Jamaica, 1835–1855." *Slavery and Abolition* 36, no. 1 (2015): 136–59.

Daut, Marlene. "The 'Alpha and Omega' of Haitian Literature: Baron de Vastey and the U.S. Audience of Haitian Political Writing." *Comparative Literature* 64, no. 1 (2012): 49–72.

Davidson, Basil. *The Black Man's Burden: Africa and the Curse of the Nation-State*. New York: Random House, 1992.

Davis, Martha Ellen. "Afro-Dominican Religious Brotherhoods: Structure, Ritual, Music." PhD diss., University of Illinois, 1976.

———. "Asentamiento y vida económica de los inmigrantes afroamericanos de Samaná: Testimonio de la profesora Martha Willmore (Leticia)." *Boletín General de la Nación* 32, no. 119 (2007): 709–34.

———. "La historia de los inmigrantes afro-americanos y sus iglesias en Samaná según el reverendo Nehemiah Willmore." *BAGN* 36, no. 129 (2011): 237–45.

Dayan, Joan. *Haiti, History, and the Gods*. Berkeley: University of California Press, 1995.

De Barros, Juanita. *Reproducing the British Caribbean: Sex, Gender and Population Projects after Slavery*. Chapel Hill: University of North Carolina Press, 2014.

de Bona, Félix. *Cuba, Santo Domingo y Puerto-Rico*. Madrid: Imprenta de Manuel Galiano, 1861.

de Granda, Germán. "Un caso de planeamiento lingüístico frustrado en el Caribe hispánico: Santo Domingo, 1822–1844." *Boletín de Filología de la Universidad de Chile* 34 (1993–94): 187–225.

Deive, Carlos Esteban. *Diccionario de dominicanismos*. Santo Domingo: Ediciones Manatí, 2002 [1977].

———. *Los guerrilleros negros: Esclavos fugitivos y cimarrones en Santo Domingo*. Santo Domingo: Fundación Cultural Dominicana, 1985.

———. *Vodú y magia en Santo Domingo*. Santo Domingo: Museo del Hombre Dominicano, 1975.

de la Fuente, Ariel. *Children of Facundo: Caudillo and Gaucho Insurgency during the Argentine State-Formation Process (La Rioja, 1853–1870)*. Durham, NC: Duke University Press, 2000.

de la Gándara y Navarro, José. *Anexión y guerra de Santo Domingo*. Madrid: Impresora de "el correo militar," 1884.

de la Rosa Garabito, Emiliano. *San Cristóbal en la historia dominicana*. Santo Domingo: Editora Alfa y Omega, 1983.

Delutis-Eichenberger, Angela. "National Consciousness and Shared Americanism in Hero Formation: Representations of Andrés Bello in Nineteenth-Century Chile." *Bulletin of Spanish Studies* 92 (2015): 1–25.

Derby, Lauren. "Haitians, Magic, and Money: Raza and Society in the Haitian-Dominican Borderlands, 1900–1937." *Society for Comparative Study of Society and History* 36, no. 3 (1994): 488–526.

———. "Male Heroism, Demonic Pigs, and Memories of Violence in the Dominican-Haitian Borderlands." *UCLA Center for the Study of Women Update Newsletter* (2010): 1–14.

Dewey, L. D., and Jean-Pierre Boyer. *Correspondence Relative to the Emigration to Hayti of the Free People in the United States*. New York: Mahlon Day, 1824.

Dhormoys, Paul. *Une visite chez Soulouque: Souvenirs d'un voyage dans l'Île d'Haïti*. Paris: Librairie Nouvelle, 1859.

Díaz Jáquez, Leonardo. "Puerto Plata y los censos de 1871, 1875 y 1879." In *Areíto, Sección sabatina del diario Hoy*. 1 September 2007. Accessed 11 June 2011. http://www.idg.org.do/capsulas/septiembre2007/septiembre20071.htm.

Díaz-Stevens, Ana María. "The Saving Grace: The Matriarchal Core of Puerto Rican Catholicism." *Latino Studies Journal* 4, no. 3 (1993): 60–78.

Dixon, Chris. *African America and Haiti: Emigration and Black Nationalism in the Nineteenth Century*. Westport, CT: Greenwood Press, 2000.

Dominguez, Jaime de Jésus. *La anexión de Santo Domingo a España*. Santo Domingo: Editora de la UASD, 1979.

Dorsey, Joseph C. "Identity, Rebellion, and Social Justice among Chinese Contract Workers in Nineteenth-Century Cuba." *Latin American Perspectives* 31, no. 3 (2004): 18–47.

———. "Seamy Sides of Abolition: Puerto Rico and the Cabotage Slave Trade to Cuba, 1848–1873." *Slavery and Abolition* 19, no. 1 (1998): 106–28.

Dubois, Laurent. *Avengers of the New World: The Story of the Haitian Revolution.* Cambridge, MA: Harvard University Press, 2004.

———. *A Colony of Citizens: Revolution and Slave Emancipation in the French Caribbean, 1787–1804.* Chapel Hill: University of North Carolina Press, 2004.

———. *Haiti: The Aftershocks of History.* New York: Metropolitan Books, 2012.

———. "Thinking Haiti's Nineteenth Century." *Small Axe* 18, no. 2 44 (2014): 72–79.

Dubois, Laurent, and John D. Garrigus. *Slave Revolution in the Caribbean: A Brief History with Documents.* New York: Bedford/St. Martin's, 2006.

Duncan, Robert H. "Maximilian and the Construction of the Liberal State, 1863–1866." In *The Divine Charter: Constitutionalism and Liberalism in Nineteenth-Century Mexico*, ed. Jaime E. Rodríquez, 133–65. New York: Rowman and Littlefield, 2005.

———. "Political Legitimation and Maximilian's Second Empire in Mexico, 1864–1867." *Mexican Studies/Estudios Mexicanos* 12, no. 1 (1996): 27–66.

Egerton, Douglas R. "Rethinking Atlantic Historiography in a Postcolonial Era: The Civil War in a Global Perspective." *Journal of the Civil War Era* 1, no. 1 (2011): 79–95.

Eller, Anne. "'All Would Be Equal in the Effort': Santo Domingo's 'Italian Revolution,' Independence, and Haiti, 1809–1822." *Journal of Early American History* 1, no. 2 (2011): 105–41.

———. "Awful Pirates and Hordes of Jackals: Santo Domingo/The Dominican Republic in Nineteenth-Century Historiography." *Small Axe* 18, no. 2 44 (2014): 80–94.

Elliott, E. N., ed. *Cotton Is King and Pro-slavery Arguments.* Augusta, GA: Pritchard, Abbott and Loomis, 1860.

Escolano Giménez, Luis Alfonso. "La insurrección dominicana de febrero de 1863: Sus causas e implicaciones internacionales." *Clío* 179 (2010): 71–108.

———. "La organización de la provincia de Santo Domingo entre 1861 y 1865: Un modelo para el estudio del sistema administrativo español en las Antillas." *BAGN*, no. 133 (2012): 325–66.

———. *La rivalidad internacional por la Republica Dominicana y el complejo proceso de su anexión a España, 1858–1865.* Santo Domingo: Archivo General de la Nación, 2013.

Espaillat y Quiñones, Ulises Francisco. *Escritos.* Santo Domingo: Sociedad Dominicana de Bibliófilos, 1987.

Espinal Estévez, Piero, and Nicanor Jiménez. *Santiago de los Caballeros: Apuntes inéditos de Nicanor Jiménez.* Santo Domingo: Editorial Letra Gráfica, 2008.

Espinal Hernández, Edwin Rafael. "Familiaridad y consanguinidad en el movimiento independentista." Instituto Dominicano de Genealogía, February 2005. Accessed February 2009. http://www.idg.org.do/charlas/2005/febrero2.htm.

———. "Geopolítica y armamentos en la Guerra Restauradora." Clío 183 (2012): 126–90.

Evanson, Philip. "The Third Dominican-Haitian War and the Return of General Pedro Santana: Part of a Long Story." Caribbean Studies 4, no. 1 (1964): 13–23.

Eyal, Yonatan. *Young America Movement and the Transformation of the Democratic Party*. New York: Cambridge University Press, 2007.

Fabens, Joseph Warren. *Facts about Santo Domingo, Applicable to the Present Crisis: An Address Delivered before the American Geographical and Statistical Society at New York, 3 April 1862*. New York: F. Taylor, 1862.

Fabens, Joseph Warren, Cora Montgomery (Jane Cazneau), and Richard Burleigh Kimball. *In the Tropics: By a Settler in Santo Domingo*. New York: Carleton, 1863.

Fanning, Sara. *Caribbean Crossing: African Americans and the Haitian Emigration Movement*. New York: NYU Press, 2015.

Faye, Stanley. "Commodore Aury." Louisiana Historical Quarterly 3 (July 1941): 1–87.

Febres-Cordero Carrillo, Francisco. "La anexión y la Guerra de Restauración dominicana desde las filas españolas (1861–5)." PhD diss., University of Puerto Rico, 2008.

Ferrer, Ada. *Freedom's Mirror: Cuba and Haiti in the Age of Revolutions*. New York: Cambridge University Press, 2014.

———. "Haiti, Free Soil, and Antislavery in the Revolutionary Atlantic." American Historical Review 117, no. 1 (2012): 40–66.

———. *Insurgent Cuba: Race, Nation, and Revolution, 1868–1898*. Chapel Hill: University of North Carolina Press, 1999.

———. "Talk about Haiti." In *Tree of Liberty: The Haitian Revolution in the Atlantic World*, edited by Doris L. Garraway, 21–40. Charlottesville: University of Virginia Press, 2008.

Ferrer de Couto, José. *Reincorporación de Santo Domingo a España*. Madrid: Imprenta de Manuel Galiano, 1861.

Fiallo Billini, José Antinoe. "La construcción antillanista: Insinuaciones para una estrategía geopolítica." Paper presented at "El Primer Seminario Internacional sobre Pensamiento Antillanista," Santo Domingo, 25 November 2004.

Figueroa, Luís. *Sugar, Slavery, and Freedom in Nineteenth-Century Puerto Rico*. Chapel Hill: University of North Carolina Press, 2005.

Finch, Aisha K. *Rethinking Slave Rebellion in Cuba: La Escalera and the Insurgencies of 1841–44*. Chapel Hill: University of North Carolina, 2015.

Finke, Carlos Manuel. "Puerto Plata en la Gesta Restauradora." Clío 170 (2005): 115–48.

Fischer, Sibylle. "Bolívar in Haiti: Republicanism in the Revolutionary Atlantic." In *Haiti and the Americas*, edited by Carla Calargé, Raphael Dalleo, Luis

Duno-Gottberg, and Clevis Headly, 24–53. Jackson: University Press of Mississippi, 2013.

———. *Modernity Disavowed: Haiti and the Cultures of Slavery in the Age of Revolution.* Durham, NC: Duke University Press, 2004.

Fleszar, Mark J. " 'My Laborers in Haiti Are Not Slaves': Proslavery Fictions and a Black Colonization Experiment on the Northern Coast, 1835–1846." *Journal of the Civil War Era* 2, no. 4 (2012): 478–510.

Fontecha Pedraza, Antonio, and Eduardo González Calleja. *Una cuestión de honor: La polémica sobre la anexión de Santo Domingo vista desde España (1861–1865).* Santo Domingo: Fundación García Arévalo, 2005.

Fradera, Josep. "Reading Imperial Transitions: Spanish Contraction, British Expansion, and American Irruption." In *Colonial Crucible: Empire in the Making of the Modern American State,* edited by Alfred W. McCoy and Francisco A. Scarano, 34–62. Madison: University of Wisconsin Press, 2009.

———. "Why Were Spain's Special Overseas Laws Never Enacted?" In *Spain, Europe and the Atlantic: Essays in Honour of John H. Elliott,* edited by Richard L. Kagan and Geoffrey Parker, 334–49. New York: Cambridge University Press, 1995.

François, Marie E. "Laundering Identities in the Americas: The Production of Individuals and Class in the Eighteenth and Nineteenth Centuries." Presentation at the annual meeting of Council on Latin American History, San Diego, 9 January 2010.

Franco Pichardo, Franklin José. *Los negros, los mulatos y la nación dominicana.* Santo Domingo: Editora Nacional, 1970.

———. *El pensamiento dominicano, 1780–1940.* Santo Domingo: UASD, 2001.

———. "Remanentes ideológicos de la esclavitud en République Dominicana." *Clío* 167 (2004): 79–98.

———. *Sobre racismo y antihaitianismo (y otros ensayos).* Santo Domingo: Impresora Vidal, 1997.

Franklin, James. *Present State of Hayti (St. Domingo): With Remarks on Its Agriculture, Commerce, Laws, Religion, Finances, and Population, etc.* London: John Murray, 1828.

Franks, Julie Cheryl. "Transforming Property: Landholding and Political Rights in the Dominican Sugar Region, 1880–1930." PhD diss., SUNY Stony Brook, 1997.

Frazer, Robert W. "The Role of the Lima Congress, 1864–1865, in the Development of Pan-Americanism." *Hispanic American Historical Review* 29, no. 3 (1949): 319–48.

Fryar, Christienna. "The Moral Politics of Cholera in Postemancipation Jamaica." *Slavery and Abolition* 34, no. 4 (2013): 598–618.

Fusté, José I. "Possible Republics: Tracing the 'Entanglements' of Race and Nation in Afro-Latino/a Caribbean Thought and Activism, 1870–1930." PhD diss., University of California, San Diego, 2012.

Gaffield, Julia. *Haitian Connections in the Atlantic World: Recognition after Revolution.* Chapel Hill: University of North Carolina Press, 2015.

Gage, Frances D. "The Market Woman of San Domingo." *Friends' Intelligencer* 20, no. 45 (16 January 1864): 717–18.

Gaillard, Roger. *Le cacoisme bourgeois contre Salnave, 1867–1870.* Finalized by Gusti-Klara Gaillard-Pourchet. Port-au-Prince: Fondation Roger Gaillard, 2003.

Galván, Manuel de Jésus. "El General don Pedro Santana y la anexión de Santo Domingo a España." New York: Imprenta de Gaspar Robertson, 1862.

Garavaglia, Juan Carlos, and Juan Marchena Fernández. *América Latina de los orígenes a la Independencia.* Madrid: Editorial Crítica, 2005.

García, José Gabriel. *Compendio de la Historia de Santo Domingo.* 2 vols. Santo Domingo: Imprenta de García Hermanos, 1893.

García Tamayo, Eduardo. "Cultura campesina en la frontera norte." *Estudios Sociales* 17, no. 55 (enero–marzo 1984), 43–57.

Garraway, Doris L., ed. *Tree of Liberty: The Haitian Revolution in the Atlantic World.* Charlottesville: University of Virginia Press, 2008.

Garrido, Victor. *Los Puello.* Santo Domingo: Editora Taller, 1974.

Gaspar, David Barry. *Bondsmen and Rebels: A Study of Master-Slave Relations in Antigua.* Durham, NC: Duke University Press, 1993 [1985].

Gaztambide-Géigel, Antonio. "La geopolítica del antillanismo en el Caribe de fines del siglo XIX." *Ciencia y Sociedad* 29, no. 4 (2004): 570–615.

———. "La geopolítica del antillanismo en el Caribe del siglo XIX." Paper presented at the annual meeting of the Latin American Studies Association, Rio de Janeiro, 11–14 June 2009. http://lasa.international.pitt.edu/members/congresspapers/lasa2009/files/GaztambideGeigelAntonio.pdf.

Geggus, David Patrick, ed. *The Impact of the Haitian Revolution in the Atlantic World.* Columbia: University of South Carolina Press, 2001.

———. "The Naming of Haiti." *New West Indian Guide* 71 (1997): 43–68.

Gil, Guido. *Origenes y proyecciones de la revolución restauradora.* Santo Domingo: Editora Nacional, 1964.

Giusti-Cordero, Juan. "Beyond Sugar Revolutions: Rethinking the Spanish Caribbean in the Seventeenth and Eighteenth Centuries." In *Empirical Futures: Anthropologists and Historians Engage the Work of Sidney W. Mintz*, edited by George Baca, Aisha Khan, and Stephan Palmié, 58–83. Chapel Hill: University of North Carolina Press, 2009.

Gobat, Michel. *Confronting the American Dream: Nicaragua under US Imperial Rule.* Durham, NC: Duke University Press, 2005.

———. "The Invention of Latin America: A Transnational History of Anti-imperialism, Democracy, and Race." *American Historical Review* 118, no. 5 (2013): 1345–75.

Gómez, Alejandro. "Entwining the Revolutions in the French Caribbean and the Spanish Mainland: From Del Valle to Bolivar, 1790–1826." Lecture given at New York University, 11 April 2011.

González, Johnhenry. "The War on Sugar: Forced Labor, Commodity Production and the Origins of the Haitian Peasantry, 1791–1843." PhD diss., University of Chicago, 2012.

González, Raymundo. "Bonó, un crítico del liberalism dominicano en el siglo XIX (Apuntes para la biografía de un intelectual de los pobres." *Ciencia y Sociedad* 10, no. 4 (1985): 472–89.

———. *De esclavos a campesinos: Vida rural en Santo Domingo colonial*. Santo Domingo: Archivo General de la Nación, 2011.

———. "La figura social del montero en la formación histórica del campesinado dominicano." *Clío*, no. 168 (2004): 74–96.

———. "Ideologia del progreso y campesinado en el siglo XIX." *Ecos* 2 (1993): 25–43.

González Canalda, María Filomena. "Importancia de los protocolos notariales en la investigación histórica: Caso del período de la unificación política de la isla de Santo Domingo, 1822–1844." *Caribbean Studies* 42, no. 1 (2014): 101–29.

González Tablas, Ramón. *Historia de la dominación y ultima guerra de España en Santo Domingo*. Madrid, 1870.

Grandin, Greg. "The Liberal Traditions in the Americas: Rights, Sovereignty, and the Origins of Liberal Multilateralism." *American Historical Review* 117, no. 1 (2012): 68–91.

Greenberg, Amy S. *Manifest Manhood and the Antebellum American Empire*. New York: Cambridge University Press, 2005.

Guardino, Peter. "Gender, Soldiering, and Citizenship in the Mexican-American War of 1846–1848." *American Historical Review* 119, no. 1 (2014): 23–46.

Guerra Sosa, Antonio José Ignacio. "Familias Haitianas al servicio de nuestra independencia." *Seccion Sabatina del Diario Hoy*, 10 December 2005. Accessed January 2010. http://www.idg.org.do/capsulas/diciembre2005/diciembre200510.htm.

Guerrero, José G. "El pensamiento conservador en el siglo XIX." In *Retrospectiva y perspectiva del pensamiento político dominicano*, 79–138. Santo Domingo: Editora Corripio, 2009.

Guerrero Cano, Magdalena. *Disciplina y laxitud: La iglesia dominicana en tiempos de anexión*. Cádiz: Universidad de Cádiz, 1984.

Guridi, Javier Ángulo. *La campana del higo: Tradición dominicana*. Santo Domingo, 1866.

Hagemann, Karen, and Jane Rendall. "Introduction: Gender, War and Politics: Transatlantic Perspectives on the Wars of Revolution and Liberation, 1775–1830." In *Gender, War and Politics: Transatlantic Perspectives, 1775–1830*, edited by Karen Hagemann, Gisela Mettele, and Jane Rendall, 1–40. New York: Palgrave Macmillan, 2010.

Hahn, Steven. "'Extravagant Expectations' of Freedom: Rumour, Political Struggle, and the Christmas Insurrection Scare of 1865 in the American South." *Past and Present* 157 (1997): 122–58.

Hall, Bruce. *A History of Race in Muslim West Africa, 1600–1900*. New York: Cambridge University Press, 2011.

Hall, Catherine. *Civilising Subjects: Metropole and Colony in the English Imagination, 1830–1867*. Chicago: University of Chicago Press, 2002.

———. "The Nation Within and Without." In *Defining the Victorian Nation: Class, Race, Gender and the British Reform Act of 1867*, edited by Keith McClelland Hall and Jane Rendall, 179–233. New York: Cambridge University Press, 2000.

Harris, Dennis J. "A Summer on the Borders of the Caribbean Sea." In *Black Separatism and the Caribbean 1860*, edited by Howard H. Bell, 69–184. Ann Arbor: University of Michigan Press, 1970.

Hauch, Charles Christian. "Attitudes of Foreign Governments towards the Spanish Reoccupation of the Dominican Republic." *Hispanic American Historical Review* 27, no. 2 (1947): 247–68.

———. "The Dominican Republic and Its Foreign Relations, 1844–82." PhD diss., University of Chicago, 1942.

Hazard, Samuel. *Santo Domingo, Past and Present, with a Glance at Hayti*. 3rd ed. Santo Domingo: Editora de Santo Domingo, 1974 [1873].

Helg, Aline. "The Aftermath of Slavery in the Spanish-Speaking Caribbean: Historiography and Methodology." In *Beyond Fragmentation: Perspectives on Caribbean History*, edited by Juanita De Barros, Audra Diptee, and David V. Trotman, 141–68. Princeton, NJ: Markus Wiener, 2006.

———. *Liberty and Equality in Caribbean Colombia, 1775–1830*. Chapel Hill: University of North Carolina Press, 2004.

———. "Simón Bolívar and the Spectre of *Pardocracia*: José Padilla in Post-independence Cartagena." *Journal of Latin American Studies* 35 (2003): 447–71.

Henriquez Ureña, Max. *La independencia efímera*. Santo Domingo: Libreria Dominicana, Editora, 1962 [1938].

———. *Panorama histórico de la literatura dominicana*. Rio de Janeiro: Companhia Brasileira de Artes Gráficas, 1945.

Henríquez Ureña, Pedro. *La cultura y las letras coloniales en Santo Domingo*. Barcelona: Red Ediciones, 2015.

Hepburn, Robert S. *Haiti as It Is: Being Notes of a Five Months' Sojourn in the North and North-west of Haiti*. Kingston: A. Decordova and Nephew, 1861.

Hernández Flores, Ismael. *Luperón, héroe y alma de la Restauración: Haití y la Revolución Restauradora*. Santo Domingo: Lotería Nacional, 1983.

———. *Pedro Santana: Totalmente negativo*. Santo Domingo: Editora Alfa y Omega, 1984.

Herrera R., Rafael Darío. *Montecristi entre campeche y bananos*. Santo Domingo: Academia Dominicana de la Historia, 2006.

Hidalgo, Dennis. "From North America to Hispaniola: First Free Black Emigration and Settlements in Hispaniola." PhD diss., Central Michigan University, 2001.

Hispaniola, Hayti, Saint Domingo. London: W. S. Johnson, 1851.

Hoefte, Rosemarijn. "Labour in the Caribbean in the Long Nineteenth Century." *International Review of Social History* 57 (2012): 257–68.

Hoetink, Harry. "Americans in Samaná." *Caribbean Studies* 2, no. 1 (1962): 3–22.

———. *The Dominican People, 1850–1900: Notes for a Historical Sociology*. Translated by Stephen Ault. Baltimore: Johns Hopkins University Press, 1982 [1972].

Holden, Robert H. *Armies without Nations: Public Violence and State Formation in Central America, 1821–1960*. New York: Oxford University Press, 2004.

Holt, Thomas C. "'An Empire over the Mind': Emancipation, Race, and Ideology in the British West Indies and the American South." In *Region, Race, and Reconstruction: Essays in Honor of C. Vann Woodward*, edited by J. Morgan Kousser and James McPherson, 283–313. New York: Oxford University Press, 1982.

———. *The Problem of Freedom: Race, Labor, and Politics in Jamaica and Britain, 1832–1938*. Baltimore: Johns Hopkins University Press, 1991.

Hopkins, A. G. *An Economic History of West Africa*. New York: Routledge, 2014 [1973].

Hostos, Eugenio María de. *Eugenio M. Hostos: Ofrendas a su memoria*. Santo Domingo: Imprenta Oiga, 1905.

———. *La Peregrinación de Bayoán*. 2nd ed. Santiago de Chile: Imprenta de Sud-América, 1873.

Hulme, Peter. *Cuba's Wild East: A Literary Geography of Oriente*. Liverpool: Liverpool University, 2011.

———. *Remnants of Conquest: The Island Caribs and Their Visitors, 1877–1998*. New York: Oxford University Press, 2000.

Huner, Michael Kenneth. "Toikove Ñane Retã! Republican Nationalism at the Battlefield Crossings of Print and Speech in Wartime Paraguay, 1867–68." In *Building Nineteenth-Century Latin America: Re-rooted Cultures, Identities, and Nations*, edited by William G. Acree and Juan Carlos González Espitia, 79–97. Nashville, TN: Vanderbilt University Press, 2009.

Ibsen, Kristine. *Maximilian, Mexico, and the Invention of Empire*. Nashville, TN: Vanderbilt University Press, 2010.

Illás, Juan José. "El terremoto del 7 de mayo del año 1842." In *Reseña histórico-crítica de la poesía en Santo Domingo: Notas y adiciones de Vetilio Alfau Durán*, edited by César Nicolás Penson, 23. Santo Domingo: Editora Taller, 1980.

Inikori, Joseph. "English versus Indian Cotton Textiles: The Impact of Imports on Cotton Textile Production in West Africa." In *How India Clothed the World: The World of South Asian Textiles, 1500–1850*, edited by Giorgio Riello and Turthankar Roy, 85–114. Leiden: Brill, 2009.

James, C. L. R. *The Black Jacobins: Toussaint Louverture and the San Domingo Revolution*. New York: Penguin, 2001 [1938].

Janvier, Louis-Joseph. *Haïti et ses visiteurs, 1840–1882*. Paris: Marpon et Flammarion, 1883.

Jimenes Grullón, Juan-Isidro. *El mito de los padres de la patria*. Santo Domingo: Editora Cultural Dominicana, 1971.

———. *La Républica Dominicana: Una ficción*. Merida: Talleres Gráficos Universitarios, 1965.

———. *Sociología política dominicana, 1844–1996*. Vol. 1, 1844–1898. Santo Domingo: Editora Alfa y Omega, 1982.

Johnson, Rashauna. *Slavery's Metropolis: Unfree Labor in New Orleans during the Age of Revolutions*. New York: Cambridge University Press, 2016.

Johnson, Sara E. *The Fear of French Negroes: Transcolonial Collaboration in the Revolutionary Americas*. Berkeley: University of California Press, 2012.

———. "The Integration of Hispaniola: A Reappraisal of Haitian-Dominican Relations in the 19th and 20th Centuries." *Journal of Haitian Studies* 8, no. 2 (2002): 4–29.

Jung, Moon-Ho. *Coolies and Cane: Race, Labor and Sugar in the Age of Emancipation*. Baltimore: Johns Hopkins University Press, 2006.

Kachun, Mitch. " 'Our Platform Is as Broad as Humanity': Transatlantic Freedom Movements and the Idea of Progress in Nineteenth-Century African American Thought and Activism." *Slavery and Abolition* 24, no. 3 (2003): 1–23.

Kaisary, Philip. "Human Rights and Radical Universalism: Aimé Césaire's and CLR James's Representations of the Haitian Revolution." *Law and Humanities* 6, no. 2 (2012): 197–216.

Kale, Madhavi. *Fragments of Empire: Capital, Slavery, and Indian Indentured Labor in the British Caribbean*. Philadelphia: University of Pennsylvania Press, 1998.

Karp, Matthew. "The World the Slaveholders Craved: Proslavery Internationalism in the 1850s." In *The World of the Revolutionary American Republic: Land, Labor, and the Conflict for a Continent*, edited by Andrew Shankman, 414–32. New York: Routledge, 2014.

Kaye, Anthony E. "The Second Slavery: Modernity in the Nineteenth-Century South and the Atlantic World." *Journal of Southern History* 75, no. 3 (2009): 627–50.

Kazanjian, David. *The Brink of Freedom: Improvising Life in the Nineteenth-Century Atlantic World*. Durham, NC: Duke University Press, 2016.

Keim, De Benneville Randolph. *San Domingo: Pen Pictures and Leaves of Travel, Romance and History, from the Portfolio of a Correspondent in the American Tropics*. Philadelphia: Claxton, Temson and Haffelfinger, 1870.

Kenny, Gale L. *Contentious Liberties: American Abolitionists in Post-emancipation Jamaica, 1834–1836*. Athens: University of Georgia Press, 2010.

Kerr-Ritchie, Jeffrey R. *Freedom's Seekers: Essays on Comparative Emancipation*. Baton Rouge: Louisiana State University Press, 2013.

Kinsbruner, Jay. *Not of Pure Blood: The Free People of Color and Racial Prejudice in Nineteenth-Century Puerto Rico*. Durham, NC: Duke University Press, 1996.

Knöbl, Wolfgang. "State Building in Western Europe and the Americas in the Long Nineteenth Century: Some Preliminary Considerations." In *State and Nation Making in Latin America and Spain: Republics of the Possible*, edited by Miguel A.

Centeno and Augustin E. Ferraro, 56–75. New York: Cambridge University Press, 2013.

Krug, Jessica. "Healing Politics and the Politics of Healing: Global African Intellectual Histories of Resistance, c. 1520–1760." Paper presented at the annual meeting of the Latin American Studies Association, San Juan, Puerto Rico, 29 May 2015.

Lambert, David. *Mastering the Niger: James MacQueen's African Geography and the Struggle over Atlantic Slavery.* Chicago: University of Chicago Press, 2013.

Landolfi, Ciriaco. *Evolución cultural dominicana, 1844–1899.* Santo Domingo: Editora de la UASD, 1981.

Laroche, Léon. *Haïti: Une page d'histoire.* Paris: Arthur Rousseau, 1885.

Larrazábal Blanco, Carlos. *Los negros y la esclavitud.* Santo Domingo: Julio D. Postigo e Hijos Editores, 1975.

Larson, Brooke. *The Trials of Nation Making: Liberalism, Race, and Ethnicity in the Andes, 1810–1910.* New York: Cambridge University Press, 2004.

Lasso, Marixa. *Myths of Harmony: Race and Republicanism during the Age of Revolution, Colombia, 1795–1831.* Pittsburgh: University of Pittsburgh Press, 2007.

Lauderbaugh, George M. *History of Ecuador.* Santa Barbara, CA: Greenwood Press, 2012.

Laviña, Javier. "Puerto Rico: 'Atlantización,' and Culture during the 'Segunda Esclavitud.'" In *The Second Slavery: Mass Slaveries and Modernity in the Americas and in the Atlantic Basin,* edited by Javier Laviña and Michael Zeuske, 93–112. Zürich: Lit Verlag, 2014.

Leary, John Patrick. "Cuba in the American Imaginary: Literature and National Culture in Cuba and the United States, 1848–1958." PhD diss., New York University, 2009.

LeFlouria, Talitha. *Chained in Silence: Black Women and Convict Labor in the New South.* Chapel Hill: University of North Carolina Press, 2015.

Lespinasse, Pierre Eugène de, Jean Price-Mars, and Augustín Ferrer Gutiérrez. *Haïti et la restauration de l'indépendance dominicaine.* Port-au-Prince: Bibliothèque Nationale d'Haïti, 2013.

Lester, Alan. *Imperial Networks: Creating Identities in Nineteenth-Century South Africa.* New York: Routledge, 2001.

Levy, Claude. *Emancipation, Sugar, and Federalism: Barbados and the West Indies, 1833–1876.* Gainesville: University Press of Florida, 1980.

Levy, Juliette. *The Making of a Market: Credit, Henequen, and Notaries in Yucatán, 1850–1900.* College Park: Penn State University Press, 2012.

Lightfoot, Natasha. *Troubling Freedom: Antigua and the Aftermath of British Emancipation.* Durham, NC: Duke University Press, 2015.

Lizardo, Fradique. *Cultura Africana en Santo Domingo.* Santo Domingo: Editora Taller, 1979.

———. *Danzas y bailes folklóricos dominicanos.* Santo Domingo: Fundación García Arevalo, 1974.

Lockward, Alfonso. *La Constitución Haitiano-Dominicana de 1843*. Santo Domingo: Taller Isabel la Católica, 1995.

———. *Documentos para la historia de las relaciones dominico-americanas*. Vol. 1, 1837–1860. Santo Domingo: Editora Corripio, 1987.

Logan, Rayford W. *The Diplomatic Relations of the United States with Haiti, 1776–1891*. Chapel Hill: University of North Carolina Press, 1941.

López, Cathy. *Chinese Cubans: A Transnational History*. Chapel Hill: University of North Carolina Press, 2013.

López-Alves, Fernando. "Visions of the National: Natural Endowments, Futures, and the Evils of Men." In *State and Nation Making in Latin America and Spain: Republics of the Possible*, edited by Miguel A. Centeno and Augustin E. Ferraro, 282–306. New York: Cambridge University Press, 2013.

López Morillo, Adriano. *Memorias sobre la segunda reincorporación de Santo Domingo a España*. Santo Domingo: Sociedad Dominicana de Bibliófilos, 1983.

Lora Hugi, Quisqueya. "Las mujeres anónimas de inicios del siglo XIX dominicano." *Clío* 176 (2008): 81–122.

———. "El sonido de la libertad: 30 años de agitaciones y conspiraciones en Santo Domingo (1791–1821)." *Clío* 182 (2011): 109–40.

———. *Transición de la esclavitud al trabajo libre en Santo Domingo: El caso de Higüey (1822–1827)*. Santo Domingo: Academia Dominicana de Historia, 2012.

Lugo Lovatón, Ramón. "La junta económica anexionista de 1861." *BAGN*, no. 64 (1950): 109–18.

———. "Tomás Bobadilla Briones." *BAGN*, no. 70 (1951): 291–347.

Luis-Brown, David. *Waves of Decolonization: Discourses of Race and Hemispheric Citizenship in Cuba, Mexico, and the United States*. Durham, NC: Duke University Press, 2008.

Lundias, Jan, and Mats Lundahl. *Peasants and Religion: A Socioeconomic Study of Dios Olivorio and the Palma Sola Movement in the Dominican Republic*. New York: Routledge, 2000.

Luperón, Gregorio. *Notas autobiográficas y apuntes históricos*. 3 vols. 2nd ed. Santiago: Editorial El Diario, 1939.

Mackenzie, Charles. *Notes on Haiti Made during a Residence in That Republic*. 2 vols. London: Henry Coleburn and Richard Bentley, 1830.

Macleod, Donald. "Narratives of Belonging and Identity in the Dominican Republic." In *Caribbean Narratives of Belonging*, edited by Jean Besson and Karen Fog Olwig, 97–114. Oxford: Macmillan, 2005.

Madiou, Thomas. *Histoire d'Haïti*. Vol. 8, 1843–6. Port-au-Prince: H. Deschamps, 1985.

Madureira, Luís. *Cannibal Modernities: Postcoloniality and the Avant-Garde in Caribbean and Brazilian Literature*. Charlottesville: University of Virginia Press, 2005.

Main, Gloria L. *Tobacco Colony: Life in Early Maryland, 1650–1720*. Princeton, NJ: Princeton University Press, 1982.

Malamud, Carlos, ed. *Ruptura y reconciliación: España y el reconocimiento de las independencias latinoamericanas.* Madrid: Taurus, Fundación Mapfre, 2012.

Mallon, Florencia. *Peasant and Nation: The Making of Postcolonial México and Peru.* Berkeley: University of California Press, 1995.

Mamdani, Mahmood. *Define and Rule: Native as Political Identity.* Cambridge, MA: Harvard University Press, 2013.

Mamigonian, Beatriz. "To Be a Liberated African in Brazil: Labour and Citizenship in the Nineteenth Century." PhD diss., University of Waterloo, 2002.

Manning, William R. *Diplomatic Correspondence of the United States: Inter-American Affairs, 1831–1860.* Vol. 6. Washington: Carnegie Endowment for International Peace, 1935.

Manuel, Peter. "Cuba: From Contradanza to Danzón." In *Creolizing Contradance in the Caribbean*, edited by Peter Manuel, 51–112. Philadelphia: Temple University Press, 2011.

Marquese, Rafael, and Tâmis Parron. "Atlantic Constitutionalism and the Ideology of Slavery: The Cádiz Experience in Comparative Perspective." In *The Rise of Constitutional Government in the Iberian Atlantic World: The Impact of the Cádiz Constitution of 1812*, edited by Scott Eastman et al., 177–93. Tuscaloosa: University of Alabama Press, 2015.

Marsh, Kate. " 'Rights of the Individual,' Indentured Labour and Indian Workers: The French Antilles and the Rhetoric of Slavery Post 1848." *Slavery and Abolition* 33, no. 2 (2012): 221–31.

Marte, Roberto. *Correspondencia consular inglesa sobre la anexión de Santo Domingo a España.* Santo Domingo: Archivo General de la Nación, 2012.

———. "Noticias consulares histórico-estadísticas sobre el comercio exterior dominicano (1855–1883)." *BAGN*, no. 132 (2012): 99–150.

———. "La oralidad sobre el pasado insular y el concepto de nación en el mundo rural dominicano del siglo XIX." Accessed 4 January 2012. http://www.cielonaranja.com/robertomarte-oralidad.pdf. Originally published in *BAGN*, no. 123 (2009): 83–172.

Martín Casares, Aurelia, and Margarita García Barranco. "Legislation on Free Soil in Nineteenth-Century Spain: The Case of Slave Rufino and Its Consequences, 1858–1879." *Slavery and Abolition* 32, no. 2 (2011): 461–76.

Martínez, Rufino. *Diccionario biográfico-histórico dominicano, 1821–1930.* Santo Domingo: Editora de la Universidad Autónoma de Santo Domingo, 1971.

———. *Gregorio Luperón.* Santo Domingo: Universidad CETEC, 1982.

Martínez, Samuel. "Not a Cockfight: Rethinking Haitian-Dominican Relations." *Latin American Perspectives* 30, no. 3 (2003): 80–101.

Martínez-Fernández, Luís. "Caudillos, Annexationism, and the Rivalry between Empires in the Dominican Republic, 1844–1874." *Diplomatic History* 17, no. 4 (1993): 571–98.

---. "The Sword and the Crucifix: Church-State Relations and Nationality in the Nineteenth-Century Dominican Republic." *Latin American Research Review* 30, no. 1 (1995): 69–93.

---. *Torn between Empires: Economy, Society, and Patterns of Political Thought in the Hispanic Caribbean, 1840–1878*. Athens: University of Georgia Press, 1994.

Martínez Paulino, Marcos Antonio. *Publicaciones periódicas dominicanas desde la colonia*. Santo Domingo: Editora del Caribe, 1973.

Matibag, Eugenio. *Haitian-Dominican Counterpoint: Nation, State, and Race on Hispaniola*. New York: Palgrave Macmillan, 2003.

Matos Rodríguez, Félix M. "Street Vendors, Pedlars, Shop-Owners and Domestics: Some Aspects of Women's Economic Roles in Nineteenth-Century San Juan, Puerto Rico, 1820–1870." In *Engendering History: Caribbean Women in Historical Perspective*, edited by Verene Shepherd, Bridget Brereton, and Barbara Bailey, 176–93. New York: St. Martin's, 1995.

May, Robert E. "Lobbyists for Commercial Empire: Jane Cazneau, William Cazneau, and U.S. Caribbean Policy, 1846–1878." *Pacific Historical Review* 48, no. 3 (1979): 383–412.

---. "'Plenipotentiary in Petticoats': Jane M. Cazneau and American Foreign Policy in the Mid-Nineteenth Century." In *Women and American Foreign Policy: Lobbyists, Critics, and Insiders*, edited by Edward P. Crapol, 19–67. Westport, CT: Rowman and Littlefield, 1987.

---. *Slavery, Race, and Conquest in the Tropics: Lincoln, Douglas, and the Future of Latin America*. New York: Cambridge University Press, 2013.

Mayes, April. *The Mulatto Republic: Class, Race, and Dominican National Identity*. Gainesville: University of Florida Press, 2014.

McGraw, Jason. "From a Mulato Caribbean to a Black Pacific: Changing Locations of Racialization in Nineteenth- and Twentieth-Century Colombia." Paper presented at the 129th annual meeting of the American Historical Association, New York City, 4 January 2015.

---. *The Work of Recognition: Caribbean Colombia and the Postemancipation Struggle for Citizenship*. Chapel Hill: University of North Carolina Press, 2014.

McGuinness, Aims. "Searching for 'Latin America.'" In *Race and Nation in Modern Latin America*, edited by Nancy P. Appelbaum, Anne S. Macpherson, and Karin Alejandra Rosemblatt, 87–107. Chapel Hill: University of North Carolina Press, 2003.

Meagher, Arnold. *The Coolie Trade: The Traffic of Chinese Laborers in Latin America, 1847–1874*. Bloomington: Xlibris, 2008.

Mella SJ, Pablo. *Los espejos de Duarte*. Santo Domingo: Instituto Filosófico Pedro Francisco Bonó, 2013.

Méndez, Cecilia. *The Plebeian Republic: The Huanta Rebellion and the Making of the Peruvian State*. Durham, NC: Duke University Press, 2005.

Méndez Jiminián, Jesús. *Apuntes sobre las dos visitas de Martí a La Vega*. Santo Domingo: Editora Búho, 2008.

Mignolo, Walter. *Local Histories/Global Designs: Coloniality, Subaltern Cultures, and Border Thinking*. Princeton, NJ: Princeton University Press, 2000.

Mintz, Sidney. *Caribbean Transformations*. New York: Columbia University Press, 1989.

Monción, Benito. "De capotillo a Santiago: Relación histórica." *Clío* 82, no. 186 (2013): 9–46.

Montulé, Édouard de. *A Voyage to North America, and the West Indies in 1817*. London: Sir Richard Phillips & Co., 1821.

Morales, José. "The Hispaniola Diaspora, 1791–1850: Puerto Rico, Cuba, Louisiana and Other Host Societies." PhD diss., University of Connecticut, 1986.

Morillo-Alicea, Javier. "'Aquel laberinto de oficinas': Ways of Knowing Empire in Late Nineteenth-Century Spain." In *After Spanish Rule: Postcolonial Predicaments of the Americas*, edited by Mark Thurner and Andrés Guerrero, 111–40. Durham, NC: Duke University Press, 2003.

———. "Uncharted Landscapes of 'Latin America': The Philippines in the Spanish Imperial Archipelago." In *Interpreting Spanish Colonialism: Empires, Nations, and Legends*, edited by Christopher Schmidt-Nowara and John M. Nieto-Phillips, 25–54. Albuquerque: University of New Mexico Press, 2005.

Moya Pons, Frank. *The Dominican Republic: A National History*. Princeton, NJ: Markus Wiener, 1995.

———. *Historia colonial de Santo Domingo*. Santiago: Universidad Católica Madre y Maestra, 1976.

———. "The Land Question in Haiti and Santo Domingo: The Sociopolitical Context of the Transition from Slavery to Free Labor, 1801–1843." In *Between Slavery and Free Labor: The Spanish-Speaking Caribbean in the Nineteenth Century*, edited by Manuel Moreno Fraginals, Frank Moya Pons, and Stanley L. Engerman, 181–214. Baltimore: Johns Hopkins University Press, 1985.

———. *Manual de historia dominicana*. Santo Domingo: Caribbean Publishers, 1992.

———. "Las ocho fronteras de Haití y la República Dominicana." In *La Frontera: Prioridad en la agenda nacional*, edited by Socrates Suazo Ruiz, 441–46. Santo Domingo: Secretaría de Estado de las Fuerzas Armadas, 2003.

Murphy, Martin F. *Dominican Sugar Plantations: Production and Foreign Labor Integration*. New York: Praeger, 1991.

Nelson, William Javier. "The Crisis of Liberalism in the Dominican Republic, 1865–1882." *Revista de Historia de América* 104 (July–December 1987): 19–29.

———. "The Haitian Political Situation and Its Effect on the Dominican Republic, 1849–1877." *The Americas* 45, no. 2 (1988): 227–35.

Neptune, Harvey. "Romance, Tragedy and, Well, Irony: Some Thoughts on David Scott's *Conscripts of Modernity*." *Social and Economic Studies* 57, no. 1 (2008): 165–81.

———. "Savaging Civilization: Michel-Rolph Trouillot and the Anthropology of the West." *Cultural Dynamics* 26, no. 2 (2014): 219–34.

Nessler, Graham. *An Island-Wide Struggle for Freedom: Revolution, Emancipation, and Re-enslavement in Hispaniola, 1789–1809*. Chapel Hill: University of North Carolina Press, 2016.

———. " 'The Shame of the Nation': The Force of Re-enslavement and the Law of 'Slavery' under the Regime of Jean-Louis Ferrand in Santo Domingo, 1804–1809." *New West Indian Guide* 86, nos. 1–2 (2012): 5–28.

Newton, Melanie. *The Children of Africa in the Colonies: Free People of Color in Barbados in the Age of Emancipation*. Baton Rouge: Louisiana State University Press, 2008.

Nicholls, David. *Economic Dependence and Political Autonomy: The Haitian Experience*. Montreal: McGill University Centre for Developing Area Studies, 1974.

———. *From Dessalines to Duvalier: Race, Colour and National Independence in Haiti*. New Brunswick, NJ: Rutgers University Press, 1996 [1979].

———. "A Work of Combat: Mulatto Historians and the Haitian Past, 1847–1867." *Journal of Interamerican Studies and World Affairs* 16, no. 1 (1974): 15–38.

Northrup, David. "Indentured Indians in the French Antilles: Les immigrants indiens engagés aux Antilles Françaises." *Revue Française d'Histoire d'Outre-Mer* 87 (2000): 326–27.

Nouel, Carlos. "El terremoto de 1842." In *Antología de la prosa dominicana, 1844–1944*, edited by Vincente Lloréns, 93–104. 2nd ed. Santo Domingo: Sociedad Dominicana de Bibliofilos, 1987.

Núñez de Arce, Gaspar. *Santo Domingo*. Madrid: Imprenta de Manuel Minuesa, 1865.

Núñez Grullón, José. *Evolución constitucional dominicana 1844–2010*. Edición al cuidado del autor, 2010.

N'Zengou-Tayo, Marie-José. " 'Famn Se Poto Mitan': Haitian Woman, the Pillar of Society." *Feminist Review* 59 (1998): 118–42.

Ojeda Reyes, Félix. *El desterrado de París: Biografía del Dr. Ramón Emeterio Betances (1827–1898)*. San Juan: Ediciones Puerto, 2001.

Ojeda Reyes, Félix, and Paul Estrade, eds. *Pasión por la libertad: Actas del Coloquio Internacional "El independentismo puertorriqueño, de Betances a nuestros días," efectuado en París en septiembre de 1988*. San Juan: Instituto de Estudios del Caribe y Editorial de la Universidad de Puerto Rico, 2000.

Otero y Pimentel, Luis. *Reflejos de la vida militar*. Havana: Imprenta y Papeleria "La Universal" de Ruiz y Hermano, 1894.

Pani, Erika. "Ciudadanos precarios: Naturalización y extranjería en el México decimonónico." *Historia Mexicana* 62, no. 2 (2012): 627–74.

———. "Dreaming of a Mexican Empire: The Political Projects of the 'Imperialistas.' " *Hispanic American Historical Review* 82, no. 1 (2002): 1–31.

———. *El segundo imperio: Pasados de usos múltiples*. Mexico City: Centro de Investigación y Docencia Económicas, 2004.

Paredes Vera, María Isabel. "La Constitución de 1812: La génesis de la Independencia Efímera de Núñez de Cáceres y los primeros periódicos dominicanos." *Clío* 184 (2012): 99–143.

Paton, Diana. *No Bond but the Law: Punishment, Race, and Gender in Jamaican State Formation, 1780–1870*. Durham, NC: Duke University Press, 2004.

———. "Revisiting *No Bond but the Law*." *Small Axe* 15, no. 1 34 (March 2011): 176–86.

Patterson, Tiffany, and Robin D. G. Kelley. "Unfinished Migrations: Reflections on the African Diaspora and the Making of the Modern World." *African Studies Review* 43, no. 1 (2000): 11–45.

Peabody, Sue. "France's Two Emancipations in Comparative Context." In *Abolitions as Global Experience*, edited by Hideaki Suzuki, 25–49. Singapore: National University of Singapore, 2016.

Peña Gómez, José Francisco. *José Francisco Peña Gómez: Internacional, socialdemócrata e inmortal*. Santo Domingo: Editora Manatí, 2001.

Peña-Jordán, Teresa. "Cuerpo politico del deseo: Literatura, género e imaginario geocultural en Cuba y Puerto Rico (1863–2000)." PhD diss., University of Pittsburgh, 2005.

Penson, César Nicolás. *Reseña historico-crítica de la poesía en Santo Domingo: Notas y adiciones de Vetilio Alfau Durán*. Santo Domingo: Editora Taller, 1980.

Pérez Dionisio, Maritza. "Santiago de Cuba y la Guerra de la Restauración de Santo Domingo." *Clío* 179 (2010): 109–20.

Pérez Memén, Fernando. *El pensamiento dominicano en la primera república, 1844–1861*. Santo Domingo: Universidad Nacional Pedro Henríquez Ureña, 1993.

Peyrou, Florencia. "The Harmonic Utopia of Spanish Republicanism, 1840–1873." *Utopian Studies* 26, no. 2 (2015): 349–65.

Picó, Fernando. *Al filo del poder: Subalternos y dominantes en Puerto Rico, 1739–1910*. Río Piedras: Universidad de Puerto Rico, 1993.

———. *Libertad y servidumbre en el Puerto Rico del siglo XIX*. Río Piedras: Ediciones Huracán, 1981.

Pierrot, Grégory. "'Our Hero': Toussaint Louverture in British Representations." *Criticism* 50, no. 4 (2008): 581–607.

———. "The Samaná Affair." *Haiti and the Atlantic World*. 9 October 2013. https://haitidoi.com/2013/10/09/the-samana-affair-2/.

Pierrot, Grégory, and Tabitha McIntosh. "Henry/Nehri: Domestic Theater and International Stagecraft at the Royal Haitian Court." Paper presented at the annual meeting of the Haitian Studies Association, Montreal, 23 October 2015.

Pineo, Ronn F. *Ecuador and the United States: Useful Strangers*. Athens: University of Georgia Press, 2007.

Plaza, Elena. "God and Federation: The Uses and Abuses of the Idea of 'Federation' during the Federal Wars in Venezuela, 1859–1863." In *Rumours of Wars: Civil Conflict in Nineteenth-Century Latin America*, edited by Rebecca Earle, 135–49. London: Institute of Latin American Studies, 2000.

Polyné, Millery. *From Douglass to Duvalier: U.S. African Americans, Haiti, and Pan Americanism, 1870–1964*. Gainesville: University Press of Florida, 2010.

Porter, Andrew. "'Commerce and Christianity': The Rise and Fall of a Nineteenth-Century Missionary Slogan." *Historical Journal* 28, no. 3 (1985): 587–621.

Porter, David Dixon. *Diario de una misión secreta a Santo Domingo (1846)*. Santo Domingo: Editora de Santo Domingo, 1978.

Powelson, Michael. "Nineteenth-Century Latin American Imperialism from a Global Perspective." *History Compass* 9, no. 10 (2011): 827–43.

Puig Ortíz, José Agosto. *Emigración de libertos norteamericanos a Puerto Plata en la primera mitad del siglo XIX: La iglesia metodista wesleyana.* Santo Domingo: Editora Alfa y Omega, 1978.

Putnam, Lara. "Ideología racial, práctica social y estado liberal en Costa Rica." *Revista de Historia* 39 (1999): 139–86.

———. "To Study the Fragments/Whole: Microhistory and the Atlantic World." *Journal of Social History* 39, no. 3 (2006): 615–30.

Ramírez, Dixa. "At the Navel of the Americas: Transnational Dominican Narratives of Belonging and Refusal." Unpublished manuscript.

Ramsey, Kate. *The Spirits and the Law: Vodou and Power in Haiti.* Chicago: University of Chicago Press, 2011.

Ratcliffe, Barrie M. "Cotton Imperialism: Manchester Merchants and Cotton Cultivation in West Africa in the Mid-Nineteenth Century." *African Economic History* 11 (1982): 87–113.

Ravelo, Temístocles A. *Diccionario geográfico-histórico dominicano.* Santo Domingo: Archivo General de la Nación, 2012.

Raybaud, Maxime (Gustave d'Alaux). *Soulouque et son empire.* Paris: Michel Lévy, 1856.

Razack, Sherene. *Race, Space and the Law: Unmapping a White Settler Society.* Toronto: Between the Lines, 2002.

"The Rehabilitation of Spain." *Atlantic Monthly*, March 1862, 351–63.

Reid, Michele. "Protesting Service: Free Black Response to Cuba's Reestablished Militia of Color, 1854–1865." *Journal of Colonialism and Colonial History* 5, no. 2 (2004): 1–22.

Reid-Vazquez, Michele. *The Year of the Lash: Free People of Color in Cuba and the Nineteenth-Century Atlantic World.* Athens: University of Georgia Press, 2011.

Reinsel, Amy. "Poetry of Revolution: Romanticism and National Projects in Nineteenth-Century Haiti." PhD diss., University of Pittsburgh, 2008.

Renault, François. *Libération d'esclaves et nouvelle servitude: Les rachats de captifs africains pour le compte des colonies françaises après l'abolition de l'esclavage.* Abidjan: Les Nouvelles Éditions Africaines, 1976.

Rey, Terry. "Toward an Ethnohistory of Haitian Pilgrimage." *Journal de la Société des Américanistes*, no. 91-1 (2005): 161–83.

Reyes-Santos, Alaí. *Our Caribbean Kin: Race and Nation in the Neoliberal Antilles.* New Brunswick, NJ: Rutgers University Press, 2015.

Richardson, Bonham C. "Freedom and Migration in the Leeward Caribbean, 1838–48." *Journal of Historical Geography* 6, no. 4 (1980): 391–408.

Rivas Rojas, Raquel. "Del criollismo al regionalismo: Enunciación y representación en el siglo XIX venezolano." *Latin American Research Review* 37, no. 3 (2002): 101–28.

Roberts, G. W., and J. Byrne. "Summary Statistics on Indenture and Associated Migration Affecting the West Indies, 1834–1918." *Population Studies* 20, no. 1 (1966): 123–34.

Roberts, John Storm. *Black Music of Two Worlds: African, Caribbean, Latin, and African-American Traditions.* 2nd ed. New York: Schirmer Books, 1998 [1972].

Robinson, St. John. "The Chinese of Central America: Diverse Beginnings, Common Achievements." In *The Chinese in Latin America and the Caribbean*, edited by Walton Look-Lai and Tan Chee-Beng, 103–28. Boston: Brill, 2010.

Robles-Muñoz, Cristobal. *Paz en Santo Domingo, 1854–1865: El fracaso de la anexión a España.* Madrid: Centro de Estudios Históricos, Consejo Superior de Investigaciones Científicas, 1987.

Rodney, Walter. *A History of the Guyanese Working People, 1881–1905.* Baltimore: Johns Hopkins University Press, 1981.

Rodríguez, Emilio Jorge. "Encroachment of Creole Culture on the Written/Oral Discourses of the Dominican/Haitian Borderland." In *A Pepper Pot of Cultures: Aspects of Creolization in the Caribbean*, edited by Gordon Collier, 109–36. New York: Editions Rodopi, 2003.

Rodríguez Demorizi, Emilio. *Actos y doctrina del gobierno de la Restauración.* Santo Domingo: Editora del Caribe, 1964.

———. *Antecedentes de la anexion a España.* Ciudad Trujillo [Santo Domingo]: Editora Montalvo, 1955.

———. *Correspondencia del consúl de Francia en Santo Domingo, 1844–46.* 2 vols. Ciudad Trujillo [Santo Domingo]: Editora Montalvo, 1944.

———. *Cuentos de política criolla.* 2nd ed. Prólogo de Juan Bosch. Santo Domingo: Libreria Dominicana, 1977.

———. *Del vocabulario dominicano.* Santo Domingo: Editora Taller, 1983.

———. *La dominación haitiana 1822–1844.* 3rd ed. Santiago: Universidad Católica Madre y Maestra, 1978.

———. *La era de Francia en Santo Domingo: Contribución a su estudio.* Ciudad Trujillo [Santo Domingo]: Editora del Caribe, 1955.

———. *Escritos de Luperón.* Ciudad Trujillo [Santo Domingo]: Imprenta de J. R. Vida García Sues., 1941.

———. *Guerra dominico-haitiana: Documentos para su estudio.* Ciudad Trujillo [Santo Domingo]: Impresora Dominicana, 1957.

———. *Invasiones haitianas de 1801, 1805 y 1822.* Ciudad Trujillo [Santo Domingo]: Editora del Caribe, 1955.

———. *Luperón y Hostos.* 2nd ed. Santo Domingo: Editora Taller, 1975 [1939].

———. *La Marina de Guerra dominicana, 1844–1861.* Ciudad Trujillo [Santo Domingo]: Editora Montalvo, 1958.

———. *Papeles de Pedro F. Bonó.* Barcelona: Gráficas M. Pareja, 1980.

———. *Papeles dominicanos de Máximo Gómez.* Ciudad Trujillo [Santo Domingo]: Editora Montalvo, 1954.

---. *Poesía popular dominicana*. Santiago: Universidad Católica Madre y Maestra, 1973 [1938].
---. *Próceres de la Restauración*. Santo Domingo: Editora del Caribe, 1963.
---. *Relaciones dominicoespañolas (1844–1859)*. Ciudad Trujillo [Santo Domingo]: Editora Montalvo, 1959.
---. *Samaná: Pasado y porvenir*. Ciudad Trujillo [Santo Domingo]: Editora Montalvo, 1945.
---. *Santana y los poetas de su tiempo*. Santo Domingo: Academia Dominicana de la Historia, 1969.
---. *Viajeros de Francia en Santo Domingo*. Santo Domingo: Editora del Caribe, 1979.
Rodríguez Demorizi, Emilio, C. Larrazábal Blanco, and V. Alfau Durán, eds. *Apuntes de Rosa Duarte: Archivo y versos de Juan Pablo Duarte*. Santo Domingo: Editora del Caribe, 1970.
Rodríguez de Tió, Lola. *Mi libro de Cuba, poesías*. Havana: Imprenta La Moderna, 1893.
Rodríguez López, Pedro Pablo. "Las Antillas y el equilibrio del mundo en Hostos." In *Pasión por la libertad: Actas del Coloquio Internacional "El independentismo puertorriqueño, de Betances a nuestros días," efectuado en París en septiembre de 1988*, edited by Félix Ojeda Reyes and Paul Estrade, 63–74. San Juan, Instituto de Estudios del Caribe y Editorial de la Universidad de Puerto Rico, 2000.
Rodríguez Objío, Manuel. *Gregorio Luperón e historia de la Restauración*. 2 vols. Santiago: Editorial el Diario, 1939.
---. "Guerra" (August 1863). In *Reseña historico-crítica de la poesia en Santo Domingo: Notas y adiciones de Vetilio Alfau Durán*, comp. César Nicolás Penson. Santo Domingo: Editora Taller, 1980.
---. *Poesías coleccionadas por la sociedad literaria, "Amigos del País."* Santo Domingo: Imprenta de García Hermanos, 1888.
Rodríguez Silva, Ileana. *Silencing Race: Disentangling Blackness, Colonialism, and National Identities in Puerto Rico*. New York: Palgrave Macmillan, 2012.
Rojas, Rafael. *Cuba Mexicana: Historia de una anexión imposible*. Mexico City: Secretaría de Relaciones Exteriores México, 2001.
Roopnarine, Lomarsh. "A Comparative Analysis of Two Failed Indenture Experiences in Post-emancipation Caribbean: British Guiana (1838–1843) and Danish St. Croix (1863–1868)." *Iberoamericana* 1-2 (2012): 203–30.
---. "The First and Only Crossing: Indian Indentured Servitude on Danish Saint Croix, 1863–1868." *South Asian Diaspora* 1, no. 2 (2009): 113–40.
Roorda, Eric, Lauren Derby, and Raymundo González, eds. *The Dominican Republic Reader: History, Culture, Politics*. Durham, NC: Duke University Press, 2014.
Roseberry, William. "Beyond the Agrarian Question in Latin America." In *Confronting Historial Paradigms: Peasants, Labor, and the Capitalist World System in Africa and Latin America*, edited by Frederick Cooper, Allen Isaacman, Florencia

Mallon, William Roseberry and Steve Stern, 318–68. Madison: University of Wisconsin Press, 1993.

Ruffin, Edmund. *The Diary of Edmund Ruffin: Toward Independence, October 1856–April 1861*. Baton Rouge: Louisiana State University Press, 1972.

Rugemer, Edward. *The Problem of Emancipation: The Caribbean Roots of the American Civil War*. Baton Rouge: Louisiana State University Press, 2008.

Ryan, Marveta. "The Glory of Weakness: National Vulnerability in Dominican Poetry about the Conquest." Paper presented at the meeting of the Latin American Studies Association, Washington, DC, 6–8 September 2001. http://lasa.international.pitt.edu/Lasa2001/RyanMarveta.pdf.

Sáez, José Luis, comp. *Documentos inéditos de Fernando A. de Meriño*. Santo Domingo: Archivo General de la Nación, 2007.

Sagás, Ernesto. "A Case of Mistaken Identity: Antihaitianismo in Dominican Culture." *Latinamericanist* 29, no. 1 (1993): 1–5.

———. *Race and Politics in the Dominican Republic*. Gainesville: University Press of Florida, 2000.

Salvatore, Ricardo D. *Wandering Paysanos: State Order and Subaltern Experience in Buenos Aires during the Rosas Era*. Durham, NC: Duke University Press, 2003.

Samet, Elizabeth. *Willing Obedience: Citizens, Soldiers, and the Progress of Consent in America, 1776–1898*. Stanford, CA: Stanford University Press, 2004.

Sánchez Ramírez, Juan. *Diario de la Reconquista*. Ciudad Trujillo (Santo Domingo): Editora Montalvo, 1957.

Sanders, James E. *Vanguard of the Atlantic World: Creating Modernity, Nation, and Democracy in Nineteenth-Century Latin America*. Durham, NC: Duke University Press, 2014.

Sang Ben, Mu-Kien Adriana. *Buenaventura Báez, el caudillo del Sur, 1844–1878*. Santo Domingo: INTEC, 1997.

———. "Contradicciones en el liberalismo dominicano del siglo XIX: Un contraste entre el discurso y la práctica." *Ciencia y Sociedad* 16, no. 3 (1991): 240–51.

———. *La Política Exterior Dominicana, 1844–1961*. Vol. 1. Santo Domingo: Secretaría de Estado de Relaxiones Exteriores de la RD, 2000.

San Miguel, Pedro Luis. *Los campesinos del Cibao: Economía de mercado y transformación agraria en la República Dominicana, 1880–1960*. Río Piedras: Universidad de Puerto Rico, 1997.

———. *Crónicas de un embrujo: Ensayos sobre historia y cultura del Caribe hispano*. Pittsburgh: University of Pittsburgh Press, 2010.

———. *The Imagined Island: History, Identity, and Utopia in Hispaniola*. Translated by Jane Ramírez. Chapel Hill: University of North Carolina Press, 2005 [1997].

Santiago-Valles, Kelvin A. " 'Forcing Them to Work and Punishing Whoever Resisted': Servile Labor and Penal Servitude under Colonialism in Nineteenth-Century Puerto Rico." In *The Birth of the Penitentiary in Latin America: Essays on Criminology, Prison Reform, and Social Control, 1830–1940*, edited by Ricardo D. Salvatore and Carlos Aguirre, 123–68. Austin: University of Texas Press, 1996.

Sartorius, David. *Ever Faithful: Race, Loyalty, and the Ends of Empire in Spanish Cuba.* Durham, NC: Duke University Press, 2013.

———. "My Vassals: Free-Colored Militias in Cuba and the Ends of Spanish Empire." *Journal of Colonialism and Colonial History* 5, no. 2 (2004): 1–25.

Scarano, Francisco. "Slavery, Race, and Power: A Half Century of Spanish Caribbean Scholarship." In *Beyond Fragmentation: Perspectives on Caribbean History*, edited by Juanita De Barros, Audra Diptee, and David V. Trotman, 35–68. Princeton, NJ: Markus Wiener, 2006.

———. *Sugar and Slavery in Puerto Rico: The Plantation Economy of Ponce, 1800–1850.* Madison: University of Wisconsin Press, 1984.

Schmidt-Nowara, Christopher. *The Conquest of History: Spanish Colonialism and National Histories in the Nineteenth Century.* Pittsburgh: University of Pittsburgh Press, 2006.

———. *Empire and Anti-slavery: Spain, Cuba, and Puerto Rico, 1833–1874.* Pittsburgh: University of Pittsburgh Press, 1999.

———. " 'La España ultramarina': Colonialism and Nation-Building in Nineteenth-Century Spain." *European History Quarterly* 34 (2004): 191–214.

———. "Silver, Slaves, and Sugar: The Persistence of Spanish Colonialism from Absolutism to Liberalism." *Latin American Research Review* 39, no. 2 (2004): 196–210.

———. *Slavery, Freedom, and Abolition in Latin America and the Atlantic World.* Albuquerque: University of New Mexico Press, 2012.

Schneider, Elena.*The Occupation of Havana: Slavery, War, and Empire in the Eighteenth Century.* Chapel Hill: Omohundro Institute / University of North Carolina Press, forthcoming.

Schoelcher, Victor. *Abolition de l'esclavage: Examen critique du préjugé contre la couleur des africains et des sang-mêlés.* Paris: Pagnerre, 1840.

Schomburgk, R. H. "The Peninsula and Bay of Samaná, Dominican Republic." *Journal of the Royal Geographical Society of London* 23 (1853): 264–83.

Schuler, Monica. *"Alas, Alas Kongo": A Social History of Indentured African Immigration into Jamaica, 1841–1865.* Baltimore: Johns Hopkins University Press, 1980.

Scott, David. *Conscripts of Modernity: The Tragedy of Colonial Enlightenment.* Durham, NC: Duke University Press, 2004.

Scott, Julius. "The Common Wind: Currents of Afro-American Communication in the Era of the Haitian Revolution." PhD diss., Duke University, 1986.

Scott, Rebecca. "Public Rights and Private Commerce: A 19th-Century Atlantic Creole Itinerary." *Current Anthropology* 48, no. 2 (2007): 237–55.

———. *Slave Emancipation in Cuba: The Transition to Free Labor, 1860–99.* Pittsburgh: University of Pittsburgh Press, 2000.

Sepinwall, Alyssa. "Still Unthinkable? The Haitian Revolution and the Reception of Michel-Rolph Trouillot's Silencing the Past." *Journal of Haitian Studies* 19, no. 2 (2013): 75–103.

Sheina, Robert L. *Latin America's Wars: The Age of the Caudillo, 1791–1899.* Dulles, VA: Potomac Books, 2003.

Sheller, Mimi. "Army of Sufferers: Peasant Democracy in the Early Republic of Haiti." *New West Indian Guide* 74, nos. 1–2 (2000): 33–55.

———. *Citizenship from Below: Erotic Agency and Caribbean Freedom.* Durham, NC: Duke University Press, 2012.

———. *Democracy after Slavery: Black Publics and Peasant Radicalism in Haiti and Jamaica.* Gainesville: University Press of Florida, 2000.

Sluyter, Andrew. *Black Ranching Frontiers: African Cattle Herders of the Atlantic World, 1500–1900.* New Haven, CT: Yale University Press, 2012.

Smith, Benjamin. *Roots of Conservatism in Mexico: Catholicism, Society, and Politics in the Mixteca Baja, 1750–1962.* Albuquerque: University of New Mexico Press, 2012.

Smith, Caleb. *The Oracle and the Curse: A Poetics of Justice from the Revolution to the Civil War.* Cambridge, MA: Harvard University Press, 2013.

Smith, Matthew J. "Footprints on the Sea: Finding Haiti in Caribbean Historiography." *Small Axe* 18, no. 1 43 (March 2014): 55–71.

———. *Liberty, Fraternity, Exile: Haiti and Jamaica after Emancipation.* Chapel Hill: University of North Carolina Press, 2014.

Smith, Stacey L. *Freedom's Frontier: California and the Struggle over Unfree Labor, Emancipation, and Reconstruction.* Chapel Hill: University of North Carolina Press, 2013.

Sobrevilla Perea, Natalia. *The Caudillo of the Andes: Andrés de Santa Cruz.* New York: Cambridge University Press, 2011.

Sommer, Doris. *One Master for Another: Populism as Patriarchal Rhetoric in Dominican Novels.* New York: University Press of America, 1983.

Soto, Miguel. *La conspiración monárquica en México 1845–6.* Ciudad de México: EOSA, 1988.

"South America—San Domingo—Haiti." *Evangelical Magazine and Missionary Chronicle, Relating Chiefly to the Missions of the London Missionary Society* 16 (December 1838): 606–8.

Spieler, Miranda Frances. "The Legal Structure of Colonial Rule during the French Revolution." *William and Mary Quarterly* 66, no. 2 (2009): 365–408.

Stinchcombe, Arthur L. *Sugar Island Slavery in the Age of Enlightenment: The Political Economy of the Caribbean World.* Princeton, NJ: Princeton University Press, 1995.

Stasiulis, Daiva, and Nira Yuval-Davis, eds. *Unsettling Settler Societies: Articulations of Gender, Race, Ethnicity, and Class.* London: Sage, 1995.

Stephens, Michelle Ann. *Black Empire: The Masculine Global Imaginary of Caribbean Intellectuals in the United States, 1914–1962.* Durham, NC: Duke University Press, 2005.

St. John, Spenser. *Hayti: Or, the Black Republic.* Pittsburgh: Ballantyne Press, 1884.

Suárez Díaz, Ada. *El Antillano: Biografía de Dr. Ramón Emeterio Betances, 1827–1898.* San Juan: Centro de Estudios Avanzados de Puerto Rico y el Caribe, 1988.

Sundiata, I. K. *From Slaving to Neoslavery: The Bight of Biafra and Fernando Po in the Era of Abolition, 1827–1930.* Madison: University of Wisconsin Press, 1996.

Tansill, Charles Callan. *The United States and Santo Domingo, 1798–1873: A Chapter in Caribbean Diplomacy.* Baltimore: Johns Hopkins University Press, 1938.

Tejeda Ortíz, Dagoberto. "El cimarronaje, la Sarandunga y San Juan Bautista en Baní, República Dominicana." In *Fiestas y rituales*, edited by John Galán Casanova, 274–84. Lima: Dupligráficas, 2009.

———, ed. *Cultura y folklore de Samaná*. Santo Domingo: Editora Alfa y Omega, 1984.

Théodat, Jean-Marie Dulix. *Haïti et la République Dominicaine: Une île pour deux, 1804–1916*. Paris: Éditions Karthala, 2003.

Thompson, Alvin. *The Haunting Past: Politics, Economics and Race in the Caribbean*. Armonk, NY: M. E. Sharpe, 1997.

Thompson, Shirley Elizabeth. *Exiles at Home: The Struggle to Become American in Colonial New Orleans*. Cambridge, MA: Harvard University Press, 2009.

Thomson, Guy. *The Birth of Modern Politics in Spain: Democracy, Association, and Revolution, 1854–1875*. New York: Palgrave Macmillan, 2009.

———. "Garibaldi and the Legacy of the Revolutions of 1848 in Southern Spain." *European History Quarterly* 31, no. 3 (2001): 353–95.

———. "Modernities in the Hispanic World." In *When Was Latin America Modern?*, edited by Nicola Miller and Stephen Hart, 69–90. New York: Palgrave Macmillan, 2007.

Tomich, Dale. *Through the Prism of Slavery: Labor, Capital, and World Economy*. New York: Rowman and Littlefield, 2004.

———. "The Wealth of Empire: Francisco Arango y Parreño, Political Economy, and the Second Slavery in Cuba." *Comparative Studies in Society and History* 45, no. 1 (2003): 4–28.

Torrente, Mariano. *Política ultramarina, que abraza todos los puntos referentes á las relaciones de España con los Estados Unidos, con la Inglaterra y las Antillas, y señaladamente con la isla de Santo Domingo*. Madrid: Imprenta de la Compañía General de Impresores y Libreros del Reino, 1854.

Torres-Saillant, Silvio. "Before the Diaspora: Early Dominican Literature in the United States." In *Recovering the United States Hispanic Literary Heritage*, vol. 3, edited by Maria Herrera-Sobek and Virginia Sánchez-Karrol, 250–67. Houston: Arte Pública Press, 2002.

———. "Blackness and Meaning in Studying Hispaniola: A Review Essay." *Small Axe* 10, no. 1 (February 2006): 180–88.

———. "The Tribulations of Blackness: Stages in Dominican Racial Identity." *Latin American Perspectives* 25, no. 3 (May 1998): 126–46.

Townsend, Camilla. "In Search of Liberty: The Efforts of the Enslaved to Attain Abolition in Ecuador, 1822–1852." In *Beyond Slavery: The Multilayered Legacy of Africans in Latin America and the Caribbean*, edited by Darién Davis, 37–56. New York: Rowman and Littlefield, 2007.

Trouillot, Michel-Rolph. *Silencing the Past: Power and Production in History*. Boston: Beacon Press, 1995.

———. *State against Nation: The Origins and Legacy of Duvalierism*. New York: Monthly Review Press, 1990.

Turits, Richard Lee. *Foundations of Despotism: Peasants, the Trujillo Régime, and Modernity in Dominican History*. Stanford, CA: Stanford University Press, 2003.

———. "Raza, esclavitud, y libertad en Santo Domingo." *Debates y Perspectivas* 4 (2004): 69–88.

Ubiñas Renville, Guaroa. *Historias y leyendas afro-dominicanas*. Santo Domingo: Editora Manatí, 2003.

Valdez, Juan R. *Tracing Dominican Identity: The Writings of Pedro Henríquez Ureña*. New York: Palgrave, 2011.

Vallejo, Catherina. *Las madres de la Patria y las bellas mentiras: Imágenes de la mujer en el discurso literario nacional de la República Dominicana, 1844–1899*. Miami: Ediciones Universal, 1999.

Vásquez de Díaz, Elixiva María. *Antiguallas de Neyba*. Santo Domingo: Editora Alfa y Omega, 1997.

Vastey, Pompée-Valentin (baron de). *The Colonial System Unveiled*. Edited and translated by Chris Bongie. Liverpool: Liverpool University Press, 2014.

Veeser, Cyrus. *A World Safe for Capitalism: Dollar Diplomacy and America's Rise to Global Power*. New York: Columbia University Press, 2007.

Vega, Bernardo. *Breve historia de Samaná*. Santo Domingo: Fundación Cultural Dominicana, 2004.

———. *Trujillo y Haiti*. Vol. 1, 1930–1937. Santo Domingo: Fundación Cultural Dominicana, 1988.

Vega, Bernardo, and José Castillo Pichardo, eds. *Dominican Cultures: The Making of a Caribbean Society*. Princeton, NJ: Markus Wiener, 2007.

Vega Boyrie, Wenceslao. "La labor legislativa de la Junta Central Gubernativa, marzo-octubre de 1844." *Clío* 175 (2008), 199–212.

Venator Santiago, Charles R. "Race, Nation-Building and Legal Transculturation during the Haitian Unification Period (1822–1844): Towards a Haitian Perspective." *Florida Journal of International Law* 16, no. 3 (September 2004): 667–76.

———. "Race, the East, and Haitian Revolutionary Ideology: Rethinking the Role of Race in the 1844 Separation of the Eastern Part of Haiti." *Journal of Haitian Studies* 10, no. 1 (2004): 102–19.

Ventura Almonte, Juan. "Presencia de ciudadanos ilustres in Puerto Plata en el siglo XIX." *Clío* 180 (2010): 187–234.

Vertovek, Steven. "Indian Indentured Migration to the Caribbean." In *The Cambridge Survey of World Migration*, edited by Robin Cohen, 57–62. New York: Cambridge University Press, 1995.

Vicioso, Abelardo. *El freno hatero en la literatura dominicana*. Santo Domingo: Editora de la UASD, 1983.

Vinson, Ben. "African (Black) Diaspora History, Latin American History." *The Americas* 63, no. 1 (2006): 1–18.

Warner-Lewis, Maureen. *Central Africa in the Caribbean: Transcending Time, Transforming Cultures*. Mona: University of West Indies Press, 2003.

Watts, Isaac. *The Cotton Supply Association: Its Origin and Progress.* Manchester: Tubbs and Brook, 1871.

Welles, Sumner. *Naboth's Vineyard: The Dominican Republic, 1844–1924.* New York: Arno Press, 1972 [1928].

White, Ashli. *Encountering Revolution: Haiti and the Making of the Early Republic.* Baltimore: Johns Hopkins University Press, 2010.

White, Luise. *Speaking with Vampires: Rumor and History in Colonial Africa.* Berkeley: University of California Press, 2000.

Williams, Brackette F. *Stains on My Name, War in My Veins: Guyana and the Politics of Cultural Struggle.* Durham, NC: Duke University Press, 1991.

Williams, Eric. *Capitalism and Slavery.* Chapel Hill: University of North Carolina Press, 1994 [1944].

Wipfler, William L. "The Catholic Church and the State in the Dominican Republic, 1930–1960." In *Christianity in the Caribbean: Essays on Church History,* edited by Armando Lampe, 191–229. Kingston: University of the West Indies, 2001.

Wolfe, Justin. *The Everyday Nation-State: Community and Ethnicity in Nineteenth-Century Nicaragua.* Lincoln: University of Nebraska Press, 2007.

Yingling, Charlton. "Colonialism Unraveling: Radicalism and Religion, Race and Nation in Santo Domingo during the Age of Revolutions, 1784–1822." PhD diss., University of South Carolina, 2016.

———. "The Maroons of Santo Domingo in the Age of Revolutions: Adaptation and Evasion, 1783–1800." *History Workshop* 79 (2015): 25–51.

Yuengling, David, ed. *Highlights in the Debates in the Spanish Chamber of Deputies Relative to the Abandonment of Santo Domingo.* Washington, DC: Murray and Heister, 1941.

Zahler, Reuben. *Ambitious Rebels: Remaking Honor, Law, and Liberalism in Venezuela, 1780–1850.* Tucson: University of Arizona Press, 2013.

Zeller, Neici. *Discursos y espacios femininos en República Dominicana, 1880–1961.* Santo Domingo: Editorial Letra Gráfica, 2011.

Index

Abbot, William Henry, 174
abolitionism: annexation and, 72–76; antislavery societies, in Separation era, 36; cabotage and, 271n112; in Caribbean, 8–11; constitutional implementation of, 266n9; "freedmen of the Palm" and, 1; indentured labor and, 90–91, 278n33, 288n209; postindependence growth of, 230–36; Spanish Empire in Caribbean and, 62–67; unification of Hispaniola and, 23–24
Act of Independence (Acta de Independencia), 188–92, 211
Africa: cotton production in, 276n13; Spanish settlements in, 76–77, 272n142
African Americans: emigration to Haiti by, 10, 14, 35, 39–40, 90; perceptions of Santo Domingo from, 10–11
African Battalion, 5–6, 28
African Methodist church, in Dominican Republic, 39–40
Afro-Dominican organizations, 35–40
agriculture: Dominican annexation and, 92–94; expansion in postannexation period, 103–6, 277n26; postannexation immigration and indenture for, 106–8; rural identity and politics and, 41–48, 239n28, 247n20, 255n173
Alba, Joaquín Manuel del, 104
Alcantara, Valentín, 57, 265n385
Alfau, Antonio Abad, 55, 68–69, 164–65

Alfau, Felipe, 55, 68–69, 196
alliances: Caribbean region initiatives for, 233–36; Dominican independence movement and, 207–8; Haitian-Dominican military alliances, 196–204; mass mobilization and social mobility of, 188–92
Alonso y Colmenares, Eduardo, 124–25
Álvarez, Luis, 63
Álvarez, Mariano, 66–70, 74, 140–43, 190, 299n180, 333n28
amnesty for rebels, during War of Restoration, 152, 304n68
Ángulo de Guridi, Francisco Javier, 112, 228
animal impressment, Spanish policy of, 132–33, 194
annexation: discipline and leisure following, 108–11; Dominican resistance to, 144–77; elite embrace of, 11–14, 54–56, 261n281; erosion of Spanish support for, 123–29; establishment in Dominican Republic of, 11–14, 54–56, 59–60, 261n281; immigration and indenture following, 106–8; imposition of Spanish civil code following, 94–97; international reception of, 83–86; labor policies and, 87–91, 103–6; military structure following, 87–94, 97–101; opposition to, 117–43; press establishment following, 111–13; religious reform following, 101–3;

annexation (*continued*)
　Separation era and ideology of, 54–56, 260n281; slavery and, 71–76, 146–77; Spanish reaction to, 76–82
"Another Pirate" (anon.), 53
anticolonialism: Dominican independence and growth of, 215–17, 230–36; Haitian organization in Dominican Republic of, 117; in Separation-era Dominican Republic, 40; War of Restoration and, 17–18
anti-emancipation narrative: annexationism and, 71–76; Caribbean independence movement and, 8–11; in Separation era, 32–40
antigaming laws, passage of, 109–11
anti-Haitianism: Dominican annexation and, 12–14, 60, 67–71, 117, 240n71; in Dominican press, 112–13, 121–23; of early Dominican elites, 10–11, 25–31; narratives of, 239n8; opposition to annexation and, 122–23, 140–43; in postindependence era, 235–36; in Separation era, 33–40, 261n298
"Antillean Nationality" proposal, 234
antislavery societies, in Separation era, 36
Argentina, Paraguayan border conflict with, 3
Argudín (Senator), 9
Asia, Spanish intervention in, 76
Asian labor: in Cuba, 72–73; in Dominican Republic, 158–59
Atlantic Monthly, 84–85
Ayiti, 2

Báez, Buenaventura: annexation and, 53–54, 162; anti-Haitianism and, 142; postindependence return of, 231–35; Provisional Government and, 192–93; "regeneration" narrative and, 182–84; resistance to annexation and, 181, 308nn142–43; rural politics and, 44; in Separation era, 21–22, 26, 31, 33, 38, 42, 51; Spanish influence and, 49
bagaje system, 132–33

Barbados, 232–33
Bart, Laguerre, 198
Basora, Francisco, 216
Basora, Santiago, 28
Batista, Doña Antonia, 181–84
benevolence narrative, imperialism in Caribbean and, 12–14
Betances, Ramón Emeterio, 36, 191, 216–17, 234
biembienes (maroon people), 43
black Dominicans: rebellion against annexation and, 161; in regiments during Separation era, 23, 28–31, 35–40; religious brotherhoods of, 44–45; in rural settlements, 36–37; Spanish military focus on during War of Restoration, 174–77
Bobadilla, Tomas, 235
Boletín Oficial, 158, 186, 188, 199–200, 220–21
Bolivia, support for Dominican independence by, 210
Bona, Félix de, 80
Bonó, Pedro Francisco, 37–38, 176, 179, 188–89, 196, 315n4
Bosch, Juan, 189, 191, 244n115
Boyer, Jean-Pierre: collapse of regime of, 7, 21, 24–25; Dominican support for, 5, 239n21, 240n32; invitation to African Americans from, 10, 35, 39–40; land rights and, 251n85; Rural Code of, 247n21; *terrenos comuneros* rights and, 42; Tree of Liberty planting and, 1, 19–20; unification of Hispaniola and, 23
Brazil, Paraguayan border conflict with, 3
British empire: abolitionism and, 8–9; annexationism and, 11–14; cotton production and, 87–90, 276n13; Dominican annexation and, 85–86, 105; filibuster efforts opposed by, 65; indentured labor in colonies of, 88–94, 277n26; independence of Dominican Republic and, 209, 211–12, 233; intervention during Separation era of, 22–23; recognition of Domini-

can Republic by, 49; Separation-era opposition to, 33, 40; U.S. cotton production and, 62, 87–88
Brotherhood of Saint Antoine, 45
Buceta, Manuel, 130, 155, 162, 181, 192, 222, 295n124, 307n138
Buchanan, James, 84

Caballero, Juan, 225
Cabral, José Maria, 120–23, 149, 183–84, 196, 216, 308n142, 333n37
call-and-response music, 45
Caminero, José María, 250n70
Camp, Stephanie, 148
Cap-Haïtien: British attack on, 233; commercial ties in, 38–39, 46; family ties in, 155; naval blockade of, 155–56; political alliances in, 22, 180, 197–202; U.S. steamships in, 174, 217
capital projects, in postannexation Dominican Republic, 104–6, 278n30
Cappa, Mariano, 125
Cap separatism, 27
Caribbean region: alliance initiatives in, 233–36; annexationism in, 11–14; colonial empires in, 3–4; Dominican independence supported in, 209; indentured labor in, 89–94; independence movements in, 8–12, 62–67, 231–36; Spanish empire in, 61–67
Carmen Rodríguez, José del, 46
Catholic Church: in Dominican Republic, 67–68, 95; opposition to annexation and, 134–36; postannexation disarray of, 101–3, 283n104
caudillo literature, rural identity and politics in, 42–48
Cazneau, Jane Storm, 51–52, 55, 64–65, 67
Cazneau, William, 51–52, 65, 67, 107–8, 208
Chicago Tribune, 84
Chile, Spanish conflict with, 77
Chincha Islands dispute, 77, 210
Civil War (U.S.), 83–85, 88–89, 191, 204; Spanish support of Confederacy in, 134

class divisions, during Separation era, 27–31, 34–40
Classification Committee, Spanish military establishment of, 100, 128–29
Clayton-Bulwer treaty, 62
Cofradía of San Juan Bautista, 35
Colombia: Atlantic identity of, 10; support for Dominican independence in, 210, 232
colonialism: annexationism and, 11–16; Dominican Republic and influence of, 16; filibuster operations and, 40, 50–51; geopolitics in Spanish empire and, 61–67; influence in Separation era of, 22–23; Latin American independence projects and, 3; postindependence indenture and unfree labor and, 9–11
Comercio de Cádiz, 208
Confederate ships, presence in Caribbean ports of, 141, 150
conscription, rural resistance to, 44, 249n50, 262n324
"Conspiracies, Seen from One Side, The," 50
Contreras, José, 149
Contreras, Teodisio, 168
Correspondiente de España newspaper, 78
Costa Rica, Atlantic identity of, 10
Cotton Association of Manchester, 106
cotton production, 62, 87–90, 106, 276n13
Cristo, Moreno del, 124
Crónica de Ambos Mundos newspaper, 74–75
Cruzat, Manuel, 65–66, 85–86, 122, 125, 288n209
Cuba: annexationism in, 12–14, 71; colonial government in, 60–67, 77–79, 94–97, 280n59; Dominican annexation and, 16–17, 33, 59, 64–76, 86–87, 94–97, 112–13, 130–36, 153–61; exiled Dominicans in, 32, 214, 225–28; fugitive slaves in Santo Domingo from, 35, 91–94, 113–16; independence movement in, 230–36; independence of Dominican Republic and, 207–9, 212–17, 220–21,

INDEX | 371

Cuba (continued)
  223; religious practices in, 101; Santana's relations with, 123–29; slavery and indenture in, 9–11, 72–76; "Spanishness" ideology in, 60; trade expansion and, 103–6; U.S. threat to, 62; War of Africa participation by, 80–81
Cuello, Juan Francisco, 214
Curaçao, 207–8
Curiel, Pedro, 125
Curiel, Ricardo, 191

Danbon, Nicolas, 225
death penalty, Dominican abolition of, 230
"Decree of Police and Governance," 111
de la Cruz, José, 168
de la Gándara, José, 136, 159–61, 171–72, 184–86, 203–4, 221, 224–27, 330n133
de Leon, Domingo, 214
Delmonte, Félix María, 185–87, 216
Del Monte, Manuel Joaquín, 23, 67
de los Santos, Honorio, 225
de los Santos, Miguel, 131–32
democratization, Dominican discourse on, 185–87
Desgrotte, Etienne, 25
Dessalines, Jean-Jacques, 2
Díaz, Modesto, 133
Díaz, Ramón, 176–77
Dolores, Francisco de los, 161
Dominican Republic: anti-Haitian campaign in, 10–11; collaborative revolution with Haiti, 56–58, 150–77, 180–81; democratization in, 185–87; devastation following independence in, 227–28; Haitian population in, 23, 27–31; Haitian Revolution and, 4–6; historical timeline for, ix–xi; marginalization of rural population in, 14–18; opposition to annexation in, 117–43; in postindependence period, 229–36; Provisional Government of, 17–18; Puerto Rican alliance with, 5; rebellion against annexation in, 144–77; reform constitution adopted by, 29–31; regional and international support for independence in, 211–17; rural rebellion in, 15–18; in Separation era, 7–11, 21–58; soldiers in postannexation period in, 97–100; Spanish identity in, 69–71; Spanish influence in, 12–14, 64–67; War of Restoration in, 16–18, 144–48, 244n115. See also annexation; independence movements; Santo Domingo
drumming practices, 45
Duarte, Juan Pablo, 19, 27–28, 210, 245n144, 252n98
Dulce, Domingo, 212
Dusablon, Estanislao, 173

economic conditions: budget expansion in Dominican Republic and, 129–36; in postannexation period, 103–6, 125–29; during Separation era, 7, 21–22, 30–31, 34–40, 48–54, 56–58; Spanish empire in Caribbean and, 61–67; during War of Restoration, 192–95
Ecuador, territorial cessions by, 266n5
"El Chivo" (caudillo leader), 190
El Clamor Público newspaper, 78
El Contemporáneo newspaper, 77–79
El Dominicano newspaper, 30–32, 50, 251n83, 253n125
Elie, Auguste, 202–3
elites of Dominican Republic: annexation and, 11–14, 54–56, 93–94, 117–18, 260n281; anti-Haitianism of, 33–40; Cuban ties with, 32; disillusionment with annexation and, 181–84; independence and, 5–6; loyalty to Spain during War of Restoration and, 162–72; narrative of War of Restoration by, 19–20, 244n115; political power in Separation era of, 21–22, 31–40; race and class discourse of, 14–18, 27–28; in rural settlements, 37–38; during Separation era, 7–8, 21–22, 27–31; slavery practiced by, 2–4, 114–16; Spanish military forces and, 136–40; Spanishness embraced by, 12–14, 32–40; War

of Africa supported by, 80–82; white supremacist and imperial pressures on, 10–11
Elliot, Jonathan, 55
El Museo de Ambas Américas, 61
El Oasis newspaper, 49, 52, 66
El Redactor de Santiago de Cuba, 212
El Tiempo, 235
emancipation movements: independence of Dominican Republic and, 222–28; Separation opposition to, 33–40; War of Restoration and, 18, 146–48, 204
Enriquez, Julieta, 115
Espaillat, Ulises, 185, 200–201, 205
ethnic identity, in Dominican Separation era, 22
Evangelista, Marcos, 139

Fabens, Joseph, 84
federalism, in Dominican Republic, 3
Feliz, Manuel ("Cabulla"), 142–43
Feliz, Manuel ("Quiri"), 142–43
Fernández de Castro, Felipe, 66, 125
Fernando Po (Bioko), 76–77, 272n142
filibuster aggression: in Dominican Republic, 50–52, 64–67; in Haiti, 66; in Nicaragua, 62; by United States, 216–17
Finch, Aisha, 147–48
Flag of Lares (Puerto Rico), 230–32
Florentino, Pedro, 140, 159–61, 190
France: annexation in Dominican Republic and, 12–14, 67–71; Ecuadorean monarchy in, 266n5; filibuster efforts opposed by, 65; Haitian indemnity payments to, 2, 6–7, 23, 40; independence of Dominican Republic and, 209; influence in Separation era of, 22–23, 26–27, 32–33, 36, 40, 48–52, 55–56, 246n16, 252n123; Mexican intervention by, 59–60; reaction to Dominican annexation in, 83
"freedmen of the Palm," 1
Freemasons: in Dominican Republic, 102–3; in postindependence period, 230

free-soil ideology: annexationist discourse and, 12–13; anti-emancipation discourse and, 33–40

Gaceta de la Habana, 86
Gaceta de Santo Domingo, 100, 111, 224
Gaceta Oficial, 103, 213, 225
Galván, Manuel de Jesús, 93, 112, 162, 187–88
Gantreau, María de Jésus, 227
García, Don Juan Francisco, 166
García, Madame, 181–84
García Moreno, Gabriel, 266n5
García Paredes, Victoriano, 125
Garibaldi, Giuseppe, 7, 185–87
Gaspar, David Barry, 41
Geffrard, Cora, 141
Geffrard, Fabre Nicholas, 244n127, 278n28; anticolonialism of, 56–57, 83, 86; cotton production in Haiti and, 88; Dominican annexation and, 67–68, 92–94, 113, 316n24; indentured labor and, 90; independence of Dominican Republic and, 222, 224; nationalist discourse and, 185–87; opposition to annexation and, 117, 119–23, 180–81; slavery rumors and, 150; Spanish presence in Haiti and, 141–43; War of Restoration and, 195–204
General Overseas Directorate (Dirección General de Ultramar), 61
geopolitics, Spanish Caribbean empire and, 61–67
George, Victor, 316n24
Gleaner newspaper, 83
Gómez, Máximo, 228
González, Raymundo, 14
government structure: Dominican annexation and, 94–97; in postannexation period, 108–11; rural identity and politics and, 43–44; in Separation era, 21–22; during War of Restoration, 192–95; War of Restoration and threat to, 166–72
Gran Colombia, 5

Grito de Capotillo (Cry of Capotillo), 145, 155, 191
Guerrero, Manuel, 167–68
Guridi, Alejandro, 42, 130–31, 207
Guzmán, Nicolás, 175–76

Haiti: annexation in Dominican Republic and, 12–14, 67–71; civil division in, 21–22; collaboration with Dominicans in, 56–58, 83–86, 153–77, 180–81, 195–204; cotton production in, 88; democratization in, 185–87; Dominican anti-Haitianism and, 21–22; Dominican family ties in, 46–48, 121–23, 132–33; earthquake of 1842 in, 24; elites in, 30–31; etymology of, 238n5; historical timeline for, ix–xi; opposition to annexation in, 117–43; privileging of black citizenship in, 11–14; Provisional Government and, 17–18, 195–204; religious practices in, 45–46; resistance to annexation and, 144–48, 180–81; revolutionary movement in, 200–204; in Separation era, 7–11, 26–31; Spanish presence in, 140–43, 292n54; War of Restoration supported in, 17–18, 196–204
Haitian-Dominican Constitution, drafting of, 25
Haitian National Guard, 44
Haitian Revolution, 2, 4–5; Caribbean independence movements and, 8–11; rural identity and politics and, 42–43; transformation of labor in, 88–89; War of Restoration and influence of, 17–18
Heneken, Teodoro, 38
Hispaniola: colonial division of, 1–4; competing coalitions on, 18–20; emancipation movements in, 18; etymology of, 238n5; settlement map of, 6–7; Spanish occupation of, 63–67; towns and rural settlements, ca. 1830, 7; unification of, 23–25, 28–31; U.S. interests in, 63–67
Hispano-American confederation proposal, 66, 82, 245n138

Histoire d'Haïti (Madiou), 33
Hungria, José, 152, 155–56, 162, 165

immigration policies: African and Asian migrant labor and, 72–73; in postannexation period, 106–8
indemnity debt to France, burden of, 2, 6–7, 23, 27, 247n23
indenture: assimilation and, 72–76; cabotage and, 271n112; Caribbean independence and growth of, 9; in Cuba, 271n116; expansion in Caribbean of, 87–94; in postannexation period, 106–8
independence movements: in Caribbean region, 62–67, 231–36; coalition for Dominican independence, 207–9; end of Spanish rule in Dominican Republic and, 221–28; growing strength in Dominican Republic of, 218–21; international and regional response to Dominican independence, 210–17
inequality, in Spanish Caribbean territories, 62–67
inter-Caribbean migration, 18
investment, in postannexation Dominican Republic, 104–6
Isabella II (Queen of Spain), 59–60, 77
Isidor, Pablo, 202

Jaeger, William, 208
Jamaica: independence movement in, 208, 232; reaction to Dominican annexation in, 83
Jean-Joseph, François, 90
Jiménez, Blas C., 132
Jiménez, Nicasio, 46
judicial system, rural identity and politics and, 43–44

Kock, Bernard, 278n30

La América, 80
L'Abeille de la Nouvelle-Orléans, 83
labor: Dominican annexation and changes in, 72–76, 86–87, 103–6,

108–11; morality linked to control of, 92–94, 108–11; in rural Dominican Republic, 15; Separation-era migration agreements for, 55–56. *See also* indenture; migrant labor; slavery

La campana del higo (Ángulo de Guridi), 228

La Discusión, 78–79, 208

La Época, 78

La España, 78–79

La idea de valor en Santo Domingo, 224

Landais, M., 141

land rights: in postannexation period, 104–6, 107–8; rural identities and politics and, 41–48, 248n35, 251n85, 251n87, 255n175

LaPlace, Anna María, 46

La Razón, 112, 121–22, 142, 159–64; antislavery rhetoric in, 149; Dominican independence movement and, 208, 224

La Regeneración, 229

La Revista Española de Ambos Mundos, 61

"Las Colonias Españolas y la República Dominicana" (Macías), 216

Las Novedades, 79

Latin America: geopolitics in Spanish empire and, 61–67; independence of Dominican Republic and, 209–10

Lavastida, Miguel, 101, 125

legal structure: Dominican annexation and, 94–97, 104–6, 124–29, 281n63, 295n121; nationalist discourse and, 184–85; opposition to annexation and burden of, 132–36

legend of Don Melchor, 43

Legros, Aimé, 199

leisure activity, postannexation regulation of, 108–11

Lema, Marques de, 222

Le Moniteur Haïtien, 83–86, 120, 123, 195, 231, 264n360

Liberal Union Party (Spain), 61, 186

Lima Congress of 1847, 61

limpieza de sangre documents, 118, 289n6

Lincoln, Abraham, 84, 209

literary culture in Dominican Republic, 38

Longuefosse, Ogé, 202

López, Narcisco, 51, 62, 65

Lora, Gregorio, 140, 165

Lora, Jacinto de, 139–40

Los Mina: as free black town, 36, 174–75; Spanish presence in, 174, 314n241

Louverture, Toussaint, 4–5

Luperón, Gregorio, 156, 179, 184, 191–93, 204–5, 216, 233–36, 320n98, 333n37

Luperón, José Gabriel, 191

Macajauc, M., 198

Macías, Juan Manuel, 216

Madiou, Thomas, 33

mail system in Santo Domingo, 95–96, 126

Malo de Molina, José, 74–76, 95–96, 104–5, 114–16, 281n63

Marcy, William, 65

maroon Dominicans, rural settlements of, 36–37

martial law, imposition in Dominican Republic of, 150–51

Martínez, Manuel, 138–40

Marzán, Huberto, 198

mass mobilization, for Dominican independence, 188–92

Mateo, Segundo, 121

matriarchal core, in rural society, 45

Medicine Committee, postannexation formation of, 109–11

Medina, Victoria, 225

Mella, Ildefonso, 215

Mella, Pablo, 27

Mella, Ramón, 26, 182, 186–87, 190, 198, 308n142

merengue, anti-Haitian rhetoric about, 34

Meriño, Fernando Arturo de (Archbishop), 67–68, 135, 191, 215–16, 303n67, 327n61

Merriman, Alexander, 153

Mexican-American War. *See* War of U.S. Intervention

Mexico: annexationism and, 11–14; French intervention in, 59–60, 231; imperial intervention in, 12; territorial losses to United States by, 13–14

INDEX | 375

migrant labor: in postannexation period, 106–8, 278n30; Separation-era demand for, 32–40, 55–56

military forces: annexation and arrival of Spanish forces, 94–97; black Dominicans in, 23, 28–31, 35–40, 247n18; Caribbean colonies' requests for, 62–67; evacuation from independent Dominican Republic, 222–28; Haitian-Dominican military alliances, 196–97; hardships during independence struggle of, 218–21; independence movement and, 213–21; opposition to annexation and, 117–18, 120–24, 132–40; in postannexation period, 97–100, 136–40; rural politics and, 44–48, 248n24, 249n50, 258n234, 260n293, 261n298; violence and criminality of, 150–55, 172–73, 189–92, 319n89; War of Restoration mobilization of, 188–92

Militia of Color, 97

miscegenation, Spanish colonial policies concerning, 61

Moca Constitution, 205, 230

Monroe Doctrine: annexation of, 84; Dominican Provisional Government and, 185–87

Monte Cristi: commercial trade in, 39, 104, 198, 211, 216; Cuban presence in, 174; earthquake in, 24; migration into, 39; rebellion in, 144–45, 155, 180, 191, 205, 220

Monzón, Bienvenido, 103

morality: labor control and, 92–94, 108–11; postannexation religious reform and, 101–3

Morant Bay Rebellion (Jamaica), 232

Morcelo, Sebastian, 218

Morning Journal, 83

Morris, William, 290n31

multilingualism: rural identity and politics and, 43, 48; in Separation-era Dominican Republic, 40

Napoleon III, 76, 266n6

nationalist rhetoric: annexationism and, 12–15; Provisional Government and, 181–85; "regeneration" narrative and, 182–84

Neiba, 48, 121–22, 142–44, 147, 157, 196, 198, 307n126

New Grenada, 210

New York Times, 84

Nicaragua: armed conspiracies in, 12; Clayton-Bulwer treaty and, 62; support for Dominican independence by, 210

Nissage-Saget, Jean-Nicolas, 234

Noël, Philanthrope, 196

Nolasco, Pedro, 196–97

North Haiti–Dominican union, proposal for, 27

"Noticias Nacionales," newspaper publication of, 112

Núñez, Petronila, 224–25

Núñez de Cáceres, José, 69–71

O'Donnell, Leopoldo, 61, 76–79, 85, 209, 273n173

Oquendo, Candelario, 211

Overseas Ministry (Ministerio de Ultramar), 61

Ovidio, Rudolfo, 46

Padilla, Enrique, 99–100

Páez, José, 314n241

palos de muerte, 45

papabocó ritual experts, 45

papalúa ritual experts, 45

Paraguay, border conflicts with Brazil and Argentina, 3

passports, in postannexation Dominican Republic, 132

Paton, Diana, 8

Peláez y Campomanes, Antonio, 69–70

Peña, Lucas Evangelista de, 191, 321n134

Peralta y Rodríguez, Federico, 24–25

Pérez, José Maria, 313n226

Peru: Spanish conflict with, 77; support for Dominican independence by, 210

Philippines, Spanish influence in, 60

Pichardo, Franklin Franco, 248n35

Pierce, Franklin, 62

Pierre, José, 291n40
Pierrot, Jean-Louis Michel, 29–30
Pimentel, Pedro Antonio, 205, 231
Pine and Palm (Redpath), 84
Pineda, Pedro, 131–32
Polanco, Gaspar, 140, 179–80, 184, 189, 193–95, 199, 204–6, 235, 311n208
Política ultramarina (Overseas Politics, 1854) (Torrente), 71–72
politics: Dominican annexation and, 94–97; instability during Separation era, 48–54; mass mobilization for independence, 188–92; in postindependence period, 229–36; rural identity and, 41–48; town politics and geography and, 31–40
Polk, James, 62
Ponce de Léon, Manuel, 211
Ponthieux, Alcius, 25
Port-au-Prince: communication in, 213; constitutional convention in, 24–25, 29; Cuban exiles in, 66; Dominicans in, 26, 117, 132, 225; earthquake in, 24; martial law in, 123; newspapers in, 30, 47, 83, 119, 150, 198; political alliances in, 3, 50, 196; rebellion in, 56; slavery issues in, 120; Spanish presence in, 121–22, 140–42, 190, 203, 292n54; trade activity in, 6, 48, 197
Portes, Thomas de, 29, 250n75
Pouget, Alexandre, 198
press coverage of Dominican Republic: independence from Spain and, 208–9, 213; opposition to annexation in, 119–23, 162–72; postannexation establishment of Dominican newspapers, 111–13; in postindependence period, 229–36; Spanish coverage of annexation, 77–82, 84–86, 272n151, 273n154
Prim, Juan, 63
prison system, postannexation expansion of, 110–11, 287n184
Protestantism: opposition to annexation and oppression of, 133–36; postannexation religious reform and, 102–3

Provincial Reserves, 138–40, 151; establishment of, 100; rebellion against annexation and, 173, 179
Provisional Government: growing strength of, 218–21; Haitian support for, 195–204; independence coalition-building by, 207–8; international recognition sought for, 216–17; leadership struggles within, 192–95; mass mobilization by, 188–92; nationalist discourse and, 184–87; "regeneration" narrative of, 181–84; Venezuelan links with, 210–11; War of Restoration and, 146–48, 155, 177, 179–81
public health provisions, postannexation formation of, 109–11
Puello, Eusebio, 165
Puello, Gabino, 29
Puello, José Joaquín, 28–29, 49
Puerto Plata: antislavery sympathies in, 40, 58, 150; Catholic Church in, 101; commercial activity in, 38–39, 105–6, 180, 187, 216, 281n69; cosmopolitanism of, 39; government structure in, 126, 130, 153–54, 162, 165, 208, 215, 283n106; as ideological center, 230; migrants in, 39–40, 46, 94, 136; political alliances in, 24, 40–41, 54, 118, 191, 198, 239n20, 248n35; Protestant population in, 102; rebellion in, 128, 139–40, 145, 151, 156–62, 169–74, 189, 210–14, 236; Spanish presence in, 55, 64, 97, 133–34, 155, 195–96, 226–27, 311n208; women leaders in, 164
Puerto Rico: alliance with Dominicans, 5, 33, 112; annexationism in, 9, 12–14, 71; colonial government in, 94, 280n59, 287n174; Dominican annexation and, 59, 73–76, 94–97, 104–6, 125, 155–61; exiled Dominicans in, 225; fugitive slaves in Santo Domingo from, 35–36, 113–16; independence of Dominican Republic supported by, 208–9, 212–17, 220–21, 238, 328n77; postindependence Dominican Republic and, 230–36; slave labor in,

Puerto Rico (continued)
9–11, 72; Spanish influence in, 60, 62, 69–70, 79; U.S. sugar industry in, 62
Pulien, Carlos, 216

Quisqueya, 1–2, 238n5

racism: annexationist discourse and, 11–14; Caribbean independence movement resurgence of, 8–11; Dominican annexation and role of, 67–71, 150–52; Dominican independence and, 209, 222–28; in Dominican military structure, 100, 150–55; elites of Dominican Republic and, 117–18; geography and, 31–40; immigration and indenture linked to, 107–8; politics of Separation era and, 31–40; rural identities and politics and, 41–48; during Separation era, 27–31; Spanish empire in Caribbean and, 61–67
Ramírez y Parmantier, Domingo, 57–58, 121–22, 196, 235, 265n385
ranching, by Dominicans of color, 41
Raybaud, Maxime, 52
raza hispana, 12, 61–62, 82, 97
Real Audiencia of Santo Domingo, 95–97, 125–27, 288n198
Recio, Ramona, 121
Redpath, James, 84, 278n28
regeneration of Dominican Republic, elites' embrace of, 181–84
religious brotherhoods, 34, 44–45
religious practices: opposition to annexation and oppression of, 133–36, 297n152; postannexation reform of, 101–3, 129, 283n104; rural identity and politics and, 44–46
republican universalism, elite Dominicans' embrace of, 32–40
revolution, during Separation era, 48–54
Revolutionary Puerto Rican Committee, 231
Ricart y Torres, Pedro, 96–97, 125
Risorgimento (Italy), 185

Rivero, Felipe, 129, 148, 150–51, 153, 155, 162, 164–66, 174
Rivière-Hérard, Charles, 26–27, 29
Rodríguez, Santiago, 198, 231
Rodríguez Objío, Manuel, 1, 144, 178, 191–92, 204–5, 210, 227–28, 233–36, 238n5
Rojas, Pedro José, 211
Roman, Josefa, 225
Rondón, Juan, 189–90
Roolt, Edward, 260n284
Roumain, Ernest, 204, 205
Royal Standard and Gazette of the Turks and Caicos Islands, 211
Rubalcaba, Joaquín, 122
Rural Code (Dominican Republic), 92–93, 274n21
rural Dominican Republic: annexation impact on, 91–94; elite marginalization of, 14–18, 34–40; identities and politics in, 41–48, 255n173; political consensus in, 14–16; rebellion against annexation and, 16–18, 178–79; during Separation era, 22–23, 26–31; sugar slavery and black settlement in, 36–40

Saint-Domingue: French colony of, 2, 4–5; fugitive slaves in, 113–16
Saint Martin (Soualiga), 4
saint veneration, in rural communities, 45–46
Salcedo, José, 192–93, 205, 320n98
Salnave, Sylvain, 198–99, 233
Sam, Simon, 321n134
Samaná: colonial ambitions in, 48–51; commercial activity in, 67, 79, 128–29; filibuster organizing in, 64–65; French presence in, 13, 26–27, 40, 50; government structure in, 126–27, 167; migrants to, 39–40, 55, 174; prisoners in, 108–11, 159; Protestants in, 133–34; rebellion in, 227–28; slavery in, 141; Spanish presence in, 97–106, 118, 169–70, 192, 216, 219–20; U.S. presence in, 51–52, 79, 84

San Carlos, as black settlement, 36, 161, 174–75, 214
Sánchez, Francisco del Rosario, 56–58, 117, 120–22, 149, 179, 187–88, 290n31, 291n40
Sánchez, José Maria, 46
Sánchez, Socorro, 218
San Just, Eduardo, 65
Santana, Pedro, 176; annexation and, 59–60, 67–71, 73, 77–78, 81–86, 104; antigaming bill signed by, 109; anti-Haitianism of, 141–42; Catholic Church and, 67–68, 215, 327n61; death penalty called for, 183; defeat of, 178–81, 209; executions and injustice of, 120, 290n31, 291n33; immigration and indenture policies of, 107–8; land rights and, 42; military forces under, 44, 96, 139–40; opposition to annexation and, 117, 119–23, 128–29, 215; "regeneration" narrative concerning, 182–84; religious reforms of, 101–3, 215, 327n61; rural politics and, 38; Separation-era power struggle and, 21–22, 26–30, 52–58; Spanish view of, 49–50, 65–66, 77–82, 123–29, 165; War of Restoration and, 148, 308n142
Santana de los Reyes, Pablo, 176
"Santana's Great Treason," 317n48
Santiago de Cuba, 32, 103–5, 156, 208–9, 213, 249n55
Santiago de los Caballeros, xii; destruction of, 145, 156, 204, 231; economic and trade development in, 37–38, 46; government structure in, 177, 181, 189; rebellion in, 53, 142, 145, 150–58, 168–69, 191–92, 210; regional conflict and, 3, 198–202, 204, 231; Spanish presence in, 73, 96–97, 130–31
Santo Domingo: fugitive slaves in, 113–16; Haitian family ties in, 46–48; Haitian Revolution and, 1, 4–5; Haitians in, 5–7; immigration and indenture in, 72–73, 106–8; Latin American perceptions of, 10–11; military forces during annexation in, 136–40; opposition to annexation in, 159–61; racial inequality in, 35; Real Audiencia of, 95–97; rural identities and politics in, 41–48; Separation-era economy and politics in, 21–22, 24–31; Spanish abandonment of, 222–28; in Unification era, 23–25, 28–31, 63. *See also* annexation
Santo Domingo and España (Guridi), 131, 207
Segovia, Antonio Maria, 66
Segundo, Macsimo, 159
self-determination, Dominican resistance and, 184–85
Separation era: geography, racism, and politics during, 31–40; governmental power struggles in, 7–8, 21–22; political reform movements and, 23–31; provocation, instability, and revolution in, 48–54; "regeneration" narrative about, 181–84; unrest and annexation during, 54–56
Serra, José María de, 215–16
Serrano, Francisco: Cuban trade practices and, 66–67; Dominican annexation and, 59, 73–78; labor policies and, 103–4; opposition to annexation and, 124, 139, 308n142; postannexation government structure and, 95–96; retirement of, 129, 209; Spanish identity embraced by, 69, 71
Seward, William E., 84
Sierra Leone, 8
Simoneau, Gabino, 291n40
slavery: annexation and, 71–76, 85–86, 113–16; cabotage and, 271n112; Caribbean emancipation dates, 90–92; in Caribbean territories, 62–67, 90–92; in early Dominican Republic, 16–17; emancipation after Haitian Revolution, 5–6; Haiti as refuge from, 5–7; in postindependence Caribbean countries, 8–11; self-emancipation from, 113–16; Separation-era opposition to, 33–40; War of Restoration and fear of, 18, 146–48, 177

social mobility, mobilization for independence and, 188–92
Sociedad Democrática de los Amigos de América, 216
Society of the Rights of Man and Citizen, 24–25
Soto, María Lucas, 114
Soulouque, Faustin, 49–50, 52, 56, 62, 65–67, 248n37, 262n324, 266n6, 267n39, 318n80
Spain: annexation of Dominican Republic by, 1–4, 11–14, 54–56, 59, 67–71, 87–97, 117–19, 129–36; anticolonialism in colonies of, 230–36; Antillean geopolitics and empire of, 61–67; antislavery decrees from, 114–16; Caribbean annexationism and, 71–76; colonial policies in Latin America and, 186–87, 266n9; Dominican nationalist discourse and, 185–87; end of Dominican rule by, 221–28; exiled Dominicans in, 214–15; fines imposed on Dominicans by, 131–32; forced labor in Caribbean colonies of, 9–11; Haitian relations with, 117–19, 140–42, 195–204; immigration and indenture policies of, 107–8; imperialist ambitions of, 76–82; indemnity demands of, 140–43; independence of Dominican Republic from, 207–28; military forces in Dominican Republic from, 97–100, 136–40, 218–21; opposition to annexation in, 122–29, 146–77; press coverage of annexation in, 77–82, 84–86, 272n151, 273n154; pro-Confederate sentiments in, 134; Separation era and influence of, 22–23, 32–40, 48–49, 54–56, 252n123; U.S. support of Dominican independence and, 216–17; Venezuelan links with, 211; War of Restoration and defeat of, 17–18, 146–77
Spanish Abolitionist Society, 231
"Spanish Haitians," 5, 121, 238n5
Spanish identity: Cuban embrace of, 60; Dominican elites' embrace of, 12–14, 32–40, 69–71, 112–13

Suero, Juan, 140, 148, 165
sugar plantations: slavery on, 2, 36–40; U.S.-Spanish colonial rivalry and, 62

Tassara, Gabriel, 84
taxation: expansion of, 129–36; in postannexation period, 103–6
terrenos comuneros rights, 42
tobacco production: annexation politics and, 93; colonialism and, 53; government support of, 23; in postannexation Dominican Republic, 106; rural Dominican Republic and, 22, 38–39, 42
Torrente, Mariano, 71–72
trade practices: annexation in Caribbean and, 66–67; cross-border trade, 47–48; Haitian-Dominican trade during War of Restoration, 197–99; in postannexation period, 104–6; in Separation-era Dominican Republic, 39–40; Spanish blockade of Dominican coast and, 208
Treaty of Aranjuez, 47–48, 51, 262n313
Tree of Liberty, 1, 5
Trinitarios society, 24–26, 29, 182, 215–16
Turkes and Caicos Islands, support for Dominican independence in, 211–12

Unification period in Hispaniola, 23–25, 28–31, 238n1; racist order during, 35; suppression in Dominican history of, 68–69
Unión Liberal, 77
United States: Caribbean independence movements and, 9–11; Dominican annexation and, 67, 83–85, 88–94; Dominican opposition to, 55–56; expansion in Caribbean of, 11–14, 60, 71; filibuster operations in Dominican Republic, 50–53; independence of Dominican Republic and, 208–9, 212–13, 216–17; intervention during Separation era of, 22–23, 40, 48–51; postindependence Dominican Republic and, 233–36; reaction to Dominican annexation in, 83–84; Spanish empire

380 | INDEX

in Caribbean and, 13–14, 61–67; War of Restoration supported by, 198. *See also* Confederate ships
Ureña, Salomé, 235
Uruguay, Garibaldi in, 185

Valverde, Pedro, 93–94, 108, 114–16, 125, 289n218
Vanderhurst, Peter, 174
Vargas, Carlos de, 166–67, 170–71, 179–81
Velázquez, Cayetano, 144, 157
Venezuela: civil war in, 3–4, 112, 210; Dominican annexation and, 105; support for Dominican independence in, 210–11
vernacular citizenship, history of, 5
Villaverde, Cirilo, 207
Virgin Mary, rural veneration of, 45
Virgin of Altagracia, 45, 258n251
Vives, Guillerma, 225

Walker, William, 65
War in Africa (Souvestre), 111
War of Africa, 76–82, 84, 273n173
War of Restoration, 16–18, 244n115; competing coalitions in aftermath of, 18–20; end of, 204–6; Haitian-Dominican collaboration during, 195–204; mass mobilization for, 188–92; nationalist discourse during, 184–87; origins of, 144–48; Provisional Government and, 181–84, 192–95
War of U.S. Intervention, 62
White, Luise, 146–48
white hierarchy: annexation of Dominican Republic and, 67–71, 117–18; postannexation immigration and indenture and, 107–8; in rural settlements, 37–38; Separation-era politics and, 31–40
women: Dominican independence and role of, 218, 224–25, 330n129; emancipation movements and, 147–48; opposition to annexation from, 135–36, 137–40, 157–61; postannexation religious reform and targeting of, 101–3; Provisional Government and, 181–84; status in Separation era of, 250n70; War of Restoration and, 162–64, 167–68
"Word to Dominicans, a Word to Haitians, A," 200
World as It Will Be in Year 3000, The (Souvestre), 111

Ysnaga, José, 216

www.ingramcontent.com/pod-product-compliance
Lightning Source LLC
Chambersburg PA
CBHW061342300426
44116CB00011B/1951